Rave reviews for
Bed & Breakfast U.S.A.:

T5-AXE-245

"One of the bibles of the business."—*Chicago Tribune*

"There must be a dozen B&B guidebooks published by my company and numerous others. The one that I wish I had published is the acknowledged leader among them, *Bed and Breakfast U.S.A.* by Betty Rundback."—*Arthur Frommer, on his TV show, "The Travel Almanac"*

"A best-selling travel book."—*Reader's Digest*

"An excellent, readable travel guide."—*Washington Post*

"A valuable source of information."—*New York Times*

"Extremely useful, well-organized guide."—*ALA Booklist*

"Many a first-time B&B guest vows never again to stay in a motel . . . business travelers—particularly women traveling alone—have found this personal touch just the ticket."—*Karen Bure, TWA Ambassador*

"The best overall view . . . Betty Rundback is so enthusiastic that she even gives readers pointers on how to start their own B&Bs."—*Detroit News*

"Squeezed budgets get relief at B&Bs. . . . *Bed and Breakfast U.S.A.* [is] an extensive list of establishments."—*United Press International*

"Especially helpful . . . especially valuable."—*New York Daily News*

"The most comprehensive B&B guide."—*Savvy*

Bed
&
Breakfast
U.S.A. 1993

Betty Revits Rundback
Updated by Peggy Ackerman
Assisted by Leslie Jay and Michael Ackerman

Tourist House Association of America

A PLUME BOOK

With great pride, our entire family remembers the love and enthusiasm Betty Revits Rundback put into this book every year. She touched many hearts. May her warmth and wisdom never be forgotten.

PLUME
Published by the Penguin Group
Penguin Books USA Inc., 375 Hudson Street, New York, New York 10014, U.S.A.
Penguin Books Ltd, 27 Wrights Lane, London W8 5TZ, England
Penguin Books Australia Ltd, Ringwood, Victoria, Australia
Penguin Books Canada Ltd, 10 Alcorn Avenue, Toronto, Ontario, Canada
M4V 3B2
Penguin Books (N.Z.) Ltd, 182–190 Wairau Road, Auckland 10, New Zealand

Penguin Books Ltd, Registered Offices:
Harmondsworth, Middlesex, England

Published by Plume, an imprint of New American Library,
a division of Penguin Books USA Inc.

First Printing, January, 1993

10 9 8 7 6 5 4 3 2

Permission to use photographs on the back cover is gratefully acknowledged to Suit's Us (Rockville, Indiana) and Twin Hollies Retreat (Danville, Kentucky).

 REGISTERED TRADEMARK—MARCA REGISTRADA

LC card number: 86-649303

Printed in the United States of America

Set in Palatino and Optima
Designed by Stanley S. Drate/Folio Graphics Co. Inc.

Contents

Reservation service organizations appear here in boldface type.

Reservation service organizations appear here in boldface type.

Reservation service organizations appear here in boldface type.

Reservation service organizations appear here in boldface type.

Reservation service organizations appear here in boldface type.

Reservation service organizations appear here in boldface type.

Reservation service organizations appear here in boldface type.

xii • CONTENTS

Reservation service organizations appear here in boldface type.

Reservation service organizations appear here in boldface type.

Reservation service organizations appear here in boldface type.

Reservation service organizations appear here in boldface type.

Reservation service organizations appear here in boldface type.

Reservation service organizations appear here in boldface type.

Reservation service organizations appear here in boldface type.

Reservation service organizations appear here in boldface type.

Reservation service organizations appear here in boldface type.

Reservation service organizations appear here in boldface type.

Reservation service organizations appear here in boldface type.

Reservation service organizations appear here in boldface type.

Reservation service organizations appear here in boldface type.

Reservation service organizations appear here in boldface type.

Reservation service organizations appear here in boldface type.

Reservation service organizations appear here in boldface type.

Reservation service organizations appear here in boldface type.

Reservation service organizations appear here in boldface type.

Reservation service organizations appear here in boldface type.

Reservation service organizations appear here in boldface type.

Reservation service organizations appear here in boldface type.

Reservation service organizations appear here in boldface type.

Reservation service organizations appear here in boldface type.

Reservation service organizations appear here in boldface type.

5.   Canada

Reservation service organizations appear here in boldface type.

Reservation service organizations appear here in boldface type.

Preface

If you are familiar with earlier editions of *Bed & Breakfast U.S.A.*, you know that this book has always been a labor of love. It is personally gratifying to see how it has grown from the first sixteen-page edition, titled *Guide to Tourist Homes and Guest Houses*, which was published in 1975 and contained 40 individual listings. Seventeen years later, the sixteenth revised edition lists 1,152 homes and 111 reservation agencies, giving travelers access to over 11,000 host homes. This spectacular success indicates how strongly the revived concept of the guest house has recaptured the fancy of both travelers and proprietors.

On the other hand, what was welcomed as a reasonably priced alternative to the plastic ambience of motel chains has, in some instances, lost its unique qualities. Our mailbox is crammed with letters from grand hotels, condominium rental agencies, campground compounds, and chic inns with nightly tariffs topping the $100 mark. All share a common theme—they all serve breakfast and they all want to be listed in *Bed & Breakfast U.S.A.* Who can blame them? Since 1976, over half a million people have bought this best-selling guide.

We also receive a substantial amount of mail from our readers and we have tailored our book to meet their needs. We have given a great deal of thought to what we feel a B&B should be and are again focusing on our original definition: an owner-occupied residence with breakfast included at a fair rate, where the visitor is made to feel more like a welcome guest then a paying customer.

Because of personal experience, and comments from our readers, the 1994 edition of *Bed & Breakfast U.S.A.* will go back to the basics. We will no longer accept any bed & breakfast over $85 for a double occupancy, or with rates exceeding $40 when there are five guests sharing one bath; or if they do not offer breakfast (When paying $35–$40, no one wants to go out to a restaurant for breakfast—no matter how close it may be, it's just not the same as breakfast "at home.") For those of you who do not mind paying a higher rate, the reservation services listed in *B&B U.S.A.* will gladly help you.

As a result of these new guidelines, we will regretfully have to delete a great number of listings that have been on our roster for years. This does not imply in any way that these B&Bs aren't nice;

it simply means that, in our opinion, they do not fit the traditional B&B experience. I'm sure we will be receiving hundreds of letters from irate members disputing our opinion and pointing out that rising operating expenses must be reflected in their charges. Newcomers to the business decry our stand and tell us of the high costs that must somehow be recouped. While we sympathize and fully understand their positions, we must, in all fairness, be firm.

This is not a project for which listings have been compiled just for the sake of putting a book together; bigger isn't necessarily better. *Bed & Breakfast U.S.A.* is a product of a membership organization whose credo is "Comfort, cleanliness, cordiality, and fairness of cost." We solicit and rely on the comments of our readers. For this purpose, we include a tear-out form on page 735. If we receive negative reports, that member is dropped from our roster. Also for our 1994 edition of *Bed & Breakfast U.S.A.* we are looking for B&Bs set up to accommodate handicapped guests. See pages 733–34 for more information. We genuinely appreciate comments from guests—negative if necessary, positive when warranted. We want to hear from you!

All of the B&Bs described in this book are members of the Tourist House Association of America, RD 1 Box 12A, Greentown, Pennsylvania 18426. THAA dues are $35 annually. We share ideas and experiences by way of our newsletter and sometimes arrange regional seminars and conferences. To order a list of B&Bs that joined after this edition went to press, use the form in the back of this book.

PEGGY ACKERMAN
Tourist House Association of America

January 1993

Even after careful editing and proofreading, errors occasionally occur. We regret any inconvenience to our readers and members.

Acknowledgments

A special thanks to all the travel writers and reporters who have brought us to the attention of their audiences. Watch for 1994! Also to Bob Rundback for allowing us to continue to publish this book.

To my family, Mike Ackerman, Travis Kali, and Justin Ackerman, the three men in my life—thank you for all the encouragement and support you have shown; to Mary Kristyak Donnelly, a superb mother, grandmother, and best friend—I admire you so; to Bill Donnelly, dad and joke teller; to the grandmothers, Ann Revits and Helen Kristyak.

Deep appreciation goes to very eager and very patient staff members: Grace and Sheri Schweisguth, Courtney Sears, Venice Anns, and all the employees at the Greentown Post Office headed by Postmaster Karen Zane.

A final note of thanks to my editor, Leslie Jay, for her deeply appreciated assistance. Never too much, always a smile.

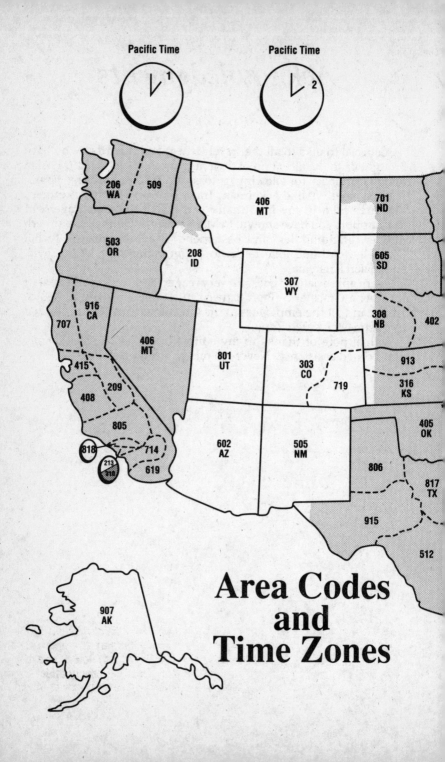

Pacific Time 1

Pacific Time 2

206
WA

509

503
OR

208
ID

406
MT

701
ND

605
SD

307
WY

308
NB

402

916
CA

707

406
MT

801
UT

303
CO

719

913

316
KS

415

209

408

805

818

213
818

714

619

602
AZ

505
NM

405
OK

806

817
TX

915

512

907
AK

**Area Codes
and
Time Zones**

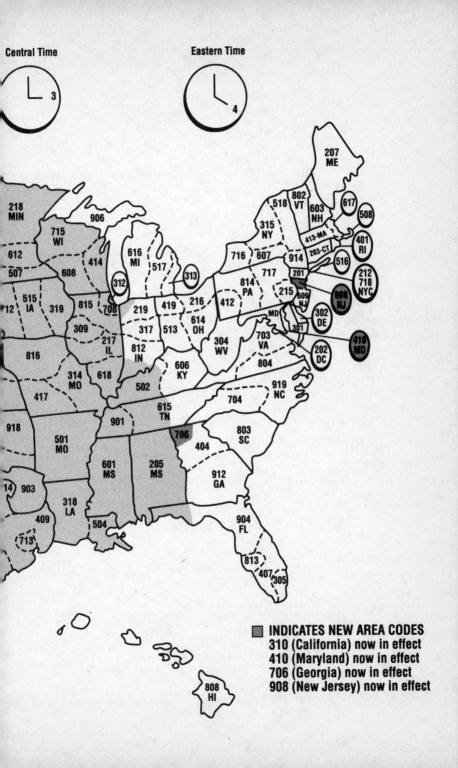

Central Time

3

Eastern Time

4

207
ME

218
MIN

715
WI

802
VT

518

315
NY

603
NH

617

508

612

906

616
MI

716

607

413-MA

203-CT

401
RI

507

608

517

313

914

516

212
718
NYC

515
IA

319

815

414

312

716

717

201

219

419

216

412

215

609
NJ

908
NJ

309

708

317

513

614
OH

304
WV

MD

302
DE

816

217
IL

812
IN

606
KY

703
VA

301

410
MD

314
MO

618

502

804

202
DC

417

615
TN

704

919
NC

918

901

706

803
SC

501
MO

601
MS

205
MS

404

912
GA

903

318
LA

409

504

904
FL

713

813

407

305

808
HI

■ **INDICATES NEW AREA CODES**
310 (California) now in effect
410 (Maryland) now in effect
706 (Georgia) now in effect
908 (New Jersey) now in effect

1

Introduction

Bed and Breakfast is the popular lodging alternative to hotel high rises and motel monotony. B&Bs are either private residences where the owners rent spare bedrooms to travelers, or small, family-operated inns offering a special kind of warm, personal hospitality. Whether large or small, B&Bs will make you feel more like a welcome guest than a paying customer.

The custom of opening one's home to travelers dates back to the earliest days of Colonial America. Hotels and inns were few and far between in those days, and wayfarers relied on the kindness of strangers to provide a bed for the night. Which is why, perhaps, there is hardly a Colonial-era home in the mid-Atlantic states that does not boast: "George Washington Slept Here!"

During the Depression, the tourist home provided an economic advantage to both the traveler and the host. Travelers always drove through the center of town; there were no superhighways to bypass local traffic. A house with a sign in the front yard reading "Tourists" or "Guests" indicated that a traveler could rent a room for the night and have a cup of coffee before leaving in the morning. The usual cost for this arrangement was $2. The money represented needed income for the proprietor as well as the opportunity to chat with an interesting visitor.

In the 1950s, the country guest house became a popular alternative to the costly hotels in resort areas. The host compensated for the lack of hotel amenities, such as private bathrooms, by providing comfortable bedrooms and bountiful breakfasts at a modest price. The visitors enjoyed the home-away-from-home atmosphere; the hosts were pleased to have paying houseguests.

The incredible growth in international travel that has occurred over the past 30 years has provided yet another stimulus. Millions of Americans now vacation annually in Europe, and travelers have become enchanted with the bed and breakfast concept so popular in England, Ireland, and other parts of the Continent. In fact, many well-traveled Americans are delighted to learn that we "finally" have B&Bs here. But, as you now know, they were always here—just a rose by another name.

Bed and breakfasts are for

- **Parents of college kids:** Tuition is costly enough without the added expense of Parents' Weekends. Look for a B&B near campus.
- **Parents traveling with children:** A family living room, playroom, or backyard is preferable to the confines of a motel room.
- **"Parents" of pets:** Many proprietors will allow your well-behaved darling to come, too. This can cut down on the expense and trauma of kenneling Fido.
- **Business travelers:** Being "on the road" can be lonely and expensive. It's so nice, after a day's work, to return to a home-away-from-home.
- **Women traveling alone:** Friendship and conversation are the natural ingredients of a guest house.
- **Skiers:** Lift prices are lofty, so it helps to save some money on lodging. Many mountain homes include home-cooked meals in your room rate.
- **Students:** A visit with a family is a pleasant alternative to camping or the local "Y."
- **Visitors from abroad:** Cultural exchanges are often enhanced by a host who can speak your language.
- **Carless travelers:** If you plan to leave the auto at home, it's nice to know that many B&Bs are convenient to public transportation. Hosts will often arrange to meet your bus, plane, or train for a nominal fee.
- **Schoolteachers and retired persons:** Exploring out-of-the-way places is fun and will save you money.
- **History buffs:** Many B&Bs are located in areas important to our country's past. A number have the distinction of being listed on the National Register of Historic Places.
- **Sports fans:** Tickets to championship games are expensive. A stay at a B&B helps to defray the cost of attending out-of-town events.
- **Antique collectors:** Many hosts have lovely personal collections, and nearby towns are filled with undiscovered antique shops.
- **House hunters:** It's a practical way of trying out a neighborhood.
- **Relocating corporate executives:** It's more comfortable to stay in a real home while you look for a permanent residence. Hosts will often give more practical advice than professional realtors.
- **Relatives of hospitalized patients:** Many B&Bs are located near

major hospitals. Hosts will offer tea and sympathy when visiting
hours are over.
• **Convention and seminar attendees:** Staying at a nearby B&B is
less expensive than checking into a hotel.

And everyone else who has had it up to here with plastic motel
monotony!

What It Is Like to Be a Guest in a B&B

The B&B descriptions provided in this book will help you choose
the places that have the greatest appeal to you. A firsthand insight
into local culture awaits you; imagine the advantage of arriving in
New York City or San Francisco and having an insider to help you
sidestep the tourist traps and direct you to that special restaurant
or explore the countryside, where fresh air and
home-cooked meals beckon. Your choice is as wide as the U.S.A.

Each bed and breakfast listed offers personal contact, a real
advantage in unfamiliar environments. You may not have a phone
in your room or a TV on the dresser. You may even have to pad
down the hall in robe and slippers to take a shower, but you'll
discover that little things count.

• In Williamsburg, Virginia, a visitor from Germany opted to
stay at a B&B to help improve her conversational English.
When the hostess saw that she was having difficulty under-
standing directions, she personally escorted her on a tour of
Old Williamsburg.
• In Pennsylvania, the guests mistakenly arrived a week prior to
their stated reservation date and the B&B was full. The hostess
made a call to a neighbor who accommodated the couple. (By
the way, the neighbor has now become a B&B host!)
• In New York City, a guest was an Emmy Award nominee and
arrived with his tuxedo in need of pressing. The hostess
pressed it; when he claimed his award over nationwide TV, he
looked well groomed!

Expect the unexpected, such as a pot of brewed coffee upon
your arrival, or fresh flowers on a nightstand. At the very least,
count on our required standard of cleanliness and comfort. Al-

though we haven't personally visited all of the places listed, they have all been highly recommended by chambers of commerce or former guests. We have either spoken to or corresponded with all of the proprietors; they are a friendly group of people who enjoy having visitors. They will do all in their power to make your stay memorable.

Our goal is to enable the traveler to crisscross the country and stay only at B&Bs along the way. To achieve this, your help is vital. Please take a moment to write us of your experiences; we will follow up on every suggestion. Your comments will serve as the yardstick by which we can measure the quality of our accommodations. For your convenience, an evaluation form is included at the back of this book.

Cost of Accommodations

Bed and Breakfast, in the purest sense, is a private home, often referred to as a "homestay," where the owners rent their spare bedrooms to travelers. These are the backbone of this book.

However, American ingenuity has enhanced this simple idea to include more spectacular homes, mansions, small inns, and intimate hotels. With few exceptions, the proprietor is the host and lives on the premises.

There is a distinction between B&B homestays and B&B inns. Inns are generally defined as a business and depend upon revenue from guests to pay expenses. They usually have six or more guest rooms, and may have a restaurant that is open to the public. The tariff at inns is usually higher than at a homestay because the owners must pay the mortgage, running expenses, and staff, whether or not guests come.

Whether plain or fancy, all B&Bs are based on the concept that people are tired of the plastic monotony of motels and are disappointed that even the so-called budget motels can be quite expensive. Travelers crave the personal touch, and they sincerely enjoy "visiting" rather than just "staying."

Prices vary accordingly. There are places listed in this book where lovely lodging may be had for as low as $20 a night, and others that feature an overnight stay with a gourmet breakfast in a canopied bed for $85. Whatever the price, if you see the sign **○**, it means that the B&B has guaranteed its rates through 1993 to holders of this book, so be sure to mention it when you call or write! (If there is a change in ownership, the guarantee may not apply. Please notify us in writing if any host fails to honor the guaranteed rate.)

Accommodations vary in price depending upon the locale and the season. Peak season usually refers to the availability of skiing in winter and water sports in summer; in the Sunbelt states, winter months are usually the peak season. Some B&Bs require a two-night weekend minimum during peak periods, and three nights on holiday weekends. Off-season rate schedules are usually reduced. Resorts and major cities are generally more expensive than out-of-the-way places. However, B&Bs are always less expensive than hotels and motels of equivalent caliber in the same area. A weekly rate is usually less expensive than a daily rate. Special reductions are sometimes given to families (occupying two rooms) or senior citizens. Whenever reduced rates are available, you will find this noted in the individual listings.

Meals

Breakfast: *Continental* refers to fruit or juice, rolls, and a hot beverage. Many hosts pride themselves on home-baked breads, homemade preserves, as well as imported teas and cakes, so their Continental breakfast may be quite deluxe. Several hosts have regular jobs outside the home, so you may have to adjust your schedule to theirs. A "full" breakfast includes fruit, cereal and/or eggs, breakfast meats, breads, and a hot beverage. The table is set family-style and is often the highlight of a B&B's hospitality. Either a Continental breakfast or full breakfast is included in the room rate unless otherwise specified.

Other Meals: If listed as "available," you can be assured that the host takes pride in his or her cooking skills. The prices for lunch or dinner are usually reasonable but are not included in the quoted room rate unless clearly specified as "included."

Making Reservations

• Reservations are a MUST or you may risk missing out on the accommodations of your choice. Reserve *early* and confirm with a deposit equal to one night's stay. If you call to inquire about reservations, please remember the difference in time zones.

When dialing outside of your area, remember to dial the digit "1" before the area code.

- Many individual B&Bs now accept charge cards. This information is indicated in the listings by the symbols MC for Master-Card, AMEX for American Express, etc. A few have a surcharge for this service, so inquire as to the policy.
- Cash or traveler's checks are the accepted method of paying for your stay. Be sure to inquire whether or not tax is included in the rates quoted so that you will know exactly how much your lodging will cost.
- Rates are based on single or double occupancy of a room as quoted. Expect that an extra person(s) in the room will be charged a small additional fee. Inquire when making your reservation what the charge will be.
- If a listing indicates that children or pets are welcome, it is expected that they will be well behaved. All of our hosts take pride in their homes and it would be unfair to subject them to circumstances in which their possessions might be abused or the other houseguests disturbed by an unruly child or animal.
- Please note that many hosts have their own resident pets. If you are allergic or don't care to be around animals, inquire before making a reservation.
- In homes where smoking is permitted, do check to see if it is restricted in any of the rooms. Most hosts object to cigars.
- Where listings indicate that social drinking is permitted, it usually refers to your bringing your own beverages. Most hosts will provide ice; many will allow you to chill mixers in the refrigerator, and others offer complimentary wine and snacks. A few B&B inns have licenses to sell liquor. Any drinking should not be excessive.
- If Yes is indicated in the listings for airport/station pickup, it means that the host will meet your plane, bus, or train for a fee.
- Feel free to request brochures and local maps so that you can better plan for your visit.
- Do try to fit in with the host's house rules. You are on vacation; he or she isn't!
- A reservation form is included at the back of this book for your convenience; just tear it out and send it in to the B&B of your choice.

Cancellations

Cancellation policies vary from one B&B to another, so be sure to read the fine print on the reservation form. Many require a 15-day notice to refund the entire deposit, after which they will refund only if the room is rebooked. When a refund is due, most keep a processing fee and return the balance. A few keep the deposit and apply it to a future stay.

While these policies may seem harsh, please keep in mind that B&Bs are not hotels, which commonly overbook and where no-show guests can easily be replaced. Your host may have turned down a prospective guest, and may have bought special breakfast food in anticipation of your visit and should not be penalized. If you feel you've been unfairly treated in a cancellation situation, please do let us know.

B&B Reservation Services

There are many host families who prefer not to be individually listed in a book, and would rather have their houseguests referred by a coordinating agency. The organizations listed in this book are all members of the Tourist House Association. They all share our standards regarding the suitability of the host home as to cordiality, cleanliness, and comfort.

The majority do a marvelous job of matching host and guest according to age, interests, language, and any special requirements. To get the best match, it is practical to give them as much time as possible to find the host home best tailored to your needs.

Many have prepared descriptive pamphlets describing the homes on their rosters, the areas in which the homes are located, and information regarding special things to see and do. *Send a self-addressed, stamped, business-size envelope to receive a descriptive directory by return mail along with a reservation form for you to complete.* When returning the form, you will be asked to select the home or homes listed in the brochure that most appeal to you. (The homes are usually given a code number for reference.) The required deposit should accompany your reservation. Upon receipt, the coordinator will make the reservation and advise you of the name, address, telephone number, and travel instructions for your host.

A few agencies prepare a descriptive directory and *include* the host's name, address, and telephone number so that you can contact the host and make your arrangements directly. They charge anywhere from $2 to $11 for the directory.

Several agencies are *membership* organizations, charging guests an annual fee ranging from $5 to $25 per person. Their descriptive directories are free to members and a few of them maintain toll-free telephone numbers for reservations.

Most reservation services have a specific geographic focus. The coordinators are experts in the areas they represent. They can often make arrangements for car rentals, theater tickets, and touring suggestions, and offer information in planning a trip best suited to your interests.

Most work on a commission basis with the host, and that fee is included in the room rates quoted in each listing. Some make a surcharge for a one-night stay; others require a two- or three-night minimum stay for holiday periods or special events. Some will accept a credit card for the reservation, but the balance due must be paid to the host in cash or traveler's checks.

All of their host homes offer a Continental breakfast, and some may include a full breakfast.

Many reservation services in the larger cities have, in addition to the traditional B&Bs, a selection of apartments, condominiums, and houses *without hosts in residence*. This may be appealing to those travelers anticipating an extended stay in a particular area.

Statewide services are listed first in the section for each state. City or regionally based organizations are listed first under the heading for that area. For a complete description of their services, look them up under the city and state where they're based.

NOTE: When calling, do so during normal business hours (for that time zone), unless otherwise stated. Collect calls are not accepted.

2

How to Start Your Own B&B

What It's Like to Be a Host

Hosts are people who like the idea of accommodating travelers and sharing their home and the special features of their area with them. They are people who have houses too large for their personal needs and like the idea of supplementing their income by having people visit. For many, it's a marvelous way of meeting rising utility and maintenance costs. For young families, it is a way of buying and keeping that otherwise-too-large house, as well as a way of furnishing it, since many of the furnishings may be tax deductible. Another advantage is that many state and local governments have recognized the service that some host families perform. In browsing through this book you will note that some homes are listed on the National Historic Register. Some state governments allow owners of landmark and historical houses a special tax advantage if they are used for any business purpose. Check with the Historical Preservation Society in your state for details.

If you have bedrooms to spare, if you sincerely like having overnight guests, if your home is clean and comfortable, this is an opportunity to consider. It is a unique business because *you* set the time of the visit and the length of stay. (Guest houses are not boarding homes.) You invite the guests at *your* convenience, and the extras, such as meals, are entirely up to you. You can provide a cup of coffee, complete meals, or just a room and shared bath. Remember that your income may be erratic and should not be depended upon to pay for monthly bills. However, it can afford you some luxuries.

Although the majority of hosts are women, many couples are finding pleasure in this joint venture. The general profile of a typical host is a friendly, outgoing, flexible person who is proud of his or her home and hometown. The following information and suggestions represent a guideline to consider in deciding whether becoming a B&B host is really for you.

There are no set rules for the location, type, or style of a B&B. Apartments, condos, farmhouses, town houses, beach houses, vacation cottages, houseboats, mansions, as well as the traditional one-family dwelling are all appropriate. The important thing is for the host to be on the premises. The setting may be urban, rural, or suburban, near public transportation or in the hinterlands. Location is only important if you want to have guests every night. Areas where tourism is popular, such as resort areas or major cities, are often busier than out-of-the-way places. However, if a steady stream of visitors is not that important or even desirable, it doesn't matter where you are. People will contact you if your rates are reasonable and if there is something to see and do in your area, or if it is near a major transportation route.

Setting Rates

Consider carefully four key factors in setting your rates: location, private versus shared bath, type of breakfast, and your home itself.

Location: If you reside in a traditional resort or well-touristed area, near a major university or medical center, or in an urban hub or gateway city, your rates should be at least 40% lower than those of the area's major motels or hotels. If you live in an out-of-the-way location, your rates must be extremely reasonable. If your area has a "season"—snow sports in winter, water sports in summer—offer off-season rates when these attractions are not available. Reading through this book will help you to see what is the going rate in a situation similar to yours.

The Bath: You are entitled to charge more for a room with private bath. If the occupants of two rooms share one bath, the rate should be less. If more than five people must share one bathroom, you may have complaints, unless your rates are truly inexpensive.

The Breakfast: Figure the approximate cost of your ingredients, plus something for your time. Allow about $1 to $2 for a Continental breakfast, $2 to $3 for a full American breakfast, and then *include* it in the rate.

Your Home: Plan on charging a fair and reasonable rate for a typical B&B home, one that is warm and inviting, clean and comfortable. If your home is exceptionally luxurious, with king-size beds, Jacuzzi baths, tennis courts, or hot tubs, you will find guests who are willing to pay a premium. If your home is over 75 years old, well restored, with lots of antiques, you may also be able to charge a higher rate.

The Three Bs—Bed, Breakfast, and Bath

The Bedroom: The ideal situation for a prospective host is the possession of a house too large for current needs. The children may be away at college most of the year or may have left permanently, leaving behind their bedrooms and, in some cases, an extra bath. Refurbishing these rooms does not mean refurnishing; an extraordinary investment need not be contemplated for receiving guests. Take a long, hard look at the room. With a little imagination and a little monetary outlay, could it be changed into a bedroom *you'd* be pleased to spend the night in? Check it out *before* you go any further. Are the beds comfortable? Is the carpet clean? Are the walls attractive? Do the curtains or shades need attention? Are there sturdy hangers in the closet? Would emptying the closet and bureau be an impossible task? Is there a good light to read by? A writing table and comfortable chair? Peek under the bed to see if there are dust balls or old magazines tucked away. While relatives and friends would "understand" if things weren't perfect, a paying guest is entitled to cleanliness and comfort.

Equip the guest bureau or dresser with a good mirror, and provide a comfortable chair and good reading light. The clothes closet should be free from your family's clothing and storage items, and stocked with firm, plastic hangers, a few skirt hangers, and some hooks. Sachet hung on the rod will chase musty odors. Provide room darkening shades or blinds on the windows. And, if your house is located on a busy street, it is wise to have your guest bedrooms in the rear. Paying guests are entitled to a good night's rest! If your tap water is not tasty, it is thoughtful to supply bottled water.

If the idea of sprucing up the room has you overwhelmed, forget the idea and continue to be a guest rather than a host! If, however, a little "spit and polish," replacement of lumpy mattresses, sagging springs, and freshening the room in general presents no problem, continue!

Mattresses should be firm, covered with a mattress pad, attractive linens, and bedspread. Although seconds are OK, good-quality linens are a wise investment, since cheap sheets tend to pill. Offer a selection of pillows of various firmnesses—a choice of down or fiberfill is the ultimate in consideration! Twin beds are often preferred, since many people do not wish to share a bed. Sofa beds are really not comfortable and should be avoided. Is there a bedside lamp and night table on each side of the bed? Bulbs should be at least 75 watts for comfortable reading. A luggage rack is convenient for guests and keeps the bedspread clean. Provide a varied assortment of books, current magazines in a rack, a local newspaper, and some information on what's doing in your town along with a map. If yours is a shared-bath accommodation, do provide a well-lit mirror and convenient electric outlet for makeup and shaving purposes. It will take the pressure off the bathroom! A fresh thermos of ice water and drinking glasses placed on an attractive dresser tray is always appreciated. Put it in the room while the guest is out to dinner, right next to the dish of hard candy or fruit. A fancy candlestick is a pretty accessory and a useful object in case of a power failure. Dresser drawers should be clean and lined with fresh paper. A sachet, flashlight, and a pad and pencil are thoughtful touches. For safety's sake, prohibit smoking in the bedroom. Besides, the odor of tobacco clings forever. Always spray the bedroom with air freshener a few minutes before the guest arrives. On warm or humid days, turn on the air conditioner as well.

From time to time sleep in each guest room yourself. It's the best test.

The Breakfast: Breakfast time can be the most pleasant part of a guest's stay. It is at the breakfast table with you and the other guests that suggestions are made as to what to see and do, and exchanges of experiences are enjoyed. From a guest's point of view, the only expected offering is what is known as a Continental breakfast, which usually consists of juice, roll, and coffee or tea.

Breakfast fare is entirely up to you. If you are a morning person who whips out of bed at the crack of dawn with special recipes for muffins dancing in your head, muffins to be drenched with your homemade preserves followed by eggs Benedict, an assortment of imported coffees or exotic teas—hop to it! You will play to a most appreciative audience. If, however, morning represents an awful intrusion on sleep, and the idea of talking to anyone before noon is difficult, the least you should do is to prepare the breakfast table the night before with the necessary mugs, plates, and silverware. Fill the electric coffeepot and leave instructions that the first one up should plug it in; you can even hook it up to a timer so that it will brew automatically!

Most of us fall somewhere in between these two extremes. Remember that any breakfast at "home" is preferable to getting dressed, getting into a car, and driving to some coffee shop. Whether you decide upon a Continental breakfast or a full American breakfast, consisting of juice or fruit, cereal or eggs, possibly bacon or sausage, toast, rolls, and coffee or tea, is up to you. It is most important that whatever the fare, it be included in your room rate. It is most awkward, especially after getting to know and like your guests, to present an additional charge for breakfast.

With so many of us watching calories, caffeine, and cholesterol, be prepared to offer unsweetened and/or whole grain breads, oat-bran cereals and muffins, and brewed decaf coffee or tea. It is also thoughtful to inquire about your guests' dietary restrictions and allergies. Whatever you serve, do have your table attractively set.

Some Suggestions

- Don't have a messy kitchen. If you have pets, make sure their food dishes are removed after they've eaten. If you have cats, make sure they don't walk along the countertops, and be certain that litter boxes are cleaned without fail. Sparkling clean surroundings are far more important than the decor.
- Let guests know when breakfast will be served. Check to see if they have any allergies, diet restrictions, or dislikes. Vary the menu if guests are staying more than one night.
- Do offer one nonsweet bread for breakfast.
- Consider leaving a breakfast order sheet in each room with a request that it be returned before guests retire. It might read:

We serve breakfast between 7 AM and 10 AM. Please check your preference and note the time at which you plan to eat.

☐ Coffee ☐ Tea ☐ Decaf ☐ Milk ☐ Toast ☐ Muffins
☐ Sweet Rolls ☐ Orange Juice ☐ Tomato Juice ☐ Fruit Cup

The Bath: This really is the third B in B&B. If you are blessed with an extra bathroom for the exclusive use of a guest, that's super. If guests will have to share the facilities with others, that really presents no problem. If it's being shared with your family, the family must always be "last in line." Be sure that they are aware of the guest's importance; the guest, paying or otherwise, always comes first. No retainers, used Band-Aids, or topless toothpaste tubes are to be carelessly left on the sink. The tub, shower, floor, and toilet bowl are to be squeaky clean. The mirrors and chrome should sparkle, and a supply of toilet tissue, fresh soap, and unfrayed towels goes a long way in reflecting a high standard of cleanliness. Make sure that the grout between tiles is free of mildew and that the shower curtain is unstained; add nonskid tape to the tub. Cracked ceilings should be repaired. Paint should be free of chips, and if your bath is wallpapered, make certain no loose edges mar its beauty.

Although it is your responsibility to check out the bath at least twice a day, most guests realize that in a share-the-bath situation they should leave the room ready for the next person's use. It is a thoughtful reminder for you to leave tub cleanser, a cleaning towel or sponge, and bathroom deodorant handy for this purpose. A wastepaper basket, paper towels, and paper cups should be part of your supplies. Needless to say, your hot water and septic systems should be able to accommodate the number of guests you'll have without being overtaxed. Call the plumber to fix any clogged drains or dripping faucets. Make sure that there are enough towel bars and hooks to accommodate the towels of all guests. Extra bathroom touches:

• Use liquid soap dispensers in lieu of bar soap on the sink.
• Provide a place for guests' personal toilet articles; shelves add convenience and eliminate clutter.
• Give different colored towels to each guest.
• Supply each guest room with its own bath soap in a covered soap dish.

• Provide guests with one-size-fits-all terry robes.

The B&B Business

Money Matters: Before embarking upon any business, it's a good idea to discuss it with an accountant and possibly an attorney. Since you'll be using your home for a business enterprise there are things with which they are familiar that are important for you to know. For instance, you may want to incorporate, so find out what the pros and cons are. Ask about depreciation. Deductible business expenses may include refurbishing, furnishings, supplies, printing costs, postage, etc. An accountant will be able to guide you with a simple system of record keeping. Accurate records will help you analyze income and expense, and show if you are breaking even or operating at a profit or a loss.

Taxes: Contact your state department of taxation requesting specific written information regarding tax collection and payment schedules. Get a sales tax number from your county clerk. If you rent rooms less than 15 days a year, you need not report the B&B income on your federal return. Income after the fourteenth day is taxable, and you can take deductions and depreciation allowances against it. If the revenues from running the B&B are insignificant, you can call it "hobby income" and avoid taxes. However, you can't qualify as a business and may lose other tax advantages.

Record Keeping: Open a B&B checking account and use it to pay expenses and to deposit all income, including sales tax associated with the B&B. Write checks whenever possible for purchases; get dated receipts when you can. Estimate the cost of serving breakfast and multiply it by the number of guests you feed annually; keep track of extra expenses for household supplies and utilities.

The Case for Credit Cards: Many guests prefer to stay now and pay later; business travelers like the easy record keeping for their expense sheets. Even if you don't wish to accept them on a regular basis, credit cards give you the opportunity to take a deposit over the phone when there isn't time to receive one by mail. The cost is negligible, generally 4%.

If you do accept a last-minute reservation without a credit card number to guarantee it, make certain the caller understands that if they don't show up, and you have held the room for them, you will have lost a night's rent. You may also remind the caller that if they aren't there by a mutually agreed upon time, you may rent the room to someone else. Needless to say, it is equally important for you to remain at home to receive the guests or to be on hand for a phone call should they get lost en route to your home.

Insurance: It is important to call your insurance broker. Some homeowner policies have a clause covering "an occasional overnight paying guest." See if you will be protected under your existing coverage and, if not, what the additional premium would be. As a member of the THAA, you may participate in our group liability policy under the auspices of Brown, Schuck, Townshend, and Associates.

Every home should be equipped with smoke detectors and fire extinguishers. All fire hazards should be eliminated; stairways and halls should be well lit and kept free of clutter. If you haven't already done so, immediately post prominently the emergency numbers for the fire department, police, and ambulance service.

Safety Reminders: Equip guest bedrooms and bathrooms with nightlights. Keep a flashlight (in working order!) in each bedroom, in case of power failure. Bathrooms should have nonslip surfaces in the tub and shower, and handholds should be installed in bathtubs. Keep a well-stocked first aid kit handy and know how to use it. Learn the Heimlich Maneuver and CPR (cardiopulmonary resuscitation). Periodically test smoke detectors and fire extinguishers to make certain they are in working order.

Regulations: If you have read this far and are still excited about the concept of running a B&B, there are several steps to take at this point. As of this writing, there don't seem to be any specific laws governing B&Bs. Since guests are generally received on an irregular basis, B&Bs do not come under the same laws governing hotels and motels. And since B&Bs aren't inns where emphasis is on food rather than on lodging, no comparison can really be made in that regard either. As the idea grows, laws and regulations will probably be passed. Refer to the back of *Bed & Breakfast U.S.A.* to write to your state's office of tourism for information. The address and phone number are listed for your convenience. You might even call or write to a few B&Bs in your state and ask the host about his or her experience in this regard. Most hosts will be happy to give you the benefit of their experience, but keep in mind that they are busy people and it would be wise to limit your intrusion upon their time.

If you live in a traditional, residential area and you are the first in your neighborhood to consider operating a B&B, it would be prudent to examine closely the character of houses nearby. Do physicians, attorneys, accountants, or psychologists maintain offices in their residences? Do dressmakers, photographers, cosmeticians, or architects receive clients in their homes? These professions are legally accepted in the most prestigious communities as "customary house occupations." Bed and breakfast has been tested in many communities where the question was actually brought to court. In towns from La Jolla, California, to Croton-on-Hudson, New York, bed and breakfast has been approved and accepted.

Zoning boards are not always aware of the wide acceptance of the B&B concept. Possibly the best evidence that you could present to them is a copy of *Bed & Breakfast U.S.A.*, which indicates that it is an accepted practice throughout the entire country. It illustrates the caliber of the neighborhoods, the beauty of the homes, and the fact that many professionals are also hosts. Reassure the zoning board that you will accept guests only by advance reservation. You will not display any exterior signs to attract attention to your home. You will keep your home and grounds properly maintained, attractive, and in no way detract from the integrity of your neighborhood. You will direct guests to proper parking facilities and do nothing to intrude upon the privacy of your neighbors.

After all, there is little difference between the visit of a family friend and a B&B guest, because that is the spirit and essence of a B&B. Just as a friend would make prior arrangements to be a houseguest, so will a B&B guest make a reservation in advance. Neither would just drop in for an overnight stay. We are happy to share letters from hosts attesting to the high caliber, honesty, and integrity of B&B guests that come as a result of reading about their accommodations in this book. There are over 12,000 B&Bs extending our kind of hospitality throughout the United States, and the number is increasing geometrically every day.

You should also bring along a copy of *Bed & Breakfast U.S.A.* when you go to visit the local chamber of commerce. Most of them are enthusiastic, because additional visitors mean extra business for local restaurants, shops, theaters, and businesses. This is a good time to inquire what it would cost to join the chamber of commerce.

The Name: The naming of your B&B is most important and will take some time and consideration because this is the moment when dreams become reality. It will be used on your brochures, stationery, and bills. (If you decide to incorporate, the corporation needs a name!) It should somehow be descriptive of the atmosphere you wish to convey.

Brochure: Once you have given a name to your house, design a brochure. The best ones include a reservation form and can be mailed to your prospective guests. The brochure should contain the name of your B&B, address, phone number, best time to call, your name, a brief description of your home, its ambience, a brief history of the house if it is old, the number of guest rooms, whether or not baths are shared, the type of breakfast served, rates, required deposit, minimum stay requirement if any, dates when you'll be closed, and your cancellation policy. Although widely used, the phrase "Rates subject to change without notice" should be avoided. Rather, state the specific dates when the rates will be valid. A deposit of one night's stay is acceptable, and the promise of a full refund if cancellation is received at least two weeks prior to arrival is typical. If you have reduced rates for a specific length of stay, for families, for senior citizens, etc., mention it.

The Rate Sheet should be a separate insert so that if rates change, the entire brochure need not be discarded. Mention your smoking policy. If you do allow smoking inside the house, do you reserve any bedrooms for nonsmokers? Don't forget to mention the ages of your children, and describe any pets in residence. If you don't accept a guest's pet, be prepared to supply the name, address, and phone number of a reliable local kennel.

If you can converse in a foreign language, say so, because many visitors from abroad seek out B&Bs; it's a marvelous plus to be able to chat in their native tongue. Include your policy regarding children, pets, or smokers, and whether you offer the convenience of a guest refrigerator or barbecue. It is helpful to include directions from a major route and a simple map for finding your home. It's a good idea to include a line or two about yourself and your interests, and do mention what there is to see and do in the area as well as proximity to any major university. A line drawing of your house is a good investment since the picture can be used not only on the brochure but on your stationery, postcards, and greeting cards as well. If you can't have this taken care of locally, write the Tourist House Association. We have a service that can handle it for you.

Take your ideas to a reliable printer for his professional guidance. Don't forget to keep the receipt for the printing bill since this is a business expense.

Confirmation Letter: Upon receipt of a paid reservation, do send out a letter confirming it. You can design a form letter and have it offset printed by a printer, since the cost of doing so is usually nominal. Include the dates of the stay; number of people expected; the rate, including tax; the cancellation policy; as well as explicit directions by car and, if applicable, by public transportation. A simple map reflecting the exact location of your home in relation to major streets and highways is most useful. It is a good idea to ask your guests to call you if they will be traveling and unavailable by phone for the week prior to their expected arrival. You might even want to include any of the house rules regarding smoking, pets, or whatever.

Successful Hosting

The Advantage of Hosting: The nicest part of being a B&B host is that you aren't required to take guests every day of the year. Should there be times when having guests would not be convenient, you can always say you're full and try to arrange an alternate date. But most important, keep whatever date you reserve. It is an excellent idea at the time reservations are accepted to ask for the name and telephone number of an emergency contact should you have to cancel unexpectedly. However, *never* have a guest come to a locked door. If an emergency arises and you cannot reach your prospective guests in time, do make arrangements for someone to greet them, and make alternate arrangements so that they can be accommodated.

House Rules: While you're in the thinking stage, give some thought to the rules you'd like your guests to adhere to. The last thing you want for you or your family is to feel uncomfortable in your own home. Make a list of House Rules concerning arrival and departure during the guests' stay, and specify when breakfast is served. If you don't want guests coming home too late, say so. Most hosts like to lock up at a certain hour at night, so arrange for an extra key for night owls. If that makes you uncomfortable, have a curfew on your House Rules list. If smoking disturbs you, confine the area where it's permitted.

Some guests bring a bottle of their favorite beverage and enjoy a drink before going out to dinner. Many hosts enjoy a cocktail hour too, and often provide cheese and crackers to share with guests. B&Bs cannot sell drinks to guests since this would require licensing. If you'd rather no drinks be consumed in your home, say so.

Many hosts don't mind accommodating a well-behaved pet. If you don't mind, or have pets of your own, discuss this with your guests before they pack Fido's suitcase. Your House Rules can even be included in your brochure. That way, both host and guest are aware of each other's likes and dislikes, and no hard feelings are made.

Entertaining: One of the most appealing features of being a guest at a B&B is the opportunity to visit in the evening with the hosts. After a day of sightseeing or business, it is most relaxing and pleasant to sit around the living room and chat. For many hosts, this is the most enjoyable part of having guests. However, if you are accommodating several people on a daily basis, entertaining can be tiring. Don't feel you'll be offending anyone by excusing yourself to attend to your own family or personal needs. The situation can be easily handled by having a room to which you can retreat, and offering your guests the living room, den, or other area for games, books, magazines, and perhaps the use of a television or bridge table. Most guests enjoy just talking to one another since this is the main idea of staying at a B&B.

The Telephone: This is a most important link between you and your prospective guests. As soon as possible, have your telephone number included under your B&B name in the white pages. It is a good idea to be listed in the appropriate section in your telephone directory yellow pages. If your home phone is used for a lot of personal calls, ask the local telephone company about call-waiting service, or think about installing a separate line for your B&B. If you are out a lot, give some thought to using a telephone answering device to explain your absence and time of return, and record the caller's message. There is nothing more frustrating to a prospective guest than to call and get a constant busy signal, or no answer at all. Request that the caller leave his or her name and address so that you can mail a reservation form. This will help eliminate the necessity of having to return long-distance calls. If the caller wants further information, he or she will call again at the time you said you'd be home.

B&B guests don't expect a phone in the guest room. However, there are times when they might want to use your phone for a long-distance call. In your House Rules list, suggest that any such calls be charged to their home telephone. Business travelers often have telephone charge cards for this purpose. In either case, you should keep a telephone record book and timer near your instrument. Ask the caller to enter the city called, telephone number, and length of call. Thus, you will have an accurate record should a charge be inadvertently added to your bill. Or, if you wish, you can add telephone charges to the guest bill. A telephone operator will quote the cost of the per-minute charge throughout the country for this purpose.

Maid Service: If you have several guest rooms and bathrooms, you may find yourself being a chambermaid as part of the business. Naturally, each guest gets fresh linens upon arrival. If a guest stays up to three days, it isn't expected that bed linen be changed every day. What is expected is that the room be freshened and the bath be cleaned and towels replaced every day. If you don't employ a full-time maid you may want to investigate the possibility of hiring a high school student on a part-time basis to give you a hand with the housekeeping. Many guests, noticing the absence of help, will voluntarily lend a hand, although they have the right to expect some degree of service, particularly if they are paying a premium rate.

Keys: A great many hosts are not constantly home during the day. Some do "hosting" on a part-time basis, while involved with regular jobs. There are times when even full-time hosts have to be away during the day. If guests are to have access to the house while you are not on the premises, make extra keys and attach them to an oversize key chain. It is also wise to take a key deposit of $50 simply to assure return of the key. Let me add that in the 16 years of my personal experience, as well as in the opinions of other hosts, B&B guests are the most honest people you can have. No one has ever had even a washcloth stolen, let alone the family treasures. In fact, it isn't unusual for the guest to leave a small gift after a particularly pleasant visit. On the other hand, guests are sometimes forgetful and leave belongings behind. For this reason it is important for you to have their names and addresses so that you can return their possessions. They will expect to reimburse you for the postage.

Registering Guests: You should keep a regular registration ledger for the guest to complete before checking in. The information should include the full name of each guest, home address, phone number, business address and telephone, and auto license number. It's a good idea to include the name and phone number of a friend or relative in case of an emergency. This information will serve you well for other contingencies, such as the guest leaving some important article behind, an unpaid long-distance phone call, or the rare instance of an unpaid bill. You may prefer to have this information on your guest bill, which should be designed as a two-part carbon form. You will then have a record and the guest has a ready receipt. (Receipts are very important to business travelers!)

Settling the Bill: The average stay in a B&B is two nights. A deposit equal to one night's lodging is the norm; when to collect the balance is up to you. Most guests pay upon leaving, but if they leave so early that the settling of the bill at that time is inconvenient, you can request the payment the previous night. You might want to consider the convenience of accepting a major credit card, but contact the sponsoring company first to see what percentage of your gross is expected for this service. If you find yourself entertaining more business visitors than vacationers, it might be something you should offer. Most travelers are aware that cash or traveler's checks are the accepted modes of payment. Accepting a personal check is rarely risky, but again, it's up to you. You might include your preference in your brochure.

Other Meals: B&B means that only breakfast is served. If you enjoy cooking and would like to offer other meals for a fee, make sure that you investigate the applicable health laws. If you have to install a commercial kitchen, the idea might be too expensive for current consideration. However, allowing guests to store fixings for a quick snack or to use your barbecue can be a very attractive feature for families traveling with children or for people watching their budget. If you can offer this convenience, be sure to mention it in your brochure. (And be sure to add a line to your House Rules that the guest is expected to clean up.) Some hosts keep an extra guest refrigerator on hand for this purpose.

It's an excellent idea to keep menus from your local restaurants on hand. Try to have a good sampling, ranging from moderately priced to expensive dining spots, and find out if reservations are required. Your guests will always rely heavily upon your advice and suggestions. After all, when it comes to your town, you're the authority! It's also a nice idea to keep informed of local happenings that might be of interest to your visitors. A special concert at the university or a local fair or church supper can add an extra dimension to their visit. If parents are visiting with young children they might want to have dinner out without them; try to have a list of available baby-sitters. A selection of guidebooks covering your area is also a nice feature.

The Guest Book: These are available in most stationery and department stores, and it is important that you buy one. It should contain designated space for the date, the name of the guest, home address, and a blank area for the guest's comments. They generally sign the guest book before checking out. The guest book is first of all a permanent record of who came and went. It will give you an idea of what times during the year you were busiest and which times were slow. Second, it is an easy way to keep a mailing list for your Christmas cards and future promotional mailings. You will also find that thumbing through it in years to come will recall some very pleasant people who were once strangers but now are friends.

Advertising: Periodically distribute your brochures to the local university, college, and hospital, since out-of-town visitors always need a place to stay. Let your local caterers know of your existence since wedding guests are often from out of town. If you have a major corporation in your area, drop off a brochure at the personnel office. Even visiting or relocating executives and salespeople enjoy B&Bs. Hotels and motels are sometimes overbooked; it wouldn't hurt to leave your brochure with the manager for times when there's no room for their last-minute guests. Local residents sometimes have to put up extra guests, so it's a good idea to take an ad out in your local school or church newspaper. The cost is usually minimal. Repeat this distribution process from time to time so that you can replenish the supply of brochures.

Check the back of this book for the address of your state tourist office. Write to them, requesting inclusion in any brochures listing B&Bs in the state.

The best advertising is being a member of the Tourist House Association since all member B&Bs are fully described in this book, which is available in bookstores, libraries, and B&Bs throughout the United States and Canada. In addition, it is natural for THAA members to recommend one another when guests inquire about similar accommodations in other areas. The most important reason for keeping your B&B clean, comfortable, and cordial is that we are all judged by what a guest experiences in any individual Tourist House Association home. The best publicity will come from your satisfied guests, who will recommend your B&B to their friends.

Additional Suggestions

Extra Earnings: You might want to consider a few ideas for earning extra money in connection with being a host. If guests consistently praise your muffins and preserves, you might sell attractively wrapped extras as take-home gifts. If you enjoy touring, you can plan and conduct a special outing, off the beaten tourist track, for a modest fee. In major cities, you can do such things as acquiring tickets for theater, concert, or sports events. A supply of *Bed & Breakfast U.S.A.* for sale to guests is both a source of income and gives every THAA member direct exposure to the B&B market. Think about offering the use of your washer and dryer. You may, if you wish, charge a modest fee to cover the service. Guests who have been traveling are thrilled to do their wash or have it done for them "at home" rather than wasting a couple of hours at the laundromat.

Several hosts tell me that a small gift shop is often a natural offshoot of a B&B. Items for sale might include handmade quilts, pillows, potholders, and knitted items. One host has turned his hobby of woodworking into extra income. He makes lovely picture frames, napkin rings, and footstools that many guests buy as souvenirs to take home. If you plan to do this, check with the Small Business Administration to inquire about such things as a resale license and tax collection; a chamber of commerce can advise in this regard.

Transportation: While the majority of B&B guests arrive by car, there are many who rely on public transportation. Some hosts, for a modest fee, are willing to meet arriving guests at airports, train depots, or bus stations. Do be knowledgeable about local transportation schedules in your area, and be prepared to give explicit directions for your visitors' comings and goings. Have phone numbers handy for taxi service, as well as information on car rentals.

Thoughtful Touches: Guests often write to tell us of their experiences at B&Bs as a result of learning about them through this book. These are some of the special touches that made their visit special: fresh flowers in the guest room; even a single flower in a bud vase is pretty. One hostess puts a foil-wrapped piece of candy on the pillow before the guest returns from dinner. A small decanter of wine and glasses, or a few pieces of fresh fruit in a pretty bowl on the dresser are lovely surprises. A small sewing kit in the bureau is handy. Offer guests the use of your iron and ironing board, rather than having them attempt to use the bed or dresser. Writing paper and envelopes in the desk invite the guest to send a quick note to the folks at home. If your house sketch is printed on it, it is marvelous free publicity. A pre-bed cup of tea for adults and cookies and milk for children are always appreciated.

By the way, keep a supply of guest-comment cards in the desk, both to attract compliments as well as to bring to your attention the flaws in your B&B that should be corrected.

Join the Tourist House Association: If you are convinced that you want to be a host, and have thoroughly discussed the pros and cons with your family and advisers, complete and return the membership application found at the back of this book. Our dues are $35 annually. The description of your B&B will be part of the next edition of *Bed & Breakfast U.S.A.*, as well as in the interim supplement between printings. Paid-up members receive a complimentary copy of *Bed & Breakfast U.S.A.* You will also receive the THAA's newsletter; regional seminars and conferences are held occasionally and you might enjoy attending. And, as an association, we will have clout should the time come when B&B becomes a recognized industry.

Affiliating with a B&B Reservation Agency: There are 111 agencies listed in *Bed & Breakfast U.S.A.* If you do not care to advertise your house directly to the public, consider joining one in your area. Membership and reservation fees, as well as the degree of professionalism, vary widely from agency to agency, so do check carefully.

Prediction of Success: Success should not be equated with money alone. If you thoroughly enjoy people, are well organized, enjoy sharing your tidy home without exhausting yourself, then the idea of receiving compensation for the use of an otherwise dormant bedroom will be a big plus. Your visitors will seek relaxing, wholesome surroundings, and unpretentious hosts who open their hearts as well as their homes. Being a B&B host or guest is an exciting, enriching experience.

3

B&B Recipes

The recipes that follow are B&B host originals. They've been chosen because of the raves they've received from satisfied B&B guests. The most important ingredient is the heartful of love that goes into each one.

We always have a good response to our request for favorite breakfast recipes. Although we could not publish them all this time, we will use most of them in future editions.

Mary Ellen's Breakfast Cookies

⅔ c. margarine
⅔ c. sugar
1 egg
1 tsp. vanilla
¾ c. flour
½ tsp. baking soda

½ tsp. salt
1¼ c. Quaker Oats
1 c. Cheddar cheese (4 oz.)
½ c. wheat germ
6–8 cooked bacon slices, crumbled

Beat margarine, sugar, egg, and vanilla together until well blended. Add flour, baking soda, and salt, mixing well. Stir in oats, cheese, wheat germ, and bacon. Drop by rounded tablespoonful onto greased cookie sheet. Bake in preheated 350°F oven for 12 to 14 minutes or until edges are golden brown. Cool one minute on a cookie sheet. Makes 3 dozen cookies.

Maricopa Manor, Phoenix, Arizona

Apple Tree Bed & Breakfast Blue Corn Waffles

¾ c. all-purpose flour
¾ c. blue corn flour (see *note*)
2 tsp. baking powder
½ tsp. baking soda

3 eggs, separated
¾ c. milk
¾ c. vanilla yogurt
½ c. vegetable oil

Mix together flours, baking powder, and baking soda. Combine egg yolks, milk, yogurt, and oil. Mix with the flour mixture until

smooth. Beat the egg whites until stiff peaks form and fold into
the batter. Cook waffles according to the directions of your waffle
iron. Serve with your favorite topping. Yield depends on size and
type of waffle iron.
Note: In New Mexico we can buy blue corn flour in any grocery
store. Out-of-state residents should try any Mexican specialty
store or health food store. If you cannot find it, write to us and we
will gladly send you a list of mail-order sources.

Apple Tree Bed & Breakfast, Cedar Crest, New Mexico

Banana Bread

½ c. margarine
1 c. sugar
3 very ripe bananas, mashed
3 eggs

2 c. flour
1 tsp. baking soda
½ c. chopped walnuts

Mix ingredients in listed order and bake in a greased and floured
pan for about 1 hour at 350°F. Makes 1 loaf or one 8-inch square
pan.

La Casita Guesthouse, Dixon, New Mexico

Joan's Orange-Walnut Muffins

2 large oranges
2 eggs
½ c. sugar
½ c. oil
2 c. flour

2 tsp. baking powder
½ tsp. baking soda
½ tsp. salt
½ c. chopped walnuts

Peel oranges and remove any seeds and as much white membrane
as possible. Chop fine or use a food processor. Set aside. In a
large bowl, slightly whisk the eggs. Add the sugar and oil and stir
to combine. In another bowl, combine the flour, baking powder,
baking soda, and salt. Add the oranges and the flour mixture to
the eggs and stir. Stir in the walnuts. Pour the batter into lightly
greased and floured muffin tins, filling just past the halfway
point. Bake at 350°F for about 15 to 20 minutes. Makes 12 muffins.

The Westchester House B&B, Saratoga Springs, New York

Orange Nut Bread

1 egg
1 c. orange juice
Grated rind of 1 orange
2 tbsp. melted margarine
1 tsp. vanilla
2 c. flour

1 c. sugar
1 tsp. baking soda
1 tsp. baking powder
¼ tsp. salt
1 c. walnuts or pecans
1 c. white raisins

With electric mixer beat egg well. Add and mix orange juice, orange rind, melted margarine, and vanilla. Sift flour and add all dry ingredients to above and mix. Add nuts and white raisins by hand. Bake in generously greased 9 × 5 × 2½-inch loaf pan at 350°F for 50 minutes, or until toothpick in center comes out clean. Cool in pan. Makes 1 loaf. Recipe doubles well.
Variations: Instead of raisins, add 1 c. dried apricots, cut into pieces, or 1 c. ground fresh cranberries. (With cranberries, grease and flour pan.)

Peaceful Hill Bed & Breakfast, Austin, Texas

Simon's Scones

3 c. flour (unbleached white or
    whole-wheat pastry)
⅓ c. sugar
½ tsp. baking soda

2½ tsp. baking powder
¾ c. cold butter
1 c. buttermilk
Cinnamon sugar (see *note*)

In a mixing bowl, stir together flour, sugar, baking soda, and baking powder. Add the cold butter to the flour mixture and cut in with two forks or with fingers until the mixture is about the texture of coarse cornmeal. Make a well in the center of the mixture and add the buttermilk. Stir with a fork until the mixture leaves the sides of the bowl. Add more buttermilk (about 1 tablespoon) if necessary to bind the mixture. Divide the dough into two equal portions. Shape each into a ¾-inch-high round on a greased cookie sheet. The two rounds will fit on one sheet. Score each round into 6 or 8 wedges with a knife, cutting almost to the bottom of the dough. Brush the tops of the dough with a little milk or cream, then sprinkle with cinnamon sugar until lightly covered. Bake the rounds in the oven at 375°F for 30 minutes or until golden brown. Serve warm with butter, jam, or lemon curd.

Note: To make cinnamon sugar, mix about 4 tablespoons of cinnamon into each cup of sugar. Keep this mixture in a shaker that has fine holes so that you can shake it onto the bread quickly and easily.

Old Thyme Inn, Half Moon Bay, California

Carrot-Date-Nut Muffins

3 c. flour
1 c. old-fashioned oats, uncooked
1 c. packed brown sugar
2 tbsp. baking powder
2 tsp. salt
½ c. milk

4 eggs, slightly beaten
1 c. oil
2 c. shredded carrots
1 c. chopped walnuts
1 c. chopped dates

In a large bowl, mix the flour, oats, brown sugar, baking powder, and salt. In another bowl, mix the milk, eggs, and oil. Add the wet ingredients to the dry and mix well. Blend in the carrots, walnuts, and dates. Lightly grease muffin tins and fill cups just past the halfway point and bake for 20 minutes at 400°F. Makes 18 muffins.

The Captain Ezra Nye House, Sandwich, Massachusetts

Applesauce Pancakes with Apple Cider Sauce

1 egg
1 c. flour, sifted
½ c. milk
½ c. applesauce (preferably homemade)

½ tsp. salt
3 tsp. baking powder
2 tbsp. melted butter

Combine all the ingredients, then cook on a griddle. Serve with Apple Cider Sauce. Makes 8 pancakes.

Apple Cider Sauce

1 c. pure apple cider
¼ to ½ c. sugar
1 tbsp. cornstarch

½ tsp. cinnamon
1 tbsp. fresh lemon juice
2 tbsp. butter

Mix all the ingredients, except butter, in a saucepan over moderate heat until mixture thickens. Boil for 1 minute. Remove from heat and stir in the butter. Serve hot over pancakes.

Bed & Breakfast at Walnut Hill, Kennett Square, Pennsylvania

Windyledge Honey 'n' Spice Blueberry Pancakes

1 c. flour
1 c. whole-wheat flour
1 tsp. baking powder
1 tsp. baking soda
½ tsp. salt
2 tbsp. sugar
⅛ tsp. freshly grated nutmeg

¼ tsp. ginger
¾ tsp. cinnamon
¼ c. butter, melted
2 tbsp. honey
1 egg, slightly beaten
2 c. buttermilk
1 c. blueberries

Sift the dry ingredients together. Mix the melted butter, honey, egg, and buttermilk together. Hand blend the wet ingredients into the dry. Fold in the blueberries. Preheat the griddle, then cook the pancakes, using ¼ cup of batter for each pancake. Serve on warm plates with Orange Butter.

Orange Butter

4 tbsp. butter, melted
Grated peel of 1 orange

6 tbsp. confectioners' sugar

Let the butter cool slightly. Stir in the orange peel and sugar until smooth. Refrigerate for 30 minutes. When cool, remix with a fork. Store tightly covered in the refrigerator (lasts 2 months). You can substitute lemon for the orange.

Windyledge Bed and Breakfast, Hopkinton, New Hampshire

Swedish Pancakes

4 eggs
2½ c. milk (or half-and-half)
1⅛ c. unbleached flour

½ tsp. salt
2 tbsp. melted butter or margarine
¼ c. sugar

Beat the eggs with some of the milk. Add the flour and salt. Blend until smooth. Add the remaining milk. Add the melted butter. Stir in the sugar. Let stand overnight in the refrigerator or at least 1 hour at room temperature. Cook in a crêpe skillet using slightly less than ½ cup batter for each pancake. Cook over medium heat on both sides. Makes about 12 pancakes.

The Swedish Guest House Bed & Breakfast, Tucson, Arizona

French Toast with Fried Apples

1 loaf French bread
4 eggs
2 c. half-and-half

2 tbsp. vanilla
Butter-flavored Crisco

Slice bread approximately ¾ inch thick (discard ends). Arrange in a jelly roll pan or shallow baking dish. Beat eggs, half-and-half, and vanilla together. Pour over bread and let stand until completely absorbed, turning the bread a few times. Heat butter-flavored Crisco on a griddle and fry the bread until golden brown. Serve with the topping, warm maple syrup, and country sausage. Serves 4.

Topping

4 tbsp. butter
4 large Granny Smith apples, pared
  and cut into eighths

Sugar and cinnamon to taste

Melt the butter in a large frying pan. Add sliced apples and fry until just tender. Add sugar and cinnamon to taste. Mix well and cook for another minute or two.

Irondale Inn Bed & Breakfast, Bloomsburg, Pennsylvania

Sycamore Hill House Apple Puff

Butter or shortening for greasing
  quiche dish
1 large Granny Smith apple
1 tbsp. butter
½ c. milk
½ c. flour

3 eggs
1 tsp. sugar
Dash of salt
2 tbsp. cinnamon sugar (see page 30)
2 tbsp. butter
Juice of 1 lemon

Grease a 9-inch quiche dish. Core, peel, and thinly slice the apple and sauté in 1 tablespoon butter until tender. Spread the apple slices evenly in the quiche dish. Mix together the milk, flour, eggs, sugar, and salt until well blended and pour over the apple slices. Bake at 500°F for 10 minutes. Remove from oven, dot with the 2 tablespoons butter, and sprinkle with the cinnamon sugar. Return to oven for 5 minutes. Before serving, sprinkle the lemon juice over the puff.

Sycamore Hill House & Gardens, Washington, Virginia

Patti's Puffcakes and Fruit

4 tbsp. butter
3 eggs
½ tsp. salt
½ c. flour
½ c. milk

½ c. shredded Cheddar or Swiss
   cheese (optional)
Fruit Sauce (see below)
1 to 2 c. fresh berries, sliced if large
1 tbsp. confectioners' sugar

Preheat oven to 450°F. Take 2 8-inch pans (Ecko's Bakers Secret pans work best). Melt 2 tablespoons of butter in each pan and spread over pans, especially up the sides. Beat the eggs and salt for 1 minute at high speed. Add the flour and milk in three separate additions, mixing at high speed for 1 minute. Pour the batter into the pans in equal amounts and bake for 15 minutes. Sprinkle each puffcake with cheese, if desired, and top with Fruit Sauce and fresh sliced berries (the fresh berries are added on top of the warm sauce and the cheese). Dust with confectioners' sugar.

Fruit Sauce

1 c. sugar
1 tbsp. cornstarch
1 c. fruit juice

1 c. crushed or sliced fresh fruit
   (optional)
1 tbsp. butter (optional)

Mix all ingredients in a saucepan, then cook on medium heat, stirring often, until clear.

The Tar Heel Inn, Oriental, North Carolina

Hamlet

4 eggs
Nonstick cooking spray
1 scallion, finely chopped

½ stalk celery, finely chopped
2 thin slices ham, diced
2 slices American cheese, diced

Break the eggs into a bowl and beat with a wire whisk. Add 1 tablespoon water. Preheat a 9-inch frying pan and spray with a little nonstick cooking spray. Pan should sizzle. Pour the beaten egg mixture into the pan. Sprinkle the chopped ingredients over the eggs. Lift the edges with a spatula from time to time while the eggs are cooking to let the uncooked egg run underneath. When the eggs are almost set, fold one half of the omelet over the other, then flip the folded omelet over to seal the edges. Slide the omelet out onto a large plate and cut in half. Serve with Danish pastries. Serves 2.

Shakespeare Inn, Spokane, Washington

Strata Deluxe

Nonstick cooking spray
½ lb. bacon, ham, or sausage, cut or crumbled into small pieces
1 small onion or 2 or 3 green onions, thinly sliced
2 c. frozen hash browns

5 eggs, slightly beaten
3 c. milk
½ tsp. celery seed
½ tsp. dill weed
3 c. unseasoned croutons
1 c. grated cheese

Spray a 9 × 13-inch baking pan with nonstick spray. Set aside. Cook bacon, ham, or sausage along with onion. Drain to remove grease. Cook the hash browns until reduced by half and drain. Combine beaten eggs, milk, and seasonings. Put the croutons in the bottom of the baking pan. Layer the cheese, bacon, and hash browns on top of the croutons. Pour the egg and milk mixture over the top and refrigerate overnight. Bake in a 350°F oven for approximately 1 hour, until golden brown and set. The strata may be cooked partially the day before and finished the next morning in time to serve for breakfast.

Snow Goose Inn, Grove City, Pennsylvania

Sausage-Apple Bake

24 link sausages, browned
4 apples, pared and halved
1 c. flour
1 c. sugar
1 tsp. baking powder

1 egg
Milk or water to moisten
2 tbsp. butter, melted
Cinnamon

In each of 8 small French baking dishes, place 3 sausage links and half an apple. Prepare a batter from the flour, sugar, baking powder, egg, and milk and pour over the sausage and apple. Pour butter over all and sprinkle with cinnamon. Bake at 350°F for 20 minutes or until done. Serve in the baking dishes. Serves 8.

Henniker House, Henniker, New Hampshire

Sausage-Filled Croissants

1 sheet puff pastry, cut in four pieces
1 egg, beaten

4 slices cheese
2 smoked sausages, cut in half

Brush each pastry piece with egg on all sides. Wrap the cheese around the sausage and roll up in the pastry like croissants. Bake at 400°F for 15 minutes or until golden brown.

On Golden Pond Bed & Breakfast, Arvada, Colorado

Miss Vicki's Breakfast Casserole

Nonstick cooking spray
2 c. seasoned croutons
1 lb. sausage meat, browned and
    drained
¼ c. Parmesan cheese
1 tbsp. Mrs. Dash seasoning

4 eggs
2⅔ c. milk
1 can cream of mushroom soup
1 tsp. dry mustard
1 c. shredded Cheddar cheese

Spray a 9 × 13-inch glass casserole dish with nonstick spray. Spread the croutons over the bottom of the dish. Spread the sausage over the croutons. Sprinkle with the Parmesan cheese and Mrs. Dash seasoning. Mix together eggs, milk, soup, and dry mustard. Pour the egg mixture over the sausage and croutons. Cover and refrigerate overnight. In the morning, let stand at room temperature for ½ hour. Bake at 325°F for 1 hour. Sprinkle shredded Cheddar cheese over the top. Cover with foil and let stand 15 to 25 minutes before serving. Serves 8–10.

School House Bed & Breakfast, Rocheport, Missouri

4

State-by-State Listings

ALABAMA

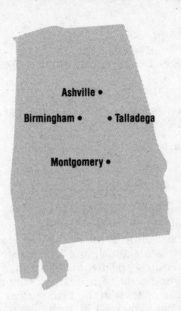

Ashville •

Birmingham •   • Talladega

Montgomery •

Roses and Lace Country Inn ✪
P.O. BOX 852, FIFTH STREET AT NINTH AVENUE SOUTH,
ASHVILLE, ALABAMA 35953

Tel: (205) 594-4366, 594-4660
Hosts: **Mark and Shirley Sparks**
Location: **40 mi. NE of Birmingham**
No. of Rooms: **4**
No. of Private Baths: **2**
Max. No. Sharing Bath: **4**
Double/pb: **$65**
Single/pb: **$55**
Double/sb: **$55**
Single/sb: **$45**

Suites: **$75**
Open: **All year**
Reduced Rates: **10% after 4 nights**
Breakfast: **Full**
Credit Cards: **MC, VISA**
Pets: **Sometimes**
Children: **Welcome**
Smoking: **No**
Social Drinking: **Permitted**

A friendly greeting awaits you at this handsome two-story Victorian
with a wraparound porch and stained-glass windows. As you cross
the threshold, your hosts Mark and Shirley will invite you to relax

with a beverage and snack. Their home, lovingly restored over a two-year period by the entire family, contains fine woodwork and many antiques. Ask about other landmark buildings in the area; St. Clair County is an old, historic part of Alabama. For modern pleasures, visit Birmingham's thoroughbred racetrack, or take a day trip to the Huntsville Space and Rocket Center.

Red Bluff Cottage

**551 CLAY STREET, MONTGOMERY, ALABAMA
(MAILING ADDRESS: P.O. BOX 1026, MONTGOMERY, ALABAMA
36101)**

Tel: **(205) 264-0056**
Best Time to Call: **9 AM–10 PM**
Hosts: **Anne and Mark Waldo**
No. of Rooms: **4**
No. of Private Baths: **4**
Double/pb: **$55**
Single/pb: **$50**
Suites: **$80**

Open: **All year**
Breakfast: **Full**
Pets: **No**
Children: **Welcome (crib)**
Smoking: **No**
Social Drinking: **Permitted**
Airport/Station Pickup: **Yes**

This raised cottage is high above the Alabama River in Montgomery's historic Cottage Hill District, close to the State Capitol, Dexter Avenue King Memorial Baptist Church, the First White House of the Confederacy, the Civil Rights Memorial, and Old Alabama Town. The Alabama Shakespeare Festival Theatre, the Museum of Fine Arts, and the expanded zoo are also nearby. The bedrooms are downstairs. Guests come upstairs to read or relax in the living rooms, to enjoy the front porch view, and to have breakfast in the dining room. Many interesting antiques and a music room, complete with harpsichord, add to the charm of this home.

Historic Oakwood Bed & Breakfast

715 EAST NORTH STREET, TALLADEGA, ALABAMA 35160

Tel: **(205) 362-0662**
Hosts: **Al and Naomi Kline**
Location: **45 mi. E of Birmingham**
No. of Rooms: **3**
No. of Private Baths: **1**
Max. No. Sharing Bath: **4**
Double/pb: **$65**
Single/pb: **$55**
Double/sb: **$55**
Single/sb: **$50**

Suites: **$95**
Open: **All year**
Breakfast: **Full**
Pets: **No**
Children: **Welcome, over 10, infants**
Smoking: **No**
Social Drinking: **Permitted**
Airport/Station Pickup: **Yes, $5–$10
fee**

This antebellum home, built in 1847, is listed on the National Register of Historic Places, and furnished with many heirloom antiques. The house was commissioned by Alexander Bowie, the first mayor of Talladega. Enjoy browsing through the antique stores in the area, visiting the International Motorsports Hall of Fame, or exploring DeSoto Caverns. The public golf course and tennis courts and beautiful Cheaha Mt. State Park are nearby. The hearty breakfast your hosts serve features homemade biscuits and southern grits. Traveling business person or vacationer, enjoy a retreat into the quiet elegance of a bygone era.

For key to listings, see inside front or back cover.

✪ This star means that rates are guaranteed through December 31, 1993, to any guest making a reservation as a result of reading about the B&B in *Bed & Breakfast U.S.A.*—1993 edition.

Important! To avoid misunderstandings, always ask about cancellation policies when booking.

Please enclose a self-addressed, stamped, business-size envelope when contacting reservation services.

For more details on what you can expect in a B&B, see Chapter 1.

Always mention *Bed & Breakfast U.S.A.* when making reservations!

If no B&B is listed in the area you'll be visiting, use the form on page 733 to order a copy of our "List of New B&Bs."

We want to hear from you! Use the form on page 735.

ALASKA

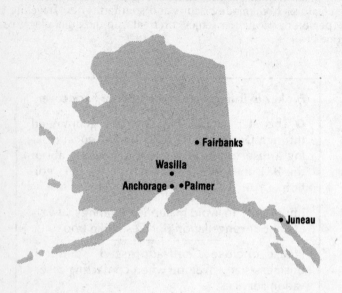

Accommodations Alaska Style—Stay With A Friend
3605 ARCTIC BOULEVARD, SUITE 173, ANCHORAGE, ALASKA 99503

Tel: (907) 278-8800; fax: (907) 272-8800
Coordinator: **Jean Parsons**
States/Regions Covered: **Anchorage, Denali, Fairbanks, Gustavus, Homer, Juneau, Kenai, Palmer, Seward, Sitka, Soldotna, Valdez, Wasilla**

Descriptive Directory: **$2**
Rates (Single/Double):
  Modest: **$40–$50**
  Average: **$45–$60**
  Luxury: **$55–$95**
Credit Cards: **MC, VISA**

Anchorage is an eclectic mix, and its frontier spirit and contemporary style always take visitors by surprise. Accommodations include statewide coverage: one B&B near a small park with views of the port and Sleeping Lady Mountain; another overlooks Cook Inlet; a third is an elegant suite where breakfast may be enjoyed on a large deck. Friendly, personal attention is how Jean has built this agency's reputation since 1981.

Alaska Bed & Breakfast Association ○
P.O. BOX 21890, JUNEAU, ALASKA 99802

Tel: (907) 586-2959
Best Time to Call: 9 AM–6 PM
Coordinator: Mavis Hanna
States/Regions Covered: Anchorage,
  Angoon, Delta Junction, Fairbanks,
  Haines, Homer, Juneau, Ketchikan,
  Sitka, Skagway, Tok, Wrangell,
  Whitehorse Yukon

Rates (Single/Double):
  Modest: $40 / $45
  Average: $50 / $70

This service extends a warm welcome to visitors to this magnificent state, which is diversified in its cultures, climate, and terrain. Gain insight into Alaska's rich history by staying in a Gold Rush bordello or a remodeled miner's cabin. Other accommodations range from urban homes to secluded waterfront retreats. Wherever you go, you'll enjoy hospitality, Alaska-style.

The Green Bough ○
3832 YOUNG STREET, ANCHORAGE, ALASKA 99508

Tel: (907) 562-4636
Best Time to Call: 7 AM–10 AM;
  4 PM–8 PM
Hosts: Jerry and Phyllis Jost
Location: 20 min. from airport
No. of Rooms: 4
Max. No. Sharing Bath: 4
Double/pb: $60
Double/sb: $50

Single/sb: $40
Suite: $70
Open: All year
Reduced Rates: Families
Breakfast: Continental
Pets: No
Children: Welcome
Smoking: No
Social Drinking: No

Even on the coldest days, you'll forget about the outside temperature in this comfortable home filled with family furnishings, needlework, and local artifacts. Breakfast features a choice of homemade breads, muffins, and scones served with seasonal fruit and plenty of hot coffee. The Green Bough is located in a quiet residential area close to colleges, shopping, bike trails, and buses. A large yard and deck are available for reading and relaxing. Your hosts have 20 years of experience in this part of the country, and they will gladly help you discover its charms. Special arrangements can be made for storing fishing and camping gear.

Snug Harbor Inn ○
1226 WEST 10TH AVENUE, ANCHORAGE, ALASKA 99501

Tel: (907) 272-6249
Hosts: Kenneth and Laurine "Sis" Hill
Location: Downtown Anchorage

No. of Rooms: 3
No. of Private Baths: 3
Double/pb: $60

Single/pb: **$60**
Open: **All year**
Reduced Rates: **Families**
Breakfast: **Full**
Other Meals: **Available**
Credit Cards: **MC, VISA**
Pets: **Sometimes**

Children: **Yes**
Smoking: **Permitted**
Social Drinking: **Permitted**
Minimum Stay: **2 nights**
Airport/Station Pickup: **Yes**
Foreign Languages: **Spanish**

This homey cottage is minutes from bus routes serving downtown Anchorage, with its parks, sports facilities, shopping areas, museum, and performing arts center. Entrance to the Coastal Bike Path—which leads to Earthquake Park—is only three blocks away; your hosts will supply bicycles. Ken, an avid outdoorsman and private pilot, likes taking guests on private tours of Alaska's mountains and glaciers. You'll get energy for these expeditions from Laurine's ample breakfasts; the menu ranges from eggs and pancakes to homemade muffins, with juice and coffee or tea.

Alaska's 7 Gables Bed & Breakfast ✪

P.O. BOX 80488, FAIRBANKS, ALASKA 99708

Tel: **(907) 479-0751**
Best Time to Call: **Evenings**
Hosts: **Paul and Leicha Welton**
Location: **2 mi. W of Fairbanks**
No. of Rooms: **7**
No. of Private Baths: **3**
Max. No. Sharing Bath: **3**
Double/pb: **$50–$90**
Single/pb: **$50–$75**
Double/sb: **$45–$75**
Single/sb: **$40–$70**
Suites: **$75–$95**
Open: **All year**

Reduced Rates: **30%, Oct.–Apr.**
Breakfast: **Full**
Other Meals: **Available**
Credit Cards: **AMEX, DC, DISC, MC, VISA**
Pets: **Sometimes**
Children: **Welcome**
Smoking: **No**
Social Drinking: **Permitted**
Minimum Stay: **2 nights**
Airport/Station Pickup: **Yes**
Foreign Languages: **Spanish**

The Weltons' large Tudor-style home is central to many city attractions—Riverboat Discovery, Cripple Creek Resort, University Museum, Alaskaland, Gold Dredge #8—and within walking distance of the University of Alaska's Fairbanks campus. Paul designed and built the house, a worthy destination in its own right. You'll enter through a floral solarium, which leads to a foyer with antique stained glass and indoor waterfall. Party planners take note: 7 Gables has a wine cellar and a wedding chapel. Guests can use the laundry facilities, library, Jacuzzi, canoe, and bikes. All rooms have telephones and cable TV; one room is accessible to wheelchair users. Ample breakfasts feature dishes like salmon quiche, crab casserole, and peachy pecan crepes.

Blueberry Lodge B&B ✪
9436 NORTH DOUGLAS HIGHWAY, JUNEAU, ALASKA 99801

Tel: (907) 463-5886
Hosts: Jay and Judy Urquhart
Location: 7 mi. N of Juneau
No. of Rooms: 5
Max. No. Sharing Bath: 4
Double/sb: $75
Single/sb: $70

Open: All year
Reduced Rates: Weekly, 10% seniors
Breakfast: Full
Pets: Sometimes
Children: Welcome
Smoking: No
Social Drinking: Permitted

Relax in a spacious handcrafted log lodge overlooking an inland ocean waterway, a wildlife refuge, and an active eagle nest. The lodge's five bedrooms, three-story living room and library, and overstuffed couches and chairs make it ideal for families to explore the great outdoors. Walk onto tidal estuaries, hike the surrounding beaches and alpine trails, fish for world-class salmon and halibut. Cross-country and downhill skiers can head to Eaglecrest, all of five minutes away. Or just savor a hearty breakfast and catch up on your laundry. Jay, a hard-rock miner, can tell you about working on Admiralty Island, which has more bears than any other place on earth.

Mat-Su Valley B&B Association ✪
2651 EAST PALMER, WASILLA HIGHWAY, WASILLA, ALASKA 99654

Tel: (907) 376-5868
Best Time to Call: 8 AM–8 PM
Coordinator: Louise Carswell
States/Regions Covered: Alaska, Mat-Su Valley, Palmer, Talkeentna, Traper Creek, Wasilla, Willow

Rates (Single/Double):
Modest: $40 / $50
Average: $45 / $60
Luxury: $70 / $95

Whether you choose an authentic log cabin or a modern lakefront home, your B&B hosts will do all they can to make your holiday in the Mat-Su Valley memorable. A one-hour drive from Anchorage, the valley—the gateway to Mt. McKinley—is a photographers' dream. Mountain vistas, glaciers, woods, and lakes abound. You can have an accessible wilderness experience by day and the creature comforts of a cozy B&B at night with excellent dining nearby. Hike, ski, fish, mush. Visit the Iditarod Race Headquarters Museum, the musk-ox farm, or the reindeer ranch. For the trip of a lifetime, board a seaplane for a personalized aerial tour of the famous Star Trek Six Glacier!

Ede Den

BOX 870365, DAVIS ROAD, WASILLA, ALASKA 99687

Tel: **(907) 376-2162**
Best Time to Call: **11 AM–8 PM**
Hosts: **Jim and Julie Ede**
Location: **45 mi. NE of Anchorage**
No. of Rooms: **2**
No. of Private Baths: **1**
Max. No. Sharing Bath: **4**
Double/pb: **$75**
Single/pb: **$65**
Double/sb: **$60**

Single/sb: **$50**
Open: **All year**
Breakfast: **Full**
Credit Cards: **MC, VISA**
Pets: **Welcome**
Children: **Welcome**
Smoking: **Permitted**
Social Drinking: **Permitted**
Airport/Station Pickup: **Yes**

Guests enjoy the privacy and charm of this scenic Matanuska Valley homestead, furnished with antiques and Alaskan art. A private entrance opens into a cozy bedroom adjoining a luxurious bath that features an artistic rock wall with a waterfall cascading into a hot tub. Breakfast includes sourdough hotcakes, local honey, and homegrown berries in season. Jim and Julie are longtime Alaskan village teachers who collect and sell antiques. They'll be happy to arrange sightseeing, fishing, river rafting, and winter dog-team trips to Mt. McKinley.

ARIZONA

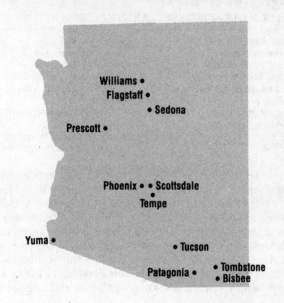

Williams •
Flagstaff •
• Sedona
Prescott •
Phoenix • • Scottsdale
• Tempe
Yuma •
• Tucson
Patagonia • • Tombstone
• Bisbee

Mi Casa–Su Casa Bed & Breakfast ✪
P.O. BOX 950, TEMPE, ARIZONA 85280-0950

Tel: **(602) 990-0682; (800) 456-0682**
Best Time to Call: **8 AM–8 PM**
Coordinator: **Ruth T. Young**
States/Regions Covered: **Arizona—
Ajo, Bisbee, Cave Creek, Flagstaff,
Fountain Hills, Mesa, Page, Prescott,
Scottsdale, Sedona, Tempe, Tucson,
Wickenburg, Yuma; New Mexico;
Utah**

Rates (Single/Double):
  Modest: **$25–$35**
  Average: **$40–$60**
  Luxury: **$75–$120**
Descriptive Directory: **$9.50**

Ruth's guest houses are located statewide; the cities listed above are only a partial listing. They are located in cities, suburbs, and rural settings, all of which are within easy driving range of canyons, national parks, Indian country, Colorado River gem country, the Mexican border area, historic mining towns, and water recreation areas. Send $9.50 for her detailed directory. Arizona State University and the University of Arizona are convenient to many B&Bs. There is a $5 surcharge for one-night stays.

The Judge Ross House ✪
605 SHATTUCK STREET, BISBEE, ARIZONA 85603

Tel: (602) 432-5597 days; 432-4120 evenings and weekends	Single/sb: **$55**
	Open: **All year**
Best Time to Call: **Evenings**	Breakfast: **Full**
Hosts: **Jim and Bonnie Douglass**	Other Meals: **Available**
Location: **25 mi. SE of Tombstone**	Credit Cards: **MC, VISA**
No. of Rooms: **3**	Pets: **No**
No. of Private Baths: **1**	Children: **Welcome, over 12**
Max. No. Sharing Bath: **4**	Smoking: **No**
Double/pb: **$65**	Social Drinking: **Permitted**
Double/sb: **$60**	Airport/Station Pickup: **Yes**

A two-story, brick home built at the turn of the century and named for its first owner, a superior court judge, the Judge Ross House has a charmingly old-fashioned look enhanced by decorative moldings, lavish wood trim, and period furniture. Jim and Bonnie are gracious hosts, welcoming visitors with fresh flowers, wine, candy, and magazines. Breakfast varies from day to day, with specialties such as Belgian waffles and eggs Benedict. Bisbee was once the Southwest's largest copper mining area, and the open pit mine remains a major attraction. Browsers will enjoy visiting the town's galleries and antique stores.

Dierker House ✪
423 WEST CHERRY, FLAGSTAFF, ARIZONA 86001

Tel: (602) 774-3249	Open: **All year**
Host: **Dorothea Dierker**	Breakfast: **Full**
No. of Rooms: **3**	Pets: **Sometimes**
Max. No. Sharing Bath: **4**	Children: **Welcome, over 12**
Double/sb: **$43.50**	Smoking: **No**
Single/sb: **$35**	Social Drinking: **Permitted**

This lovely old home in Flagstaff's historic section is located high in the mountains, at an elevation of 7,000 feet. Flagstaff is the hub of wonderful day trips to the Grand Canyon, Indian ruins and reservations, Lake Powell, Monument Valley, and many more sites. The second floor accommodations are extremely comfortable and include many amenities. In the morning, Dorothea sets out an excellent and sociable breakfast in the dining room.

The Little House
P.O. BOX 461, PATAGONIA, ARIZONA 85624

Tel: **(602) 394-2493**	Open: **All year**
Hosts: **Don and Doris Wenig**	Breakfast: **Full**
Location: **60 mi. S of Tucson**	Pets: **No**
No. of Rooms: **2**	Children: **Sometimes**
No. of Private Baths: **2**	Smoking: **No**
Double/pb: **$60**	Social Drinking: **Permitted**
Single/pb: **$50**	

The Wenigs' home is located close to the Mexican border in a small mountain town at an elevation of 4,000 feet. Comfort and privacy are assured in the adobe guest house separated from the main house by a charming courtyard. One of the bedrooms has a queen-size bed; the other has twin beds and is wheelchair accessible. Each bedroom has a fireplace, sitting area, and adjacent patio. Coffee or tea is brought to your room to start the day. Afterward, join Don and Doris for a breakfast of sausage and waffles, eggs from local hens, and home-baked breads. Birdwatching, a visit to a ghost town or silver mine, and shopping in Nogales, Mexico, are pleasant pastimes available.

Gerry's Bed & Breakfast ○
5150 NORTH 37TH AVENUE, PHOENIX, ARIZONA 85019

Tel: **(602) 973-2542**	Single/sb: **$45**
Best Time to Call: **8 AM–8 PM**	Open: **All year**
Hosts: **Gerry and Lynn Snodgres**	Breakfast: **Full**
Location: **1½ mi. W of I-17**	Pets: **No**
No. of Rooms: **3**	Children: **Welcome, over 12**
Max. No. Sharing Bath: **3**	Smoking: **No**
Double/sb: **$50**	Social Drinking: **Permitted**

The Snodgreses welcome guests to their contemporary two-story stucco with crackers, cheese, and home-baked goodies. Bring a bathing suit so you can make use of the swimming pool; your hosts will provide terry cover-ups so you can lounge in comfort. Indoor diversions include TV, pool, and other games. Gerry's full breakfasts feature specialties like cinnamon French toast and a salsa-garnished egg-and-cheese casserole.

Maricopa Manor ○
P.O. BOX 7186, 15 WEST PASADENA AVENUE, PHOENIX, ARIZONA 85011

Tel: **(602) 274-6302**	Location: **5 mi. N of downtown Phoenix**
Hosts: **Mary Ellen and Paul Kelley**	

No. of Rooms: **5 suites**
No. of Private Baths: **5**
Suites: **$69–$99**
Wheelchair Accessible: **1 Suite**
Open: **All year**
Breakfast: **Continental**

Credit Cards: **No**
Pets: **No**
Children: **Welcome**
Smoking: **No**
Social Drinking: **Permitted**

Inside this Spanish-style manor house built in 1928, you'll find beautiful art, antiques, and warm southwestern hospitality. The five private suites, spacious public rooms, decks, and gazebo spa create an intimate, Old World atmosphere in an elegant urban setting. Maricopa Manor is in the heart of the Valley of the Sun, convenient to shops, restaurants, museums, churches, and civic and government centers. Advance reservations are required.

Bed & Breakfast Scottsdale and the West
P.O. BOX 3999, PRESCOTT, ARIZONA 86302-3999

Tel: **(602) 776-1102**
Best Time to Call: **10 AM–5 PM, Mon.–Fri.**
Coordinators: **Joyce and George Thomson**
States/Regions Covered: **Arizona**

Descriptive Directory: **Free**
Rates (Single/Double):
  Modest: **$45 / $55**
  Average: **$50 / $65–$75**
  Luxury: **$65 / $75–$150**
Credit Cards: **No**

The Thomsons have a roster of friendly hosts with homes that have a relaxed atmosphere to complement the easygoing southwestern lifestyle. Many are close to Paolo Soleri's Bell Foundry, Taliesin West, fine restaurants, shops, galleries, and lively entertainment. Take along plenty of color film to capture the panoramic desert sunsets.

Betsy's Bed and Breakfast ✪
1919 ROCK CASTLE DRIVE, PRESCOTT, ARIZONA 86301

Tel: **(602) 445-0123**
Best Time to Call: **Before 9 PM**
Host: **Elizabeth "Betsy" Rominger**
Location: **100 mi. NW of Phoenix**
No. of Rooms: **2**
No. of Private Baths: **2**
Double/pb: **$48–$70**
Single/pb: **$30–$45**

Open: **All year**
Reduced Rates: **15%, over 5 days**
Breakfast: **Full**
Pets: **Sometimes**
Children: **Welcome, over 8**
Smoking: **No**
Social Drinking: **Permitted**

Perched on a rocky hillside, this contemporary redwood house affords visitors a breathtaking view of Prescott, a vibrant town with five museums, three colleges, and myriad antique shops. Betsy, a retired antiques appraiser, will be glad to discuss her own collection; you'll find many distinctive pieces in the guest bedrooms and bathrooms.

Breakfast, served at guests' convenience, may include homemade zucchini cakes, cinnamon rolls, and Betsy's own tortilla quiche.

Bed & Breakfast in Arizona
P.O. BOX 8628, SCOTTSDALE, ARIZONA 85252

Tel: **(602) 995-2831; (800) 266-7829**
Best Time to Call: **10 AM–6 PM**
Coordinator: **Stephanie Osterlitz**
States/Regions Covered: **Ajo, Bisbee, Flagstaff, Lake Havasu City, Lakeside, Oracle, Page, Phoenix, Prescott, Scottsdale, Sedona, Tucson**

Descriptive Directory of B&Bs: **$2**
Rates (Single/Double):
  Modest: **$35–$50**
  Average: **$51–$75**
  Luxury: **$76–$150**
Credit Cards: **AMEX, MC, VISA**
Minimum Stay: **Holidays; 2 nights**

Claiming more mountains than Switzerland and more forests than Minnesota, Arizona boasts spectacular scenery. It is the home of the Grand Canyon, Lake Powell, London Bridge, famous museums, and sporting opportunities. Stephanie's choices range from a modestly priced town house with a swimming pool to a historic ranch with a spa, gardens, and a pool that served as the locale for a western film. In business for ten years, this service takes pride in its growing roster of friendly hosts. Two days' advance notice is required for reservations; seven days' notice for cancellation.

Casa de Mariposa ❂
6916 EAST MARIPOSA, SCOTTSDALE, ARIZONA 85251

Tel: **(602) 947-9704, 994-9599**
Hosts: **Jo and Jim Cummings**
Location: **15 mi. N of I-10**
No. of Rooms: **1**
No. of Private Baths: **1**
Double/pb: **$70**
Open: **All year**
Reduced Rates: **20%, May 30–Sept. 30**

Breakfast: **Full**
Pets: **No**
Children: **Welcome**
Smoking: **No**
Social Drinking: **Permitted**
Airport/Station Pickup: **Yes**

Located in the original Sunkist orchards, Casa de Mariposa offers golden grapefruit fresh from the tree. This quiet residential neighborhood is in the heart of beautiful Scottsdale, in walking distance of numerous shops, restaurants, theaters, golf courses, etc. Guests are welcome to soak in the spa, use the hosts' golf clubs or their box seats at the Giants spring training games. Adjoining the large luxury guest suite is a game room with fifties memorabilia.

Valley o' the Sun Bed & Breakfast ✪
P.O. BOX 2214, SCOTTSDALE, ARIZONA 85252

Tel: (602)941-1281	Open: All year
Best Time to Call: After 5 PM	Reduced Rates: Weekly; monthly;
Host: Kay Curtis	seniors
Location: Tempe	Breakfast: Continental, Full
No. of Rooms: 3	Pets: No
No. of Private Baths: 1	Children: Welcome, over 12
Max. No. Sharing Bath: 4	Smoking: Permitted
Double/pb: $40	Social Drinking: Permitted
Double/sb:$35	Minimum Stay: 2 nights
Single/sb: $25	Airport/Station Pickup: Yes

The house is ideally located in the college area of Tempe, but is close enough to Scottsdale to enjoy its fine shops and restaurants. From the patio, you can enjoy a beautiful view of the Papago Buttes and McDowell Mountains. Local attractions include swimming at Big Surf, the Phoenix Zoo, and the Scottsdale Center for the Arts.

Cathedral Rock Lodge ✪
STAR RTE. 2, BOX 856, SEDONA, ARIZONA 86336

Tel: (602) 282-7608	Reduced Rates: Available
Host: Carol Shannon	Breakfast: Full
Location: 2.7 mi. from Rte. 89A	Credit Cards: DISC, MC, VISA
No. of Rooms: 3	Pets: No
No. of Private Baths: 3	Children: Welcome (crib)
Double/pb: $65	Smoking: No
Suites: $90	Social Drinking: Permitted
Open: All year	

Set in rock terrace gardens surrounded by tall shade trees, this rambling country home boasts spectacular views of the surrounding mountains. The suite has its own deck, built against a giant pine tree. Guest bedrooms feature family treasures and handmade quilts. Each day starts with Carol's hot breads and homemade jams; fresh fruits from local orchards are summertime treats. Lovers of the great outdoors will delight in the natural scenic beauty of the area, and browsers will enjoy the many galleries and shops. In the evening, curl up in front of the fireplace, borrow a book, or select a videotape from your host's collection.

Kennedy House ✪
HC 30, BOX 785K, 2075 UPPER RED ROCK LOOP ROAD, SEDONA, ARIZONA 86336

Tel: (602) 282-1624	Hosts: Tonya and Chuck Kennedy
Best Time to Call: 10 AM–10 PM	Location: 116 mi. N of Phoenix

No. of Rooms: **2**
No. of Private Baths: **2**
Double/pb: **$70**
Suites: **$85**
Open: **Feb.–Dec.; Closed Thanksgiving and Christmas**
Reduced Rates: **$10 less per night, after 3rd day**
Breakfast: **Full**
Credit Cards: **MC, VISA**

Pets: **No**
Children: **Welcome**
Smoking: **No**
Social Drinking: **Permitted**
Minimum Stay: **2 nights weekends, except Dec. and Feb.**
Airport/Station Pickup: **Yes**

This attractively furnished contemporary home lies within walking distance of Red Rock Crossing, the most photographed spot in Arizona. Chuck, a retired wildlife biologist, offers guests a guided nature hike and will cheerfully assist in planning picnics or giving directions to the area's many famous monuments. After a full day of sightseeing, relax with a beverage on the large deck, which overlooks the breathtaking Cathedral Rock.

Sipapu Lodge ✪
65 PIKI DRIVE, P.O. BOX 552, SEDONA, ARIZONA 86336

Tel: **(602) 282-2833**
Hosts: **Lea Pace and Vince Mollan**
Location: **100 mi. N of Phoenix**
No. of Rooms: **5**
No. of Private Baths: **3**
Max. No. Sharing Bath: **4**
Double/sb: **$68**
Suites: **$98**

Open: **All year**
Reduced Rates: **After 4th night**
Breakfast: **Full**
Pets: **Sometimes**
Children: **Welcome, over 5**
Smoking: **No**
Social Drinking: **Permitted**
Airport/Station Pickup: **Yes**

Constructed of local red rock and timber, the house is surrounded by blooming vegetation. The influence of the Anasazi Indian culture is evident with the decor of each spacious room reflecting its artifacts and memorabilia. Explore the Indian ruins or art galleries; hike Oak Creek Canyon; visit a ghost town; or just commune with nature. Lea is a former schoolteacher who loves to celebrate special occasions, and offers tea or spiced cider in the evening. Son Vince is a massage technician, craftsman, and potter.

Buford House B&B
113 EAST SAFFORD STREET, P.O. BOX 38, TOMBSTONE, ARIZONA 85638

Tel: **(602) 457-3168; (800) 355-1880**
Best Time to Call: **9 AM–noon; 5 PM–9 PM**
Hosts: **Jeanne and Charles Hagel**
Location: **87 mi. S of Tucson**

No. of Rooms: **4**
No. of Private Baths: **1**
Max. No. Sharing Bath: **4**
Double/pb: **$85**
Double/sb: **$55**

Single/sb: **$45**
Open: **All year**
Reduced Rates: **15%, 3 nights**
Breakfast: **Full**

Pets: **Sometimes**
Children: **Welcome, over 15**
Smoking: **No**
Social Drinking: **No**

Prominent Bisbee mine owner George Buford built this large two-story adobe during Tombstone's mining era. Subsequent inhabitants included two sheriffs and a bronc rider for the Indian scout John Slaughter. Today the house is listed on the National Register of Historic Places. The grounds include an herb garden and roses, which attract hummingbirds; a barbecue and hot tub are also available. Inside, guests can watch cable TV or play piano in the common room. Weather permitting, full breakfasts are served on the veranda.

Casa Tierra Bed and Breakfast Inn ✪
11155 WEST CALLE PIMA, TUCSON, ARIZONA 85743

Tel: **(602) 578-3058**
Best Time to Call: **Noon–3 PM**
Hosts: **Karen and Lyle Hymer-Thompson**
Location: **15 mi. W of Tucson**
No. of Rooms: **3**
No. of Private Baths: **3**
Double/pb: **$65–$75**
Open: **Sept.–May**

Reduced Rates: **10% after 7 days**
Breakfast: **Full**
Pets: **No**
Children: **Welcome**
Smoking: **No**
Social Drinking: **Permitted**
Minimum Stay: **2 nights**
Foreign Languages: **Spanish**

Casa Tierra is located on five acres of beautiful Sonoran desert thirty minutes from downtown Tucson. This secluded desert area has hundreds of saguaro cactus, spectacular mountain views, and brilliant sunsets. Built and designed by owners Lyle and Karen, the all-adobe house features entryways with vaulted brick ceilings, an interior arched courtyard, and Mexican furnishings. Each guest room has a private bath, queen-size bed, microwave, small refrigerator, and private patio and entrance. Nearby attractions include the Desert Museum, the Saguaro National Monument, and Old Tucson. Karen is an artist/photographer; Lyle is a designer/builder who takes tours into Mexico.

Ford's Bed & Breakfast ✪
P.O. BOX 18784, TUCSON, ARIZONA 85731

Tel: **(602) 885-1202**
Best Time to Call: **8–10 AM**
Hosts: **Sheila and Tom Ford**
Location: **12 mi. E of Tucson**
No. of Rooms: **2**
No. of Private Baths: **1**

Double/pb: **$50**
Single/pb: **$40**
Suites: **$100; sleeps 4**
Open: **All year**
Breakfast: **Continental**
Pets: **No**

Children: **No** Social Drinking: **Permitted**
Smoking: **No** Airport/Station Pickup: **Yes**

A warm welcome awaits you at this air-conditioned ranch-style home in a quiet residential cul-de-sac on Tucson's northeast side. Walk through your private entrance and enjoy a bird's-eye view of the mountains from your own garden patio. Your English-born hostess, a retired nanny and dog breeder, has lived here for 35 years and can direct you to the attractions of the area: Sabino Canyon, Mount Lemmon, Saguaro National Monument, hiking trails, and the like. For easy access, city bus lines run nearby. Guests have use of a microwave, a refrigerator, and the sitting room with a TV.

Hideaway B&B ✪
4344 EAST POE STREET, TUCSON, ARIZONA 85711

Tel: **(602) 323-8067** Reduced Rates: **Weekly**
Best Time to Call: **After 5 PM** Breakfast: **Continental**
Hosts: **Dwight and Ola Parker** Pets: **No**
No. of Rooms: **1** Children: **No**
No. of Private Baths: **1** Smoking: **No**
Guest Cottage: **$40–$52** Minimum Stay: **3 nights**
Open: **Oct.–June, special** Airport/Station Pickup: **Yes**
  arrangements for the rest of year

A cozy bungalow with its own entrance, Hideaway B&B is located in the hosts' backyard in central Tucson, just minutes from two major shopping centers. One mile away, a city park provides lots of diversions, with two golf courses, a driving range, tennis courts, and a zoo. Pima Air Museum, Davis Monthan Air Force Base, the University of Arizona, Colossal Cave, the Old Tucson movie set, and Mt. Lemmon Ski Resort are among the many sights of interest. The air-conditioned accommodations include a private bath, a bedroom, and a sitting room equipped with a TV, VCR, and stereo. Your hosts, a retired art teacher and an engineer/insurance man, enjoy big band music, gardening, and their clown ministry.

Katy's Hacienda ✪
5841 EAST 9TH STREET, TUCSON, ARIZONA 85711

Tel: **(602) 745-5695** Double/pb: **$45**
Host: **Katy Gage** Single/pb: **$35**
Location: **8 mi. from Rte. 10, Grant or** Double/sb: **$45**
  Kolb exit Single/sb: **$35**
No. of Rooms: **2** Open: **All year**
No. of Private Baths: **1** Reduced Rates: **10% weekly**
Max. No. Sharing Bath: **3** Breakfast: **Full**

Pets: **No**	Social Drinking: **Permitted**
Children: **Welcome, over 8**	Minimum Stay: **2 nights**
Smoking: **Permitted**	Airport/Station Pickup: **Yes**

An ornamental iron guard protects this adobe brick house filled with charming antiques and glass. Guests can unwind in the backyard and the patio area, or come inside and enjoy the living room and television room. Katy's Hacienda is within walking distance of the bus line, fine restaurants, theaters, and a hospital. The El Con shopping area, the Randolph Golf Course, and the zoo are three miles away.

Mesquite Retreat ✪
3770 NORTH MELPOMENE WAY, TUCSON, ARIZONA 85749

Tel: **(602) 749-4884**	Open: **All year**
Best Time to Call: **Evenings**	Breakfast: **Full**
Hosts: **Jan and Curt Albertson**	Pets: **No**
No. of Rooms: **2**	Children: **Welcome, over 12**
Max. No. Sharing Bath: **4**	Smoking: **Permitted**
Double/sb: **$50**	Social Drinking: **Permitted**
Single/sb: **$45**	

At the base of Mt. Lemmon sits this spacious ranch-style house, shaded by mesquite trees in the serene quiet of the desert. Traditional furnishings are accented with antiques and collectibles. All of the sights of Tucson—interesting caves, missions, monuments, and museums—are not far, and fine dining is just 10 minutes away. Save time to enjoy the Albertsons' beautiful pool and spa surrounded by lush vegetation and mountain views.

Natural Bed and Breakfast ✪
3150 EAST PRESIDIO ROAD, TUCSON, ARIZONA 85716

Tel: **(602) 881-4582**	Single/sb: **$35**
Best Time to Call: **Mornings**	Open: **All year**
Host: **Marc Haberman**	Reduced Rates: **5% seniors**
No. of Rooms: **2**	Breakfast: **Full**
No. of Private Baths: **1**	Other Meals: **Available**
Max. No. Sharing Bath: **2**	Pets: **Sometimes**
Double/pb: **$45**	Children: **Welcome**
Single/pb: **$35**	Smoking: **No**
Double/sb: **$45**	Social Drinking: **Permitted**

Marc Haberman is a holistic health practitioner, and his B&B is natural in all senses of the word: it's a simply furnished, water-cooled home that provides a nontoxic, nonallergenic environment. The grounds are landscaped with palm and pine trees. Only whole-grain and natural foods are served here and the drinking water is purified. Soothing professional massages are available by request.

Redbud House Bed & Breakfast ○
7002 EAST REDBUD ROAD, TUCSON, ARIZONA 85715

Tel: **(602) 721-0218**
Hosts: **Ken and Wanda Mayer**
Location: **7 mi. from Rte. 10**
No. of Rooms: **1**
No. of Private Baths: **1**
Double/pb: **$45**
Single/pb: **$37**

Open: **Sept.–May**
Breakfast: **Full**
Pets: **No**
Children: **No**
Smoking: **No**
Social Drinking: **Permitted**

The Mayers' comfortable ranch-style brick home is on a residential street bordered by tall pines and palm trees. There is a view of the Catalina Mountains from the porch. Local attractions are the Saguaro National Monument, the Arizona Sonora Desert Museum, Kitt Peak National Observatory, and Sabino Canyon. You are welcome to use the bicycles, barbecue, and TV, or to just relax on the patio. Several fine restaurants and a recreation complex with Olympic-sized swimming pool are nearby.

The Johnstonian B&B ○
321 WEST SHERIDAN AVENUE, WILLIAMS, ARIZONA 86046

Tel: **(602) 635-2178**
Best Time to Call: **Before 8 AM, after 1 PM**
Hosts: **Bill and Pidge Johnston**
Location: **55 mi. S of Grand Canyon National Park**
No. of Rooms: **4**
Max. No. Sharing Bath: **4**
Double/pb: **$65**
Single/pb: **$60**

Double/sb: **$50**
Single/sb: **$45**
Suites: **$108**
Open: **All year**
Breakfast: **Full**
Pets: **No**
Children: **Welcome**
Smoking: **No**
Social Drinking: **Permitted**

As old as the century, this two-story Victorian has been carefully restored and decorated in period style. You'll admire the antique oak furniture and the lovely floral wallpapers. In the winter, guests cluster around the wood-burning stove. Pidge's breakfast specialties include Ukrainian potato cakes, blueberry pancakes, and homemade breads.

Casa de Osgood ✪
11620 IRONWOOD DRIVE, YUMA, ARIZONA 85365

Tel: **(602) 342-0471**
Best Time to Call: **7:30–8:30 AM;**
 8:00–9:00 PM
Hosts: **Chris and Vickie Osgood**
Location: **12 mi. E of Yuma**
No. of Rooms: **1**
No. of Private Baths: **1**
Double/pb: **$65**

Open: **All year**
Breakfast: **Continental**
Pets: **No**
Children: **No**
Smoking: **No**
Social Drinking: **No**
Airport Pickup: **Yes**

Casa de Osgood offers wonderful views round the clock. From the dining room, sundeck, or hacienda-style front veranda of this B&B, you can see the Gila Mountains. Feel like a night of stargazing? Arrangements can be made for guests to sleep under the sky in the double bed. If you prefer a roof over your head, you'll appreciate the spacious bedroom with its fireplace and big picture window. Yuma's attractions include museums, community arts groups, and state parks. Fans of waterfront sports can head out for several lakes as well as the Colorado River. Camping, hunting, fishing, and hiking are permitted nearby throughout the Kofa, Chocolate, and Castle Dome mountain ranges.

ARKANSAS

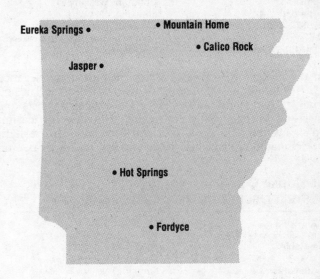

Eureka Springs •   • Mountain Home

• Calico Rock

Jasper •

• Hot Springs

• Fordyce

Arkansas and Ozarks Bed & Breakfast ✪
HC 61, BOX 72, CALICO ROCK, ARKANSAS 72519

Tel: (501) 297-8764, 297-8211
Coordinator: **Carolyn S. Eck**
States/Regions Covered: **Batesville, Calico Rock, Des Arc, Fayetteville, Fort Smith, Gassville, Harrison, Hot Springs, Mountain Home, Mountain View, Norfolk, Ozark, Yellville**

Rates (Single/Double):
  Modest: **$25 / $35**
  Average: **$30 / $65**
  Luxury: **$65 / $95**
Credit Cards: **MC, VISA**

North-central Arkansas boasts an enviable combination of natural scenic beauty in its forests, rivers, and caves, as well as the homespun fun of hootenannies, square dancing, and craft shops. Carolyn's homes include contemporary houses, restored Victorians, Colonials, and log cabins in the mountains.

59

Bridgeford House B&B
263 SPRING STREET, EUREKA SPRINGS, ARKANSAS 72632

Tel: (501) 253-7853
Best Time to Call: 10 AM–10 PM
Hosts: Denise and Michael McDonald
No. of Rooms: 4
No. of Private Baths: 4
Double/pb: $70–$90
Open: All year
Reduced Rates: 10% less, Jan.–Feb.

Breakfast: Full
Credit Cards: MC, VISA
Pets: No
Children: Welcome
Smoking: No
Social Drinking: Permitted
Minimum Stay: 2 nights weekends, holidays

A stay at the Bridgeford House is a step into the quiet elegance of yesterday. It is located in the historic district, where Victorian homes line charming streets, and old-fashioned trolleys carry guests to and fro. Denise and Michael will pamper you with coffee or tea in the afternoon or evening. Breakfast is a real eye-opener of fresh fruit, homemade cinnamon rolls, Ozark ham, and delicious egg casseroles.

Harvest House ✪
104 WALL STREET, EUREKA SPRINGS, ARKANSAS 72632

Tel: (501) 253-9363
Best Time to Call: 9 AM–1 PM
Host: Lynne Goble
No. of Rooms: 3
No. of Private Baths: 3
Double/pb: $45–$65
Open: All year

Breakfast: Full
Wheelchair Accessible: Yes
Pets: Sometimes
Children: Welcome
Smoking: No
Social Drinking: Permitted

This green-and-white Victorian house is furnished with antiques, collectibles, and family favorites. The guest rooms are downstairs, with private entrances. Located in the Ozark Mountains, the scenery is lovely. Homemade surprise snacks are always available. Lynne will do everything possible to make your stay pleasant.

Singleton House Bed and Breakfast ✪
11 SINGLETON, EUREKA SPRINGS, ARKANSAS 72632

Tel: (501) 253-9111
Best Time to Call: Anytime
Host: Barbara Gavron
No. of Rooms: 4
No. of Private Baths: 4
Double/pb: $55–$65
Single/pb: $55–$65
Guest Cottage: $85–$95; open Apr.–Nov.

Suites: $65–$75
Open: All year
Reduced Rates: After 3rd night
Breakfast: Full
Credit Cards: AMEX, DISC, MC, VISA
Pets: No
Children: Welcome
Smoking: No
Social Drinking: Permitted

You'll find a hidden garden, winding stone paths, and more than fifty birdhouses on the grounds of this Victorian home in Eureka Springs' historic district. For help in identifying your various feathered friends, consult the titles in Singleton House's small nature library. Full breakfasts are served on the balcony overlooking the wildflower garden and lily-filled goldfish pond. After your meal, take a one-block stroll on the historic walking tour footpath to the city's shops, galleries, and cafés. If you prefer, there's an old-fashioned trolley that stops right at Singleton Street. At a second historic district address, your hosts maintain a private cottage with a full kitchen.

Wynne Phillips House ✪
412 WEST FOURTH STREET, FORDYCE, ARKANSAS 71742

Tel: **(501) 352-7202**
Best Time to Call: **Morning**
Hosts: **Colonel and Mrs. James H. Phillips**
Location: **60 mi. S of Little Rock**
No. of Rooms: **4**
No. of Private Baths: **4**
Double/pb: **$55**

Open: **All year**
Breakfast: **Full**
Credit Cards: **MC, VISA**
Pets: **No**
Children: **Yes**
Smoking: **No**
Social Drinking: **Permitted**

A gracious Colonial Revival mansion listed on the National Register of Historic Places, the Wynne Phillips House is filled with antiques and oriental rugs. Mrs. Phillips grew up here, and the bedrooms are furnished with family heirlooms. This is a place where you can enjoy old-fashioned pleasures, such as singing around the piano, or watching the sunset from the wraparound porch. A swimming pool is on the premises; tennis courts are nearby. The generous, Southern-style breakfasts feature fresh fruit, homemade biscuits, eggs, sausage, and grits.

Stillmeadow Farm ✪

111 STILLMEADOW LANE, HOT SPRINGS, ARKANSAS 71913

Tel: **(501) 525-9994**
Hosts: **Gene and Jody Sparling**
Location: **4 mi. S of Hot Springs**
No. of Rooms: **4**
No. of Private Baths: **2**
Max. No. Sharing Bath: **4**
Double/pb: **$50**
Single/pb: **$40**

Suites: **$80**
Open: **All year**
Breakfast: **Continental**
Pets: **No**
Children: **Welcome, over 12**
Smoking: **No**
Social Drinking: **Permitted**

Stillmeadow Farm is a reproduction of an 18th-century New England saltbox, set in 75 acres of pine forest with walking trails and an herb garden. The decor is of early country antiques. Your hosts provide homemade snacks and fruit in the guest rooms. For breakfast, freshly baked pastries and breads are served. Hot Springs National Park, Lake Hamilton, the Mid-America Museum, and a racetrack are nearby.

Vintage Comfort B&B Inn ✪

303 QUAPAW AVENUE, HOT SPRINGS, ARKANSAS 71901

Tel: **(501) 623-3258**
Host: **Helen Bartlett**
No. of Rooms: **4**
No. of Private Baths: **4**
Double/pb: **$60–$75**
Single/pb: **$50–$60**
Open: **All year**

Breakfast: **Full**
Credit Cards: **AMEX, DISC, MC, VISA**
Pets: **No**
Children: **Welcome, over 6**
Smoking: **No**
Social Drinking: **Permitted**
Airport/Station Pickup: **Yes**

This handsome turn-of-the-century Queen Anne–style home has been faithfully restored, attractively appointed, and air-conditioned. The theme here is comfort and southern hospitality. Breakfast treats include biscuits and sausage gravy, grits, and regional hot breads. Afterwards, enjoy a short stroll to the famed Bath House Row or a brisk walk to the park, where miles of hiking trails will keep you in shape. Helen will be happy to direct you to the studios and shops of local artists and craftspeople. You are welcome to relax in the old-world sitting room and parlor or on the lovely veranda shaded by magnolia trees.

Williams House Bed & Breakfast Inn ✪
420 QUAPAW AVENUE, HOT SPRINGS, ARKANSAS 71901

Tel: **(501) 624-4275**
Hosts: **Mary and Gary Riley**
Best Time to Call: **9–11 AM; evenings**
Location: **50 mi. SW of Little Rock**
No. of Rooms: **6**
No. of Private Baths: **4**
Max. No. Sharing Bath: **4**
Double/pb: **$65–$80**
Single/pb: **$60–$75**
Double/sb: **$55**

Single/sb: **$50**
Suites: **$75–$80**
Open: **All year**
Breakfast: **Full**
Credit Cards: **AMEX, MC, VISA**
Pets: **No**
Children: **Welcome, over 7**
Smoking: **Permitted**
Social Drinking: **Permitted**

This Victorian mansion, with its stained-glass and beveled-glass windows, is a nationally registered historical place. The atmosphere is friendly, and the marble fireplace and grand piano invite congeniality. Breakfast menu may include quiche, toast amandine, or exotic egg dishes. Gary and Mary will spoil you with special iced tea, snacks, and mineral spring water. World health experts recognize the benefits of the hot mineral baths in Hot Springs National Park. The inn is within walking distance of Bath House Row. There's a two-night minimum stay on weekends during March and April.

Brambly Hedge Cottage
HC 31, BOX 39, JASPER, ARKANSAS 72641

Tel: **(501) 446-5849**
Best Time to Call: **Anytime**
Hosts: **Bill and Jacquelyn Smyers**

Location: **24 mi. S of Harrison**
No. of Rooms: **2**
No. of Private Baths: **2**

Double/pb: **$55**
Open: **All year**
Breakfast: **Full**
Pets: **No**

Children: **No**
Smoking: **No**
Social Drinking: **Permitted**

Delight in a gourmet breakfast served on the deck while you watch the clouds drift by in the valley below. From the back of this Ozark Mountain home you can see clear to Missouri. Brambly Hedge is a two-story stucco house built around a hundred-year-old cabin; the original logs frame the thick-walled living room. Your hosts favor country French decor with Victorian accents, pairing plush furnishings with the lace your hostess tats herself. Tea lovers should ask Jacquelyn about her collection of Russian and Turkish samovars. The lovely upstairs bedroom has a king-size bed and a sitting area. Nearby are hiking trails, craft shops, river float trips, and the famous town of Dogpatch, while Eureka Springs and Branson, Missouri, are an hour and a half away.

Mountain Home Country Inn ✪
1501 HIGHWAY 201 NORTH, MOUNTAIN HOME, ARKANSAS 72653

Tel: **(501) 425-7557**
Hosts: **Ellen and Robert Ritlinger**
Location: **100 mi. N of Little Rock**
No. of Rooms: **4**
No. of Private Baths: **4**
Double/pb: **$35–$45**
Open: **March–Dec.**

Reduced Rates: **10% business travelers**
Breakfast: **Continental**
Pets: **No**
Children: **Welcome, over 5**
Smoking: **No**
Social Drinking: **Permitted**

Located just south of the Missouri border, this 80-year-old Colonial-style home is surrounded by huge oak trees and lush green lawns. Centrally air-conditioned, the guest rooms are attractively furnished in a country motif, with a lot of wicker, pretty quilts, and craft accessories. Ellen and Robert offer a snack and beverage upon your arrival. Robert, an avid angler, willingly shares his secrets about where the fish are biting. Most months feature activities of special interest, ranging from special fairs and flower festivals to music shows. Ellen graciously offers the use of her laundry facility to freshen your travel duds.

CALIFORNIA

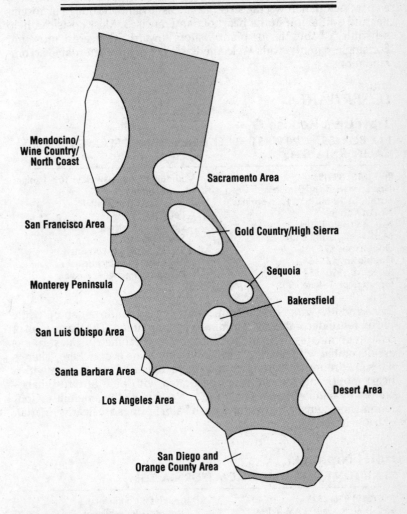

Mendocino/
Wine Country/
North Coast

Sacramento Area

San Francisco Area

Gold Country/High Sierra

Sequoia

Monterey Peninsula

Bakersfield

San Luis Obispo Area

Santa Barbara Area

Desert Area

Los Angeles Area

San Diego and
Orange County Area

Kids Welcome
730 CATALINA AVENUE, SEAL BEACH, CALIFORNIA 90740

Tel: **(310) 493-6837; (800) 383-3513**
Coordinator: **Robin Nahin**
States/Regions Covered: **Entire state**

Rates (Family):
  Modest: **$50**
  Average: **$60–$75**
  Luxury: **$85–$100**
Credit Cards: **MC, VISA**

Travelers with children can bed-and-breakfast in California with the assistance of this reservation network geared especially to families. For a $10 membership fee, guests receive a list of hosts and unlimited reservation assistance. The roster includes a hot springs spa in Ukiah, a cozy Victorian down the street from Disneyland, a cottage in Yosemite, and a little inn in the heart of San Francisco. Most hosts can help schedule a babysitter or point visitors toward the nearest museum. For single parents, Kids Welcome has a list of very affordable accommodations.

DESERT AREA

Travellers Repose ✪
P.O. BOX 655, 66920 FIRST STREET, DESERT HOT SPRINGS, CALIFORNIA 92240

Tel: (619) 329-9584
Hosts: Marian and Sam Relkoff
Location: 12 mi. N of Palm Springs
No. of Rooms: 3
No. of Private Baths: 1
Max. No. Sharing Bath: 4
Double/pb: $75
Double/sb: $55–$60
Single/sb: $50–$54
Open: Sept. 1–June 30

Reduced Rates: Weekly; 10% families on 2nd room
Breakfast: Continental
Pets: No
Children: Welcome, over 12
Smoking: No
Social Drinking: Permitted
Airport/Station Pickup: Yes
Foreign Languages: Russian

Bay windows, gingerbread trim, stained-glass windows, and a white picket fence decorate this charming Victorian home. The warm look of oak predominates in floors, wainscoting, and cabinetry. Guest rooms are decorated with hearts, dolls, and teddy bears everywhere. There's a rose bedroom with antiques and lace, a blue-and-white room with a heart motif, and a green room decorated with pine furniture handcrafted by Sam. A patio, pool, and spa complete the amenities. Golf, tennis, museums, galleries, and posh Palm Springs are nearby. Marian graciously serves tea at 4 PM.

Hotel Nipton ✪
72 NIPTON ROAD, NIPTON, CALIFORNIA 92364

Tel: (619) 856-2335
Best Time to Call: 9 AM–6 PM
Hosts: Jerry and Roxanne Freeman
Location: 10 mi. from I-15
No. of Rooms: 4
Max. No. Sharing Bath: 4
Double/sb: $45
Open: All year
Reduced Rates: Group

Breakfast: Continental
Other Meals: Available
Credit Cards: MC, VISA
Pets: No
Children: Welcome
Smoking: Permitted
Social Drinking: Permitted
Foreign Languages: Spanish

The population of Nipton is 30! The recently restored hotel, with its foot-thick adobe walls, was built in 1904 and is located in the East Mohave National Scenic Area. Nipton is in the heart of gold-mining territory, 30 minutes from Lake Mohave's Cottonwood Cove. You are welcome to relax on the porch or in the outdoor Jacuzzi. Continental breakfast is served in the lobby at your convenience.

GOLD COUNTRY/HIGH SIERRA

The Matlick House ✪
1313 ROWAN LANE, BISHOP, CALIFORNIA 93514

Tel: **(619) 873-3133**
Best Time to Call: **8 AM–8 PM**
Host: **Nanette Robidart**
Location: **1 mi. N of Bishop**
No. of Rooms: **5**
No. of Private Baths: **5**
Suites: **$65–$75**
Open: **All year**

Reduced Rates: **Corporate discounts**
Breakfast: **Full**
Pets: **No**
Children: **Welcome, over 10**
Smoking: **No**
Social Drinking: **Permitted**
Airport/Station Pickup: **Yes**

Hikers, backpackers, fishermen, and skiers are drawn to this turn-of-the-century ranch house in Owens Valley, which separates the White Mountains from the Sierra Nevadas. Energetic guests can reserve bicycles and picnic lunches and explore the area on their own. Of course, you may not be hungry for hours after a full breakfast of eggs, bacon, sausage, fresh-squeezed orange juice, sweet bread, homemade biscuits, and coffee or tea. Nanette has deftly combined authentic antiques with modern amenities to assure you a comfortable stay. A gallery showcasing local artists and a fine dinner restaurant are within walking distance.

Country Living Bed and Breakfast ✪
40068 ROAD 88, DINUBA, CALIFORNIA 93618

Tel: (209) 591-6617
Host: **Barbara Richardson**
Location: **30 mi. SE of Fresno**
No. of Rooms: **2**
Max. No. Sharing Bath: **4**
Double/sb: **$45–$55**
Open: **Sept.–June**

Breakfast: **Full**
Other Meals: **Available**
Pets: **No**
Children: **Welcome**
Smoking: **No**
Social Drinking: **No**

Once the guest house to the Tagus Ranch Historical site in Tulare, California, this home was moved to its present site in 1959. David and Barbara remodeled the house; inside, you'll see Barbara's own batik works. (Demonstrations and lessons available upon request, for an extra fee.) This area, known as the fruit basket of the world, bursts into bloom in late February and early March. Your map will show you easy access to Sequoia National Park, 40 miles away. Experience the snow and skiing areas in the Sierras, then return to Country Living for a hot shower and cozy bed.

The Heirloom ✪
P.O. BOX 322, 214 SHAKLEY LANE, IONE, CALIFORNIA 95640

Tel: (209) 274-4468
Hosts: **Melisande Hubbs and Patricia Cross**
Location: **35 mi. E of Sacramento**
No. of Rooms: **6**
No. of Private Baths: **4**
Max. No. Sharing Bath: **2**
Double/pb: **$69–$85**
Single/pb: **$65–$80**
Double/sb: **$55–$69**

Single/sb: **$50–$65**
Open: **All year**
Reduced Rates: **Weekly**
Breakfast: **Full**
Pets: **No**
Children: **Welcome, over 10**
Smoking: **No**
Social Drinking: **Permitted**
Airport/Station Pickup: **Yes**

Nestled in the Sierra foothills, yet close to the historic gold mines, wineries, antique shops, and museums, this 1863 mansion, with its lovely balconies and fireplaces, is a classic example of antebellum architecture. It is furnished with a combination of family treasures and period pieces. Patricia and Melisande's hearty breakfast includes such delights as quiche, crêpes, soufflé, and fresh fruits. Afternoon refreshments are always offered.

Chaney House ✪

4725 WEST LAKE BOULEVARD, P.O. BOX 7852, TAHOE CITY, CALIFORNIA 96145

Tel: **(916) 525-7333**
Hosts: **Gary and Lori Chaney**
Location: **50 mi. W of Reno, Nevada**
No. of Rooms: **3**
No. of Private Baths: **2**
Max No. Sharing Bath: **4**
Double/pb: **$85**
Double/sb: **$85**
Suites: **$95**

Guest Apartment: **$110**
Open: **All year**
Breakfast: **Full**
Pets: **No**
Children: **Welcome, over 12**
Smoking: **No**
Social Drinking: **Permitted**
Minimum Stay: **2 nights weekends**

Built on the Lake Tahoe shore by Italian stonemasons, Chaney House has an almost medieval quality, with its dramatically arched windows, extra thick walls, and enormous fireplace. The rear of the house faces the waterfront, where the Chaneys' private beach and pier beckon to guests. A water-skiing boat will even be placed at your disposal, by advance arrangement. Winter visitors can choose from 19 nearby ski areas. All the bedrooms have wood paneling and antique furniture. Breakfasts feature such foods as French toast and quiche.

Cort Cottage ✪
P.O. BOX 245, THREE RIVERS, CALIFORNIA 93271

Tel: (209) 561-4671
Best Time to Call: **Before 9 PM**
Hosts: **Gary and Catherine Cort**
Location: **5 mi. W of Sequoia National Park**
Guest Cottage: **$75; sleeps 2**
Open: **All year**

Breakfast: **Continental**
Pets: **No**
Children: **Welcome**
Smoking: **No**
Social Drinking: **Permitted**
Minimum Stay: **2 nights**

Hidden in the Sierra foothill village of Three Rivers, you will find this private guest cottage, ten minutes away from the entrance to Sequoia National Park. Built by Gary and Catherine as a house for Grandma, the cottage fits snugly into the hillside and has a panoramic view of mountains and sky. It offers an outdoor hot tub, a fully equipped kitchen, and full bath with step-down tub. Your hosts work as an architect/artist and a part-time nurse, have interests in gardening, crafts, and photography, and own a local art gallery.

LOS ANGELES AREA

Bed & Breakfast of Los Angeles
730 CATALINA AVENUE, SEAL BEACH, CALIFORNIA 90740

Tel: (310) 493-6837; (800) 383-3513
Coordinator: **Mario Voce**
States/Regions Covered: **Los Angeles, San Diego, Santa Barbara, San Luis Obispo, Ventura**

Rates: (Single/Double):
Modest: **$45 / $50**
Average: **$55 / $60**
Luxury: **$75 / $85**
Credit Cards: **MC, VISA**

Bed & Breakfast of Los Angeles has more than 130 accommodations stretching from San Diego to the Oregon border. Want to stay in a Malibu beach house, a Yosemite cottage, or a Victorian near Disneyland? Mario will send you a directory of hosts in the area you want to visit and make recommendations based on your special needs or interests. All hosts are happy to help with local arrangements, and many provide special amenities such as pools, hot tubs, bicycles, afternoon tea, or late night sherry.

El Camino Real Bed & Breakfast ✪
P.O. BOX 5475, SHERMAN OAKS, CALIFORNIA 91413-5475

Tel: (818) 785-8351
Best Time to Call: **Evenings**
Coordinator: **Lisa Reinstein**
States/Regions Covered: **Anaheim, Beverly Hills, Malibu, Palm Springs, San Diego, San Fernando Valley; Sun Valley, ID; Zion, UT**

Rates (Single/Double):
Modest: **$40–45 / $45–50**
Average: **$45–$55 / $55–$75**
Luxury: **N/A $115**
Credit Cards: **No**
Minimum Stay: **2 nights**

This service brings the tradition of California hospitality begun with the Franciscan missions to the present-day traveler. Homes are in beach communities conveniently located to such attractions as Disneyland, Knotts Berry Farm, and the movie studios. Average accommodations are in upper-middle-class homes with swimming pools/spas, except in hilly areas. Lisa offers modest apartments with simple furnishings and a luxurious private guest house on an estate with a hot tub and swimming pool. All hosts are longtime residents of California, familiar with the restaurants, tourist attractions, and the best ways of getting to them.

Martha Mueller's B&B
1154 DEERCREST DRIVE, DEVORE, CALIFORNIA 92407

Tel: **(714) 384-8119, 880-8028**
Hosts: **Ed and Jan Mueller**
Location: **15 mi. N of San Bernardino**
No. of Rooms: **3**
No. of Private Baths: **1**
Max. No. Sharing Bath: **4**
Double/pb: **$75**
Single/pb: **$70**
Double/sb: **$55–$65**
Single/sb: **$50–$60**

Open: **All year**
Reduced Rates: **10% seniors and families**
Breakfast: **Full**
Pets: **Sometimes**
Children: **Welcome, over 12**
Smoking: **No**
Social Drinking: **Permitted**
Airport/Station Pickup: **Yes**

Sited high above San Bernardino, in the foothills of the San Bernardino Forest, this recently built Victorian-style farmhouse has a panoramic view of both the city and the mountains. The local animal life is pretty spectacular, too: a llama farm is next door, and many people own horses. Cowboys and cowgirls of all ages will want to mosey on over to the Roy Rogers Museum, less than an hour away. If you're interested in classic examples of four-wheeled horsepower, be sure to ask Ed about his nostalgia car shop specializing in models from the fifties and sixties.

Black Rabbit Chateaux ✪
3146 CADET COURT, HOLLYWOOD HILLS, CALIFORNIA 90068

Tel: **(213) 851-8470**
Best Time to Call: **8–11 AM, 4–6 PM**
Hosts: **Francie and Morgan Neiman**
Location: **5 mi. SW of Beverly Hills**
No. of Rooms: **1**
No. of Private Baths: **1**
Double/pb: **$85**
Open: **Mar.–Oct.**

Breakfast: **Full**
Credit Cards: **AMEX**
Pets: **No**
Children: **Welcome, over 12**
Smoking: **No**
Social Drinking: **No**
Airport/Station Pickup: **Yes**

Retreat from L.A. at this quiet B&B three minutes from Hollywood Bowl and within walking distance of Universal Studios. Guests step through a private entrance into a bedroom furnished with antique pine, a fine feather bed, and exquisite linens; the screenless French windows let in fresh air from the canyon. Full gourmet breakfasts are served in the French country kitchen.

Casablanca Villa ✪
449 NORTH DETROIT STREET, LOS ANGELES, CALIFORNIA 90036

Tel: **(213) 938-4794**
Host: **Suzanne Moultout**
No. of Rooms: **2**
Max. No. Sharing Bath: **3**
Double/sb: **$60**
Single/sb: **$50**
Open: **All year**

Breakfast: **Continental**
Pets: **No**
Children: **No**
Smoking: **No**
Social Drinking: **No**
Foreign Languages: **French**

Suzanne Moultout welcomes you to her Spanish-style house located on a quiet, attractive street. Here, guests can enjoy the convenience of being close to West Hollywood, downtown, and Beverly Center, while having a comfortable home base. Your hostess offers an attractive guest room and a shady yard with fruit trees. She will gladly direct you to such nearby sights as Hollywood Hills, CBS Studios, and the beaches. Even if you don't have a car, the area is quite convenient, with a bus stop located within walking distance. This home is not wheelchair accessible.

Casa Larronde ✪
P.O. BOX 86, MALIBU, CALIFORNIA 90265-0086

Tel: **(310) 456-9333**
Best Time to Call: **Mornings**
Host: **Charlou Larronde**
Location: **40 mi. NW of Los Angeles**
No. of Rooms: **1 suite**
No. of Private Baths: **1**
Suite: **$115**

Open: **All year**
Breakfast: **Full**
Pets: **No**
Children: **Sometimes**
Smoking: **No**
Social Drinking: **Permitted**

The guest suite has a fireplace and color TV, but if you walk down the beach you may get to see the stars live; Flip Wilson and Bruce Willis are the neighborhood people here on Millionaires' Row. This house is 4,000 square feet of spectacular living space. It has floor-to-ceiling glass, ocean decks, a private beach, and a planter that's two stories high. Charlou, world traveler, enjoys entertaining, and her gourmet breakfast ranges from Scotch eggs to French toast made with Portuguese sweet bread. Champagne, cocktails, and snacks are complimentary refreshments. Pepperdine College is two miles away. The Getty Museum is a five-minute drive away.

Marina Bed & Breakfast ○
P.O. BOX 11828, MARINA DEL REY, CALIFORNIA 90295

Tel: (310) 821-9862
Best Time to Call: 5 PM–10 PM
Hosts: Peter and Carolyn Griswold
Location: 10 mi. SW of Los Angeles
No. of Rooms: 1
No. of Private Baths: 1
Suites: $50–$80
Open: All year

Reduced Rates: Weekly
Breakfast: Continental
Pets: No
Children: Welcome, over 12
Smoking: No
Social Drinking: Permitted
Minimum Stay: 2 nights

Peter and Carolyn's two-story house has a spacious studio with a separate entrance, full kitchen, color TV, private bathroom, and two full beds. Have a leisurely breakfast in your room or on the large rooftop yard. Then stroll across the street and admire the thousands of boats and yachts moored in the marina. Nearby, Fisherman's Village offers fine dining, shopping, and harbor cruises. Or you can borrow your hosts' bicycles and strike out for the bike path that runs from Malibu Beach in the north all the way down to San Pedro Harbor, some 35 miles away.

The Exley House "By-the-Sea" ○
4273 PALOS VERDES DRIVE SOUTH, RANCHO PALOS VERDES, CALIFORNIA 90274

Tel: (310) 377-2113
Hosts: Ruth and Earl Exley
Location: 5 mi. SW of Los Angeles
No. of Rooms: 2
No. of Private Baths: 2
Double/pb: $50
Single/pb: $35
Open: All year

Reduced Rates: 10% seniors
Breakfast: Full
Other Meals: Available
Pets: Sometimes
Children: Welcome
Smoking: Permitted
Social Drinking: Permitted
Airport/Station Pickup: Yes

This gracious ranch-style home in suburban Los Angeles has an unobstructed ocean view. Ruth and Earl belong to a private beach club across the road, and you can use the facilities there. It is close to Marineland, Disneyland, and Hollywood. Ruth's breakfast specialties include honey-baked ham, French toast, and quiche. Your hosts offer you hors d'oeuvres with other pre-dinner refreshments. California State–Dominguez Hills is close by.

Sea Breeze Bed & Breakfast ○
122 SOUTH JUANITA, REDONDO BEACH, CALIFORNIA 90277

Tel: (310) 316-5123
Best Time to Call: 6–10 PM

Hosts: Norris and Betty Binding
Location: 19 mi. S of Los Angeles

No. of Rooms: 2	Breakfast: **Continental**
No. of Private Baths: **2**	Pets: **No**
Double/pb: **$40–$50**	Children: **Welcome, over 5**
Single/pb: **$30–$35**	Smoking: **Permitted**
Open: **All year**	Social Drinking: **Permitted**
Reduced Rates: **10% seniors**	Airport/Station Pickup: **Yes**

The welcome mat is out in front of the lovely stained-glass Colonial doors at Norris and Betty's modest home. A patio-garden is just outside the large guest room, where you may relax after seeing the sights in the area. The Getty Museum and the Pasadena Rose Bowl are within easy reach. Their beach is the start of 22 miles of the Redondo-to-Pacific Palisades bicycle path, and tennis courts are within walking distance. Provisions are available if you prefer to fix breakfast yourself. You are welcome to use the Jacuzzi and TV. UCLA, USC, and Loyola Marymount University are nearby.

The Whites' House ✪
17122 FAYSMITH AVENUE, TORRANCE, CALIFORNIA 90504

Tel: **(310) 324-6164**	Open: **All year**
Host: **Margaret White**	Reduced Rates: **Weekly, monthly**
Location: **5 mi. S of Los Angeles Intl.**	Breakfast: **Continental**
Airport	Pets: **No**
No. of Rooms: 2	Children: **No**
No. of Private Baths: **2**	Smoking: **No**
Double/pb: **$30–$35**	Social Drinking: **Permitted**
Single/pb: **$25**	

This contemporary home, with its fireplaces, deck, and patio, is located on a quiet street in an unpretentious neighborhood. The airport and lovely beaches are 15 minutes away. Disneyland, Knotts Berry Farm, Universal Studio Tours, and Hollywood are 30 minutes from the door. Use the laundry facilities or kitchen; Margaret wants you to feel perfectly at home.

MENDOCINO/WINE COUNTRY/NORTH COAST

The Plantation House ✪
1690 FERRY STREET, ANDERSON, CALIFORNIA 96007

Tel: **(916) 365-2827**	Open: **All year**
Best Time to Call: **Anytime**	Breakfast: **Full**
Hosts: **Vi and Bob Webb**	Pets: **No**
Location: **8 mi. S of Redding**	Children: **No**
No. of Rooms: 2	Smoking: **No**
No. of Private Baths: **2**	Social Drinking: **Permitted**
Double/pb: **$50**	Airport/Station Pickup: **Yes**
Suite: **$90**	

Stay in a sumptuous suite with its own romantic balcony or in one of two elegantly furnished rooms at this antique-filled Queen Anne Victorian. Vi and Bob dress in elaborate Civil War fashions to greet you. Their complimentary hors d'oeuvres, served at your convenience, are so ample that guests have no room for dinner afterward. Schedule breakfast whenever you want it. For this meal, your hosts are decked out in turn-of-century style: bustle dress for Vi, frocked coat, striped morning trousers, and cravat for Bob.

Hillcrest B&B ○
3225 LAKE COUNTY HIGHWAY, CALISTOGA, CALIFORNIA 94515

Tel: (707) 942-6334
Best Time to Call: After 8 PM
Host: Debbie O'Gorman
Location: 2 mi. N of Calistoga
No. of Rooms: 6
No. of Private Baths: 3
Max. No. Sharing Bath: 4
Double/pb: $80–$90

Double/sb: $45–$70
Open: All year
Breakfast: Continental
Pets: Sometimes
Children: No
Smoking: Permitted
Social Drinking: Permitted

Despite its name, Hillcrest is located near the base—not the top—of Mt. St. Helena, in an area famed for its wineries and spas. Without leaving the B&B's 36-acre property, guests can hike, swim, fish, or stay indoors and play the Steinway grand piano. The house was built by Debbie's great-great-grandfather, and you'll see cherished family heirlooms at every turn. An elegant Continental breakfast of juice, coffee, fresh fruit, and baked goods is served on antique china and silver.

Scarlett's Country Inn ○
3918 SILVERADO TRAIL NORTH, CALISTOGA, CALIFORNIA 94515

Tel: (707) 942-6669
Best Time to Call: 9 AM–5 PM
Host: Scarlett Dwyer
Location: 75 mi. N of San Francisco;
   30 mi. from I-80, Napa exit
No. of Rooms: 3
No. of Private Baths: 3
Double/pb: $85
Single/pb: $70

Suites: $95–$125
Guest Cottage: $220; sleeps 6
Open: All year
Breakfast: Continental
Pets: No
Children: Welcome
Smoking: Permitted
Social Drinking: Permitted
Foreign Languages: Spanish

This inn is an intimate retreat tucked away in a small canyon in the heart of the famed Napa Valley, just minutes away from wineries and spas. Tranquillity, green lawns, and a refreshing swimming pool await you in this peaceful woodland setting. An ample breakfast, featuring freshly squeezed juice, sweet rolls, and freshly ground coffee, is served on the deck, at poolside, or in your own sitting room. All rooms have separate entrances, queen-size beds, and luxurious linens.

Muktip Manor ✪
12540 LAKESHORE DRIVE, CLEARLAKE, CALIFORNIA 95422

Tel: (707) 994-9571	Breakfast: **Full**
Hosts: **Jerry and Nadine Schiffman**	Pets: **Welcome**
Location: **101 mi. N of San Francisco**	Children: **Sometimes**
No. of Rooms: **1 suite**	Smoking: **Permitted**
No. of Private Baths: **1**	Social Drinking: **Permitted**
Suite: **$50**	Foreign Languages: **French, Spanish**
Open: **All year**	

Jerry traded the often-frenzied San Francisco life-style for an uncomplicated existence by the largest lake in the state. He does not offer Victoriana, priceless antiques, or gourmet food. He does provide comfortable accommodations in his unpretentious beach house, a place to relax on the deck, and the use of his private beach and bicycles. He enjoys windsurfing and canoeing, and has been known to give instruction to interested guests. The motto of Muktip Manor is, "If you wish company, I'm a conversationalist; if you wish privacy, I'm invisible."

Inn Oz ✪
13311 LAKESHORE DRIVE, P.O. BOX 1046, CLEARLAKE PARK, CALIFORNIA 95424

Tel: (707) 995-0853	Reduced Rates: **10% seniors**
Best Time to Call: **Between 9 AM and 5 PM**	Breakfast: **Full, Continental**
	Wheelchair accessible: **Yes**
Hosts: **Pauline and Charley Stephanski**	Pets: **Yes**
Location: **100 mi. N of San Francisco**	Children: **Welcome**
No. of Rooms: **1**	Smoking: **Permitted**
No. of Private Baths: **1**	Social Drinking: **Permitted**
Double/pb: **$60**	Station Pickup: **Yes**
Open: **All year**	

On the shores of California's largest freshwater lake, two hours north of San Francisco by automobile (and faster by house in a cyclone), you'll find country so beautiful it could have inspired L. Frank Baum's tales of the land of Oz. Savor unsurpassed sunsets, full moons, and starry heavens over Clearlake from your bed or on your private patio. Your spacious chamber has a wheelchair-accessible private entrance, a wood-burning fireplace, and a fully equipped kitchenette; the bathroom has a shower and a tub with a portable whirlpool. Pianists are encouraged to tickle the ivories of the upright Steinway. For additional fun, ask your hosts to show you the doll's house Pauline's grandfather built in 1938.

An Elegant Victorian Mansion ✪
1406 'C' STREET, EUREKA, CALIFORNIA 95501

Tel: **(707) 444-3144, 442-5594**	Reduced Rates: **20% Jan.–May,** **except holidays**
Best Time to Call: **11 AM–7 PM**	Breakfast: **Full**
Hosts: **Doug and Lily Vieyra**	Credit Cards: **MC, VISA**
No. of Rooms: **4**	Pets: **No**
No. of Private Baths: **1**	Children: **Welcome, over 15**
Max. No. Sharing Bath: **4**	Smoking: **No**
Double/pb: **$110**	Social Drinking: **Permitted**
Single/pb: **$100**	Airport/Station Pickup: **Yes**
Double/sb: **$75–$95**	Foreign Languages: **Dutch, French,**
Single/sb: **$65–$75**	**German**
Open: **All year**	

Just a few blocks from Eureka's historic Old Town, on a rise overlooking the city and Humboldt Bay, sits An Elegant Victorian Mansion. Opulent and gracious, it is one of Eureka's most luxurious homes, offering spirited camaraderie and five-star service. A visit here is like a festive vacation with one's best friends. Warm and friendly hosts serve an acclaimed gourmet breakfast in the regal splendor of a national historic landmark.

Gingerbread Mansion

400 BERDING STREET, FERNDALE, CALIFORNIA 95536

Tel: (707) 786-4000
Host: **Ken Torbert**
Location: **15 mi. S of Eureka**
No. of Rooms: **9**
No. of Private Baths: **9**
Double/pb: **$70–$175**
Single/pb: **$55–$160**
Suites: **$85–$175**
Open: **All year**

Reduced Rates: **Available**
Breakfast: **Continental**
Credit Cards: **MC, VISA**
Pets: **No**
Children: **Welcome, over 10**
Smoking: **No**
Social Drinking: **Permitted**
Minimum Stay: **2 nights Saturday,
    holidays, and special events**

Painted peach and yellow, surrounded by English gardens, this striking Victorian landmark is one of northern California's most photographed homes. Guests have a choice not only of bedrooms, but of parlors as well: two are stocked with books and games, a third is set up for afternoon tea, and the fourth displays the inn's own 1,000-piece jigsaw in various stages of completion. In your bedroom there are a bathrobe in the dresser and a hand-dipped chocolate by the bedside. Forgot your raingear? Not to worry, umbrellas and rubber boots are available. In good weather, borrow a house bicycle. For breakfast, homemade muffins, fruit, local cheeses, hard-boiled eggs, and beverages are served in the formal dining room overlooking the garden.

Avalon House

561 STEWART STREET, FORT BRAGG, CALIFORNIA 95437

Tel: (707) 964-5555
Best Time to Call: **9 AM–noon**
Host: **Anne Sorrells**
Location: **One block off Hwy. 1, Fir
    St. exit**
No. of Rooms: **6**
No. of Private Baths: **6**
Double/pb: **$70–$125**

Open: **All year**
Breakfast: **Full**
Credit Cards: **AMEX, DISC, MC, VISA**
Pets: **No**
Children: **Welcome**
Smoking: **No**
Social Drinking: **Permitted**

Located three blocks from the ocean and one block from the Skunk Train depot, this redwood California Craftsman house makes a great home base for visitors to Mendocino County. Anne, a designer who specializes in historic renovations, drew on her own travels to create an appealing B&B. Her furniture is an eclectic mix of antiques and wicker pieces. The more luxurious rooms have fireplaces and whirlpool baths. Breakfasts are ample: a typical meal might consist of hominy grits with eggs, ham, fried apples, and biscuits or perhaps sour cream pancakes.

Campbell Ranch Inn
1475 CANYON ROAD, GEYSERVILLE, CALIFORNIA 95441

Tel: (707) 857-3476	Open: **All year**
Best Time to Call: **10 AM–8 PM**	Breakfast: **Full**
Hosts: **Mary Jane and Jerry Campbell**	Credit Cards: **DISC, MC, VISA**
Location: **1.6 mi. from Rte. 101,**	Pets: **No**
Canyon Road Exit	Children: **Welcome, over 10**
No. of Rooms: **5**	Smoking: **No**
No. of Private Baths: **5**	Social Drinking: **Permitted**
Double/pb: **$90–$125**	Minimum Stay: **2 nights weekends**
Single/pb: **$80–$115**	Airport/Station Pickup: **Yes**
Guest Cottage: **$145**	

"Spectacular!" and "charming!" are expressions most often used when guests describe their stay at this picture-perfect hilltop home surrounded by 35 acres in the heart of the Sonoma County wine country. The spacious bedrooms, each with a king-size bed, are handsomely furnished; several have balconies where views of mountains and vineyards are a backdrop to the colorful flower gardens. Breakfast, beautifully served, features a selection of fresh fruit, choice of gourmet egg dishes, homemade breads and cakes, and a variety of beverages. You can burn off the calories on the Campbells' tennis court or in their swimming pool, or borrow a bike to tour the wineries. Water sports and fishing are less than four miles away. Jerry will be happy to make your dinner reservations at one of the area's fine restaurants, but leave room for Mary Jane's dessert, always served "at home."

Moorings ✪
8 PINE HILL DRIVE, P.O. BOX 35, INVERNESS, CALIFORNIA 94937

Tel: (415) 669-1464	Open: **All year**
Hosts: **John and Lee Boyce-Smith**	Breakfast: **Full**
Location: **45 mi. N of San Francisco**	Pets: **No**
No. of Rooms: **1**	Children: **No**
No. of Private Baths: **1**	Smoking: **No**
Double/pb: **$75**	Social Drinking: **Permitted**
Single/pb: **$70**	Foreign Languages: **German**

Sailors and hikers will feel right at home here. From the open-air decks of this modern, cedar-shingled home, visitors can admire both Tomales Bay and Inverness Ridge. Your hosts will be glad to tell you about nearby parks and beaches. You'll have the stamina to explore the area after a hearty breakfast, served in the dining room overlooking the bay. Standard offerings range from Belgian waffles and Dutch babies to scrambled eggs with chopped ham.

Palisades Paradise B&B
1200 PALISADES AVENUE, REDDING, CALIFORNIA 96003

Tel: **(916) 223-5305**
Best Time to Call: **4–6 PM**
Host: **Gail Goetz**
Location: **1¼ mi. from Rte. I-5 Exit Hilltop Dr.**
No. of Rooms: **2**
Max. No. Sharing Bath: **4**
Double/sb: **$60–$70**
Single/sb: **$55–$65**

Open: **All year**
Reduced Rates: **Available**
Breakfast: **Full**
Credit Cards: **AMEX, MC, VISA**
Pets: **No**
Children: **Welcome, over 6**
Smoking: **No**
Social Drinking: **Permitted**

Enjoy breathtakingly beautiful views from the patio and spa deck of this contemporary riverside home near Shasta College and Simpson College. Stay in either the Cozy Retreat or the Sunset Suite, both aptly named. In the morning, Gail serves ample breakfasts, with gourmet coffee, pastries, and her own Palisades fruit puffs.

The Hidden Oak
214 EAST NAPA STREET, SONOMA, CALIFORNIA 95476

Tel: **(707) 996-9863**
Best Time to Call: **9 AM–5 PM**
Host: **Catherine Cotchett**
Location: **45 mi. N of San Francisco**
No. of Rooms: **3**
No. of Private Baths: **3**
Double/pb: **$90–$115**
Single/pb: **$85–$105**

Open: **All year**
Reduced Rates: **weekly**
Breakfast: **Full**
Pets: **No**
Children: **Welcome, over 12**
Smoking: **On front porch only**
Social Drinking: **Permitted**
Airport/Station Pickup: **No**

This brown-shingled bungalow makes a great home base for forays into wine country. In fact, Catherine will lend you a bicycle to discover several wineries just a short ride away. Upon your return, you can select a book from the library and sit by the fire. The spacious bedrooms are furnished with antiques and wicker pieces. Breakfasts, served at 9:30, include egg entrées, fresh fruit, and baked goods hot out of the oven; early risers will find coffee and a newspaper in the parlor after 7:30. Feel free to specify what you cannot eat. Catherine will happily create a meal that adheres to your dietary restrictions.

Vichy Springs
2605 VICHY SPRINGS ROAD, UKIAH, CALIFORNIA 95482

Tel: **(707) 462-9515**
Best Time to Call: **9 AM–9 PM**
Host: **Gilbert Ashoff**
Location: **105 mi. N of San Francisco**
No. of Rooms: **15**
No. of Private Baths: **15**
Double/pb: **$115**
Single/pb: **$80**
Guest Cottage: **$145–$160**

Open: **All year**
Breakfast: **Continental**
Credit Cards: **AMEX, DC, MC, VISA**
Pets: **No**
Children: **Welcome**
Smoking: **No**
Social Drinking: **Permitted**
Airport Pickup: **Yes**
Foreign Languages: **Spanish**

Choose between twelve individually decorated rooms and two self-contained cottages at this B&B spa. Vichy features naturally sparkling, 90-degree mineral baths, a 104-degree pool, and an Olympic-size pool, along with 700 private acres with trails and roads for hiking, jogging, picnicking, and mountain biking. Staff members offer Swedish massage, reflexology, herbal facials, and acupressure. Set amid native oak, madrone, manzanita, bay, fir, pine, and buckeye, this quiet resort will leave you refreshed and invigorated.

MONTEREY PENINSULA
Happy Landing Inn ❂
P.O. BOX 2619, CARMEL, CALIFORNIA 93921

Tel: **(408) 624-7917**
Best Time to Call: **8:30 AM–9 PM**
Hosts: **Robert and Carol Ballard and Dick Stewart**
Location: **120 mi. S of San Francisco**
No. of Rooms: **7**
No. of Private Baths: **7**
Double/pb: **$90–145**
Open: **All year**

Breakfast: **Continental**
Credit Cards: **MC, VISA**
Pets: **No**
Children: **Welcome, over 12**
Smoking: **No**
Social Drinking: **Permitted**
Minimum Stay: **2 nights weekends**
Foreign Languages: **Japanese**

Located on Monte Verde between 5th and 6th, this Hansel and Gretel–style inn is a charming and romantic place to stay. Rooms with cathedral ceilings open onto a beautiful garden with gazebo, pond, and flagstone paths. Lovely antiques and personal touches, including breakfast served in your room, make your stay special.

Unicorn ✪
BOX 1540, PEBBLE BEACH, CALIFORNIA 93953

Tel: **(408) 624-5717**	Open: **All year**
Best Time to Call: **After 6 PM**	Breakfast: **Continental**
Host: **Ingo**	Pets: **No**
Location: **3 mi. W of Carmel**	Children: **No**
No. of Rooms: **1**	Smoking: **No**
No. of Private Baths: **1**	Social Drinking: **Permitted**
Double/pb: **$85**	Foreign Languages: **German**

Located in an exclusive area on the magnificent Monterey Peninsula, this lovely home on two acres is just a quarter-mile from the beach. The guest bedroom has ocean and forest views, and it is quite private because it is separated by two hallways from the main section of the house. The only thing you'll hear is the sound of ocean, and seals. Two nights preferred, one night $10 extra.

Babbling Brook Inn ✪
1025 LAUREL STREET, SANTA CRUZ, CALIFORNIA 95060

Tel: **(408) 427-2437; (800) 866-1131**	Reduced Rates: **Available**
Best Time to Call: **7 AM–11 PM**	Breakfast: **Full**
Host: **Helen King**	Credit Cards: **AMEX, DISC, MC, VISA**
Location: **2 blocks from Hwy. 1**	Pets: **No**
No. of Rooms: **12**	Children: **Welcome, over 12**
No. of Private Baths: **12**	Smoking: **No**
Double/pb: **$85–$135**	Minimum Stay: **2 nights weekends**
Open: **All year**	Foreign Languages: **French, Spanish**

Cascading waterfalls, a brook, gardens, and redwood trees surround this country inn. The oldest part of the house was built in 1909 on what was once a tannery and flour mill. Over the years, the house was changed by a number of owners, including the counsel to a czar and a woman known as the countess, who added several rooms and a balcony. It is a rustic, rambling retreat decorated in French country furnishings. Most rooms have a cozy fireplace, private deck, and outside entrance. Your host has owned restaurants and hotels in South America and is an expert in making 2 people or 100 feel equally at home. Helen is a gourmet cook, as you will see from her breakfast repertoire of omelets, stratas, and frittatas. This historic inn is walking distance from the ocean, boardwalk, shops, and tennis courts.

Blue Spruce Inn
2815 MAIN STREET, SOQUEL, CALIFORNIA 95073

Tel: **(408) 464-1137**	Hosts: **Pat and Tom O'Brien**
Best Time to Call: **Afternoons**	Location: **60 mi. S of San Francisco**

No. of Rooms: **5**
No. of Private Baths: **5**
Double/pb: **$80–$115**
Single/pb: **$75–$110**
Open: **All year**
Reduced Rates: **15% Sun. thru Thurs.;**
  15% Corporate; Nov.–Mar., 10%
  seniors
Breakfast: **Full**
Credit Cards: **AMEX, MC, VISA**

Pets: **No**
Children: **Welcome**
Smoking: **No**
Social Drinking: **Permitted**
Minimum Stay: **2 nights weekends**
Airport/Station Pickup: **Yes**
Foreign Languages: **Spanish**

The O'Briens' 1873 farmhouse, where beds are graced with Amish quilts and walls are hung with original local art, blends the flavor of yesterday with the luxury and privacy of today. From these accommodations on the crest of Monterey Bay, guests can easily enjoy beaches, unique shops, and superb dining. There are excellent local wineries, many antique shops, and state parks with miles of hiking and biking trails. Pat sets out a bountiful breakfast of fresh fruit, homemade breads, and exceptional entrees to fuel guests for the day's activities; for the perfect day's end, she recommends soaking in the hot tub under the stars.

Knighttime Bed and Breakfast ✪
890 CALABASAS ROAD, WATSONVILLE, CALIFORNIA 95076

Tel: **(408) 684-0528**
Best time to Call: **8–10 AM;**
  5–7 PM
Hosts: **Diane Knight and Ray Miller**
Location: **90 mi. S of San Francisco**
No. of Rooms: **1**
No. of Private Baths: **1**
Double/pb: **$60**

Single/pb: **$50**
Open: **All year**
Breakfast: **Full**
Other Meals: **Available**
Pets: **Sometimes**
Children: **Welcome**
Smoking: **No**
Social Drinking: **Permitted**

A wooden home with a pitched roof and wide porches, Knighttime is set on 26 wooded acres just a few minutes' drive from the beaches between Santa Cruz and Monterey. Sunlight bathes the interior filled with art, pine cabinetry, and country comforts. Eclectic furnishings include some antiques as well as reproductions and wicker. The main floor has a country French flavor while the upper floor—the private guest area—is strongly influenced by shells and the sea. This spacious guest area comprises a sitting room, large bath, large bedroom, and a second bedroom that can sleep two additional people in the same party.

SACRAMENTO AREA

The Inn at Shallow Creek Farm ☯
ROUTE 3, BOX 3176, ORLAND, CALIFORNIA 95963

Tel: **(916) 865-4093**	Reduced Rates: **$10 less after 3rd**
Best Time to Call: **Evenings**	**night**
Hosts: **Mary and Kurt Glaeseman**	Breakfast: **Continental**
Location: **3 mi. from I-5**	Pets: **No**
No. of Rooms: **4**	Children: **Sometimes**
No. of Private Baths: **2**	Smoking: **No**
Max. No. Sharing Bath: **4**	Social Drinking: **Permitted**
Double/pb.: **$60**	Airport/Station Pickup: **Yes**
Double/sb: **$45**	Foreign Languages: **French, German,**
Guest Cottage: **$75; sleeps 2–4**	**Spanish**
Open: **All year**	

The orchards of Shallow Creek Farm are known for mandarin and navel oranges and sweet grapefruit. Luscious berries, fresh garden produce, and a collection of exotic poultry, including rare silver guinea hens and African geese, are quite extraordinary. The inn, a gracious turn-of-the-century farmhouse, offers airy, spacious rooms furnished with carefully chosen antiques and family heirlooms, combining nostalgia with country comfort. Breakfast features homemade baked goods and jams, and a generous assortment of fresh fruits or juices and hot beverages.

The Feather Bed ☯
542 JACKSON STREET, QUINCY, CALIFORNIA 95971

Tel: **(916) 283-0102**	Open: **All year**
Hosts: **Chuck and Dianna Goubert**	Reduced Rates: **10% less on 3rd night**
Location: **70 mi. NW of Reno, Nevada**	Breakfast: **Full**
No. of Rooms: **7**	Credit Cards: **AMEX, MC, VISA**
No. of Private Baths: **7**	Pets: **No**
Double/pb: **$65**	Children: **Welcome**
Single/pb: **$60**	Smoking: **No**
Suite: **$75**	Social Drinking: **Permitted**
Separate Cottage: **$90; sleeps 3**	Airport/Station Pickup: **Yes**

This charming Queen Anne was built in 1893 and renovated at the turn of the century. The rooms feature vintage wallpaper, antique furnishings, and charming baths; most have clawfoot tubs. Enjoy a glass of cider in the parlor, or a cool iced tea on the front porch. A full three-course breakfast is served on the patio or in the dining room. The inn is convenient to water sports, snowmobiling, hiking, tennis, and skiing. Your hosts offer complimentary bicycles to help you explore beautiful Plumas National Forest and historic downtown Quincy. Restaurants and the county museum are close by.

SAN DIEGO AND ORANGE COUNTY AREA

Coronado Village Inn ✪
1017 PARK PLACE, CORONADO, CALIFORNIA 92118

Tel: **(619) 435-9318**
Best Time to Call: **To 10 PM**
Hosts: **Brent and Elizabeth Bogh**
Location: **3 mi. W of San Diego**
No. of Rooms: **14**
No. of Private Baths: **14**
Double/pb: **$50–$60**
Single/pb: **$50–$60**
Suites: **$70; sleeps 4**

Open: **All year**
Reduced Rates: **Winter weekly rate—7th night free**
Breakfast: **Continental**
Credit Cards: **AMEX, MC, VISA**
Pets: **No**
Children: **Welcome**
Smoking: **Yes**
Social Drinking: **Permitted**

Enjoy the ambience of yesteryear at this small, European-style hotel. Within easy walking distance are tennis courts, golf courses, boating facilities, quaint shops, fine restaurants, and the white sandy beaches of the Pacific Ocean. San Diego and Mexico are just a short drive away, boasting numerous attractions.

The Blue Door ✪
13707 DURANGO DRIVE, DEL MAR, CALIFORNIA 92014

Tel: **(619) 755-3819**
Best Time to Call: **7 AM–10 PM**
Hosts: **Bob and Anna Belle Schock**
Location: **20 mi. N of San Diego**
No. of Rooms: **1 suite**
No. of Private Baths: **1**
Suite: **$50–$60**

Open: **All year**
Reduced Rates: **After 5th night**
Breakfast: **Full**
Pets: **No**
Children: **No**
Smoking: **No**
Social Drinking: **Permitted**

Enjoy New England charm in a quiet southern California setting overlooking exclusive Torrey Pines State Reserve. A garden-level two-room suite with wicker accessories and king or twin beds is yours. The sitting room has a couch, a desk, and a color TV. Breakfast is served in the spacious country kitchen or in the dining room warmed by the fire on chilly days. Anna Belle prides herself on creative breakfast menus featuring homemade baked goods. Breakfast specialties include blueberry muffins, Swedish oatmeal pancakes, and Blue Door orange French toast. Your hosts will gladly direct you to the nearby racetrack, beach, zoo, or University of California at San Diego. There is a $10 surcharge for one-night stays.

Gulls Nest
12930 VIA ESPERIA, DEL MAR, CALIFORNIA
(MAILING ADDRESS: P.O. BOX 1056, DEL MAR, CALIFORNIA 92014)

Tel: **(619) 259-4863**
Best Time to Call: **Before 8:30 AM**
Hosts: **Connie and Mike Segel**
Location: **20 mi. N of San Diego**
No. of Rooms: **2**
No. of Private Baths: **2**
Double/pb: **$60**

Suite: **$75**
Open: **All year**
Breakfast: **Full**
Pets: **No**
Children: **Welcome, over 6**
Smoking: **No**
Social Drinking: **Permitted**

Gulls Nest is a contemporary wood home surrounded by pine trees. The house boasts a beautiful view of the ocean and a bird sanctuary from two upper decks. Guest accommodations consist of a comfortable, quiet room with queen-size bed, TV, private bath, and patio. The suite has a king-size bed and a sitting room that can accommodate a third person for $10 more. Breakfast is served outdoors, weather permitting, and features fresh-squeezed juice, eggs, homemade breads, and coffee cake. Great swimming and surfing are three blocks away at Torrey State Beach. Golf, shops, and restaurants are a 5-minute drive, and Tijuana and the international border are 40 minutes away.

Inncline B&B ✪
121 NORTH VULCAN, ENCINITAS, CALIFORNIA 92024

Tel: **(619) 944-0318**
Host: **Kirsten Cline**
Location: **23 mi. N of San Diego**
No. of Rooms: **5**
No. of Private Baths: **5**
Double/pb: **$75–150**
Double/sb: **$85**
Suite: **$95**

Open: **All year**
Reduced Rates: **10% weekly, seniors, families**
Breakfast: **Continental**
Pets: **No**
Children: **Welcome (playpen)**
Smoking: **Permitted**
Social Drinking: **Permitted**

Choose among a separate apartment, three queen bedrooms, and a penthouse with a private spa, whirlpool tub, and shower in this contemporary two-story home filled with furniture the Clines built themselves. Sunbathe in privacy on the deck overlooking the Pacific, or stroll down to Moonlight Beach for a refreshing ocean dip. It's a short walk to downtown Encinitas, which boasts many fine restaurants. Mt. Palomar Observatory, Sea World, Del Mar Race Track, and the Mexican border are about a half hour away by car. Guests have use of a kitchenette. Continental breakfasts consist of muffins, fresh fruit, yogurt, and coffee, tea, or hot chocolate.

Hidden Village Bed & Breakfast ✪
9582 HALEKULANI DRIVE, GARDEN GROVE, CALIFORNIA 92641

Tel: **(714) 636-8312**	Suites: **$75**
Best Time to Call: **8 AM–9 PM**	Open: **All year**
Hosts: **Dick and Linda O'Berg**	Reduced Rates: **$10 less, Sun.–Thurs.**
Location: **3 mi. S of Anaheim**	Breakfast: **Full**
No. of Rooms: **4**	Wheelchair Accessible: **Yes**
No. of Private Baths: **2**	Pets: **Sometimes**
Max. No. Sharing Bath: **2**	Children: **Welcome (crib)**
Double/pb: **$55**	Smoking: **No**
Single/pb: **$45**	Social Drinking: **Permitted**
Double/sb: **$50**	Airport/Station Pickup: **Yes**
Single/sb: **$40**	

Linda has decorated this large Colonial home with lacy draperies and handmade quilts; she's a professional weaver, and guests are welcome to browse in her studio. When you're done looking at fabrics, Disneyland, the Anaheim Convention Center, and Orange County's lovely beaches are just minutes away. Couch potatoes can watch tapes on the VCR, while the energetic can borrow the O'Bergs' bicycles and go for a spin. In the mornings, you'll savor a full breakfast of fresh fruit, homemade apple muffins, and quiche or omelets.

Country Comfort Bed and Breakfast ✪
5104 EAST VALENCIA DRIVE, ORANGE, CALIFORNIA 92669

Tel: **(714) 532-2802**	Reduced Rates: **10% less after 3rd night**
Best Time to Call: **Evenings**	Breakfast: **Full**
Hosts: **Geri Lopker and Joanne Angell**	Other Meals: **Available**
Location: **5 mi. E of Anaheim**	Pets: **By arrangement**
No. of Rooms: **3**	Children: **Welcome**
No. of Private Baths: **3**	Smoking: **No**
Double/pb: **$60**	Social Drinking: **Permitted**
Single/pb: **$55**	
Open: **All year**	

Located in a quiet residential area, Geri and Joanne have furnished their home with your comfort and pleasure in mind. It is handicapped-accessible with adaptive equipment available. Amenities include a swimming pool, cable TV and VCR, an atrium, fireplace, and the use of bicycles, including one built for two. Breakfast often features delicious Scotch eggs, stuffed French toast and hash, along with fruits and assorted beverages. Vegetarian selections are also available. Disneyland and Knotts Berry Farm are less than seven miles away.

Betty S. Bed & Breakfast ✪
3742 ARIZONA STREET, SAN DIEGO, CALIFORNIA 92104

Tel: **(619) 692-1385**
Host: **Betty Spiva Simpson**
No. of Rooms: **2**
Max. No. Sharing Bath: **2**
Single/sb: **$25–$30**
Open: **All year**
Reduced Rates: **Long-term stay**

Breakfast: **Full**
Pets: **No**
Children: **No**
Smoking: **Permitted**
Social Drinking: **Permitted**
Airport/Station Pickup: **Yes**

Betty offers clean, comfortable accommodations in an attractive bungalow. The guest rooms are furnished comfortably with tasteful pieces, carpeting, and a ceiling fan. You are welcome to relax in the den or on the patio, and can feel free to store snacks and beverages in the guest refrigerator. Betty will gladly direct you to nearby Balboa Park, San Diego Zoo, and tennis courts.

The Cottage ✪
P.O. BOX 3292, SAN DIEGO, CALIFORNIA 92163

Tel: **(619) 299-1564**
Best Time to Call: **9 AM–5 PM**
Hosts: **Robert and Carol Emerick**
Location: **1 mi. from Rte. 5**
No. of Rooms: **2**
No. of Private Baths: **2**
Double/pb: **$49–$80**
Guest Cottage: **$65–$80; sleeps 3**

Open: **All year**
Breakfast: **Continental**
Credit Cards: **AMEX, MC, VISA**
Pets: **No**
Children: **Welcome**
Smoking: **No**
Social Drinking: **Permitted**

Located in the Hillcrest section, where canyons and old houses dot the landscape, this private hideaway offers a cottage with a king-size bed in the bedroom, a single bed in the living room, full bath, and fully equipped kitchen. Decorated with turn-of-the-century furniture, the wood-burning stove and oak pump organ evoke memories of long ago. It's two miles to the zoo, less to Balboa Park, and it is within easy walking distance of restaurants, shops, and theater. The University of California and the University of San Diego are nearby.

E's Inn
3776 HAWK STREET, SAN DIEGO, CALIFORNIA 92103

Tel: **(619) 295-5622**	Breakfast: **Continental**
Host: **Erene Rallis**	Other Meals: **Available**
Location: **½ mi. from US 5 and 8**	Pets: **Sometimes**
No. of Rooms: **2**	Children: **Welcome**
No. of Private Baths: **2**	Smoking: **Porch and patio only**
Double/pb: **$45**	Social Drinking: **Permitted**
Single/pb: **$35**	Airport/Station Pickup: **Yes**
Open: **All year**	Foreign Languages: **Greek**
Reduced Rates: **Weekly; 10% seniors**	

On a quiet street in Mission Hills, this gray-and-white cedar-sided home welcomes the visitor with its inviting pillared porch and French doors. The house is decorated with a blend of Greek antiques, armoires, and modern Dansk pieces, complemented by original paintings, ceramics, and enamels. Your host loves to cater to her guests, and provides baskets of fresh fruit and flowers in each room. In the evening, she places a tiny surprise under each pillow. Breakfast specialties include seven-grain breads. On weekends Greek and Mexican omelets are served. E's is close to Balboa Park, the Gaslight District, and beautiful beaches.

Vera's Cozy Corner
2810 ALBATROSS STREET, SAN DIEGO, CALIFORNIA 92103

Tel: **(619) 296-1938**	Open: **All year**
Best Time to Call: **Before 10 AM;**	Reduced Rates: **Weekly; 10% seniors**
after 5 PM	Breakfast: **Continental**
Host: **Vera V. Warden**	Pets: **No**
No. of Rooms: **1**	Children: **No**
No. of Private Baths: **1**	Smoking: **No**
Double/pb: **$50**	Social Drinking: **Permitted**
Single/pb: **$40**	Foreign Languages: **French, German**

This crisp white Colonial with black shutters sits on a quiet cul-de-sac overlooking San Diego Bay. Guest quarters consist of a separate cottage with private patio entrance. Vera offers fresh-squeezed juice from her own fruit trees in season as a prelude to breakfast, served in the Wardens' old-world dining room. The house is convenient to local shops and restaurants, and is a mile from the San Diego Zoo.

SAN FRANCISCO AREA

American Family Inn ☉
P.O. BOX 420009, SAN FRANCISCO, CALIFORNIA 94142

Tel: (415) 479-1913
Best Time to Call: 9:30 AM–5 PM
Coordinators: **Susan and Richard Kreibich**
States/Regions Covered: **Carmel, Marin County, Monterey, Napa, San Francisco, Sonoma (wine country)**

Descriptive Directory: **$2**
Rates (Single/Double):
  Modest: **$45 / $55**
  Average: **$50 / $55**
  Luxury: **$65 / $75–$200**
Credit Cards: **AMEX, DC, MC, VISA**
Minimum Stay: **2 nights**

The San Francisco locations are near all of the famous sights, such as Fisherman's Wharf and Chinatown. Many are historic Victorian houses. Some homes offer hot tubs and sun decks; a few are on yachts and houseboats.

Bed & Breakfast International—San Francisco ☉
P.O. BOX 282910, SAN FRANCISCO, CALIFORNIA 94128

Tel: (415) 696-1690
Best Time to Call: 8:30 AM–5 PM
Coordinator: **Sharene Z. Klein**
States/Regions Covered: **California— Berkeley, Los Angeles, Palo Alto, San Francisco and the Bay Area, Monterey, Napa Valley, Lake Tahoe, San Diego, Santa Barbara; Yosemite; Las Vegas**

Rates (Single/Double):
  Modest: **$40–$44 / $44–$58**
  Average: **$54–$72 / $60–$78**
  Luxury: **$74 and up / $80 and up**
Credit Cards: **AMEX, MC, VISA**
Minimum Stay: **2 nights, generally**

Bed and Breakfast International is the oldest reservation service in the United States. Accommodations range from a town house apartment to a villa, with a private pool, above an ocean beach. Others are located near the seashore, at a marina, in a redwood forest, by a mountain stream, in the middle of a vineyard, as well as in city neighborhoods and downtown areas. A $10 surcharge is made by those who accept one-night stays.

Burlingame B&B ☉
1021 BALBOA AVENUE, BURLINGAME, CALIFORNIA 94010

Tel: (415) 344-5815
Hosts: **Joe and Elnora Fernandez**

Location: **½ mi. from Rte. 101**
No. of Rooms: **1**

No. of Private Baths: **1**
Double/pb: **$50**
Single/pb: **$40**
Open: **All year**
Breakfast: **Continental**
Pets: **No**

Children: **Welcome**
Smoking: **No**
Social Drinking: **No**
Airport/Station Pickup: **Yes**
Foreign Languages: **Italian, Spanish**

Located in a pleasantly quiet neighborhood, with San Francisco only minutes away by good public transportation. The house offers the privacy of upstairs guest quarters with a view of a creek and native flora and fauna. It's all very clean and cheerfully decorated. Joe and Elnora will direct you to restaurants and shops to suit your budget.

Lore's Haus ✪
22051 BETLEN WAY, CASTRO VALLEY, CALIFORNIA 94546

Tel: **(415) 881-1533**
Host: **Lore Bergman**
Location: **25 mi. SE of San Francisco**
No. of Rooms: **2**
No. of Private Baths: **1**
Max. No. Sharing Bath: **4**
Double/pb: **$60**
Single/pb: **$55**
Double/sb: **$55**
Single/sb: **$50**

Open: **All year**
Breakfast: **Full**
Pets: **No**
Children: **Welcome, over 14**
Smoking: **Permitted**
Social Drinking: **Permitted**
Airport/Station Pickup: **Yes**
Foreign Languages: **French, German**
Minimum Stay: **2 nights**

Lore's Haus is an attractive ranch home on a quiet street, with a large, beautiful garden. Lore was born in Germany and has spent the last 30 years in Castro Valley. She prides herself on offering Americans a true European atmosphere, with a lot of plants, books, comfortable furnishings, and oriental rugs. Breakfast includes French Brie, fresh German black bread, homemade jams, cold cuts, and eggs. If you like, tours of the Bay Area, Napa Valley, or anyplace else are available in German, French, or English. If you'd like to venture out on your own, the city center is 25 minutes away via car or rapid transit. After a day of touring, come back to Lore's and enjoy a glass of wine.

Old Thyme Inn ✪
779 MAIN STREET, HALF MOON BAY, CALIFORNIA 94019

Tel: **(415) 726-1616**
Best Time to Call: **8 AM–10 PM**
Hosts: **Anne and Simon Lowings**
Location: **30 mi. S of San Francisco**
No. of Rooms: **7**
No. of Private Baths: **7**
Double/pb: **$65–$135**
Single/pb: **$60–$130**
Suites: **$145–$210**

Open: **All year**
Breakfast: **Full**
Credit Cards: **AMEX, DISC, MC, VISA**
Pets: **Sometimes**
Children: **Welcome, over 6**
Smoking: **No**
Social Drinking: **Permitted**
Minimum Stay: **Holiday weekends**
Foreign Languages: **French**

The Old Thyme Inn is a restored Victorian house located on the Pacific coast just 35 minutes south of San Francisco. Some rooms have fireplaces, some have baths with double-size whirlpool tubs, and all are decorated with antiques. Your hosts Anne and Simon hail from England. They invite you to stroll in Anne's herb garden; if you like, you can have a cutting kit and take samples home for your own use. Simon's breakfast includes his justly celebrated buttermilk scones.

Zaballa House ✪
324 MAIN STREET, HALF MOON BAY, CALIFORNIA 94019

Tel: **(415) 726-9123**	Reduced Rates: **Mon.–Thurs.**
Best Time to Call: **7 AM–9 PM**	Breakfast: **Continental, plus**
Hosts: **Sharon Tedrow and Linda Malone**	Credit Cards: **AMEX, DISC, MC, VISA**
Location: **35 mi. S of San Francisco**	Pets: **By arrangement**
No. of Rooms: **9**	Children: **Welcome, over 6**
No. of Private Baths: **9**	Smoking: **No**
Double/pb: **$65–$135**	Social Drinking: **Permitted**
Single/pb: **$60–$130**	Minimum Stay: **2 nights holiday weekends**
Open: **All year**	

Built in 1859 by Estanislao Zaballo, the community's first city planner, this bed-and-breakfast inn is the oldest house in Half Moon Bay. The inn is located on the same block as two of the coast's finest restaurants and enjoys a wonderful garden setting. Sharon loves flower arranging, and the local gardens provide her with an abundance of flowers for all the rooms. She is also expert in neighborhood lore—ask her to tell you about the ghost. In the evenings, guests are invited to share complimentary drinks around the fireplace; in the mornings, all-you-can-eat buffet breakfasts are served.

Montara Bed & Breakfast ✪
P.O. BOX 493, MONTARA, CALIFORNIA 94037

Tel: **(415) 728-3946**	Open: **All year**
Best Time to Call: **Evenings**	Reduced Rates: **Weekly**
Hosts: **Bill and Peggy Bechtell**	Breakfast: **Full**
Location: **20 mi. S of San Francisco**	Credit Cards: **MC, VISA**
No. of Rooms: **1**	Pets: **Sometimes**
No. of Private Baths: **1**	Children: **No**
Double/pb: **$80**	Smoking: **No**
Single/pb: **$70**	Social Drinking: **Permitted**

Relax in a California-style contemporary set in a coastal hamlet on scenic Highway 1. Montara is a rural area, yet it's just 20 miles from San Francisco. Guest accommodations are newly remodeled and feature a private entrance that opens onto a redwood deck. Guests have exclusive use of an adjacent sitting room with a fireplace and an ocean view. Breakfast is served in a solarium overlooking the garden. Your hosts serve a variety of specialties along with honey from their beehives. Local activities include playing in the waves at the state beach, wandering the hiking trails at McNee Ranch State Park, or riding on Miramar Beach. There are numerous seafood restaurants to choose from, as well as cuisine from Italy, Germany, and Mexico.

Casa Arguello
225 ARGUELLO BOULEVARD, SAN FRANCISCO, CALIFORNIA 94118

Tel: **(415) 752-9482**	Open: **All year**
Best Time to Call: **10 AM–6 PM**	Breakfast: **Continental**
Host: **Emma Baires**	Pets: **No**
No. of Rooms: **4**	Children: **Welcome, over 7**
No. of Private Baths: **2**	Smoking: **No**
Max. No. Sharing Bath: **3**	Social Drinking: **Permitted**
Double/pb: **$67–$77**	Minimum Stay: **2 nights**
Double/sb: **$50**	Foreign Languages: **Spanish**
Suites: **$101 for 4**	

This spacious duplex has an elegant living room, dining room, and cheerful bedrooms that overlook neighboring gardens. Tastefully decorated with modern and antique furnishings, it is convenient to Golden Gate Park, Golden Gate Bridge, Union Square, and fine shops and restaurants. The University of California Medical School is nearby. Excellent public transportation is close by.

Casita Blanca ✪
330 EDGEHILL WAY, SAN FRANCISCO, CALIFORNIA 94127

Tel: **(415) 564-9339**	Pets: **No**
Host: **Joan Bard**	Children: **No**
No. of Rooms: **1 cottage**	Smoking: **No**
No. of Private Baths: **1**	Social Drinking: **Permitted**
Guest Cottage: **$80; sleeps 2**	Minimum Stay: **2 nights**
Open: **All year**	Foreign Languages: **French, Spanish**
Breakfast: **Continental**	

Casita Blanca is a guest cottage perched high on a hill, not far from Golden Gate Park. In this delightful hideaway, nestled among giant trees, you'll find twin beds, a private bath with a stall shower, and a complete kitchen stocked for your convenience with all the necessary items. If you tire of sightseeing and shopping, then just curl up in front of the little fireplace, have a glass of wine, and listen to the birds singing outside. Joan also offers accommodations in Carmel-by-the-Sea, Lake Tahoe, Sonoma, Palm Desert, and Maui.

Chez Duchéne
1075 BROADWAY, SAN FRANCISCO, CALIFORNIA 94133

Tel: (415) 441-3160	Open: **All year**
Best Time to Call: **Early AM—evening**	Breakfast: **Continental**
Host: **Jay Duchéne**	Pets: **No**
No. of Rooms: **1**	Children: **Welcome**
No. of Private Baths: **1**	Smoking: **No**
Double/pb: **$90**	Social Drinking: **Permitted**
Single/pb: **$90**	Minimum Stay: **2 nights**

Experience true San Francisco style in this charming three-story Victorian row home. Your bedroom offers breathtaking views of the bay and the city skyline. An exhilarating walk or cable car ride will take you from this Russian Hill hideaway to the heart of the downtown and waterfront bustle. Cross the Golden Gate Bridge, sail on the bay, or simply make yourself at home at Chez Duchéne.

Rancho San Gregorio ✪
ROUTE 1, BOX 54, SAN GREGORIO, CALIFORNIA 94074

Tel: (415) 747-0810; fax: (415) 747-0184	Reduced Rates: **Available**
	Breakfast: **Continental, full**
Hosts: **Bud and Lee Raynor**	Pets: **No**
Location: **35 mi. S of San Francisco**	Children: **Welcome**
No. of Rooms: **4**	Smoking: **No**
No. of Private Baths: **4**	Social Drinking: **Permitted**
Double/pb: **$65–$135**	Airport/Station Pickup: **Yes**
Open: **All year**	

Graceful arches and bright stucco characterize this Spanish Mission home set on 15 wooded acres. Rooms are decorated with American antiques and family pieces. Your hosts, Bud and Lee, are glad to share a snack and a beverage. On weekdays they serve a Continental breakfast; on Saturdays and Sundays a full feast features eggs or pancakes, fresh fruit and breads, and a variety of meats. The atmosphere is relaxing, and guests are welcome to borrow a book from the library, or play the organ. Rancho San Gregorio is close to the beach, horseback riding, and golf. San Francisco, Half Moon Bay, and a variety of state parks and recreational areas are within an hour's drive.

Mrs. "K's" Retreat ✪
14497 NEW JERSEY AVENUE, SAN JOSE, CALIFORNIA 95124

Tel: (408) 371-0593	Double/pb: **$50**
Hosts: **Barbara and George Kievlan**	Single/pb: **$40**
Location: **3 mi. E of Hwy. 17**	Open: **All year**
No. of Rooms: **3**	Reduced Rates: **Weekly**
No. of Private Baths: **3**	Breakfast: **Continental**

Pets: **No**   Smoking: **No**
Children: **Welcome**   Social Drinking: **Permitted**

This sprawling ranch-style home is nestled at the base of Blossom Valley, once famous for its orchards. Guest rooms are furnished with flair and boast separate entrances. Your hosts invite you to enjoy the living room fireplace, family room, spa, and adjacent patio, with pool and spacious yard. Those interested in stained glass will surely want to visit the studio on the premises. Handicap facilities are available.

Madison Street Inn ✪
1390 MADISON STREET, SANTA CLARA, CALIFORNIA 95050

Tel: **(408) 249-5541**
Hosts: **Theresa and Ralph Wigginton**
Location: **1½ mi. from Rte. 880**
No. of Rooms: **5**
No. of Private Baths: **3**
Max. No. Sharing Bath: **4**
Double/pb: **$75–$85**
Double/sb: **$60**
Single/sb: **$60**

Open: **All year**
Reduced Rates: **15% seniors**
Breakfast: **Full**
Other Meals: **Available**
Credit Cards: **AMEX, DC, MC, VISA**
Pets: **No**
Children: **Welcome**
Smoking: **No**
Social Drinking: **Permitted**

This restored, vintage Queen Anne is furnished with oriental rugs and museum-quality antiques, including brass beds and tubs-for-two. Landscaped gardens, a swimming pool, and a hot tub grace the grounds, and a sunny meeting room is available for business gatherings. Belgian waffles or eggs Benedict are often on the breakfast menu. Exciting dinners can be arranged, prepared by Ralph, an accomplished cook. It is convenient to Santa Clara University and San Jose State University.

SAN LUIS OBISPO AREA

Megan's Friends B&B Reservation Service
1776 ROYAL WAY, SAN LUIS OBISPO, CALIFORNIA 93405

Tel: **(805) 544-4406**
Best Time to Call: **Noon–4 PM; 6–10 PM; Mon.–Sat.**
Coordinator: **Joyce Segor**
States/Regions Covered: **Arroyo Grande, Baywood Park, Cambria, Los Osos, Morro Bay, Paso Robles, San Luis Obispo, Solvang, Sunset Palisades**

Rates (Single/Double):
  Average: **$50–$85 / $55–$85**
  Luxury: **$100–$125**

Joyce has exclusive listings no other reservation agency has. She is sure to accommodate you in a B&B best suited to your interests and purse; these range from a contemporary showplace to a cozy country cottage. A $10 onetime membership fee, for which you receive a detailed list describing the accommodations, is required. Local attractions include the beaches, wineries, farmers market, and Hearst Castle. Transatlantic travelers take note: through her association with an English B&B reservation service, Joyce can provide clients with lodging in the central London area west or north of Hyde Park and Kensington Gardens. Call or write for more information.

Baywood Bed & Breakfast Inn ✪
1370 SECOND STREET, BAYWOOD PARK, CALIFORNIA 93402

Tel: (805) 528-8888
Best Time to Call: 7 AM–8 PM
Hosts: Pat and Alex Benson and Pam and John Cutmore
Location: 12 mi. W of San Luis Obispo
No. of Rooms: 15
No. of Private Baths: 15
Double/pb: $80–$140
Suites: $120–$140
Open: All year

Reduced Rates: Available
Breakfast: Continental
Other Meals: Available
Credit Cards: MC, VISA
Pets: No
Children: Welcome
Smoking: No
Social Drinking: Permitted
Minimum Stay: 2 days on holiday weekends

This waterfront establishment lies on a tiny peninsula that projects into Morro Bay. Outdoor types will find plenty to do here; the options include kayaking, golfing, hiking, bicycling, and picnicking. Several shops and restaurants are right in town, and Montano De Oro State Park, San Luis Obispo, and Hearst Castle are only minutes away. Each Baywood suite has bay views, cozy seating areas, and a wood-burning fireplace. Guests are treated to afternoon wine and cheese, room tours, and breakfast in bed.

Gerarda's Bed & Breakfast ✪
1056 BAY OAKS DRIVE, LOS OSOS, CALIFORNIA 93402

Tel: (805) 528-3973
Host: Gerarda Ondang
Location: 10 mi. from Hwy. 101
No. of Rooms: 3
No. of Private Baths: 1
Max. No. Sharing Bath: 4
Double/pb: $41.34
Single/pb: $26.50
Double/sb: $41.34
Single/sb: $26.50

Open: All year
Breakfast: Full
Pets: Welcome
Children: Welcome
Smoking: No
Social Drinking: Permitted
Airport/Station Pickup: Yes
Foreign Languages: Dutch, Indonesian

When you stay at Gerarda's, you are in for a veritable Dutch treat! Located in a pleasant, quiet neighborhood, the house is surrounded by interesting landscaping and lovely flower beds. This is a simple home comfortably furnished, with charm and warmth. Breakfast features Dutch delicacies such as honeycake, jams, and breads. Hearst Castle, Morro Bay, and San Luis Obispo are within a half hour's drive. Gerarda has thoughtfully placed a TV in each guest bedroom.

SANTA BARBARA AREA

Carpinteria Beach Condo ✪
1825 CRAVENS LANE, CARPINTERIA, CALIFORNIA 93013

Tel: **(805) 684-1579**
Best Time to Call: **7 AM–9 PM**
Hosts: **Bev and Don Schroeder**
Location: **11 mi. SE of Santa Barbara**
Guest Condo: **$60–$75; sleeps 2 to 4**
Open: **All year**
Reduced Rates: **Available**

Breakfast: **Continental**
Pets: **No**
Children: **Welcome**
Smoking: **No**
Social Drinking: **Permitted**
Station Pickup: **Yes**

You may view majestic mountains from this one-bedroom condo across the street from the beach. If you tire of the ocean, there is also a swimming pool. Play a set of tennis at the local Polo and Racquet Club, visit your hosts' avocado and lemon ranch less than two miles away, or take a ten-minute drive into Santa Barbara. Breakfast is a do-it-yourself affair in the condo's complete minikitchen.

Long's Seaview Bed & Breakfast
317 PIEDMONT ROAD, SANTA BARBARA, CALIFORNIA 93105

Tel: **(805) 687-2947**
Best Time to Call: **Before 6 PM**
Host: **LaVerne Long**
Location: **1½ mi. from Hwy. 101**
No. of Rooms: **1**
No. of Private Baths: **1**
Double/pb: **$70–$75**
Single/pb: **$70**

Open: **All year**
Breakfast: **Full**
Pets: **No**
Children: **No**
Smoking: **No**
Social Drinking: **Permitted**
Airport/Station Pickup: **Yes**

Overlooking Santa Barbara's prestigious north side, this ranch-style home is in a quiet, residential neighborhood. Breakfast is usually served on the patio, where you can see the ocean, Channel Islands, and citrus orchards. Convenient to the beach, Solvang, and Santa Ynez Valley, the large, airy bedroom is cheerfully furnished with antiques and king-size bed. The breakfast menu varies from Southern dishes to Mexican specialties.

Ocean View House ○

P.O. BOX 20065, SANTA BARBARA, CALIFORNIA 93102

Tel: **(805) 966-6659**
Best Time to Call: **8 AM–5 PM**
Hosts: **Bill and Carolyn Canfield**
Location: **2 mi. from Hwy. 101**
No. of Rooms: **2**
No. of Private Baths: **1**
Double/pb: **$50**
Suite: **$70 for 4**

Open: **All year**
Breakfast: **Continental**
Pets: **Sometimes**
Children: **Welcome**
Smoking: **No**
Social Drinking: **Permitted**
Airport/Station Pickup: **Yes**
Minimum Stay: **2 nights**

This California ranch house features a guest room furnished with a queen-size bed and antiques. The adjoining paneled den, with double-bed divan and TV, is available together with the guest room as a suite. While you relax on the patio, you can look out at the sailboats on the ocean. It's a short walk to the beach and local shops. There is a $10 surcharge for one-night stays.

SEQUOIA AREA

Kern River Inn Bed & Breakfast ○

P.O. BOX 1725, 119 KERN RIVER DRIVE, KERNVILLE, CALIFORNIA 93238

Tel: **(619) 376-6750**
Best Time to Call: **8 AM–8 PM**
Hosts: **Mike Meehan and Marti Andrews**
Location: **50 mi. NE of Bakersfield**
No. of Rooms: **6**
No. of Private Baths: **6**
Double/pb: **$79–$89**
Single/pb: **$69–$79**

Open: **All year**
Reduced Rates: **Available**
Breakfast: **Full**
Credit Cards: **MC, VISA**
Pets: **No**
Children: **Welcome, over 12**
Smoking: **No**
Social Drinking: **Permitted**

Stay in a charming riverfront B&B in a quaint western town within Sequoia National Forest. Marti and Mike specialize in romantic, relaxing getaways. Nearby activities include golf, hiking, biking, whitewater rafting, downhill skiing, and year-round fishing in front of the inn. It's an easy stroll to shops, restaurants, and parks, and a short drive to the giant redwood trees. Your hosts love to fish and hike and can direct you to some of their favorite locations.

Road's End at Poso Creek ✪
RR 1, P.O. BOX 450, POSEY, CALIFORNIA 93260

Tel: **(805) 536-8668**
Best Time to Call: **9 AM–9 PM**
Host: **Jane Baxter**
Location: **55 mi. NE of Bakersfield**
No. of Rooms: **2**
No. of Private Baths: **1**
Max. No. Sharing Bath: **3**
Double/pb: **$135**
Single/pb: **$75**
Double/sb: **$120**

Single/sb: **$60**
Open: **All year**
Reduced Rates: **Weekly**
Breakfast: **Full**
Other Meals: **Available**
Pets: **No**
Children: **Yes**
Smoking: **No**
Social Drinking: **Permitted**
Minimum Stay: **Weekends, holidays**

Road's End is a restful streamside hideaway tucked into Sequoia National Forest. In this rustic setting, you can soak in a hot tub, fish for trout, and hike wilderness trails; in the winter, sledding and cross-country skiing await you. Jane prepares sumptuous meals, flavored with herbs and vegetables from her hillside garden. Her breakfast specialties include orange pecan waffles and, in homage to Dr. Seuss, green eggs and ham (the coloring comes from pesto).

For key to listings, see inside front or back cover.

✪ This star means that rates are guaranteed through December 31, 1993, to any guest making a reservation as a result of reading about the B&B in *Bed & Breakfast U.S.A.*—1993 edition.

Important! To avoid misunderstandings, always ask about cancellation policies when booking.

Please enclose a self-addressed, stamped, business-size envelope when contacting reservation services.

For more details on what you can expect in a B&B, see Chapter 1.

Always mention *Bed & Breakfast U.S.A.* when making reservations!

If no B&B is listed in the area you'll be visiting, use the form on page 733 to order a copy of our "List of New B&Bs."

We want to hear from you! Use the form on page 735.

COLORADO

Fort Collins •
Estes Park •
• Greeley

Winter Park •
Arvada
• • Denver
Glenwood Springs •
Vail •
• Golden
Georgetown
Pine
Grand Junction
Snowmass •
• Breckenridge
•
Aspen •
Minturn
• Cedaredge
Buena Vista •
Manitou Springs
• •
Hotchkiss •
• Gunnison
Colorado Springs

Ouray •

• Silverton

Durango •
• Pagosa Springs

Bed & Breakfast—Rocky Mountains
906 SOUTH PEARL STREET, DENVER, COLORADO 80209

Tel: **(800) 733-8415**
Best Time to Call: 8:30 AM–5:30 PM
  Mon.–Fri.; 9 AM–1 PM Sat. (MST)
Coordinator: **Cheryl Carroll**
States/Regions Covered: **Colorado,
  New Mexico, Utah**

Descriptive Directory: **$4.50**
Rates (Single/Double):
  Modest: **$20 / $35**
  Average: **$28 / $65**
  Luxury: **$50 / $120**
Credit Cards: **MC, VISA**

A free reservation service for Colorado, New Mexico, and Utah representing over 200 inns and homestays.

On Golden Pond Bed & Breakfast ✪
7831 ELDRIDGE, ARVADA, COLORADO 80005

Tel: (303) 424-2296
Best Time to Call: Anytime
Hosts: John and Kathy Kula
Location: 15 mi. W of Denver
No. of Rooms: 5
No. of Private Baths: 5
Double/pb: $50–$80
Single/pb: $40–$70
Suites: $80; sleeps 4
Open: All year

Reduced Rates: 10% Mar., Apr., Nov.; midweek; seniors, families
Breakfast: Full
Credit Cards: MC, VISA
Pets: Sometimes
Children: Welcome
Smoking: No
Social Drinking: Permitted
Airport/Station Pickup: Yes
Foreign Languages: German

A secluded retreat tucked into the Rocky Mountain foothills, this custom-built, two-story brick home has dramatic views of mountains, prairies, and downtown Denver. Birds and other wildlife are drawn to the ten-acre grounds, which have a fishing pond and hiking trails. After a full breakfast, stroll along the garden path, bicycle by the creek, swim laps in the pool, or ride horses into the foothills. Then join John and Kathy for a late afternoon kaffeeklatsch. Conclude the day with a soak in the hot tub.

The Tree House ✪
6650 SIMMS STREET, ARVADA, COLORADO 80004

Tel: (303) 431-6352
Hosts: Don and Sue Thomas
Location: 10 mi. W of Denver
No. of Rooms: 5
No. of Private Baths: 5
Double/pb: $49–$79
Open: All year

Breakfast: Full
Credit Cards: MC, VISA
Pets: No
Children: Welcome
Smoking: No
Social Drinking: Permitted
Airport/Station Pickup: Yes

The name of this bed-and-breakfast is inspired by its location, a ten-acre forest on the west side of Denver. Trails allow visitors to get an intimate view of Colorado's wildflowers, other plants, and woodland animals. Guest rooms are furnished with brass beds, handmade quilts, and antiques; most bedrooms have fireplaces. You are welcome to use the kitchen and laundry facilities. The Tree House also has a generous common area with a fireplace and oak and leather furniture.

Cotten House
102 SOUTH FRENCH STREET, P.O. BOX 387, BRECKENRIDGE, COLORADO 80424

Tel: (303) 453-5509
Hosts: Peter and Georgette Contos

Location: 85 mi. W of Denver
No. of Rooms: 3

No. of Private Baths: **1**
Max. No. Sharing Bath: **4**
Double/pb: **$90**
Single/pb: **$70–$75**
Open: **All year**
Reduced Rates: **$35–$40; less during summer months**

Breakfast: **Full**
Other Meals: **Available**
Pets: **No**
Children: **Welcome**
Smoking: **No**
Social Drinking: **Permitted**
Foreign Languages: **Greek, French**

Get the feel of Breckenridge's mining days in this restored 1886 Victorian listed on the National Historic Register. Peter and Georgette can tell you about their town's past with the help of period photographs mounted on their walls. The common room—equipped with a TV, VCR, books, and games—is a favorite gathering place, but shopping, restaurants, and evening entertainments will lure you to Main Street, two blocks away. Breckenridge's stunning mountain setting is appealing throughout the year. Admire wildflowers in the spring, attend special summer events, see the aspens change color in the fall; higher rates apply in the winter, when you have access to cold weather activities from the free shuttle bus that stops at the B&B's front door.

Trout City Inn ✪
BOX 431, BUENA VISTA, COLORADO 81211

Tel: **(719) 495-0348**
Best Time to Call: **After 6 PM**
Hosts: **Juel and Irene Kjeldsen**
Location: **5 mi. E of Buena Vista on Hwy. 24**
No. of Rooms: **4**
No. of Private Baths: **4**
Double/pb: **$35–$40**

Open: **June 1–Oct. 1**
Breakfast: **Full**
Other Meals: **Available**
Credit Cards: **MC, VISA**
Pets: **No**
Children: **Welcome, over 10**
Smoking: **No**
Social Drinking: **Permitted**

Trout City Inn is a historic site on the famous South Park Narrow Gauge Railroad, and is located at the edge of a trout stream. It is an accurate reconstruction of a mountain railroad depot, with authentic private rail cars containing Pullman berths. The depot rooms feature Victorian decor, high ceilings, and four-poster or brass beds. Glass doors open onto a deck with views of the 14,000-foot peaks of the Continental Divide. Hiking, biking, panning for gold, and fly-fishing are within steps of the front door; white-water rafting is minutes away. Social-hour snacks are served in the depot "waiting room."

Cedars' Edge Llamas Bed and Breakfast
2169 HIGHWAY 65, CEDAREDGE, COLORADO 81413

Tel: **(303) 856-6836**
Hosts: **Ray and Gail Record**
Location: **50 mi. E of Grand Junction**

No. of Rooms: **2**
No. of Private Baths: **2**
Double/pb: **$45–$55**

Single/pb: **$35–$45**
Open: **All year**
Breakfast: **Full**
Pets: **Sometimes**

Children: **Welcome**
Smoking: **No**
Social Drinking: **Permitted**
Airport/Station Pickup: **Yes**

Nestled on the southern slope of the Grand Mesa, this modern cedar home offers a panoramic view of several mountain ranges, plus the unique opportunity to share life on a llama-breeding ranch. The accommodations are immaculate. Cheerful rooms are tastefully decorated in pastel shades, with exposed beams, hanging plants, and light streaming in from many windows. Sportsmen and sportswomen can fish for trout, hunt deer and elk, or go cross-country and downhill skiing. After a filling breakfast, guests can join Ray and Gail in feeding or grooming well-behaved four-footed friends—a rewarding experience for all.

Griffin's Hospitality House ✪
4222 NORTH CHESTNUT, COLORADO SPRINGS, COLORADO 80907

Tel: **(719) 599-3035**
Best Time to Call: **Mornings, after 6 PM**
Hosts: **John and Diane Griffin**
Location: **5 mi. N of Colorado Springs**
No. of Rooms: **3**
No. of Private Baths: **1**
Max. No. Sharing Bath: **4**
Double/pb: **$45**
Single/pb: **$25**

Double/sb: **$35**
Open: **All year**
Breakfast: **Full**
Pets: **No**
Children: **Welcome (crib)**
Smoking: **No**
Social Drinking: **Permitted**
Airport/Station Pickup: **Yes**
Minimum Stay: **2 nights**

The welcome mat is always out at Diane and John's house. It's close to Pikes Peak, the Air Force Academy, and the Garden of the Gods. You can use the picnic table, TV, washing machine, and dryer. You will enjoy a fine view of Pikes Peak while eating a bountiful breakfast. In the evening, you are invited to relax in the living room with wine and good conversation. The University of Colorado is four miles away.

Holden House—1902 Victorian Bed & Breakfast Inn
1102 WEST PIKES PEAK AVENUE, COLORADO SPRINGS, COLORADO 80904

Tel: **(719) 471-3980**
Best Time to Call: **AM; after 4 PM**
Hosts: **Sallie and Welling Clark**
No. of Rooms: **5**
No. of Private Baths: **5**
Double/pb: **$60–$62**
Suites: **$90–$95**

Open: **All year**
Breakfast: **Full**
Credit Cards: **AMEX, DISC, MC, VISA**
Pets: **No**
Children: **No**
Smoking: **No**
Social Drinking: **Permitted**

Built by Isabel Holden, this 1902 storybook Victorian and 1906 carriage house are centrally located near historic Old Colorado City. The inn, lovingly restored by the Clarks in 1985, is filled with antiques and family heirlooms. Named for mining towns, guest rooms are furnished with queen beds, period furnishings, and down pillows. The inn also boasts three romantic suites with tubs for two, mountain views, fireplaces, and more! Gourmet breakfasts, served in summer on the veranda, might include carob chip muffins, Sallie's famous Eggs Fiesta, fresh fruit, gourmet coffee, tea, and juice. Complimentary refreshments, homemade cookies, and turndown service are just some of the Holden House's special touches. Sallie and Welling will be happy to help in planning your itinerary around the many activities in Pikes Peak Region. Friendly cat Mingtoy in residence.

The Painted Lady Bed & Breakfast Inn ✪
1318 WEST COLORADO AVENUE, COLORADO SPRINGS, COLORADO 80904

Tel: **(719) 473-3165**	Open: **All year**
Best Time to Call: **After 5 PM**	Reduced Rates: **10% seniors**
Hosts: **Kenneth and Stacey Kale**	Breakfast: **Full**
No. of Rooms: **4**	Credit Cards: **DISC, MC, VISA**
No. of Private Baths: **2**	Pets: **No**
Max. No. Sharing Bath: **4**	Children: **No**
Double/pb: **$65–$75**	Smoking: **No**
Double/sb: **$45–$55**	Social Drinking: **No**

Kenneth and Stacey lovingly restored this fanciful Victorian home built in 1894. You'll admire the exterior, with its gingerbread trim and wraparound porch and balcony. In good weather, breakfast and afternoon tea are served on the veranda overlooking the Colorado Mountains. Inside, you'll find period-style furnishings, such as brass or four-poster beds, lacy curtains, and even a pedestal sink. To immerse yourself further in the past, walk a few blocks to historic Old Colorado City, with its specialty shops and restaurants.

Queen Anne Inn ✪
2147 TREMONT PLACE, DENVER, COLORADO 80205

Tel: **(303) 296-6666; (800) 432-INNS**	Open: **All year**
[4667]	Breakfast: **Continental**
Best Time to Call: **Afternoons**	Credit Cards: **AMEX, DISC, MC, VISA**
Hosts: **Ann and Charles Hillestad**	Pets: **No**
No. of Rooms: **10**	Children: **Welcome, over 15**
No. of Private Baths: **10**	Smoking: **No**
Double/pb: **$64–$124**	Social Drinking: **Permitted**
Single/pb: **$54–$114**	

Located in the residential Clements Historic District, this three-story house, built in 1879, faces Benedict Fountain and Park. Decorated in the Queen Anne style, the luxurious bedrooms offer a choice of mountain or city views along with such touches as heirloom antiques, air-conditioning, and writing desks. Fine art, good books, and unobtrusive chamber music provide a lovely backdrop. The Hillestads offer a generous breakfast, including seasonal fruits, assorted breads, juice, homemade granola, and a special blend of coffee. The Central Business District, museums, shopping, and diverse restaurants are within walking distance. You are always welcome to help yourself to fruit, candy, soft drinks, and a glass of sherry. Ann and Charles will be happy to lend you their bikes for local touring.

Country Sunshine B&B
35130 HIGHWAY 550 NORTH, DURANGO, COLORADO 81301

Tel: (303) 247-2853; (800) 383-2853	Open: **All year**
Best Time to Call: **Anytime**	Reduced Rates: **Multiday stays and**
Hosts: **Jim and Jill Anderson**	**groups**
No. of Rooms: 5	Breakfast: **Full**
No. of Private Baths: 3	Credit Cards: **MC, VISA**
Max. No. Sharing Bath: 4	Pets: **No**
Double/pb: **$70**	Children: **Welcome, over 5**
Single/pb: **$60**	Smoking: **No**
Double/sb: **$55**	Social Drinking: **Permitted**
Single/sb: **$45**	Airport/Station Pickup: **Yes**

From this spacious ranch home nestled below rocky bluffs, there's a spectacular view of the San Juan Mountains. In summer, breakfast of homemade breads, jams, and blackberry pancakes with pure maple syrup is served on the large deck in view of the narrow-gauge train. In cooler weather, it is set family style in front of the dining room's wood stove.

Logwood—The Verheyden Inn ✪
35060 HIGHWAY 550, DURANGO, COLORADO 81301

Tel: (303) 259-4396; (800) 369-4082	Open: **All year**
Best Time to Call: **After 11 AM**	Breakfast: **Full**
Hosts: **Debby and Greg Verheyden**	Credit Cards: **MC, VISA**
Location: 212 mi. NW of	Pets: **No**
Albuquerque, New Mexico	Children: **Welcome, over 7**
No. of Rooms: 5	Smoking: **No**
No. of Private Baths: 5	Social Drinking: **Permitted**
Double/pb: **$65–$75**	Minimum Stay: **Holidays**
Single/pb: **$55–$65**	

Debby and Greg and their sons Michael and Alan invite you to come home to Logwood—an appealing rough-hewn cedar log retreat with a wraparound porch. All five rooms have that perfect western style, complete with home-stitched country quilts. A full breakfast and homemade award-winning desserts are served for your enjoyment.

Penny's Place ✪
1041 COUNTY ROAD 307, DURANGO, COLORADO 81301 ✪

Tel: **(303) 247-8928**	Open: **All year**
Best Time to Call: **Mornings**	Reduced Rates: **10% seniors**
Host: **Penny O'Keefe**	Breakfast: **Full**
Location: **11 mi. SE of Durango**	Credit Cards: **MC, VISA**
No. of Rooms: **3**	Pets: **No**
No. of Private Baths: **1**	Children: **Sometimes**
Max. No. Sharing Bath: **4**	Smoking: **No**
Double/pb: **$65–$75**	Social Drinking: **Permitted**
Double/sb: **$50–$55**	

Penny's Place rests on 26 acres of rolling countryside overlooking the spectacular La Plata Mountains. With a hot tub, satellite TV, and wood-burning stove, the large common room offers the perfect place for sharing ideas with other guests. Early risers can glimpse a deer or a meadowlark while inhaling the aroma of freshly brewed coffee. Penny prides herself on her hearty breakfasts, which may include blueberry muffins, quiche, or waffles, all served with jam and choke-cherry syrup made from the fruit of her own trees. A stay of several days is recommended so you can take advantage of Durango's attractions, such as the narrow-gauge train, Mesa Verde, hiking trails and bridle paths, and excellent fishing.

River House B & B ✪
495 ANIMAS VIEW DRIVE, DURANGO, COLORADO 81301

Tel: **(303) 247-4775**	Breakfast: **Full**
Host: **Crystal Carroll**	Other Meals: **Available**
No. of Rooms: **6**	Credit Cards: **DISC, MC, VISA**
No. of Private Baths: **6**	Pets: **No**
Double/pb: **$55**	Children: **Welcome**
Single/pb: **$40**	Smoking: **No**
Open: **All year**	Social Drinking: **Permitted**
Reduced Rates: **10% Mar. and Oct.**	Airport/Station Pickup: **Yes**

Healthful gourmet breakfasts are served in this B&B's spectacular, 900-square-foot atrium featuring eight skylights, a goldfish pond, and a cascading waterfall. From the bedrooms, views of the Animas River Valley often include elk, deer, geese, and eagles. Skiers enjoy the warmth of three fireplaces, while the large-screen TV is alive with nature videos. The house is often reserved for weddings, reunions, and retreats. Massage and hypnotherapy are offered by appointment.

Scrubby Oaks Bed & Breakfast ✪
P.O. BOX 1047, DURANGO, COLORADO 81302

Tel: **(303) 247-2176**
Best Time to Call: **Early mornings; evenings**
Host: **Mary Ann Craig**
Location: **4 mi. from junction 160 and 550**
No. of Rooms: **7**
No. of Private Baths: **3**
Max. No. Sharing Bath: **4**
Double/pb: **$65**

Single/pb: **$50**
Double/sb: **$55**
Single/sb: **$40**
Open: **All year**
Breakfast: **Full**
Pets: **No**
Children: **Welcome**
Smoking: **No**
Social Drinking: **Permitted**

There's a quiet country feeling to this two-story home set on 10 acres overlooking the spectacular Animas Valley and surrounding mountains. Trees and gardens frame the patios where breakfast is apt to be served. All breads and preserves are homemade, and strawberry Belgian waffles are a specialty. On chilly mornings, the kitchen fireplace is the cozy backdrop for your wake-up cup of coffee or cocoa. You are made to feel part of the family and are welcome to play pool, take a sauna, read a book, watch a VCR movie, or simply take in the crisp air.

Emerald Manor ✪
441 CHIQUITA LANE, P.O. BOX 3592, ESTES PARK, COLORADO 80517

Tel: **(303) 586-8050**
Best Time to Call: **8 AM–8 PM**
Hosts: **Reggie and Maura Fowler**

Location: **65 mi. NW of Denver**
No. of Rooms: **4**
Max. No. Sharing Bath: **4**

Double/sb: **$55–$65**
Single/sb: **$50–$60**
Open: **All year**
Breakfast: **Full**
Pets: **No**

Children: **No**
Smoking: **No**
Social Drinking: **Permitted**
Airport/Station Pickup: **Yes**

Every window of this Tudor pioneer home affords a beautiful view of the Rocky Mountains. The house is set on two acres in a quiet estate neighborhood within walking distance of downtown. Your hosts have decorated with comfortable wood furnishings, antiques, fine china, and crystal. Guest rooms are furnished in a variety of styles, from western to Victorian, and all have fine linens and lace-trimmed towels. Your hosts invite you to relax in a beamed living room in front of a cozy fire, or in a tropical room with indoor heated pool and sauna. They serve a complete gourmet breakfast, different every morning.

Wanek's Lodge at Estes ✪

P.O. BOX 898, 560 PONDEROSA DRIVE, ESTES PARK, COLORADO 80517

Tel: **(303) 586-5851**
Best Time to Call: **Evenings**
Hosts: **Jim and Pat Wanek**
Location: **71 mi. NW of Denver**
No. of Rooms: **3**
Max. No. Sharing Bath: **4**
Double/sb: **$44–$49**
Single/sb: **$37–$40**

Suite: **$98–$108**
Open: **All year**
Breakfast: **Continental**
Other Meals: **Available**
Pets: **No**
Children: **Welcome, over 10**
Smoking: **No**
Social Drinking: **Permitted**

Jim and Pat invite you to share their modern mountain inn, located on a ponderosa pine-covered hillside just minutes away from Rocky Mountain National Park. The wood beams, stone fireplace, plants, and beautiful scenery provide a comfortable and relaxed atmosphere. Former educators, your hosts are people-oriented, and staying with them is like being with old friends.

Elizabeth Street Guest House ✪

202 EAST ELIZABETH, FORT COLLINS, COLORADO 80524

Tel: **(303) 493-BEDS [2337]**
Hosts: **John and Sheryl Clark**
Location: **65 mi. N of Denver**
No. of Rooms: **3**
Max. No. Sharing Bath: **4**
Double/pb: **$61**
Single/pb: **$51**
Double/sb: **$47**
Single/sb: **$41**

Open: **All year**
Breakfast: **Full**
Credit Cards: **AMEX, MC, VISA (for deposits only)**
Pets: **No**
Children: **Welcome, over 8**
Smoking: **No**
Social Drinking: **Permitted**

This completely renovated and restored 1905 brick American four-square has leaded windows and oak woodwork. Family antiques, plants, old quilts, and handmade touches add to its charm. All of the bedrooms have sinks. It is close to historic Old Town Square, Estes Park, Rocky Mountain National Park, and a block away from Colorado State University. John and Sheryl will spoil you with their special brand of hospitality and homemade treats.

Hardy House
P.O. BOX 0156, GEORGETOWN, COLORADO 80444

Tel: **(303) 569-3388**	Suites: **$45–$65**
Best Time to Call: **After 10 AM**	Open: **All year**
Host: **Sarah M. Schmidt**	Breakfast: **Full**
Location: **50 mi. W of Denver**	Other Meals: **Available**
No. of Rooms: **4**	Pets: **No**
No. of Private Baths: **4**	Children: **Welcome, over 10**
Double/pb: **$57–$72**	Smoking: **No**
Single/pb: **$47–$62**	Social Drinking: **Permitted**

Back in the 1870s this bright red Victorian, surrounded by a white picket fence, was the home of a blacksmith. Inside you can relax by the potbelly parlor stove, sleep under feather comforters, and wake up to savory breakfast dishes such as waffle cheese strata and coffee cake. Guest quarters range from a two-bedroom suite to rooms with king-size or twin beds. In the evening, Sarah serves coffee and tea. Hardy House is located in the heart of the Historic District, half a block from the shops of Main Street. It is also close to hiking, skiing, and is walking distance from the Loop Railroad. Perhaps the best way to explore the town is on Sarah's six-speed tandem mountain bike, which she will gladly lend.

Bedsprings ○
830 BLAKE, GLENWOOD SPRINGS, COLORADO 81601

Tel: **(303) 945-0350**	Open: **All year**
Best Time to Call: **8 AM–8 PM**	Breakfast: **Full**
Host: **Emmy Hesse**	Credit Cards: **MC, VISA**
Location: **170 mi. W of Denver**	Pets: **No**
No. of Rooms: **2**	Children: **Welcome**
No. of Private Baths: **2**	Smoking: **Permitted**
Double/pb: **$50–$55**	Social Drinking: **Permitted**
Single/pb: **$40–$45**	Airport/Station Pickup: **Yes**

With its generous wraparound porch, this big, gabled home says welcome. Glenwood Springs is a resort community famous for its hot-springs pool. Depending on the season, visitors may ski, hike, or go river rafting. And the stores and restaurants are open year round. Of course, after a full breakfast of fresh fruit, Belgian waffles, and home-made muffins, you may not be hungry for hours.

The Kaiser House
932 COOPER AVENUE, GLENWOOD SPRINGS, COLORADO 81601

Tel: (303) 945-8827
Best Time to Call: 9 AM–5 PM
Hosts: Ingrid and Glen Eash
Location: 160 mi. W of Denver
No. of Rooms: 7
No. of Private Baths: 7
Double/pb: $58–$88
Single/pb: $42–$70
Open: All year
Reduced Rates: 10% for 4 nights or more

Breakfast: Full
Credit Cards: MC, VISA
Pets: No
Children: Welcome, over 8
Smoking: No
Social Drinking: Permitted
Minimum Stay: 2 nights summer weekends and holidays
Station Pickup: Yes

Located in the center of Glenwood Springs, the "Spa of the Rockies," Kaiser House combines turn-of-the-century charm and modern comforts. Each bedroom, decorated in Victorian style, has a private bath. In the winter, before hitting the ski slopes, savor a gourmet breakfast in either the spacious dining room or the sunny breakfast nook. In the summer, enjoy brunch on the private patio. From Kaiser House, it's an easy walk to parks, shopping, fine restaurants, and the hot-springs pool and vapor caves.

The Dove Inn
711 14TH STREET, GOLDEN, COLORADO 80401-1906

Tel: (303) 278-2209
Hosts: Sue and Guy Beals
Location: 10 mi. W of downtown Denver
No. of Rooms: 6
No. of Private Baths: 6
Double/pb: $46–$64
Single/pb: $41–$59

Open: All year
Reduced Rates: 10% weekly
Breakfast: Full
Credit Cards: AMEX, DC, MC, VISA
Pets: No
Children: Welcome (crib)
Smoking: No
Social Drinking: Permitted

The Dove Inn is a charming Victorian on grounds beautifully landscaped with decks, walkways, and huge trees. The house has many bay windows, dormers, and angled ceilings; each room is individually decorated with pretty wallpapers and Victorian touches. Breakfast specialties such as cinnamon rolls and fresh fruit compotes are served. This delightful inn is located in the foothills of West Denver in one of the state's most beautiful valleys, yet it is just minutes from downtown Denver, historic Golden, and many other Rocky Mountain attractions. No unmarried couples, please.

The Cider House ✪
1126 GRAND AVENUE, GRAND JUNCTION, COLORADO 81501

Tel: **(303) 242-9087**
Host: **Helen Mills**
Location: **2 mi. from I-70**
No. of Rooms: **3**
No. of Private Baths: **1**
Max. No. Sharing Bath: **4**
Double/pb: **$42**
Single/pb: **$32**
Double/sb: **$38**
Single/sb: **$28**

Open: **All year**
Reduced Rates: **Available**
Breakfast: **Full**
Other Meals: **Available**
Credit Cards: **MC**
Pets: **Sometimes**
Children: **Welcome**
Smoking: **Permitted**
Social Drinking: **Permitted**
Airport/Station Pickup: **Yes**

Nestled in the heart of Grand Junction is this two-story frame house built at the start of the century. It is comfortably decorated with period furnishings, old-fashioned wallpapers, and nostalgic touches. Lace curtains and French doors add to the elegance of the living room. Sumptuous breakfasts of locally grown fruit, homemade breads, jams, special waffles, and beverages are served in the adjoining dining room. Nearby attractions include the Grand Mesa, river rafting, dinosaur digs, and some of the best winter skiing in the country.

Sterling House Bed & Breakfast Inn ✪
818 12TH STREET, GREELEY, COLORADO 80631

Tel: **(303) 351-8805**
Host: **Lillian Peeples**
Location: **55 mi. N of Denver**
No. of Rooms: **2**
No. of Private Baths: **2**
Double/pb: **$39–$49**
Single/pb: **$34**
Open: **All year**
Reduced Rates: **Weekly**

Breakfast: **Full**
Other Meals: **Available**
Pets: **No**
Children: **Welcome, over 10**
Smoking: **Restricted**
Social Drinking: **Permitted**
Minimum Stay: **2nd week in May only**
Airport Pickup: **Yes**
Foreign Languages: **German**

One of Greeley's pioneers, cattle baron and banker Asa Sterling built this home for his family in 1886. Under its current ownership, the house retains its Victorian charm, thanks to the period decor and furniture. Downtown Greeley and the University of Northern Colorado are within walking distance, and it's an easy drive to Rocky Mountain National Park. Guests rave about Lillian's full breakfasts, with specialties like German apple pancakes and crêpes Benedict. Romantic candlelight dinners can also be arranged.

Mary Lawrence Inn ✪
601 NORTH TAYLOR, GUNNISON, COLORADO 81230

Tel: (303) 641-3343	Suites: $78–$102; sleep 2–4
Hosts: Les and Tom Bushman	Open: All year
Location: 195 mi. W and S of Denver	Breakfast: Full
No. of Rooms: 5	Other Meals: Available
No. of Private Baths: 3	Credit Cards: DISC, MC, VISA
Max. No. Sharing Bath: 4	Pets: No
Double/pb: $63	Children: Welcome
Single/pb: $58	Smoking: No
Double/sb: $50	Social Drinking: Permitted
Single/sb: $45	Airport/Station Pickup: Yes

An Italianate frame house with spacious, antique-filled guest rooms and comfortable common areas, the Mary Lawrence Inn is located in a well-kept neighborhood inside Gunnison's city limits. Surrounded by wilderness and Forest Service land, this B&B is a haven for sportspeople of all types; the Black Canyon of the Gunnison, the Alpine Tunnel, the town of Crested Butte, and many spectacular mountain vistas are all within an hour's drive. Les is a full-time innkeeper, while her husband Tom teaches mathematics at a nearby college.

Ye Ole Oasis Bed and Breakfast ✪
3142 J ROAD, HOTCHKISS, COLORADO 81419

Tel: (303) 872-3794	Open: Oct.–Aug.
Best Time to Call: Mornings; late evenings	Reduced Rates: Available
Hosts: Dwight and Rosemarie Ward	Breakfast: Full
Location: 1 mi. from Rte. 92	Other Meals: Available
No. of Rooms: 3	Credit Cards: MC, VISA
Max. No. Sharing Bath: 4	Pets: Sometimes
Double/sb: $40–$45	Children: Welcome, over 6
Single/sb: $30–$35	Smoking: No
	Social Drinking: Permitted

The Wards welcome you to their restored farmhouse set on the Rodgers Mesa at an elevation of 5,200 feet. They have a 17-acre working farm. The house is filled with antiques of all types, including many family heirlooms. Bedrooms have hand-crocheted and quilted spreads, wood furnishings, and period wallpapers. Before retiring, you can take a long soak in the claw-foot tub. On winter mornings, Rosemarie uses an antique wood stove to prepare special dishes such as Swedish-style French toast and New England fruit duffy. The farm is close to swimming at Glenwood Springs, skiing at Powderhorn and Aspen, and over 80 lakes for swimming and fishing.

Onaledge Bed & Breakfast Inn ✪
336 EL PASO BOULEVARD, MANITOU SPRINGS, COLORADO 80829

Tel: **(719) 685-4265; (800) 530-8253**
Best Time to Call: **6 AM–10 PM**
Hosts: **Mel and Shirley Podell**
Location: **4 mi. from I-25, Exit 141**
No. of Rooms: **4**
No. of Private Baths: **4**
Double/pb: **$75–$90**
Single/pb: **$75**
Suites: **$95–$120**

Open: **All year**
Breakfast: **Full**
Credit Cards: **AMEX, MC, VISA**
Pets: **No**
Children: **Welcome, over 12**
Smoking: **Permitted**
Social Drinking: **Permitted**
Airport/Station Pickup: **Yes**

Located on a hill overlooking historic Manitou Springs, this rock-and-frame Tudor-style home was built by a millionaire in 1912. Approximately $75,000 was spent on the garden area alone. The inn boasts unusual copper hardware and light fixtures, a large copper fireplace, and lovely hardwood floors. The spacious bedrooms have large windows framing lovely views of the mountains and Pikes Peak. In warm weather, breakfast may be enjoyed on one of the flowery patios. The cranberry muffins are legend, and guests have been known to give Mel's Western Omelet a standing ovation. For those watching their diet, a Heart's Delight low-fat breakfast may be ordered. Downtown Manitou Springs and Garden of the Gods Park are within walking distance.

Two Sisters Inn ✪
TEN OTOE PLACE, MANITOU SPRINGS, COLORADO 80829

Tel: **(719) 685-9684**	Double/sb: **$52**
Best Time to Call: **Evenings**	Guest Cottage: **$80**
Hosts: **Sharon Smith and Wendy Goldstein**	Open: **All year**
	Breakfast: **Full**
Location: **4 mi. W of Colorado Springs**	Credit Cards: **MC, VISA**
No. of Rooms: **5**	Pets: **No**
No. of Private Baths: **3**	Children: **Welcome**
Max. No. Sharing Bath: **4**	Smoking: **No**
Double/pb: **$65**	Social Drinking: **Permitted**

Built in 1919 as a boardinghouse, this rose-colored Victorian bungalow has been lovingly restored with four bedrooms and a honeymoon cottage in the back garden. Family collectibles, antiques, and fresh flowers fill the sunny rooms. Your hosts, former caterers, set out a gourmet breakfast of home-baked muffins, freshly ground coffee, fresh fruit, and a hot entrée. The inn is located at the base of Pikes Peak, in Manitou Springs' historic district. Nearby attractions include the Garden of the Gods, the cog railway, the U.S. Air Force Academy, and the Olympic Training Center.

The Eagle River Inn
145 NORTH MAIN, BOX 100, MINTURN, COLORADO 81645

Tel: **(303) 827-5761; (800) 344-1750**	Reduced Rates: **April–Nov.**
Best Time to Call: **7 AM–10 PM**	Breakfast: **Full**
Hosts: **Beverly Rude and Richard Galloway**	Credit Cards: **AMEX, MC, VISA**
	Pets: **No**
Location: **100 mi. W of Denver**	Children: **Welcome, over 12**
No. of Rooms: **12**	Smoking: **No**
No. of Private Baths: **12**	Social Drinking: **Permitted**
Double/pb: **$79–$175**	Minimum Stay: **5 nights Dec. 26–**
Single/pb: **$69–$165**	**Jan. 2**
Open: **All year**	

The inn's adobe facade and decor are fashioned after the historic inns of Santa Fe. The living room is warm and cozy, accented by an authentic beehive fireplace and a view of the river. The guest rooms are furnished in a southwestern mode, each with a king-size bed. Minutes away are the slopes of Vail and Beaver Creek. A ski shuttle stops across the street. You are invited to join your hosts for wine and cheese each afternoon. An outdoor Jacuzzi has been added for guests' enjoyment.

Ouray 1898 House ✪
322 MAIN STREET, P.O. BOX 641, OURAY, COLORADO 81427

Tel: (303) 325-4871
Best Time to Call: **Afternoons**
Hosts: **Kathy and Lee Bates**
Location: **On Hwy. 550**
No. of Rooms: **3**
No. of Private Baths: **3**
Double/pb: **$58–$78**
Open: **May 25–Sept. 25**

Reduced Rates: **Singles, off-season**
Breakfast: **Full**
Credit Cards: **MC, VISA**
Pets: **No**
Children: **Welcome, over 5**
Smoking: **No**
Social Drinking: **Permitted**

This 90-year-old house has been carefully renovated and combines the elegance of the 19th century with the comfortable amenities of the 20th. Each guest room features a spectacular view of the San Juan Mountains from its private deck. Breakfast is beautifully served on antique china. Jeep trips, horseback riding, hiking, browsing in the many quaint shops, and relaxing in the hot springs are but a few of the local diversions.

The Yellow Rose ✪
P.O. BOX 725—#5 MUNN PARK, OURAY, COLORADO 81427

Tel: (303) 325-4175
Best Time to Call: **8 AM–5 PM**
Hosts: **Ed and Edith Roark**
No. of Rooms: **2**
Max. No. Sharing Bath: **4**
Double/sb: **$50**
Single/sb: **$45**
Open: **May 1–Oct. 1**

Reduced Rates: **Available**
Breakfast: **Full**
Credit Cards: **MC, VISA**
Pets: **No**
Children: **Welcome**
Smoking: **No**
Social Drinking: **Permitted**

From every window, you'll enjoy magnificent views of the San Juan Mountains; step outside in this quiet neighborhood and you'll hear the continuous whisper of the Uncompahgre River. At night, sit by the TV in the common room and catch a movie on cable. The Roarks offer incomparable Texas hospitality, with afternoon tea and a full breakfast of your choice.

Davidson's Country Inn ✪
BOX 87, PAGOSA SPRINGS, COLORADO 81147

Tel: (303) 264-5863
Hosts: **The Davidson Family**
Location: **On US Hwy. 160**
No. of Rooms: **8**
No. of Private Baths: **3**
Max. No. Sharing Bath: **2**
Double/pb: **$55**

Single/pb: **$42**
Double/sb: **$44**
Single/sb: **$36**
Open: **All year**
Breakfast: **Full**
Credit Cards: **MC, VISA**
Pets: **Sometimes**

Children: **Welcome**   Social Drinking: **No**
Smoking: **No**

You're sure to enjoy the beautiful Rocky Mountain scenery surrounding the 32 acres of this log inn's grounds. Some months bring the deer and elk to graze neaby. There's a natural hot spring in town and the San Juan River flows close by. You are invited to play horseshoes, or use the solarium and library. For the children, there's a full toy chest and sandbox. Family heirlooms, handmade quilts, and lovely paintings enhance the comfortable decor. Wolf Creek ski area is 18 miles away.

Meadow Creek B&B Inn
13438 HIGHWAY 285, PINE, COLORADO 80470

Tel: **(303) 838-4167, 838-4899**
Best Time to Call: **10 AM–6 PM**
Hosts: **Pat and Dennis Carnahan; Judy and Don Otis**
Location: **25 mi. SW of Denver**
No. of Rooms: **6**
No. of Private Baths: **6**
Double/pb: **$69–$99**
Open: **All year**
Reduced Rates: **6th night free; 5% seniors**

Breakfast: **Full**
Other Meals: **Available**
Credit Cards: **MC, VISA**
Pets: **No**
Children: **Welcome, over 12**
Smoking: **Permitted**
Social Drinking: **Permitted**
Minimum Stay: **2 nights weekends**

Nestled in a secluded meadow surrounded by stone outcroppings and aspen and pine trees, along a spring-fed creek, this rustic mountain retreat is balm for stress. Don't forget your camera as you wander the 35 acres, home to elk, birds, and other wildlife. The historically significant house, barn, and outbuildings have been faithfully restored. Omelets and fresh baked cinnamon bread are breakfast specialties. The relaxing hot tub and the parlor fireside are both favorite gathering spots; fruit, beverages, homemade treats, and sherry are graciously served.

The Alma House ✪
220 EAST 10TH STREET, SILVERTON, COLORADO 81433

Tel: **(303) 387-5336**
Hosts: **Christine and Terry Payne**
Location: **50 mi. N of Durango**
No. of Rooms: **10**
Max. No. Sharing Bath: **3**
Double/sb: **$48**
Single/sb: **$43**
Suite: **$70**

Open: **All year**
Breakfast: **Continental**
Credit Cards: **AMEX, MC, VISA**
Pets: **Yes**
Children: **Welcome**
Smoking: **Restricted**
Social Drinking: **Permitted**

This 1898 stone-and-frame building has been lovingly restored and comfortably updated. Each spacious room has a deluxe queen-size bed, luxurious linens, antique dresser, and special touches. The plumbing in the bathrooms is up-to-date, but the brass-and-walnut fixtures are faithful to a day gone by. Ride the Durango-Silverton Narrow Gauge Railroad. Silverton retains the flavor of the old Western town it is.

Starry Pines
2262 SNOWMASS CREEK ROAD, SNOWMASS, COLORADO 81654

Tel: (303) 927-4202	Open: All year
Best Time to Call: 7 AM–9 AM, 4 PM–9 PM	Reduced Rates: Available
	Breakfast: Continental
Host: Shelley Burke	Children: Welcome, over 6
Location: 200 mi. W of Denver	Smoking: No
No. of Rooms: 2	Social Drinking: Permitted
Max. No. Sharing Bath: 4	Minimum Stay: 2 nights ski season
Double/sb: $80–$90	Airport Pickup: Yes
Single/sb: $75–$85	

On 70 private acres with its own trout stream and a panoramic view of the Rockies, Starry Pines offers you year-round activities and hospitality. Enjoy the Aspen summer music festival, ballet, and theater. Try hot air balloon rides landing in the B&B's fields, or biking, hiking, jeeping, and riding in the back country. For quieter moments, there's a secluded picnic site with horseshoes and a hammock by the stream. Fall unveils spectacular aspen foliage. Winter and spring bring world-renowned skiing at four mountains only 25 minutes away, plus snowshoeing and cross-country skiing at Starry Pines's own door. At the end of the day, bathe in the hot tub on the patio, then sit around the living room fireplace or watch a movie on the VCR.

Alpen Rose ✪
244 FOREST TRAIL, P.O. BOX 769, WINTER PARK, COLORADO 80482

Tel: (303) 726-5039	Reduced Rates: 10% seniors
Best Time to Call: Mornings; evenings	Breakfast: Full
Hosts: Robin and Rupert Sommeraver	Credit Cards: AMEX, MC, VISA
Location: 62 mi. W of Denver	Pets: Sometimes
No. of Rooms: 5	Children: Welcome, over 10
No. of Private Baths: 5	Smoking: No
Double/pb: $65–$95	Social Drinking: Permitted
Single/pb: $45–$85	Airport/Station Pickup: Yes
Open: All year	Foreign Languages: Austrian, German

Surrounded by aspen and pine trees, this woodsy retreat is much like the chalets Rupert remembers from his days as an Austrian Ski School instructor. If you want to go skiing, the Winter Park slopes are just 2 miles away. Hiking, fishing, mountain biking, rafting, and golfing are the main summer activities in this area. Throughout the year, a memorable breakfast with Austrian specialties awaits you in the morning; after the day's adventures, a crackling fire, hot tea, and cookies beckon you home.

Engelmann Pines ✪
P.O. BOX 1305, WINTER PARK, COLORADO 80482

Tel: (303) 726-4632; (800) 992-9512	Open: **All year**
Hosts: **Heinz and Margaret Engel**	Reduced Rates: **10% seniors, families**
Location: **67 mi. W of Denver**	Breakfast: **Full**
No. of Rooms: **6**	Credit Cards: **AMEX, MC, VISA**
No. of Private Baths: **2**	Pets: **Sometimes**
Max. No. Sharing Bath: **4**	Children: **Welcome**
Double/pb: **$65–$95**	Smoking: **No**
Single/pb: **$55–$85**	Social Drinking: **Permitted**
Double/sb: **$45–$85**	Airport/Station Pickup: **Yes**
Single/sb: **$35–$75**	Foreign Languages: **German**

From its Rocky Mountain perch, this spacious modern lodge offers spectacular views of the Continental Divide. Bathrooms are equipped with Jacuzzis, and there is a complete kitchen for guests' use. A free bus ferries skiers from the front door to some of Colorado's best ski slopes; cross-country ski aficionados will find a trail just across the road. When the snow melts, it's time to go golfing, hiking, fishing, and horseback riding. In the morning, eager sportsmen and -women can fill up on marzipan cake, muesli, and fresh fruit crêpes.

CONNECTICUT

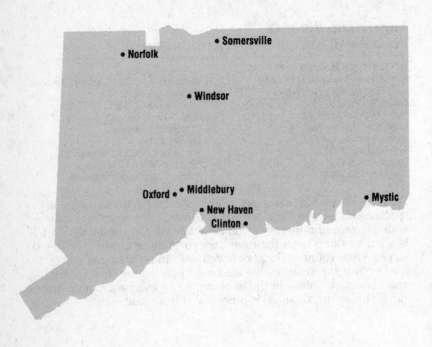

● Somersville
● Norfolk
● Windsor
Oxford ● ● Middlebury
● New Haven
Clinton ●
● Mystic

Bed and Breakfast, Ltd. ✪
P.O. BOX 216, NEW HAVEN, CONNECTICUT 06513

Tel: (203) 469-3260
Best Time to Call: **Sept.–June 5 PM–
9:30 PM weekdays, July–Aug.;
weekends, anytime**
Coordinator: **Jack Argenio**
States/Regions Covered: **Statewide;
Rhode Island—Providence, Newport**

Rates (Single/Double):
  Modest: **$45 / $50**
  Average: **$50 / $60**
  Luxury: **$60 / $75 and up**
Credit Cards: **No**

Whether you plan to visit one of Connecticut's many fine colleges—
including Trinity, Yale, Wesleyan, or the Coast Guard Academy—the
Mystic Seaport, picturesque country villages, theater, opera, fine
restaurants, it is always pleasant to return to one of Jack's homes-

away-from-home with congenial hosts ready to extend warmth and hospitality. They now have 125 listings statewide and offer great variety in host homes and personalized service to guests.

Covered Bridge Bed & Breakfast ✪
P.O. BOX 447A, MAPLE AVENUE, NORFOLK, CONNECTICUT 06058

Tel: **(203) 542-5944; (800) 488-5690**
Best Time to Call: **9 AM–6 PM**
Coordinator: **Diane Tremblay**
States/Regions Covered:
  Connecticut—Statewide; New York—Amenia, Cherry Plains, Dover Plains; Massachusetts—The Berkshires, Rhode Island

Descriptive Directory: **$3**
Rates (Single/Double):
  Modest: **$60–$80 / $60–$80**
  Average: **$80–$95 / $80–$95**
  Luxury: **$100–$160 / $100–$160**
Credit Cards: **AMEX, MC, VISA**
Minimum Stay: **2 nights holidays, weekends**

If you enjoy historic homes, charming farmhouses, Victorian estates, picture-postcard New England scenery, unsurpassed fall foliage, music festivals, theater, antiquing, auto racing, skiing, white-water rafting, or hiking, call Diane.

Captain Dibbell House ✪
21 COMMERCE STREET, CLINTON, CONNECTICUT 06413

Tel: **(203) 669-1646**
Hosts: **Ellis and Helen Adams**
Location: **21 mi. E of New Haven**
No. of Rooms: **4**

No. of Private Baths: **4**
Double/pb: **$75–$85**
Single/pb: **$65–$75**
Open: **All year, except Jan.**

Reduced Rates: **Weekly; 10% seniors,
3 or more nights**
Breakfast: **Full**
Credit Cards: **AMEX, MC, VISA**
Pets: **No**
Children: **Welcome, over 14**

Smoking: **No**
Social Drinking: **Permitted**
Airport/Station Pickup: **Yes**

Ellis and Helen fell in love with this piece of Connecticut shore years ago when they used to come from their home in New York to spend the weekend sailing. They liked it so much, in fact, that they bought this sea captain's home, located just one-half mile from the shore and marinas and a short drive from the town beach, and converted it into a B&B. Clinton is ideally situated for exploring the Connecticut coast; not far away you'll find Hammonassett State Beach, Mystic Seaport and Aquarium, Gillette Castle, the Goodspeed Opera House, the Essex Steam Train, Long Wharf Theater, and Yale. In order to help you enjoy the Connecticut shore they love so much, the Adamses are happy to lend you their bicycles and beach chairs.

Tucker Hill Inn
96 TUCKER HILL ROAD, MIDDLEBURY, CONNECTICUT 06762

Tel: **(203) 758-8334**
Best Time to Call: **9 AM–noon; after
4 PM**
Hosts: **Richard and Susan Cebelenski**
Location: **5 mi. W of Waterbury**
No. of Rooms: **4**
No. of Private Baths: **2**
Max. No. Sharing Bath: **4**
Double/pb: **$70–$90**

Double/sb: **$55–$65**
Open: **All year**
Reduced Rates: **Weekly**
Breakfast: **Full**
Credit Cards: **MC, VISA**
Pets: **No**
Children: **Welcome**
Smoking: **Permitted**
Social Drinking: **Permitted**

Built in 1920, this large Colonial-style home, just down from the village green, exemplifies warm hospitality and charm. The spacious guest rooms are bright and airy, decorated with fine linens and pretty accessories. Breakfast features such caloric creations as pancakes, waffles, and omelets. Facilities for antiquing, music, theater, golf, tennis, water sports, and cross-country skiing are nearby.

Comolli's House ✪
36 BRUGGEMAN PLACE, MYSTIC, CONNECTICUT 06355

Tel: **(203) 536-8723**
Host: **Dorothy M. Comolli**
Location: **1 mi. from I-95, Exit 90**
No. of Rooms: **2**
No. of Private Baths: **1**
Double/pb: **$75–$90**
Single/pb: **$75–$90**

Open: **All year**
Breakfast: **Continental**
Pets: **No**
Children: **Welcome, over 12**
Smoking: **No**
Social Drinking: **Permitted**

This immaculate home on a quiet hill overlooking Mystic Seaport is convenient to the sights of Olde Mistick Village and the Aquarium. Dorothy caters to discriminating adults who appreciate a simple, homey atmosphere. The guest rooms are cozy in winter and cool in summer. She is pleased to provide information on sightseeing, sporting activities, shopping, and restaurants.

Pequot Hotel Bed and Breakfast ✪
711 COW HILL ROAD, MYSTIC, CONNECTICUT 06355

Tel: **(203) 572-0390**
Best Time to Call: **8 AM–8 PM**
Host: **Nancy Mitchell**
Location: **135 mi. NE of New York**
No. of Rooms: **3**
No. of Private Baths: **3**
Double/pb: **$90**
Suites: **$80**
Open: **All year**

Reduced Rates: **10% Jan.–Mar.**
Breakfast: **Full**
Other Meals: **Available**
Pets: **Sometimes**
Children: **Welcome, over 10**
Smoking: **No**
Social Drinking: **Permitted**
Airport/Station Pickup: **Yes**

The Pequot Hotel is an authentically restored 1840 stagecoach stop, in the center of the Burnett's Corners Historic District, just 2½ miles from the charming New England seacoast village of Mystic, Connecticut. This large, comfortable Greek Revival–style inn is situated on 23 wooded acres convenient to the Mystic Seaport Museum, the Mystic Aquarium, and the new Foxwoods Gambling Casino. At the end of a busy day, guests are free to relax on the large screened porch or in one of the elegant fireplaced parlors. Recommendations and reservations for dinner at one of the area's fine restaurants are provided by the innkeeper, Nancy. In the morning a full country breakfast, including fresh local fruits and vegetables, is ready when you are. Nancy, a resident for 18 years, has 23 years' experience as an international flight attendant.

Weaver's House ✪
GREENWOODS ROAD, NORFOLK, CONNECTICUT 06058

Tel: **(203) 542-5108**
Hosts: **Judy and Arnold Tsukroff**
Location: **39 mi. NW of Hartford**
No. of Rooms: **4**
Max. No. Sharing Bath: **4**
Double/sb: **$45**
Single/sb: **$40**

Open: **All year**
Breakfast: **Full**
Pets: **No**
Children: **Welcome**
Smoking: **No**
Social Drinking: **Permitted**
Foreign Languages: **German**

Weaver's House is a turn-of-the-century Victorian facing the Yale Summer School of Music and Art Estate. In the 1930s, it was used as an annex to the Norfolk Inn. The guest rooms are simply decorated with handwoven rag rugs. Your hostess is a talented weaver, who will gladly display her loom for you. There are concerts and art shows in the summer, and two state parks are nearby with blazed hiking trails. Judy offers vegetarian choices at breakfast.

Butterbrooke Farm ✪
78 BARRY ROAD, OXFORD, CONNECTICUT 06483

Tel: **(203) 888-2000**
Best Time to Call: **4–10 PM**
Host: **Tom Butterworth**
Location: **10 mi. SW of Waterbury**
No. of Rooms: **1**
No. of Private Baths: **1**
Double/pb: **$65**
Single/pb: **$55**
Open: **All year**
Reduced Rates: **15% after 1 week; 10% seniors; $10 less per night, Sun–Thurs.**

Breakfast: **Full**
Pets: **Yes**
Children: **Welcome, over 2**
Smoking: **Permitted**
Social Drinking: **Permitted**
Foreign Languages: **German**
Airport/Station Pickup: **Yes**

Butterbrooke Farm, a Colonial saltbox dating to 1711, has been restored and furnished in period style. From the guest-suite windows, you can survey the four-acre property, which boasts authentic 18th-century plantings: Tom, a biology professor at Connecticut State University, is interested in both historic and organic gardening. He'll also direct you to the best antique outlets. But first, he'll whip up a batch of multigrain pancakes, topped by freshly picked, home-grown berries.

The Old Mill Inn ✪
63 MAPLE STREET, SOMERSVILLE, CONNECTICUT 06072

Tel: **(203) 763-1473**
Best Time to Call: **9 AM–9 PM**
Hosts: **Ralph and Phyllis Lumb**
Location: **10 mi. S of Springfield, Mass.**
No. of Rooms: **4**
No. of Private Baths: **2**
Max. No. Sharing Bath: **4**
Double/pb: **$60**
Single/pb: **$60**

Double/sb: **$54**
Single/sb: **$54**
Open: **All year**
Reduced Rates: **10% seniors**
Breakfast: **Continental**
Pets: **No**
Children: **Welcome**
Smoking: **No**
Social Drinking: **Permitted**
Airport/Station Pickup: **Yes**

Originally built in the 1850s, this comfortable home was enlarged and renovated many years later by the owner of the woolen mill next door. Today the old mill is a place to shop for gifts and furniture, while the house provides cozy lodgings for the traveler. Guest quarters are located on the second floor with bedrooms, baths, and a sitting room with cable TV, books, and a refrigerator. Bedrooms feature twin or

full-size beds and comfortable furnishings. Downstairs in the gracious guest living room, you may relax by the fire, read, or listen to the stereo. Breakfast is served in a beautiful dining room with hand-painted walls overlooking the lawn. The Old Mill Inn is minutes from golf, the Basketball Hall of Fame, museums, restaurants, and shops.

The Charles R. Hart House
1046 WINDSOR AVENUE, WINDSOR, CONNECTICUT 06095

Tel: **(203) 688-5555**	Open: **All year**
Best Time to Call: **4–8 PM**	Breakfast: **Full**
Hosts: **Dorothy and Bob McAllister**	Pets: **No**
Location: **6 mi. N of Hartford**	Children: **Welcome, over 12**
No. of Rooms: **3**	Smoking: **No**
No. of Private Baths: **3**	Social Drinking: **No**
Double/pb: **$75–$85**	Station Pickup: **Yes**
Single/pb: **$65–$75**	

Hartford merchant Charles Hart added luxurious wallcoverings, ceramic tiled fireplaces, and an elegant Palladian window to this farm-house in 1896, some thirty years after it was built. By the 1940s, the property was serving as a pheasant farm. The current owners have restored it and furnished it with exquisite period pieces. You can hear the past as well as see it, thanks to an antique music box. Local cultural sites span many eras, from the Mark Twain House and Old Newgate Prison to the New England Air Museum at Bradley International Airport. Modern distractions include shopping in Hartford and golf at the challenging Tournament Players Course, home of the Greater Hartford Open.

DELAWARE

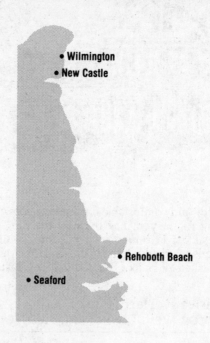

- • Wilmington
- • New Castle
- • Rehoboth Beach
- • Seaford

William Penn Guest House ✪
206 DELAWARE STREET, NEW CASTLE, DELAWARE 19720

Tel: **(302) 328-7736**
Best Time to Call: **After 5 PM**
Hosts: **Mr. and Mrs. Richard Burwell**
Location: **2 mi. from I-95**
No. of Rooms: **4**
Max. No. Sharing Bath: **4**
Double/pb: **$65**
Double/sb: **$45**

Single/sb: **$45**
Open: **All year**
Breakfast: **Continental**
Pets: **No**
Children: **Welcome, over 3**
Smoking: **No**
Social Drinking: **Permitted**
Foreign Languages: **Italian**

If you're a history buff, perhaps a stay in a 1682 house named for William Penn is what you've been seeking. Located in the heart of New Castle's historic district, the accommodations here are most comfortable. A lovely park for strolling and for the children to play in borders the Delaware shore, just two blocks away. The University of Delaware is 15 minutes from the house.

Tembo Guest House ✪
100 LAUREL STREET, REHOBOTH BEACH, DELAWARE 19971

Tel: (302) 227-3360
Hosts: **Don and Gerry Cooper**
Location: ¾ mi. from DE 1
No. of Rooms: 6
Max. No. Sharing Bath: 4
Double/pb: **$100**
Double/sb: **$80**
Open: **All year**

Reduced Rates: **Off-season, weekdays**
Breakfast: **Continental**
Pets: **Sometimes**
Children: **Welcome, over 12**
Smoking: **No**
Social Drinking: **Permitted**
Airport/Station Pickup: **Yes**

This white two-story frame beach cottage, set among old shade trees, is one block from the Atlantic Ocean. The house is surrounded by brick walks and gardens, and a private yard with chaise lounges for relaxing. The living room has a fireplace, hand-braided rugs, and an unusual collection of hand-carved shore birds and elephants. Each bedroom has an antique bureau, rocking chair, and either twin or full-size beds. Breakfast is served on a large enclosed front porch with rockers and swing. In colder weather, homemade muffins and scones are served in the kitchen, with its antique chandelier, butter churn, and coffee grinder. Don and Gerry will gladly direct you to local sights, such as the restored Homestead, historic Port Lewes, and the Zwaanendael Museum.

Riverview B&B ✪
P.O. BOX 528, 9 RIVER ROAD, SEAFORD, DELAWARE 19973-0528

Tel: (302) 629-2201; fax: (302) 629-3388
Best Time to Call: **Anytime**
Hosts: **Phil and Phillys Livingston**
No. of Rooms: 1
No. of Private Baths: 1
Double/pb: **$50**

Open: **All year**
Breakfast: **Continental**
Pets: **No**
Children: **No**
Smoking: **No**
Social Drinking: **Permitted**

Phil and Phillys' home is nestled on more than nine acres along the Nanticoke River, a tidal waterway off the Chesapeake Bay's Eastern Shore. The property has its own bulkhead, pier, and dock. Have breakfast on the screened porch as you watch sailboats, tugboats, and other small craft head out to sea. You're also likely to see osprey, seagulls, cranes, and deer. As you would imagine, excellent beaches are nearby; so are factory outlets, colleges, the Delaware and Maryland state capitols, Dover Air Force Base, and the U.S. Naval Academy at Annapolis.

Bed & Breakfast of Delaware
3650 SILVERSIDE ROAD BOX 177, WILMINGTON, DELAWARE 19810

Tel: **(302) 479-9500; (800) 233-4689**
Best Time to Call: **9 AM–5 PM Mon.–Fri.**
Coordinator: **Millie Alford**
States/Regions Covered: **Delaware—Bridgeville, Dover, Laurel, Lewis, Middletown, Milford, New Castle, Newark, Odessa, Wilmington; Pennsylvania—Chadds Ford, Landenberg, Oxford**

Rates (Single/Double):
  Modest: **$35–$55 / —**
  Average: **$45 / $65–$75**
  Luxury: **$80 / $90–$120**
Credit Cards: **MC, VISA**

Whether you are vacationing or traveling on business, Bed & Breakfast of Delaware gives you a choice of quality accommodations with a wide range of facilities. Our lifelong knowledge of Delaware and adjacent areas—a region rich in history, recreation, and corporate activity—allows us to place you where you will feel most welcome according to your life-style and budget.

The Boulevard Bed & Breakfast ✪
1909 BAYNARD BOULEVARD, WILMINGTON, DELAWARE 19802

Tel: **(302) 656-9700**
Hosts: **Charles and Judy Powell**
Location: **½ mi. from I-95, Exit 8**
No. of Rooms: **6**
No. of Private Baths: **4**
Max. No. Sharing Bath: **3**
Double/pb: **$65–$70**
Single/pb: **$60**
Double/sb: **$55**
Single/sb: **$50**

Open: **All year**
Reduced Rates: **Corporate**
Breakfast: **Full**
Credit Cards: **AMEX, MC, VISA**
Pets: **No**
Children: **Welcome**
Smoking: **Permitted**
Social Drinking: **Permitted**
Airport/Station Pickup: **Yes**

This beautifully restored city mansion was built in 1913 and has earned a place on the National Register of Historic Places. Upon entering, you'll be struck by the impressive foyer and magnificent staircase, leading to a landing complete with a window seat and large leaded-glass windows flanked by 15-foot-tall fluted columns. Breakfast is served in the formal dining room or on the screened-in porch. Although Baynard Boulevard is a quiet and peaceful street, it's just a short walk away from the downtown business district. Parks are close by, and it's just a short drive to Hagley, Winterthur, the Delaware Natural History or Art Museum; or head for nearby Chadds Ford, Pennsylvania, and the famous Brandywine River Museum.

A Small Wonder B&B ✪
213 WEST CREST ROAD, WILMINGTON, DELAWARE 19803

Tel: **(302) 764-0789; (800) 373-0781**
Best Time to Call: **After 4 PM**
Hosts: **Dot and Art Brill**
Location: **½ mi. from I-95, Exit 9**
No. of Rooms: **2**
No. of Private Baths: **2**
Double/pb: **$60**
Single/pb: **$50**

Open: **All year**
Breakfast: **Full**
Other Meals: **Available**
Credit Cards: **AMEX, MC, VISA**
Pets: **No**
Children: **Welcome, over 9**
Smoking: **No**
Social Drinking: **Permitted**

The Brills describe their area as "a microcosm of American history and cosmopolitan trends." They live in a quiet suburb surrounded by things they enjoy—piano, organ, books, paintings, plants, outdoor swimming pool and spa set in an award-winning garden—all of which they share with guests. Learn of historic New Castle, Winterthur, Longwood, Bellevue, Nemours, Hagley and Eleutherian Mills, Rockwood, the Wyeths, Pyle, and more at breakfast, by the pool, or over drinks by the fire. The Brills' warm, considerate style has earned a national award for B&B comfort and hospitality. There's a $5 surcharge for one-night stays.

DISTRICT OF COLUMBIA

Bed 'n' Breakfast Ltd. of Washington, D.C.
P.O. BOX 12011, WASHINGTON, D.C. 20005

Tel: **(202) 328-3510; fax (202) 332-3885**
Best Time to Call: **10 AM–5 PM Mon.–Fri.; 10 AM–1 PM Sat.**
Coordinator: **Anna Earle**
States/Regions Covered: **Washington, D.C.; Virginia and Maryland suburbs**

Rates: (Single/Double):
  Average: **$40–$150 / $50–$150**
Credit Cards: **AMEX, DC, MC, VISA**
Minimum Stay: **2 nights**

This service has a network of 75 homes, apartments, guest houses, and inns. Most of the accommodations are convenient to public transportation. Several of the homes are historic properties. There is a wide range of accommodations, from budget to luxury.

The Bed & Breakfast League/Sweet Dreams and Toast ✪
P.O. BOX 9490, WASHINGTON, D.C. 20016

Tel: **(202) 363-7767**
Coordinators: **Martha Black and
   Millie Groobey**
States/Regions Covered: **Washington,
   D.C.; Maryland—Bethesda, Chevy
   Chase, Rockville; Virginia—
   Arlington**

Rates (Single/Double):
   Modest: **$35–$50 / $45–$60**
   Average: **$50–$65 / $60–$75**
   Luxury: **$75–$115 / $85–$130**
Credit Cards: **AMEX, DC, MC, VISA**
Minimum Stay: **2 nights**

The Bed & Breakfast League/Sweet Dreams and Toast reservation services were merged in 1988. They offer accommodations in privately owned homes and apartments. Many are in historic districts; all are in good, safe sections of the city within easy walking distance of an excellent public transportation system. Gracious hosts will cheerfully direct you to points of interest, monuments, museums, shops, and restaurants. The office of this service is closed on federal holidays, Thanksgiving, and Christmas. A $10 fee is charged for each reservation.

The Stableford Inn ✪
WOODLEY PARK, WASHINGTON, D.C. 20008

Tel: **(202) 333-7159**
Best Time to Call: **8 AM–8 PM**
Host: **Jean Stableford**
No. of Rooms: **3**
No. of Private Baths: **1**
Max. No. Sharing Bath: **4**
Double/pb: **$75**
Single/pb: **$65**
Double/sb: **$65**

Single/sb: **$55**
Open: **All year**
Breakfast: **Full**
Credit Cards: **AMEX, MC, VISA**
Pets: **No**
Children: **Welcome, over 5**
Smoking: **Restricted**
Social Drinking: **Permitted**
Minimum Stay: **2 nights**

Enjoy the pleasure of staying in a splendid old Georgian home with high ceilings and a lovely central hall. The spacious living and dining rooms contain artworks, antiques, and treasures from around the world. Outside, relax or smoke in a pretty garden patio or on the balcony or porch. The inn is located in Woodley Park, renowned for its beauty, convenience, and safety; it is home to members of Congress and the media. It is a 15-minute walk to the zoo or the metro stop located near the Sheraton and Shoreham hotels, but your hostess is happy to take guests to the subway in the morning. Washington National Cathedral is across the street. A thirty-minute walk leads the visitor to Georgetown or to Dupont Circle along Embassy Row. Public transportation is available in any direction.

FLORIDA

Havana •
• Pensacola
• Seaside
• Panama City
• Amelia Island
• Jacksonville
• St. Augustine
• Crescent City
Gainesville •
Ocala • Lake • Daytona Beach
Helen • • New Smyrna Beach
• Winter Park
Bushnell • • Orlando
• Cocoa Beach
Tarpon Springs •
Palm Harbor •
Indian Shores • • Ruskin
• St. Petersburg
Holmes Beach • • Madeira Beach
Sarasota Springs
Jupiter •
• Lake Park
Palm Beach •
Palm Beach Gardens •
Fort Myers • Lake Worth • West Palm Beach
Delray Beach •
Naples • • Fort Lauderdale
Miami Beach •
• Key Largo
• Islamorada
Big Pine Key •
Key West • • Summerland Key

A & A Bed & Breakfast of Florida, Inc. ✪
P.O. BOX 1316, WINTER PARK, FLORIDA 32790

Tel: **(407) 628-3233**
Best Time to Call: **9 AM–6 PM**
Coordinator: **Brunhilde (Bruni) Fehner**
States/Regions Covered: **Orlando area—Disney World, Epcot; Altamonte Springs, Cape Canaveral (Kennedy Space Center), Maitland, New Smyrna Beach, Sea World, Winter Park, Delray Beach, Ft. Myers, St. Augustine**

Rates (Single/Double):
  Modest: **$35 / $40**
  Average: **$40 / $55**
  Luxury: **$65 / $125**
Credit Cards: **No**
Minimum Stay: **2 nights**

132

You should allow several days to really savor all this area has to offer. Bruni's hosts will suggest hints on getting the most out of the major attractions, wonderful un-touristy restaurants, and tips on where to shop for unique gifts to take home. All of her homes have a certain "touch of class" to make you delighted with your visit. Rollins College is close by. There is a surcharge of $10 for one-night stays.

Bed & Breakfast Co.—Tropical Florida ✪
P.O. BOX 262, SOUTH MIAMI, FLORIDA 33243

Tel: (305) 661-3270
Best Time to Call: 9 AM–5 PM Mon.–Fri.
Coordinator: Marcella Schaible
States/Regions Covered: Statewide

Rates (Single/Double):
  Modest: $27–$35 / $32–$40
  Average: $35–$55 / $40–$60
  Luxury: $55–$150 / $60–$170
Credit Cards: AMEX, MC, VISA

Native Floridians, Marcella's hosts live in mansions on historic properties, in homes along the ocean and Gulf of Mexico, in woodland retreats, and on private residential islands. They exude southern hospitality and want you to come stay in their accommodations that range from a charming cottage to a contemporary condo to unhosted accommodations. The decor may be simple or wildly extravagant. They are ready to direct you to famous attractions or to an undiscovered, special restaurant or shop that only a resident knows about. There is a $5 surcharge for each night stayed less than three.

Open House Bed & Breakfast Registry—Gold Coast ✪
P.O. BOX 3025, PALM BEACH, FLORIDA 33480

Tel: (407) 842-5190
Best Time to Call: Evenings; weekends
Coordinator: Peggy Maxwell
States/Regions Covered: Boca Raton, Boynton Beach, Delray, Jupiter, Lake Worth, Lantana, Palm Beach, West Palm Beach

Rates (Single/Double):
  Average: $40 / $45–$55
  Luxury: $50 / $60–$110

Peggy's roster includes classic contemporaries as well as beautifully restored mansions in south Florida's historic districts; there's even an ocean villa. Most of the homes boast swimming pools. All are located in the most desirable residential areas. Guest comment cards rave about our hosts' generous hospitality, extending to guided tours of the many local attractions. Special weekly, monthly, and summer rates. Free brochure.

The 1735 House ✪
584 SOUTH FLETCHER, AMELIA ISLAND, FLORIDA 32034

Tel: (904) 261-5878; (800) 872-8531	Reduced Rates: **Weekly; 5% seniors**
Best Time to Call: **9 AM–6 PM**	Breakfast: **Continental**
Hosts: **Gary and Emily Grable**	Credit Cards: **AMEX, DISC, MC, VISA**
Location: **35 mi. NE of Jacksonville**	Pets: **No**
No. of Rooms: **5 suites**	Children: **Welcome, over 3**
No. of Private Baths: **5**	Smoking: **Permitted**
Suites: **$55–$150**	Social Drinking: **Permitted**
Guest Cottage: **$75–$125; sleeps 2–4**	Airport/Station Pickup: **Yes**
Open: **All year**	

This century-old country inn is situated right on the beach of a beautiful North Florida barrier island; each of the suites has an ocean view. A special treat is the free-standing lighthouse with four levels of living area, including two bedrooms and two baths. The decor throughout is wicker and rattan accented with nautical antiques. Breakfast, complete with freshly baked treats from the Grables' galley, is delivered to your suite along with the morning newspaper. Historic Fernandina Beach, with its lovely restored Victorian homes and shops, is nearby. Gary and Emily can suggest boat charters for those who wish to try their skill at landing a big one.

The Barnacle
ROUTE 1, BOX 780 A, LONG BEACH ROAD, BIG PINE KEY, FLORIDA 33043

Tel: (305) 872-3298	Open: **All year**
Best Time to Call: **Before 9 PM**	Breakfast: **Full**
Hosts: **Wood and Joan Cornell**	Pets: **No**
Location: **Mile marker 33**	Children: **No**
No. of Rooms: **4**	Smoking: **Permitted**
No. of Private Baths: **4**	Social Drinking: **Permitted**
Double/pb: **$70–$100**	Foreign Languages: **French**

The ultimate in privacy is the self-contained cottage—a tropical tree house with stained-glass windows and private terrace. Rooms overlook the ocean or the atrium, with its hot tub and lush plants. One room has a private entrance and opens onto the beach. Every detail in and around their home reflects Wood and Joan's taste, attention to detail, and artistic flair. The structure was built to frame their eclectic collection of statuary, tapestries, and art. Their emphasis is on the sun and sea, with warm hospitality offered in abundance. You can snorkel or fish right off "your own" beach. Bahia Honda State Park and Key West are close by.

Bed & Breakfast-on-the-Ocean "Casa Grande" ✪
P.O. BOX 378, BIG PINE KEY, FLORIDA 33043

Tel: **(305) 872-2878**
Hosts: **Jon and Kathleen Threlkeld**
Location: **30 mi. E of Key West**
No. of Rooms: **3**
No. of Private Baths: **3**
Double/pb: **$85**

Open: **All year**
Breakfast: **Full**
Pets: **No**
Children: **No**
Smoking: **Permitted**
Social Drinking: **Permitted**

This spectacular Spanish-style home, facing the ocean, was custom-designed to suit the natural beauty of the Keys. The large landscaped garden patio, with panoramic beach views, is where you'll enjoy Jon and Kathleen's bountiful breakfast. It is also the site of the hot tub/Jacuzzi for relaxing by day or under a moonlit sky. The large and airy guest rooms are comfortably cooled by Bahama fans or air-conditioning. Key deer and birds abound. From the private beach, you'll enjoy swimming, fishing, snorkeling, bicycling, and jogging. There's a picnic table, gas grill, hammock, and Windsurfer for guests to use, compliments of the gracious hosts.

Canal Cottage Bed & Breakfast
P.O. BOX 266, BIG PINE KEY, FLORIDA 33043

Tel: **(305) 872-3881**
Best Time to Call: **Evenings**
Hosts: **Dean and Patti Nickless**
Suites: **$85 for 2**
Open: **All year**
Breakfast: **Continental**

Pets: **No**
Children: **Welcome**
Smoking: **Permitted**
Social Drinking: **Permitted**
Minimum Stay: **2 nights**

Get away and relax! You can be self-sufficient in this unusual wood stilt house. Your accommodations are nestled in the trees and consist of a bedroom with a queen-size bed, a bathroom, a living room with sleeping space for two, and a kitchen stocked for your breakfast, which you can prepare at leisure and enjoy on the porch. Take advantage of local diving, snorkeling, and fishing charters, or bring your own boat to launch at the neighborhood ramp and tie it up at your backyard dock. There are bicycles for those so inclined, and a gas grill to cook your catch. You'll probably see a Key deer, too.

Deer Run ✪

LONG BEACH ROAD, P.O. BOX 431, BIG PINE KEY, FLORIDA 33043

Tel: (305) 872-2015, 872-2800
Best Time to Call: **Anytime before 10 PM**
Host: **Sue Abbott**
Location: **33 mi. E of Key West**
No. of Rooms: **2**
No. of Private Baths: **2**
Double/pb: **$85–$95**
Single/pb: **$75**

Open: **All year**
Breakfast: **Full**
Pets: **No**
Children: **No**
Smoking: **No**
Social Drinking: **Permitted**
Airport/Station Pickup: **Yes**
Minimum Stay: **2 nights**

Deer Run is a Florida Cracker–style home nestled among lush native trees on the ocean. The house is beautifully designed, with skylights, high ceilings, central air-conditioning, and Bahama fans. The decor boasts many paintings, artifacts, and antiques to compliment wicker and rattan furnishings. Upstairs each room has French doors that open onto a large veranda. Breakfast is served outside overlooking the ocean, where you may spot Key deer walking along the beach. Looe Key Coral Reef, Bahia Honda State Park, and Key West are all within easy reach, or you can relax and soak up the rays in the free-form deep spa, where there's room for eight.

Cypress House Bed and Breakfast ✪

R.R. 1, BOX 70 W.F., BUSHNELL, FLORIDA 33513

Tel: (904) 568-0909
Best Time to Call: **8 AM–10 PM**
Hosts: **Jan and Walt Fessler and Thelma Schaum**
Location: **50 mi. N of Tampa**
No. of Rooms: **2**
Max. No. Sharing Bath: **4**
Double/sb: **$40**
Single/sb: **$30**

Suites: **$70; sleeps 4**
Open: **All year**
Reduced Rates: **Seniors, 10%**
Breakfast: **Continental**
Other Meals: **Available**
Pets: **Sometimes**
Children: **Welcome**
Smoking: **No**
Social Drinking: **Permitted**

A new log home built in the gracious old Florida style, Cypress House is set on wooded farmland. From the oak rockers on the wide wrap-

around veranda, you can see oak trees draped with moss. The Webster
Flea Market (Mondays only) and Brooksville's Christmas House are
nearby, and Disney World and Busch Gardens are an hour away. You
won't have to travel far to browse for antiques, fish, hike, ride horseback, or go canoeing. To bolster your energy, your hosts offer a
generous Continental breakfast buffet, plus coffee and snacks round-
the-clock.

Frank's Guest House ✪
295 ANDROS AVENUE, COCOA BEACH, FLORIDA 32931

Tel: **(407) 783-4977**
Best Time to Call: **2 PM–5 PM**
Hosts: **Frank and Angie Percival**
Location: **50 mi. E of Orlando**
No. of Rooms: **3**
No. of Private Baths: **1**
Max. No. Sharing Bath: **4**
Double/pb: **$60**
Single/pb: **$50**

Double/sb: **$50**
Single/sb: **$40**
Open: **All year**
Reduced Rates: **10% seniors**
Breakfast: **Continental**
Pets: **No**
Children: **Welcome**
Smoking: **No**
Social Drinking: **Permitted**

Stay in a spacious two-story home in an exclusive residential neighborhood right on the waterfront. Do your laps in the in-ground swimming
pool, or try your luck fishing on the back dock. It's an hour drive to
Disney World and the Universal Studios, and a half-hour drive to
Kennedy Space Center (your host's deck is a great place to see shuttle
launches). Of course, beaches are within biking or walking distance.

Sprague House Inn
125 CENTRAL AVENUE, CRESCENT CITY, FLORIDA 32012

Tel: **(904) 698-2430**
Hosts: **Terry and Vena Moyer**
Location: **75 mi. N of Orlando**
No. of Rooms: **5**
No. of Private Baths: **5**
Double/pb: **$60**
Suite: **$75–$125**
Open: **All year**

Breakfast: **Full**
Other Meals: **Available**
Credit Cards: **MC, VISA**
Pets: **No**
Children: **No**
Smoking: **No**
Social Drinking: **Permitted**
Airport/Station Pickup: **Yes**

A Steamboat Gothic inn, Sprague House Inn has been welcoming
guests since 1905. The comfortably air-conditioned guest rooms are
highlighted in antiques. Accents of stained glass and handsome woods
are found throughout. The wraparound porches both upstairs and
down boast rockers and swings from which you may enjoy the views
of the lake. A public boat ramp and dock are a stone's throw away.
You are welcome to borrow a cane fishing pole (no license required) or
grab your net and try your luck at blue crabs. This one-stoplight town,

unspoiled by plastic and neon, claims to be "the bass capital of the world." Terry is the gourmet cook for their on-premises restaurant.

Bed 'n Breakfast of Greater Daytona Beach ✪
P.O. BOX 1081, ORMOND BEACH, FLORIDA 32175

Tel: **(904) 673-2232**	Rates (Single/Double):
Coordinator: **Rusty Reed**	Average: **$35–$75**
States/Regions Covered: **Daytona**	Credit Cards: **No**
Beach, Ormond Beach, Pt. Orange,	Minimum Stay: **2 nights Speed/Bike**
Wilbur-by-the-Sea	**weeks in Feb. and Mar.**

The host homes, each with its own special amenities and charm, are located throughout the greater Daytona area and pride themselves on catering to the needs of each guest. The Space Center and Disney World are within 60 miles. Closer to home, Daytona offers deep-sea fishing, golf, tennis, jai alai, dog racing, theater, and Halifax River cruises. A Daytona International Speedway tour and a drive on "the world's most famous beach" are a must. Yacht enthusiasts will be interested in the new 600-slip Halifax Marina, where they can dock, and then bed-and-breakfast nearby.

Hutch's Haven ✪
811 NORTH WEST 3RD AVENUE, DELRAY BEACH, FLORIDA 33444

Tel: **(407) 276-7390**	Open: **All year**
Best Time to Call: **Evenings**	Reduced Rates: **10% June–Sept.,**
Host: **Jean Hutchison**	**weekly**
Location: **30 mi. S of Palm Beach**	Breakfast: **Continental**
No. of Rooms: **2**	Pets: **No**
No. of Private Baths: **2**	Children: **Welcome, over 6**
Double/pb: **$60**	Smoking: **No**
Single/pb: **$55**	Social Drinking: **Permitted**

Hidden in a beautiful tropical garden is this charming artist's home. Guests can pick their own citrus fruits to go with homemade muffins and jellies for their Continental breakfast. This B&B is 1½ miles from the ocean; bicycles are supplied, along with umbrellas and hats. Golf and tennis facilities are nearby.

Dolan House ✪
1401 NORTHEAST 5 COURT, FT. LAUDERDALE, FLORIDA 33301

Tel: **(305) 462-8430**	No. of Private Baths: **2**
Hosts: **Tom and Sandra Dolan**	Max. No. Sharing Bath: **4**
Location: **5 mi. from I-95**	Double/pb: **$60**
No. of Rooms: **4**	Single/pb: **$50**

Double/sb: **$60**
Single/sb: **$50**
Open: **Oct. 1–July 31**
Reduced Rates: **20% less May–July, Oct.**
Breakfast: **Continental**

Pets: **No**
Children: **Welcome**
Smoking: **Permitted**
Social Drinking: **Permitted**
Airport/Station Pickup: **Yes**

All the comforts of home—if your home has a hot tub large enough to fit 19! Set right in the heart of Fort Lauderdale, and only two miles from the city's famed beach, the Dolan House offers privacy (it's completely fenced in) and convenience. When the weather's balmy, guests sit out on the large deck; when the nights are cool, they can move indoors and enjoy the large coquina fireplace. The Dolans have lived in the area for 30 years, and they're eager to tell you all about it. Ask them about the Galleria Shopping Center, the new Riverwalk historic section, Holiday Park, and all the nearby theaters and museums.

Windsong Garden & Art Gallery ✪
5570–4 WOODROSE COURT, FORT MYERS, FLORIDA 33907

Tel: **(813) 936-6378**
Host: **Embe Burdick**
No. of Rooms: **2**
No. of Private Baths: **2**
Double/pb: **$55**
Suite: **$55**
Open: **All year**

Breakfast: **Continental**
Pets: **No**
Children: **No**
Smoking: **No**
Social Drinking: **Permitted**
Minimum Stay: **2 nights**

This modern clear-shake-and-brick town house has a private courtyard and balcony for your enjoyment. The spacious combination bedroom-and-sitting room is most comfortable. Embe's varied interests include arts, crafts, music, and her household cats. It's close to Sanibel and Captiva islands, Ft. Myers Beach, fine shopping, good restaurants, and the University of Florida. You are welcome to use the pool.

Country Meadows ✪
9506 SOUTH WEST 81 WAY, GAINESVILLE, FLORIDA 32608

Tel: **(904) 495-2699**
Best Time to Call: **3–11 PM**
Hosts: **Allene and Orville Higgs**
Location: **10 mi. SW of Gainesville**
No. of Rooms: **2**
No. of Private Baths: **2**
Double/pb: **$38–$40**
Single/pb: **$32–$35**

Open: **All year**
Breakfast: **Continental**
Other Meals: **Available**
Pets: **No**
Children: **Welcome**
Smoking: **Permitted**
Social Drinking: **Permitted**
Airport/Station Pickup: **Yes**

Country Meadows is a Colonial-style home set on an acre and a half. The house is surrounded by pine trees, and has a fenced-in yard for relaxing. The country-style decor consists of comfortable furnishings and lots of handmade craft items. The Higgses enjoy entertaining and are glad to prepare either a Continental breakfast or a larger meal for guests. They will gladly direct you to nearby nature parks, horse farms, and museums.

Gaver's Bed & Breakfast ✪
301 EAST SIXTH AVENUE, HAVANA, FLORIDA 32333

Tel: **(904) 539-5611**
Hosts: **Shirley and Bruce Gaver**
Location: **12 mi. N of Tallahassee**
No. of Rooms: **1**
No. of Private Baths: **1**
Double/pb: **$55**
Open: **All year**
Reduced Rates: **15% after 3rd night, Mon.–Thurs.**

Breakfast: **Full**
Pets: **No**
Children: **Welcome, over 8**
Smoking: **No**
Social Drinking: **Permitted**
Airport/Station Pickup: **Yes**

This B&B, situated on a quiet residential street two blocks from the center of town, is a likely stop for collectors—at last count, Havana had twelve antique shops. Tallahassee, the state capital and home of Florida State University, is only ten minutes away by car. A restored 1907 frame house, Gaver's has two large screened porches, and guests are welcome to watch cable TV or play the piano. For breakfast, your hosts will design a menu to suit your preferences.

Harrington House B&B Inn ✪
5626 GULF DRIVE, HOLMES BEACH, FLORIDA 34217

Tel: **(813) 778-5444**
Best Time to Call: **Noon–8 PM**
Hosts: **Jo Davis and Betty Spangler**
Location: **40 mi. SW of Tampa**
No. of Rooms: **7**
No. of Private Baths: **7**
Double/pb: **$79–$139**
Open: **All year**
Breakfast: **Full**

Credit Cards: **MC, VISA**
Pets: **No**
Children: **Welcome, over 12**
Smoking: **No**
Social Drinking: **Permitted**
Minimum Stay: **2 nights weekends, Feb.–Apr.**
Airport/Station Pickup: **Yes**

Surrounded by tropical foliage and the gulf's blue waters, this gracious Florida home, built in 1925, has the beach for its backyard. Each of the seven eclectically furnished guest rooms has its own charm and character. Relax by the pool, baste on the beach, take a moonlight stroll, or just let the sound of the surf lull you to sleep. Whatever your pleasure, the warm hospitality will ensure that your stay is a memorable one.

Meeks B&B on the Gulf Beaches ✪
19418 GULF BOULEVARD, #407, INDIAN SHORES, FLORIDA 34635

Tel: (813) 596-5424
Best Time to Call: 7 AM–10 PM
Hosts: Greta and Bob Meeks
Location: 35 min. from Tampa Airport
No. of Rooms: 2
No. of Private Baths: 2
Double/pb: $50–$60
Single/pb: $45–$55

Suites: $75–$85
Open: All year
Breakfast: Full or Continental
Pets: No
Children: Welcome
Smoking: No
Social Drinking: Permitted

Beach! Pool! Sunsets! Enjoy your stay in this beach condo overlooking the Gulf of Mexico. A beach cottage is sometimes available. Choose your breakfast, then bask in the sun, swim in the gulf, and catch spectacular sunsets from your balcony. Dine at nearby seafood restaurants and visit the local seabird sanctuary, sunken gardens, and the Dali Museum. Other nearby attractions are Busch Gardens in Tampa and sponge diving in Tarpon Springs. This B&B is located between Clearwater and St. Petersburg Beach, only two hours from Walt Disney World. Your hostess is a real estate broker.

Bed & Breakfast of Islamorada
81175 OLD HIGHWAY, ISLAMORADA, FLORIDA 33036

Tel: (305) 664-9321
Host: Dottie Saunders
Location: 87 mi. S of Miami
No. of Rooms: 2
No. of Private Baths: 2
Double/pb: $50–$55
Single/pb: $45
Open: All year

Reduced Rates: Available
Breakfast: Full
Credit Cards: MC, VISA
Pets: Sometimes
Children: Welcome
Smoking: Permitted
Social Drinking: Permitted

Make the most of the Florida Keys while staying in this one-story house. Bicycles, snorkeling gear, and a hot tub are at your disposal, and sailing trips on a historic old boat can be arranged. John Pennecamp Coral Reef State Park, 40 minutes away, is a great place for snorkeling and diving, and the whole family can ride in the glass-bottomed boats. Your hostess has had a varied career, from cooking on a freighter to selling real estate; she enjoys waterfront activities, gardening, and photography.

Judge Gray's House ✪

2814 ST. JOHNS AVENUE, JACKSONVILLE, FLORIDA 32205

Tel: **(904) 388-4248; (800) 654-3095**
Best Time to Call: **Anytime**
Hosts: **Bill and Yvonne Edmonds**
No. of Rooms: **3**
No. of Private Baths: **3**
Double/pb: **$50–$65**
Single/pb: **$45–$50**

Open: **All year**
Reduced Rates: **7th night free**
Breakfast: **Continental**
Pets: **No**
Children: **No**
Smoking: **No**
Social Drinking: **Permitted**

This splendid riverfront Victorian was once the residence of a local justice. Built in 1911, the house is a testimonial to the Queen Anne style, with its latticed window sashes, fluted veranda columns, and two-story bay and pedimented gable with a fanlight window. Inside, the guest rooms boast high ceilings, antiques, and Whistler etchings. But there are plenty of modern amenities, such as TVs, phones, and central air-conditioning. Bill and Yvonne will happily direct you to the Gator Bowl, the Civic Auditorium, and the numerous other sights Jacksonville has to offer.

Innisfail ✪

134 TIMBER LANE, JUPITER, FLORIDA 33458

Tel: **(407) 744-5905**
Best Time to Call: **Evenings**
Hosts: **Katherine and Luke van Noorden**
Location: **20 mi. N of Palm Beach**
No. of Rooms: **1**
No. of Private Baths: **1**
Double/pb: **$51–$60**
Open: **All year**

Reduced Rates: **10% weekly; 10% seniors**
Breakfast: **Continental**
Other Meals: **Available**
Pets: **Welcome**
Children: **Yes**
Smoking: **No**
Social Drinking: **Permitted**
Airport/Station Pickup: **Yes**

A contemporary ranch framed by palm trees, Innisfail—Gaelic for "the abode of peace and harmony"—doubles as a gallery. The van Noordens are sculptors, and guests are welcome to watch them work in their home studio. While you don't have to be an art lover to visit, it helps to be a pet lover; Katherine and Luke's four-footed family comprises four dogs and two cats. Jupiter has wonderful beaches, but you can get an equally good tan lounging by the van Noordens' swimming pool. In the morning, a Continental breakfast of coffee or tea, fresh citrus fruit, and muffins or cereal is served.

Hibiscus House ✪
345 WEST ENID DRIVE, KEY BISCAYNE, FLORIDA 33149

Tel: **(305) 361-2456**	Reduced Rates: **May 1–Dec. 15**
Best Time to Call: **9 AM–5 PM**	Breakfast: **Full**
Hosts: **Bernice and Earl Duffy**	Wheelchair Accessible: **Yes**
Location: **10 mi. SE of Miami**	Pets: **No**
No. of Rooms: **2**	Children: **No**
No. of Private Baths: **2**	Smoking: **Permitted**
Double/pb: **$65**	Social Drinking: **Permitted**
Single/pb: **$60**	Minimum Stay: **2 nights**
Open: **All year**	

Welcome to an island paradise only 15 minutes from downtown Miami and 20 minutes from Miami International Airport. Key Biscayne features two lushly landscaped parks, a championship golf course, and miles of white sandy beaches; your hosts offer private beach privileges. Tennis courts and bicycle paths are in plentiful supply. Add to this the famous Miami Seaquarium and easy access to Greater Miami's many attractions and you have all of the ingredients for a very pleasant visit.

Papaya Paradise ✪
305 ST. THOMAS AVENUE, KEY LARGO, FLORIDA 33037

Tel: **(305) 451-5629**	Open: **All year**
Best Time to Call: **8 AM–8 PM**	Breakfast: **Continental**
Hosts: **Gina and Peter Cunningham-Eves**	Pets: **Sometimes**
Location: **55 mi. S of Miami**	Children: **Welcome**
No. of Rooms: **2 guest cottages**	Smoking: **Permitted**
Guest Cottage: **$75; Sleeps 3**	Social Drinking: **Permitted**
	Minimum Stay: **2 nights**

Enjoy boating, snorkeling, fishing, and swimming just off the premises of this oceanside inn adjacent to John Pennekamp Coral Reef State Park. Peter, a licensed boat captain, knows the local waters. When he's not at the helm, he's in front of an easel: both Peter and Gina are artists, and you'll see their work displayed on B&B walls. Accommodations are fully equipped efficiency studios with private entrances and baths. Continental breakfast, served by the water, includes oranges, bananas, mangoes, and yes, papayas from your hosts' walled garden.

Clauser's Bed & Breakfast ✪
201 EAST KICKLIGHTER ROAD, LAKE HELEN, FLORIDA 32744

Tel: **(904) 228-0310**	Location: **30 mi. NE of Orlando; 20 mi. W of Daytona Beach**
Best Time to Call: **7 AM–10 PM**	No. of Rooms: **2**
Hosts: **Marge and Tom Clauser**	

No. of Private Baths: **2**
Double/pb: **$70–$75**
Single/pb: **$60–$65**
Open: **All year**
Reduced Rates: **10% seniors; $10 less
     midweek**
Breakfast: **Full**
Credit Cards: **DISC, MC, VISA**
Pets: **No**

Children: **No**
Smoking: **No**
Social Drinking: **Permitted**
Minimum Stay: **Required during
     special events**
Airport/Station Pickup: **Yes**

Clauser's, a two-and-a-half-story, tin-roofed Victorian home with a porch wrapping around three sides, was described by a local journalist as "everybody's grandmother's house." Heirlooms, quilts, and comforters make the interior warm and cozy. Beach and state parks are nearby, but you may never want to leave; right on the property you can play croquet, badminton, volleyball, and horseshoes, or admire horses—Tom's passion—in the family's corral. Full country breakfasts feature Marge's homemade breads, pastries, jams, and jellies.

Bed & Breakfast of the Palm Beaches ✪
909 NORTHERN DRIVE, LAKE PARK, FLORIDA 33403

Tel: **(407) 848-6320**
Best Time to Call: **6 PM–9 PM**
Host: **Jim Rawnsley**
Location: **8 mi. N of West Palm Beach**
No. of Rooms: **3**
No. of Private Baths: **1**
Max. No. Sharing Bath: **4**
Double/pb: **$45**
Single/pb: **$40**
Double/sb: **$40**

Single/sb: **$35**
Open: **All year**
Reduced Rates: **10% weekly, 5%
     seniors, 20% for 2 rooms**
Breakfast: **Continental**
Pets: **No**
Children: **Welcome, over 5**
Smoking: **No**
Social Drinking: **Permitted**
Airport/Station Pickup: **Yes**

Located in a quiet section of town, this B&B is convenient to many attractions, from beaches, golf courses, and swimming pools to restaurants and stores. Your host couldn't be more accommodating: The Colonial ranch layout is accessible to disabled guests, and visitor's guides and maps are supplied for all Palm Beach attractions. You can fish in the Atlantic Ocean or see New York stage shows at the Burt Reynolds Theatre. Or just escape from it all on your host's sheltered tropical patio. In season, you may pick yourself oranges from Jim's trees.

The Matthews B&B ✪
3150 GULFSTREAM ROAD, LAKE WORTH, FLORIDA 33461

Tel: **(407) 965-0068**
Best Time to Call: **9 AM–noon, 6–10 PM**
Hosts: **Vern and Beryl Matthews**

Location: **2 mi. off I-95, 10th Ave. N.
     exit**
No. of Rooms: **1**

No. of Private Baths: **1**
Double/pb: **$55**
Single/pb: **$45**
Open: **All year**
Reduced Rates: **Weekly**
Breakfast: **Full**

Pets: **No**
Children: **Welcome, under 2**
Smoking: **No**
Social Drinking: **No**
Airport/Station Pickup: **Yes**

As you enter this contemporary stucco ranch house, you'll be greeted with coffee and a light snack. A bowl of candies or fresh fruit will await you in the bedroom. Bicycles are at guests' disposal, but Vern and Beryl suggest renting a car for maximum enjoyment of such area attractions as jai alai, greyhound races, the Royal Poinciana Playhouse, and of course, the beach. Full breakfasts always feature Florida's famed citrus fruits and juices. You have a choice of eating areas—the kitchen, the dining room, and the sun room.

Lighthouse Bed & Breakfast ✪
13355 SECOND STREET EAST, MADEIRA BEACH, FLORIDA 33708

Tel: **(813) 391-0015**
Hosts: **Norm and Maggie Lucore**
Location: **4 mi. W of St. Petersburg**
No. of Rooms: **5**
No. of Private Baths: **5**
Double/pb: **$45–$85**
Open: **All year**

Breakfast: **Full or Continental**
Credit Cards: **MC, VISA**
Pets: **Sometimes**
Children: **Welcome**
Smoking: **Permitted**
Social Drinking: **Permitted**

This contemporary two-story home is just 300 steps, count them, from the Gulf of Mexico's sandy beaches; to the rear of the house is a classic white lighthouse. Feel free to loll about on the private sun deck, soak in the Jacuzzi, and grill dinner on the gas barbecue. Epcot Center, Busch Gardens, Sea World, and MGM tours are among the local attractions. Breakfast offerings, served either in the lighthouse or outside in the gazebo, range from fruit and pastry in summer to omelets and waffles in winter.

Inn by the Sea ✪
287 11TH AVENUE SOUTH, NAPLES, FLORIDA 33940

Tel: **(813) 649-4124**
Best Time to Call: **9 AM–9 PM**
Host: **Catlin Maser**
Location: **30 mi. S of Ft. Myers**
No. of Rooms: **6**
No. of Private Baths: **4**
Max. No. Sharing Bath: **4**
Double/pb: **$60–$120**
Double/sb: **$45–$85**
Suites: **$80–$115**

Open: **All year**
Reduced Rates: **10% weekly**
Breakfast: **Continental**
Credit Cards: **MC, VISA**
Pets: **No**
Children: **Welcome, over 16**
Smoking: **No**
Social Drinking: **Permitted**
Airport/Station Pickup: **Yes**

This inn, a beautifully appointed guest house on the National Register of Historic Places, has a tropical setting just two blocks from the beach. Decor is casually elegant, with abundant wicker, floral-print fabrics, white-iron and brass beds, and romantic ceiling fans. Much of the artwork is done by local artists; all of it is for sale to guests. Naples offers seven miles of white sand beaches, swimming, sailing, boating, and tennis. Grab a fishing pole and head for the Naples Pier, a local landmark that extends 1,000 feet into the Gulf of Mexico. Jump on one of the inn's beach cruisers and pedal through prestigious Port Royal, a neighborhood of million-dollar homes. Fabulous shopping, award-winning restaurants, and art galleries are all within walking distance.

Night Swan Intracoastal Bed & Breakfast ✪
512 SOUTH RIVERSIDE DRIVE, NEW SMYRNA BEACH, FLORIDA 32168

Tel: **(904) 423-4940**	Open: **All year**
Best Time to Call: **5–9 PM**	Reduced Rates: **Available**
Hosts: **Martha and Charles Nighswonger**	Breakfast: **Continental**
	Credit Cards: **MC, VISA**
Location: **15 mi. S of Daytona Beach**	Pets: **No**
No. of Rooms: **5**	Children: **Welcome**
No. of Private Baths: **5**	Smoking: **No**
Double/pb: **$49–$69**	Social Drinking: **Permitted**
Suites: **$89; sleeps 4**	Airport/Station Pickup: **Yes**

Come sit on Night Swan's wraparound porch or by its windows and watch pelicans, dolphins, sailboats, and yachts ply the Atlantic Intracoastal Waterway. Then enjoy the waterfront yourself: surf, swim, fish, drive, or bicycle along the bathing beach two miles to the east. This spacious three-story home in New Smyrna's historic district has a central fireplace and intricate, natural woodwork in every room, and some rooms overlook the Indian River. Continental breakfast is served in the dining room; low cholesterol dishes are a house specialty.

Neva's Bed & Breakfast ✪
520 SOUTHEAST 17TH PLACE, OCALA, FLORIDA 32671

Tel: **(904) 732-4607**	Single/sb: **$20**
Best Time to Call: **8 AM**	Open: **Sept. 1–July 31**
Host: **Neva Stanojevich**	Breakfast: **Full**
Location: **40 mi. S of Gainesville**	Pets: **No**
No. of Rooms: **2**	Children: **No**
Max. No. Sharing Bath: **4**	Smoking: **No**
Double/sb: **$40**	Social Drinking: **No**

This five-bedroom split-level is near shopping malls, churches, and hospitals. Ocala is 80 miles west of Daytona and 80 miles north of

Orlando. Attractions closer to home include numerous horse farms and Wild Waters, a six-acre water park just outside Ocala. Within city limits are the Appleton Cultural Center and the Walt Disney World Information/Reservation Center. Your host, a retired schoolteacher, is a church organist who takes great pride in her baking.

Action Center of Orlando ✪
6638 CONWAY LAKES DRIVE, ORLANDO, FLORIDA 32812

Tel: **(407) 859-8333**
Best Time to Call: **Mornings**
Hosts: **Trish and Rob Kershner**
Location: **1 mi. from Beeline 528**
No. of Rooms: **2**
Max. No. Sharing Bath: **4**
Double/pb: **$55**
Single/pb: **$40**
Suites: **$75 for 4**

Open: **All year**
Breakfast: **Full**
Pets: **Welcome**
Children: **Welcome**
Smoking: **Permitted**
Social Drinking: **Permitted**
Minimum Stay: **2 nights**
Airport/Station Pickup: **Yes**

Rob and Trish's contemporary home is furnished in a pleasant mix of past and present accented by unusual silk flower arrangements. It is accessible to all of the area's attractions, including Disney World, Epcot, and Sea World. Cape Canaveral, home of the United States space program, is less than an hour's drive; Orlando International Airport is minutes away.

PerriHouse Bed & Breakfast Inn
10417 STATE ROAD 535, ORLANDO, FLORIDA 32836

Tel: **(407) 876-4830; (800) 780-4830;**
    fax: (407) 876-0241
Best Time to Call: **9 AM–9 PM**
Hosts: **Nick and Angi Perretti**
Location: **3 mi. N of I-4 Exit 27, Lake Buena Vista, on SR 535 N**
No. of Rooms: **4**
No. of Private Baths: **4**
Double/pb: **$65–$75**
Single/pb: **$50**

Open: **All year**
Reduced Rates: **Groups, seniors, weekly**
Breakfast: **Continental**
Credit Cards: **AMEX, MC, VISA**
Pets: **No**
Children: **Welcome (crib)**
Smoking: **No**
Social Drinking: **Permitted**
Airport/Station Pickup: **Yes**

PerriHouse is a quiet, private, and secluded country estate inn conveniently nestled on 20 acres located right in the backyard of the Walt Disney World Resort area of Orlando. Because of its outstanding location, PerriHouse provides easy access to all that Disney and Orlando have to offer; it's the perfect vacation setting for families who desire a unique travel experience with a comfortable, convenient home away from home. Your hosts, Nick and Angi, heartily welcome children of all ages and specialize in accommodating vacationing families and holiday reunions. Each guest room features its own outside entrance, TV, telephone, and ceiling fans. An upscale Continental breakfast awaits you each morning with a potpourri feast of muffins, breads, and cakes; hot and cold cereals, fresh fruit bowls, and choice of beverages. After ten years of owning and operating a restaurant and nightclub, Nick and Angi instinctively offer their guests a unique blend of cordial hospitality, comfort, and friendship!

The Rio Pinar House ✪
532 PINAR DRIVE, ORLANDO, FLORIDA 32825

Tel: **(407) 277-4903**	Single/pb: **$45**
Best Time to Call: **7 AM–11 PM**	Double/sb: **$45**
Hosts: **Victor and Delores**	Single/sb: **$40**
Freudenburg	Suites: **$80 (family)**
Location: **½ mi. from E-W Expy.,**	Open: **All year**
Goldenrod exit	Breakfast: **Full**
No. of Rooms: **3**	Pets: **No**
No. of Private Baths: **2**	Children: **Welcome**
Max. No. Sharing Bath: **4**	Smoking: **No**
Double/pb: **$50**	Social Drinking: **Permitted**

Located in the quiet neighborhood near Rio Pinar Golf Course, this home features comfortably furnished rooms, antiques, and filtered air and water. Breakfast includes fresh local fruit and is served on a porch overlooking a garden of flowers and trees. The house is a 30-minute drive from the airport, Disney World, Sea World, and Universal Studios, and six miles from downtown Orlando and its Church Street Station Entertainment Complex.

The Spencer Home ✪
313 SPENCER STREET, ORLANDO, FLORIDA 32839

Tel: **(407) 855-5603**	Open: **All year**
Hosts: **Neal and Eunice Schattauer**	Breakfast: **Continental**
Location: **2 mi. from I-4**	Pets: **No**
No. of Rooms: **1 suite, 2 bedrooms**	Children: **Welcome**
No. of Private Baths: **1**	Smoking: **No**
Suites: **$50–$60; sleeps 2–4**	Social Drinking: **Permitted**
$90–$100; sleeps 4–6	Airport/Station Pickup: **Yes**

The guest suite of this comfortable neat, ranch-style house has a private entrance and consists of a bedroom with a double bed, one with a queen-size bed, a living room with a sleeper for two, and a full bathroom. It is completely air-conditioned. You are welcome to freshen your traveling duds in the laundry room and yourselves in the swimming pool. Eunice will start your day with breakfast, and Neal will be pleased to direct you to central Florida's attractions within a half hour from "home."

Heron Cay ✪
15106 PALMWOOD ROAD, PALM BEACH GARDENS, FLORIDA 33410

Tel: **(407) 744-6315**
Best Time to Call: **8 AM–10 PM**
Hosts: **Margie and Randy Salyer**
Location: **10 mi. N of West Palm Beach**
No. of Rooms: **3**
No. of Private Baths: **2**
Max. No. Sharing Bath: **4**
Double/pb: **$80–$110**
Double/sb: **$75**

Guest Yacht: **$150–$225, sleeps 4–6**
Suites: **$125**
Open: **All year**
Reduced Rates: **Available**
Breakfast: **Full or Continental**
Pets: **No**
Children: **Welcome**
Smoking: **No**
Social Drinking: **Permitted**

Heron Cay is a Key West–style home on two acres overlooking the intracoastal waterway. The Salyers' private half-acre island protects their dockage—which accommodates boats to 55 feet—and concrete boat ramp. While there are refrigerators in each room, guests also have access to a full kitchen and a laundry room. Other amenities include a Mexican-tiled patio with a swimming pool, a heated spa, and a large barbecue pit. Miles of ocean beaches are five minutes away. Randy and Margie are avid boaters who regularly invite their guests aboard their 48-foot sportfisherman for Palm Beach cruises.

Bed & Breakfast of Tampa Bay ✪
126 OLD OAK CIRCLE, OAK TRAIL, PALM HARBOR, FLORIDA 34683

Tel: **(813) 785-2342**
Best Time to Call: **7–9 AM; 6–10 PM**
Hosts: **Vivian and David Grimm**
Location: **18 mi. W of Tampa**
No. of Rooms: **4**
No. of Private Baths: **2**
Max. No. Sharing Bath: **4**
Double/pb: **$50**
Single/pb: **$40**

Double/sb: **$45**
Single/sb: **$30**
Suite: **$75**
Open: **All year**
Breakfast: **Full**
Pets: **Sometimes**
Children: **Welcome**
Smoking: **No**
Social Drinking: **Permitted**

A premier facility in a premier location: this new Art Deco residence is 1½ miles from the Gulf of Mexico and 25 minutes from Busch

Gardens, Dali Museum, and Weeki-Wachee Springs. Shopping, restaurants, churches, and public transportation are within easy walking distance. The Grimms' home has an ivory stucco exterior, with front pillars, a tile roof, and stained-glass doors. Inside, artifacts from their world travels are shown to advantage under 12-foot ceilings. Amenities include a pool and Jacuzzi, a grand piano, and bicycles for local excursions.

Gulf View Inn ✪
21722 FRONT BEACH ROAD, PANAMA CITY BEACH, FLORIDA 32413

Tel: **(904) 234-6051**
Hosts: **Raymond and Linda Nance**
Location: **3 mi. W of Panama City**
No. of Rooms: **5**
No. of Private Baths: **5**
Double/pb: **$60**
Single/pb: **$55**

Suites: **$75**
Open: **All year**
Breakfast: **Continental**
Pets: **No**
Children: **Welcome**
Smoking: **Permitted**
Social Drinking: **Permitted**

Gulf View Inn is a two-story beach house painted Cape Cod blue with cream lattice trim. Guest quarters have private entrances, TV, carpeting, and ceiling fans. In the morning, dine on the upstairs sun deck or the porch overlooking the Gulf of Mexico; homemade breads and jellies are specialties of the house. Then it's just 200 feet across the road to the white sand of Panama City Beach. Linda and Raymond's inn is near fishing, sailing, golf, tennis, and restaurants; water parks for the children are within easy reach.

Sunshine Inn ✪
508 DECATUR AVENUE, PENSACOLA, FLORIDA 32507

Tel: **(904) 455-6781**
Best Time to Call: **Early mornings**
Hosts: **The Jablonskis**

Location: **8 mi. from I-10; 4 mi. from beach**
No. of Rooms: **2**

No. of Private Baths: **1**
Max. No. Sharing Bath: **4**
Double/sb: **$35**
Suites: **$35 for 2**
Open: **All year**
Breakfast: **Full**

Pets: **No**
Children: **Welcome**
Smoking: **No**
Social Drinking: **Permitted**
Airport/Station Pickup: **Yes**
Foreign Languages: **German**

Sun and swim in the Gulf of Mexico, on the beautiful Emerald Coast of northwest Florida. Your knowledgeable hostess will provide you with all the touring advice you seek. Sunshine Inn is only minutes from the Naval Aviation Museum and the beach. The breakfast specialty is blueberry pancakes. There is a $5 surcharge for one-night stays.

Ruskin House Bed and Breakfast ✪
120 DICKMAN DRIVE S.W., RUSKIN, FLORIDA 33570

Tel: **(813) 645-3842**
Best Time to Call: **Anytime**
Host: **Arthur M. Miller, Ph.D.**
Location: **25 mi. S of Tampa; 30 mi. N of Sarasota**
No. of Rooms: **3**
No. of Private Baths: **1**
Max No. Sharing Bath: **4**
Double/pb: **$65**
Double/sb: **$45**
Suites: **$65**

Wheelchair Accessible: **Yes**
Open: **All year**
Reduced Rates: **7th day free**
Breakfast: **Continental**
Credit Cards: **MC, VISA**
Pets: **No**
Children: **Welcome, over 6**
Smoking: **No**
Social Drinking: **Permitted**
Minimum Stay: **2 nights**
Foreign Languages: **French**

A waterfront home listed on the State Register of Historic Places, this B&B, built in 1910, is graced with verandas and furnished with period antiques. The property abounds in citrus trees, and guests can help themselves to fruit in season. Your host, a poet, editor, and literature professor at New College in Sarasota, is a third-generation inhabitant of Ruskin; his grandfather cofounded the town as a Christian Socialist venture complete with Ruskin College, tuition-free for residents and their families. (The college's only surviving building, just a block from Ruskin House, is enrolled on the National Register of Historic Places.) Ruskin is no longer a utopian community, but the beach and playground are nearby, and it's an easy drive to either Tampa or Sarasota.

Carriage Way Bed & Breakfast ✪
70 CUNA STREET, ST. AUGUSTINE, FLORIDA 32084

Tel: **(904) 829-2467**
Best Time to Call: **8:30 AM–4:30 PM**
Host: **Karen Burkley**
No. of Rooms: **9**

No. of Private Baths: **9**
Double/pb: **$49–$105**
Single/pb: **$49–$105**
Open: **All year**

Reduced Rates: **10% seniors; Sun.–
  Thurs. off-season**
Breakfast: **Continental, full**
Other Meals: **Available**
Credit Cards: **DISC, MC, VISA**
Pets: **Seeing eye dogs only**

Children: **Sometimes**
Smoking: **No**
Social Drinking: **Permitted**
Airport/Station Pickup: **Yes**

This B&B, located in the heart of the historic district, is a restored Victorian built in 1883. Unique shops, museums, Castillo de San Marcos, fine restaurants, carriage tours, and the waterfront are within an easy walk. The atmosphere is leisurely and casual, in keeping with the feeling of Old St. Augustine. In addition to breakfast, Karen generously includes newspapers, wine, cookies, cordials, and dessert on Friday and Saturday evenings.

Casa de la Paz ☼
22 AVENIDA MENENDEZ, ST. AUGUSTINE, FLORIDA 32084

Tel: **(904) 829-2915**
Best Time to Call: **9 AM–9 PM**
Hosts: **Sandy Upchurch**
Location: **7 mi. from I-95**
No. of Rooms: **6**
No. of Private Baths: **6**
Double/pb: **$75–$105**
Suites: **$105–$150**
Open: **All year**

Breakfast: **Full**
Credit Cards: **AMEX, DISC, MC, VISA**
Pets: **No**
Children: **Welcome, over 9**
Smoking: **No**
Social Drinking: **Permitted**
Airport/Station Pickup: **Yes**
Foreign Languages: **Spanish**

Overlooking historic Matanzas Bay in the heart of Old St. Augustine is this three-story Mediterranean-style stucco home. The rooms are comfortably furnished in a pleasant blend of the old and new. Amenities in each room include ceiling fans, central air-conditioning and heat, high-quality linens, cable TV, and complimentary sherry or wine. The veranda rooms have private entrances. Guests are welcome to use the private, walled courtyard, well-stocked library, and delightful parlor. It is central to all attractions and convenient to fine restaurants and shops.

Casa de Solana ☼
21 AVILES STREET, ST. AUGUSTINE, FLORIDA 32084

Tel: **(904) 824-3555**
Best Time to Call: **9 AM–6 PM**
Hosts: **Faye and Jim McMurry**
No. of Rooms: **4 suites**
No. of Private Baths: **4**
Suites: **$125**
Open: **All year**

Breakfast: **Full**
Credit Cards: **AMEX, DISC, MC, VISA**
Pets: **No**
Children: **No**
Smoking: **No**
Social Drinking: **Permitted**

This is a gorgeous Colonial home built in 1763. It is located in the heart of the historic area, within walking distance of restaurants, museums, and quaint shops. Some of the antique-filled suites have fireplaces, while others have balconies that overlook the lovely garden, or a breathtaking view of Matanzas Bay. Jim and Faye include cable TV, chocolates, a decanter of sherry, and the use of their bicycles.

Castle Garden ✪
15 SHENANDOAH STREET, ST. AUGUSTINE, FLORIDA 32084

Tel: **(904) 829-3839**	Reduced Rates: **20% weekly; $20 less**
Best Time to Call: **9 AM–6 PM**	**Sun.–Thurs.; 10% seniors**
Hosts: **Bruce and Joyce Kloeckner**	Breakfast: **Full**
Location: **10 mi. from I-95**	Credit Cards: **AMEX, DISC, MC, VISA**
No. of Rooms: **6**	Pets: **No**
No. of Private Baths: **6**	Children: **Welcome**
Double/pb: **$75–$150**	Smoking: **No**
Single/pb: **$75–$150**	Social Drinking: **Permitted**
Open: **All year**	Airport/Station Pickup: **Yes**

The only Moorish-revival dwelling in St. Augustine, Castle Garden dates to the late 1800s; the unusual coquina stone exterior remains virtually untouched since its completion. The interior was completely renovated, and color-coordinated draperies, linens, and wallpaper give each room a distinctive appearance. You'll want to park your car in the B&B's fenced lot and borrow bikes to tour the city, one of the nation's oldest. When you return, relax on the sunporch or stroll the lovely grounds. The Kloeckners give each guest a complimentary bottle of wine, and Joyce prides herself on preparing mouthwatering country breakfasts "just like Mom used to make."

Kenwood Inn
38 MARINE STREET, ST. AUGUSTINE, FLORIDA 32084

Tel: **(904) 824-2116**	Single/pb: **$45**
Best Time to Call: **11 AM–10 PM**	Open: **All year**
Hosts: **Mark, Kerrianne, and Caitlin**	Breakfast: **Continental**
Constant	Credit Cards: **DISC, MC, VISA**
Location: **40 mi. S of Jacksonville**	Pets: **No**
No. of Rooms: **12**	Children: **Welcome, over 8**
No. of Private Baths: **12**	Smoking: **No**
Double/pb: **$55–$85**	Social Drinking: **Permitted**

If you are to discover a Victorian building in Florida, how appropriate that it should be in the historic section of St. Augustine, the oldest city in the U.S. This New England–style inn is a rarity in the South; this one has old-fashioned beds with color-coordinated touches right down to the sheets and linens. Breakfast may be taken in your room, in the courtyard surrounded by trees, or by the swimming pool. Tour trains, waterfront shops, restaurants, and museums are within walking distance. Flagler College is three blocks away.

Old City House Inn & Restaurant ✪
115 CORDOVA STREET, ST. AUGUSTINE, FLORIDA 32084

Tel: **(904) 826-0113**
Best Time to Call: **Anytime**
Hosts: **Robert and Alice Compton**
Location: **6 mi. from I-95, Exit 95**
No. of Rooms: **5**
No. of Private Baths: **5**
Double/pb: **$60–$95**
Open: **All year**
Reduced Rates: **Weekdays**
Breakfast: **Full**

Other Meals: **Available**
Credit Cards: **AMEX, MC, VISA**
Pets: **Sometimes**
Children: **Welcome**
Smoking: **No**
Social Drinking: **Permitted**
Minimum Stay: **2 nights weekends; 3 nights some holidays**
Airport/Station Pickup: **Yes**

A majestic example of Colonial-revival architecture, the Old City House Inn & Restaurant, built in 1873, stands in the heart of St. Augustine's historic district. Each of the five cheerfully decorated bedrooms contains a queen-size bed, cable TV, and a private entrance and bath. After a full day of sightseeing, you're invited to join Robert and Alice on the veranda for a complimentary snack and beverage. They will also supply you with bicycles to help you work off the filling gourmet breakfast, which may include quiche, frittatas, pancakes, and waffles.

Old Powder House Inn ✪
38 CORDOVA STREET, ST. AUGUSTINE, FLORIDA 32084

Tel: **(904) 824-4149; (800) 447-4149**
Hosts: **Michael and Connie Emerson**
Location: **30 mi. S of Jacksonville**
No. of Rooms: **6**
No. of Private Baths: **6**
Double/pb: **$65–$85**
Suite: **$95**
Open: **All year**

Reduced Rates: **$15 less Sun.–Thurs.**
Breakfast: **Full**
Credit Cards: **MC, VISA**
Pets: **No**
Children: **Welcome, over 2**
Smoking: **No**
Social Drinking: **Permitted**
Airport/Station Pickup: **Yes**

High ceilings, spacious verandas, and elaborate woodwork distinguish this winter cottage, built in 1899 on the site of an 18th-century Spanish powder magazine. Cordova Street is in St. Augustine's historic district, and you're likely to see visitors surveying the neighborhood from a horse and buggy. If you want to take your own tour, your hosts can supply bicycles and guide maps. Of course, you're never far from the beach. The Emersons set out tea every afternoon; mornings, you'll savor juice, muffins or croissants, soufflé, fruit, cereal, and tea or coffee.

St. Francis Inn ☯
279 ST. GEORGE STREET, ST. AUGUSTINE, FLORIDA 32084

Tel: **(904) 824-6068**	Breakfast: **Continental**
Host: **Jeanette Boerema**	Credit Cards: **MC, VISA**
Location: **2 mi. from US 1**	Pets: **No**
No. of Rooms: **13**	Children: **Welcome (crib)**
No. of Private Baths: **13**	Smoking: **No**
Double/pb: **$52–$95**	Social Drinking: **Permitted**
Guest Cottage: **$130; sleeps 4–6**	Airport/Station Pickup: **Yes**
Open: **All year**	

Built in 1791, the inn is a Spanish Colonial structure with a private courtyard and garden, located in the center of the restored part of town. Balconies are furnished with rocking chairs, and the swimming pool is a great cooling-off spot. The building is made of coquina, a limestone made of broken shells and coral. Due to its trapezoidal shape, there are no square or rectangular rooms. All of St. Augustine's historic and resort activities are within a three-mile radius.

Bayboro House on Old Tampa Bay
1719 BEACH DRIVE SOUTHEAST, ST. PETERSBURG, FLORIDA 33701

Tel: **(813) 823-4955**	Breakfast: **Continental**
Hosts: **Gordon and Antonia Powers**	Credit Cards: **MC, VISA**
Location: **½ mi. from I-275, Exit 9**	Pets: **No**
No. of Rooms: **3**	Children: **No**
No. of Private Baths: **3**	Smoking: **No**
Double/pb: **$69–$79**	Social Drinking: **Permitted**
Open: **All year**	

A unique three-story Queen Anne with airy, high-ceilinged rooms, and a wraparound veranda in view of Tampa Bay, Bayboro House is graced with antique furniture plus tropical plants and flowers. It is the ideal spot for sunning and beachcombing. Visit unusual shops, fine restaurants, the Sunken Gardens, or the Salvador Dali museum. Tampa is 20 minutes away; Walt Disney World and Epcot are 1½ hours away. The Suncoast Dome is five minutes from the door. A self-contained apartment is also available.

Crescent House

459 BEACH ROAD, SIESTA KEY, SARASOTA, FLORIDA 34242

Tel: **(813) 346-0857**
Hosts: **Paulette and Bob Flaherty**
Location: **10 mi. from Sarasota**
No. of Rooms: **3**
No. of Private Baths: **3**
Double/pb: **$95**
Double/sb: **$55**
Open: **All year**

Reduced Rates: **May–Nov.**
Breakfast: **Continental**
Pets: **No**
Children: **Welcome**
Smoking: **Permitted**
Social Drinking: **Permitted**
Airport/Station Pickup: **Yes**
Foreign Languages: **French, Spanish**

This lovely, over-70-year-old home has been fully restored and furnished with comfortable antiques. Breakfast specialties include freshly squeezed Florida orange juice, homemade muffins, scones, and freshly ground coffee. Sunbathe on a spacious wood deck, or step across the street to a white sandy beach and cool off in the Gulf of Mexico. The house is located within a short walk of Siesta Village and Pavilion, with its many restaurants, quaint shops, tennis courts, and public beach. Your hosts specialize in European service and hospitality, and will gladly guide you to fine dining and sailboat and watersporting gear rentals.

Hardisty Inn on the Bay ✪

621 GULF STREAM AVENUE, SARASOTA, FLORIDA 34236

Tel: **(813) 955-4683**
Best Time to Call: **8 AM—8 PM**
Hosts: **Mike and Penny Livingston**
Location: **56 mi. S of Tampa**
No. of Rooms: **3**
No. of Private Baths: **3**
Double/pb: **$75–$89**
Open: **All year**

Breakfast: **Continental**
Pets: **No**
Children: **Welcome, over 12**
Smoking: **No**
Social Drinking: **Permitted**
Minimum Stay: **2 nights mid-Jan.–
    mid-Apr.**
Airport Pickup: **Yes**

True to its name, Hardisty Inn overlooks Sarasota's bay. It's a 1940s cypress-wood house that your British-born hosts have carefully restored to capture the feel of old Florida. The inn is within walking distance of antique shops, boutiques, and the theater-and-arts district, with its many restaurants and night spots. In your spare time lounge on the lanai or watch TV in the sitting room.

The Pepperberry House

P.O. BOX 841, SARASOTA, FLORIDA 34240

Tel: **(813) 955-2823**
Best Time to Call: **Early mornings;
    evenings**

Host: **Lorraine Yerdonek**
No. of Rooms: **4**
No. of Private Baths: **2**

Max. No. Sharing Bath: **2**	**Dec. 14**
Double/pb: **$85**	Breakfast: **Continental**
Double/sb: **$55**	Pets: **No**
Suites: **$85**	Children: **Welcome**
Open: **All year**	Smoking: **No**
Reduced Rates: **30–40% May 15–**	Social Drinking: **Permitted**

This two-story Key West house right on the Hudson Bayou has its own dock for launching boating and fishing expeditions. Landlubbers can catch rays on the spacious sun deck. Inside, the house is light and airy, with coral fireplaces, honey oakwood floors, and pickled cypress walls hung with Lorraine's own artwork. In addition to beaches, Sarasota's attractions include the Ringling Mansion and Museum, the Selby Botanical Gardens, the Van Wetzel Performing Arts Center, and many excellent restaurants. Continental breakfasts consist of fresh-squeezed juice, locally grown fruit, cereal, yogurt, and muffins and breads hot from the oven.

Phillippi Crest Inn ✪
2549 ASHTON ROAD, SARASOTA, FLORIDA 34231

Tel: **(813) 924-2396**	Single/pb: **$45**
Best Time to Call: **Anytime**	Open: **All year**
Hosts: **Frank and Cheryl Herbold**	Breakfast: **Continental, plus**
Location: **1 mi. S of Sarasota**	Pets: **No**
No. of Rooms: **2**	Children: **Welcome, over 13**
No. of Private Baths: **2**	Smoking: **Permitted**
Double/pb: **$65**	Social Drinking: **Permitted**

Step inside this Old Florida clapboard and you'll see knotty-pine paneling, wood floors, and lots of English chintz. You're welcome to have breakfast on the latticed porch, which is furnished with a wrought-iron dining table and wicker chairs; as you dine, you can watch Japanese carp dart around in the pond below. Then sunbathe on the deck and relax until you're warm enough to jump in the pool.

The Dolphin Inn at Seaside ✪
107 SAVANNAH STREET, SEASIDE, FLORIDA 32459

Tel: **(904) 231-5477; (800) 443-3146**	Open: **All year**
Best Time to Call: **Anytime**	Breakfast: **Continental**
Hosts: **Richard "Mac" McCullen and**	Other Meals: **Available**
Nancy Judkins	Credit Cards: **MC, VISA**
Location: **25 mi. W of Panama City**	Pets: **No**
No. of Rooms: **2**	Children: **Welcome**
Max. No. Sharing Bath: **4**	Smoking: **Permitted**
Double/sb: **$85**	Social Drinking: **Permitted**

Seaside, a unique new community, recaptures the charm and tranquility of turn-of-the-century resort towns with its pastel-hued Victorian houses, white picket fences, brick streets, sugar white beaches, and clear blue waters. The Dolphin Inn is a pink three-story Victorian cottage with stained-glass windows and dolphin-shaped gingerbread trim; inside, a 1909 piano adds to the nostalgia. Guest rooms open onto a veranda with a breathtaking view of the Gulf of Mexico. Mac is a scuba instructor and Nancy also dives, so there is a nautical air to their furnishings, including Nancy's striking shell collection. If you share Mac's passion for old cars, you'll admire his restored 1961 Impala convertible.

Florida Keys House ✪
P.O. BOX 41, SUMMERLAND KEY, FLORIDA 33042

Tel: **(800) 833-9857**	Credit Cards: **MC, VISA**
Best Time to Call: **Anytime**	Pets: **No**
Hosts: **Captain Dave Wiley and Camille Wiley**	Children: **Welcome**
	Smoking: **No**
Location: **27 mi. E of Key West**	Social Drinking: **Permitted**
Suites: **$79, sleeps 2**	Minimum Stay: **2 nights**
Open: **All year**	Foreign Languages: **French, Spanish**
Breakfast: **Continental**	

Set among an abundance of palm trees, Florida Keys House boasts a one-hundred-foot dock where you can barbecue, swim, or relax under the tiki hut. If you'd like to dive or snorkel in nearby Looe Key Marine Sanctuary, take in the sunset, or fish for Capt. Dave's specialty, the mighty tarpon, your host can arrange a personalized charter cruise with dockside pickup. Private guest quarters consist of two bedrooms, a bathroom, living room, and large kitchen stocked with breakfast selections which you may prepare at your convenience.

Knightswood
P.O. BOX 151, SUMMERLAND KEY, FLORIDA 33042

Tel: **(305) 872-2246; (800) 437-5402**	Open: **All year**
Hosts: **Chris and Herb Pontin**	Breakfast: **Full**
Location: **26 mi. E of Key West**	Pets: **No**
No. of Rooms: **2**	Children: **No**
No. of Private Baths: **2**	Smoking: **No**
Double/pb: **$85**	Social Drinking: **Permitted**
Single/pb: **$70**	Minimum Stay: **2 nights**

Knightswood boasts one of the loveliest water views in the Keys. The guest apartment is self-contained and very private. Snorkeling, fishing, and boating can be enjoyed right from the Pontins' dock. You are welcome to swim in the freshwater pool, relax in the spa, or sunbathe on the white sand beach. Trips to protected Looe Key Coral Reef can be arranged. Fine dining and Key West nightlife are within easy reach.

Fiorito's Bed & Breakfast ○
421 OLD EAST LAKE ROAD, TARPON SPRINGS, FLORIDA 34689

Tel: **(813) 937-5487**
Best Time to Call: **8 AM–9 PM**
Hosts: **Dick and Marie Fiorito**
Location: **2 mi. E of US 19**
No. of Rooms: **1**
No. of Private Baths: **1**
Double/pb: **$40**
Single/pb: **$35**

Open: **All year**
Breakfast: **Full**
Pets: **No**
Children: **No**
Smoking: **Restricted**
Social Drinking: **Permitted**
Airport/Station Pickup: **Yes**

Just off a quiet road that runs along Lake Tarpon's horse country, this meticulously maintained home on two-and-a-half acres offers respite for the visitor. The guest room and bath are decorated in tones of blue, enhanced with beautiful accessories. Fresh fruit, cheese omelet, homemade bread and jam, and a choice of beverage is the Fioritos' idea of breakfast. It is beautifully served on the tree-shaded, screened terrace. They'll be happy to direct you to the Greek Sponge Docks, deep-sea fishing opportunities, golf courses, beaches, and great restaurants.

Heartsease
272 OLD EAST LAKE ROAD, TARPON SPRINGS, FLORIDA 34689

Tel: **(813) 934-0994**
Best Time to Call: **5 PM–10 PM**
Hosts: **Gerald and Sharon Goulish**
No. of Rooms: **1 cottage**
No. of Private Baths: **1**
Double/pb: **$55**
Single/pb: **$45**
Open: **All year**

Reduced Rates: **Available**
Breakfast: **Continental**
Pets: **No**
Children: **No**
Smoking: **No**
Social Drinking: **Permitted**
Airport Pickup: **Yes**

You'll find plenty of "heartsease," meaning peace of mind and tranquillity, at Gerald and Sharon's guest cottage. Wicker and pine furniture and a green and mauve color scheme create a light, airy feeling. Amenities include a private entrance, a mini-kitchen stocked with a microwave and breakfast fixings, cable TV, private bath, tennis court, and a deck overlooking the in-ground pool. Pluck an orange or a grapefruit from one of the many fruit trees and then settle in the gazebo, an ideal place for observing the bald eagles that nest nearby. Golf courses, Tampa's Old Hyde Park, Harbour Island, and Tarpon Springs' famed sponge docks are all within a short drive.

Spring Bayou Inn

32 WEST TARPON AVENUE, TARPON SPRINGS, FLORIDA 34689

Tel: **(813) 938-9333**
Best Time to Call: **9 AM–9 PM**
Hosts: **Ron and Cher Morrick**
Location: **2 mi. W of US 19**
No. of Rooms: **5**
No. of Private Baths: **4**
Max. No. Sharing Bath: **2**
Double/pb: **$65–$85**
Single/pb: **$55–$75**

Double/sb: **$55–$70**
Single/sb: **$45–$60**
Open: **Oct. 1–Aug. 15**
Breakfast: **Continental**
Reduced Rates: **Apr. 16–Dec. 15**
Pets: **No**
Children: **No**
Smoking: **No**
Social Drinking: **Permitted**

This large, comfortable Victorian was built in 1905. Located in the Historic District, it has architectural details of the past combined with up-to-date conveniences. You will enjoy relaxing on the porch or in the courtyard to take in the sun. The parlor is a favorite gathering place, offering informal atmosphere, complimentary wine, music, books, and games, and the opportunity to make new friends. The fireplace chases the chill on winter evenings. Tarpon Springs is the sponge capital of the world, and the nearby sponge docks are interesting to visit. The area is known for its excellent restaurants and variety of shops.

West Palm Beach Bed & Breakfast

419 32ND STREET, OLD NORTHWOOD HISTORIC DISTRICT,
WEST PALM BEACH, FLORIDA 33407

Tel: **(800) 736-4064**
Hosts: **Dennis Keimel and Ron Seltz**
Location: **3 mi from Palm Beach International Airport**
No. of Rooms: **3**
No. of Private Baths: **3**
Double/pb: **$65–$85**
Open: **All year**

Reduced Rates: **$10 less weekly, May–Nov.**
Breakfast: **Continental**
Pets: **Sometimes**
Children: **Welcome**
Smoking: **No**
Social Drinking: **Permitted**
Airport/Station Pickup: **Yes**

This enchanting Key West–style cottage is generally located in the Old Northwood Historic District, one block from the intracoastal waterway. The B&B's colorful Caribbean decor will remind you of the islands. With its own kitchenette, living area, and tropical pool area, the carriage house is perfect for a private weekend getaway.

GEORGIA

Fort Oglethorpe •
• Helen
• Dahlonega
Commerce •
• Danielsville
• Atlanta
Newnan •
• Senoia
• Perry
Savannah •
• Blakely

Bed & Breakfast Atlanta ✪
1801 PIEDMONT AVENUE NORTHEAST, SUITE 208, ATLANTA,
GEORGIA 30324

Tel: **(404) 875-0525; (800) 96-PEACH**
Best Time to Call: **9 AM–5 PM Mon.–
Fri.**
Coordinators: **Madalyne Eplan and
Paula Gris**
States/Regions Covered: **Alpharetta,
Atlanta, Brookhaven, Buckhead,
Decatur, Dunwoody, Marietta,
Roswell, Sandy Springs, Smyrna,
Stone Mountain, Tucker**

Rates (Single/Double):
Modest: **$32–$40 / $40–$44**
Average: **$44–$56 / $48–$56**
Luxury: **$60–$80 / $60–$100**
Credit Cards: **AMEX, MC, VISA**
Descriptive Directory of B&Bs: **$3**

Visit one of America's most gracious cities, site of the 1996 Olympics,
and experience the hospitality for which Atlanta is famous. Since 1979,

Madalyne and Paula have been carefully selecting accommodations for fortunate travelers, weighing transportation and language needs as well as other personal preferences. There are B&Bs near all major educational, medical, industrial, and convention complexes, such as the Georgia World Congress Center, Emory University, and the Centers for Disease Control. Special rates for long-term relocation and temporary duty assignments can be arranged. There is an $8 surcharge for one-night stays.

Quail Country Bed & Breakfast, Ltd. ✪
1104 OLD MONTICELLO ROAD, THOMASVILLE, GEORGIA 31792

Tel: **(912) 226-7218, 226-6882**
Coordinators: **Mercer Watt and Kathy Lanigan**
States/Regions Covered: **Thomas County, Thomasville**

Rates (Single/Double):
  Average: **$30 / $40**
  Luxury: **$40 / $50**
Credit Cards: **No**

Mercer and Kathy have a wide selection of homes, several with swimming pools, in lovely residential areas. There's a lot to see and do, including touring historic restorations and plantations. Enjoy the Pebble Hill Plantation museum, historic Glen Arven Country Club, and the April Rose Festival. There is a $5 surcharge for one-night stays.

Layside ✪
611 RIVER STREET, BLAKELY, GEORGIA 31723

Tel: **(912) 723-8932**
Best Time to Call: **8:30 AM–11 PM**
Hosts: **Ted and Jeanneane Lay**
Location: **½ mi. from Rte. 27**
No. of Rooms: **4**
Max. No. Sharing Bath: **4**
Double/sb: **$38**
Single/sb: **$30**

Open: **All year**
Reduced Rates: **10% seniors over 60**
Breakfast: **Continental**
Pets: **No**
Children: **Welcome, over 10**
Smoking: **No**
Social Drinking: **Permitted**

Layside is a southern Colonial dating back to the turn of the century. Spend the night in a queen-size bed and wake up to homemade muffins, jams, and coffee. State parks, Indian burial grounds, good fishing, and boating are all nearby attractions. The 60-foot-long front porch is a fine place to relax after a day of touring.

The Pittman House ✪
103 HOMER STREET, COMMERCE, GEORGIA 30529

Tel: **(404) 335-3823**	Single/sb: **$45**
Best Time to Call: **7 AM–9 PM**	Open: **All year**
Hosts: **Tom and Dot Tomberlin**	Breakfast: **Full**
Location: **60 mi. NE of Atlanta**	Credit Cards: **MC, VISA**
No. of Rooms: **4**	Pets: **No**
No. of Private Baths: **3**	Children: **Welcome**
Max. No. Sharing Bath: **4**	Smoking: **No**
Double/pb: **$55**	Social Drinking: **No**
Double/sb: **$50**	

This gracious white Colonial, built in 1890, is decorated throughout with period pieces. If the furniture inspires you, visit Granny's Old Things, an antique shop right next door. Other points of interest include Château Elan Winery, in neighboring Braselton, and the Crawford W. Long Museum—honoring the doctor who discovered the use of ether as an anesthetic—in the town of Jefferson. Swimmers and sailors have their choice of Lake Lanier and Lake Hartwell; Hurricane Shoals is another lovely outdoor recreational area.

The Mountain Top Lodge ✪
ROUTE 7, BOX 150, DAHLONEGA, GEORGIA 30533

Tel: **(706) 864-5257**	Suites: **$80–$125**
Best Time to Call: **10 AM–6 PM**	Open: **All year**
Host: **David Middleton**	Breakfast: **Full**
Location: **70 mi. N of Atlanta**	Pets: **No**
No. of Rooms: **13**	Children: **Welcome, over 12**
No. of Private Baths: **13**	Smoking: **No**
Double/pb: **$65–$75**	Social Drinking: **Permitted**
Single/pb: **$45–$55**	

Flanked by porches and decks, this gambrel-roofed, rustic cedar lodge is a secluded rural retreat on 40 acres, with a 360-degree mountain view. Decorated with art and antiques, the pine furniture and accessories made by mountain craftsmen add to the charm. Dahlonega was the site of America's first gold rush, and nature buffs will appreciate the Chattahoochee National Forest and Amicalola Falls State Park. Rafting, hiking, and horseback riding are all nearby. Don't miss the "Alpine village" of Helen, Georgia, only 30 minutes away.

Royal Guard Inn ✪
203 SOUTH PARK STREET, DAHLONEGA, GEORGIA 30533

Tel: **(404) 864-1713**	Location: **50 mi. N of Atlanta**
Best Time to Call: **Anytime**	No. of Rooms: **5**
Hosts: **John and Farris Vanderhoff**	No. of Private Baths: **5**

Double/pb: **$65–$70**
Open: **All year**
Reduced Rates: **10% seniors, Sun.–
  Thurs.**
Breakfast: **Full**

Credit Cards: **MC, VISA**
Pets: **No**
Children: **Welcome**
Smoking: **No**
Social Drinking: **Permitted**

Located in the northeast Georgia mountains, Dahlonega is where the first major U.S. gold rush occurred in 1828. Dahlonega Gold Museum, Price Memorial Hall—on the site of one of the first U.S. branch mints—and gold-panning areas are all in the heart of the historic downtown. Royal Guard Inn, a half-block from the old town square, is a restored and enlarged old home. John and Farris serve complimentary wine and cheese on the great wraparound porch. Breakfast, served on fine china and silver on crisp white linen, includes a casserole, pastries, or hotcakes from an old family recipe, and fresh fruit and whipped cream.

Honey Bear Hideaway Farm ○

ROUTE 4, BOX 4106, ROGERS MILL ROAD, DANIELSVILLE, GEORGIA 30633

Tel: **(404) 789-2569**
Best Time to Call: **After 4 PM**
Hosts: **Ray and Natachia Dodd**
Location: **12 mi. N of Athens**
No. of Rooms: **5**
No. of Private Baths: **5**
Double/pb: **$50**
Single/pb: **$45**
Open: **All year**

Breakfast: **Full**
Other Meals: **Available**
Credit Cards: **MC, VISA**
Pets: **No**
Children: **Welcome, over 12**
Smoking: **No**
Social Drinking: **Permitted**
Airport/Station Pickup: **Yes**

This 125-year-old farmhouse is nestled among pecan and walnut trees, with a lake nearby. Ray and Natachia are artists who converted the property's two barns into studios. The house is a virtual gallery of antiques and curios; one bedroom is decorated with old-fashioned purses. Visitors will wake up to a Southern, country-style breakfast, with farm-fresh eggs, ham or sausage, and homemade breads and jellies.

Captain's Quarters B&B Inn
13 BARNHARDT CIRCLE, FORT OGLETHORPE, GEORGIA 30742

Tel: (706) 858-0624
Hosts: Ann Gilbert and Pam Humphrey
Location: 5 mi. S of Chattanooga, Tenn.
No. of Rooms: 4
No. of Private Baths: 4
Double/pb: $60–$85

Open: All year
Reduced Rates: 10% seniors
Breakfast: Full
Credit Cards: AMEX, MC, VISA
Pets: No
Children: No
Smoking: No
Social Drinking: No

This grand home, with its twin porches and winding staircase, was originally built for two army officers and their families when Fort Oglethorpe was regarded as one of the army's most elite posts. Ann and Pam have transformed and restored it to a vision that could easily grace the pages of any magazine. A charming sitting room with TV is a comfortable spot to spend a relaxing evening. Breakfast is served in the large dining room, where one can imagine officers and their ladies being graciously served. Museums, Chickamauga battlefield, and Lookout Mountain are close by.

Hilltop Haus
P.O. BOX 154, CHATTAHOOCHEE STREET, HELEN, GEORGIA 30545

Tel: (404) 878-2388
Hosts: Frankie Tysor and Barbara Nichols
Location: 60 mi. from I-85
No. of Rooms: 5
No. of Private Baths: 3
Max. No. Sharing Bath: 3
Double/pb: $40–$65
Single/pb: $35–$50
Double/sb: $35–$60

Single/sb: $30–$45
Suite: $50–$75
Open: All year
Breakfast: Full
Credit Cards: MC, VISA
Pets: No
Children: Welcome
Smoking: Permitted
Social Drinking: Permitted

This contemporary split-level overlooks the Alpine town of Helen and the Chattahoochee River. It is near the foothills of the Smoky Mountains, six miles from the Appalachian Trail. Rich wood paneling and fireplaces create a homey atmosphere for the traveler. Guests may choose a private room or the efficiency cottage with separate entrance. Each morning a hearty breakfast includes homemade biscuits and preserves. Your hostess will direct you to many outdoor activities and sights.

Parrott-Camp-Soucy House ✪
155 GREENVILLE STREET, NEWNAN, GEORGIA 30263

Tel: (404) 253-4846
Hosts: **Chuck and Doris Soucy**
Location: **25 mi. SW of Atlanta**
No. of Rooms: **3**
No. of Private Baths: **1**
Max. No. Sharing Bath: **4**
Double/pb: **$75**
Single/pb: **$65**

Double/sb: **$70**
Single/sb: **$60**
Open: **All year**
Breakfast: **Full**
Pets: **No**
Children: **No**
Smoking: **Permitted**
Social Drinking: **Permitted**

This extraordinary Second Empire mansion, listed on the National Register of Historic Places, is a brilliant example of Victorian–French Mansard architecture. It took two years to restore it to its original elegance. For example, the fireplace in the front hall is surrounded by tiles that depict characters from the Robin Hood legend, and the magnificent grand staircase is lit by beautiful stained-glass windows. It is no surprise that the house is furnished entirely in antiques. The surprise is that it is so comfortable. You are certain to enjoy the formal gardens, swimming pool and spa, and the game room with its 1851 Brunswick pool table. If you can tear yourself away, Warm Springs, Callaway Gardens, and Atlanta are within easy reach.

The Swift Street Inn B&B ✪
1204 SWIFT STREET, PERRY, GEORGIA 31069

Tel: (912) 987-3428
Best Time to Call: **Before 12 noon**
Hosts: **Wayne and Jane Coward**
Location: **20 mi. S of Macon**
No. of Rooms: **4**
No. of Private Baths: **4**
Double/pb: **$55–$75**
Single/pb: **$45–$65**
Open: **All year**

Reduced Rates: **20% seniors**
Breakfast: **Full**
Credit Cards: **AMEX, DISC, MC, VISA**
Pets: **Yes**
Children: **Welcome, over 12**
Smoking: **No**
Social Drinking: **No**
Airport Pickup: **Yes**

Experience the elegance and warmth of a small inn in a growing southern town. Enter this antebellum coastal plantation-style home and you'll enjoy the charm, romance, and luxury of the mid-nineteenth century. Each spacious antique-filled guest room has its own character. With homemade jams, jellies, and baked goods, Georgia peaches and pecans, herbal teas, and specially ground coffees, the gourmet breakfast is a wonderful treat.

R.S.V.P. Savannah—B&B Reservation Service ○
417 EAST CHARLTON STREET, SAVANNAH, GEORGIA 31401

Tel: **(912) 232-7787; (800) 729-7787;**
  fax: (912) 236-2880; toll free fax:
  from France 0590 0371, Germany
  0130 81 6523, England 0800 89
  6288
Best Time to Call: **9:30 AM–5:30 PM**
  Mon.–Fri.
Coordinator: **Alan Fort**
States/Regions Covered: **Georgia—**
  Atlanta, Brunswick, Darien, Macon,
  St. Marys, St. Simons Island,
  Savannah, Swainsboro, Tybee Island;
  South Carolina—Beaufort,
  Charleston

Rates (Single/Double):
  Modest: **$50 / $65**
  Average: **$65 / $100**
  Luxury: **$100 / $225**
Credit Cards: **AMEX, MC, VISA**

Alan's accommodations include elegantly restored inns, guest houses, private homes, and even a villa on the water. They're located in the best historic districts as well as along the coast, from South Carolina's Low Country to Georgia's Sea Islands. A special blend of cordial hospitality, comfort, and services is provided. All are air-conditioned in the summer. Facilities for children and the handicapped are often available. Please note that while some hosts accept credit cards, most do not.

Joan's on Jones
17 WEST JONES STREET, SAVANNAH, GEORGIA 31401

Tel: **(912) 234-3863**
Hosts: **Joan and Gary Levy**
Location: **140 mi. N of Jacksonville, FL**
No. of Rooms: **2**
No. of Private Baths: **2**
Double/pb: **$85–$95**
Single/pb: **$55–$65**
Suites: **$85–$95; sleeps 2–4**
Open: **All year**

Reduced Rates: **Weekly**
Breakfast: **Continental**
Pets: **Sometimes**
Children: **Welcome**
Smoking: **No**
Social Drinking: **Permitted**
Minimum Stay: **3 days for St. Patrick's**
  Day week only
Airport/Station Pickup: **Yes**

Clip-clopping along the brick streets of the city's historic district, horse-drawn carriages take you back to a more serene and elegant era. This bed and breakfast maintains the old-fashioned mood, with its original heart-pine floors, antique furnishings, and Savannah grey brick walls. (Note the late nineteenth-century documents that slipped behind one of the fireplace mantels.) All the historic places of interest, including the famous squares, are a short walk away. Joan and Gary, former restaurateurs, live upstairs and invite you to tour their home if you're staying at least two nights.

The Culpepper House

P.O. BOX 462, BROAD AT MORGAN, SENOIA, GEORGIA 30276

Tel: **(404) 599-8182**	Open: **All year**
Best Time to Call: **7 AM–10 PM**	Reduced Rates: **10% families**
Host: **Mary A. Brown**	Breakfast: **Full**
Location: **37 mi. S of Atlanta**	Credit Cards: **No**
No. of Rooms: **4**	Pets: **No**
No. of Private Baths: **1**	Children: **Welcome, over 10 and**
Max. No. Sharing Bath: **4**	**infants**
Double/pb: **$60**	Smoking: **Permitted**
Double/sb: **$55**	Social Drinking: **Permitted**
Single/sb: **$50**	Airport/Station Pickup: **Yes**

This Queen Anne Victorian was built in 1871. Gingerbread trim, stained glass, sliding doors, bay windows, and provincial furnishings re-create that turn-of-the-century feeling. Snacks and setups are offered. Your host will gladly direct you to surrounding antique and craft shops, state parks, and gardens.

Four Chimneys ✪

2316 WIRE ROAD, THOMSON, GEORGIA 30824

Tel: **(706) 597-0220**	Open: **All year**
Best Time to Call: **Before 11 AM**	Breakfast: **Continental**
Hosts: **Ralph and Maggie Zieger**	Credit Cards: **MC, VISA**
Location: **35 mi. W of Augusta**	Pets: **No**
No. of Rooms: **4**	Children: **Welcome, over 12**
No. of Private Baths: **3**	Smoking: **Permitted**
Double/pb: **$45**	Social Drinking: **Permitted**
Single/pb: **$40**	

Escape from the modern world at this early 1800s plantation manor house with a Colonial herb garden and landscaping. Period antique and reproduction furniture complement the original heart pineplank floors, ceilings, and walls. All guest rooms feature four-poster beds and working fireplaces.

HAWAII

Bed & Breakfast—Hawaii ✪
P.O. BOX 449, KAPAA, HAWAII 96746

Tel: **(808) 822-7771; (800) 733-1632;**
  fax: (808) 822-2723
Best Time to Call: **8:30 AM–4:30 PM**
Coordinators: **Evie Warner (Elvrine,**
  Nancy, Patty)
States/Regions Covered: **All of the**
  Hawaiian Islands

Descriptive Directory: **$10.95**
Rates (Single/Double):
  Modest: **$35 / $35**
  Average: **$45 / $55**
  Luxury: **— / $80**
Credit Cards: **MC, VISA**
Minimum Stay: **2 nights**

Hawaii is a group of diverse islands offering traditional warmth and hospitality to the visitor through this membership organization. Some are separate units; others are in the main house. Most have private baths. The University of Hawaii at Oahu is convenient to many B&Bs.

Haikuleana B&B, Plantation Style ✪
69 HAIKU ROAD, HAIKU, MAUI, HAWAII 96708

Tel: **(808) 575-2890**
Best Time to Call: **8 AM–8 PM**
Host: **Frederick J. Fox, Jr.**
Location: **12 mi. E of Kahului**
No. of Rooms: **3**
No. of Private Baths: **3**
Double/pb: **$75–$85**
Single/pb: **$65–$70**
Open: **All year**

Reduced Rates: **After 5th night**
Breakfast: **Full**
Pets: **No**
Children: **Welcome, over 6**
Smoking: **No**
Social Drinking: **Permitted**
Minimum Stay: **2 nights**
Foreign Languages: **Swedish**

Experience the real feelings of "aloha" in an 1850s Hawaiian plantation home. Set in the agricultural district, close to secluded waterfalls and beautiful beaches, Haikuleana is a convenient way station for visitors headed to Hana and Haleakala Crater. Swimming ponds, the world's best windsurfing, and golf courses are all nearby. Fred completely renovated the house; you'll admire its high ceilings, plank floors, porch, and lush Hawaiian gardens. The cool, tropical rooms are furnished with drapes, ticking comforters, wicker, and antiques.

Pilialoha Bed & Breakfast Cottage ✪
255 KAUPAKALUA ROAD, HAIKU, MAUI, HAWAII 96708

Tel: **(808) 572-1440**
Best Time to Call: **9 AM–9 PM**
Hosts: **Bill and Machiko Heyde**
Location: **10 mi. E of Kahului**
Guest Cottages: **$75, sleeps 2–5**
Open: **All year**
Reduced Rates: **Weekly**

Breakfast: **Continental**
Pets: **No**
Children: **Welcome**
Smoking: **No**
Social Drinking: **Permitted**
Minimum Stay: **2 nights**
Foreign Languages: **Japanese**

Pilialoha, in Hawaiian, means "friendship." Located in lush, cool upcountry Maui on a two-acre property, with half-century-old eucalyptus trees and a cottage garden, Pilialoha is convenient to North Shore beaches, Haleakala National Park, and the road to Hana. This is a separate small house for one group of guests, most comfortable for two people but accommodates up to five. The cottage has a fully equipped kitchen with complimentary assortment of coffee and teas, a cable TV, and private telephone in the living room. Bill enjoys ham radio and welcomes other hams to operate his station. Machiko is an artist and avid gardener.

HAWAII • 171

Bev & Monty's Bed & Breakfast
4571 UKALI STREET, HONOLULU, OAHU, HAWAII 96818

Tel: **(808) 422-9873**
Best Time to Call: **7 AM–9 PM**
Hosts: **Bev and Monty Neese**
Location: **4½ mi. from airport**
No. of Rooms: **2**
Max. No. Sharing Bath: **4**
Double/sb: **$50**
Single/sb: **$40**

Open: **All year**
Reduced Rates: **Weekly**
Breakfast: **Continental**
Pets: **No**
Children: **Welcome**
Smoking: **Permitted**
Social Drinking: **Permitted**
Airport/Station Pickup: **Yes**

This typical Hawaiian home is convenient to many of Hawaii's most popular attractions. Bev and Monty are just a mile above historic Pearl Harbor, and the Arizona Memorial can be seen from their veranda. They enjoy sharing a Hawaiian aloha, for a convenient overnight stay or a long vacation where they can share their favorite places with you. This comfortable home is just off the access road leading east to Honolulu and Waikiki, or west to the North Shore beaches, sugar plantations, and pineapple fields. Good hiking country as well as city entertainment and shopping centers are located nearby.

Akamai Bed & Breakfast ✪
172 KUUMELE PLACE, KAILUA, OAHU, HAWAII 96734

Tel: **(808) 261-2227**
Best Time to Call: **8 AM–8 PM**
Host: **Diane Van Ryzin**
No. of Rooms: **2**
No. of Private Baths: **2**
Double/pb: **$60**
Single/pb: **$60**

Open: **All year**
Breakfast: **Full**
Pets: **No**
Children: **Welcome, over 7**
Smoking: **Permitted**
Social Drinking: **Permitted**
Minimum Stay: **3 nights**

Guests at Akamai stay in a separate wing of the house; each room has a private entrance, bath, cable TV, and radio. Honolulu and Waikiki are within a half-hour drive, but you may prefer to lounge by your host's pool or take the eight-minute stroll to the beach. No meals are served here, but your refrigerator is stocked with breakfast foods and the kitchen area is equipped with light cooking appliances, dishes, and flatware. Laundry facilities are also available.

Ali'i Bed & Breakfast ✪
237 AWAKEA ROAD, KAILUA OAHU, HAWAII 96734

Tel: **(800) 262-9545**
Best Time to Call: **5:30–7:00 AM;**
  3:00–9:00 PM
Host: **Earlene Sasaki**

Location: **10 mi. E of Honolulu**
No. of Rooms: **2**
Max. No. Sharing Bath: **4**
Double/sb: **$45**

Single/sb: **$40**
Guest Apartment: **$65–$85, sleeps 2–4**
Open: **All year**
Reduced Rates: **Extended stays**
Breakfast: **Continental**
Pets: **No**

Children: **Welcome**
Smoking: **Permitted**
Social Drinking: **Permitted**
Minimum Stay: **3 nights**
Foreign Languages: **Japanese**

On the windward side of Oahu, the white-sand Kailua Beach is a famous swimming and windsurfing retreat. Ali'i's self-sufficient guest units have private entrances, ceiling fans or air conditioners, refrigerators, microwaves, coffee pots, cable TV, and phones for local calls. The cozy cottage has its own little yard with a picnic table. The one-bedroom apartment, furnished with oak and rattan, is wheelchair accessible. The guest rooms offer twins or king beds. The B&B is within walking distance of the beach, bus stop, restaurants, and shopping centers. Ali'i's breakfasts feature Hawaiian fruit and fruit juices, and fresh muffins.

Papaya Paradise ✪
395 AUWINALA ROAD, KAILUA, OAHU, HAWAII 96734

Tel: **(808) 261-0316**
Best Time to Call: **7 AM–8 PM**
Hosts: **Bob and Jeanette Martz**
Location: **10 mi. E of Honolulu**
No. of Rooms: **2**
Double/pb: **$65–$70**
Open: **All year**

Breakfast: **Full**
Pets: **No**
Children: **Welcome, over 6**
Smoking: **Permitted**
Social Drinking: **Permitted**
Minimum Stay: **3 nights**

The Martz paradise is on the windward side of Oahu, miles from the high-rise hotels, but just 20 miles from the Waikiki/Honolulu airport. Their one-story home is surrounded by a papaya grove and tropical plants and flowers. Each guest room has two beds, a ceiling fan, air-conditioning, cable TV, and its own private entrance. Bob loves to cook, and serves breakfast on the lanai overlooking the pool and Jacuzzi. Kailua Beach, a beautiful white sandy beach four miles long, is within easy walking distance.

Kauai Calls B&B
5972 HEAMOI PLACE, KAPAA, KAUAI, HAWAII 96746

Tel: **(808) 822-9699**
Hosts: **Earle and Joy Schertell**
Location: **About 5 mi. NE of Lihue Airport**
No. of Rooms: **2**
No. of Private Baths: **2**

Double/pb: **$60**
Single/pb: **$55**
Guest Apartment: **$75 double, $70 single, $80 for one night**
Open: **All year**
Reduced Rates: **10% seniors, weekly**

Breakfast: **Full**
Pets: **No**
Children: **Welcome, over 13**
Smoking: **No**

Social Drinking: **Permitted**
Minimum Stay: **3 nights, guest apt. 2 nights**

Whether you choose to stay in the main house or the apartment, you'll be minutes away from beaches and mountain hiking trails; your hosts will lend you beach mats and towels. Earle, a dedicated shell collector, will tell you his favorite haunts. The studio apartment has a microwave oven and refrigerator, so you can be self-sufficient. At the end of the day, you can survey the stunning Hawaiian landscape while relaxing in the hot tub. Joy's Aloha Breakfasts feature locally grown fruit, macadamia nut pastries, and, of course, freshly brewed Kona coffee.

The Orchid Hut ✪
6402 KAAHELE STREET, KAPAA, KAUAI, HAWAII 96746

Tel: **(808) 822-7201; fax: (808) 822-7201**
Hosts: **Norm and Leonora Ross**
Location: **10 mi. E of Lihue Airport**
No. of Rooms: **1**
No. of Private Baths: **1**
Double/pb: **$75**
Open: **All year**
Reduced Rates: **10% weekly**

Breakfast: **Continental**
Pets: **No**
Children: **No**
Smoking: **No**
Social Drinking: **Permitted**
Minimum Stay: **3 nights**
Foreign Languages: **French, Danish, Dutch, Indonesian, Malaysian**

Bring your camera and escape to tropical tranquillity at a romantic, private hideaway on Kauai, known as "The Garden Island." Norm and Leonora offer the use of their completely equipped three-room contemporary cottage perched high above the Wailua River, encompassing spectacular island and water views. It's a short drive to the beach, shopping, golf, tennis, and fine dining. Local tropical fruit, a variety of cold cereals, tea, and coffee are stocked in your kitchen so you can enjoy breakfast at your own pace and leisure. Guests fly into Lihue Airport, where a car can be rented for the 15-minute drive to the "hut."

Merryman's ✪
P.O. BOX 474, KEALAKEKUA, HAWAII 96750

Tel: **(808) 323-2276**
Hosts: **Don and Penny Merryman**
No. of Rooms: **3**
No. of Private Baths: **1**
Max. No. Sharing Bath: **4**
Double/pb: **$80**
Single/pb: **$70**
Double/sb: **$65**

Single/sb: **$55**
Open: **All year**
Breakfast: **Full**
Credit Cards: **MC, VISA**
Pets: **No**
Children: **Welcome**
Smoking: **No**
Social Drinking: **Permitted**

Don and Penny left the snows of Alaska to settle in this lovely tropical retreat a few minutes from the Captain Cook Monument at Kealakekua Bay, where you'll also find an underwater sealife park. Your hosts' cedar home, situated on an acre of lush grounds, has open beams, wood floors, antique furniture, and wonderful ocean views. Breakfasts are highlighted by Kona coffee and fresh local fruit.

Whale Watch House ✪
726 KUMULANI DRIVE, KIHEI, MAUI, HAWAII 96753

Tel: **(808) 879-0570**
Best Tme to Call: **8 AM–8 PM**
Hosts: **Patricia and Patrick Lowry**
No. of Rooms: **4**
No. of Private Baths: **2**
Max. No. Sharing Bath: **4**
Double/sb: **$55**
Single/sb: **$50**
Guest Cottage: **$85, sleeps 2; $100, sleeps 4; studio, $75**

Open: **All year**
Reduced Rates: **10% less June, July, Sept., Oct.**
Breakfast: **Continental**
Pets: **No**
Children: **Welcome**
Smoking: **Yes**
Social Drinking: **Permitted**
Minimum Stay: **2 nights**

Whale Watch House is located at the very edge of Ulapalakua Ranch on Haleakala, Maui's 10,228-foot dormant volcano. At every turn there are wonderful views of the ocean, the mountains, and the neighboring islands, Lanai and Kahoolawe. Your hosts' lush tropical garden is filled with fruits and flowers, and the swimming pool is large enough for laps. Sunbathe on the large decks around the house, cottage, and pool, or drive down to the beach—you'll be there in five minutes.

Hale Ho'o Maha ✪
P.O. BOX 422, KILAUEA, KAUAI, HAWAII 96754

Tel: **(808) 826-1130**
Best Time to Call: **7 AM–7 PM**
Hosts: **Kirby and Toby Searles**
Location: **28 mi. N of Lihue Airport**
No. of Rooms: **2**
No. of Private Baths: **1**
Max. No. Sharing Bath: **4**
Double/pb: **$65**
Double/sb: **$50**

Open: **All year**
Reduced Rates: **10% after 5th night**
Breakfast: **Continental**
Pets: **No**
Children: **No**
Smoking: **Permitted**
Social Drinking: **Permitted**
Foreign Languages: **Spanish**

Escape to a B&B that lives up to its name, which means "house of rest" in Hawaiian. This single-story home is perched on the cliffs along Kauai's north shore. Sandy beaches, rivers, waterfalls, and riding stables are five minutes away. Ask your hosts to direct you to "Queens Bath"—a natural saltwater whirlpool. Guests have full use of the kitchen, gas grill, cable TV, and Boogie boards. When in Rome, do as the Romans: Kirby will teach you to dance the hula and make leis, and Toby will instruct you in scuba diving.

Ahinahina Farm Bed & Breakfast ✪
210 AHINAHINA PLACE, KULA, MAUI, HAWAII 96790

Tel: **(808) 878-6096; (800) 241-MAUI [6184]**
Hosts: **Mike and Annette Endres**
Location: **16 mi. SE of Kahului**
Guest Cottage: **$90–$140**
Suites: **$75–$85**

Open: **All year**
Breakfast: **Continental**
Pets: **No**
Children: **Welcome, over 12**
Smoking: **No**
Social Drinking: **Permitted**

Stay on a working farm in upcountry Maui, where the Endreses grow seedless limes and other fruit. Feel free to wander around, pick limes and bananas, gather fresh flowers, or just sit on the decks and admire the view. Haleakala National Park, Tedeschi Winery, and two botanical gardens are nearby, and windward fishing and swimming areas are 20 minutes away. A 40-minute drive will take you to the parks and beaches on the island's leeward side. Couples will prefer the efficiency studio with a queen-size bed; a futon is on hand, so there's room for one more. Parties of four can rent the two-bedroom cottage, where the well-equipped kitchen has a washer, dryer, and dishwasher. Whichever you choose, beach towels, mats, chairs, and a cooler are provided on request. Mike and Annette will also supply warm vests and windbreakers for hikers headed to Mt. Haleakala. Whether your adventures take place on land or by the sea, you'll begin the day with fresh fruit, cereal, home-baked breads or muffins, juice, and coffee or tea.

Kula Cottage ✪
206 PUAKEA PL., KULA, HAWAII 96790

Tel: **(808) 871-6230**
Best Time to Call: **8 AM–5 PM**
Hosts: **Larry and Cecilia Gilbert**
Location: **18 mi. E of Kahului**
Guest Cottage: **$85, sleeps 2**
Open: **All year**
Breakfast: **Continental**

Pets: **No**
Children: **No**
Smoking: **Permitted**
Social Drinking: **Permitted**
Minimum Stay: **2 nights**
Foreign Languages: **Spanish**

Once the exclusive domain of farmers and cowboys, Kula has lately acquired a fashionable air, and this B&B makes a perfectly cozy retreat. A modern, fully equipped one-bedroom cottage, it has a wood-burning fireplace to warm the cool evenings and a breathtaking view of the ocean and West Maui mountains. The beach and windsurfing are only half an hour away by car, and restaurants are even closer.

Kula View Bed and Breakfast ✪

140 HOLOPUNI ROAD (MAILING ADDRESS: P.O. BOX 322), KULA, HAWAII 96790

Tel: **(808) 878-6736**	Open: **All year**
Best Time to Call: **8 AM–6 PM**	Reduced Rates: **10% weekly**
Host: **Susan Kauai**	Breakfast: **Continental**
Location: **16 mi. E of Kahului**	Pets: **No**
No. of Rooms: **1**	Children: **No**
No. of Private Baths: **1**	Smoking: **No**
Double/pb: **$75**	Social Drinking: **Permitted**
Single/pb: **$75**	Minimum Stay: **2 nights**

The fragrances of island fruits and flowers fill the fresh mountain air at this B&B 2,000 feet above sea level, on the slopes of the dormant volcano Haleakala. The upper level guest room has its own private entrance and a spacious deck that faces majestic Haleakala Crater, where the sunrises are nothing short of magical. Breakfast is served at a sun-warmed wicker table overlooking a flower and herb garden. Kula View is surrounded by two acres of lush greenery, yet it is close to Kahului Airport, shopping centers, parks, and beaches.

Victoria Place

P.O. BOX 930, LAWAI, KAUAI, HAWAII 96765

Tel: **(808) 332-9300**	Open: **All year**
Host: **Edee Seymour**	Breakfast: **Continental**
No. of Rooms: **4**	Pets: **No**
No. of Private Baths: **4**	Children: **No**
Double/pb: **$65–$75**	Smoking: **No**
Single/pb: **$55**	Social Drinking: **Permitted**
Guest Apartment: **$95**	

Perched high in the lush hills of southern Kauai, overlooking the thick jungle, cane fields, and the Pacific, Victoria Place promises an oasis of pampered comfort and privacy. The guest rooms, located in one wing of this spacious skylit home, open directly through glass doors onto the pool area, which is surrounded by flower gardens. Edee, a former Michigan native, will direct you to nearby attractions, including the resort beaches of Poipu, the National Tropical Botanical Gardens, Spouting Horn geyser, open-air markets, boutiques, and ethnic restaurants, all within minutes of the house. There is a $10 surcharge for one-night stays.

Chalet Kilauea at Volcano ✪
P.O. BOX 998, VOLCANO, HAWAII 96785

Tel: **(808) 967-7786; (800) 937-7786**
Hosts: **Lisha and Brian Crawford**
Location: **2 mi. NE of Hawaii**
   Volcanoes National Park
No. of Rooms: **7**
Max. No. Sharing Bath: **4**
Double/sb: **$75–$85**
Single/sb: **$75**
Guest Cottage: **$65–$100**

Open: **All year**
Breakfast: **Full**
Pets: **Sometimes**
Children: **Welcome**
Smoking: **No**
Social Drinking: **Permitted**
Foreign Languages: **Dutch, French,**
   Portuguese, Spanish

Chalet Kilauea is moments from Hawaii Volcanoes National Park, at an elevation of 3,800 feet. Guests can examine treasures from around the world in rooms inspired by Pacific, African, and European themes. Relax in the hot tub, enjoy the fireplace, peruse books from the library, and wake up to a gourmet breakfast in the art deco dining room.

Hale Kilauea
P.O. BOX 28, VOLCANO, HAWAII 96785

Tel: **(808) 967-7591**
Best Time to Call: **6 AM–9 PM**
Hosts: **Maurice Thomas and Jean Lai**
Location: **28 mi. NE of Hilo**
No. of Rooms: **10**
No. of Private Baths: **10**
Double/pb: **$55–$65**
Open: **All year**

Reduced Rates: **10% seniors**
Breakfast: **Continental**
Credit Cards: **AMEX, MC, VISA**
Pets: **Sometimes**
Children: **Welcome**
Smoking: **Permitted**
Social Drinking: **Permitted**

Hale Kilauea is a quiet place near the heart of Volcano Village, just outside Hawaii Volcanoes National Park, the world's only "drive-in volcano." Colorful, exotic native birds live in the towering pines and ohia trees that surround this B&B. After a day of climbing mountains and peering into craters, enjoy an evening of conversation around the living room fireplace. Your host Maurice, a lifelong Volcano resident, has neighbors and friends who know about volcano geology and the history and tradition of old Hawaii.

IDAHO

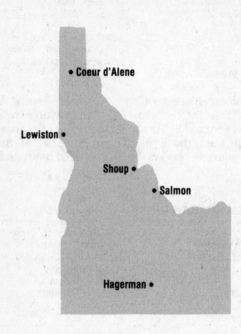

• Coeur d'Alene

Lewiston •

Shoup •

• Salmon

Hagerman •

Cricket on the Hearth ✪
1521 LAKESIDE AVENUE, COEUR d'ALENE, IDAHO 83814

Tel: **(208) 664-6926**
Best Time to Call: **9 AM–8 PM**
Hosts: **Al and Karen Hutson**
Location: **30 mi. E of Spokane**
No. of Rooms: **5**
No. of Private Baths: **3**
Max. No. Sharing Bath: **4**
Double/pb: **$65–$75**

Double/sb: **$45–$55**
Open: **All year**
Reduced Rates: **$5 less after 2nd night**
Breakfast: **Full**
Pets: **No**
Children: **Welcome, over 10**
Smoking: **Permitted**
Social Drinking: **Permitted**

Cricket on the Hearth, Coeur d'Alene's first bed-and-breakfast inn, is a comfortable 1920s cottage with second-story dormer windows and a large front porch. Guests can unwind in the library and the game room; musicians should ask Al about the antique pump organ, which has been in his family since 1916. Lake Coeur d'Alene, just a mile away, is a great place for boating and fishing. The area's many golf courses will lure duffers, and the snow-covered slopes will challenge skiers. Morning meals feature fruit, oven-fresh muffins and breads, and main courses like deep-dish French toast with huckleberry sauce.

Inn the First Place ✪
509 NORTH 15TH STREET, COEUR d'ALENE, IDAHO 83814

Tel: **(208) 667-3346**	Breakfast: **Full**
Best Time to Call: **7 AM–11:30 PM**	Other Meals: **Available**
Hosts: **Tom and Lois Knox**	Credit Cards: **MC, VISA**
Location: **30 mi. E of Spokane, Wash.**	Pets: **No**
No. of Rooms: **3**	Children: **Welcome, over 12**
Max. No. Sharing Bath: **4**	Smoking: **No**
Double/sb: **$40**	Social Drinking: **Permitted**
Open: **All year**	Airport/Station Pickup: **Yes**
Reduced Rates: **Available**	

Tom and Lois welcome you to their unusual home, which was once a grocery store. The guest rooms, located on the second floor, are decorated attractively, with wood paneling or country wallpaper, coordinating quilts, and a smattering of crafts and collectibles. The large living room and fully equipped kitchen are available to guests. In the morning, you can look forward to Lois's specialties, such as stuffed French toast or quiche. The inn is a mile away from beautiful Lake Coeur d'Alene, famous for fishing, swimming, and day cruises.

The Sleeping Place of the Wheels
3308 LODGEPOLE ROAD, COEUR d'ALENE, IDAHO
(MAILING ADDRESS: P.O. BOX 5273, COEUR d'ALENE, IDAHO 83814)

Tel: **(208) 765-3435**	Open: **May 1–Sept. 30**
Host: **Donna Bedord**	Breakfast: **Full**
Location: **1 mi. from I-90**	Pets: **No**
No. of Rooms: **2**	Children: **Welcome**
Max. No. Sharing Bath: **4**	Smoking: **No**
Double/sb: **$35**	Social Drinking: **No**
Single/sb: **$22.50**	Airport/Station Pickup: **Yes**

Wagon wheels mark the entrance to Donna's home, which is surrounded by tall pines and pretty flower gardens. Raspberries, strawberries, plums, and cherries are yours for the picking. Children will delight in the special playhouse with its fireman's slide, swing, and sandbox. Donna enjoys quilting, gardening, and reading.

The Cary House ✪
17985 U.S. 30 NORTH, HAGERMAN, IDAHO 83332

Tel: **(208) 837-4848**
Best Time to Call: **8 AM–10 PM**
Hosts: **Darrell and Linda Heinemann**
Location: **90 mi. SE of Boise**
No. of Rooms: **4**
No. of Private Baths: **4**
Double/pb: **$55–$75**

Open: **All year**
Breakfast: **Full**
Pets: **No**
Children: **Welcome, over 12**
Smoking: **No**
Social Drinking: **Permitted**
Airport Pickup: **Yes**

This beautifully restored two-story farmhouse from the late Victorian era is richly furnished with locally obtained antiques. Your hosts, Idaho natives, combine country-style hospitality with gourmet cooking to ensure that your stay is pleasurable. Cary House is located in the lower portion of the Shoshone Gorge of the Snake River, where the abundance of spring water makes for excellent hiking, fishing, and bird watching. Several splendid golf courses lie within easy driving distance, and day trips can be made to Sun Valley, Craters of the Moon National Monument, and the Sawtooth National Forest.

Shiloh Rose B&B ✪
3414 SELWAY DRIVE, LEWISTON, IDAHO 83501

Tel: **(208) 743-2482**
Best Time to Call: **Before 10 AM**
Host: **Dorothy Mader**
Location: **100 mi. S of Spokane, Wash.**
No. of Rooms: **1**
Double/pb: **$65**
Open: **All year**
Reduced Rates: **10% seniors**

Breakfast: **Full**
Credit Cards: **MC, VISA**
Pets: **Sometimes**
Children: **Welcome, over 10**
Smoking: **No**
Social Drinking: **Permitted**
Airport/Station Pickup: **Yes**

Shiloh Rose has one spacious suite. Lovely wallpapers, lace curtains, and fine bed linens give the bedroom a warm, country-Victorian feel. The cozy private sitting room has a wood-burning stove, overflowing bookshelves, and an upright grand piano, as well as a TV and VCR. Breakfasts feature fresh fruit, home-baked muffins, gourmet casseroles, and your choice of coffee or tea. On warm summer evenings, you'll share the backyard with quail and pheasant families. Golf and water sports are available much of the year. The surrounding area is a hunting and fishing paradise and the river levees provide eight miles of hiking and biking trails. But top priority should be given to a day-long jet-boat trip up Hells Canyon, the deepest gorge in the Northwest.

Heritage Inn ✪
510 LENA STREET, SALMON, IDAHO 83467

Tel: (208) 756-3174
Best Time to Call: 6 AM–9 PM
Host: Audrey Nichols
Location: ½ mi. from Hwy. 93
No. of Rooms: 5
Max. No. Sharing Bath: 3
Double/sb: $30–$32
Single/sb: $22–$27

Suites: $35–$40
Open: All year
Breakfast: Continental, plus
Credit Cards: MC, VISA
Pets: No
Children: Welcome
Smoking: Restricted
Social Drinking: Permitted

This 100-year-old Victorian farmhouse is set in a valley, surrounded by mountains and pine trees. In the old days, this was a cozy stopover for those traveling by stagecoach. The Heritage has since been lovingly restored and decorated with many antiques. Enjoy a cool drink on the glassed-in sun porch while you enjoy the quiet of this pretty neighborhood. The River of No Return is just half a mile away, and it's just a mile to the city park and swimming pool. Your hostess serves homemade muffins and jams in the sunny dining room or on the porch each morning. She is a native of Salmon and can gladly direct you to restaurants within walking distance, nearby ghost towns, and other places of historic or cultural interest.

Smith House Bed & Breakfast ✪
49 SALMON RIVER ROAD, SHOUP, IDAHO 83469

Tel: (208) 394-2121; (800) 238-5915
Best Time to Call: 9 AM–5 PM
Hosts: Aubrey and Marsha Smith
Location: 50 mi. N of Salmon
No. of Rooms: 6
No. of Private Baths: 2
Max. No. Sharing Bath: 4
Double/pb: $54
Double/sb: $35–$42
Single/sb: $35

Open: All year
Reduced Rates: Weekly; groups
Breakfast: Full
Other Meals: Available
Credit Cards: MC, VISA
Pets: No
Children: Welcome
Smoking: No
Social Drinking: Permitted
Airport/Station Pickup: Yes

Located on the Salmon River and adjoining a wilderness area, Smith House is a dream come true. Aubrey and Marsha vacationed here 11 years ago and fell in love with the constantly changing scenery. They sold their Florida house and built their dream log home, which they enjoy sharing with their guests. Marsha enjoys pampering people with such breakfast creations as hash-brown quiche, buttermilk scones, or wheat French toast with homemade fruit topping. Meals are served underneath the dining room skylight. Recreational opportunities include white-water rafting, fishing, hunting, and hiking. Visit the nearby ghost town or restored gold mine, then come "home" to relax in the hot tub.

ILLINOIS

Galena •   Mundelein • • Winnetka
   West Dundee • Oak Park
      Sycamore • • • Chicago

Rock Island •

Navuoo •   • Mossville   • Danforth
Quincy •   • Champaign
   Williamsville •   • Decatur

      • Arcola

   • Maeystown

Bed & Breakfast/Chicago, Inc.
P.O. BOX 14088, CHICAGO, ILLINOIS 60614-0088

Tel: (312) 951-0085
Coordinator: **Mary Shaw**
States/Regions Covered: **Downtown Chicago, Hyde Park, Near North, North Shore Suburbs**

Rates (Single/Double):
 Modest: **$55 / $65**
 Average: **$65 / $75–$85**
Credit Cards: **AMEX, MC, VISA**

Mary welcomes you to midwestern hospitality in the "windy city" and its North Shore suburbs. Discover Chicago's outdoor sculpture plazas on foot, shop world-famous Marshall Field's, or observe the skyline from the top of the Sears Tower while staying in one of the over 150 different guest rooms, unhosted furnished apartments, or inns represented by this service. There is a two-night minimum on most accommodations.

B&B Midwest Reservations (formerly B&B Northwest Suburban–Chicago) ✪
P.O. BOX 95503, HOFFMAN ESTATES, ILLINOIS 60195-0503

Tel: (800) 34 B AND B [342-2632]
Best Time to Call: 9 AM–5 PM Mon.–Fri.
Coordinator: Martha McDonald-Swan
States/Regions Covered: Illinois—Galena, Geneva, Gurnee, Hinsdale, Mt. Morris, Mundelein, Oak Park, Oregon, Wadsworth, West Dundee; Indiana—Knightstown; Ohio—Cincinnati, Milan; Kentucky

Descriptive Directory of B&Bs: Free
Rates (Single/Double):
  Modest: $40 / $50
  Average: $50 / $100
  Luxury: $110 / $175
Credit Cards: DISC, MC, VISA

B&B Midwest Reservations (formerly B&B Northwest Suburban–Chicago) has expanded beyond northern Illinois to include southern Illinois, Indiana, Kentucky, and Ohio. Most homes are on historic registers. Hosts enjoy sharing beautiful antiques, handwork, and lots of TLC with their guests. Many also offer numerous special activities and theme weekends, available from suburban locations to country farms.

Curly's Corner ✪
RR 2, BOX 590, ARCOLA, ILLINOIS 61910

Tel: (217) 268-3352
Best Time to Call: Anytime
Hosts: Warren and Maxine Arthur
Location: 35 mi. S of Champaign; 5 mi. from I-57
No. of Rooms: 4
No. of Private Baths: 2
Max. No. Sharing Bath: 3
Double/pb: $50–$60

Single/sb: $40
Open: All year
Breakfast: Full
Pets: No
Children: Welcome, over 10
Smoking: No
Social Drinking: No
Airport/Station Pickup: Yes

This ranch-style farmhouse is located in a quiet Amish community. Your hosts are dedicated to cordial hospitality and will gladly share information about the area or even take you on a tour. They offer comfortable bedrooms with king- or queen-size beds. In the morning, enjoy a wonderful breakfast of homemade biscuits, apple butter, fresh country bacon, and eggs. Curly's Corner is a half mile from beautiful Rockome Gardens.

The Golds ✪

RR 3, BOX 69, CHAMPAIGN, ILLINOIS 61821

Tel: (217) 586-4345	Open: **All year**
Best Time to Call: **Evenings**	Reduced Rates: **15% weekly**
Hosts: **Bob and Rita Gold**	Breakfast: **Continental**
Location: **6 mi. W of Champaign**	Pets: **No**
No. of Rooms: **3**	Children: **Welcome**
Max. No. Sharing Bath: **4**	Smoking: **No**
Double/sb: **$45**	Social Drinking: **Permitted**
Single/sb: **$40**	Airport/Station Pickup: **Available**

One of the most beautiful views in Champaign County is yours from the deck of this restored farmhouse. The house is set on six acres surrounded by prime central Illinois farmland. Inside you'll find country antiques, complemented by beautiful wainscoting. An open walnut stairway leads to bedrooms decorated with four-poster beds, handmade quilts, and oriental rugs. Guests can relax by the living room wood stove or enjoy a glass of wine on the deck. Bob and Rita offer garden fruits and cider for breakfast, served with homemade jams, muffins, and coffee cakes. The Golds is two miles from Lake of the Woods, and 20 minutes from the University of Illinois campus. Shopping and restaurants are also within easy reach.

City Bed and Breakfast ✪

P.O. BOX 14119, CHICAGO, ILLINOIS 60614

Tel: (312) 472-2893	Single/sb: **$50**
Best Time to Call: **9 AM–9 PM**	Open: **All year**
Host: **Bea Gray**	Breakfast: **Continental**
Location: **1 mi. from I-94, Lake Shore Drive exit**	Pets: **No**
No. of Rooms: **2**	Children: **Welcome**
Max. No. Sharing Bath: **3**	Smoking: **No**
Double/sb: **$65**	Social Drinking: **Permitted**
	Minimum Stay: **2 nights**

This 100-year-old house is located in the heart of trendy Lincoln Park, an area known for its tree-lined streets, renovated old homes, fine restaurants and shops, and easy access to downtown. Guests can walk to Lake Michigan beaches, Lincoln Park Zoo, jogging and cycling paths, restaurants, theaters, movie houses, and great shopping. Excellent public transportation will take you to Orchestra Hall, the Art Institute, Northwestern Memorial Hospital, and McCormick Convention Center.

Fannie's House ✪

300 NORTH FRONT STREET, P.O. BOX 194, DANFORTH, ILLINOIS 60930

Tel: **(815) 269-2145**
Best Time to Call: **After 5:30 PM**
Hosts: **Mary and Don Noonan**
Location: **85 mi. S of Chicago**
No. of Rooms: **2**
No. of Private Baths: **2**
Double/pb: **$60**
Single/pb: **$50**
Open: **All year**

Reduced Rates: **10% seniors and families, $10 less after 2 nights**
Breakfast: **Continental**
Pets: **No**
Children: **Welcome, over 8**
Smoking: **No**
Social Drinking: **Permitted**
Station Pickup: **Yes**

Escape to this one-hundred-year-old home in a small country town just two hours south of Chicago's Loop. Both bedrooms have queen-size beds. Complimentary snacks are provided, and a stove and refrigerator are available for your use should you want to prepare some special treats. Or let someone else do the cooking—good restaurants are within five to ten minutes by car. Mary and Don can give you a list of interesting things to see and do nearby. Your hosts will also supply good maps to the well-marked country roads that are ideal for bicycling, running, or just strolling.

Weedon's Bed & Breakfast

919 WEST WILLIAM STREET, DECATUR, ILLINOIS 62522

Tel: **(217) 422-4930**
Best Time to Call: **9 AM–9 PM**
Host: **Joyce M. Weedon**
Location: **36 mi. E of Springfield**
No. of Rooms: **3**
No. of Private Baths: **1**
Max. No. Sharing Bath: **4**
Double/pb: **$45**
Single/pb: **$40**
Double/sb: **$40**

Single/sb: **$35**
Open: **All year**
Reduced Rates: **10% seniors**
Breakfast: **Full**
Credit Cards: **MC, VISA**
Pets: **Sometimes**
Children: **No**
Smoking: **No**
Social Drinking: **Permitted**
Airport Pickup: **Yes**

Ray and Joyce welcome you to their three-story, 13-room prairie-style mansion, built in 1904 for industrialist Thomas T. Roberts. This B&B is located in Decatur's historic district, near Lake Decatur and Millikin University, and there are many other distinctive homes in the area. Inside Weedon's, you'll find five fireplaces, lots of antique crystal chandeliers, handsome mahogany and oak woodwork, and period furniture. Breakfast is served in the large, elegant dining room with a palladium window. Your hosts also set out afternoon tea in the marble-floored sunroom, which is furnished in white wicker.

Aldrich Guest House
900 THIRD STREET, GALENA, ILLINOIS 61036

Tel: **(815) 777-3323**
Host: **Judy Green**
Location: **¼ mi. from Rte. 20**
No. of Rooms: **5**
No. of Private Baths: **3**
Max. No. Sharing Bath: **4**
Double/pb: **$75–$95**
Single/pb: **$70–$90**
Double/sb: **$65–$75**

Single/sb: **$60–$70**
Suites: **$139–$159**
Open: **All year**
Breakfast: **Full**
Credit Cards: **AMEX, DISC, MC, VISA**
Pets: **No**
Children: **Welcome, over 6**
Smoking: **Restricted**
Social Drinking: **Permitted**

George Washington didn't sleep here, but Ulysses S. Grant was entertained in the spacious double parlors of this elegant 1845 home. Throughout the house, period decor, antiques, and some reproductions harmonize effectively. Centrally air-conditioned for summer comfort, the house is convenient to all of the historic sites. Judy's hearty breakfasts include fresh fruit salads and entrées such as pancakes or egg dishes.

Avery Guest House ✪
606 SOUTH PROSPECT STREET, GALENA, ILLINOIS 61036

Tel: **(815) 777-3883**
Best Time to Call: **9 AM–9 PM**
Hosts: **Flo and Roger Jensen**

Location: **15 mi. E of Dubuque, Iowa**
No. of Rooms: **4**
Max. No. Sharing Bath: **4**

Double/sb: **$55**
Single/sb: **$50**
Open: **All year**
Reduced Rates: **10% seniors, $10 less weekdays**
Breakfast: **Continental**

Credit Cards: **MC, VISA**
Pets: **No**
Children: **Welcome (crib, high chair)**
Smoking: **No**
Social Drinking: **Permitted**
Airport/Station Pickup: **Yes**

This spacious, 140-year-old home is located two blocks from historic downtown Galena. Enjoy the view of bluffs and Victorian mansions from an old-fashioned porch swing overlooking the Galena River Valley. Your hosts welcome you to use the piano or bring your own instrument and join them in chamber music. Enjoy delicious home-made muffins and breads along with cheeses and jams each morning. Flo and Roger will gladly direct you to Grant's home, antique shops, and other interesting sights in the historic district.

Corner George Inn ✪
CORNER OF MAIN AND MILL, P.O. BOX 103, MAEYSTOWN, ILLINOIS 62256

Tel: **(618) 458-6660; (800) 458-6020**
Best Time to Call: **9 AM–9 PM**
Hosts: **David and Marcia Braswell**
No. of Rooms: **5**
No. of Private Baths: **5**
Double/pb: **$65–$95**
Open: **All year**

Breakfast: **Full**
Credit Cards: **MC, VISA**
Pets: **No**
Children: **Welcome, over 12**
Smoking: **No**
Social Drinking: **Permitted**
Foreign Languages: **German**

A frontier Victorian structure built in 1884—when it was known as the Maeystown Hotel and Saloon—the Corner George Inn has been pains-takingly restored. In addition to the five antique-filled guest rooms, there are two sitting rooms, a wine cellar, and an elegant ballroom, where David and Marcia serve breakfast. Maeystown is a quaint 19th-century village; guests can tour it on a bicycle built for two or aboard a horse-drawn carriage. Nearby are St. Louis, Fort de Chartres, Fort Kaskaskia, and the scenic bluff road that hugs the Mississippi.

Old Church House Inn ✪
1416 EAST MOSSVILLE ROAD, MOSSVILLE, ILLINOIS 61552

Tel: **(309) 579-2300**
Hosts: **Dean and Holly Ramseyer**
Location: **5 mi. N of Peoria**
No. of Rooms: **2**
No. of Private Baths: **1**
Max. No. Sharing Bath: **4**
Double/pb: **$85**
Single/pb: **$65 (Mon.–Thurs. only)**
Double/sb: **$65**

Single/sb: **$49**
Open: **All year**
Breakfast: **Continental, plus**
Credit Cards: **MC, VISA**
Pets: **No**
Children: **Welcome, over 10**
Smoking: **No**
Social Drinking: **No**

Nestled in the scenic Illinois River Valley 5 miles north of Peoria, Old Church House Inn welcomes you to the plush warmth of the Victorian era. Curl up to a crackling fire, take tea in the flower garden, sink deep into the queen-size featherbeds, and enjoy being pampered. Listed on the National Historic American Building Survey, this 1869 church still boasts soaring 18-foot ceilings, tall arched windows, and an "elevated library." Victorian antiques, period furnishings, pedestal sinks, quilts, thick robes, and fine soaps allow guests to relax in luxury. Swiss chocolates, a house specialty, are placed on pillows during chamber service. Bicycling and cross-country skiing on the Rock Island Trail is just five minutes away, while nearby Peoria features riverboat cruises, cultural attractions, antiquing, and a full choice of restaurants to suit your taste!

Round-Robin Guesthouse ✪
231 EAST MAPLE AVENUE, MUNDELEIN, ILLINOIS 60060

Tel: **(708) 566-7664**	Open: **All year**
Hosts: **George and Laura Loffredo**	Reduced Rates: **10% seniors, families**
Location: **38 mi. NW of Chicago**	Breakfast: **Full**
No. of Rooms: **5**	Credit Cards: **MC, VISA**
No. of Private Baths: **2**	Pets: **No**
Max. No. Sharing Bath: **4**	Children: **Welcome**
Double/pb: **$60**	Smoking: **Restricted**
Double/sb: **$40–$50**	Social Drinking: **Permitted**
Suite: **$110**	

This handsome red Victorian with white trim takes its name from the letters circulated by your hosts' relatives for more than 70 years; to encourage you to write friends and family, George and Laura will provide you with paper, pen, and stamps. The many local diversions ensure that you'll have plenty to write about. Six Flags Great America, the Volo Auto Museum, and the antique village of Long Grove are barely fifteen minutes away by car, and you're never far from golf, swimming, and horseback riding. During the summer, the Chicago Symphony is in residence at nearby Ravinia Park. Or you can enjoy Laura's renditions of classical and ragtime music on the piano. You'll wake up to the aroma of fresh-brewed coffee; coffee cake, muffins, and homemade jam are served between 7:30 and 9:00 AM.

The Ancient Pines Bed & Breakfast ✪
2015 PARLEY STREET, NAUVOO, ILLINOIS 62354

Tel: **(217) 453-2767**	No. of Rooms: **3**
Best Time to Call: **9 AM–9 PM**	Max. No. Sharing Bath: **3**
Host: **Genevieve Simmens**	Double/sb: **$35**
Location: **225 mi. SW of Chicago**	Single/sb: **$30**

Open: **All year**
Reduced Rates: **15% weekly**
Breakfast: **Full**
Pets: **Sometimes**

Children: **Welcome**
Smoking: **No**
Social Drinking: **Permitted**

This turn-of-the-century brick home is rich in detail inside and out, from the stained-glass windows and etched-glass front door to the tin ceilings, open staircase, and carved woodwork. Wander through herb and flower gardens, play badminton on the lawn, or listen to music in the library. Local attractions include wineries (Nauvoo holds its own grape festival), Civil War reenactments, historic Mormon homes, and Nauvoo State Park. Whatever your itinerary, you'll wake to the aroma of baking bread, served with eggs and sausage or ham. Special low-cholesterol menus are available upon request.

Toad Hall Bed & Breakfast House
301 NORTH SCOVILLE AVENUE, OAK PARK, ILLINOIS 60302

Tel: **(708) 386-8623**
Host: **Cynthia Mungerson**
Location: **5 mi. from Chicago Loop**
No. of Rooms: **3**
No. of Private Baths: **3**
Double/pb: **$55**
Single/pb: **$50**

Suites: **$65 for 2; $85 for 3**
Open: **Feb.–Dec.**
Breakfast: **Full**
Pets: **No**
Children: **No**
Smoking: **No**
Social Drinking: **Permitted**

Built in 1909, and carefully maintained and restored, this gracious home is furnished with Victorian antiques, Oriental rugs, and Laura Ashley wallpapers. Guest rooms have comfortable reading chairs, luxurious linens, television, and air-conditioning. You are welcome to relax in the wicker on the porches, picnic on the sun deck, or curl up near a fireplace with a book. Breakfast is served in the oak-paneled dining room; afternoon tea and evening brandy and sweets are offered. Centrally located in the Frank Lloyd Wright Historic District, it is within walking distance of 25 Wright masterpieces, dozens of architecturally significant buildings, the Ernest Hemingway home, and lovely shops and restaurants.

The Kaufmann House
1641 HAMPSHIRE, QUINCY, ILLINOIS 62301

Tel: **(217) 223-2502**
Best Time to Call: **Noon–9 PM**
Hosts: **Emery and Bettie Kaufmann**
Location: **100 mi. W of Springfield**
No. of Rooms: **3**
No. of Private Baths: **1**

Max. No. Sharing Bath: **4**
Double/pb: **$60**
Single/pb: **$50**
Double/sb: **$40–$50**
Single/sb: **$35**
Reduced Rates: **10% 3 nights or more**

Open: **All year**
Breakfast: **Continental, plus**
Pets: **No**
Children: **Welcome (crib)**

Smoking: **No**
Social Drinking: **No**
Airport/Station Pickup: **Yes**

History buffs will remember Quincy, set right on the Mississippi River, as the scene of the famous Lincoln-Douglas debates, while architecture buffs will be attracted to the town's feast of Victorian styles—Greek Revival, Gothic Revival, Italianate, and Richardsonian. The Kaufmann House was built 100 years ago, and the owners have been careful to maintain its "country" feeling. Guests may enjoy breakfast in the Ancestor's Room, on a stone patio, or at a picnic table under the trees. They are invited to play the piano, watch TV, or enjoy popcorn by the fire. The Kaufmanns describe themselves as "Christians who have a love for God, people, nature, and life."

The Potter House Bed & Breakfast Inn ✪
1906 7 AVENUE, ROCK ISLAND, ILLINOIS 61201

Tel: **(309) 788-1906; (800) 747-0339**
Best Time to Call: **10 AM–9 PM**
Hosts: **Gary and Nancy Pheiffer**
No. of Rooms: **5**
No. of Private Baths: **5**
Double/pb: **$60–$95**
Guest Cottage: **$100, sleeps 4**
Suites: **$70, sleeps 3**
Open: **All year**
Reduced Rates: **Available**

Breakfast: **Full**
Credit Cards: **AMEX, DC, DISC, MC, VISA**
Pets: **No**
Children: **No**
Smoking: **No**
Social Drinking: **Permitted**
Minimum Stay: **Special event weekends and peak seasons**
Airport Pickup: **Yes**

Stay in either the main house or the adjacent cottage at this turn-of-the-century property listed on the National Register of Historic Places. Look for the old-fashioned details, from porcelain doorknobs to embossed leather wallcovering and stained- and leaded-glass windows. Even the bathrooms are distinctive: one has its original nickel-plated hardware. You'll notice other historic homes in the neighborhood, which you can tour on foot or aboard a horse-drawn carriage. Gamblers will want to stroll six blocks to the Mississippi, where a riverboat casino is moored. Those who like less risky games can play croquet or shoot baskets on the inn grounds.

Top o' the Morning ✪
1505 19TH AVENUE, ROCK ISLAND, ILLINOIS 61201

Tel: **(309) 786-3513**
Best Time to Call: **After 5 PM**
Hosts: **Sam and Peggy Doak**
Location: **1½ mi. from Rte. 92, 18th Ave. Exit**

No. of Rooms: **3**
No. of Private Baths: **3**
Double/pb: **$50–$60**
Open: **All year**
Breakfast: **Full**

Pets: **No**	Smoking: **Permitted**
Children: **Welcome**	Social Drinking: **Permitted**

Sam and Peggy welcome you to their country estate, set on a bluff overlooking the Mississippi River, near the center of the Quad Cities area. The 18-room mansion is situated at the end of a winding drive on three acres of lawn, orchards, and gardens. The guest rooms, graced with lovely chandeliers and oriental rugs, command a spectacular view of the cities and river. The parlor, with its grand piano and fireplace, is an inviting place to relax. Local attractions are Mississippi River boat rides, harness racing, Rock Island Arsenal, Black Hawk State Park, Augustana College, and St. Ambrose University.

The Country Charm Inn ✪
ROUTE 2, QUIGLEY ROAD, SYCAMORE, ILLINOIS 60178

Tel: **(815) 895-5386**	Breakfast: **Full weekends, Continental weekdays**
Hosts: **Howard and Donna Petersen**	Pets: **No**
Location: **55 mi. W of Chicago**	Children: **Welcome, over 3**
No. of Rooms: **3**	Smoking: **No**
No. of Private Baths: **3**	Social Drinking: **No**
Double/pb: **$35–$55**	Minimum Stay: **Only for local weekend events**
Open: **All year**	
Reduced Rates: **20% weekly**	

This rambling, three-story stucco farmhouse is a great place to bring kids—they can wander around the grounds and pet all the animals. The Petersens are happy to put Champ, the resident trick horse, through his paces. Meanwhile, adults can borrow a title from the 2,000-book library, or play golf and tennis at a nearby park. In good weather, a hearty country breakfast is served on the front porch. House specialties range from egg-and-cheese dishes to peach cobbler, with special designer pancakes for youthful visitors.

Ironhedge Inn Bed & Breakfast ✪
305 OREGON, WEST DUNDEE, ILLINOIS 60118

Tel: **(708) 426-7777**	Suites: **$159**
Hosts: **Sarah and Frank Hejhal**	Open: **All year**
Location: **35 mi. NW of Chicago**	Reduced Rates: **10% seniors, families**
No. of Rooms: **6**	Breakfast: **Continental**
No. of Private Baths: **3**	Credit Cards: **AMEX, DISC, MC, VISA**
Max. No. Sharing Bath: **4**	Pets: **No**
Double/pb: **$69**	Children: **Welcome, over 12**
Double/sb: **$59**	Smoking: **No**
Single/sb: **$49**	Social Drinking: **Permitted**

Ironhedge Inn, named for the hand-wrought iron fence surrounding the property, is a 28-room Tudor-style mansion in the heart of the historic district, where many homes date back to the 1800s. Walk to quaint shops and restaurants to satisfy every taste. Bikes and picnic lunches are available for the scenic hiking/biking trails along the beautiful Fox River. Inside enjoy a Victorian vision of velvet and lace in the romantic parlor and sip tea in front of the fireplace while listening to turn-of-the-century musical instruments. Floral Tiffany-style windows adorn window seats and rooms, including the dining and breakfast rooms where breakfast is served formally. The library, with French doors opening onto a veranda, is perfect for corporate meetings, seminars, and retreats, and the formally landscaped lawn with large gazebo is perfect for weddings and receptions. It's half an hour to O'Hare International Airport.

Bed and Breakfast at Edie's ✪
233 EAST HARPOLE, P.O. BOX 351, WILLIAMSVILLE, ILLINOIS 62693

Tel: **(217) 566-2538**
Best Time to Call: **After 5 PM**
Host: **Edith L. Senalik**
Location: **10 mi. N of Springfield**
No. of Rooms: **3**
Max. No. Sharing Bath: **4**
Double/sb: **$45**
Single/sb: **$35**

Open: **All year**
Reduced Rates: **Available**
Breakfast: **Continental**
Pets: **No**
Children: **Welcome**
Smoking: **No**
Social Drinking: **Permitted**

Just ten minutes north of the state capital, Springfield, the friendly village of Williamsville offers the peace, quiet, and safety of a small town. Edie's is a 75-year-old mission-style house where guests have use of a formal living room, dining room, and a TV room equipped with cable TV and a video library. Springfield offers the Abraham Lincoln attractions, Springfield Theater Centre, Old State Capitol, Lincoln Land Community College, and Sangamon State University. Historic Petersburg and New Salem, 20 miles to the west, are easily accessible.

Chateau des Fleurs ✪
552 RIDGE ROAD, WINNETKA, ILLINOIS 60093

Tel: **(708) 256-7272**
Best Time to Call: **Mornings**
Host: **Sally Ward**
Location: **15 mi. N of Chicago**
No. of Rooms: **3**
No. of Private Baths: **3**
Double/pb: **$90**
Single/pb: **$80**

Open: **All year**
Reduced Rates: **15% weekly**
Breakfast: **Continental plus**
Pets: **No**
Children: **Welcome, over 11**
Smoking: **No**
Social Drinking: **Permitted**
Foreign Languages: **Limited Spanish**

At Chateau des Fleurs, guests may enjoy the elegance of a French country home and still be only 30 minutes from Chicago's Loop.

Antique shops, Lake Michigan, and commuter trains are within walking distance. But there's so much to do at this luxurious B&B, you may not want to leave. Swim in the pool, screen movies on Sally's 50-inch television, tickle the ivories of a Steinway baby grand, or admire the terraced yard and carefully tended gardens. You'll enjoy the generous Continental breakfasts of muffins, fresh fruit, yogurt, toast, and hot and cold cereals.

The Chateau's garden is pictured on our back cover.

For key to listings, see inside front or back cover.

○ This star means that rates are guaranteed through December 31, 1993, to any guest making a reservation as a result of reading about the B&B in *Bed & Breakfast U.S.A.*—1993 edition.

Important! To avoid misunderstandings, always ask about cancellation policies when booking.

Please enclose a self-addressed, stamped, business-size envelope when contacting reservation services.

For more details on what you can expect in a B&B, see Chapter 1.

Always mention *Bed & Breakfast U.S.A.* when making reservations!

If no B&B is listed in the area you'll be visiting, use the form on page 733 to order a copy of our "List of New B&Bs."

We want to hear from you! Use the form on page 735.

INDIANA

Chesterton •

• Peru   • Decatur

Rockville •   • Knightstown

Morgantown •
     • Nashville

Paoli •

• Grandview

Evansville •

Indiana Homes Bed & Breakfast, Inc.
1431 ST. JAMES COURT, LOUISVILLE, KENTUCKY 40208

Tel: (502) 635-7341
Best Time to Call: 8 AM–noon
Coordinators: JoAnn Jenkins and
   Carson G. Jenkins
States/Regions Covered: Indiana—
   Corydon, Indianapolis, Paoli,
   Washington, West Baden

Descriptive Directory: $1
Rates (Single/Double):
   Average: $65 / $90
Reduced Rates: After 7th night
Credit Cards: AMEX, MC, VISA
   (deposit only)

Moving south from the Indianapolis Museum of Art and the Indy 500 racetrack, leave the Interstate for a true view of Middle America. Traverse rolling hills past the famous stone quarries in Bedford and head for historic Corydon, the state's original capital city. Tour the cave systems, canoe the Blue River, and explore Wyandotte Woods. Wherever you decide to stop, you can be assured of a hearty welcome and pleasant surroundings.

195

Gray Goose Inn ✪

350 INDIAN BOUNDARY ROAD, CHESTERTON, INDIANA 46304

Tel: **(219) 926-5781**
Best Time to Call: **After 4 PM**
Hosts: **Tim Wilk and Charles Ramsey**
Location: **60 mi. E of Chicago**
No. of Rooms: **5**
No. of Private Baths: **5**
Double/pb: **$75–$85**
Single/pb: **$65–$75**
Suites: **$85**

Open: **All year**
Reduced Rates: **10% seniors**
Breakfast: **Full**
Credit Cards: **AMEX, DISC, MC, VISA**
Pets: **No**
Children: **Welcome, over 12**
Smoking: **Permitted**
Social Drinking: **Permitted**

Elegant accommodations await you in this English country-style home overlooking a 30-acre lake. Guest rooms feature canopied four-poster beds, fine linens, and thick, fluffy towels. Some rooms are decorated in Williamsburg style, and some have a fireplace. Enjoy a quiet moment in the common room, or relax with a cup of coffee on the screened-in porch. Take long walks beside the shady oaks, or feed the Canada geese and wild ducks. The Gray Goose is five minutes from Dunes State and National Lakeshore parks. Swimming, canoeing down the Little Calumet River, hiking, and fishing on Lake Michigan are all within easy reach. Dining and weekend entertainment are within walking distance.

Cragwood Inn B&B ✪

303 NORTH SECOND STREET, DECATUR, INDIANA 46733

Tel: **(219) 728-2000**
Hosts: **George and Nancy Craig**
Location: **15 mi. S of Ft. Wayne**
No. of Rooms: **4**
No. of Private Baths: **2**
Max. No. Sharing Baths: **4**
Double/pb: **$55**
Single/pb: **$50**
Double/sb: **$45–$55**
Single/sb: **$40–$50**
Suites: **$75, sleeps four**
Open: **All year**
Reduced Rates: **Weekdays, extended stays, families**

Breakfast: **Continental weekdays, full weekends**
Other Meals: **Available**
Credit Cards: **MC, VISA**
Pets: **No**
Children: **Welcome, over 12**
Smoking: **No**
Social Drinking: **Permitted**
Airport/Station Pickup: **Yes**
Foreign Languages: **Limited Spanish and German**

Built in 1900, this Queen Anne home is distinguished by red oak woodwork, parquet floors, tin ceilings, and stained and beveled glass. If this whets your appetite for antiques, good shops are within walking distance. With ready access to a golf course, a fitness center, a swimming pool, a lake, bike paths, and tennis courts, fitness buffs won't be bored. Also of note are the Swiss Amish settlements in Berne and Amishville. The Continental breakfast consists of juice, coffee or tea, fruit, and homemade breads and muffins; the weekend menu includes French toast or strata. George and Nancy host several murder mystery parties during the year.

Brigadoon Bed & Breakfast Inn
1201 SOUTH EAST 2ND STREET, EVANSVILLE, INDIANA 47713

Tel: **(812) 422-9635; (800) 321-7647**	Open: **All year**
Host: **Kathee Forbes**	Reduced Rates: **Families**
Location: **1 mi. from Hwy. 41**	Breakfast: **Full**
No. of Rooms: **4**	Other Meals: **Sometimes**
No. of Private Baths: **2**	Credit Cards: **MC, VISA**
Max. No. Sharing Bath: **4**	Pets: **Sometimes**
Double/pb: **$40**	Children: **Welcome (baby-sitter)**
Single/pb: **$35**	Smoking: **Permitted**
Double/sb: **$40**	Social Drinking: **Permitted**
Single/sb: **$35**	Airport/Station Pickup: **Yes**

Brigadoon is a white frame Victorian with a gingerbread porch. The inn was built in 1892 and has been thoroughly renovated by the Forbes family. Four fireplaces, original parquet floors, and beautiful stained-glass windows have been lovingly preserved. Modern baths and a country eat-in kitchen have been added. Bedrooms are large and sunny, with accents of lace and ruffles, floral wallpapers, and antique furnishings. Guests are welcome to relax in the parlor or library. Breakfast specialties change daily, and can include a soufflé or quiche served with a lot of homemade breads, jams, and apple butter. This charming Victorian getaway is close to the Historic Preservation area, restaurants, the riverfront, antique shops, the University of Southern Indiana, and the University of Evansville.

The River Belle Bed & Breakfast
P.O. BOX 669, HIGHWAY 66, GRANDVIEW, INDIANA 47615

Tel: **(812) 649-2500**	Guest Cottage: **$60, sleeps 4**
Hosts: **Don and Pat Phillips**	Open: **All year**
Location: **33 mi. E of Evansville**	Reduced Rates: **Weekly**
No. of Rooms: **6**	Breakfast: **Continental**
No. of Private Baths: **2**	Credit Cards: **MC, VISA**
Max. No. Sharing Bath: **4**	Pets: **No**
Double/pb: **$65**	Children: **Welcome**
Single/pb: **$60**	Smoking: **No**
Double/sb: **$45–$55**	Social Drinking: **Permitted**
Single/sb: **$40**	

Guests may choose from a selection of accommodations in an 1866 white painted brick steamboat-style house, an 1898 redbrick Italianate house, or an 1860 cottage with full kitchen. These adjacent beauties on the Ohio River have been carefully restored by Pat and Don to serve as their B&B complex. The guest rooms are large and airy, furnished with timeless heirlooms and graced by lace curtains and Oriental rugs. You may choose to walk along the riverfront, sit quietly and watch the white squirrels play among the magnolia, pecan, and dogwood trees, or take a side trip to the nearby Lincoln Boyhood National Memorial, Lincoln State Park, the "Young Abe Lincoln" Drama, and Holiday World (the nation's oldest theme amusement park).

Lavendar Lady B&B ✪

130 WEST MAIN, KNIGHTSTOWN, INDIANA 46148

Tel: (317) 345-5400	Breakfast: Full
Best Time to Call: Mornings	Credit Cards: MC, VISA
Hosts: Judith and Clyde Larrew	Pets: No
Location: 32 mi. E of Indianapolis	Children: Welcome, over 6
No. of Rooms: 3	Smoking: No
No. of Private Baths: 3	Social Drinking: Permitted
Double/pb: $60	Airport/Station Pickup: Yes
Open: All year	

This recently restored Victorian has all its original charm, with modern baths and air-conditioning added for present-day comfort. For guests' amusement, the upstairs gallery is stocked with cards, games, and books. While you're here, you'll want to ride the vintage train, walk around historic Knightstown, and visit the area's many antique shops.

Old Hoosier House ✪

7601 SOUTH GREENSBORO PIKE, KNIGHTSTOWN, INDIANA 46148

Tel: (317) 345-2969	Reduced Rates: 10% seniors
Hosts: Tom and Jean Lewis	Breakfast: Full
Location: 30 mi. E of Indianapolis	Pets: No
No. of Rooms: 4	Children: Welcome
No. of Private Baths: 4	Smoking: No
Double/pb: $55–$65	Social Drinking: Permitted
Single/pb: $45–$55	Airport/Station Pickup: Yes
Open: All year	

The Old Hoosier House takes you back more than 100 years, when the livin' was easier. The rooms are large, with high ceilings, arched windows, antiques, and mementos. A library and patio are available for your pleasure. In the morning you'll wake to the aroma of home-made rolls and coffee. Golfers will enjoy the adjoining golf course, while antique buffs will be glad to know there are hundreds of local dealers in the area. The cities of Anderson and Richmond are close by, and the Indianapolis 500 is within an hour's drive.

Olde Country Club
P.O. BOX 115, KNIGHTSTOWN, INDIANA 46148

Tel: (317) 345-5381
Best Time to Call: Noon–5 PM
Hosts: Dick and Norma Firestone
Location: 35 mi. E of Indianapolis
No. of Rooms: 2
No. of Private Baths: 2
Double/pb: $60
Single/pb: $55

Open: All year
Reduced Rates: Available
Breakfast: Full
Pets: No
Children: Welcome
Smoking: No
Social Drinking: Permitted

Dick and Norma, who own one of Knightstown's antique shops, purchased this property in 1961 and expanded it over the years, adding a family room, greenhouse, herb garden, and fish pond. The house once belonged to the Knightstown golf course, and you can practice your chip shots on your hosts' short par three. Rooms are decorated with paisley and floral wallpapers, lace curtains, and, of course, antique furniture. When you're not prowling for antiques of your own—there are lots of shops in town—you can play golf on an eighteen-hole course or ride an old-fashioned train.

The Rock House ✪
380 WEST WASHINGTON STREET, MORGANTOWN, INDIANA 46160

Tel: (812) 597-5100
Hosts: George and Donna Williams
Location: 32 mi. S of Indianapolis
No. of Rooms: 6
No. of Private Baths: 2
Max. No. Sharing Bath: 4
Double/pb: $65
Single/pb: $55
Double/sb: $55

Single/sb: $45
Open: All year
Reduced Rates: 10% seniors
Breakfast: Full
Pets: No
Children: Welcome
Smoking: No
Social Drinking: No

The Rock House was built in the 1890s by James Smith Knight. He used concrete blocks years before they were popular, but it's the way he used them that made him an innovator. Before the concrete dried, Knight embedded in it rocks, seashells, dishes, and jewelry collected as souvenirs from 48 states. The result is spectacular, drawing many sightseers to the house. Inside, guests will find a homey atmosphere and comfortable furnishings. Your hosts will gladly direct you to such local attractions as Lake Monroe, Ski World, and Little Nashville Opry.

Allison House ✪

90 SOUTH JEFFERSON STREET, P.O. BOX 546, NASHVILLE, INDIANA
47448

Tel: (812) 988-0814	Open: **All year**
Best Time to Call: **9 AM–9 PM**	Reduced Rates: **10% after 2nd night**
Host: **Tammy Galm**	Breakfast: **Continental, plus**
Location: **50 mi. S of Indianapolis**	Pets: **No**
No. of Rooms: 5	Children: **Welcome, over 12**
No. of Private Baths: 5	Smoking: **No**
Double/pb: **$85**	Social Drinking: **No**

Allison House is a fully restored Victorian located in the heart of
Nashville. Tammy has filled the house with a blend of old mementos
and new finds from the local arts and crafts colony. The artisans are
quite famous in this area, and they are located within walking distance. Tammy offers a light breakfast of home-baked goods.

Plain and Fancy/Traveler's Accommodations & Country Store ✪

STATE ROAD 135N, R.R. 3, BOX 62, NASHVILLE, INDIANA 47448

Tel: (812) 988-4537	Reduced Rates: **30% 2-night**
Best Time to Call: **9AM–5PM**	**minimum, Dec.–Feb.**
Host: **Suanne Shirley**	Breakfast: **Continental**
Location: **18 mi. W of I-65 South**	Credit Cards: **MC, VISA**
No. of Rooms: 2	Pets: **Sometimes**
Max. No. Sharing Bath: 4	Children: **Welcome**
Double/sb: **$60–$65**	Smoking: **Permitted**
Single/sb: **$50–$55**	Social Drinking: **Permitted**
Open: **Fri., Sat., and Sun. only**	Minimum Stay: **2 nights Oct.**

Enjoy an intimate stay at Suanne's turn-of-the-century log home set
among four wooded acres. A variety of wildlife can be viewed from
the comfort of a shaded deck or while strolling the property's walking
trails. This secluded B&B is easily accessible to area attractions. Just
minutes away, Brown County State Park, Indiana's largest, offers a
full range of recreational activities. Nashville, one of the nation's
oldest artists' colonies, boasts a playhouse, a country music hall, and
an assortment of quaint shops—among them Suanne's own emporium, which features a wide array of unique handicrafts and *objets
d'art*, and is conveniently located on the B&B premises.

Braxtan House Inn B&B ✪

210 NORTH GOSPEL STREET, PAOLI, INDIANA 47454

Tel: (812) 723-4677	Location: **45 mi. S of Bloomington**
Best Time to Call: **6 PM–8 PM**	No. of Rooms: 6
Hosts: **Terry and Brenda Cornwell**	No. of Private Baths: 6

Double/pb: **$50–$70**
Single/pb: **$45–$55**
Open: **All year**
Reduced Rates: **10% seniors**
Breakfast: **Full**
Pets: **No**

Children: **Welcome, over 10**
Smoking: **Permitted**
Social Drinking: **Permitted**
Minimum Stay: **2 nights ski season
and Kentucky Derby weekend**

This Queen Anne Victorian was built in 1893. The original cherry, oak, and walnut woodwork is still evident in many of the 21 rooms. Terry and Brenda have carefully refurbished the mansion and decorated with lovely antiques. The dining room, with its original wainscoting and wide-plank floors, is where pecan pancakes with a variety of fruit toppings are on the breakfast menu. Paoli Peaks, a ski resort, is 2 miles away, and it's 15 miles to Patoka, the second largest lake in the state. Coffee, tea, and snacks are graciously offered.

Rosewood Mansion ✪
54 NORTH HOOD, PERU, INDIANA 46970

Tel: **(317) 472-7151; fax (317) 472-5575**
Best Time to Call: **8 AM–5 PM**
Hosts: **Carm and Zoyla Henderson**
No. of Rooms: **9**
No. of Private Baths: **9**
Double/pb: **$68**
Single/pb: **$60**
Suites: **$75–$115**
Open: **All year**
Reduced Rates: **10% weekly, seniors, families, business travelers (midweek)**

Breakfast: **Full**
Other Meals: **Available by request**
Credit Cards: **AMEX, DC, DISC, MC, VISA**
Pets: **Sometimes**
Children: **Welcome**
Smoking: **Restricted**
Social Drinking: **Permitted**
Airport/Station Pickup: **Yes**
Foreign Languages: **Spanish**

Rosewood Mansion is a stately brick Georgian residence constructed in 1862. A winding wooden staircase connects each floor, and stained-glass windows accent each landing. The house is decorated in period style, with floral wallpaper and antique furniture. Because this B&B is located three blocks from downtown Peru, restaurants, shops, public parks, and numerous sports facilities are just minutes away. Guests breakfast on coffee, tea, juice, fresh fruit, freshly baked breads or muffins, and quiche or eggs Benedict. Upon request snacks are served in the afternoon, with a round of hot chocolate at bedtime. Each room has a TV and VCR.

Suit's Us❂

514 NORTH COLLEGE, ROCKVILLE, INDIANA 47872

Tel: **(317) 569-5660**	Double/sb: **$45**
Hosts: **Bob and Ann McCullough**	Open: **All year**
Location: **50 mi. W of Indianapolis**	Breakfast: **Continental, plus**
No. of Rooms: **4**	Pets: **No**
No. of Private Baths: **2**	Children: **Welcome**
Max. No. Sharing Bath: **4**	Smoking: **No**
Double/pb: **$55**	Social Drinking: **Permitted**

This classic plantation-style home, with its widow's walk and generous front porch, dates to the early 1880s. The Strausses, a locally prominent family, bought the house about twenty years later; their overnight guests included Woodrow Wilson, Annie Oakley, James Whitcomb Riley, and John L. Lewis. Today, Ann and Bob extend their hospitality to you. There are books and a color TV in each room, and some even have stereos. Turkey Run Park is ten miles away, while five universities—Indiana State, DePauw, Wabash, St. Mary-of-the-Woods, and Rose-Hulman—are within a thirty-mile radius. Also, Rockville sponsors its own annual event, the Covered Bridge Festival.

Suit's Us is pictured on this year's back cover (top photograph).

IOWA

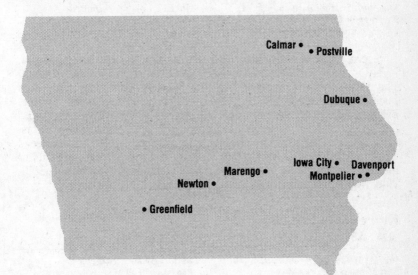

Bed and Breakfast in Iowa, Ltd. ✪
BOX 430, PRESTON, IOWA 52069

Tel: **(319) 689-4222**
Coordinator: **Wilma Bloom**
States/Regions Covered: **Statewide**
Descriptive Directory: **$2**

Rates (Single/Double):
  Modest: **$25 / $35**
  Average: **$30 / $50**
  Luxury: **$50 / $65**
Credit Cards: **No**

Wilma has a vast variety of accommodations, some of which are on the National Register of Historic Places. Travelers' interests, including cultural, historic, sports, and crafts, as well as fairs and festivals, can be easily satisfied. The University of Iowa, Iowa State, and Drake University are close to several homes. Some B&Bs impose a surcharge for one-night stays.

Calmar Guesthouse
RR 1, BOX 206, CALMAR, IOWA 52132

Tel: **(319) 562-3851**
Hosts: **Art and Lucille Kruse**
Location: **10 mi. S of Decorah**
No. of Rooms: **5**
Max. No. Sharing Bath: **5**
Double/sb: **$35–$40**
Open: **All year**

Breakfast: **Full**
Pets: **No**
Children: **Welcome**
Smoking: **No**
Social Drinking: **Permitted**
Airport/Station Pickup: **Yes**

A recent guest reports that "The Calmar Guesthouse is a spacious, lovely, newly remodeled Victorian home located on the edge of town. The atmosphere is enhanced by the friendly, charming manner of Lucille, who made us feel right at home. The rooms were comfortable, private, and pretty. After a peaceful night's sleep, we were served a delicious breakfast of fresh farm eggs with ham and cheeses, croissants with butter and jam, homemade cinnamon rolls, and coffee. I would recommend it to anyone visiting the area." Nearby points of interest include Lake Meyer, the world's smallest church, and Spillville, home of hand-carved Bily Bros. Clocks.

River Oaks Inn ✪
1234 EAST RIVER DRIVE, DAVENPORT, IOWA 52803

Tel: **(319) 326-2629; (800) 352-6016**
Best Time to Call: **9 AM–5 PM**
Hosts: **Bill and Suzanne Pohl; Ron and Mary Jo Pohl**
Location: **2 mi. from I-80**
No. of Rooms: **5**
No. of Private Baths: **5**
Double/pb: **$49–$69**
Suites: **$79**
Open: **All year**

Reduced Rates: **Available**
Breakfast: **Full**
Credit Cards: **MC, VISA**
Pets: **Sometimes**
Children: **Welcome**
Smoking: **Restricted**
Social Drinking: **Permitted**
Airport/Station Pickup: **Yes**
Foreign Languages: **Spanish**

Abner Davison combined Italianate, Victorian, and Prairie architecture when he built his home back in the 1850s. The house is situated on a rolling lot that still shows evidence of the original carriage drive. Choose from a suite with king-size bed, sun porch, and dressing room; the Ambrose Fulton Room, with double bed and garden view; the Mississippi Room, with queen-size bed and window seat; or the Abner Davison Room, which has twin beds or a king-size bed and a bay window. Breakfast is served in the dining room, or out on the deck in warm weather. The inn is located one block from riverboat rides, and is convenient to many area attractions, such as Historic Rock Island Arsenal and the village of East Davenport.

The Richards House ✪
1492 LOCUST STREET, DUBUQUE, IOWA 52001

Tel: (319) 557-1492	Open: All year
Host: Michelle Delaney	Reduced Rates: 10% Nov.–Apr.; 40%
No. of Rooms: 5	Sun.–Thurs.
No. of Private Baths: 4	Breakfast: Full
Max. No. Sharing Bath: 2	Credit Cards: AMEX, DISC, MC, VISA
Double/pb: $45–$75	Pets: Sometimes
Single/pb: $45–$75	Children: Welcome (crib)
Double/sb: $40–$55	Smoking: Restricted
Single/sb: $40–$55	Social Drinking: Permitted
Suites: $50–$85	Airport/Station Pickup: Yes

Inside and out, this four-story Victorian is a feast for the eyes, with its gabled roof, stained-glass windows, gingerbread trim, and elaborate woodwork. Rooms are furnished in period style. Guests can continue their journey back in time with a ride on the Fenelon Place Cable Car, the shortest inclined railway in the country. Then it's time to pay respects to another form of transportation at the Woodward Riverboat Museum. You're welcome to use the kitchen for light snacks; in the morning, Michelle takes over, setting out fresh fruit, waffles, pancakes, sausage, and homemade breads.

The Wilson Home ✪
RR 1, BOX 132, GREENFIELD, IOWA 50849

Tel: (515) 743-2031	Double/pb: $75
Best Time to Call: 5–10 PM	Open: Jan. 15–Oct. 15
Hosts: Wendy and Henry Wilson	Breakfast: Full
Location: 1 mi. E of Greenfield on	Pets: Sometimes
Hwy. 92	Children: Welcome (crib)
No. of Rooms: 2	Smoking: Permitted
No. of Private Baths: 2	Social Drinking: Permitted

Enjoy the quiet, simple life at The Wilson Home, set in the rolling countryside. The poolhouse encloses a huge indoor pool; a two-level deck filled with plants, wicker and iron furniture, a beverage-stocked kitchenette; and two spacious guestrooms. Breakfasts are served in the sunny dining room of the Wilsons' 1918 farmhouse, which is beautifully decorated with family antiques. Nearby you will find golf, fishing, antiquing, an airplane museum, covered bridges, and John Wayne's birthplace. Pheasant hunting packages available.

Bella Vista Place
2 BELLA VISTA PLACE, IOWA CITY, IOWA 52245

Tel: (319) 338-4129	Location: 20 mi. S of Cedar Rapids
Host: Daissy Owen	No. of Rooms: 2

Max. No. Sharing Bath: **4**	Pets: **No**
Double/sb: **$45**	Children: **Welcome, over 8**
Single/sb: **$40**	Smoking: **No**
Open: **All year**	Social Drinking: **Permitted**
Reduced Rates: **Weekly**	Airport Pickup: **Yes**
Breakfast: **Full**	Foreign Languages: **Spanish**

Daissy has furnished her lovely 1920s home with antiques and artifacts she acquired on her travels in Europe and Latin America. Downtown Iowa City and the University of Iowa are within walking distance of Bella Vista Place; the Hoover Library, the Amana Colonies, and the Amish center of Kalona are all nearby. Full breakfasts feature fruit, orange juice, croissants, jams, eggs, and either coffee or cappuccino.

The Golden Haug ✪
517 EAST WASHINGTON, IOWA CITY, IOWA 52240

Tel: **(319) 338-6452; 354-4284**	Open: **All year**
Best Time to Call: **Evenings**	Reduced Rates: **Available**
Hosts: **Nila Haug and Dennis Nowotny**	Breakfast: **Full**
Location: **2 mi. from I-80, Exit 244**	Pets: **No**
No. of Rooms: **4**	Children: **Welcome**
No. of Private Baths: **4**	Smoking: **No**
Double/pb: **$65–$90**	Social Drinking: **Permitted**
Single/pb: **$65–$90**	Airport Pickup: **Yes**
Suites: **$65–$90**	

Nila and Dennis's 1920s Arts-and-Crafts house has been restored and updated to provide comfortable accommodations and modern conveniences. Guests can retreat to the comfort of their suites or enjoy the camaraderie of other visitors. With refreshments upon your arrival, evening snacks, and brunch-sized breakfasts, you won't go away hungry. The convenient Iowa City location puts you within walking distance of the University of Iowa, restaurants, stores, and houses of worship.

Loy's Bed and Breakfast ✪
RR 1, BOX 82, MARENGO, IOWA 52301

Tel: **(319) 642-7787**	Double/sb: **$50**
Best Time to Call: **7 AM; noon; 6 PM**	Open: **All year**
Hosts: **Loy and Robert Walker**	Breakfast: **Full**
Location: **3 mi. from I-80, Exit 216**	Other Meals: **Available**
No. of Rooms: **3**	Pets: **If caged**
No. of Private Baths: **2**	Children: **Welcome**
Max. No. Sharing Bath: **4**	Smoking: **No**
Double/pb: **$50–$60**	Social Drinking: **Permitted**
Single/pb: **$35**	

The Walkers invite you to visit their contemporary farmhouse in the heartland of rural Iowa. Enjoy the peaceful surroundings of a large lawn, gardens, and patio. The rooms are furnished in modern and refinished pieces. Guests are welcome to relax in the family room by the fire or to stop by the rec room for a game of shuffleboard or pool, and a treat from the snack bar. If they are not busy with the harvest, your hosts will gladly take you on day trips. Tours may include Plum Grove, Iowa City, Brucemore Mansion, and Herbert Hoover's birthplace. A visit to the nearby lakes is recommended, and a take-along lunch can be arranged. The Amana Colonies is right there and shouldn't be missed.

Varners' Caboose Bed & Breakfast
204 EAST SECOND STREET, P.O. BOX 10, MONTPELIER, IOWA 52759

Tel: **(319) 381-3652**
Best Time to Call: **Afternoons**
Hosts: **Bob and Nancy Varner**
Location: **11 mi. W of Davenport**
No. of Rooms: **1**
No. of Private Baths: **1**
Double/pb: **$55**

Open: **All year**
Breakfast: **Full**
Pets: **Sometimes**
Children: **Welcome**
Smoking: **No**
Social Drinking: **Permitted**
Airport/Station Pickup: **Yes**

Bob and Nancy offer their guests the unique experience of staying in a genuine Rock Island Line caboose. Their home, located close to the Mississippi, was the original Montpelier Depot, and the caboose is a self-contained unit with bath, shower, and kitchen set on its own track behind the house. It sleeps four, with a queen-size bed and two singles in the cupola. The rate is increased to $65 when more than two occupy the caboose. A fully prepared egg casserole, fruit, homemade breads, juice, and coffee or tea are left in the kitchen to be enjoyed at your leisure. Enjoy this quiet town while being a few minutes downstream from the heart of the Quad Cities.

LaCorsette Maison Inn ✪
629 FIRST AVENUE EAST, NEWTON, IOWA 50208

Tel: **(515) 792-6833**
Host: **Kay Owen**
Location: **25 mi. E of Des Moines**
No. of Rooms: **5**
No. of Private Baths: **5**
Double/pb: **$60–$100**
Suites: **$80–$165**
Open: **All year**

Breakfast: **Full**
Other Meals: **Available**
Pets: **Sometimes**
Children: **Yes**
Smoking: **No**
Social Drinking: **Permitted**
Airport/Station Pickup: **Yes**

Bringing a touch of Spanish architecture to the American heartland, this 21-room mansion has all the hallmarks of the Mission style, from

its stucco walls and red-tiled roof to its interior oak woodwork. Six nights a week, Kay doubles as a chef, preparing elaborate six-course dinners for as many as 48 scheduled guests; the first caller to make reservations selects the entrée, and a house tour precedes the meal. Overnight guests wake up to a full breakfast accented by the herbs and vegetables Kay grows in the backyard. If you want to work off the calories, tennis courts and a pool are in the area.

Old Shepherd House ✪

256 W. TILDEN STREET, BOX 251, POSTVILLE, IOWA 52162

Tel: **(319) 864-3452**	Single/sb: **$30**
Best Time to Call: **10 AM–10 PM**	Open: **All year**
Host: **Rosalyn Krambeer**	Breakfast: **Full**
Location: **25 mi. SE of Decorah**	Pets: **Sometimes**
No. of Rooms: **4**	Children: **Welcome**
No. of Private Baths: **1**	Smoking: **Permitted**
Max. No. Sharing Bath: **2**	Social Drinking: **Permitted**
Double/sb: **$45–$50**	

Postville, a town of 1,500 with four quaint craft shops and a fabulous antiques emporium, is in northeast Iowa in an area known as the state's Little Switzerland. Within a thirty-mile radius you can canoe the Iowa River, or visit sites like the Vesterheim Museum, Effigy Mounds, Villa Louis, Spook Cave, and Bily Brothers clock museum. Shepherd House, built in the early 1880s, is furnished entirely with antique and Victorian pieces. Your hostess is an interior decorator, and she's filled her home with unusual window treatments, restored trunks, and crafts work.

KANSAS

- WaKeeney

Kansas City

Abilene •

Tonganoxie • •

Modoc •

Fort Scott •

Balfours' House
ROUTE 2, ABILENE, KANSAS 67410

Tel: **(913) 263-4262**
Best Time to Call: **After 5 PM**
Hosts: **Gilbert and Marie Balfour**
Location: **2¼ mi. S of Abilene**
Suites: **$40–$50**
Open: **All year**
Breakfast: **Continental**

Credit Cards: **MC, VISA**
Pets: **Sometimes**
Children: **Welcome**
Smoking: **Restricted**
Social Drinking: **Permitted**
Airport/Station Pickup: **Sometimes**

Gilbert and Marie Balfour welcome you to their modern, cottage-style home, set on a hillside. The house is located on just over two acres, and has a spacious yard. Guests have their own private entrance into the family room, which includes a fireplace, piano, and TV. The main attraction of the house is a hexagonal recreation room that has a built-in swimming pool, spa, and dressing area with shower. A separate southwestern-style bungalow is also available. Your hosts will gladly direct you to the Eisenhower Museum, Greyhound Hall of Fame, and old historic mansions.

Country Quarters ✪

ROUTE 5, BOX 80, FORT SCOTT, KANSAS 66701

Tel: (316) 223-6012	Open: All year
Host: Marilyn McQuitty	Breakfast: Full
Location: 2 mi. S of Fort Scott	Pets: No
No. of Rooms: 2	Children: Welcome
Max. No. Sharing Bath: 4	Smoking: Permitted
Double/sb: $25	Social Drinking: Permitted

Marilyn McQuitty welcomes you to a real working farm located outside a charming Victorian town. Her 100-year-old farmhouse is furnished with comfortable family pieces. While you're sitting by the fire, ask to hear the story behind the 100-year-old hearth and hand-carved mantelpiece. Guests are welcome to relax on the porch or visit the ceramic shop located on the premises. There is easy access to the Fort Scott Lake, Gunn Park, and the Fort Scott National Historic Site, an authentically restored military fort dating back to 1892. Downtown you can drive past the magnificent old homes, browse through antiques stores, and visit a one-room schoolhouse.

Krause House ✪

ROUTE 1, BOX 9, MODOC, KANSAS 67866

Tel: (316) 379-4627	Open: All year
Hosts: Paul and Merilyn Krause	Reduced Rates: Families
Location: 13 mi. W of Scott City	Breakfast: Full
No. of Rooms: 2	Other Meals: Available
No. of Private Baths: 1	Pets: Sometimes
Max. No. Sharing Bath: 4	Children: Welcome
Double/pb: $35	Smoking: No
Single/pb: $25	Social Drinking: No
Double/sb: $35	Airport/Station Pickup: Available
Single/sb: $25	

Experience a working grain farm in the western Kansas countryside. Paul and Merilyn Krause have a remodeled farmhouse surrounded by tall shade trees. Breakfast specialties such as egg casseroles, homemade breads, and cinnamon rolls are served on the glassed-in patio overlooking the flowers and greenery. Krause House is 25 miles from Scott County State Park, where you may fish, boat, hunt for fossils, and see Indian ruins.

Almeda's Inn ✪

BOX 103, 220 SOUTH MAIN, TONGANOXIE, KANSAS 66086

Tel: (913) 845-2295	Hosts: Almeda and Richard Tinberg
Best Time to Call: Before 9 AM; after	Location: 20 mi. W of Kansas City
6 PM	No. of Rooms: 7

No. of Private Baths: **2**
Max. No. Sharing Bath: **4**
Double/pb: **$40**
Double/sb: **$30**
Single/sb: **$30**
Suite: **$60**

Open: **All year**
Breakfast: **Continental**
Pets: **No**
Children: **Welcome, over 10**
Smoking: **Permitted**
Social Drinking: **Permitted**

Located in a picturesque small town, and made a designated Historical Site in 1983, the inn dates back to World War I. You are welcome to sip a cup of coffee at the unique stone bar in the room once used as a bus stop in 1930. In fact, this room was the inspiration for *Bus Stop*. Almeda and Richard will be happy to direct you to the golf course, swimming facilities, the Starlight Theatre, or the University of Kansas at Lawrence.

Thistle Hill ✪
ROUTE 1, BOX 93, WAKEENEY, KANSAS 67672

Tel: **(913) 743-2644**
Best Time to Call: **6–8 AM; evenings**
Hosts: **Dave and Mary Hendricks**
Location: **1½ mi. from I-70, Exit 120**
No. of Rooms: **3**
No. of Private Baths: **2**
Max. No. Sharing Bath: **4**
Double/pb: **$50–$55**
Single/pb: **$40**

Double/sb: **$50–$55**
Single/sb: **$40**
Open: **All year**
Breakfast: **Full**
Pets: **Sometimes**
Children: **Welcome**
Smoking: **Restricted**
Social Drinking: **Permitted**
Airport/Station Pickup: **Yes**

The entry of this weathered wood country house sets the hospitable tone of this B&B located 325 miles west of Kansas City, or the same distance east of Denver, Colorado. Seasonal wreaths, an Early American bench, antique lanterns, and a big sign saying, "Welcome to Thistle Hill" are the Hendrickses' way of saying they're glad you've come to visit. They're anxious to share with you the pleasures of their rural life, which include cooking, restoring antiques, and working with their team of draft horses. A varied breakfast often includes country fresh eggs, breakfast meats, fresh baked breads, or hotcakes made with whole wheat from their own wheat fields. On chilly mornings it is served near the fireplace. Cedar Bluff Reservoir, for fishing, is 30 miles away; pheasant, waterfowl, and deer roam 10,000 acres of public hunting land nearby.

KENTUCKY

Carrollton • • Ghent
Louisville •
• Georgetown
• Versailles • Mt. Sterling
Bardstown •
Springfield • Perryville
• • Danville
• Paducah • Bowling Green • Somerset
Murray •

Bluegrass Bed & Breakfast ✪
2964 McCRACKEN PIKE, VERSAILLES, KENTUCKY 40383

Tel: **(606) 873-3208**
Coordinator: **Betsy Pratt**
States/Regions Covered: **Berea,
Georgetown, Lexington, Louisville,
Midway, Perryville, Versailles**

Rates (Single/Double):
Modest: **$50**
Average: **$60**
Luxury: **$100**

Most of Betsy's B&Bs are in beautiful old houses that grace the country roads of the area. You may choose among a stone house built in 1796, a turreted Victorian in downtown Lexington, or a country home where your bedroom windows look out on thoroughbred horses. Visit Shakertown, where weavers, smiths, and woodworkers display their skills in an 1839 restored village. Take a ride on the winding Kentucky River in a paddlewheel boat. Tour exquisite historic mansions or see the picturesque homes of such Derby winners as Secretariat and Seattle Slew. And don't miss the 1,000-acre Kentucky Horse Park that includes a theater, museum, track, barns, and hundreds of horses. You may even take a horseback ride, because this place will inspire you.

Kentucky Homes Bed & Breakfast, Inc. ❂
1431 ST. JAMES COURT, LOUISVILLE, KENTUCKY 40208

Tel: **(502) 635-7341**
Best Time to Call: **4–8 PM**
Coordinators: **JoAnn Jenkins and Carson G. Jenkins**
States/Regions Covered: **Kentucky— Bardstown, Danville, Lexington, Louisville; S. Indiana—Corydon, Indianapolis, Paoli**

Descriptive Directory: **Free**
Rates (Single/Double):
  Average: **$65 / $90**
Reduced Rates: **Weekly**
Credit Cards: **AMEX, MC, VISA**

JoAnn and Carson cordially invite you to be a guest in friendly Kentucky at one of dozens of host homes. Fish in spectacular lakes, visit Mammoth Cave, drop in on Shakertown at Pleasant Hill, or reserve early and assure yourself a spot at the next running of the Kentucky Derby (held the first Saturday in May). Stay in a gorgeous turn-of-the-century home in restored old Louisville, or a dairy farm that boards and trains racehorses, or many comfortable choices in between.

Jailer's Inn ❂
111 WEST STEPHEN FOSTER AVENUE, BARDSTOWN, KENTUCKY 40004

Tel: **(502) 348-5551**
Best Time to Call: **10 AM–5 PM**
Hosts: **Challen and Fran McCoy**
Location: **35 mi. S of Louisville**
No. of Rooms: **5**
No. of Private Baths: **5**
Double/pb: **$55–$80**
Open: **Mar.–Dec.**

Reduced Rates: **Available**
Breakfast: **Continental**
Credit Cards: **MC, VISA**
Pets: **No**
Children: **Welcome**
Smoking: **No**
Social Drinking: **Permitted**

For the ultimate in unusual experiences, spend the night in "jail" without having committed a crime. Built in 1819, this former jailer's residence originally housed prisoners upstairs, and has been completely remodeled and furnished with fine antiques and oriental rugs. An adjacent building, once used as the women's cell, has been transformed into a charming suite, where bunk beds are suspended from a brick wall and the decor is black and white checks instead of stripes. The town is famous for *The Stephen Foster Story*, an outdoor musical production. Take time to visit the Getz Museum of Whiskey History and a Civil War museum, and take a tour of My Old Kentucky Home conducted by guides in antebellum costumes.

Alpine Lodge ✪
5310 MORGANTOWN ROAD, BOWLING GREEN, KENTUCKY 42101

Tel: (502) 843-4846
Best Time to Call: 9 AM–9 PM
Hosts: Dr. and Mrs. David Livingston
Location: 60 mi. N of Nashville, Tenn.
No. of Rooms: 5
No. of Private Baths: 3
Max. No. Sharing Bath: 4
Double/pb: $50
Single/pb: $40
Double/sb: $45
Single/sb: $35
Guest Cottage: $150, sleeps 6

Suites: $75
Open: All year
Reduced Rates: Weekly
Breakfast: Full
Other Meals: Available
Pets: Dogs welcome
Children: Welcome
Smoking: Permitted
Social Drinking: Permitted
Airport/Station Pickup: Yes
Foreign Languages: Spanish

The lush bluegrass area of Kentucky is the setting for this spacious Swiss chalet-style home that's situated on four lovely acres and furnished with many antiques. A typical Southern breakfast of eggs, sausage, biscuits and gravy, fried apples, grits, coffee cake, and beverage starts your day. If you can manage to get up from the table, stroll the grounds complete with nature trails and gardens or take a swim in the pool. Afterwards, take in the sights and sounds of Opryland, Mammoth Cave, or the battlefields of historic Bowling Green. In the evening, relax in the living room, where Dr. Livingston, a music professor, may entertain you with selections played on the grand piano.

Bowling Green Bed & Breakfast ✪
1415 BEDDINGTON WAY, BOWLING GREEN, KENTUCKY 42104

Tel: (502) 781-3861
Best Time to Call: Early AM; evenings
Hosts: Dr. Norman and Ronna Lee
  Hunter
Location: 2.5 mi. from I-65, Exit 22
No. of Rooms: 2
No. of Private Baths: 1
Max. No. Sharing Bath: 4
Double/pb: $55
Single/pb: $45

Double/sb: $55
Single/sb: $45
Open: All year
Reduced Rates: 20% families
Breakfast: Full
Pets: No
Children: Welcome, over 14
Smoking: No
Social Drinking: Permitted
Station Pickup: Yes

You will feel most welcome in this new one-story brick home in an exclusive neighborhood in south-central Kentucky. It is an easy drive to Mammoth Cave or Nashville, Tennessee, and many restaurants are nearby. The home, furnished with antiques, features lovely hardwood floors, a cozy fireplace, and tray ceilings with fans, mirrors, and tile. Delicious breakfasts are served in the dining room, next to the bay window. Or, in the summer, guests may prefer the lovely patio or deck. Your hosts, a chemistry professor and a nurse, have many interests, including travel, photography, theater, bowling, and working with exchange students.

P. T. Baker House Bed & Breakfast ✪
406 HIGHLAND AVENUE, CARROLLTON, KENTUCKY 41008

Tel: (502) 732-4210 weekends;
(800) 74 BAKER [742-1537], outside
Kentucky
Hosts: Bill and Judy Gants
Location: 5 mi. N of I-71, Exit 44
No. of Rooms: 3
No. of Private Baths: 3
Double/pb: $60
Single/pb: $45
Open: All year

Guest Cottage: $110, sleeps 6
Reduced Rates: 10% seniors
Breakfast: Full
Credit Cards: MC, VISA
Pets: No
Children: Welcome, over 10
Smoking: Permitted
Social Drinking: Permitted
Airport/Station Pickup: Yes

Upon entering this large Victorian home, listed on the National Register of Historic Places, one gets the feeling of having stepped back to the 1800s. The high ceilings, heavy walnut doors, hand-carved cherry staircase, oil lamp chandeliers, and elegant antiques embellish the careful restoration of this ornate house. Upon arrival, you are graciously welcomed wth a snack and beverage. A bowl of fresh fruit in your room, a potpourri gift, and breakfast served on antique china and crystal are just some of the special touches. Recreational diversions abound in this area located midway between Cincinnati and Louisville.

Twin Hollies Retreat ✪
406 MAPLE AVENUE, DANVILLE, KENTUCKY 40422

Tel: (606) 236-8954
Best Time to Call: 9 AM–1 PM
Host: Mary Joe Bowling
No. of Rooms: 3
No. of Private Baths: 1
Max. No. Sharing Bath: 4
Double/pb: $75
Single/sb: $75
Open: All year

Reduced Rates: 20% seniors and
families
Breakfast: Continental
Wheelchair Accessible: Yes
Pets: No
Children: Welcome, over 10
Smoking: Permitted
Social Drinking: Permitted
Airport/Station Pickup: Yes

Welcome to the bluegrass region! Your host promises that this setting is so peaceful you'll want to stay forever. Her fine old antebellum home—a designated Kentucky Landmark that is listed on the National Register of Historic Places—features spacious rooms, elegant antiques, and genuine Southern hospitality. This is horse country, with lots of farms to visit. But you'll also want to take a walking tour of historic Danville, with its many gracious houses.

Twin Hollies Retreat is pictured on this year's back cover (bottom photograph).

Breckinridge House B&B ✪
201 SOUTH BROADWAY, GEORGETOWN, KENTUCKY 40324

Tel: **(502) 863-3163**
Hosts: **Annette and Felice Porter**
No. of Rooms: **2 suites**
Suites: **$65–$85**
Open: **All year**
Breakfast: **Full**

Credit Cards: **VISA**
Pets: **Sometimes**
Children: **Welcome**
Smoking: **Permitted**
Social Drinking: **Permitted**
Airport/Station Pickup: **Yes**

This charming Georgian home was the residence of John C. Breckin-ridge, a former vice-president who ran against Abraham Lincoln for the presidency. (After losing the election, Breckinridge became a leading Confederate general.) Each antique-filled suite has a bedroom, sitting room, kitchen, and bath. Breakfast features homemade breads, pecan rolls, fresh fruit, and bacon and eggs.

Jordan Farm Bed & Breakfast ✪
4091 NEWTOWN PIKE, GEORGETOWN, KENTUCKY 40324

Tel: **(502) 863-1944, 868-9002**
Best Time to Call: **Anytime**
Hosts: **Harold and Becky Jordan**
Location: **8 mi. N of Lexington**
No. of Rooms: **2**
Double/sb: **$60**
Suites: **$75–$85, sleeps 2**
Open: **All year**

Breakfast: **Full**
Pets: **No**
Children: **Welcome**
Smoking: **Permitted**
Social Drinking: **Permitted**
Minimum Stay: **2 nights weekends Apr. and Oct.**
Airport/Station Pickup: **Yes**

Derby fans will want to stay on this 100-acre thoroughbred farm in the middle of Kentucky's legendary horse country. Indeed, the Kentucky Horse Park is only five minutes away. From the guest room's private deck, you can watch the Jordans' horses cavort in the fields. Or drop a line into the fishing pond and try your luck.

Log Cabin Bed and Breakfast ✪
350 NORTH BROADWAY, GEORGETOWN, KENTUCKY 40324

Tel: **(502) 863-3514**
Hosts: **Clay and Janis McKnight**
Location: **10 mi. N of Lexington**
No. of Rooms: **2**
No. of Private Baths: **1**
Guest Cottage: **$64 for 2**

Open: **All year**
Breakfast: **Continental**
Pets: **Welcome**
Children: **Welcome**
Smoking: **Permitted**
Social Drinking: **Permitted**

This rustic log cabin was built, circa 1809, with a shake shingle roof and chinked logs. Inside, the living room is dominated by a huge fieldstone fireplace. The master bedroom and bath are on the ground floor and a loft bedroom will sleep additional people with ease. The house has been fully restored and air-conditioned by the McKnights, and is filled with period furnishings. The dining-kitchen wing is equipped with all new appliances and modern amenities. The Log Cabin is located in a quiet neighborhood close to Kentucky Horse Park, Keeneland, and many other historic places. This is the perfect spot to bring the kids and give them a taste of authentic American tradition.

Ghent House B&B ○

411 MAIN STREET, U.S. 42, GHENT, KENTUCKY 41045

Tel: **(502) 347-5807 weekends; (606) 291-0168 weekdays**	Single/pb: **$55–$60**
Best Time to Call: **After 6 PM; weekends**	Suites: **$110**
	Open: **All year**
Hosts: **Wayne and Diane Young**	Reduced Rates: **Available**
Location: **12 mi. N and E of I-71, Exit 44**	Breakfast: **Full**
	Pets: **No**
No. of Rooms: **3**	Children: **Welcome (crib)**
No. of Private Baths: **3**	Smoking: **No**
Double/pb: **$65–$70**	Social Drinking: **Permitted**
	Airport/Station Pickup: **Yes**

Ghent House is a gracious antebellum residence, built in the usual style of the day—a central hall with rooms on either side and the kitchen and dining room in the rear. A beautiful fantail window and two English coach lights enhance the front entrance. Guests can look out over the Ohio River and imagine the time when steamboats regularly traveled the waterways. The view includes the lovely homes of the Vevay, Indiana, side of the river.

The Trimble House ○

321 NORTH MAYSVILLE STREET, MT. STERLING, KENTUCKY 40353

Tel: **(606) 498-6561, 498-7078**	Double/sb: **$55**
Best Time to Call: **9 AM–10 PM**	Open: **All year**
Hosts: **Jim and June Hyska**	Reduced Rates: **10% seniors**
Location: **29 mi. E of Lexington**	Breakfast: **Full**
No. of Rooms: **4**	Credit Cards: **AMEX, MC, VISA**
No. of Private Baths: **3**	Pets: **No**
Max. No. Sharing Bath: **4**	Children: **Welcome, over 12**
Double/pb: **$60**	Smoking: **Permitted**
Single/pb: **$45**	Social Drinking: **Permitted**

An "Old South" plantation-style home located in Mt. Sterling's historic district, the Trimble House (1872) is listed on the Kentucky Historic Register. Visitors can enjoy air-conditioning, comfortable beds, Granny's handmade quilts, and antiques. Pool, exercise room, Jacuzzi, bicycles, and limo available for horse racing events and bluegrass horse farm tours.

Diuguid House Bed & Breakfast ✪
603 MAIN STREET, MURRAY, KENTUCKY 42071

Tel: (502) 753-5470
Best Time to Call: 4–10 PM
Hosts: Karen and George Chapman
Location: 45 mi. S of Paducah
No. of Rooms: 3
Max. No. Sharing Bath: 6
Double/sb: $35
Open: All year

Reduced Rates: Seventh night free
Breakfast: Full
Credit Cards: MC, VISA
Pets: No
Children: Welcome
Smoking: No
Social Drinking: Permitted
Airport/Station Pickup: Yes

Upon walking into this 1890s Queen Anne, listed on the National Register of Historic Places, guests see an impressive sweeping oak staircase and unusual hallway fretwork. In addition to their rooms, visitors have use of the parlor, TV lounge, and dining room. Murray State University houses a local history museum, an art gallery, and the National Boy Scout Museum. The town, a top-rated retirement community, offers lots of theatrical and musical events. For outdoor activities, take the twenty-minute drive to Land Between the Lakes, where you can hike, hunt, fish, admire the resident buffalo herd, or see a working historical farm.

The Victorian Secret Bed & Breakfast ✪
1132 SOUTH FIRST STREET, OLD LOUISVILLE, KENTUCKY 40203

Tel: (502) 581-1914
Hosts: Nan and Steve Roosa
Location: 1 mi. S of downtown
  Louisville
No. of Rooms: 3
No. of Private Baths: 1
Max. No. Sharing Bath: 4
Double/pb: $53

Double/sb: $53
Open: All year
Reduced Rates: Weekly
Breakfast: Continental
Pets: No
Children: Welcome
Smoking: Permitted
Social Drinking: Permitted

An elegant brick Victorian with lavish woodwork, this B&B has modern amenities like an exercise room with a bench press and a rowing machine, and color TVs in guest rooms. The Louisville area is rich in historic homes. Railbirds and would-be jockeys will want to make pilgrimages to the famous tracks at Churchill Downs (site of the Kentucky Derby) and Louisville Downs (home of harness races).

Ehrhardt's B&B ✪
285 SPRINGWELL LANE, PADUCAH, KENTUCKY 42001

Tel: (502) 554-0644
Best Time to Call: 7–9 AM; 4–6 PM
Hosts: Eileen and Phil Ehrhardt

Location: 1 mi. from I-24
No. of Rooms: 2
Max. No. Sharing Bath: 4

Double/sb: **$35**
Single/sb: **$30**
Open: **All year**
Reduced Rates: **10% seniors**
Breakfast: **Full**
Other Meals: **Available**

Pets: **No**
Children: **Welcome, over 12**
Smoking: **Permitted**
Social Drinking: **Permitted**
Airport/Station Pickup: **Yes**

This brick Colonial ranch home is just a mile off I-24, which is famous for its beautiful scenery. Your hosts hope to make you feel at home in antique-filled bedrooms and a den with a fireplace. Homemade biscuits and jellies, and country ham and gravy are breakfast specialties. Enjoy swimming in the Ehrhardts' pool and boating at nearby Lake Barkley, Ky Lake, and Land Between the Lakes. Paducah features quarterhorse racing from June through November, and the National Quilt Show in April.

Elmwood Inn ✪
205 EAST FOURTH STREET, PERRYVILLE, KENTUCKY 40468

Tel: **(606) 332-2400**
Hosts: **Bruce and Shelley Richardson**
Location: **35 mi. SW of Lexington**
No. of Rooms: **2 suites**
Suites: **$79**
Open: **All year**
Breakfast: **Full**

Other Meals: **Available**
Credit Cards: **MC, VISA**
Pets: **No**
Children: **No**
Smoking: **No**
Social Drinking: **Permitted**

Escape the hectic pace of the modern world at this beautifully restored 1842 Greek Revival mansion along a quiet river in the heart of one of Kentucky's most historic small towns. Listed on the National Register of Historic Places—it served as a Civil War field hospital—the inn features guest suites with private sitting rooms, antiques, fireplaces, and a well-stocked library. Join area residents in the dining room for an authentic English afternoon tea Thursday through Saturday. Don't be surprised to find Civil War soldiers or a brass band on the front lawn. Perryville was the site of the only major Civil War battle fought in Kentucky. Perryville Battlefield, Shakertown, Bardstown, and Keeneland are all close by.

Shadwick House ✪
411 SOUTH MAIN STREET, SOMERSET, KENTUCKY 42501

Tel: **(606) 678-4675**
Best Time to Call: **Anytime**
Host: **Ann Epperson**
Location: **84 mi. S of Lexington**
No. of Rooms: **4**
Max. No. Sharing Bath: **4**
Double/sb: **$30**
Single/sb: **$25**

Open: **All year**
Breakfast: **Full**
Credit Cards: **MC, VISA**
Pets: **No**
Children: **Welcome**
Smoking: **No**
Social Drinking: **Permitted**

Shadwick House has been known for its southern hospitality for more than seventy years—the home was built in 1920 by Nellie Stringer Shadwick, great-grandmother of the present owners. The first floor has been converted into an antique and craft shop. Kentucky ham and biscuits are served for breakfast in the original dining room. This B&B is tucked into the Cumberland Mountain foothills, near Lake Cumberland. Other local attractions are Renfro Valley, Cumberland Falls State Park, Tombstone Junction, and Big South Fork National Park.

Maple Hill Manor B&B ✪
ROUTE 3B, BOX 20, PERRYVILLE ROAD, SPRINGFIELD, KENTUCKY 40069

Tel: **(606) 336-3075**
Hosts: **Bob and Kay Carroll**
No. of Rooms: **7**
No. of Private Baths: **7**
Double/pb: **$55–$80**
Single/pb: **$45**
Open: **All year**
Reduced Rates: **After 1st night; 10% families**

Breakfast: **Full**
Credit Cards: **MC, VISA**
Pets: **No**
Children: **Welcome (crib)**
Smoking: **No**
Social Drinking: **Permitted**
Minimum Stay: **2 nights Derby weekend**

This hilltop manor house built in 1851 is situated on 14 tranquil acres in the scenic Bluegrass Region of Kentucky. Listed on the National Register of Historic Places, its Italianate design features 13-foot ceilings, 9-foot windows and doors, a profusion of fireplaces, and a solid cherry spiral staircase. The bedrooms are large, airy, and beautifully decorated with carefully chosen antique furnishings. The romantic honeymoon bed chamber has a canopy bed and Jacuzzi bath. In the evening, Bob and Kay graciously offer complimentary beverages and homemade dessert. Within an hour of Lexington and Louisville, you can visit Perryville Battlefield and Shaker Village and take a tour of distilleries.

Bed and Breakfast at Sills Inn ✪
270 MONTGOMERY AVENUE, VERSAILLES, KENTUCKY 40383

Tel: **(606) 873-4478; (800) 526-9801;** fax: **(606) 873-4726**	Breakfast: **Full**
Host: **Tony Sills**	Other Meals: **Available**
Location: **7 mi. W of Lexington**	Credit Cards: **AMEX, DC, DISC, MC, VISA**
No. of Rooms: **6**	Pets: **No**
No. of Private Baths: **6**	Children: **Welcome**
Double/pb: **$55**	Smoking: **No**
Guest Cottage: **$175 weekly**	Social Drinking: **Permitted**
Suites: **$85**	Airport/Station Pickup: **Yes**
Open: **All year**	
Reduced Rates: **20% corporate, 10% AAA, 10% seniors**	

Sills Inn is steeped in Kentucky's thoroughbred tradition—this state attracts horse owners and admirers from around the world. Come and see why royalty, governors, businesspersons, honeymooners, and friends continue to visit this B&B. Antique shops, art studios, cafes, and quaint restaurants are within a short walk or drive. All rooms have private baths; two suites have double Jacuzzis; a full gourmet breakfast, served formally in the main dining room each morning, is included with each room.

Shepherd Place ✪
31 HERITAGE ROAD (U.S. 60), VERSAILLES, KENTUCKY 40383

Tel: **(606) 873-7843**	Breakfast: **Full**
Hosts: **Marlin and Sylvia Yawn**	Credit Cards: **MC, VISA**
Location: **10 mi. W of Lexington**	Pets: **No**
No. of Rooms: **2**	Children: **Welcome, over 12**
No. of Private Baths: **2**	Smoking: **Restricted**
Double/pb: **$65–$70**	Social Drinking: **Permitted**
Single/pb: **$60**	Airport/Station Pickup: **Yes**
Open: **All year**	

Marlin and Sylvia encourage you to make yourself comfortable in their pre–Civil War home, built around 1815. Rest in a spacious, beautifully decorated bedroom or relax in the parlor. Enjoy the lovely scenery while sitting on the patio or the porch swing. You might even want to pet the resident ewes, Abigail and Victoria. Brochures, menus, and plenty of ideas will be available to help you plan the rest of your stay.

For key to listings, see inside front or back cover.

✪ This star means that rates are guaranteed through December 31, 1993, to any guest making a reservation as a result of reading about the B&B in *Bed & Breakfast U.S.A.*—1993 edition.

Important! To avoid misunderstandings, always ask about cancellation policies when booking.

Please enclose a self-addressed, stamped, business-size envelope when contacting reservation services.

For more details on what you can expect in a B&B, see Chapter 1.

Always mention *Bed & Breakfast U.S.A.* when making reservations!

If no B&B is listed in the area you'll be visiting, use the form on page 733 to order a copy of our "List of New B&Bs."

We want to hear from you! Use the form on page 735.

LOUISIANA

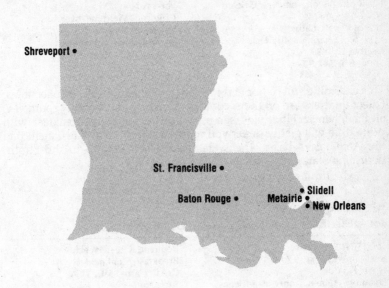

Southern Comfort Bed & Breakfast
2856 HUNDRED OAKS, BATON ROUGE, LOUISIANA 70808

For information: **(504) 346-1928,
928-9815; for reservations: (800)
749-1928**
Best Time to Call: **8 AM–8 PM**
Coordinators: **Susan Morris and Helen
Heath**
States/Regions Covered: **Alabama—
Mobile; Louisiana—statewide;
Mississippi—Natchez, Vicksburg,
Port Gibson; Texas—Houston**

Descriptive Directory: **$3.50**
Rates (Single/Double):
   Modest: **$40–45 / $45–$55**
   Average: **$50–$60 / $60–$85**
   Luxury: **$65–$140 / $90–$160**
Credit Cards: **AMEX, MC, VISA**
Minimum Stay: **3–5 nights in New
Orleans during Mardi Gras, Jazz
Festival, Sugar Bowl, Super Bowl**

Susan and Helen offer you the best of the old and the new South with
hosts in urban and rural areas. The above is only a sample list. Special
attractions are Civil War and other historic sites; fabulous New Orleans; Acadian (Cajun) country; sports, deep-sea fishing, and racetracks in Louisiana. There's a $5 surcharge for one-night stays.

223

Joy's B&B ✪
4920 PERKINS ROAD, BATON ROUGE, LOUISIANA 70808

Tel: (504) 766-2291
Best Time to Call: 6 AM–noon
Host: Joy Robinson
Location: 85 mi. from New Orleans
No. of Rooms: 2
No. of Private Baths: 1
Max. No. Sharing Bath: 4
Double/sb: $55
Single/sb: $47.50

Open: **All year**
Reduced Rates: **15% seniors**
Breakfast: **Full**
Pets: **No**
Children: **Welcome, over 12**
Smoking: **Permitted**
Social Drinking: **Permitted**
Airport/Station Pickup: **Yes**

This charming stucco home is furnished with antiques and collectibles. Guest quarters are on the second floor and feature a family room, TV, and kitchen facilities. Joy serves a hearty, Southern breakfast with pride. She will gladly direct you to interesting nearby sites, including the Atchafalaya basin, the largest hardwood swamp in the South. Louisiana State University is five minutes away.

Metairie Meadows
141 METAIRIE COURT, METAIRIE, LOUISIANA 70001

Tel: (504) 525-3983
Best Time to Call: 9 AM–5 PM
Host: Flo Cairo
Location: 15 min. from New Orleans
No. of Rooms: 3
No. of Private Baths: 3
Double/pb: $75–$125
Open: **All year**

Reduced Rates: **Weekly**
Breakfast: **Continental**
Credit Cards: **MC, VISA**
Pets: **No**
Smoking: **No**
Social Drinking: **Permitted**
Minimum Stay: **2 nights**

Flo offers you quiet, peaceful accommodations in a pleasant neighborhood just 15 minutes away from New Orleans' famous French Quarter. Bedrooms are large and tastefully decorated; one features an antique bed and armoire. The many local attractions include plantations, Mississippi riverboats, antique shops, the French market, Bourbon Street, and wonderful five-star restaurants.

Bed & Breakfast, Inc.—New Orleans ✪
1021 MOSS STREET, BOX 52257, NEW ORLEANS, LOUISIANA 70152-2257

Tel: (504) 488-4640; (800) 749-4640
Coordinator: **Hazell Boyce**
States/Regions Covered: **New Orleans**
Descriptive Directory: **Free**

Rates (Single/Double):
   Modest: **$25–$40 / $35–$50**
   Average: **$35–$75 / $40–$75**
   Luxury: **$60 and up / $60 and up**
Credit Cards: **No**

New Orleans is called The City That Care Forgot. You are certain to be carefree, visiting the French Quarter, taking Mississippi riverboat rides, taking plantation tours, as well as dining in fine restaurants and attending jazz concerts. Hazell's hosts, many with historic properties along the streetcar line and in the French Quarter, will help you get the most out of your stay.

New Orleans Bed & Breakfast and Accommodations
P.O. BOX 8163, NEW ORLEANS, LOUISIANA 70182-8163

Tel: **(504) 838-0071, 838-0072, 838-0073**
Best Time to Call: **8:30 AM–4:30 PM**
Coordinator: **Sarah-Margaret Brown**
States/Regions Covered: **Louisiana— Covington, Jeanerette, Lafayette, Mandeville, New Iberia, New Orleans**

Rates (Single/Double):
  Modest: **$30–$45 / $40–$45**
  Average: **$45–$50 / $50–$55**
  Luxury: **$65–$200**
Credit Cards: **AMEX, DISC, MC, VISA (For deposit only)**
Minimum Stay: **5 nights Mardi Gras, Jazz Festival; 3 nights Sugar Bowl**

Sarah-Margaret offers a range from the youth-hostel type for the backpacker crowd, to modest accommodations in all areas of the city, to deluxe B&Bs in lovely and historic locations. If the past intrigues you, treat yourself to an overnight stay in a great Louisiana plantation home. Rates increase during Mardi Gras, Jazz Fest, Sugar Bowl; decrease for longer stays.

Beau Séjour
1932 NAPOLEON AVENUE, NEW ORLEANS, LOUISIANA 70115

Tel: **(504) 897-3746**
Best Time to Call: **10 AM–8 PM**
Hosts: **Gilles and Kim Gagnon**
No. of Rooms: **5**
No. of Private Baths: **5**
Double/pb: **$75**
Single/pb: **$65**
Suites: **$100**
Open: **All year**

Breakfast: **Continental**
Credit Cards: **MC, VISA**
Pets: **No**
Children: **Welcome**
Smoking: **Permitted**
Social Drinking: **Permitted**
Minimum Stay: **2 nights**
Foreign Languages: **French**

Kim and Gil recently restored their 1906 Beau Séjour house to its original character, with beautiful detailing and wood floors. It is decorated in the best New Orleans style, blending country and European antiques with Louisiana and New Orleans touches. Located in one of the most picturesque neighborhoods of New Orleans, surrounded by lush tropical plantings, and on the Mardi Gras parade route, the mansion is convenient to convention and tourist attractions. Kim and Gil are dedicated to New Orleans preservation and enjoy sharing their knowledge of local restaurants, excursions, and the culture of the "big easy."

Jensen's Bed & Breakfast ✪
1631 SEVENTH STREET, NEW ORLEANS, LOUISIANA 70115

Tel: **(504) 897-1895**
Best Time to Call: **6–9 PM**
Hosts: **Shirley, Joni, and Bruce Jensen**
No. of Rooms: **5**
Max. No. Sharing Bath: **4**
Double/sb: **$55**
Single/sb: **$45**

Open: **All year**
Breakfast: **Continental**
Pets: **No**
Children: **Welcome**
Smoking: **Permitted**
Social Drinking: **Permitted**

Your hosts have drawn on their backgrounds as an interior decorator, piano teacher, and renovator of vintage homes, to restore this Victorian mansion. Stained glass, 12-foot-high alcove ceilings, antiques, a grand piano, raised-panel-pocket doors, and carefully chosen furnishings enhance the mansion. Located across the street from the Garden District, an area famed for its lovely homes, it is just a block to the trolley, which will whisk you to the French Quarter, Audubon Park, the zoo, or Tulane University. Breakfast is likely to feature banana cornbread, muffins, seasonal fruit, and Louisiana-style coffee. The mansion is air-conditioned for your summer comfort, and there's a TV in each bedroom. Rates increase during Mardi Gras, the Jazz Festival, and other special events.

The Levee View ✪
39 HENNESEY COURT, NEW ORLEANS, LOUISIANA 70123

Tel: **(504) 737-5471**
Hosts: **Jack and Clemmie Devereux**
No. of Rooms: **2**
No. of Private Baths: **1**
Max. No. Sharing Bath: **4**
Double/pb: **$35**
Single/pb: **$30**
Double/sb: **$30**
Single/sb: **$25**

Suites: **$50**
Open: **All year**
Reduced Rates: **10% weekly, seniors**
Breakfast: **Continental**
Pets: **No**
Children: **Welcome**
Smoking: **Permitted**
Social Drinking: **Permitted**
Airport/Station Pickup: **Yes**

The Devereuxs welcome you to their contemporary home, located in a convenient residential suburb of New Orleans. The house is large and attractive, with comfortable family furnishings. Guest quarters are located in a two-story wing with separate entrance, ensuring visitors plenty of privacy and quiet. Breakfast specialties include homemade breads, croissants, and plenty of hot coffee. If you like, you can relax outside on the patio or sip a drink in the gazebo. The levee bordering the Mississippi River is less than 100 feet from the house; many lovely plantation homes are also located nearby. Your hosts will gladly guide you to the best restaurants and shops, and will occasionally baby-sit for the kids while you go out on the town.

Sully Mansion
2631 PRYTANIA STREET, NEW ORLEANS, LOUISIANA 70130

Tel: **(504) 891-0457**
Best Time to Call: **7 AM–10 PM**
Hosts: **Maralee Prigmore**
No. of Rooms: **7**
No. of Private Baths: **7**
Double/pb: **$65–$150**
Open: **All year**
Reduced Rates: **June 15–Sept. 1**

Breakfast: **Continental**
Credit Cards: **MC, VISA**
Pets: **Sometimes**
Children: **No**
Smoking: **No**
Social Drinking: **Permitted**
Minimum Stay: **2 nights weekends, 5
   nights special events**

A Queen Anne named to honor its architect, Sully Mansion shows his discerning eye in its 12-foot ceilings, 10-foot doors, grand staircase, and stained glass. The house is furnished with a blend of yesterday's antiques and today's comfortable pieces, and most of the bedrooms have fireplaces. Other architectural jewels fill the surrounding historic Garden District; board the St. Charles streetcar for a 15-minute ride to New Orleans's main attractions.

Terrell House ✪
1441 MAGAZINE STREET, NEW ORLEANS, LOUISIANA 70130

Tel: **(504) 524-9859**
Host: **Harry Lucas and Sally Cates**
Location: **½ mi. from I-10**
No. of Rooms: **9**
No. of Private Baths: **9**
Double/pb: **$60–$90**
Suites: **$100**

Open: **All year**
Breakfast: **Continental**
Credit Cards: **AMEX, MC, VISA**
Pets: **No**
Children: **Welcome**
Smoking: **Permitted**
Social Drinking: **Permitted**

Built in 1858, this faithfully restored mansion offers antique furnishings and modern conveniences. The twin parlors and the formal dining room, with gas chandeliers, gold mirrors, marble mantels, and period furnishings, capture the grace of yesteryear. All of the guest rooms open onto balconies and the landscaped courtyard. They all have telephones, color television, and central air-conditioning. Located in the historic Lower Garden District, it's convenient to public transportation. The French Quarter is five minutes away. Complimentary cocktails and other refreshments are graciously offered.

Barrow House B&B ✪
**P.O. BOX 1461, 524 ROYAL STREET, ST. FRANCISVILLE, LOUISIANA
70775**

Tel: **(504) 635-4791**
Hosts: **Lyle and Shirley Dittloff**
Location: **25 mi. N of Baton Rouge**

No. of Rooms: **5**
No. of Private Baths: **3**
Max. No. Sharing Bath: **4**

Double/pb: **$75–$85**
Single/pb: **$65**
Suites: **$95–$125**
Open: **All year, except Dec. 21–25**
Breakfast: **Continental**

Wheelchair Accessible: **Yes**
Pets: **No**
Children: **Welcome**
Smoking: **Permitted**
Social Drinking: **Permitted**

A saltbox erected in 1809, with a Greek Revival wing that was added some four decades later, Barrow House is listed on the National Register of Historic Places. Appropriately enough, Lyle and Shirley have furnished their B&B with 19th-century pieces from the American South. Other notable homes are in the area; the Dittloffs like to send guests on a cassette walking tour of the neighborhood. Afterward, sit on the screened front porch and sip a glass of wine or iced tea. Breakfast options range from a simple Continental meal to a full-course New Orleans spread. Shirley is a fabulous cook, and private candlelight dinners, featuring Cajun and Creole specialties, can also be arranged.

Wolf-Schlesinger House—The St. Francisville Inn ☉
118 NORTH COMMERCE, DRAWER 1369, ST. FRANCISVILLE, LOUISIANA 70775

Tel: **(504) 635-6502; (800) 488-6502**
Hosts: **Patrick and Laurie Walsh**
Location: **24 mi. N of Baton Rouge**
No. of Rooms: **9**
No. of Private Baths: **9**
Double/pb: **$65–$70**
Single/pb: **$55–$60**
Open: **All year**
Reduced Rates: **10% seniors**

Breakfast: **Full**
Other Meals: **Available**
Credit Cards: **AMEX, DC, DISC, MC, VISA**
Pets: **No**
Children: **Welcome (crib)**
Smoking: **Permitted**
Social Drinking: **Permitted**

The St. Francisville Inn is located in the heart of plantation country in a town that is listed on the National Register of Historic Places. The inn is a Victorian Gothic known as the Wolf-Schlesinger House, built circa 1880. The air-conditioned guest rooms are furnished in lovely antiques, and each opens onto a New Orleans–style courtyard out back.

Fairfield Place
2221 FAIRFIELD AVENUE, SHREVEPORT, LOUISIANA 71104

Tel: **(318) 222-0048**
Host: **Janie Lipscomb**
Location: **½ mi. from I-20**
No. of Rooms: **6**
No. of Private Baths: **6**
Double/pb: **$75–$105**
Single/pb: **$65–$75**
Suite: **$145**

Open: **All year**
Breakfast: **Continental**
Credit Cards: **AMEX, MC, VISA**
Pets: **No**
Children: **Sometimes**
Smoking: **No**
Social Drinking: **Permitted**

You will enjoy this elegant 1900s inn, where the legendary hospitality of the Deep South rings true. Begin your day with New Orleans coffee, croissants and strawberry butter, and French pastries. Janie's home features lambskin rugs, king-size beds, 19th-century paintings, Swedish crystal, designer sheets and linens, and allergy-proofed European feather beds. It is located in the beautiful Highland Historical Restoration District, convenient to the business district, medical center, and airport. Louisiana Downs Racetrack is minutes away.

2439 Fairfield "A Bed and Breakfast Inn" ✪
2439 FAIRFIELD AVENUE, SHREVEPORT, LOUISIANA 71104

Tel: **(318) 424-2424**
Best Time to Call: **7 AM–10 PM**
Hosts: **Jimmy and Vicki Harris**
Location: **½ mi from I-20**
No. of Rooms: **4**
No. of Private Baths: **4**
Double/pb: **$85–$105**
Single/pb: **$85–$105**
Open: **All year**

Reduced Rates: **Available**
Breakfast: **Full**
Credit Cards: **AMEX, MC, VISA**
Pets: **No**
Children: **No**
Smoking: **No**
Social Drinking: **Permitted**
Airport Pickup: **Yes**

2439 Fairfield is a meticulously restored three-story Victorian mansion located in the Highland historic district and was featured on the front cover of the 1992 edition of *Bed & Breakfast U.S.A.* This home is surrounded by century-old oaks, rose gardens, and azaleas—you can enjoy the scenic view from your own private balcony complete with porch swings and rocking chairs. The gracious guest rooms are furnished with antiques, Amish quilts, quality linens, feather beds, and down pillows and comforters. Each guest bath has a whirlpool tub. Hearty English breakfasts are served in the morning room. Then it's off to the races at nearby Louisiana Downs. The Strand Theatre, art galleries, and fine restaurants are all within reasonable driving distances.

Salmen-Fritchie House ✪
127 CLEVELAND AVENUE, SLIDELL, LOUISIANA 70458

Tel: **(504) 643-1405**
Best Time to Call: **Mornings**
Hosts: **Homer and Sharon Fritchie**
Location: **30 mi. N of New Orleans**
No. of Rooms: **5**
No. of Private Baths: **5**
Double/pb: **$75–$95**
Single/pb: **$75–$85**
Suites: **$150**

Open: **All year**
Reduced Rates: **Available**
Breakfast: **Full**
Credit Cards: **AMEX, MC, VISA**
Pets: **No**
Children: **Welcome, over 12**
Smoking: **No**
Social Drinking: **Permitted**
Station Pickup: **Yes**

You'll feel the sense of history as you step inside this magnificent sixteen-room house listed on the National Register of Historic Places. From the front door to the back, the great hall measures twenty feet wide and eighty-five feet long! All the rooms are filled with beautiful antiques, reminiscent of days gone by; your hosts own a large antique shop on the adjoining property. Hospitality is a way of life here. Arrive by 4 PM and you can join your hosts for tea in the parlor and afterward, a tour of the house and grounds. In the morning, you'll receive fresh hot coffee in your room. Then you'll enjoy a full Southern breakfast in the bright, cheery breakfast room.

MAINE

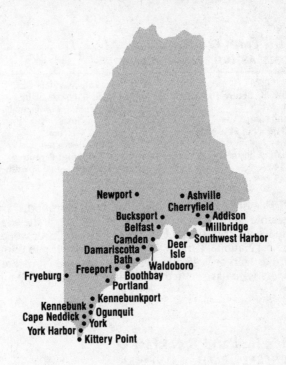

Newport •
• Ashville
Cherryfield
Bucksport •
• Addison
Belfast •
• Millbridge
Camden • •
Deer
Southwest Harbor
Damariscotta • •
Isle
Bath •
Freeport • •
Waldoboro
• Boothbay
Fryeburg •
Portland
• Kennebunkport
Kennebunk •
Cape Neddick • • Ogunquit
York Harbor • • York
• Kittery Point

Pleasant Bay Bed and Breakfast ✪
BOX 222 WEST SIDE ROAD, ADDISON, MAINE 04606

Tel: **(207) 483-4490**
Hosts: **Leon and Joan Yeaton**
Location: **42 mi. N of Ellsworth**
No. of Rooms: **3**
No. of Private Baths: **1**
Max. No. Sharing Bath: **4**
Double/pb: **$60**
Single/pb: **$55**
Double/sb: **$50**

Single/sb: **$40**
Open: **All year**
Breakfast: **Full**
Credit Cards: **MC, VISA**
Pets: **No**
Children: **Welcome**
Smoking: **No**
Social Drinking: **Permitted**

The Yeatons' 110-acre llama farm rests on a knoll by the shores of
Pleasant Bay and the Pleasant River. Watch shorebirds and seals play

231

in the rising and falling tides. Explore the shoreline in seclusion or meander along rustic trails, accompanied by a gentle llama. Relax before the hearth at sunset. In the morning, you'll wake up to a full down east breakfast made with farm-fresh eggs laid by your hosts' own chickens.

Green Hill Farm ✪
RR 1, BOX 328, ASHVILLE, MAINE 04607

Tel: (207) 422-3273	Open: **Late May–late Oct.**
Best Time to Call: **Before 10 AM;**	Reduced Rates: **Available**
after 4 PM	Breakfast: **Full, Continental**
Hosts: **Ted and Nuna Cass**	Pets: **Sometimes**
Location: **17 mi. N of Ellsworth**	Children: **Welcome**
No. of Rooms: **2**	Smoking: **Restricted**
Max. No. Sharing Bath: **5**	Social Drinking: **Permitted**
Double/sb: **$40**	Foreign Languages: **Spanish**
Single/sb: **$35**	

Stay in an 1820s home in a rural neighborhood, surrounded by fields, a large vegetable garden, and a small apple orchard on the edge of the forest. From its 35 acres, Green Hill Farms looks out over woods to the peaks of Acadia National Park. It's a convenient day trip to Campobello Island, and Bar Harbor is 45 minutes away. Ted and Nuna are experienced travelers who have settled down here to raise sheep, spin, knit, and garden.

Elizabeth's Bed and Breakfast ✪
360 FRONT STREET, BATH, MAINE 04530

Tel: (207) 443-1146	Single/sb: **$40**
Best Time to Call: **Anytime**	Open: **Apr. 15–Jan. 1**
Host: **Elizabeth Lindsay**	Breakfast: **Continental**
Location: **40 mi. up the coast from**	Pets: **No**
Portland	Children: **Welcome, over 12**
No. of Rooms: **5**	Smoking: **Permitted**
Max. No. Sharing Bath: **4**	Social Drinking: **Permitted**
Double/sb: **$50–$60**	

Elizabeth's Bed and Breakfast is a fine old Federalist house, painted a traditional white with green shutters. Each bedroom is furnished in country antiques. Bath is famed as a shipbuilding center, and the Maine Maritime Museum merits a visit. It's also fun to walk around the downtown area, which has been restored to its 19th-century glory. Breakfast includes juice, cereal, muffins, and jam. During the summer, Elizabeth prepares Sunday brunches.

Fairhaven Inn ✪
RR 2, BOX 85, NORTH BATH ROAD, BATH, MAINE 04530

Tel: **(207) 443-4391**
Hosts: **George and Sallie Pollard**
Location: **35 mi. N of Portland**
No. of Rooms: **7**
No. of Private Baths: **3**
Max. No. Sharing Bath: **4**
Double/pb: **$60–$70**
Double/sb: **$50–$60**

Single/sb: **$40–$45**
Open: **All year**
Breakfast: **Full**
Pets: **Yes**
Children: **Yes**
Smoking: **Permitted in tavern only**
Social Drinking: **Permitted**

An 18th-century Colonial mansion on a hill above the Kennebec River, Fairhaven Inn is furnished with antique and country pieces. Shaded by hemlock, birch, and pine trees, the 27-acre grounds lure cross-country skiers in the winter, and strollers year round. Around the bend, Bath Country Club is open to the public for golfing, and beaches are nearby. Birdwatchers can study migratory waterfowl at Merrymeeting Bay. You'll get stamina for the day's activities from ample breakfasts of juice, fresh fruit, home-baked breads, and main courses such as blintzes, eggs Benedict, and orange honey French toast.

"Glad II"
60 PEARL STREET, BATH, MAINE 04530

Tel: **(207) 443-1191**
Host: **Gladys Lansky**
Location: **7–10 mi. from US 1**
No. of Rooms: **3**
Max. No. Sharing Bath: **3**
Double/sb: **$40–$45**
Open: **All year**

Breakfast: **Continental**
Credit Cards: **MC, VISA**
Pets: **No**
Children: **Welcome, over 8 (in own room)**
Smoking: **No**
Social Drinking: **Permitted**

This spic-and-span white house, with its crisp green trim, is comfortable and attractively furnished. Gladys delights in pleasing her guests with breakfasts featuring fresh, homemade treats. You are welcome to play the piano, borrow a book from her library, and visit or watch TV in the parlors. It's an easy walk to the Maritime Museum, a short drive to Popham Beach, Reid State Park, Boothbay Harbor, L. L. Bean, and the Brunswick Naval Air Station. Bowdoin College is eight miles away.

Horatio Johnson House ✪
36 CHURCH STREET, BELFAST, MAINE 04915

Tel: **(207) 338-5153**
Hosts: **Helen and Gene Kirby**
Location: **30 mi. S of Bangor**
No. of Rooms: **3**

No. of Private Baths: **3**
Double/pb: **$45**
Single/pb: **$40**
Open: **All year**

Breakfast: **Full**	Smoking: **Permitted**
Pets: **No**	Social Drinking: **Permitted**
Children: **No**	

While the rest of the world is rushing ahead, the small seafaring town of Belfast is rediscovering its past. The waterfront and old town buildings are being refurbished to reflect the way things used to be. Your hosts offer good company and comfortable lodging in a 19th-century home five minutes from the ocean. The Kirbys offer a variety of breakfast specialties, such as Belgian waffles and blueberry pancakes. They will glady recommend flea markets, antique shops, and restaurants galore.

Kenniston Hill Inn ✪
ROUTE 27, P.O. BOX 125, BOOTHBAY, MAINE 04537

Tel: **(207) 633-2159; (800) 992-2915**	Open: **All year**
Best Time to Call: **Afternoons;** **evenings**	Breakfast: **Full**
	Other Meals: **MAP available**
Hosts: **Susan and David Straight**	Credit Cards: **MC, VISA**
Location: **50 mi. N of Portland**	Pets: **No**
No. of Rooms: **10**	Children: **Welcome, over 13**
No. of Private Baths: **10**	Smoking: **No**
Double/pb: **$65–$95**	Social Drinking: **Permitted**

Kenniston Hill Inn is a center-chimney Georgian Colonial dating back to 1786. The house is warm and gracious, with a large front porch and open-hearth fireplace. The bedrooms, four with fireplaces, are tastefully decorated with antiques and fresh flowers. David and Susan offer sumptuous breakfast specialties such as peaches and cream, French toast, or maple walnut pancakes with cinnamon butter. The inn is surrounded by large, shady maples and fields of flowers, but is within easy reach of the harbor, shops, restaurants, boat rides, and the beautiful Maine coastline. Fireside dining is offered during the winter months, November–April.

Harbour Towne Inn ✪
71 TOWNSEND AVENUE, BOOTHBAY HARBOR, MAINE 04538

Tel: **(207) 633-4300**	Reduced Rates: **10% seniors; 10%** **off-season**
Best Time to Call: **8 AM–8 PM**	Breakfast: **Continental**
Hosts: **Rob and Marilyn Crisp**	Wheelchair Accessible: **Yes**
Location: **60 mi. N of Portland**	Credit Cards: **MC, VISA**
No. of Rooms: **12**	Pets: **No**
No. of Private Baths: **12**	Children: **Welcome**
Double/pb: **$50–$175**	Smoking: **Permitted**
Single/pb: **$50**	Social Drinking: **Permitted**
Suites: **$175**	
Open: **All year**	

This turn-of-the-century mansion is so close to the waterfront that you can stand on the deck and take a deep breath of invigorating salt air. Boothbay's shops, galleries, and restaurants are just a few steps away; would-be sailors can rent boats and spend the day at sea. Breakfast includes juice, muffins, and breads.

L'ermitage ✪
219 MAIN STREET, BUCKSPORT, MAINE 04416

Tel: (207) 469-3361	Reduced Rates: 20% off-season
Hosts: Ginny and Jim Conklin	Breakfast: Full
Location: 19 mi. E of Bangor; 1 block from US 1	Other Meals: Available
	Credit Cards: MC, VISA
No. of Rooms: 3	Pets: By arrangement
Max. No. Sharing Bath: 2	Children: By arrangement
Double/sb: $60	Smoking: Permitted
Single/sb: $60	Social Drinking: Permitted
Open: All year	Airport/Station Pickup: Yes

L'ermitage is a 19th-century white Colonial with black shutters, dating back to the 1830s. Your hosts have patterned their inn after those found in Europe. The spacious rooms are furnished in period antiques, Oriental carpets, and collectibles. A small gourmet restaurant is on the premises and features an extensive wine list. L'ermitage is on Penobscot Bay, near Ft. Knox.

Blue Harbor House
67 ELM STREET, ROUTE 1, CAMDEN, MAINE 04843

Tel: (207) 236-3196; (800) 248-3196; fax: (207) 236-6523	Reduced Rates: $65–$85 Nov.–May 15
Hosts: Dennis Hayden and Jody Schmoll	Breakfast: Full
Location: 85 mi. NE of Portland	Credit Cards: MC, VISA
No. of Rooms: 10	Pets: By arrangement
No. of Private Baths: 10	Children: Welcome
Double/pb: $85–$125	Smoking: No
Open: All year	Social Drinking: Permitted
	Airport/Station Pickup: Yes

Camden is one of the prettiest coastal villages in New England. This 1835 Cape Cod house has been completely renovated and captures the essence of a bygone era. Each room is decorated in country antiques, stenciled walls, and handmade quilts. Guests enjoy visiting with each other in the common room, furnished with comfortable chairs and accented by antique stoneware, samplers, and folk art. The spacious dining room, with its views of Mt. Battie, is the setting for the generous breakfast that features homemade breads, delicious egg dishes, and Maine blueberries. It's a few minutes' walk to many fine restaurants, unique shops, and the famous Windjammer fleet.

Camden Maine Stay ✪
22 HIGH STREET, CAMDEN, MAINE 04843

Tel: (207) 236-9636	Single/sb: $64
Best Time to Call: 8 AM–9 PM	Open: All year
Hosts: Peter and Donny Smith, Diana Robson	Reduced Rates: Off-season
	Breakfast: Full
Location: 85 mi. NE of Portland	Credit Cards: MC, VISA
No. of Rooms: 8	Pets: No
Max. No. Sharing Bath: 4	Children: Welcome, over 10
Double/pb: $89	Smoking: No
Double/sb: $76	Social Drinking: Permitted

A comfortable bed, a hearty breakfast, and a friendly innkeeper are found in this treasured old Colonial home. Listed on the National Register of Historic Places and located in Camden's historic district, the inn is a five-minute walk from the harbor, shops, and restaurants. Whether you relax by a crackling log fire, sit on the deck overlooking a wooded glen, or stroll by the brook behind the barn, you will find the Maine Stay to be the perfect base from which to explore midcoast Maine.

The Elms Bed and Breakfast
84 ELM STREET, ROUTE 1, CAMDEN, MAINE 04843

Tel: (207) 236-6250	Suite: $75
Best Time to Call: 9:30 AM–9:30 PM	Open: All year
Host: Joan A. James	Reduced Rates: Off-season
Location: 150 mi. N of Boston, Mass.	Breakfast: Full
No. of Rooms: 6	Credit Cards: MC, VISA
No. of Private Baths: 3	Pets: No
Max. No. Sharing Bath: 4	Children: Welcome, over 12
Double/pb: $85	Smoking: No
Double/sb: $65	Social Drinking: Permitted

Joan keeps candles burning in the windows to welcome you to her lovingly restored Colonial home, built in 1806. Inside, period-style furnishings will take you back two centuries. Camden offers sailing, hiking, and skiing, and the fall foliage is spectacular. Or just stroll over to the city harbor, with its shops, galleries, and restaurants. Breakfast always consists of home-baked breads and such memorable entrées as French toast stuffed with puréed peaches and sour cream.

Hawthorn Inn
9 HIGH STREET, CAMDEN, MAINE 04843

Tel: (207) 236-8842	Location: On Rte. 1, 150 mi. N of Boston
Best Time to Call: 9 AM–8 PM	No. of Rooms: 10
Hosts: Pauline and Brad Staub	

No. of Private Baths: **10**
Double/pb: **$70–$140**
Suites and 2 Apartments: **$90–$225**
Open: **All year**
Reduced Rates: **$10 less daily
  Nov. 1–May 25**
Breakfast: **Full**

Credit Cards: **MC, VISA**
Pets: **No**
Children: **Welcome, over 10**
Smoking: **Permitted**
Social Drinking: **Permitted**
Airport/Station Pickup: **Yes**

The airy rooms of this Victorian inn are an elegant mixture of the old and the new. Guests are welcome to coffee while relaxing on the deck or getting warm by the fire. Tea is served at 4 PM. All rooms overlook either Mt. Battie or Camden Harbor. A score of sports can be enjoyed in the area, and shops and restaurants are a short walk away.

Ricker House
PARK STREET, P.O. BOX 256, CHERRYFIELD, MAINE 04622

Tel: **(207) 546-2780**
Hosts: **William and Jean Conway**
Location: **32 mi. E of Ellsworth**
No. of Rooms: **3**
Max. No. Sharing Bath: **4**
Double/sb: **$50**
Single/sb: **$45**
Open: **All year**

Reduced Rates: **Available**
Breakfast: **Full**
Pets: **No**
Children: **Welcome (crib)**
Smoking: **No**
Social Drinking: **Permitted**
Airport/Station Pickup: **Yes**

Built in 1803, this comfortable Federal Colonial has grounds that border the Narraguagus River, one of the best salmon rivers in the States. The village is quaint and historic, and it is fun to tour it on foot or by bike. Reasonable restaurants offer great menus, and all feature fabulous local lobster. Your hosts will be pleased to direct you to a fresh water lake and the best places to canoe and mountain climb.

Brannon-Bunker Inn ✪
HCR 64, BOX 045L, DAMARISCOTTA, MAINE 04543

Tel: **(207) 563-5941**
Hosts: **Jeanne and Joseph Hovance**
No. of Rooms: **7**
No. of Private Baths: **4**
Max. No. Sharing Bath: **3**
Double/pb: **$65**
Single/pb: **$60**
Double/sb: **$55**
Single/sb: **$50**

Suites: **$70–$110**
Open: **All year**
Breakfast: **Continental**
Credit Cards: **AMEX, MC, VISA**
Pets: **No**
Children: **Welcome**
Smoking: **No**
Social Drinking: **Permitted**

The Brannon-Bunker Inn is an informal, relaxing inn, ideally situated in rural, coastal Maine. Guests may choose from accommodations in the main 1820 Cape House, the 1900 converted barn, or the carriage house across the stream. Each room is individually decorated in styles ranging from Colonial to Victorian. Hosts Jeanne and Joseph Hovance will help you plan your days over breakfast. Nearby activities include golf, ocean swimming at Pemaquid Beach Park, and fishing on the Damariscotta River.

Laphroaig Bed and Breakfast
STATE ROUTE 15, P.O. BOX 489, DEER ISLE, MAINE 04627

Tel: (207) 348-6088	Suites: $75–$110
Hosts: John and Andrea Maberry	Open: All year
Location: 50 mi. S of Bangor	Breakfast: Full
No. of Rooms: 2	Pets: No
No. of Private Baths: 2	Children: No
Double/pb: $85	Smoking: No
Single/pb: $75	Social Drinking: Permitted

In the Scottish language, Laphroaig means "the beautiful hollow by the broad bay." True to its name, this lovely 1854 Greek Revival sits on a hill across a two-lane road from Penobscot Bay. Among the extras you can expect in the large sunny suites are cable TV, AM-FM radio, window fans in the summer, apples in the winter, and hard candies year-round. Full breakfasts feature island seafood, homemade breads, freshly ground coffees, and other delights. Afterward, borrow a book from the library, curl up in a porch swing or rocker, or settle on a secluded garden bench and enjoy peace and quiet.

Isaac Randall House
5 INDEPENDENCE DRIVE, FREEPORT, MAINE 04032

Tel: (207) 865-9295	Open: All year
Best Time to Call: 10 AM–10 PM	Reduced Rates: Off-season
Hosts: Cynba and Shannon Ryan	Breakfast: Full
Location: Rte. 1 South side of town	Pets: Sometimes
No. of Rooms: 8	Children: Welcome (crib)
No. of Private Baths: 6	Smoking: No
Max. No. Sharing Bath: 4	Social Drinking: Permitted
Double/pb: $90–$105	Airport/Station Pickup: Yes
Double/sb: $70	Foreign Languages: French

One hundred seven years ago, this Federal-style farmhouse was built as a wedding gift for Isaac Randall, Jr., and his young bride. It later became a stopover on the Underground Railroad, and then a Depression-era dance hall. Today, guests are welcomed to a charming, air-conditioned, antique-filled home set on five wooded acres. The grounds include a spring-fed pond, perfect for ice skating. Hiking and cross-country ski trails start at the front door. Breakfast specialties such as fruit compote, homemade breads, blueberry pancakes, coffee, and assorted teas are served in the country kitchen. Downtown Freeport, home of L. L. Bean, is within walking distance. Maine's beautiful coast, summer theater, Bowdoin College, and Freeport Harbor are just a short drive away. After a day of activity, join your hosts for an evening snack back at the inn.

The Oxford House Inn ✪
105 MAIN STREET, FRYEBURG, MAINE 04037

Tel: **(207) 935-3442**
Best Time to Call: **Anytime**
Hosts: **John and Phyllis Morris**
Location: **50 mi. W of Portland**
No. of Rooms: **5**
No. of Private Baths: **5**
Double/pb: **$65–$85**
Single/pb: **$50**

Open: **All year**
Breakfast: **Full**
Other Meals: **Available**
Credit Cards: **AMEX, DC, MC, VISA**
Pets: **No**
Children: **Welcome**
Smoking: **No**
Social Drinking: **Permitted**

Located in a Colonial village and surrounded by lakes and mountains, this charming 1913 Edwardian home has served as an inn and restaurant since 1985. Spacious guest rooms are tastefully decorated with old-fashioned flair. A full hearty breakfast is served on the enclosed back porch with panoramic mountain views. Gourmet dinners are served from 6 to 9 PM by reservation. In addition to fine dining, Oxford House offers easy access to many local activities; scenic drives, antiquing, hiking, canoeing, skiing, and tax-free outlet shopping are only minutes away.

The Alewife House

1917 ALEWIVE ROAD, KENNEBUNK, MAINE 04043

Tel: **(207) 985-2118**
Best Time to Call: **8 AM–11 PM**
Hosts: **Maryellen and Tom Foley**
Location: **25 mi. S of Portland**
No. of Rooms: **2**
No. of Private Baths: **2**
Double/pb: **$70**

Open: **All year**
Breakfast: **Continental**
Credit Cards: **MC, VISA**
Pets: **No**
Children: **Welcome, over 12**
Smoking: **No**
Social Drinking: **Permitted**

Step back in time as you enter this 1756 farmhouse, located on six acres of rolling hills and gardens. Inside, the house is decorated with antiques; more are sold in the on-site shop. Awaken to the aroma of hot muffins, fresh fruit, and fresh-perked coffee served on the sunporch each morning. Then explore the area's coastline or the many nearby lakes.

Arundel Meadows Inn

P.O. BOX 1129, KENNEBUNK, MAINE 04043

Tel: **(207) 985-3770**
Best Time to Call: **9 AM–9 PM**
Hosts: **Mark Bachelder and Murray Yaeger**
Location: **2 mi. N of Kennebunk**
No. of Rooms: **7**
No. of Private Baths: **7**
Double/pb: **$75–$95**

Suites: **$95–$135**
Open: **All year**
Breakfast: **Full**
Pets: **Sometimes**
Children: **Welcome, over 11**
Smoking: **No**
Social Drinking: **Permitted**

The Arundel Meadows Inn is situated on three and a half acres next to the Kennebunk River. Murray, a retired professor, and Mark, a professional chef, have always loved this area, and it is a dream come true for them to watch others enjoy it. They renovated this 165-year-old house themselves, and meticulously planned the decor. Several guest rooms have fireplaces and two suites sleep four. Mark's beautifully prepared breakfast specialties are the perfect start for your day. It's just three minutes to the center of town, and about ten to Kennebunk Beach. In the afternoon, come back to the inn for tea and enjoy pâtés, homemade sweets, and beverages.

English Meadows Inn ✪

141 PORT ROAD, KENNEBUNK, MAINE 04043

Tel: **(207) 967-5766**
Best Time to Call: **Mornings**
Host: **Charlie Doane**
Location: **35 mi. S of Portland**
No. of Rooms: **13**

No. of Private Baths: **9**
Max. No. Sharing Bath: **4**
Double/pb: **$85**
Double/sb: **$70**
Guest Cottage: **$115; sleeps 4**

Suites: **$115**
Open: **All year**
Reduced Rates: **25% Nov.–Apr.; 10%
   May–June**
Breakfast: **Full**
Credit Cards: **MC, VISA**

Pets: **Sometimes**
Children: **Welcome, over 10**
Smoking: **No**
Social Drinking: **No**
Airport/Station Pickup: **Yes**

Inside this Victorian farmhouse, period antiques and reproductions transport visitors to a bygone time. But prominently displayed works of local painters and craftspeople demonstrate why Kennebunkport is known as a haven for artists, artisans, and authors. Your host is a native New Englander and retired naval officer; the specialty of the day, in addition to the sumptuous breakfasts, is sharing your experiences with Charlie and his family.

Lake Brook Guest House ✪
57 WESTERN AVENUE, KENNEBUNK, MAINE 04043

Tel: **(207) 967-4069**
Best Time to Call: **9 AM–9 PM**
Host: **Carolyn A. McAdams**
Location: **25 mi. S of Portland**
No. of Rooms: **4**
No. of Private Baths: **3**
Max. No. Sharing Bath: **3**
Double/pb: **$75–$80**
Single/pb: **$60**

Double/sb: **$60**
Single/sb: **$50**
Open: **All year**
Breakfast: **Full**
Pets: **No**
Children: **Welcome**
Smoking: **No**
Social Drinking: **Permitted**
Foreign Languages: **Spanish**

Lake Brook is an appealing turn-of-the-century New England farmhouse. Its wraparound porch is equipped with comfortable rocking chairs, and flower gardens stretch right down to the tidal brook that feeds the property. The shops and restaurants of Dock Square are within easy walking distance, and Kennebunk Beach is a little more than one mile away. Breakfasts include such main dishes as quiche, baked French toast, and Mexican chili eggs and cheese.

Captain Fairfield Inn ✪
CORNER PLEASANT AND GREEN STREETS, P.O. BOX 1308, KENNEBUNKPORT, MAINE 04046

Tel: **(207) 967-4454**
Best Time to Call: **9 AM–8 PM**
Hosts: **Bonnie Dunn and Dennis
   Tallagnon**
Location: **24 mi. S of Portland**
No. of Rooms: **9**
No. of Private Baths: **9**
Double/pb: **$75–$135**
Single/pb: **$65–$125**
Suites: **$135**
Open: **All year**

Reduced Rates: **5% seniors**
Breakfast: **Full**
Credit Cards: **AMEX, MC, VISA**
Pets: **Sometimes**
Children: **Welcome, over 10**
Smoking: **No**
Social Drinking: **Permitted**
Minimum Stay: **2 nights weekends,
   June–Nov.**
Airport/Station Pickup: **Yes**

From this gracious sea captain's mansion in Kennebunkport's historic district, you can walk to the village green and harbor, Dock Square marinas, shops, restaurants, and beaches. Period furnishings and wicker lend tranquility and charm to the bright, beautiful bedrooms; some have fireplaces. Guests may relax in the living room and study, or stroll the tree-shaded grounds. You'll awaken to birdsong, the smell of sea air, and the aroma of gourmet coffee, followed by a wonderful breakfast prepared by chef/owner Dennis.

The Green Heron Inn
P.O. BOX 2578, OCEAN AVENUE, KENNEBUNKPORT, MAINE 04046

Tel: **(207) 967-3315**
Best Time to Call: **Noon–6 PM**
Hosts: **Charles and Elizabeth Reid**
Location: **4½ mi. from US 1**
No. of Rooms: **10**
No. of Private Baths: **10**
Double/pb: **$60–$86**
Single/pb: **$50–$76**

Guest Cottage: **$96–$115**
Reduced Rates: **Weekly**
Breakfast: **Full**
Pets: **Sometimes**
Children: **Welcome (crib)**
Smoking: **Permitted**
Social Drinking: **Permitted**

This immaculate inn, circa 1908, with its inviting porch and striped awnings, furnished simply and comfortably, is located between the river and the ocean in this Colonial resort village. The full Yankee breakfast is a rib-buster! This is a saltwater fisherman's heaven, close to shops and galleries, with boating, golf, swimming, and tennis all nearby.

Gundalow Inn ✪
6 WATER STREET, KITTERY, MAINE 03904

Tel: **(207) 439-4040**
Hosts: **Cevia and George Rosol**
Location: **50 mi. N of Boston**
No. of Rooms: **6**
No. of Private Baths: **6**
Double/pb: **$75–$95**
Single/pb: **$65–$85**

Open: **All year**
Breakfast: **Full**
Credit Cards: **MC, VISA**
Pets: **No**
Children: **Welcome, over 16**
Smoking: **No**
Social Drinking: **Permitted**

Gundalow Inn is a wonderful brick Victorian overlooking Portsmouth harbor. Guest rooms are comfortably furnished with antiques; most have water views. Savor a hearty home-cooked breakfast by the fireplace or on the patio. Stroll over to Colonial Portsmouth, a town noted for its museums, theaters, restaurants, cafés, gardens, festivals, boat tours, and antique and craft shops. Strawbery Banke and Prescott Park are within walking distance. It's a ten-minute drive to beaches and factory outlets, and the White Mountains are two hours away. Of

course, you can always relax with a book on the porch or patio or in the parlor.

Harbour Watch
6 FOLLETT LANE, KITTERY POINT, MAINE 03905

Tel: **(207) 439-3242**
Hosts: **Marian and Robert Craig**
Location: **50 mi. N of Boston**
No. of Rooms: **4**
Max. No. Sharing Bath: **4**
Double/sb: **$65**

Open: **May–Oct.**
Breakfast: **Continental**
Pets: **No**
Children: **Welcome, over 14**
Smoking: **No**
Social Drinking: **Permitted**

This charming sea captain's house has been in Marian's family since the 1700s. Recently recommended by *New York Times* travel writers, Harbour Watch presents an ever-changing panorama of sailboat races, lobstermen pulling their traps, and cocktail cruises (either in the harbor or to the historic Isles of Shoals). For your added pleasure, your hostess often presents an evening of baroque music with harpsichord and recorders. While nearby beaches abound, you should save time to see the Strawbery Banke restoration in Portsmouth and the Prescott Park Art and Theater Series.

Moonraker Bed & Breakfast ✪
MAIN STREET, ROUTE 1, MILBRIDGE, MAINE 04658

Tel: **(207) 546-2191**
Best Time to Call: **9 AM–9 PM**

Hosts: **Bill and Ingrid Handrahan**
Location: **29 mi. N of Ellsworth**

No. of Rooms: **5**
Max. No. Sharing Bath: **4**
Double/sb: **$45**
Single/sb: **$40**
Open: **All year**
Breakfast: **Full**

Other Meals: **Available**
Credit Cards: **MC, VISA**
Pets: **No**
Children: **Welcome**
Smoking: **No**
Social Drinking: **Permitted**

This Queen Anne mansion offers an in-town location in a rural village setting. Rooms, on the second and third story, have outstanding views and turn-of-the-century mahogany furnishings. Restaurants, light shopping, and an inexpensive movie theater are a short walk from the doorstep. It's a pleasant stroll to the Narraguagus River, where you may see seals sunning themselves. Your hosts serve full breakfasts as well as four o'clock tea, so you'll have energy to explore the area.

Black Friar Inn ✪
10 SUMMER STREET, BAR HARBOR, MT. DESERT ISLAND, MAINE 04609

Tel: **(207) 288-5091; (215) 449-6114**
Best Time to Call: **12–3 PM; evenings**
Hosts: **Barbara and Jim Kelly**
No. of Rooms: **6**
No. of Private Baths: **6**
Double/pb: **$85–$105**
Single/pb: **$80–$100**
Open: **May–Nov.**
Reduced Rates: **May 1–June 15**

Breakfast: **Full**
Credit Cards: **MC, VISA**
Pets: **No**
Children: **Welcome, over 12**
Smoking: **No**
Social Drinking: **Permitted**
Minimum Stay: **2 nights July 1–
  Columbus Day**
Airport/Station Pickup: **Yes**

This uniquely restored Victorian incorporates beautiful woodwork, mantels, and tin from area churches and homes. Afternoon refreshments are served in the sunroom, which is paneled in cyprus and embossed tin, or by the fireside in the intimate English pub. Full breakfasts include fresh fruit, juice, eggs, Belgian waffles, and home-baked breads, rolls, and muffins, served in the dining area, featured on the back cover of the 1992 edition of *Bed & Breakfast U.S.A.* Guests have a short walk to shops, restaurants, and the waterfront; it's an easy drive to Acadia National Park.

Hearthside B&B
7 HIGH STREET, BAR HARBOR, MT. DESERT ISLAND, MAINE 04609

Tel: **(207) 288-4533**
Hosts: **Susan and Barry Schwartz**
No. of Rooms: **9**
No. of Private Baths: **9**
Max. No. Sharing Bath: **4**
Double/pb: **$75–$110**
Double/sb: **$65**
Open: **All year**

Reduced Rates: **Before June 15**
Breakfast: **Full**
Credit Cards: **MC, VISA**
Pets: **No**
Children: **Welcome, over 10**
Smoking: **No**
Social Drinking: **Permitted**

On a quiet street, just a short walk to town, is this gracious home, recently redecorated in the manner of a country cottage. Breakfast is served buffet-style, featuring home-baked muffins and cakes, eggs, pancakes, hot cereal, a fresh fruit bowl, and beverages. You are invited to share the special ambience of a living room with a cozy fireplace and brimming with books. Some rooms have a balcony or a fireplace.

The Kingsleigh ✪
P.O. BOX 1426, 100 MAIN STREET, SOUTHWEST HARBOR, MT. DESERT ISLAND, MAINE 04679

Tel: (207) 244-5302	Reduced Rates: Available
Hosts: Nancy and Tom Cervelli	Breakfast: Full
Location: 45 mi. E of Bangor	Credit Cards: AMEX, MC, VISA
No. of Rooms: 8	Pets: No
No. of Private Baths: 8	Children: Welcome, over 12
Double/pb: $85–$95	Smoking: No
Suite: $155	Social Drinking: Permitted
Open: All year	

Built at the turn of the century, the Kingsleigh is a shingled and pebble-dash Colonial revival. The house is set high on a knoll overlooking magnificent Southwest Harbor, where generations of boatbuilders and fishermen have earned their living. Waverly wall coverings, lace window treatments, plush carpeting, and period furnishings provide a comfortable blend of the old and new. Afternoon tea is served on a wraparound porch overlooking the harbor, while you relax in a white wicker chair. Your hosts serve fresh coffee, imported teas, country omelets, oatmeal pancakes, and other specialties for breakfast. They take pleasure in welcoming you to Mt. Desert Island, and will gladly direct you to swimming, hiking, fishing expeditions, whale-watching, restaurants, and shopping.

The Lamb's Ear ✪
P.O. BOX 30, CLARK POINT ROAD, SOUTHWEST HARBOR, MT. DESERT ISLAND, MAINE 04679

Tel: (207) 244-9828	Breakfast: Full
Hosts: Elizabeth and George Hoke	Wheelchair Accessible: Yes
Location: 45 mi. E of Bangor	Credit Cards: MC, VISA
No. of Rooms: 6	Pets: No
No. of Private Baths: 6	Children: Welcome, over 10
Double/pb: $65–$85	Smoking: No
Suite: $125	Social Drinking: Permitted
Open: May–Nov.	

A stately home that dates to the mid-19th century, The Lamb's Ear overlooks the waterfront of Southwest Harbor, a quaint fishing village. While swimming, sailing, and fishing are the primary activities here, you'll want to set aside time to explore nearby galleries, museums, and Acadia National Park. After a full breakfast of eggs, Belgian waffles, fresh fruit, and muffins, you'll be ready for the day's adventures.

Lindenwood Inn ✪
P.O. BOX 1328, SOUTHWEST HARBOR, MT. DESERT ISLAND, MAINE 04679

Tel: (207) 244-5335	Open: **All year**
Hosts: **Gardiner and Marilyn Brower**	Reduced Rates: **Nov. 1–June 1**
No. of Rooms: **7**	Breakfast: **Full**
No. of Private Baths: **3**	Pets: **No**
Max. No. Sharing Bath: **4**	Children: **Welcome, over 12 in inn;**
Double/pb: **$75–$115**	**over 6 in cottage**
Double/sb: **$55–$70**	Smoking: **No**
Guest Cottage: **$105 for 2; $145 for 4**	Social Drinking: **Permitted**

Built at the turn of the century as a sea captain's home, the inn derives its name from the stately linden trees that line the front lawn. Most rooms have fine harbor views, and all are comfortably furnished. Cool mornings are warmed by the glowing fireplace in the dining room, where you can enjoy a hearty breakfast. You are welcome to relax on the shaded porch, enjoy the pleasures of a good book, or play the harpsichord in the parlor. You can explore the wonders of Acadia National Park by car, bicycle, hiking, or sailing.

Penury Hall ✪
BOX 68, MAIN STREET, SOUTHWEST HARBOR, MT. DESERT ISLAND, MAINE 04679

Tel: (207) 244-7102	Breakfast: **Full**
Hosts: **Gretchen and Toby Strong**	Pets: **No**
No. of Rooms: **3**	Children: **Welcome, over 16**
Max. No. Sharing Bath: **3**	Smoking: **No**
Double/sb: **$55**	Social Drinking: **Permitted**
Single/sb: **$45**	Minimum Stay: **2 nights June 15–**
Open: **All year**	**Oct. 1**
Reduced Rates: **Oct. 1–June 1**	Airport/Station Pickup: **Yes**

This gray frame house is on the quiet side of Mt. Desert Island. Built in 1830, it is comfortably furnished with traditional pieces, antiques, and original art. Gretchen and Toby are cosmopolitan and cordial. Their motto is: "Each guest is an honorary member of the family," and you'll soon feel at home. Knowledgeable about the area's highlights, they'll direct you to special shops and restaurants and all of the best things to see and do. Breakfast often features eggs Benedict and blueberry pancakes or cinnamon waffles. You are welcome to use the canoe or sail the 19-foot day sailor. There's a $10 surcharge for one-night stays.

Pointy Head Inn ✪
HCR 33 BOX 2A, BASS HARBOR, MT. DESERT ISLAND, MAINE 04653

Tel: **(207) 244-7261**
Best Time to Call: **9:30 AM–3 PM**
Hosts: **Doris and Warren Townsend**
Location: **18 mi. S of Bar Harbor**
No. of Rooms: **6**
No. of Private Baths: **1**
Max. No. Sharing Bath: **4**
Double/pb: **$70**
Double/sb: **$60**

Single/sb: **$45**
Open: **May 15–Oct.**
Breakfast: **Full**
Pets: **No**
Children: **Welcome, over 10**
Smoking: **No**
Social Drinking: **Permitted**
Airport/Station Pickup: **Yes**

In Colonial times a sea captain made his home here, overlooking beautiful Bass Harbor. Today, this sprawling inn is a haven for artists and photographers who appreciate the quiet side of Mount Desert Island. The house is decorated with nautical accents and homey furnishings. One of its special qualities is the beautiful sunsets that can be enjoyed from your room or the comfortable porch. The inn is set in a quaint fishing village bordering Acadia National Park. Swimming, canoeing, nature trails, fishing, and mountain climbing are just a few of the activities that can be enjoyed locally. A variety of restaurants, shops, and galleries are within walking distance.

Lake Sebasticook B&B ✪
P.O. BOX 502, 8 SEBASTICOOK AVENUE, NEWPORT, MAINE 04953

Tel: **(207) 368-5507**
Hosts: **Bob and Trudy Zothner**
Location: **1 mi. off I-95, Exit 39**
No. of Rooms: **3**

Max. No. Sharing Bath: **3**
Double/sb: **$50**
Single/sb: **$37.50**
Open: **May–Oct.**

B. Ramsey
8-88

Breakfast: **Full**	Smoking: **No**
Pets: **No**	Social Drinking: **No**
Children: **No**	Airport/Station Pickup: **Yes**

This gracious white Victorian, with its front wraparound porch and screened-in second-story sun porch, stands so near to Lake Sebasticook that guests can hear the calls of ducks and loons. In summer, the lake is a haven for swimmers and fishermen; in winter, it freezes, providing an outlet for cross-country skiers. Bob and Trudy, who love the outdoors, will direct you to the best locations. Full country breakfasts, with homemade breads and jams, will supply you with the energy to enjoy the great outdoors.

Morning Dove Bed and Breakfast
30 BOURNE LANE, OGUNQUIT, MAINE 03907

Tel: **(207) 646-3891**	Breakfast: **Continental**
Hosts: **Peter and Eeta Sachon**	Credit Cards: **AMEX, DISC**
Location: **75 mi. N of Boston**	Pets: **No**
No. of Rooms: **3**	Children: **Welcome, over 12**
No. of Private Baths: **3**	Smoking: **Permitted**
Double/pb: **$70–$105**	Social Drinking: **Permitted**
Open: **All year**	Minimum Stay: **2 nights July, Aug.,**
Reduced Rates: **Off-season**	**holiday weekends**

The Morning Dove is a restored farmhouse dating back to the 1860s. The airy rooms feature antiques, luxurious towels, and fresh garden flowers. At night, handmade chocolates are placed on the pillows. Breakfast is served on the Victorian porch or in the elegant dining room. The house is within walking distance of beaches, a busy harbor for fishing and boating, and the Marginal Way, a cliff-top path along the edge of the ocean. Restaurants, art galleries, and the trolley stop are just a few steps away.

West End Inn ✪
146 PINE STREET, PORTLAND, MAINE 04102

Tel: **(207) 772-1377**	Breakfast: **Full**
Best Time to Call: **Anytime**	Credit Cards: **AMEX, MC, VISA**
Hosts: **Hilary and Tom Jacobs**	Pets: **No**
No. of Rooms: **4**	Children: **Welcome, over 10**
No. of Private Baths: **4**	Smoking: **No**
Double/pb: **$90**	Social Drinking: **Permitted**
Single/pb: **$80**	Airport/Station Pickup: **Yes**
Open: **All year**	
Reduced Rates: **10% Columbus**	
weekend–Memorial weekend	

A comfortable Victorian town house, the West End Inn is in Portland's Western Promenade Historic District, a neighborhood noted for its fine turn-of-the-century homes. Guests can stroll to downtown Portland, the picturesque Old Port, the Portland Art Museum, and many fine restaurants. Beaches, state parks, and lighthouses are nearby, and there are many wonderful jogging and walking paths. Year round, the coastal scenery is spectacular.

Harbour Woods Lodging
P.O. BOX 1214, SOUTHWEST HARBOR, MAINE 04679

Tel: **(207) 244-5388**
Best Time to Call: **Anytime**
Hosts: **Margaret Eden and James Paviglianite**
Location: **20 mi. S of Ellsworth**
No. of Rooms: **3**
No. of Private Baths: **3**
Double/pb: **$60–$105**
Single/pb: **$55–$100**

Guest Cottage: **$85–$105; sleeps 6**
Open: **All year**
Reduced Rates: **Available**
Breakfast: **Full**
Pets: **No**
Children: **Welcome, in cottage**
Smoking: **No**
Social Drinking: **Permitted**

Built in the mid-1800s, this rambling farmhouse combines today's comforts with yesterday's charms. Shops, restaurants, and the harbor front are all within walking distance. Each spacious guest room has either a garden or a harbor view, plus a queen-size bed, plush carpet, and a private bath stocked with oversized towels and luxurious soaps. Snack on afternoon refreshments by the hearth in winter, or on the porch in summer; for an extra warm-weather treat, you'll get to see hummingbirds dart around the flowers. Breakfast is guaranteed to please, thanks to entrées like Margaret's herb-baked eggs and her melon salad served with lime-mint dressing.

Broad Bay Inn & Gallery
MAIN STREET, P.O. BOX 607, WALDOBORO, MAINE 04572

Tel: **(207) 832-6668**
Hosts: **Jim and Libby Hopkins**
Location: **80 mi. N of Portland**
No. of Rooms: **5**
Max. No. Sharing Bath: **4**
Double/sb: **$40–$70**
Single/sb: **$35–$60**
Open: **All year**

Breakfast: **Full**
Credit Cards: **MC, VISA**
Pets: **No**
Children: **Welcome, over 12**
Smoking: **Restricted**
Social Drinking: **Permitted**
Foreign Languages: **French**

The inn, set in a charming midcoast village, is a classic Colonial, circa 1830, with light, airy, handsomely decorated rooms. Some guest rooms have canopy beds, and all have Victorian furnishings. There's a large deck on which to sip afternoon tea or sherry, and the Hopkins' garden is lovely enough to be included in local Garden Club tours. This is a convenient base from which to enjoy the quaint fishing villages, the lighthouse, and the Audubon Sanctuary. Guests can swim at Damariscotta Lake, and morning or evening sailboat cruises are easily arranged. A sumptuous breakfast often includes crêpes and herbed cheese omelets. Jim and Libby are theater buffs and retired commercial artists; their inn doubles as a gallery that showcases watercolors by local painters.

Tide Watch Inn
P.O. BOX 94, PINE STREET, WALDOBORO, MAINE 04572

Tel: **(207) 832-4987**	Single/pb: **$50**
Best Time to Call: **Anytime**	Double/sb: **$50**
Hosts: **Mel and Cathy Hanson**	Single/sb: **$40**
Location: **62 mi. N of Portland; 1⁷⁄₁₆**	Open: **All year**
mi. from Rte. 1	Breakfast: **Full**
No. of Rooms: **3**	Pets: **No**
No. of Private Baths: **1**	Children: **Welcome**
Max. No. Sharing Bath: **4**	Smoking: **Permitted**
Double/pb: **$60**	Social Drinking: **Permitted**

Built in 1850, this twin Colonial home is located on the shore of the Medomac River. The first five-masted schooners were crafted right by the inn. You are welcome to bring your boat or canoe, or just watch the local fishermen sail with the tide. Cathy's forte is keeping the inn shipshape, and guests comment on the comfortable ambience she's created. Mel's talent as a retired chef is evident in the ambitious and delicious breakfasts that might include asparagus cordon bleu.

Terra Field Bed & Breakfast ◎
BRANN ROAD BOX 1950, WEST LEVANT, MAINE 04456

Tel: **(207) 884-8805**	Open: **All year**
Hosts: **William and Carol Terra**	Reduced Rates: **15% weekly**
Location: **12 mi. NW of Bangor**	Breakfast: **Full**
No. of Rooms: **3**	Pets: **Yes**
Max. No. Sharing Bath: **4**	Children: **Welcome**
Double/pb: **$65**	Smoking: **Permitted**
Single/pb: **$55**	Social Drinking: **Permitted**
Double/sb: **$40–$55**	Airport/Station Pickup: **Yes**
Single/sb: **$35–$50**	
Guest Cottage: **$65 sleeps 2, $10**	
each additional guest	

Talk about happy landings! Terra Field, a 102-acre hay farm near Bangor, has its own sod runway suitable for single-engine and small

twin-engine planes. Bill constructed his elegant contemporary home with wood and fieldstone from the premises. You're welcome to wander in the fields, swim or canoe in the large pond, hike along wooded trails, or just take in the sights from the sunny deck. For breakfast, the specialty is eggs Penobscot, made with local fiddlehead ferns.

The Cape Neddick House ✪
1300 ROUTE 1, P.O. BOX 70, CAPE NEDDICK (YORK), MAINE 03902

Tel: **(207) 363-2500**
Hosts: **The Goodwin family**
Location: **12 mi. N of Portsmouth,
N.H.**
No. of Rooms: **6**
Max. No. Sharing Bath: **4**
Double/sb: **$55–$70**

Single/sb: **$50–$65**
Open: **All year**
Reduced Rates: **Weekly**
Breakfast: **Full**
Pets: **No**
Children: **Welcome, over 5**
Social Drinking: **Permitted**

The Goodwins inherited this late-19th-century farmhouse from a relative. While cleaning up the place for resale, they fell in love with it and decided to move in. The bedrooms are furnished with antique pieces, handmade quilts, and family keepsakes. If you want a souvenir or two, there's a craft shop on the premises. Whatever your interest, Cape Neddick has something to tempt you, from swimming, biking, and cross-country skiing to browsing in numerous local boutiques, antique shops, and factory outlets. Dianne is so proud of her cooking that she prints up recipe cards; cinnamon popovers, strawberry scones, and ham apple biscuits are a few of her specialties.

The Wild Rose of York B&B
78 LONG SANDS ROAD, YORK, MAINE 03909

Tel: **(207) 363-2532**	Open: **All year**
Best Time to Call: **6–10 PM**	Reduced Rates: **Oct. 16–May 31**
Hosts: **Fran and Frank Sullivan**	Breakfast: **Full**
No. of Rooms: **3**	Pets: **No**
No. of Private Baths: **3**	Children: **Welcome**
Double/pb: **$60**	Smoking: **No**
Single/pb: **$50**	Social Drinking: **Permitted**
Suites: **$80 for 3**	

This handsome house, built in 1814, sits high on a hill within easy range of the ocean breezes. The bedrooms are cozy, with antique beds, patchwork quilts, fireplaces, and Fran's special artistic touches. Breakfast is special and may feature peach pancakes or nut waffles. In summer, an old-fashioned trolley will take you to the beach. Deep-sea fishing, golf, hiking, shops, galleries, and factory outlets are nearby diversions. In winter, sledding, skating, and cross-country skiing are all fun. An art gallery is literally on the drawing board for this B&B.

Canterbury House
432 YORK STREET, P.O. BOX 881, YORK HARBOR, MAINE 03911

Tel: **(207) 363-3505**	Breakfast: **Full, Continental**
Best Time to Call: **Early mornings**	Other Meals: **Available**
Hosts: **James T. Pappas and Jim S. Hager**	Credit Cards: **MC, VISA**
	Pets: **No**
Location: **50 mi. N of Boston**	Children: **Welcome, over 12**
No. of Rooms: **7**	Smoking: **Restricted**
No. of Private Baths: **2**	Social Drinking: **Permitted**
Max. No. Sharing Bath: **4**	Minimum Stay: **2 nights in season**
Double/pb: **$75**	Airport/Station Pickup: **Yes**
Double/sb: **$59–$69**	Foreign Languages: **French, Greek, German**
Open: **All year**	
Reduced Rates: **7th night free**	

A lovely white Victorian overlooking unspoiled York Harbor, Canterbury House is within walking distance from the beach and other local attractions. Guests enjoy large hotel amenities while being pampered in a homey atmosphere. A scrumptious breakfast, served on fine Royal Albert china in either the dining room or, weather permitting, the scenic front porch, features hot muffins fresh from your hosts' own bakery.

MARYLAND

Oakland •

Smithsburg • Cascade
Hagerstown • • Taneytown
Sharpsburg • • Funkstown • Westminster
Frederick • Lutherville • • Elkton
Stevenson • • • North East
Ellicott City • • Baltimore
Poolesville • • Chestertown
Olney • Burtonsville
• Annapolis
Bethesda • • • St. Michaels
Chevy Chase Harwood

• Vienna

Scotland •

The Traveller in Maryland, Inc. ✪
P.O. BOX 2277, ANNAPOLIS, MARYLAND 21404-2277

Tel: **(410) 269-6232**
Best Time to Call: **9 AM–5 PM**
Coordinator: **Greg Page**
States/Regions Covered: **Annapolis, Baltimore, Central Maryland, Eastern and Southern shore, Western Maryland, London, England, United Kingdom**

Descriptive Directory: **$5**
Rates (Single/Double):
  Modest: **$55 / $60**
  Average: **$60 / $70**
  Luxury: **$80 / $100**
Credit Cards: **AMEX, MC, VISA**

Maryland is the home of Annapolis, site of the United States Naval Academy; Baltimore, home to the restored Inner Harbor and locale of historic Fort McHenry of "Star-Spangled Banner" fame; and Chesapeake Bay, known for its excellent harbors and fabulous fishing. Greg's carefully selected hosts are anxious to show off their expertise in helping you discover all of those special places that will make your visit memorable.

College House Suites ✪

ONE COLLEGE AVENUE, ANNAPOLIS, MARYLAND 21401

Tel: **(410) 263-6124**	Credit Cards: **MC, VISA**
Best Time to Call: **10 AM–4 PM**	Pets: **No**
Hosts: **Jo Anne and Don Wolfrey**	Children: **No**
Suites: **$130–$155**	Smoking: **No**
Open: **All year**	Social Drinking: **Permitted**
Breakfast: **Continental**	Minimum Stay: **2 nights**

This brick town house is nestled between the U.S. Naval Academy and St. John's College. The Annapolitan suite has a fireplace, Laura Ashley decor, and a private entrance through the ivy-covered courtyard. The Colonial suite has superb oriental rugs, antiques, and views of the Academy. The hosts pay close attention to details such as fresh flowers, fruit baskets, and chocolates. College House Suites is a short walk to the city dock, Paca House and Gardens, fine restaurants, fascinating shops and boutiques, art and antique galleries, museums, historic buildings, churches, and theater. A "breakfast-out" option is available.

Mulberry House

111 WEST MULBERRY STREET, BALTIMORE, MARYLAND 21201

Tel: **(410) 576-0111**	Breakfast: **Full**
Hosts: **Charlotte and Curt Jeschke**	Pets: **No**
No. of Rooms: **4**	Children: **Welcome, over 16**
Max. No. Sharing Bath: **4**	Smoking: **No**
Double/sb: **$65**	Social Drinking: **Permitted**
Open: **All year**	Foreign Languages: **German**

Mulberry House, in downtown Baltimore, was built circa 1830 as a Federal-period town house. Over the years a fourth floor and a courtyard were added, and a painstaking restoration has now taken place. The owners have added special touches, such as leaded glass in first-floor transoms, fan windows, and needlepoint cushions from 19th-century wallpaper designs. Guests may choose from the Victorian, Far East, Federal, and Pineapple rooms, all professionally decorated. Guests are treated like old friends, and are welcome to relax in the sitting room with its grand piano, sofa, and fireplace. A sumptuous breakfast is served at an 18th-century banquet table each morning. The house is within walking distance of many shops, museums, restaurants, historic sights, and the waterfront area.

The Winslow Home ✪
8217 CARAWAY STREET, CABIN JOHN, BETHESDA, MARYLAND 20818

Tel: (301) 229-4654	Open: All year
Best Time to Call: After 5 PM	Reduced Rates: Seniors, families
Host: Jane Winslow	Breakfast: Full
Location: 7 mi. W of Washington, D.C.	Pets: Welcome
No. of Rooms: 2	Children: Welcome
Max. No. Sharing Bath: 4	Smoking: No
Double/sb: $40	Social Drinking: No
Single/sb: $30	Airport/Station Pickup: Yes

You may enjoy the best of two worlds while staying at Jane's. This comfortable home is located in a lovely residential section of Bethesda, just 20 minutes from downtown Washington, D.C. Imagine touring the capital with some extra pocket money saved on high hotel costs. You are welcome to use the kitchen, laundry facilities, and piano. Georgetown, George Washington, and American universities are close by. There's a $5 surcharge for one-night stays.

The Taylors' B&B ✪
P.O. BOX 238, BURTONSVILLE, MARYLAND 20866-0238

Tel: (301) 236-4318	Open: All year
Best Time to Call: 9–11 AM; 7–9 PM	Breakfast: Continental
Hosts: Ruth and Fred Taylor	Pets: No
Location: 30 min. from Washington, D.C., and the Inner Harbor	Children: No
No. of Rooms: 1	Smoking: No
No. of Private Baths: 1	Social Drinking: Permitted
Double/pb: $60	Foreign Languages: French

This gracious two-story Colonial home offers a breath of fresh country air just 45 minutes from Washington, D.C., and Baltimore's Inner Harbor district. Guests can enjoy the grand piano, the extensive collection of books in the library, and Ruth's paintings. In warm weather, cool drinks are served in the gazebo; in winter, guests gather by the fireplace in the family room. Both of your hosts are retired. Ruth likes to read, sew, paint, and cook; Fred enjoys reading, writing, history, and music. They've traveled extensively and know how to make guests feel welcome. Tennis courts, horseback riding, and nature trails are nearby.

Bluebird on the Mountain ○

14700 EYLER AVENUE, CASCADE, MARYLAND 21719

Tel: **(301) 241-4161**
Best Time to Call: **9 AM–7 PM**
Host: **Edie Smith-Eley**
Location: **65 mi. N of Washington,**
  D.C.
No. of Rooms: **4**
No. of Private Baths: **4**
Suites: **$85–$105**
Open: **All year**
Reduced Rates: **10% seniors; $10 less**
  Mon.–Thurs.

Breakfast: **Continental**
Wheelchair Accessible: **Yes**
Credit Cards: **MC, VISA**
Pets: **No**
Children: **Welcome, over 12**
Smoking: **Permitted in common rooms**
  and on porches
Social Drinking: **Permitted**

Lovingly restored to its former elegance, this 1890 Georgian Colonial mansion has four separate guest suites. Your host is an award-winning nature photographer; her work—and that of her friends—is displayed throughout the house. Once a fashionable resort area, Blue Ridge Summit remains an appealing hideaway year-round. Depending on the season, you can ski, golf, or take foliage tours. You can plan your itinerary over such breakfast fare as apple dumplings, cranberry nut bread, and other home-baked goodies brought right to your suite.

Radcliffe Cross ○

8046 QUAKER NECK ROAD, ROUTE 289, CHESTERTOWN,
MARYLAND 21620

Tel: **(410) 778-5540**
Hosts: **Dan and Marge Brook**
No. of Rooms: **2**
No. of Private Baths: **2**
Double/pb: **$70–$75**
Open: **All year**

Breakfast: **Full**
Pets: **No**
Children: **Welcome, infants and over**
  10
Smoking: **No**
Social Drinking: **Permitted**

This pre-Revolutionary white brick Colonial, situated on 28 acres, is appropriately furnished with Early American antiques. A unique hanging spiral staircase rises from the center hall to the third floor. Each room boasts its own fireplace. Guests rave about Marge's puff pastries, muffins, and coffee cakes. Coffee, tea, and soft drinks are always available. Reserve well in advance for the popular Chestertown Tea Party Festival in May, or the Candlelight Walking Tour of Historic Chestertown in September.

Chevy Chase Bed & Breakfast
6815 CONNECTICUT AVENUE, CHEVY CHASE, MARYLAND 20815

Tel: **(301) 656-5867**
Best Time to Call: **Anytime**
Host: **S. C. Gotbaum**
Location: **1 mi. N of Washington**
No. of Rooms: **2**
No. of Private Baths: **2**
Double/pb: **$55–$65**
Single/pb: **$50–$55**

Single/sb: **$45**
Open: **All year**
Reduced Rates: **Families**
Breakfast: **Continental**
Pets: **No**
Children: **Welcome**
Smoking: **Permitted**
Social Drinking: **Permitted**

Enjoy the convenience of being close to the transportation and sights of Washington, D.C., while staying at a relaxing country-style house just outside the city. Rooms have beamed ceilings and are filled with rare tapestries, oriental rugs, baskets, copperware, and native crafts from Mexico to the Mideast. Your host is a sociologist with a private consulting business. For breakfast she offers homemade muffins, jams, pancakes, French toast, and a special blend of Louisiana coffee. When you want to take a break from touring, a quiet backyard and garden will relax you. Tennis courts and a swimming pool are nearby.

The Garden Cottage at Sinking Springs Herb Farm ✪
234 BLAIR SHORE ROAD, ELKTON, MARYLAND 21921

Tel: **(410) 398-5566**
Best Time to Call: **8 AM–8 PM**
Hosts: **Ann and Bill Stubbs**
Location: **4½ mi. from Rte. 40**
No. of Rooms: **1**
No. of Private Baths: **1**
Guest Cottage: **$85; sleeps 3**
Open: **All year**
Reduced Rates: **5% seniors**

Breakfast: **Full**
Credit Cards: **MC, VISA**
Other Meals: **Available**
Pets: **Sometimes**
Children: **Welcome**
Smoking: **No**
Social Drinking: **Permitted**
Airport/Station Pickup: **Yes**

Guests frequently comment on the peaceful beauty of this 128-acre historical farm. The garden cottage has a sitting room and fireplace adjoining the bedroom. Breakfast features coffee ground from organically grown beans, herbal teas, homemade buns, fruit, and juice. A full country breakfast prepared with unprocessed food fresh from the farm is available at no extra charge. Lectures on herbs and craft classes are available, and a gift shop is on the premises. Longwood Gardens and the famed Winterthur Museum are close by. Historic Chesapeake City is five minutes away.

Hayland Farm
5000 SHEPPARD LANE, ELLICOTT CITY, MARYLAND 21043

Tel: **(410) 531-5593**	Double/sb: **$40**
Host: **Dorothy Mobley**	Single/sb: **$25**
Location: **Bet. Baltimore and D.C.**	Open: **All year**
No. of Rooms: **3**	Breakfast: **Full**
No. of Private Baths: **1**	Pets: **No**
Max. No. Sharing Bath: **4**	Children: **No**
Double/pb: **$50**	Smoking: **No**
Single/pb: **$40**	Social Drinking: **Permitted**

When you breathe the country-fresh air, it may surprise you that Baltimore and Washington, D.C., are only a short drive away. At Hayland Farm you will find gracious living in a large manor house furnished in a handsome, yet comfortable, style. Dorothy is retired and has traveled extensively. She enjoys sharing conversation with her guests. In warm weather, the 20- by 50-foot swimming pool is a joy.

Middle Plantation Inn ✪
9549 LIBERTY ROAD, FREDERICK, MARYLAND 21701

Tel: **(301) 898-7128**	Open: **All year**
Best Time to Call: **6–10 PM**	Breakfast: **Continental**
Mon.–Fri.; Weekends anytime	Credit Cards: **MC, VISA**
Hosts: **Shirley and Dwight Mullican**	Pets: **No**
Location: **5 mi. E of Frederick**	Children: **Welcome, over 15**
No. of Rooms: **4**	Smoking: **No**
No. of Private Baths: **4**	Social Drinking: **Permitted**
Double/pb: **$85–$95**	

Dwight and Shirley have furnished their handsome stone and log home with antiques collected on their travels. Their rustic B&B will appeal to Civil War buffs, since Gettysburg, Pennsylvania, Sharpsburg, Maryland, and Harpers Ferry, West Virginia, are all 40 minutes away by car. Closer to home, Frederick's 33-block historic district boasts a fascinating mix of museums, galleries, antique shops, and eateries. And for more antiquing, guests should head to nearby New Market.

Edmar Manor ✪
SIX SOUTH HIGH STREET, FUNKSTOWN, MARYLAND 21734

Tel: **(301) 416-7270**	No. of Rooms: **4**
Best Time to Call: **10 AM–4 PM**	No. of Private Baths: **2**
Hosts: **Ed and Marina Gossart**	Max. No. Sharing Bath: **4**
Location: **70 mi. NW of Washington,**	Double/pb: **$70**
D.C.	Double/sb: **$60**

Single/sb: **$50**
Open: **All year**
Reduced Rates: **Weddings and family
  reunions**
Breakfast: **Full**

Credit Cards: **MC, VISA**
Pets: **No**
Children: **By special arrangement**
Smoking: **No**
Social Drinking: **Permitted**

On a quiet street in historic Funkstown, Edmar Manor (built in 1790) offers the elegance and charm of a bygone era. Enjoy a refreshing champagne punch on the veranda in summer, or fragrant mulled cider before one of the seven fireplaces in winter; drinks are paired with culinary delights offered by the mistress of the manor. Enchanting rooms are decorated with an array of laces, and four-poster and canopy beds. The town offers many historic homes, some housing antique and craft shops. Nearby attractions include Antietam Battlefield and Harpers Ferry, West Virginia. Edmar Manor is only minutes away from Black Rock and Beaver Creek golf courses, Whitetail ski resort, as well as theaters, museums, and shopping outlets.

Beaver Creek House Bed and Breakfast ✪
20432 BEAVER CREEK ROAD, HAGERSTOWN, MARYLAND 21740

Tel: **(301) 797-4764**
Best Time to Call: **Anytime**
Hosts: **Don and Shirley Day**
Location: **4 mi. E of Hagerstown**
No. of Rooms: **5**
No. of Private Baths: **3**
Max. No. Sharing Bath: **4**
Double/pb: **$85**
Single/pb: **$75**
Double/sb: **$85**

Single/sb: **$75**
Open: **All year**
Reduced Rates: **$10 less Mon.–Thurs.**
Breakfast: **Full**
Credit Cards: **MC, VISA**
Pets: **No**
Children: **Welcome, over 12**
Smoking: **No**
Social Drinking: **Permitted**
Airport/Station Pickup: **Yes**

This turn-of-the-century country home enjoys a wonderful view of South Mountain. Start your day with a bountiful country breakfast served on the wraparound screened porch. Then it's off to South Mountain for a hike along the Appalachian Trail. Or perhaps you'd rather bicycle along the scenic country roads. Civil War buffs will want to visit nearby historic parks like Antietam Battlefield and Harpers Ferry, while duffers can choose between two professional courses. Whatever your pleasure, save time to explore the beautifully maintained B&B grounds, with their gardens, fish pond, and patio.

Lewrene Farm B&B ✪
9738 DOWNSVILLE PIKE, HAGERSTOWN, MARYLAND 21740

Tel: **(301) 582-1735**
Hosts: **Lewis and Irene Lehman**

Location: **3½ mi. from I-70 and I-81**
No. of Rooms: **6**

No. of Private Baths: **3**
Max. No. Sharing Bath: **4**
Double/pb: **$65–$78**
Double/sb: **$45–$55**
Suites: **$75**
Open: **All year**

Breakfast: **Full**
Children: **Welcome**
Smoking: **No**
Social Drinking: **No**
Foreign Languages: **Spanish**

Lewis and Irene will help you discover the peaceful beauty of their 125-acre farm located in a historic area near the Antietam Battlefield. Guests are treated like old friends and are welcome to lounge in front of the fireplace or to play the piano in the Colonial-style living room. You're invited to enjoy snacks and a video in the evening. Harpers Ferry, Fort Frederick, the C&O Canal, and Gettysburg are nearby. Irene sells antiques and collectibles on the premises.

Oakwood

4566 SOLOMONS ISLAND ROAD, P.O. BOX 99, HARWOOD, MARYLAND 20776

Tel: **(301) 261-5338**
Hosts: **Dennis and Joan Brezina**
Location: **10 mi. S of Annapolis**
No. of Rooms: **2**
Max. No. Sharing Bath: **4**
Double/sb: **$65**
Single/sb: **$60**

Open: **Mar. 1–Nov. 30**
Breakfast: **Full**
Pets: **No**
Children: **Welcome, over 12**
Smoking: **Permitted**
Social Drinking: **Permitted**

This elegant antebellum manor house, featured on Maryland House Tours, has six fireplaces, 11-foot ceilings, and handmade rugs. Guests are welcome to relax on the veranda or stroll in the terraced gardens. Your hosts serve an English-style breakfast in the open-hearthed kitchen. They are happy to advise on day trips to Washington, D.C., or nearby Chesapeake Bay and Annapolis.

Twin Gates Bed and Breakfast Inn ✪

308 MORRIS AVENUE, LUTHERVILLE, MARYLAND 21093

Tel: **(800) 635-0370**
Best Time to Call: **Anytime**
Hosts: **Gwen and Bob Vaughan**
Location: **3 mi. N of Baltimore**
No. of Rooms: **5**
No. of Private Baths: **5**
Double/pb: **$85–$95**

Open: **All year**
Breakfast: **Full**
Credit Cards: **AMEX, MC, VISA**
Pets: **No**
Children: **Welcome, over 12**
Smoking: **No**
Social Drinking: **Permitted**

Soft music and fresh flowers are the order of the day at this stately mansion located in a serene area on the northern outskirts of Baltimore. In the richly appointed guest rooms, queen-size beds, ceiling fans, and air-conditioning ensure a peaceful night's sleep. Ask your hosts to arrange free tours of local wineries and historic mansions and to direct you to some of the area's best seafood restaurants. The expressway will whisk you to Baltimore's famous Inner Harbor and exciting museums and galleries. After a day's activity, join Bob and Gwen for some refreshments. Then relax by the living room fireplace with a book from the library and let the world pass by.

The Mill House B&B ✪
102 MILL LANE, NORTH EAST, MARYLAND 21901

Tel: **(410) 287-3532**	Single/sb: **$50–$60**
Best Time to Call: **Before 9 AM; after**	Open: **All year**
4 PM	Breakfast: **Full**
Hosts: **Lucia and Nick Demond**	Credit Cards: **MC, VISA**
Location: **40 mi. NE of Baltimore**	Pets: **No**
No. of Rooms: **2**	Children: **Welcome, over 12**
Max. No. Sharing Bath: **4**	Smoking: **No**
Double/sb: **$55–$65**	Social Drinking: **Permitted**

A genuine mill house that dates to the early 18th century, this B&B is furnished entirely in antiques. You'll see picturesque mill ruins and wildflowers on the grounds, but you won't see the parlor's original Queen Anne paneling; that was purchased by Henry Francis Du Pont and installed in his Winterthur estate bedroom. The Winterthur Museum and the Brandywine River Museum are less than an hour's drive away, as is Baltimore's Inner Harbor. Sightseers will be sustained with a full breakfast, including homemade breads fresh from the oven.

Red Run Inn ✪
ROUTE 5, BOX 5108, OAKLAND, MARYLAND 21550

Tel: **(301) 387-6606**	Open: **All year**
Host: **Ruth Umbel**	Breakfast: **Continental**
Location: **180 mi. W of Baltimore**	Credit Cards: **AMEX, MC, VISA**
No. of Rooms: **5**	Pets: **No**
No. of Private Baths: **5**	Children: **Welcome**
Double/pb: **$65–$85**	Smoking: **Permitted**
Single/pb: **$35**	Social Drinking: **Permitted**
Suites: **$100**	Airport/Station Pickup: **Yes**

Nestled in a wooded setting on 18 acres, Red Run overlooks the expansive blue waters of Deep Creek Lake. The grounds and structures have been carefully planned to preserve the unspoiled atmosphere. The property includes a swimming pool, tennis courts, horseshoe pits, dock facilities, and a cross-country ski trail.

The Thoroughbred Bed & Breakfast
16410 BATCHELLORS FOREST ROAD, OLNEY, MARYLAND 20832

Tel: **(301) 774-7649**
Best Time to Call: **8 AM–7 PM**
Host: **Helen M. Polinger**
Location: **12 mi. N of Washington, D.C.**
No. of Rooms: **13**
No. of Private Baths: **7**
Max. No. Sharing Bath: **4**
Double/pb: **$65–$115**
Double/sb: **$75–$85**

Open: **All year**
Breakfast: **Full**
Credit Cards: **MC, VISA ($5 surcharge)**
Pets: **No**
Children: **Welcome, over 12**
Smoking: **No**
Social Drinking: **Permitted**

This beautiful estate is surrounded by 175 acres of rolling hills, fields, and pastures. Helen breeds some of the finest racehorses in the country. You may choose to stay in either her modern country-style home, the farmhouse annex, or the carriage house. Amenities include a swimming pool, hot tub, and champion-size pool table. Two rooms have their own fireplaces and whirlpool tubs. It's only 12 miles to the attractions of Washington, D.C., easily reached by Metrorail, only 6 miles away.

Rocker Inn ✪
17924 ELGIN ROAD, POOLESVILLE, MARYLAND 20837

Tel: **(301) 972-8543**
Best Time to Call: **After 5:30 PM**
Hosts: **Bob and Nancy Hopkinson**
Location: **25 mi. NW of Washington, D.C.**
No. of Rooms: **1**
No. of Private Baths: **1**
Double/pb: **$45**

Single/pb: **$40**
Open: **All year**
Breakfast: **Continental**
Pets: **Sometimes**
Children: **Welcome**
Smoking: **No**
Social Drinking: **Permitted**

Built in 1915 as a local telephone house, Rocker Inn takes its name from the rocking chairs and two swings that fill its 48-foot front porch. Inside, the home is decorated in an informal country mode. Walking tours of Poolesville and Frederick, along with a hike on the C&O Canal, are minutes away. For more ambitious excursions, Harpers Ferry, Gettysburg Battlefield, and historic Leesburg are within an hour's drive.

Parsonage Inn ✪
210 NORTH TALBOT STREET, ST. MICHAELS, MARYLAND 21663

Tel: **(800) 234-5519**
Hosts: **David and Gina Hawkins**

Location: **11 mi. off Rte. 50**
No. of Rooms: **8**

No. of Private Baths: **8**
Double/pb: **$92–$108**
Open: **All year**
Reduced Rates: **10% seniors; $10 less
  midweek, off-season**
Breakfast: **Full**
Wheelchair Accessible: **Yes**

Credit Cards: **MC, VISA**
Pets: **No**
Children: **Welcome**
Smoking: **Permitted**
Social Drinking: **Permitted**

Built in the 1880s with bricks fired in the St. Michaels brickyard, the Parsonage Inn was completely restored in 1985. This striking Victorian B&B is part of the town's historic district, and it's an easy stroll to shops, restaurants, and the Chesapeake Bay Maritime Museum. More ambitious guests may borrow the inn's 12-speed bicycles and venture farther afield.

St. Michael's Manor B&B ✪
ST. MICHAEL'S MANOR, SCOTLAND, MARYLAND 20687

Tel: **(301) 872-4025**
Hosts: **Joe and Nancy Dick**
Location: **9 mi. S of St. Marys City**
No. of Rooms: **4**
Max. No. Sharing Bath: **4**
Double/sb: **$60**
Open: **All year**

Reduced Rates: **Nov. 1–Apr. 1**
Breakfast: **Full**
Pets: **No**
Children: **By arrangement**
Smoking: **Downstairs**
Social Drinking: **Permitted**

St. Michael's Manor was built in 1805 on land patented to Leonard Calvert during the seventeenth century. Today, the white stucco manor home on picturesque Long Neck Creek is included in the state's Pilgrimage Tour. The beautiful handcrafted woodwork has been preserved and is complemented by antiques and handcrafts. Your hosts offer you the use of a canoe, paddleboat, bikes, and swimming pool. Estate wine tasting is also available. The manor house is near Point Lookout State Park, the Chesapeake Bay, and historic St. Marys City.

Jacob Rohrbach Inn ✪
P.O. BOX 607, SHARPSBURG, MARYLAND 21782

Tel: **(301) 432-5079**
Best Time to Call: **9 AM–9 PM**
Host: **Denise Yeager**
Location: **70 mi. NW of Washington**
No. of Rooms: **3**
No. of Private Baths: **3**
Double/pb: **$75**
Single/pb: **$65**

Open: **All year**
Reduced Rates: **10% seniors**
Breakfast: **Full**
Pets: **No**
Children: **Welcome**
Smoking: **No**
Social Drinking: **Permitted**

This great brick and stone house survived the Battle of Antietam with relatively minor damage only to have its owner murdered by Confederate raiders in 1864. Today, the Jacob Rohrbach Inn looks much as it did during the Civil War, permitting patrons a unique view into the past. Antietam Battlefield surrounds the inn and Harpers Ferry Historical Park is just twenty minutes away. Tour the battlefield, bicycle the C&O Canal, visit quaint country shops, or just curl up with a book in front of a warm fire. White-water rafting, horseback riding, and skiing are nearby; if you'd rather travel by car, a leisurely one-hour trip leads through the Shenandoah Valley to the Skyline Drive.

Blue Bear Bed & Breakfast ✪

ROUTE 2, BOX 378, HOLIDAY DRIVE, SMITHSBURG, MARYLAND 21783

Tel: **(301) 824-2292**
Best Time to Call: **After 4 PM**
Host: **Ellen Panchula**
Location: **6 mi. from I-70, Exit 35**
No. of Rooms: **2**
Max. No. Sharing Bath: **4**
Double/sb: **$45**
Single/sb: **$40**

Open: **July 1–Aug. 31; weekends Apr.–June, Sept.–Dec.**
Breakfast: **Continental**
Pets: **No**
Children: **Welcome, over 12**
Smoking: **No**
Social Drinking: **Permitted**

Ellen is a full-time schoolteacher from September through June, so she can entertain guests during the week only in July and August; during the school year it's strictly weekends only. Her home is decorated in an informal country mode, with several antiques complementing the decor. Smithsburg is located in apple and peach country. It is convenient to the Antietam Battlefield in Sharpsburg, and to many fine restaurants in Hagerstown. Homemade breads, coffee cakes, quiche, fresh fruit, and beverages constitute the breakfast menu. Snacks, dessert, and wine and cheese are generously offered in the evenings.

Gramercy Bed & Breakfast ✪
1400 GREENSPRING VALLEY ROAD, BOX 119, STEVENSON, MARYLAND 21153

Tel: **(410) 486-2405**	Open: **All year**
Host: **Anne Pomykala**	Breakfast: **Full**
Location: **10 mi. NW of Baltimore**	Credit Cards: **MC, VISA**
No. of Rooms: **3**	Pets: **No**
No. of Private Baths: **3**	Children: **Welcome**
Double/pb: **$90–$110**	Smoking: **Permitted**
Suites: **$100–$135**	Social Drinking: **Permitted**

Gramercy Bed & Breakfast, a historic mansion built by Alexander Cassatt, brother of the artist Mary Cassatt, is located on 45 acres in the Greenpoint Valley of Baltimore County. Choose a working fireplace or Jacuzzi in your bedroom. Enjoy the pool, tennis courts, flower and herb gardens, woodland trails and stream, and paulownia wood sculptures. Anne's house collie enjoys hiking with guests and sometimes flushes deer, fox, or rabbit. While you're here, you can learn about fresh herbs and take some home.

Null's Bed & Breakfast ✪
4910 BAPTIST ROAD, TANEYTOWN, MARYLAND 21787

Tel: **(410) 756-6112**	Double/sb: **$50**
Hosts: **Francis and Betty Null**	Single/sb: **$45**
Location: **8 mi. S of Gettysburg, Penn.**	Open: **All year**
No. of Rooms: **2**	Breakfast: **Full**
No. of Private Baths: **1**	Pets: **No**
Max. No. Sharing Bath: **4**	Children: **Welcome**
Double/pb: **$55**	Smoking: **Permitted**
Single/pb: **$50**	Social Drinking: **Permitted**

Francis Null grew up in this blue farmhouse, which has always been in his family. While it is no longer a working farm, the property's 22 acres invite exploration. Ask your hosts about the furniture; some pieces are genuine antiques, others are artful reproductions Francis created in his woodworking shop. Taneytown is about nine miles from Gettysburg, and Baltimore, Washington, D.C., and Amish country are all accessible by car. Homemade bread and jam accompany Betty's full breakfasts.

The Tavern House ☉

111 WATER STREET, P.O. BOX 98, VIENNA, MARYLAND 21869

Tel: **(410) 376-3347**
Hosts: **Harvey and Elise Altergott**
Location: **15 mi. NW of Salisbury**
No. of Rooms: **4**
Max. No. Sharing Bath: **4**
Double/sb: **$65–$75**
Single/sb: **$60–$70**
Open: **All year**

Reduced Rates: **After 1st night**
Breakfast: **Full**
Credit Cards: **MC, VISA**
Pets: **No**
Children: **Welcome, over 12**
Smoking: **Permitted**
Social Drinking: **Permitted**
Foreign Languages: **German, Spanish**

Vienna is a quiet little town on the Nanticoke River, where one can escape the stress of the 20th century. Careful restoration has brought back the simple purity of this Colonial tavern. The stark white "lime, sand, and hair" plaster accents the authentic furnishings. This is a place for those who enjoy looking at the river and marshes, watching an osprey, or taking a leisurely walk. Days begin with fruits of the season and end with complimentary cheese and wine. For the sports minded, there's tennis, boating, and flat roads for bicycling, all within easy reach. This is an excellent base for exploring the Eastern Shore, interesting small towns, and Blackwater National Wildlife Refuge.

Winchester Country Inn
430 SOUTH BISHOP STREET, WESTMINSTER, MARYLAND 21157

Tel: **(410) 876-7373**
Best Time to Call: **8 AM–7 PM**
Hosts: **Estella Williams and Alina McCarron**
Location: **35 mi. NW of Baltimore**
No. of Rooms: **5**
No. of Private Baths: **3**
Max. No. Sharing Bath: **4**
Double/pb: **$65–$75**
Single/pb: **$60–$70**
Double/sb: **$60–$70**

Single/sb: **$55–$65**
Open: **All year**
Reduced Rates: **10% seniors, business rate Sun.–Thurs. double $45, single $40**
Breakfast: **Full**
Credit Cards: **MC, VISA**
Pets: **No**
Children: **Welcome, over 6**
Smoking: **No**
Social Drinking: **Permitted**

Built in the 1760s, this inn is one of the oldest inns in Carroll County. It is furnished with period antiques that enhance the interior. It is only a quarter of a mile to the historic Carroll County Farm Museum, which is the site of special events such as the Maryland Wine Festival. It is within walking distance of the Farmers Market, where produce, flowers, and crafts may be bought. Breakfast includes farm-fresh eggs and country sausage or ham.

MASSACHUSETTS

Rockport
Essex •
Gloucester
Salem •
Greenfield
Buckland
Cambridge • Marblehead
Cummington • Ashfield
Harvard •
Boston • Swampscott
Peru •
Sudbury •
Needham • N. Scituate
Amherst
Scituate
Lenox
Ware
Norwell •
Tyringham
Great Barrington

Mendon •
Yarmouth
Eastham
Attleboro •
Plymouth • Port
Dennis • E. Orleans
Barnstable
South Dennis
Rehoboth •
Sandwich •
West Harwic
Wareham •
Harwich Por
South Dartmouth •
Centerville
Woods Hole
Falmouth
Cape Cod
Edgartown
Nantucket
Martha's Vineyard

Pineapple Hospitality, Inc. ✪
P.O. BOX F 821, NEW BEDFORD, MASSACHUSETTS 02742

Tel: **(508) 990-1696; 990-1798**
Best Time to Call: **Winter 9 AM–5 PM; Summer 9 AM–7 PM**
Coordinator: **Rob Mooz**
States/Regions Covered: **Connecticut, Maine, Massachusetts, New Hampshire, Rhode Island, Vermont**

Descriptive Directory: **$6.95**
Rates (Single/Double):
  Modest: **$50 / $60**
  Average: **$55 / $65**
  Luxury: **$75 / $145**
Credit Cards: **AMEX, MC, VISA**

The pineapple has been the symbol of rare hospitality since early Colonial days, and the host homes on Rob's roster personify this spirit. They are located in cities and in the countryside, at beach resorts and lakeside communities, in historic districts and near hundreds of schools and colleges; you are bound to find just the spot to call home. There's a $10 processing fee.

268

Bed & Breakfast Associates—Bay Colony, Ltd. ✪
P.O. BOX 57166, BABSON PARK, BOSTON, MASSACHUSETTS 02157-0166

Tel: (617) 449-5302; (800) 347-5088;
fax: (617) 449-5958
Best Time to Call: 10 AM–12:30 PM;
1:30–5 PM
Coordinators: Arline Kardasis and
Marilyn Mitchell
States/Regions Covered: Boston,
Brookline, Cambridge, Cape Cod,
Concord, Framingham, Gloucester,
Newton, North Shore, South Shore

Descriptive Directory: $6
Rates (Single/Double):
  Modest: $45–$50 / $55–$60
  Average: $55–$65 / $65–$75
  Luxury: $70–$100 / $80–$125
Credit Cards: AMEX, MC, VISA
Minimum Stay: 2 nights

A wide variety of 150 host homes, inns, and apartments is available in the city, in the country, and at the shore. They range from historic brownstones to contemporary condominiums. Many are convenient to the major colleges and universities. There's a $10 surcharge for one-night stays.

Bed & Breakfast Marblehead & North Shore
P.O. BOX 35, NEWTONVILLE, MASSACHUSETTS 02160

Tel: (617) 964-1606; (800) 832-2632
outside Massachusetts
Best Time to Call: 8:30 AM–9 PM
Mon.–Fri., 9 AM–noon Sat., 7 PM–9
PM Sun.
Coordinator: Sheryl Felleman
States/Regions Covered:
Massachusetts—Beverly, Danvers,
Gloucester, Hamilton, Manchester,
Marblehead, Middleton,
Newburyport, Peabody, Plum Island,
Rockport, Salem, Swampscott,
Topsfield; Maine; New Hampshire;
Vermont

Rates (Single/Double):
  Modest: $45–$55 / $55–$65
  Average: $55–$70 / $65–$80
  Luxury: $70–$100 / $85–$150
Credit Cards: AMEX, MC, VISA

Come home to the history and culture of New England! Stay in one of the beautiful B&B homes, small inns, or furnished apartments in historic oceanside towns on Massachusetts' North Shore. This area is known for its rich past, beautiful beaches and harbors, recreational activities, wonderful restaurants, and friendly New England hospitality. Easy access by public transportation to Boston. Selected B&Bs in fall foliage and ski areas elsewhere in New England. Daily, weekly, or monthly rates.

Bed & Breakfast in Minuteman Country
P.O. BOX 665, CAMBRIDGE, MASSACHUSETTS 02140

Tel: **(617) 576-2112; (800) 888-0178**
Coordinators: **Tally and Pamela Carruthers**
States/Regions Covered: **Arlington, Bedford, Boston, Brookline, Cambridge, Concord, Lexington, Sudbury, Waltham, Winchester**

Rates (Single/Double):
Average: **$50 / $80**
Luxury: **$60 / $100**
Credit Cards: **AMEX, MC, VISA**
Minimum Stay: **2 nights**

Tally and Pamela can place you in host homes convenient to historic Lexington and Concord, downtown Boston, or in Cambridge. Many are close to Harvard and MIT, Lahey Clinic, historic Wright Tavern, Emerson's home, Walden Pond, and the Charles River. Unusual restaurants, specialty shops, and cultural happenings abound. Just tell your host about your interests and you will be assured of excellent advice. There's a $6 surcharge for one-night stays.

B&B/Inns of New England ✪
P.O. BOX 146, MAIN STREET, ASHFIELD, MASSACHUSETTS 01330

Tel: **(800) 582-0853**
Best Time to Call: **9 AM–8 PM**
Coordinator: **Ernie Taddei**
States/Regions Covered: **Connecticut, Maine, Massachusetts, New Hampshire, Rhode Island, Vermont**

Descriptive Directory: **$2**
Rates (Single/Double):
Modest: **$35–$45**
Average: **$50–$55**
Luxury: **$80–$85**
Credit Cards: **MC, VISA**

Stay anywhere in New England, near historic sites, natural attractions, and schools and colleges. Vacation on the seacoast, in the Berkshires, or even on a 125-acre maple sugar farm. This reservation service has something for everyone; the more than 100 guest homes range from an 18th-century Colonial to a stately Georgian mansion.

Be Our Guest Bed & Breakfast, Ltd.
P.O. BOX 1333, PLYMOUTH, MASSACHUSETTS 02362

Tel: **(617) 837-9867**
Coordinators: **Diane Gillis and Mary Gill**
States/Regions Covered: **Boston, Cohasset, Duxbury, Falmouth, Hanover, Kingston, Marshfield, Plymouth, Sandwich, Scituate, Quincy**

Descriptive Directory: **$1**
Rates (Single/Double):
Modest: **$38 / $65**
Average: **$50 / $75**
Luxury: **$110**
Credit Cards: **AMEX, MC, VISA**

The homes range from historic to traditional New England style. Some are in private settings; others are surrounded by tourist activities. A few have commanding views of the waterfront. All are hosted by people who are dedicated to making certain that you enjoy your visit. Don't miss Plymouth Rock, the *Mayflower*, the Wax Museum, and winery tours. If you enjoy the sea, whale watching, deep-sea fishing, and sailing are all available.

BOSTON AREA

Bed & Breakfast Greater Boston & Cape Cod
A Division of Bed & Breakfast Marblehead & North Shore
P.O. BOX 35, NEWTONVILLE, MASSACHUSETTS 02160

Tel: (617) 964-1606; (800) 832-2632 outside Massachusetts
Best Time to Call: 8:30 AM–9 PM, Mon.–Fri., 9 AM–noon Sat., 7 PM–9 PM Sun.
Coordinator: Suzanne Ross
States/Regions Covered: Boston, Brookline, Cambridge, Chestnut Hill, Concord, Newton, Cape Cod

Rates (Single/Double):
Modest: $45–$55 / $55–$65
Average: $55–$70 / $65–$80
Luxury: $70–$100 / $85–$150
Credit Cards: AMEX, MC, VISA

Explore the city and the many tourist attractions this region offers, then escape to the beautiful beaches of Cape Cod. Whether you choose an antique Victorian, restored inn, classic Colonial, charming ocean-view apartment, cozy carriage house, or contemporary condo, you will experience the finest New England hospitality. Many accommodations close to area colleges and universities and public transportation.

Greater Boston Hospitality ✪
P.O. BOX 1142, BROOKLINE, MASSACHUSETTS 02146

Tel: (617) 277-5430
Coordinator: Kelly Simpson
States/Regions Covered: Boston, Brookline, Cambridge, Gloucester, Lexington, Marblehead, Needham, Newton, Wellesley, Winchester

Descriptive Directory: Free
Rates (Single/Double):
Modest: $35 / $45
Average: $45 / $55
Luxury: $55 / $100
Credit Cards: MC, VISA

Kelly's accommodations are convenient to many of the 75 colleges and universities in the greater Boston area. They're in inns, condos, or self-serve apartments. Many include parking, most are near public transportation. What a boon it is for people applying to school, and to parents visiting undergrads, to have a home-away-from-home nearby. There's a $10 surcharge for one-night stays.

Host Homes of Boston ✪
P.O. BOX 117, WABAN BRANCH, BOSTON, MASSACHUSETTS 02168

Tel: **(617) 244-1308; fax: (617) 244-5156**
Best Time to Call: **9 AM–noon; 1:30–4:30 PM weekdays**
Coordinator: **Marcia Whittington**
States/Regions Covered: **Boston, Brookline, Cambridge, Lexington, Marblehead, Milton, Newton, Wellesley, Westwood, Weymouth**

Descriptive Directory: **Free**
Rates (Single/Double):
   Modest: **$45–$55 / $54–$57**
   Average: **$55–$65 / $57–$68**
   Luxury: **$68–$95 / $68–$125**
Credit Cards: **AMEX, MC, VISA**
Minimum Stay: **2 nights**

Since 1982, Marcia has culled a variety of select private homes in excellent areas near major hotels and institutions, historic sites, and good public transportation. Hosts offer free parking (except downtown), hearty breakfasts, and a cordial welcome to their city of colleges, universities, museums, and cultural life. To fax your reservation request, please use the form in the directory.

Hamilton House ✪
335 PEARL STREET, CAMBRIDGE, MASSACHUSETTS 02139

Tel: **(617) 491-0274**
Host: **Charlotte Goldberg**
No. of Rooms: **3**
Max. No. Sharing Bath: **4**
Double/sb: **$50**
Single/sb: **$45**
Open: **All year**
Reduced Rates: **Weekly**

Breakfast: **Continental**
Credit Cards: **AMEX, DISC, MC, VISA**
Pets: **No**
Children: **Welcome, over 5**
Smoking: **No**
Social Drinking: **Permitted**
Airport/Station Pickup: **Yes**
Foreign Languages: **French, German**

A day at Hamilton House begins around 8 or 8:30 AM, with juice, fresh fruit, cereal, muffins, and tea and coffee. Often the conversation is so stimulating that guests linger at the table until 10 AM or later. Then it's time to go sightseeing and shopping. In the evening, guests start returning at 9:30 PM, when they're welcome to join Charlotte—a full-time hostess with a penchant for literature, languages, and complicated knitting—for a jigsaw puzzle, a lively discussion, or an account of their day.

George Fuller House
148 MAIN STREET, ESSEX, MASSACHUSETTS 01929

Tel: (508) 768-7766	Reduced Rates: **$10 less Nov. 1–May**
Best Time to Call: **10 AM–10 PM**	**31**
Hosts: **Cindy and Bob Cameron**	Breakfast: **Full**
Location: **3 mi. off Rte. 128, Exit 15**	Credit Cards: **AMEX, DISC, MC, VISA**
No. of Rooms: **6**	Pets: **No**
No. of Private Baths: **6**	Children: **Welcome, over 6**
Double/pb: **$75–$85**	Smoking: **No**
Suites: **$110**	Social Drinking: **Permitted**
Open: **All year**	Airport/Station Pickup: **Yes**

This handsome Federalist home retains much of its 19th-century paneling and woodwork; two of the guest rooms have working fireplaces. The Camerons have decorated the house with antique beds, handmade quilts, braided rugs, and caned Boston rockers. Three hundred years ago, Essex was a shipbuilding center; today, appropriately enough, Bob—a licensed captain—teaches sailing and takes guests for cruises on his 30-foot yacht. Among landlubbers, Essex's main claim to fame is its antique shops. Whether you venture out on sea or on land, you'll be fortified by Cindy's versions of breakfast classics, such as her French toast drizzled with brandied lemon butter.

Williams Guest House ✪
136 BASS AVENUE, GLOUCESTER, MASSACHUSETTS 01930

Tel: (508) 283-4931	Guest Cottage: **$450 weekly for 2**
Best Time to Call: **8 AM–9 PM**	Open: **May 1–Nov. 1**
Host: **Betty Williams**	Reduced Rates: **Off-season, before**
Location: **30 mi. N of Boston**	**June 17 and after Labor Day**
No. of Rooms: **7**	Breakfast: **Continental**
No. of Private Baths: **5**	Pets: **No**
Max. No. Sharing Bath: **4**	Children: **Welcome, in cottage**
Double/pb: **$50–$55**	Smoking: **Permitted**
Double/sb: **$45–$50**	Social Drinking: **Permitted**

Located five miles from Rockport, and one and a half miles from Rocky Neck, Gloucester is a quaint fishing village on the North Shore. Betty's Colonial Revival house borders the finest beach, Good Harbor. The guest rooms are furnished with comfort in mind. Betty will be happy to suggest many interesting things to do, such as boat tours, sport fishing, whale-watching trips, sightseeing cruises around Cape Ann, the Hammond Castle Museum, and the shops and galleries of the artist colony.

The Thistle

31 FAIRFIELD STREET, NEEDHAM, MASSACHUSETTS 02192

Tel: **(617) 444-5724**	Open: **All year**
Best Time to Call: **Anytime**	Reduced Rates: **Seniors 10%**
Hosts: **Leo and Susan Rainville**	Breakfast: **Continental**
Location: **10 mi. SW of Boston**	Pets: **No**
No. of Rooms: **2**	Children: **No**
No. of Private Baths: **1**	Smoking: **No**
Max. No. Sharing Bath: **4**	Social Drinking: **Permitted**
Double/pb: **$60**	Station Pickup: **Yes**
Single/pb: **$50**	
Double/sb: **$55**	
Single/sb: **$45**	

Relax in this peaceful setting on a tree-lined street just a few blocks off Route 128 and Interstate 95. The Thistle offers easy access to colleges, business districts, restaurants, and golf courses, not to mention the many historic tourist sites in Boston, Lexington, Concord, Quincy, and Plymouth. Ask your hosts to suggest activities; Leo enjoys woodworking and deep-sea fishing, while Susan likes sightseeing, walking, and swimming.

Rasberry Ink ✪

748 COUNTRY WAY, NORTH SCITUATE, MASSACHUSETTS 02060

Tel: **(617) 545-6629**	Single/sb: **$60**
Best Time to Call: **Evenings**	Open: **All year**
Hosts: **Frances Honkonen and Carol Hoban**	Breakfast: **Full**
	Pets: **Sometimes**
Location: **25 mi. SE of Boston**	Children: **No**
No. of Rooms: **2**	Smoking: **No**
No. of Private Baths: **1**	Social Drinking: **Permitted**
Max. No. Sharing Bath: **4**	Minimum Stay: **2 nights in season**
Double/sb: **$65**	Airport/Station Pickup: **Yes**

This 19th-century farmhouse is set in a small seaside town rich in Colonial and Victorian history. Frances and Carol have restored the house and furnished the rooms with antiques and lace. Guest quarters are located on the second floor and feature a private sitting room. Rasberry Ink is five minutes from the beach and is conveniently located on a bus line, midway between Boston and the Cape Cod Canal. In season, fresh raspberries are offered at breakfast.

1810 House Bed & Breakfast ✪

147 OLD OAKEN BUCKET ROAD, NORWELL, MASSACHUSETTS 02061

Tel: **(617) 659-2532**	Open: **All year**
Best Time to Call: **8 AM–noon**	Reduced Rates: **25% families taking 2 rooms**
Hosts: **Susanne and Harold Tuttle**	Breakfast: **Full**
Location: **20 mi. S of Boston**	Pets: **No**
No. of Rooms: **3**	Children: **Welcome, over 6**
No. of Private Baths: **1**	Smoking: **No**
Max. No. Sharing Bath: **4**	Social Drinking: **No**
Double/pb: **$55**	
Double/sb: **$50**	

The 1810 House is located in Norwell, a beautiful historic town halfway between Boston and Plymouth. The antique half-Cape boasts wide pine floors, stenciled walls, beamed ceilings, three working fireplaces, plus oriental rugs and lovely antiques. Harold is a woodworker who did extensive restoration in the house, while Susanne is a seamstress who created the custom window treatments. A tour of the area in their 1915 Model T depot hack adds to the feeling of a bygone era and is part of the fun of staying at the 1810 House.

Mooringstone for Nonsmokers ✪

12 NORWOOD AVENUE, ROCKPORT, MASSACHUSETTS 01966

Tel: **(508) 546-2479**	Reduced Rates: **Available**
Best Time to Call: **9 AM–9 PM**	Breakfast: **Continental**
Hosts: **David and Mary Knowlton**	Credit Cards: **AMEX, MC, VISA**
Location: **35 mi. N of Boston**	Pets: **No**
No. of Rooms: **3**	Children: **No**
No. of Private Baths: **3**	Smoking: **No**
Double/pb: **$72–$81**	Social Drinking: **Permitted**
Single/pb: **$72–$81**	Minimum Stay: **2 nights**
Open: **May 15–Oct. 15**	Airport/Station Pickup: **Yes**

David and Mary expanded their home in 1987 to establish this contemporary, smoke-free B&B. Each of the quiet, comfortable, ground-floor rooms has cable TV, a refrigerator, a microwave oven, and room-controlled air-conditioning and heat, while bed sizes range from twin to king. There's parking for all guests. A great base for day trips to Boston, Salem, and Newburyport, Rockport is a notable destination in its own right: Walt Disney Productions named the harbor—a great site for whale watching—one of the ten "most scenic places in the country." And Mary promises that once you eat one of her muffins, you'll come back for more.

Five o'Clock Tea at the Allen House ✪
18 ALLEN PLACE, SCITUATE, MASSACHUSETTS 02066

Tel: (617) 545-8221
Best Time to Call: **Mornings; evenings**
Hosts: **Christine and Iain Gilmour**
Location: **32 mi. SE of Boston**
No. of Rooms: **4**
No. of Private Baths: **2**
Max. No. Sharing Bath: **4**
Double/pb: **$85**
Double/sb: **$75**

Open: **All year**
Breakfast: **Full**
Pets: **No**
Children: **Welcome, over 16**
Smoking: **No**
Social Drinking: **Permitted**
Airport/Station Pickup: **Yes**
Foreign Languages: **Limited French, German, Spanish**

With views of the village center, this white gabled Victorian overlooks the yacht harbor, where Scituate's commercial fishermen unload lobster and cod. When the Gilmours came to the United States in 1976, they brought along the lovely furniture of their native Great Britain. English antiques fill the house. They also imported British rituals: high tea is a frequent celebration. For breakfast, Christine, a professional caterer, offers standards such as waffles, pancakes, and homemade breads as well as gourmet treats. Allen House is distinguished by good music and good food. Iain, an accomplished musician, cheerfully shares the large library of classical music.

Checkerberry Corner
5 CHECKERBERRY CIRCLE, SUDBURY, MASSACHUSETTS 01776

Tel: (508) 443-8660
Best Time to Call: **Evenings**
Hosts: **Stuart and Irene MacDonald**
Location: **20 mi. W of Boston**
No. of Rooms: **3**
Max. No. Sharing Bath: **4**
Double/sb: **$55–$65**
Single/sb: **$50–$55**

Open: **All year**
Reduced Rates: **10% families**
Breakfast: **Full**
Pets: **No**
Children: **Welcome**
Smoking: **No**
Social Drinking: **Permitted**

Checkerberry Corner is a classic Colonial with stained-glass entry windows, red doors, and a large porch. The rooms are tastefully decorated with traditional mahogany furnishings and comfortable Colonial accents. Beverages and snacks are always available. Stuart and Irene serve breakfast on fine china in the dining room. Homemade muffins, jams, and coffee cakes are specialties of the house. This charming Colonial is located in a historic district, close to the Lexington Minuteman Statue, Old North Bridge, the homes of Louisa May Alcott, Hawthorne, and Emerson, and Longfellow's Wayside Inn.

Marshall House ✪
11 EASTERN AVENUE, SWAMPSCOTT, MASSACHUSETTS 01907

Tel: (617) 595-6544
Hosts: Pat and Al Marshall
Location: 10 mi. N of Boston
No. of Rooms: 3
Max. No. Sharing Bath: 4
Double/sb: $60–$65
Single/sb: $50–$55
Open: All year

Reduced Rates: 10% seniors
Breakfast: Continental
Credit Cards: AMEX, MC, VISA
Pets: No
Children: Welcome, over 6
Smoking: No
Social Drinking: Permitted
Airport/Station Pickup: Yes

Marshall House, built circa 1900, is located just a short walk from the beaches of the North Shore. The many porches of this spacious home offer salty breezes and an ocean view. Inside, the rooms are decorated with country furnishings, some cherished antiques, and accents of wood and stained glass. The bedrooms have modern amenities such as color televisions and refrigerators. Guests are welcome to relax in the common room and warm up beside the wood stove. This B&B is located ten miles from Logan International Airport. Pat and Al will gladly direct you to nearby restaurants, historic seacoast villages, and popular bicycle touring routes.

Oak Shores ✪
64 FULLER AVENUE, SWAMPSCOTT, MASSACHUSETTS 01907

Tel: (617) 599-7677
Best Time to Call: 5–8 PM
Host: Marjorie McClung
Location: 13 mi. N of Boston
No. of Rooms: 2
Max. No. Sharing Bath: 4
Double/sb: $60

Single/sb: $50
Open: Apr. 1–Dec. 1
Breakfast: Continental
Pets: No
Children: Welcome, over 9
Smoking: No
Social Drinking: Permitted

This 60-year-old Dutch Colonial is located on Boston's lovely North Shore. Enjoy rooms filled with fine restored furniture, and sleep in the comfort of old brass and iron beds. Relax in the private, shady garden, on the deck, or take a two-block stroll to the beach. Swampscott was the summer White House of Calvin Coolidge. It is a convenient place to begin tours of nearby Marblehead, birthplace of the United States Navy, and Salem, famous for its witch trials. Marjorie is glad to help with travel plans, and has an ample supply of maps and brochures.

CAPE COD/MARTHA'S VINEYARD

Bed & Breakfast Cape Cod

P.O. BOX 341, WEST HYANNISPORT, MASSACHUSETTS 02672

Tel: **(508) 775-2772**; fax: **(508) 775-2884**
Best Time to Call: **8:30 AM–7:30 PM**
Coordinator: **Clark Diehl**
States/Regions Covered: **Cape Cod, Martha's Vineyard, Nantucket; Boston Area—Cape Ann, Gloucester, Cohasset, Marshfield, Scituate**

Descriptive Directory: **Free**
Rates (Single/Double):
  Modest: **$38 / $50**
  Average: **$55 / $65**
  Luxury: **$85 / $185**
Credit Cards: **AMEX, DISC, MC, VISA**
Minimum Stay: **2 nights in season**

It's a little over an hour's drive from Boston to the charm, history, and relaxation of Cape Cod and the islands. Choose from more than eighty of Clark's inspected and approved, restored sea captains' houses, host homes, or small inns. Enjoy the warm-water beaches on Nantucket Sound and golf, biking, and other recreational activities. Don't miss the discount shopping. Your hosts can direct you to things to do, including whale watches and antiques. Seafood restaurants and pleasant evening entertainment at a theater are at your disposal. There is a $5 surcharge for one-night stays. Write, call, or fax for the free descriptive directory.

House Guests—Cape Cod and the Islands ✪

BOX 1881, ORLEANS, MASSACHUSETTS 02653

Tel: **(508) 896-7053**; **(800) 666-HOST**
Best Time to Call: **8 AM–7 PM**
Coordinator: **Richard Griffin**
States/Regions Covered: **Cape Cod, Martha's Vineyard, Nantucket**
Descriptive Directory: **$3.95**

Rates (Single/Double):
  Modest: **$40 / $48–$58**
  Average: **$50–$60 / $59–$75**
  Luxury: **$60–$150 / $76–$187**
Credit Cards: **AMEX, MC, VISA**
Minimum Stay: **2 nights Memorial Day weekend through Columbus Day**

Richard's accommodations range from a simple single bedroom with shared bath to historic homes furnished with antiques. Some are on the ocean; others are in wooded country areas. There are even a few self-contained guest cottages on private estates. A $15 booking fee is waived for members of Richard's service, who pay $25 annual dues.

Orleans Bed & Breakfast Associates ✪

P.O. BOX 1312, ORLEANS, MASSACHUSETTS 02653

Tel: **(508) 255-3824**; **(800) 541-2662**
Best Time to Call: **8 AM–8 PM**
Coordinator: **Mary Chapman**

States/Regions Covered: **Cape Cod— Brewster, Chatham, Harwich, Orleans, Truro, Wellfleet**

Descriptive Directory: **Free**
Rates (Single/Double):
  Modest: — / **$60**
  Average: — / **$70**
  Luxury: — / **$90**

Credit Cards: **AMEX, MC, VISA**
Minimum Stay: **2 nights**

Mary offers a variety of accommodations with a diversity of styles, and guests may choose from historic to contemporary houses, all compatible with the atmosphere of the Cape. The fine reputation this service enjoys is largely due to the attitude of the host to the guest. Under Mary's direction, hosts meet regularly to share experiences, role-play B&B situations, and tour member homes. Each host is aware that a guest's experience reflects on the association as a whole. We applaud the professionalism of this organization! A $10 booking fee is charged per reservation.

Bacon Barn Inn ✪

P.O. BOX 621, 3400 MAIN STREET, BARNSTABLE, MASSACHUSETTS 02630

Tel: **(508) 362-5518**
Best Time to Call: **8 AM–8 PM**
Hosts: **Mary and Robert Guiffreda**
Location: **3 mi. off Rte. 6, Exit 6**
No. of Rooms: **3**
No. of Private Baths: **3**
Double/pb: **$85–$95**
Single/pb: **$65–$75**
Open: **All year**

Reduced Rates: **Lower rates Nov. 15–May 15**
Breakfast: **Full**
Pets: **No**
Children: **Welcome, over 14**
Smoking: **No**
Social Drinking: **Permitted**
Minimum Stay: **2 nights during peak season**

You can still see the original posts and beams in this beautifully restored barn, which dates to the 1820s. For more examples of early-19th-century architecture (and fine 20th-century dining), stroll over to Barnstable Village. Snacks and afternoon tea are served at Bacon Barn Inn, and there is a refrigerator for guests' use. Full breakfasts feature juice, coffee, muffins, and French toast or pancakes.

Thomas Huckins House ✪

2701 MAIN STREET (ROUTE 6A), P.O. BOX 515, BARNSTABLE, MASSACHUSETTS 02630

Tel: **(508) 362-6379**
Hosts: **Burt and Eleanor Eddy**
Location: **2 mi. from Rte. 6, Exit 6**
No. of Rooms: **3**
No. of Private Baths: **3**
Double/pb: **$75–$105**
Suites: **$85–$135**

Open: **Apr. 15–Oct. 15**
Breakfast: **Continental, plus**
Credit Cards: **AMEX, MC, VISA**
Pets: **No**
Children: **Welcome, over 12**
Smoking: **Permitted**
Social Drinking: **Permitted**

Located in the historic district, which is less crowded and less commercial than much of the Cape, the house, circa 1705, has all the privacy and charm of a small country inn. Each bedroom has a small sitting area and a four-poster bed with canopy. Two rooms have working fireplaces. The parlor is comfortably furnished with antiques and handmade reproductions. It's a short walk to a small beach, boat ramp, and the inlet that overlooks the dunes of Sandy Neck. Whale watching, the Nantucket ferry, the Sandwich Glass Museum, and Plimoth Plantation are but 15 minutes away. Eleanor loves to garden, and the jam served at breakfast is literally the fruits of her labor. Breakfast is served in the original keeping room in front of the fireplace. Banana pancakes and Cape Cod cranberry muffins are two favorites.

Copper Beech Inn on Cape Cod ✪
497 MAIN STREET, CENTERVILLE, MASSACHUSETTS 02632

Tel: **(508) 771-5488**	Breakfast: **Full**
Best Time to Call: **8:30 AM–5:30 PM**	Credit Cards: **AMEX, MC, VISA**
Host: **Joyce Diehl**	Pets: **No**
Location: **4 mi. W of Hyannis**	Children: **Welcome, over 11**
No. of Rooms: 3	Smoking: **Permitted**
No. of Private Baths: 3	Social Drinking: **Permitted**
Double/pb: **$80–$85**	Airport/Station Pickup: **Yes**
Open: **All year**	

Home of the largest European beech tree in Cape Cod, the inn, listed on the National Register of Historic Places, is set in the heart of town amid private estates and vintage homes. It features traditional furnishings, formal parlors, and well-kept grounds with sunning areas. Golf, tennis, fishing, sailing, and swimming are available nearby; Craigville Beach is less than a mile away. The Hyannis ferry to Nantucket and Martha's Vineyard is four miles away. All rooms have air-conditioning.

Isaiah Hall B&B Inn ✪
152 WHIG STREET, DENNIS, MASSACHUSETTS 02638

Tel: **(508) 385-9928; (800) 736-0160**	Single/sb: **$48**
Best Time to Call: **8 AM–10 PM**	Open: **Apr. 1–Oct. 26**
Host: **Marie Brophy**	Breakfast: **Continental, plus**
Location: **7 mi. E of Hyannis**	Credit Cards: **AMEX, MC, VISA**
No. of Rooms: 11	Pets: **No**
No. of Private Baths: 10	Children: **Welcome, over 7**
Max. No. Sharing Bath: 4	Smoking: **Permitted (6 nonsmoking**
Double/pb: **$71–$99**	**rooms)**
Single/pb: **$58–$89**	Social Drinking: **Permitted**
Double/sb: **$55**	

This Cape Cod farmhouse built in 1857 offers casual country living on the quiet, historic northside. The house is decorated in true New England style with quilts, antiques, and oriental rugs. Four rooms have balconies and one has a fireplace. Within walking distance are the beach, good restaurants, the Cape Playhouse, and countless antique and craft shops. It is also close to freshwater swimming, bike paths, and golf.

Great Pond House ✪
P.O. BOX 351, EASTHAM, MASSACHUSETTS 02642

Tel: **(802) 988-4300**	Open: **May–Aug.**
Best Time to Call: **Evenings**	Breakfast: **Continental**
Hosts: **The Mead Family**	Pets: **No**
Location: **90 mi. SE of Boston**	Children: **No**
No. of Rooms: 2	Smoking: **No**
No. of Private Baths: 2	Social Drinking: **Permitted**
Double/pb: **$75**	Minimum stay: **2 nights**
Single/pb: **$75**	Airport/Station Pickup: **Yes**

Have your choice of waterfront activities at this traditional two-story home on the shore of Great Pond, just two miles from Cape Cod Bay and three miles from the ocean beaches. You'll see the lake as you enjoy breakfast in the dining room or on the deck. Then go whale watching, charter a fishing trip, participate in a seaside nature walk, or head into town and explore the many local shops, galleries, and restaurants. At the end of the day, relax in the TV room or tickle the ivories of the 1927 grand piano in the living room.

The Over Look Inn ✪
ROUTE 6, 3085 COUNTY ROAD, P.O. BOX 771, EASTHAM, MASSACHUSETTS 02642

Tel: **(508) 255-1886; (800) 356-1121** (in Mass.)	Breakfast: **Full**
	Credit Cards: **AMEX, MC, VISA**
Hosts: **Ian and Nan Aitchison**	Pets: **No**
Location: **90 mi. E of Boston**	Children: **Welcome, over 12**
No. of Rooms: 10	Smoking: **Permitted**
No. of Private Baths: 10	Social Drinking: **Permitted**
Double/pb: **$60–$110**	Airport/Station Pickup: **Yes**
Open: **All year**	Foreign Languages: **French**
Reduced Rates: **10% off-season; 10% seniors**	

From its site opposite the entrance to the Cape Cod National Seashore, Over Look Inn offers immediate access to more than 30 miles of unspoiled beaches. The Aitchisons are happy to arrange such activities as bike tours, hikes, clambakes, and deep-sea fishing expeditions. The inn itself is a grand Queen Anne–style mansion with wraparound porches and landscaped gardens; inside, period furniture complements the rich mahogany woodwork. On the walls you'll see paintings by the innkeepers' younger son. In the evenings guests are welcome to browse in the library or shoot pool in the game room. Breakfasts feature Scottish dishes like kedgeree.

The Penny House
P.O. BOX 238, ROUTE 6, EASTHAM, MASSACHUSETTS 02651

Tel: (508) 255-6632
Hosts: Bill and Margaret Keith
No. of Rooms: 10
No. of Private Baths: 10
Double/pb: $80–$110
Open: All year
Reduced Rates: $55–$85 Sept.–June

Breakfast: Full
Credit Cards: AMEX, MC, VISA
Pets: No
Children: Welcome, over 8
Smoking: Permitted
Social Drinking: Permitted

Back in 1751, Captain Isiah Horton built the Penny House and crowned it with a shipbuilder's bow roof. She has weathered many a storm, but this spacious Cape just gets more charming. The rooms have wide-pine floors and are decorated with a blend of antiques and country accents. Your hosts provide special treats in the public room, where beautiful old wooden beams provide a sense of nostalgia. The Penny House is five minutes from National Seashore Park, and is just as convenient to the warm waters off Cape Cod Bay.

The Parsonage
202 MAIN STREET, P.O. BOX 1501, EAST ORLEANS,
MASSACHUSETTS 02643

Tel: (508) 255-8217
Best Time to Call: 10 AM–6 PM
Hosts: Ian and Elizabeth Browne
Location: 90 mi. SE of Boston
No. of Rooms: 7
No. of Private Baths: 7
Double/pb: $65–$80
Suites: $85

Open: All year
Reduced Rates: Oct.–May
Breakfast: Continental
Credit Cards: MC, VISA
Pets: No
Children: Welcome, over 6
Smoking: No
Social Drinking: Permitted

This quiet, romantic inn is housed in a charming 18th-century parsonage just one-and-a-half miles from the sparkling waters at Nauset Beach. Bike trails, lakes, galleries, fine stores, and restaurants are all nearby. Delicious continental breakfasts are served in the morning; in the evening, your hosts set out complimentary hors d'oeuvres in the parlor. And fresh floral arrangements add a special touch to the comfortable, tastefully decorated rooms.

The Arbor ✪
222 UPPER MAIN STREET, P.O. BOX 1228, EDGARTOWN, MARTHA'S VINEYARD, MASSACHUSETTS 02539

Tel: **(508) 627-8137**
Best Time to Call: **8 AM–8PM**
Host: **Peggy Hall**
Location: **7 mi. SE of Woods Hole Ferry**
No. of Rooms: **10**
No. of Private Baths: **8**
Max. No. Sharing Bath: **4**
Double/pb: **$85–$125**
Double/sb: **$80–$90**

Open: **May 1–Oct. 31**
Reduced Rates: **May 1–June 14; Sept. 16–Oct. 30**
Minimum stay: **3 nights in season**
Breakfast: **Continental**
Credit Cards: **MC, VISA**
Pets: **No**
Children: **Welcome, over 12**
Smoking: **Permitted**
Social Drinking: **Permitted**

This turn-of-the-century guest house offers island visitors a unique experience in comfort and charm. The house is a short distance from downtown, and at the same time provides the feeling of being away from it all. Relax in a hammock, enjoy tea on the porch, and retire to a cozy room filled with the smell of fresh flowers. Peggy provides setups and mixers at cocktail time, and will gladly direct you to unspoiled beaches, walking trails, sailing, fishing, and the delights of Martha's Vineyard.

Captain Tom Lawrence House—1861 ✪
75 LOCUST STREET, FALMOUTH, MASSACHUSETTS 02540

Tel: **(508) 540-1445, 548-9178**
Best Time to Call: **8 AM–noon**
Host: **Barbara Sabo**
Location: **67 mi. S of Boston**
No. of Rooms: **6**
No. of Private Baths: **6**
Double/pb: **$85–$99**
Open: **All year**

Reduced Rates: **Off-season**
Breakfast: **Full**
Credit Cards: **MC, VISA**
Pets: **No**
Children: **Welcome, over 11**
Smoking: **No**
Social Drinking: **Permitted**
Foreign Languages: **German**

Captain Lawrence was a successful whaler in the 1800s. When he retired from the sea, he built himself a town residence on Locust Street. Today, the house remains much as he left it, including the original hardwood floors, circular stairwell, high ceilings, and antique furnishings. In the morning, Barbara serves a hearty breakfast of fruit and creative entrées. Her Black Forest bread and Belgian waffles are truly special. She grinds her own flour from organically grown grain. She will gladly help you get around town—it's half a mile to the beach, a short walk to downtown Falmouth, and four miles to Woods Hole Seaport.

Mostly Hall B&B Inn ✪
27 MAIN STREET, FALMOUTH, MASSACHUSETTS 02540

Tel: (508) 548-3786; (800) 682-0565	Reduced Rates: Nov. 1–Apr. 30
Best Time to Call: 10 AM–9 PM	Breakfast: Full
Hosts: Caroline and Jim Lloyd	Credit Cards: MC, VISA
Location: 73 mi. SE of Boston on Rte. 28	Pets: No
	Children: Welcome, over 16
No. of Rooms: 6	Smoking: No
No. of Private Baths: 6	Social Drinking: Permitted
Double/pb: $95–$105	Foreign Languages: German
Single/pb: $75–85	
Open: Mid-Feb. through New Year's Day	

This B&B got its name when a young child walked through the front door, surveyed the atrium and staircases, and gasped, "It's mostly hall!" Built in 1849 by a sea captain who wanted to please his New Orleans–born bride, the house has a distinctly Southern ambience, with its wide, wraparound porch, high ceilings, and garden gazebo. History buffs should note that the church in the Village Green has a bell cast by Paul Revere. Cyclists will want to borrow the inn's bicycles and follow the Shining Sea Bikeway that connects Falmouth to the Woods Hole ferry docks. Mostly Hall's breakfasts are sure to provide stamina: juice, fruit, and home-baked goods are always served, plus an entrée such as stuffed French toast or cheese blintz muffins.

Palmer House Inn ✪
81 PALMER AVENUE, FALMOUTH, MASSACHUSETTS 02540

Tel: (508) 548-1230; (800) 472-2632	Reduced Rates: Off-season
Best Time to Call: 11 AM–10 PM	Breakfast: Full
Hosts: Ken and Joanne Baker	Credit Cards: AMEX, DC, DISC, MC, VISA
Location: 1 block from Rte. 28	
No. of Rooms: 8	Pets: No
No. of Private Baths: 8	Children: Welcome, over 12
Double/pb: $85–$125	Smoking: No
Single/pb: $75–$115	Social Drinking: Permitted
Open: All year	

Warmth and charm are evident in this turn-of-the-century Victorian home, with its stained-glass windows, soft warm wood, antiques, and collectibles. Centrally located within the Historic District, it is convenient to recreational diversions, miles of sandy beaches, ferries, and Woods Hole. Guests rave about breakfast entrées such as pain perdue with orange cream and Vermont maple syrup, Belgian waffles with honey butter, or Finnish pancakes and strawberry soup served in the dining room on fine linen, china, and crystal. Return from your afternoon activities and enjoy a glass of lemonade in a rocker on the front porch. Spend your after-dinner hours relaxing before the fireplace or sampling theater offerings close by.

Village Green Inn ✪
40 WEST MAIN STREET, FALMOUTH, MASSACHUSETTS 02540

Tel: **(508) 548-5621**
Hosts: **Linda and Don Long**
Location: **15 mi. S of Bourne Bridge**
No. of Rooms: **5**
No. of Private Baths: **5**
Double/pb: **$75–$90**
Suites: **$90–$110**
Open: **All year**

Reduced Rates: **20% Nov. 1–**
 Memorial Day
Breakfast: **Full**
Pets: **No**
Children: **No**
Smoking: **No**
Social Drinking: **Permitted**
Airport/Station Pickup: **Yes**

This lovely Victorian is located on Falmouth's Village Green. Feel free to relax on the outdoor porch or in the parlor. Breakfast is a treat that includes hot, spiced fruit, eggs Mornay, homemade breads and muffins, and freshly ground coffee. Linda and Don look forward to pampering you with such delights as sherry, cordials, lemonade, fresh flowers, and sinfully delicious chocolates.

The Coach House ✪
74 SISSON ROAD, HARWICH PORT, MASSACHUSETTS 02646

Tel: **(508) 432-9452**
Hosts: **Sara and Cal Ayer**
Location: **1 mi. from Rtes. 39 and 124**
No. of Rooms: **2**

No. of Private Baths: **2**
Double/pb: **$65–$70**
Single/pb: **$65**
Open: **May–Oct.**

Breakfast: **Continental**
Credit Cards: **AMEX, MC, VISA**
Pets: **No**

Children: **No**
Smoking: **Permitted**
Social Drinking: **Permitted**

Built in 1909, The Coach House was the original barn of one of Cape Cod's old estates. In the mid-1950s, the barn was fully converted into a lovely Cape Cod home. The rooms are quiet and elegant, and guests may choose from king- and queen-size beds. A breakfast of fresh fruit compote, home-baked muffins, coffee cake, and croissants is served in the dining room each morning. Enjoy three picturesque harbors, beautiful beaches, sailing, windsurfing, golf, and tennis. A 21-mile hard-surface bike trail will take you through the scenic woods and cranberry bogs to the National Seashore. Your hosts will gladly recommend shops, museums, fine restaurants, and summer theater.

Dunscroft By-The-Sea ✪
24 PILGRIM ROAD, HARWICH PORT, MASSACHUSETTS 02646

Tel: **(508) 432-0810**
Best Time to Call: **7 AM–11 PM**
Hosts: **Alyce and Wally Cunningham**
Location: **80 mi. SE of Boston**
No. of Rooms: **9**
No. of Private Baths: **9**
Double/pb: **$75–$125**
Guest Cottage: **$115–$150**

Open: **All year**
Breakfast: **Full**
Credit Cards: **AMEX, MC, VISA**
Pets: **No**
Children: **Welcome, over 12**
Smoking: **Restricted**
Social Drinking: **Permitted**

Its cedar shingles weathered a traditional waterfront grey, this Colonial inn offers everything you'd expect from a Cape Cod B&B: flower gardens, spacious grounds, an enclosed sun porch, a piano in the living room, and a private mile-long beach. Harwich Port's shops, galleries, theater, and restaurant are within easy walking distance. You'll awaken to the aroma of freshly ground coffee as Alyce prepares a full, generous breakfast.

The Inn on Bank Street ✪
88 BANK STREET, HARWICH PORT, MASSACHUSETTS 02646

Tel: **(508) 432-3206**
Best Time to Call: **8 AM–10 PM**
Hosts: **Arky and Janet Silverio**
Location: **85 mi. S of Boston**
No. of Rooms: **6**
No. of Private Baths: **6**
Double/pb: **$60–$80**
Single/pb: **$55–$75**
Open: **Apr. 1–Nov. 30**

Reduced Rates: **Available**
Breakfast: **Continental**
Credit Cards: **MC, VISA**
Pets: **No**
Children: **Welcome, over 7**
Smoking: **Permitted**
Social Drinking: **Permitted**
Airport/Station Pickup: **Yes**
Foreign Languages: **Italian, Spanish**

This contemporary, sprawling Cape is set in a quaint old town named after an English village. The main house has a large living room and library, with a fine selection of vacation reading. Guest rooms are decorated with comfortable country-style modern pieces. In the morning, breakfast is served on the sun porch or outdoors on the shady grounds where the roses grow wild. Specialties of the house include cranberry crisp, French toast, and fresh-baked breads. The ocean is a five-minute walk from the inn, and you can bike the paved trails for a closer look at Harwich Port. Restaurants, art galleries, and a movie theater are also within walking distance.

Foxglove Cottage ✪
101 SANDWICH ROAD, PLYMOUTH, MASSACHUSETTS 02360

Tel: **(508) 747-6576**
Best Time to Call: **After 5 PM**
Hosts: **Charles and Michael Cowan**
Location: **35 mi. S of Boston**
No. of Rooms: **2**
No. of Private Baths: **2**
Double/pb: **$70**
Single/pb: **$70**
Open: **All year**

Reduced Rates: **10% families; 10% after 4 nights**
Breakfast: **Full**
Other meals: **Available**
Credit Cards: **AMEX, MC, VISA**
Pets: **No**
Children: **Welcome, over 12**
Smoking: **No**
Social Drinking: **Permitted**
Station Pickup: **Yes**

Just five minutes from downtown Plymouth, the *Mayflower II*, and Plimoth Plantation, you'll find this restored 1820 Cape-style home, with its eight fireplaces and two beehive ovens. The house is tastefully furnished with American and English antiques. There is a large common room with a fireplace and deck for guests' use. In good weather, breakfast is served al fresco overlooking the pastoral forty-acre property; in cooler temperatures, you'll have your morning meal in the dining room. Michael, a nurse, and Charles, the president and CEO of a chemical distribution firm, are interested in design and architecture. Your hosts have traveled internationally and enjoy sharing their experiences with their guests.

Barclay Inn ✪
40 GROVE STREET, SANDWICH, MASSACHUSETTS 02563

Tel: (508) 888-5738	Single/sb: $45
Best Time to Call: 10 AM–8 PM	Guest Cottage: $425 weekly
Hosts: Patricia and Gerald Barclay	Open: All year
Location: 50 mi. S of Boston	Breakfast: Continental
No. of Rooms: 2	Pets: No
No. of Private Baths: 1	Children: No
Max. No. Sharing Bath: 4	Smoking: No
Double/pb: $75	Social Drinking: Permitted
Single/pb: $60	Minimum Stay: 1 week for cottage
Double/sb: $55	Airport/Station Pickup: Yes

Located near the center of Sandwich, Cape Cod's oldest town, this bed-and-breakfast makes an ideal home base whether you plan to hunt for antiques or just work on a tan. Local museums house everything from hand-blown glass to military artifacts, and the beach is only a few minutes away. Barclay Inn has two guest rooms; those desiring extra privacy may prefer to stay at the Kelman House, a one-bedroom cottage overlooking Peter's Pond. Whichever you choose, you'll savor Continental breakfasts that include glazed orange rolls, coffee cake, and raspberry cream cheese.

The Captain Ezra Nye House ✪
152 MAIN STREET, SANDWICH, MASSACHUSETTS 02563

Tel: (800) 388-2278; fax: (508) 888-2940	Open: All year
	Reduced Rates: 10% over 6 days; lower rates winter
Best Time to Call: 9 AM–9 PM	Breakfast: Full
Hosts: Elaine and Harry Dickson	Credit Cards: AMEX, DISC, MC, VISA
Location: 60 mi. SE of Boston	Pets: No
No. of Rooms: 7	Children: Welcome, over 6
No. of Private Baths: 5	Smoking: No
Max. No. Sharing Bath: 4	Minimum Stay: 2 nights in season, weekends, and all holidays
Double/pb: $55–$85	Airport/Station Pickup: Yes
Single/pb: $55–$85	Foreign Languages: Spanish
Double/sb: $50–$65	
Single/sb: $50–$65	
Suites: $65–$75	

The Captain Ezra Nye House is a stately 1829 Federal home built by a seafarer noted for his record-breaking North Atlantic crossings and daring ocean rescues. The house sits in the heart of Sandwich, the oldest town on Cape Cod, and is within walking distance of museums, shops, and fine restaurants. Guests rooms are tastefully decorated in soft pastel tones, antiques, and an eclectic art collection. Hearty homemade breakfasts are served in the dining room. A cozy den with fireplace and parlor with piano complete the common areas.

Dillingham House ✪
71 MAIN STREET, SANDWICH, MASSACHUSETTS 02563

Tel: **(508) 833-0065**
Best Time to Call: **6–8 PM**
Host: **Kathleen Kenney**
Location: **60 mi. S of Boston**
No. of Rooms: **3**
No. of Private Baths: **3**
Double/pb: **$75**
Open: **All year**

Reduced Rates: **$20 less Nov.–Mar.;**
     $10 less Apr., May, Oct.
Breakfast: **Continental**
Pets: **Sometimes**
Children: **Welcome**
Smoking: **Permitted**
Social Drinking: **Permitted**
Minimum Stay: **2 nights off-season**

Dillingham House is named for its first owner, who helped to found Sandwich, Cape Cod's oldest town. The house has many of the hallmarks of 17th-century construction, such as wide pine floors, exposed beams and rafters, and cozy brick hearths. Kathy is a Cape native and loves to discuss local lore. Your hosts charter sailing trips and lend bicycles to landlubbers. A Continental breakfast of juice, fresh fruit, muffins, and coffee or tea will fortify you for your excursions, whether they occur on land or on sea.

Hawthorn Hill ✪
P.O. BOX 777, SANDWICH, MASSACHUSETTS 02563

Tel: **(508) 888-3333**
Best Time to Call: **Mornings**
Host: **Maxime Caron**
Location: **60 mi. S of Boston**
No. of Rooms: **2**
No. of Private Baths: **2**
Double/pb: **$65–$70**
Open: **May–Nov.**

Breakfast: **Full**
Pets: **Sometimes**
Children: **Sometimes**
Smoking: **Permitted**
Social Drinking: **Permitted**
Airport/Station Pickup: **Yes**
Foreign Languages: **German**

This rambling English country house, off Grove Street, is set on a hill surrounded by trees, with both the conveniences of an in-town location and the pleasantness of a country setting. The property has a spring-fed pond for boating and swimming, and there is plenty of space for long walks through the woods. Inside, your host welcomes you to large, sunny rooms, comfortably furnished. Hawthorn Hill is close to beaches, fishing, museums, and shops, and is adjacent to the Heritage Plantation. Maxime will gladly help plan sightseeing in this historic town or day trips to many nearby points of interest.

The Summer House ✪
158 MAIN STREET, SANDWICH, MASSACHUSETTS 02563

Tel: (508) 888-4991
Best Time to Call: 8 AM–10 PM
Hosts: David and Kay Merrell
Location: 60 mi. S of Boston
No. of Rooms: 5
No. of Private Baths: 1
Max. No. Sharing Bath: 4
Double/pb: $65–$75
Single/pb: $55–$65
Double/sb: $50–$60
Single/sb: $40–$50

Open: All year
Reduced Rates: 10% seniors; Oct.
    16–May 25, $10 less per room
Breakfast: Full
Credit Cards: AMEX, DISC, MC, VISA
Pets: No
Children: Welcome, over 6
Smoking: No
Social Drinking: Permitted
Station Pickup: Yes

An elegant 1835 Greek Revival inn in the heart of historical Sandwich Village, the Summer House has been featured in *Country Living* magazine. The large, sunny rooms of this bed and breakfast are decorated with fireplaces, antiques, hand-stitched quilts, and flowers, and the grounds boast lovely English-style gardens. Restaurants, museums, shops, a pond and gristmill, and the boardwalk to the beach are all within strolling distance. Bountiful full breakfasts are served at tables for two, while afternoon tea is served in the garden.

Little Harbor Guest House ✪
20 STOCKTON SHORTCUT, WAREHAM, MASSACHUSETTS 02571

Tel: (508) 295-6329
Hosts: Dennis and Ken
Location: 20 mi. S of Plymouth
No. of Rooms: 5
Max. No. Sharing Bath: 4
Double/sb: $65
Single/sb: $65

Open: All year
Reduced Rates: 20% Nov. 1–May 1
Breakfast: Continental
Pets: No
Children: Welcome
Smoking: Permitted
Social Drinking: Permitted

The Little Harbor Guest House is set on three acres surrounded by a lovely 18-hole golf course. The house is a rambling Cape Cod, dating back to 1703. The large, sunny rooms are comfortable and quiet, furnished in antiques, wicker, and a lot of plants. Dennis and Ken prepare a lovely breakfast, featuring many types of homemade breads. They have bicycles to lend, a pool, and will gladly give directions to local attractions. The beach is less than a half mile away, and it's just 20 minutes to Plymouth and Hyannis.

Mulberry Bed and Breakfast ✪
257 HIGH STREET, WAREHAM, MASSACHUSETTS 02571

Tel: (508) 295-0684
Host: Frances Murphy

Location: 52 mi. S of Boston
No. of Rooms: 3

Max. No. Sharing Bath: **4**
Double/sb: **$45–$55**
Open: **All year**
Reduced Rates: **15% weekly**
Breakfast: **Continental**

Pets: **No**
Children: **Welcome, over 10**
Smoking: **No**
Social Drinking: **Permitted**
Airport/Station Pickup: **Yes**

Frances Murphy welcomes you to her vintage Cape Cod home, built in 1847. The house is one and a half stories and is painted white with red shutters. It is named for the mulberry tree in the yard that attracts many birds and provides shade from the summer sun. Frances has created a home-away-from-home atmosphere, where guests can relax in a small living room with a piano, or join her in a larger living-dining area with fireplace. Spend the night in an Early American–style bedroom and have breakfast on the spacious private deck. Home-baked breads and muffins, casseroles, and fresh fruit are served with jams and jellies made from Frances's fruit trees. In the afternoon, snacks and cool drinks are served. Mulberry Bed and Breakfast is located in the historic part of town, ten minutes from the beach.

The Marlborough ☉
320 WOODS HOLE ROAD, BOX 283, FALMOUTH, WOODS HOLE, MASSACHUSETTS 02543

Tel: **(508) 548-6218**
Best Time to Call: **3–9 PM**
Host: **Diana Smith**
Location: **2½ mi. from Rte. 28**
No. of Rooms: **5**
No. of Private Baths: **5**
Double/pb: **$85–$105**

Single/pb: **$80–$95**
Open: **All year**
Breakfast: **Full**
Pets: **No**
Children: **Welcome, over 2**
Smoking: **No**
Social Drinking: **Permitted**

This faithful reproduction of a full Cape house is beautifully decorated with antiques, collectibles, fabric wall coverings, and matching bed linens. It is situated on a shaded half-acre with a paddle tennis court, swimming pool, and hammock. It's 1 mile to a private beach, where a lifeguard is on duty. Ferries to Martha's Vineyard are a mile away. Patricia serves a full gourmet breakfast year round. Teatime and hospitality hours are 3–5 PM daily.

Liberty Hill Inn ☉
77 MAIN STREET, YARMOUTH PORT, MASSACHUSETTS 02675

Tel: **(508) 362-3976; (800) 821-3977**
Best Time to Call: **8 AM–9 PM**
Hosts: **Jack and Beth Flanagan**
Location: **1 mi. off Rte. 6, Exit 7**
No. of Rooms: **5**
No. of Private Baths: **5**

Double/pb: **$110**
Single/pb: **$70**
Bridal Suite: **$125**
Open: **All year**
Reduced Rates: **Available**
Breakfast: **Full**

Other Meals: **Available**
Credit Cards: **AMEX, MC, VISA**
Pets: **No**
Children: **Welcome**

Smoking: **Permitted**
Social Drinking: **Permitted**
Airport/Station Pickup: **Yes**

This gracious house sits on a small knoll just a stone's throw away from historic Old Kings Highway. A Greek Revival mansion built by a whaling tycoon in 1825, the inn is listed on the National Register of Historic Places. The interior is richly furnished in Queen Anne style, and each guest room has its own distinctive ambience. As devotees of local history, your hosts can add extra destinations and activities to your itinerary. Breakfasts begin with juice, fresh fruit, home-baked bread, and cheese, followed by French toast, quiche, or the Flanagans' specialty, Irish apple pastry. While outstanding restaurants are within walking distance, fine dinners are served here, by reservation only.

CENTRAL/WESTERN/SOUTHERN MASSACHUSETTS

American Country Collection—Massachusetts
4 GREENWOOD LANE, DELMAR, NEW YORK 12054

Tel: **(518) 439-7001**
Best Time to Call: **10 AM–5 PM Mon.–Fri.**
Coordinator: **Arthur Copeland**
States/Regions Covered: **Amherst, Ashfield, Egremont, Lenox, Northampton, Peru, Williamstown, Worthington, West Stockbridge**

Descriptive Directory: **$5**
Rates (Single/Double):
  Modest: **$55**
  Average: **$75**
  Luxury: **$110 / $125**
Credit Cards: **AMEX, MC, VISA**

The American Country Collection offers comfortable lodging in private homes and inns throughout western Massachusetts. The hosts pride themselves on the charm and cleanliness of their establishments, and the personal attention and hospitality given to each traveler. Locations range from Victorian and Early American homes to elegant mansions and full-service country inns. From the quiet Berkshire hills to nineteenth-century Old Sturbridge and the heritage of Pioneer Valley, the accommodations appeal to both businesspeople and vacationers. In addition, this service handles reservations for eastern New York and all of Vermont.

Allen House Inn ✪
599 MAIN STREET, AMHERST, MASSACHUSETTS 01002

Tel: **(413) 253-5000**
Hosts: **Alan and Ann Zieminski**
Location: **5 mi. from Rte. 91, Exit 19**

No. of Rooms: **5**
No. of Private Baths: **5**
Double/pb: **$55–$95**

Single/pb: **$45–$85**
Open: **All year**
Breakfast: **Full**
Pets: **No**
Children: **Welcome**

Smoking: **No**
Social Drinking: **Permitted**
Minimum Stay: **College and fall foliage weekends**

This 1886 Queen Anne Stick-style Victorian features period antiques, decor, and art wall coverings by designers from the Aesthetic movement, which emphasized art in interior decoration; Charles Eastlake, Walter Crane, and William Morris are represented. Allen House is located on three scenic acres in the heart of Amherst, within walking distance of Emily Dickinson House, Amherst College, the University of Massachusetts, and innumerable galleries, museums, theaters, shops, and restaurants. Free busing is available throughout the five-college area. A full formal breakfast is served.

Emma C's B&B ✪
18 FRENCH FARM ROAD, ATTLEBORO, MASSACHUSETTS 02703

Tel: **(508) 226-6365**
Best Time to Call: **9 AM–9 PM**
Hosts: **Caroline and Jim Logie**
Location: **10 mi. N of Providence, R.I.**
No. of Rooms: **3**
No. of Private Baths: **1**
Max. No. Sharing Bath: **4**
Double/pb: **$60–$70**
Single/pb: **$50–$60**
Double/sb: **$55–$65**

Single/sb: **$45–$55**
Open: **All year**
Reduced Rates: **7th night free; 10% families, seniors**
Breakfast: **Full**
Pets: **Sometimes**
Children: **Welcome (crib)**
Smoking: **No**
Social Drinking: **Permitted**
Airport/Station Pickup: **Yes**

Folk art, decorative stencils, antique four-poster beds, and handmade quilts make this country Colonial home a warm and friendly place. Your hosts enjoy discussing their world travels with guests. Caroline's well-balanced breakfasts include her own granola, home-baked muffins, fresh fruit, and freshly ground coffee. It's only 45 minutes to Boston or Cape Cod. Emma C's is only minutes to both Wheaton College in Norton and Brown University in Providence.

1797 House ✪
1797 UPPER STREET, BUCKLAND, MASSACHUSETTS 01338

Tel: **(413) 625-2975**
Best Time to Call: **5 PM–9 PM**
Host: **Janet Turley**
Location: **13 mi. from Rte. 91, Exit 26**
No. of Rooms: **3**
No. of Private Baths: **3**
Double/pb: **$65–$75**

Single/pb: **$58**
Open: **Jan. 2–Oct. 31**
Breakfast: **Full**
Pets: **No**
Children: **No**
Smoking: **No**
Social Drinking: **Permitted**

This white, center-hall Colonial, circa 1797, has a lovely screened-in porch for summer enjoyment and four fireplaces and down quilts for cozy winter pleasure. Prestigious Deerfield Academy, Old Deerfield, Sturbridge Village, and the historic sights of Pioneer Valley are all close by. The University of Massachusetts, Smith, Amherst, and Williams are convenient to Janet's home. Sensational breakfast treats include stuffed croissants, French toast, and special casseroles, along with fresh fruit and breakfast meats.

Windfields Farm ✪
RR 1, BOX 170, WINDSOR BUSH ROAD, CUMMINGTON, MASSACHUSETTS 01026

Tel: **(413) 684-3786**	Open: **May 1–Mar. 1**
Best Time to Call: **Before 9 PM**	Breakfast: **Full**
Hosts: **Carolyn and Arnold Westwood**	Pets: **No**
Location: **20 mi. E of Pittsfield**	Children: **Welcome, over 12**
No. of Rooms: **2**	Smoking: **No**
Max. No. Sharing Bath: **4**	Social Drinking: **Permitted**
Double/sb: **$60**	Minimum Stay: **2 nights most**
Single/sb: **$45**	**weekends**

Since 1983, the Westwoods have been welcoming guests to their secluded nineteenth-century homestead in the rolling Berkshire country-side. The hundred-acre estate includes organic gardens, flower beds, wild blueberry fields, and a brook and a pond. Hiking and skiing trails, a state forest, and the Audubon Wildlife Sanctuary are within walking distance. Arnold, a retired Unitarian minister, built his own sugarhouse and greenhouse and doubles as publisher of a local monthly newspaper. Carolyn is an award-winning gardener. Both are active in community affairs and conservation, and, during the late winter mud season, they make maple syrup from their property's 500 taps.

Arrawood Bed & Breakfast
105 TACONIC AVENUE, GREAT BARRINGTON, MASSACHUSETTS 01230

Tel: **(413) 528-5868**	Open: **All year**
Hosts: **Marilyn and Bill Newmark**	Breakfast: **Full**
Location: **100 mi. W of Boston**	Pets: **No**
No. of Rooms: **4**	Children: **By arrangement**
No. of Private Baths: **2**	Smoking: **No**
Max. No. Sharing Bath: **4**	Social Drinking: **Permitted**
Double/pb: **$65–$85**	Minimum Stay: **2 nights weekends**
Double/sb: **$45–$75**	**during summer**

A beautifully restored turn-of-the-century Victorian in the quaint New England village of Great Barrington, Arrawood is handsomely and comfortably furnished. Common rooms have fireplaces, and guest rooms are decorated with four-poster, canopy, and country pine beds. Candlelight breakfasts include homemade entrees like quiche, frittata, and fruited pancakes; afternoon snacks are served on the covered front porch or fireside in the parlor. The Berkshires' natural beauty draws visitors year-round. In the summer, Tanglewood, the Berkshire Theatre Festival, and Jacob's Pillow are the main attractions. In winter, there are two ski areas, Butternut Basin and Catamount. During any season, there is an abundance of antique shops, craft stores, galleries, and outlets.

Hitchcock House ✪
15 CONGRESS STREET, GREENFIELD, MASSACHUSETTS 01301

Tel: **(413) 774-7452**
Hosts: **Elizabeth and Peter Gott**
Location: **30 mi. N of Springfield**
No. of Rooms: **3**
No. of Private Baths: **1**
Max. No. Sharing Bath: **4**
Double/pb: **$85**
Double/sb: **$60–$70**
Single/sb: **$40**

Suites: **$110–$130; sleeps 3–5**
Open: **All year**
Reduced Rates: **Available**
Breakfast: **Full**
Pets: **No**
Children: **Welcome, over 6**
Smoking: **Restricted**
Social Drinking: **Permitted**
Station Pickup: **Yes**

This 1881 Victorian gem is minutes away from tennis courts, a variety of golf courses, hiking trails, fabulous fall foliage, cross-country and downhill skiing, historic Old Deerfield, museums, and nine well-known schools and colleges. The town center and many places of worship are within easy walking distance. Wake up to a sumptuous breakfast or take the special no-meal rate. Rooms are decorated with period furniture, country quilts, and other accessories. Hitchcock House has fireplaces, porches, patios, gardens, horseshoe pitching, croquet courts, and an abundance of genial hospitality.

Garden Gables Inn ✪
141 MAIN STREET, LENOX, MASSACHUSETTS 01240

Tel: (413) 637-0193
Hosts: Lynn and Mario Mekinda
Location: 10 mi. off Mass Pike, Exit 2
No. of Rooms: 12
No. of Private Baths: 12
Double/pb: $65–$160
Single/pb: $60–$155
Open: All year
Reduced Rates: 10% weekly;
  midweek, off-season

Breakfast: Full
Credit Cards: AMEX, MC, VISA
Pets: No
Children: Welcome, over 12
Smoking: Permitted
Social Drinking: Permitted
Minimum Stay: 3 nights weekends
  July, Aug., holidays
Airport/Station Pickup: Yes

Built in 1790 and expanded a little more than a century later, this white clapboard house has dark green shutters and, true to its name, a gambrel roof with three gables. Inside, the antique furniture and floral wallpapers are reminiscent of an earlier era, but there is nothing old-fashioned about the inviting 72-foot swimming pool in the backyard. The Berkshires in summertime are rich in cultural activities, with music at Tanglewood, dance at Jacob's Pillow, and the Williamstown Theatre Festival. Winter visitors can choose between the area's downhill ski slopes and cross-country trails; spring through fall, Lenox's stables cater to the horsey set. Plan your day over a buffet-style breakfast of fresh fruit and berries, homemade bran and blueberry muffins, cereals, crumb cakes, and low-fat yogurts.

Arnold Taft House ✪
166 MILLVILLE ROAD, MENDON, MASSACHUSETTS 01756

Tel: (508) 634-8143
Hosts: Diedre and Michael Meddaugh
Location: 37 mi. SW of Boston
No. of Rooms: 3
Max. No. Sharing Bath: 4
Double/sb: $45–$55
Single/sb: $40–$50

Open: All year
Reduced Rates: Families
Breakfast: Full
Pets: No
Children: Welcome, over 5
Smoking: No
Social Drinking: Permitted

The Arnold Taft House is located in Mendon, a small rural town founded in 1667. Restored by the owners, the handsome Federal-style brick home (circa 1800) has six fireplaces and its original wide pine floors and is furnished with antiques, reproduction pieces, and Colonial decor. Each guest room has its own personality. A full breakfast is served in the country-style dining room. Guests may enjoy books and board games in the common room, play croquet, badminton, tennis, or go swimming, hiking, and biking. Local points of interest include Southwick Zoo, canoe trips on the Blackstone River, Purgatory Chasm, Willard Clock Museum, and historical tours.

Chalet d'Alicia ○
EAST WINDSOR ROAD, PERU, MASSACHUSETTS 01235

Tel: **(413) 655-8292**	Open: **All year**
Hosts: **Alice and Richard Halvorsen**	Breakfast: **Full**
Location: **15 mi. E of Pittsfield**	Pets: **Sometimes**
No. of Rooms: **3**	Children: **Welcome**
Max. No. Sharing Bath: **4**	Smoking: **Permitted**
Double/sb: **$55**	Social Drinking: **Permitted**

Chalet d'Alicia is set high in the Berkshire Mountains overlooking the majestic countryside. This Swiss chalet–style home offers a private, casual atmosphere. The large front deck is a perfect spot for reading, sunning, or chatting. Alice and Richard are proud to make everyone feel at home. For breakfast they serve homemade muffins, and jams made from local wild berries. The property has a pond and plenty of places for cross-country skiing. Tanglewood, Jacob's Pillow, and the Williamstown Theatre Festival are all within easy reach.

Perryville Inn ○
157 PERRYVILLE ROAD, REHOBOTH, MASSACHUSETTS 02769

Tel: **(508) 252-9239**	Double/sb: **$50**
Best Time to Call: **8 AM–10 PM**	Open: **All year**
Hosts: **Tom and Betsy Charnecki**	Breakfast: **Continental**
Location: **8 mi. E of Providence, R.I.**	Credit Cards: **AMEX, MC, VISA**
No. of Rooms: **5**	Pets: **No**
No. of Private Baths: **3**	Children: **Welcome**
Max. No. Sharing Bath: **4**	Smoking: **Restricted**
Double/pb: **$55–$85**	Social Drinking: **Permitted**

This 19th-century restored Victorian, listed on the National Register of Historic Places, is located on four and a half acres, featuring a quiet brook, stone walls, and shaded paths. You are welcome to use your hosts' bikes for local touring. There's a public golf course across the road. It's a short drive to antique shops, museums, and fine seafood restaurants. Don't miss a traditional New England clambake. All rooms are furnished with antiques and accented with colorful, handmade quilts. Brown University, Wheaton College, and the Rhode Island School of Design are within a 10-mile radius of the inn.

Salt Marsh Farm

322 SMITH NECK ROAD, SOUTH DARTMOUTH, MASSACHUSETTS 02748

Tel: **(508) 992-0980**
Hosts: **Larry and Sally Brownell**
Location: **5 mi. SW of New Bedford**
No. of Rooms: **2**
No. of Private Baths: **2**
Double/pb: **$70–$90**
Single/pb: **$70–$90**
Open: **All year**
Reduced Rates: **Available**
Breakfast: **Full**

Credit Cards: **MC, VISA**
Pets: **No**
Children: **Welcome, over 5**
Smoking: **No**
Social Drinking: **Permitted**
Minimum Stay: **2 nights summer, holiday weekends**
Airport/Station Pickup: **Yes, fee charged**

Surrounded by old stone walls, this colonial farmhouse, built in c. 1730, is part of a 90-acre nature preserve with a variety of wildlife. The hay fields, pine groves, freshwater pond, and wetlands afford a peaceful setting for a leisurely stroll. With its original wide-board floors, low ceilings, working fireplaces, and treasured family heirlooms, the house suggests a journey through time. Sally's scrumptious breakfast features her own organically grown fruits, prize-winning muffins, and farm-fresh eggs taken right from the nest.

The Golden Goose ✪

MAIN ROAD, BOX 336, TYRINGHAM, MASSACHUSETTS 01264

Tel: **(413) 243-3008**
Best Time to Call: **8 AM–8 PM**
Hosts: **Lilja and Joseph Rizzo**

Location: **4 mi. from Mass. Tpk., Exit 2-Lee**
No. of Rooms: **7**

No. of Private Baths: **5**
Max. No. Sharing Bath: **4**
Double/pb: **$70–$95**
Single/pb: **$65–$90**
Double/sb: **$60–$70**
Single/sb: **$55–$65**
Suites: **$95–$110**
Open: **All year**
Reduced Rates: **Available**

Breakfast: **Continental**
Pets: **No**
Children: **Welcome, in suite**
Smoking: **Permitted**
Social Drinking: **Permitted**
Minimum Stay: **2 nights weekends during Tanglewood season; 3 nights holiday weekends**

The inn lies between Stockbridge and Lenox in the Berkshires. Antique beds with firm new mattresses, and washstands, are in each bedroom. Lilja and Joseph serve hors d'oeuvres and drinks by the fireside in the two common rooms. In warm weather, you may play croquet, volleyball, badminton, hike the Appalachian Trail, or fish for trout in the brook across the street and barbecue it at "home." In summer, the cultural attractions of Tanglewood and Jacob's Pillow are nearby. Skiing is popular in winter. A $5 surcharge is added for one-night stays.

The Wildwood Inn ✪
121 CHURCH STREET, WARE, MASSACHUSETTS 01082

Tel: **(413) 967-7798**
Best Time to Call: **5–8 PM**

Hosts: **Fraidell Fenster and Richard Watson**

Location: **70 mi. W of Boston**
No. of Rooms: **7**
Max. No. Sharing Bath: **4**
Double/sb: **$38–$69**
Open: **All year**
Reduced Rates: **10% weekly**

Breakfast: **Full**
Pets: **No**
Children: **Welcome, over 6**
Smoking: **No**
Social Drinking: **Permitted**

Everything about this old-fashioned country home, with its rambling two acres, is designed to help you unwind. There's a swing on the porch, a hammock under the firs, a blazing fire in the winter, a Norman Rockwell–esque brook-fed swimming hole in the summer. Your host Fraidell has furnished her guest rooms with heirloom quilts and American primitive antiques, all of which work to spell welcome. Homemade bread and Wildwood's own peach butter and "country yummies" are included with breakfast. Sturbridge Village, Old Deerfield, and Amherst offer recreational activities that are all close by. You can stroll to the tennis court or borrow the canoe, or visit in the parlor for stimulating conversation. Fraidell does her best to spoil you.

NANTUCKET

Lynda Watts Bed & Breakfast ✪
10 UPPER VESTAL STREET, NANTUCKET, MASSACHUSETTS 02554

Tel: **(508) 228-3828**
Hosts: **Lynda and David Watts**
No. of Rooms: **2**
Max. No. Sharing Bath: **4**
Double/sb: **$65**
Open: **All year**
Reduced Rates: **20% Jan. 1–Apr. 15**

Breakfast: **Continental**
Pets: **No**
Children: **Welcome**
Smoking: **Permitted**
Social Drinking: **Permitted**
Minimum Stay: **2 nights**

Lynda and David's 15-year-old saltbox house is located on a quiet street in a residential neighborhood, only a seven-minute walk to town. It is simply furnished and guest rooms are equipped with TVs. Weather permitting, breakfast is served on the sunny patio.

Seven Sea Street Inn
7 SEA STREET, NANTUCKET, MASSACHUSETTS 02554

Tel: **(508) 228-3577**
Hosts: **Matthew and Mary Parker**
No. of Rooms: **8**
No. of Private Baths: **8**
Double/pb: **$85–$165**
Wheelchair Accessible: **4 rooms**
Open: **All year**
Reduced Rates: **Oct.–June**
Breakfast: **Continental**

Credit Cards: **MC, VISA**
Pets: **No**
Children: **Welcome, over 7**
Smoking: **No**
Social Drinking: **Permitted**
Minimum Stay: **2 nights weekends May–Oct.**
Foreign Languages: **French**

This romantic red-oak post-and-beam country inn is located on a quiet side street in the town's historic district. Each bedroom is decorated with Colonial-style furniture, fishnet canopy beds, handmade quilts, and braided rugs covering wide-plank pine floors. A small refrigerator and cable TV will please those who like to snack and view in private. Don't miss the spectacular sunset from the widow's walk overlooking the harbor and do take some time to relax in the Jacuzzi whirlpool. After a good night's sleep, you may have breakfast served to you in bed.

MICHIGAN

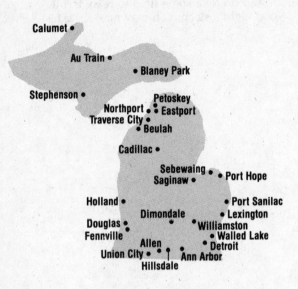

The Olde Bricke House ✪
P.O. BOX 211, ALLEN, MICHIGAN 49227

Tel: (517) 869-2349
Host: **Erma Jones**
Location: **On Rte. 12**
No. of Rooms: **4**
Max. No. Sharing Bath: **4**
Double/sb: **$50**
Single/sb: **$40**
Open: **Mar. 1–Dec. 15**
Reduced Rates: **10% Sun.–Thurs.**
Breakfast: **Continental**

Credit Cards: **MC, VISA**
Pets: **No**
Children: **Welcome, over 13**
Smoking: **Permitted**
Social Drinking: **Permitted**
Minimum Stay: **2 nights during
    Hillsdale College special weekends
    (Homecoming, Parents' Weekends,
    Graduation)**

This Victorian house, built in 1873, was recently renovated. If you are an antiques buff, spend the day browsing the fabulous shops (75 at last count) that have made Allen the Antiques Capital of Michigan. Several lakes for boating, swimming, and fishing are nearby, and Hillsdale College is 10 miles away. You are welcome to join your host for afternoon refreshments on the porch or in the library or living room.

The Urban Retreat ✪
2759 CANTERBURY ROAD, ANN ARBOR, MICHIGAN 48104

Tel: (313) 971-8110	Double/sb: $50
Best Time to Call: 5–10 PM	Single/sb: $40
Hosts: Andre Rosalik and Gloria Krys	Open: All year
Location: 40 mi. W of Detroit	Breakfast: Full
No. of Rooms: 2	Pets: No
Max. No. Sharing Bath: 4	Children: No
Double/pb: $55	Smoking: Permitted
Single/pb: $45	Social Drinking: Permitted

This 1950s ranch-style house is located on a quiet, tree-lined street, 10 minutes from downtown and the University of Michigan campus. The home is decorated with antiques and collectibles from the early 1900s, with an abundance of birdseye maple furniture. Adjacent to the property is the County Farm Park, 127 acres of meadowland with walking and jogging paths and a 13-box bluebird trail. The Retreat has been designated as a Backyard Wildlife Habitat by the National Wildlife Federation. Andre and Gloria emphasize a quiet, relaxed atmosphere and assure their guests a peaceful visit and personal attention.

Pinewood Lodge ✪
P.O. BOX 176, M28 WEST, AU TRAIN, MICHIGAN 49806

Tel: (906) 892-8300	Open: All year
Best Time to Call: 9 AM–5 PM	Reduced Rates: 10% seniors
Hosts: Jerry and Jenny Krieg	Breakfast: Full
Location: 24 mi. E of Marquette	Credit Cards: AMEX, DISC, MC, VISA
No. of Rooms: 8	Pets: Sometimes
No. of Private Baths: 6	Children: Welcome
Max. No. Sharing Bath: 4	Smoking: No
Double/pb: $80–$95	Social Drinking: Permitted
Double/sb: $40–$60	Airport/Station Pickup: Yes
Single/sb: $45	

This B&B is a pine log home on the shores of Lake Superior. Pictured Rocks National Shoreline is right down the highway, and you can see the Grand Islands from the living room. Guests can enjoy activities year-round, from swimming, diving, and boating to ice fishing, snowmobiling, and downhill and cross-country skiing.

The Windermere Inn ✪
747 CRYSTAL DRIVE, BEULAH, MICHIGAN 49617

Tel: (616) 882-9000
Best Time to Call: 8 AM–11 PM
Hosts: Anne Fitch-Clark and Cameron
  Clark
Location: 35 mi. SW of Traverse City
No. of Rooms: 4
No. of Private Baths: 4
Double/pb: $65
Single/pb: $55

Open: All year
Breakfast: Continental
Credit Cards: AMEX, MC, VISA
Pets: Sometimes
Children: Welcome, over 10
Smoking: No
Social Drinking: Permitted
Minimum Stay: 2 nights on weekends
  June–Aug.

Whether you sip lemonade on the screened porch in summer or enjoy a hot toddy by the fire in winter, the Windermere Inn on beautiful Crystal Lake makes comfort its top priority. Situated in scenic Benzie County, the inn has Sleeping Bear National Lakeshore to its north, Crystal Mountain ski resort to its south, Interlochen Arts Academy to its east, Lake Michigan and its beaches to its west, and golf courses all around. Anne and Cameron can help make your stay as eventful or relaxing as you wish. Your day begins with native fruits and muffins in summer, breakfast casseroles and breads in winter.

Celibeth House
ROUTE 1, BOX 58A, M-77 BLANEY PARK ROAD, BLANEY PARK, MICHIGAN 49836

Tel: (906) 283-3409
Host: Elsa Strom
Location: 60 mi. W of Mackinac
  Bridge
No. of Rooms: 8
No. of Private Baths: 8
Double/pb: $40–$50
Single/pb: $35–$45

Open: May 1–Dec. 1
Reduced Rates: 10% after 2nd night
Breakfast: Continental
Credit Cards: MC, VISA
Pets: No
Children: Welcome
Smoking: No
Social Drinking: Permitted

This lovely house, built in 1895, is situated on 85 acres overlooking a small lake. Many of the scenic attractions of Michigan's Upper Peninsula lie within an hour's drive. Guests may enjoy a cozy living room, a quiet reading room, a comfortably furnished porch, an outdoor deck, and lots of nature trails. Elsa is a retired personal manager who enjoys reading, gardening, traveling, and collecting antiques.

Dewey Lake Manor Bed & Breakfast ✪
11811 LAIRD ROAD, BROOKLYN, MICHIGAN 49230

Tel: (517) 467-7122
Best Time to Call: Before 11 PM

Hosts: Joe, Barb, Barry and Tandy
  Phillips

Location: **45 mi. SW of Ann Arbor**
No. of Rooms: **4**
No. of Private Baths: **4**
Double/pb: **$50–$65**
Single/pb: **$45–$60**
Open: **All year**
Reduced Rates: **Available**
Breakfast: **Continental, plus**

Other Meals: **Available**
Credit Cards: **MC, VISA**
Pets: **Sometimes**
Children: **Welcome**
Smoking: **No**
Social Drinking: **Permitted**
Minimum Stay: **2 nights on race weekends**

This 1870s Italianate home sits on the shore of Dewey Lake in the Irish Hills of southern Michigan. Four spacious, airy rooms are furnished with antiques and old-fashioned wallpapers. Guests may linger over a Continental-plus breakfast in the formal dining room or on the porch overlooking the lake. Picnics, bonfires, volleyball, or croquet may be enjoyed on the large lawn. Nearby is the Stagecoach Stop Dinner Theater, as well as golf courses, quaint towns, and many antique shops. Come experience the country with the Phillips family.

Essenmachers Bed & Breakfast ✪
204 LOCUST LANE, CADILLAC, MICHIGAN 49601

Tel: **(616) 775-3828**
Best Time to Call: **Evenings; weekends**
Hosts: **Doug and Vickie Essenmacher**
Location: **1 block from Rte. M55**
No. of Rooms: **2**
No. of Private Baths: **2**
Double/pb: **$55**

Open: **All year**
Breakfast: **Continental**
Credit Cards: **MC, VISA**
Pets: **No**
Children: **Welcome**
Smoking: **No**
Social Drinking: **No**

The large windows of this modern home take in the vista of Lake Mitchell, while the lakeside guest rooms are just steps away from year-round activities. Swim, feed the ducks, fish, boat, and toast marsh-mallows at an evening bonfire. In winter, enjoy the miles of cross-country and snowmobile trails in nearby Manistee National Forest, or go downhill skiing, just minutes away, then relax with the family in front of a crackling fire on chilly evenings. Coffee and cold drinks are always available.

Calumet House ✪
1159 CALUMET AVENUE, P.O. BOX 126, CALUMET, MICHIGAN 49913

Tel: **(906) 337-1936**
Hosts: **George and Rose Chivses**
Location: **10 mi. N of Hancock-Houghton**
No. of Rooms: **2**
Max. No. Sharing Bath: **4**
Double/sb: **$30**
Single/sb: **$25**

Open: **All year**
Breakfast: **Full**
Pets: **No**
Children: **No**
Smoking: **No**
Social Drinking: **Permitted**
Airport/Station Pickup: **Yes**
Foreign Languages: **Finnish**

The Calumet House is set in a historic old mining town, known for its clean air and scenic vistas. Built in 1895, the house boasts its original woodwork and is filled with local antique furnishings. In the morning, you're in for a treat with Rose's home cooking. Breakfast specialties include English scones, pancakes, local berries in season, and home-made jam. Calumet House is within walking distance of the village, with its opera house, museum, and antique shops. Your hosts will also direct you to local hunting and fishing, as well as to places that any botanist would call paradise. It's 10 miles north of Michigan Technological University and Suomi College.

Michigamme Lake Lodge ✪
BOX 97, CHAMPION, MICHIGAN 49814

Tel: **(906) 339-4400**	Open: **All year**
Hosts: **Frank and Linda Stabile**	Reduced Rates: **Available**
Location: **30 mi. W of US 41**	Breakfast: **Continental**
No. of Rooms: **9**	Credit Cards: **MC, VISA**
No. of Private Baths: **3**	Pets: **No**
Max. No. Sharing Bath: **2**	Children: **Welcome**
Double/pb: **$94**	Smoking: **No**
Double/sb: **$90**	Social Drinking: **Permitted**

Built in 1934, listed on the State and National Historical Register, this two-and-a-half-story lodge is a fine representative of the "great camps" that punctuated Michigan's Upper Peninsula. Guests can relax by a crackling fire in the massive stone fireplace gracing the large central hall. Lake Michigamme provides opportunities for canoeing, swimming, fishing, and boating. Depending on the season, you may go cross-country skiing, snowshoeing, hiking, and biking. With a cup of coffee in hand, enjoy sunrise from the porch, which has a pano-ramic view of the lake. Outside, birch trees line the walkways that lead to a secluded area with beautiful flower gardens.

Bannicks B&B ✪
4608 MICHIGAN ROAD, M-99, DIMONDALE, MICHIGAN 48821

Tel: **(517) 646-0224**	Open: **All year**
Hosts: **Pat and Jim Bannick**	Breakfast: **Full**
Location: **5 mi. SW of Lansing**	Pets: **No**
No. of Rooms: **2**	Children: **Welcome**
Max. No. Sharing Bath: **3**	Smoking: **No**
Double/sb: **$35**	Social Drinking: **No**
Single/sb: **$25**	

This large ranch-style home features a stained-glass entry, nautical-style basement, and a Mona Lisa bathroom. Guest accommodations consist of comfortable bedrooms and a den-TV room. Your hosts invite you to share a cup of coffee anytime. They will be happy to advise on the sights of Michigan's capital city, just five minutes away. Michigan State University is eight miles away.

Torch Lake Sunrise Bed and Breakfast ✪
BOX 52, EASTPORT, MICHIGAN 49627

Tel: **(616) 599-2706**
Host: **Betty A. Collins**
Location: **35 mi. N of Traverse City**
No. of Rooms: **3**
No. of Private Baths: **3**
Double/pb: **$70–$80**
Open: **All year**

Reduced Rates: **Available**
Breakfast: **Full**
Pets: **Sometimes**
Children: **Welcome**
Smoking: **No**
Social Drinking: **Permitted**

This B&B overlooks what *National Geographic* calls the third-most beautiful lake in the world. All rooms are furnished with antiques and have decks and private baths. Close at hand are several golf courses, tennis courts, gourmet restaurants, and ski resorts. For summer activities, a canoe, a rowboat, and paddleboards are available. In winter, cross-country skiing awaits you just outside. Wake up seeing the sunrise over the lake and smelling the wonderful aroma of fresh muffins baking! Perhaps you'll be served a frittata, or strawberry pancakes, or eggs Benedict, but always fresh fruit of the season.

Hidden Pond Bed and Breakfast ✪
5975 128TH AVENUE, FENNVILLE, MICHIGAN 49408

Tel: **(616) 561-2491**
Best Time to Call: **Anytime**
Hosts: **Larry and Priscilla Fuerst**
Location: **40 mi. SW of Grand Rapids**
No. of Rooms: **2**
No. of Private Baths: **2**
Double/pb: **$80–$110**
Open: **All year**

Reduced Rates: **Sun.–Thurs.**
Breakfast: **Full**
Pets: **No**
Children: **Welcome**
Smoking: **Permitted**
Social Drinking: **Permitted**
Airport/Station Pickup: **Yes**

Hidden Pond Bed and Breakfast is set on 28 acres of woods, perfect for birdwatching, hiking, cross-country skiing, or just relaxing in a rowboat on the pond. This sprawling 13-room house was designed to provide visitors with privacy and rest. Guests have exclusive use of seven entry-level rooms, including bedrooms and baths, a living room with a fireplace, and the dining room, den, kitchen, and breakfast porch. Priscilla and Larry, who work for rival airlines, understand the importance of a soothing, calm, and slow-paced overnight. They enjoy pleasing guests and creating an atmosphere of quiet elegance. There are no schedules; breakfast is served when you wake up. Unwind and take in the sun on the outdoor deck and patio. Behind the house is a ravine with a pond, where you might see a deer or two. Or take a brief excursion; this lovely retreat is near the beaches on Lake Michigan, the boutiques of Saugatuck, and the winery and cider mill in Fennville.

The Kingsley House ✪
626 WEST MAIN STREET, FENNVILLE, MICHIGAN 49408

Tel: **(616) 561-6425**
Hosts: **David and Shirley Witt**
Location: **6 mi. SE of Saugatuck**
No. of Rooms: **5**
No. of Private Baths: **5**
Double/pb: **$65–$125**
Open: **All year**
Reduced Rates: **10% after 4th night;
 10% seniors**

Breakfast: **Full**
Pets: **No**
Smoking: **No**
Social Drinking: **Permitted**
Airport/Station Pickup: **Yes**
Foreign Languages: **Dutch, Friesian**

Just 10 minutes south of Holland, and surrounded by 90 acres, this 1886 white clapboard house has a red tile roof and 3-story-high turret. A spacious home, it is entirely decorated with Victorian antiques. Breakfast, a bountiful feast, is served in the formal dining room. A backyard picnic area for hotdog and marshmallow roasts, a tree swing, bicycles, and a porch overlooking the Allegan National Forest are all guest favorites. Dutch Village, Tulip Gardens, Windmill Island, marinas, museums, shops, and fine dining are all nearby.

Shadowlawn Manor ○

84 UNION STREET, HILLSDALE, MICHIGAN 49242

Tel: **(517) 437-2367**	Reduced Rates: **10% Jan., Feb., Dec.;**
Hosts: **Art Young and Al Paskevich**	**weekly; 10% seniors**
Location: **90 mi. SW of Detroit**	Credit Cards: **MC, VISA**
No. of Rooms: **5**	Breakfast: **Continental**
No. of Private Baths: **1**	Pets: **No**
Max. No. Sharing Bath: **4**	Children: **No**
Double/pb: **$60**	Smoking: **No**
Double/sb: **$50**	Social Drinking: **Permitted**
Single/sb: **$40**	Airport/Station Pickup: **Yes**
Open: **All year**	

Built in 1860, Shadowlawn Manor has been restored and refurbished with your comfort in mind. Art and Al have been collecting furniture, silverware, crystal, and antique accessories for years, and they have used it all to great advantage at Shadowlawn. They will be happy to direct you to the lake, beach, golf course, or Hillsdale College's arboretum. You are welcome to relax on the screened-in porch, where, in springtime, the lilacs perfume the air.

Dutch Colonial Inn

560 CENTRAL AVENUE, HOLLAND, MICHIGAN 49423

Tel: **(616) 396-3664**	Open: **All year**
Best Time to Call: **Anytime**	Breakfast: **Full**
Hosts: **Bob and Pat Elenbaas**	Pets: **No**
Location: **30 mi. W of Grand Rapids**	Children: **Welcome, over 10**
No. of Rooms: **5**	Smoking: **No**
No. of Private Baths: **5**	Social Drinking: **No**
Double/sb: **$65–$95**	Airport/Station Pickup: **Yes**

Bob and Pat Elenbaas invite you to experience Dutch hospitality in their spacious Colonial inn. The house is set in a quiet, residential section, with a large yard and lovely sun porch. Rooms are furnished with traditional family antiques, some dating back to the 1830s. Choose from a bedroom with lovely candlewicking on the drapes, comforters, and pillow shams; a suite with Victorian furnishings and its own sitting area; or the Jenny Lind Room, with its antique beds and dusty rose accents. Breakfast specialties such as quiche, home-made rolls, and muffins are served in the formal dining room. The Elenbaases are centrally located in a beautiful city, famous for its tulip festival, original Dutch windmill, and miles of sandy beaches on Lake Michigan.

Centennial ✪
5774 MAIN STREET, P.O. BOX 54, LEXINGTON, MICHIGAN 48450

Tel: (313) 359-8762
Best Time to Call: **After 5 PM**
Hosts: **Daniel and Dilla Miller**
Location: **20 mi. N of Port Huron**
No. of Rooms: **4**
No. of Private Baths: **2**
Max. No. Sharing Bath: **4**
Double/pb: **$55**
Single/pb: **$50**
Double/sb: **$55**
Single/sb: **$50**

Open: **All year**
Reduced Rates: **Available**
Breakfast: **Full (weekends),
  Continental (midweek)**
Pets: **No**
Children: **Welcome, over 10**
Smoking: **No**
Social Drinking: **Permitted**
Minimum Stay: **2 nights holiday
  weekends**

Centennial is a warm, inviting home furnished in traditional styles. Sit on the side porch listening to the singing birds and bubbling, splashing fountain, or stroll among the well-maintained lawns and gardens. Daniel and Dilla take the greatest pleasure in making your stay special. After a great night's sleep in the comfortable bedrooms, you'll wake up to fresh-brewed coffee and a homemade breakfast. The fresh fruit comes to the table from your hosts' garden and trees.

Governor's Inn ✪
LEXINGTON, MICHIGAN 48450

Tel: (313) 359-5770
Hosts: **Jane and Bob MacDonald**
Location: **20 mi. N of Port Huron**
No. of Rooms: **3**
No. of Private Baths: **3**
Double/pb: **$50**
Single/pb: **$50**

Open: **Memorial and Labor Day
  weekends**
Breakfast: **Continental**
Pets: **No**
Children: **Welcome, over 12**
Smoking: **Permitted**
Social Drinking: **Permitted**

A handsome residence built in 1859, it is located near the shore of Lake Huron. It has been refurbished to its original "summer home" style. Wicker furniture, rag rugs, iron beds, and green plants accent the light, airy decor. You can stroll to the nearby beach, browse through interesting shops, fish from the breakwater, or play golf or tennis. Jane and Bob, both educators, look forward to sharing their quaint village surroundings with you.

Charter Cottage on the Bay ✪
8250 CAMP HAVEN ROAD, NORTHPORT, MICHIGAN 49670

Tel: (616) 386-5534
Best Time to Call: **9 AM–10 PM**
Hosts: **Kay Kingery and Jim Charter**
Location: **30 mi. N of Traverse City**

No. of Rooms: **2**
No. of Private Baths: **2**
Double/pb: **$75**
Open: **Mar. 16–Dec. 31**

Breakfast: **Full**
Pets: **No**
Children: **No**
Smoking: **No**

Social Drinking: **No**
Minimum Stay: **3 nights holidays; 2
nights July–Aug.**

Wildlife enthusiasts will appreciate this modified Cape Cod cottage designed and built by the owners to take full advantage of their wooded bayside lot. The Charters have finished their home with architectural antiques and refer to their cottage as their "new-old" house. This cozy bed and breakfast is located near the tip of Michigan's scenic Leelanau County, home of the Sleeping Bear Dunes National Lakeshore, several wineries, and a number of quaint villages. Visitors to the area also enjoy a nearby gold course, tennis courts, a sail on the tall ship *Malabar*, or a ride on the Leelanau Scenic Railroad.

Benson House B&B ○

618 EAST LAKE STREET, PETOSKEY, MICHIGAN 49770

Tel: **(616) 347-1338**
Best Time to Call: **9–12 AM**
Hosts: **Rod and Carol Benson**
No. of Rooms: **4**
No. of Private Baths: **4**
Double/pb: **$78–$98**
Single/pb: **$78–$98**
Open: **All year**

Reduced Rates: **Available**
Breakfast: **Full**
Credit Cards: **MC, VISA**
Pets: **No**
Children: **Welcome, over 6**
Smoking: **No**
Social Drinking: **Permitted**
Airport/Station Pickup: **Yes**

From the beautiful veranda of Benson House, you can admire Lake Michigan's Little Traverse Bay, just as guests did in 1878 when this Victorian inn first opened its doors. Petoskey is in the heart of Michigan's Little New England; the town's Gaslight District offers excellent shopping and dining. Mackinac Island is just a short drive away, as are numerous beaches, lakes, and other points of interest. The area's scenic roads wind through forests, valleys, and upland meadows. Five major ski resorts provide the Midwest's best downhill and cross-country skiing.

Stafford House ○

4489 MAIN STREET, PORT HOPE, MICHIGAN 48468

Tel: **(517) 428-4554**
Best Time to Call: **Mornings; evenings**
Hosts: **Bill and Dolores Grubbs**
Location: **82 mi. N of Port Huron**
No. of Rooms: **2**
No. of Private Baths: **2**
Double/pb: **$45**
Suite: **$70**

Open: **All year**
Reduced Rates: **10% less Dec.–Mar.**
Breakfast: **Full**
Pets: **Sometimes**
Children: **Welcome**
Smoking: **Restricted**
Social Drinking: **Permitted**
Minimum Stay: **Holiday weekends**

Built in 1886 by the town's founder, this classic Victorian, painted three shades of blue, has won a place on the National Register of Historic Places. Antique furnishings, marble fireplaces, and ornate woodwork enhance the decor. Lake Huron is within walking distance for boating, fishing, or just relaxing on the beach. Among the many historic attractions nearby are the Grice Museum and the Huron City museums. Dolores, a retired social service worker, enjoys refinishing antiques and baking breakfast goodies. Bill, semiretired, does wood-working and fishes in his spare time. They look forward to sharing their quiet town with you.

Raymond House Inn ○

111 SOUTH RIDGE STREET, M-25, PORT SANILAC, MICHIGAN 48469

Tel: **(313) 622-8800**	Reduced Rates: **10% seniors**
Host: **Shirley Denison**	Breakfast: **Full**
Location: **30 mi. N of Port Huron**	Pets: **No**
No. of Rooms: 7	Children: **Welcome, over 12**
No. of Private Baths: 7	Smoking: **No**
Double/pb: **$50–$70**	Social Drinking: **Permitted**
Open: **May 1–Oct. 31**	

Shirley will put you right at ease in her antique-filled inn with the conveniences of today and the ambience of 1895. Each bedroom is furnished with period furniture, brightly colored spreads, and lace curtains. There's an old-fashioned parlor and a dining room where you are served breakfast. Sport fishermen and sailboat enthusiasts will enjoy this area; cultural activities, quilting bees, and the annual summer festival are longtime traditions here. There is a pottery and sculpture gallery in the inn.

Brockway House Bed & Breakfast ○

1631 BROCKWAY, SAGINAW, MICHIGAN 48602

Tel: **(517) 792-0746**	Open: **All year**
Best Time to Call: **Mornings**	Breakfast: **Full**
Hosts: **Richard and Danice Zuehlke**	Credit Cards: **AMEX, MC, VISA**
Location: **90 mi. N of Detroit**	Pets: **No**
No. of Rooms: 4	Children: **Welcome**
No. of Private Baths: 2	Smoking: **No**
Max. No. Sharing Bath: 4	Social Drinking: **Permitted**
Double/pb: **$85**	Airport/Station Pickup: **Yes**
Double/sb: **$65**	

This stately home, with huge white pillars, was built in 1864 by a lumber baron for his family. The Zuehlkes have restored it using a charming mix of primitive antiques and Victorian furnishings. Such special touches as sun-dried linens, imaginative window treatments, artfully arranged plants and baskets, and breakfast served on heirloom dishes are pleasures you'll savor. Tennis, golf, and a visit to the Japanese Gardens are local possibilities. And, given advance notice, Richard will arrange a tour of the General Motors plant in Saginaw.

Rosemont Inn

83 LAKESHORE DRIVE, P.O. BOX 214, SAUGATUCK, MICHIGAN 49453

Tel: **(616) 857-2637**
Best Time to Call: **8 AM–10 PM**
Hosts: **Joe and Marilyn Sajdak**
Location: **10 mi. S of Holland**
No. of Rooms: **14**
No. of Private Baths: **14**
Double/pb: **$55–$105**

Open: **All year**
Breakfast: **Continental, plus**
Credit Cards: **DISC, MC, VISA**
Pets: **No**
Children: **Welcome**
Smoking: **Permitted**
Social Drinking: **Permitted**

The Rosemont is a Victorian inn with gingerbread trim. It began receiving guests in 1886 and still maintains a tradition of country living and hospitality. The air-conditioned house is furnished in country prints and antique reproductions, with fireplaces in nine of the guest rooms. On a large porch, enjoy the cool breezes from Lake Michigan, whose beaches are directly across the street. Or swim in the inn's heated pool. Your hosts will gladly supply information on boat trips, golf, and the sights of Saugatuck. Ten of the 14 bedrooms are non-smoking areas.

Rummel's Tree Haven ❂
41 NORTH BECK STREET, M-25, SEBEWAING, MICHIGAN 48759

Tel: **(517) 883-2450**	Open: **All year**
Best Time to Call: **Afternoons;**	Breakfast: **Full**
evenings	Pets: **Sometimes**
Hosts: **Carl and Erma Rummel**	Children: **Welcome (crib)**
Location: **28 mi. NE of Bay City**	Smoking: **Permitted**
No. of Rooms: **2**	Social Drinking: **Permitted**
Double/pb: **$40**	Airport/Station Pickup: **Yes**
Single/pb: **$30**	

A tree grows right through the porch and roof of this charming old home that was built by the Beck family in 1878. Guests can relax in large, airy rooms furnished with twin beds and comfortable family pieces. City dwellers are sure to enjoy the small-town friendliness and the quiet of the countryside. Saginaw Bay offers fine fishing, hunting, boating, birdwatching, or just plain relaxing. Carl and Erma offer color TV, videocassettes, and the use of the barbecue and refrigerator. They love having company and will do all they can to make you feel welcome and relaxed.

Csatlos' Csarda ❂
P.O. BOX 523, STEPHENSON, MICHIGAN 49887

Tel: **(906) 753-4638; fax: (906) 753-**	Open: **All year**
2170	Breakfast: **Continental**
Host: **Barb Upton**	Pets: **No**
Location: **70 mi. N of Green Bay,**	Children: **No**
Wisconsin	Smoking: **No**
No. of Rooms: **2**	Social Drinking: **Permitted**
Max. No. Sharing Bath: **4**	Airport/Station Pickup: **Yes**
Double/sb: **$28**	Foreign Languages: **Hungarian**
Single/sb: **$22**	

Barb offers a touch of things Hungarian to those who wish to sample the charm of a very small town. Two blocks east of the front door and you're downtown; two blocks west and you're in a farmer's field! Lakes and beaches are nearby for summer swimming and boating or winter fishing. Cross-country ski trails are plentiful. It is a perfect spot to stop for the night for those travelers going to Chicago, Milwaukee, Mackinac Island, or Canada.

Linden Lea, A B&B on Long Lake ❂
279 SOUTH LONG LAKE ROAD, TRAVERSE CITY, MICHIGAN 49684

Tel: **(616) 943-9182**	No. of Rooms: **2**
Hosts: **Jim and Vicky McDonnell**	Max. No. Sharing Bath: **4**
Location: **9 mi. W of Traverse City**	Double/sb: **$70**

Open: **All year**
Reduced Rates: **$60 Nov.–May**
Breakfast: **Full**
Pets: **Sometimes**
Children: **Welcome**

Smoking: **No**
Social Drinking: **Permitted**
Minimum Stay: **Holiday weekends**
Airport/Station Pickup: **Yes**

Linden Lea is an extensively remodeled and expanded 1900 lakeside cottage set on a private sandy beach surrounded by woods. The bedrooms are comfortably furnished in country style, accented with antiques. You are certain to enjoy the window seats and the panoramic views of Long Lake. The area offers the Interlochen Center for the Arts National Music Camp, a PGA golfcourse, and local wineries. Breakfast features local specialties, such as smoked bacon, maple syrup, and berries that make the home-baked muffins so delicious.

Peninsula Manor
8880 PENINSULA DRIVE, TRAVERSE CITY, MICHIGAN 49684

Tel: **(616) 929-1321**
Best Time to Call: **Before 10 PM**
Hosts: **Karen and Will Williamson**
Location: **3 mi. N of Traverse City**
No. of Rooms: **3**
No. of Private Baths: **1**
Max. No. Sharing Bath: **4**
Double/pb: **$85**
Double/sb: **$70**

Open: **All year**
Breakfast: **Full**
Credit Cards: **MC, VISA**
Pets: **No**
Children: **Sometimes**
Smoking: **No**
Social Drinking: **Permitted**
Minimum Stay: **Holiday weekends**
Airport Pickup: **Yes**

Peninsula Manor, located on Old Mission Peninsula, is a contemporary home with spacious rooms and beachfront property on Grand Traverse Bay. The area is home to the National Cherry Festival and the Interlochen National Music Camp and Center for the Arts. Excellent golf, tennis, skiing, water sports, and hiking and biking areas are available. Relax on a deck and enjoy the bay view or gather in the family room to watch TV, play games, or socialize. Homemade jam, muffins, and coffee cake accompany the nutritious breakfast.

The Victorian Villa Inn ✪
601 NORTH BROADWAY STREET, UNION CITY, MICHIGAN 49094

Tel: **(517) 741-3895; (800) 34 VILLA
    [348-4552]**
Host: **Ron Gibson**
Location: **20 mi. S of Battle Creek**
No. of Rooms: **10**
No. of Private Baths: **10**
Double/pb: **$85–$125**
Single/pb: **$80**
Open: **All year**

Breakfast: **Full**
Credit Cards: **MC, VISA**
Pets: **No**
Children: **Welcome**
Smoking: **No**
Social Drinking: **Permitted**
Airport/Station Pickup: **Yes**

The Victorian Villa is a 19th-century estate house furnished with antiques. Guests may choose from ten private chambers, all elegantly appointed. Chilled champagne, wine, cheese, and a private "tea for two" can be arranged. Fancy chocolates, a specialty of the house, are placed on the pillows at night. Your host will help make your visit as sparkling as you like, directing you to summer theater, museums, antique shops, and restaurants. Ask Ron about the special "getaway" weekends, including cross-country skiing, Sherlock Holmes mystery themes, a Victorian Christmas, and fun-filled Summer-Daze.

Villa Hammer ✪

3133 LINDA MARIE WAY, WALLED LAKE, MICHIGAN 48088

Tel: **(313) 624-1071**
Best Time to Call: **Evenings**
Hosts: **Veronica and Reinhold Hammer**
Location: **5 mi. N of Novi**
No. of Rooms: **1**
No. of Private Baths: **1**
Double/pb: **$45**
Single/pb: **$35**

Open: **All year**
Reduced Rates: **10% weekly**
Breakfast: **Full**
Pets: **Sometimes**
Children: **Welcome, over 12**
Smoking: **No**
Social Drinking: **Permitted**

A Tudor house set on three secluded acres on the Huron River, it is furnished in a contemporary fashion accented with lots of plants.

Veronica and Reinhold invite you to relax in the hot tub and sauna. They offer a hearty breakfast; waffles are the house specialty. The Hammers are happy to acquaint you with the delights of the Lake Region and its many recreational activities. The Villa Hammer is 20 miles from Greenfield Village and Ann Arbor.

Williamston Bed and Breakfast
3169 SOUTH WILLIAMSTON ROAD, WILLIAMSTON, MICHIGAN 48895

Tel: **(517) 655-1061**	Single/sb: **$43**
Best Time to Call: **9 AM–9 PM**	Open: **All year**
Hosts: **Colleen and Bob Stone**	Breakfast: **Continental**
Location: **18 mi. E of Lansing**	Credit Cards: **MC, VISA**
No. of Rooms: **3**	Pets: **No**
No. of Private Baths: **1**	Children: **Welcome**
Max. No. Sharing Bath: **4**	Smoking: **Restricted**
Double/pb: **$60**	Social Drinking: **Permitted**
Double/sb: **$50**	

Colleen Stone welcomes you to her 1916 farmhouse located at the edge of historic Williamston. This is a town filled with craftsmen, and your host is no exception. Colleen's basketry and primitive country landscapes accent each room. The bedrooms are decorated with antique beds and matching wood dressers and spanking white quilts and curtains. The breakfast specialties of the house are fresh fruit cup and pastries served with hot beverages. In the afternoon, wine and cheese can be enjoyed by the living room fire or outside on the porch. Antiques dealers, shops, and fine restaurants are within walking distance of the house. Michigan State University and the State Capitol are less than 20 minutes away.

MINNESOTA

- Lutsen
- North Branch
- Stacy
- Norwood
- Minneapolis/St. Paul
- Dundas
- Lake City
- Round Lake
- Spring Valley

Martin Oaks B&B ✪
107 FIRST STREET, DUNDAS, MINNESOTA 55019

Tel: **(507) 645-4644**
Best Time to Call: **Before noon or after 6 PM**
Hosts: **Marie and Frank Gery**
Location: **35 mi. S of Minneapolis and St. Paul**
No. of Rooms: **2**
Max. No. Sharing Bath: **4**
Double/sb: **$65**
Single/sb: **$45**
Open: **All year**

Breakfast: **Full**
Other Meals: **Available**
Credit Cards: **MC, VISA**
Pets: **No**
Children: **Sometimes**
Smoking: **No**
Social Drinking: **Permitted**
Minimum Stay: **2 nights during college events**
Airport/Station Pickup: **Yes**

Built in 1869 by the treasurer of the thriving Archibald Mill just across the Cannon River, Martin Oaks is listed on the National Register of

318

Historic Places. The architecture combines elements of Italianate and Greek Revival styles. Some rooms have their original pine floors, and all are furnished with comfortable antiques. Local activities abound, with options like golf, tennis, skiing, biking, hiking, canoeing, antiquing, and bookstore browsing. St. Olaf and Carleton colleges are minutes away. After serving you fresh fruit, egg dishes, and home-baked goodies, your hostess, a storyteller, will probably end breakfast by regaling you with an episode or two of local history.

Red Gables Inn ✪

403 NORTH HIGH STREET, LAKE CITY, MINNESOTA 55041

Tel: (612) 345-2605
Hosts: **Mary and Douglas De Roos**
Location: **60 mi. SE of Twin Cities**
No. of Rooms: 5
No. of Private Baths: 3
Max. No. Sharing Bath: 4
Double/pb: **$68–$75**
Double/sb: **$58–$68**

Open: **All year**
Breakfast: **Full**
Other Meals: **Available**
Credit Cards: **MC, VISA**
Pets: **No**
Children: **Welcome, over 13**
Smoking: **No**
Social Drinking: **Permitted**

Red Gables Inn is located in the Hiawatha Valley on the shore of Lake Pepin. The inn was built in 1865 by a wealthy merchant and is a mixture of Italianate and Greek Revival styles. The original pine floors, white-pine woodwork, and large windows have been carefully restored; each bedroom has an old-fashioned iron, brass, or walnut bed, antique wood wardrobe, Victorian wall coverings, and ceiling fan. A breakfast buffet of fruit specialties, sticky buns, home-baked breads, eggs, jams, and coffee is served on the screened-in porch or in the fireside dining room, and hors d'oeuvres are served in the parlor. Your hosts are also happy to assist with gourmet picnic lunches, chilled champagne in your room, and reservations for dining. They have bicycles to lend for exploring the nearby marina, antique shops, and nature trails.

Lindgren's Bed and Breakfast ✪

COUNTY ROAD 35—W-191, P.O. BOX 56, LUTSEN, MINNESOTA 55612-0056

Tel: (218) 663-7450
Best Time to Call: **Anytime**
Hosts: **Bob and Shirley Lindgren**
Location: **5**
No. of Rooms: 4
No. of Private Baths: 2
Max. No. Sharing Bath: 4
Double/pb: **$85–$110**
Single/pb: **$80–$105**

Double/sb: **$75–$85**
Single/sb: **$70–$80**
Suites: **$110; sleeps 4**
Open: **All year**
Reduced Rates: **5% seniors**
Breakfast: **Full**
Credit Cards: **MC, VISA**
Pets: **No**
Children: **Sometimes**

Smoking: **Permitted**
Social Drinking: **Permitted**
Minimum Stay: **2 nights weekends,**

3 nights holiday weekends
Airport/Station Pickup: **Yes**

Whatever the season, get away from it all at this 1920s log home on the north shore of Lake Superior. Walk along the shoreline, or just admire it from one of the B&B's 52 windows, all of them offering wonderful views. From golfing, tennis, and skiing to hiking, snowmobiling and berry picking, there is plenty to do here. Foliage fans can choose between two seasons of fall colors. Your hosts are avid outdoorspeople who can direct you to the best hunting and fishing spots.

Evelo's Bed & Breakfast
2301 BRYANT AVENUE SOUTH, MINNEAPOLIS, MINNESOTA 55405

Tel: **(612) 374-9656**
Best Time to Call: **After 4 PM**
Hosts: **David and Sheryl Evelo**
No. of Rooms: **3**
Max. No. Sharing Bath: **6**
Double/sb: **$35**
Single/sb: **$35**

Open: **All year**
Breakfast: **Full**
Credit Cards: **MC, VISA**
Pets: **No**
Children: **Welcome**
Smoking: **No**
Social Drinking: **Permitted**

Located in the historic Lowry Hill East neighborhood, on the bus line, this 1897 Victorian has one of the best-preserved interiors in the area and is furnished with fine period pieces. David and Sheryl are both schoolteachers. Breakfast, served in the formal dining room, often features quiche or egg casseroles. The house is within walking distance of the Guthrie Theater, the Walker Art Center, convention center, shops, and restaurants.

Red Pine Log B&B ✪
15140 400TH STREET, NORTH BRANCH, MINNESOTA 55056

Tel: **(612) 583-3326**
Best Time to Call: **After 5 PM**
Hosts: **Lowell and Gloria Olson**
Location: **45 mi. N of St. Paul**
No. of Rooms: **3**
No. of Private Baths: **1**
Max. No. Sharing Bath: **4**
Double/pb: **$95**
Double/sb: **$75–$80**

Single/sb: **$70**
Open: **All year**
Reduced Rates: **10% weekly; Mar.–
Apr.; 60 and older all year**
Breakfast: **Full**
Pets: **No**
Children: **Welcome, over 12**
Smoking: **No**
Social Drinking: **Permitted**

If Abe Lincoln had known log homes could look like this, he would have had second thoughts about heading for the White House! Lowell Olson handcrafted this lodge-style home in 1985. His professional

training as a log home designer is obvious from the exposed logs and
trusses throughout the house. Loft bedrooms are richly paneled and
feature country furnishings, skylights, ceiling fans, and a balcony.
Your hosts invite you for crassane and cheese in the living room,
which boasts a 26-foot-high ceiling and an antique parlor stove. You
will find the kitchen an equally cozy place with its antique harvest
table and ash cabinets. Here you can relax over Gloria's prize muffins
and special frittatas, served with plenty of fresh coffee. The Olsons
have 30 acres for you to explore, and they are within easy reach of
downhill skiing, Taylors Falls, and Wild River State Park.

The Prairie House on Round Lake ✪
RR 1, BOX 105, ROUND LAKE, MINNESOTA 56167

Tel: (507) 945-8934
Hosts: **Ralph and Virginia Schenck**
No. of Rooms: **4**
No. of Private Baths: **1**
Max. No. Sharing Bath: **4**
Double/pb: **$45–$55**
Single/pb: **$45–$55**
Double/sb: **$35–$45**

Single/sb: **$35–$45**
Open: **All year**
Breakfast: **Full**
Pets: **Welcome**
Children: **Welcome**
Smoking: **No**
Social Drinking: **Permitted**
Airport/Station Pickup: **Yes**

Built in 1879 by a prominent Chicago businessman, this farmhouse is
a retreat from the bustle of city life. It's a working horse farm:
American paint horses roam the pasture, and three barns house both
young stock in training and show horses that are exhibited all over the
world. A cupola rising from the central stairway is circled by four
dormer bedrooms on the second floor. Antique furniture accented
with equine touches reflects the spirit of the farm. Fishing, hiking,
swimming, boating, and tennis are at the doorstep.

Chatsworth Bed and Breakfast
984 ASHLAND AVENUE, ST. PAUL, MINNESOTA 55104

Tel: (612) 227-4288
Best Time to Call: **Noon–5 PM**
Hosts: **Donna and Earl Gustafson**
Location: **½ mi. from I-94**
No. of Rooms: **5**
No. of Private Baths: **3**
Max. No. Sharing Bath: **4**
Double/pb: **$80–$100**
Single/pb: **$75–$95**
Double/sb: **$60–$65**

Single/sb: **$55–$60**
Open: **All year**
Reduced Rates: **Weekly**
Breakfast: **Continental**
Pets: **No**
Children: **Welcome**
Smoking: **No**
Social Drinking: **Permitted**
Airport/Station Pickup: **Yes**

This spacious 1902 Victorian is located on a large corner lot surrounded
by maple and basswood trees. The setting is quiet and residential, but

is just a few blocks from shops, restaurants, and the governor's mansion. Guest rooms are decorated in international motifs and are located on a separate floor from your hosts' quarters. The Victorian Room features a handcarved wood bed, floral rug, lace curtains, and antiques, while the Scandinavian Room uses pine furnishings, white curtains, and matching spread to create a light and airy feeling. Guests may prefer the room with a four-poster bed and private double whirlpool bath, or the one with Afro-Asian furnishings, whirlpool bath, and adjoining porch. The Gustafsons serve breakfast in a beautifully paneled formal dining room. They also invite you to relax in the living room, where you may enjoy the library, the piano, and a roaring fire.

Chase's Bed & Breakfast ✪
508 NORTH HURON, SPRING VALLEY, MINNESOTA 55975

Tel: (507) 346-2850	Reduced Rates: 15% weekly
Hosts: Bob and Jeannine Chase	Breakfast: Full
Location: 26 mi. S of Rochester	Credit Cards: DISC, MC, VISA
No. of Rooms: 5	Pets: No
No. of Private Baths: 5	Children: Sometimes
Double/pb: $75	Smoking: No
Single/pb: $60	Social Drinking: Permitted
Open: Feb.–Dec.	Airport/Station Pickup: Yes

William H. Strong built this Second Empire–style home in 1879 for $8,000. At the time, it was considered to be the most handsome home in the county. Over the years, the house has been an office, motel, and rest home, and is now listed on the National Register of Historic Places. Guests will find elegant rooms furnished in period antiques, many of which are for sale. Bob and Jeannine serve a hearty breakfast and offer snacks and setups in the evening. Nearby activities include swimming, tennis, golf, trout fishing, and hiking. Chase's is 18 miles from the airport, and 28 miles from the Mayo Clinic. The Amish area is nearby.

Kings Oakdale Park Guest House ✪
6933 232 AVENUE NORTHEAST, STACY, MINNESOTA 55079

Tel: (612) 462-5598	Suites: $28
Hosts: Donna and Charles Solem	Open: All year
Location: 38 mi. N of St. Paul	Breakfast: Continental
No. of Rooms: 3	Pets: Sometimes
No. of Private Baths: 2	Children: No
Double/pb: $28	Smoking: Permitted
Single/pb: $25	Social Drinking: Permitted
Double/sb: $26	Foreign Languages: French
Single/sb: $23	

This comfortable home is situated on four landscaped acres on the banks of Typo Creek. The picnic tables, volleyball net, and horseshoe game are sure signs of a hospitable country place. It is a serene retreat for people on business trips to the Twin Cities. The Wisconsin border and the scenic St. Croix River, where boat trips are offered, are minutes from the house. Charles and Donna will direct you to the most reasonable restaurants in town. For late snacks, refrigerators in the bedrooms are provided.

For key to listings, see inside front or back cover.

❂ This star means that rates are guaranteed through December 31, 1993, to any guest making a reservation as a result of reading about the B&B in *Bed & Breakfast U.S.A.—1993* edition.

Important! To avoid misunderstandings, always ask about cancellation policies when booking.

Please enclose a self-addressed, stamped, business-size envelope when contacting reservation services.

For more details on what you can expect in a B&B, see Chapter 1.

Always mention *Bed & Breakfast U.S.A.* when making reservations!

If no B&B is listed in the area you'll be visiting, use the form on page 733 to order a copy of our "List of New B&Bs."

We want to hear from you! Use the form on page 735.

MISSISSIPPI

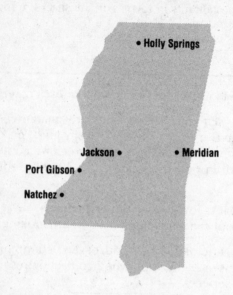

Holly Springs •

Jackson •   • Meridian
Port Gibson •

Natchez •

Lincoln, Ltd. Bed & Breakfast—Mississippi Reservation Service

P.O. BOX 3479, 2303 23RD AVENUE, MERIDIAN, MISSISSIPPI 39303

Tel: **(601) 482-5483; resv. only: (800) 633-MISS [6477]; Fax: (601) 693-7447**
Best Time to Call: **9 AM–5 PM**
Coordinator: **Barbara Lincoln Hall**
States/Regions Covered: **Statewide**

Descriptive Directory: **$3.50**
Rates (Single/Double):
  Average: **$45–$65 / $55–$75**
  Luxury: **$75–$125 / $85–$160**
Credit Cards: **AMEX, MC, VISA**

For the traveling businessperson or for the vacationer, a stay with one of Barbara's hosts offers a personal taste of the finest Southern hospitality. All rooms have private baths. Mississippi abounds with historic-house tours, called "pilgrimages," in March and April, and Natchez and Vicksburg have similar pilgrimages in autumn. In May, Meridian is host to the Jimmie Rodgers Festival. Accommodations range from a cozy, historic log cabin to an elegant antebellum mansion.

Hamilton Place
105 EAST MASON AVENUE, HOLLY SPRINGS, MISSISSIPPI 38635

Tel: **(601) 252-4368**	Open: **All year**
Best Time to Call: **After 4:30 PM**	Breakfast: **Full**
Hosts: **Linda and Jack Stubbs**	Credit Cards: **MC, VISA**
Location: **35 mi. SE of Memphis, Tenn.**	Pets: **No**
No. of Rooms: **3**	Children: **Welcome**
No. of Private Baths: **3**	Smoking: **Permitted**
Double/pb: **$65**	Social Drinking: **Permitted**
Single/pb: **$55**	Airport/Station Pickup: **Yes**
Guest Cottage: **$65**	

On the National Register of Historic Places, this antebellum home, circa 1838, is furnished with heirloom antiques. In fact, Linda and Jack have a delightful antique shop on the premises featuring furniture, china, and cut glass. Breakfast can be enjoyed on the veranda or in the garden gazebo. You'll love the taste of the homemade biscuits with strawberry or honey-lemon butter. You are welcome to use the sauna or swimming pool.

Eastport Inn Bed & Breakfast ☉
100 SOUTH PEARL STREET, IUKA, MISSISSIPPI 38852

Tel: **(601) 423-2511**	Reduced Rates: **Available**
Best Time to Call: **8 AM–10 AM, 3 PM–10 PM**	Breakfast: **Continental**
	Other Meals: **Available**
Host: **Betty Watson**	Credit Cards: **AMEX, DC, DISC, MC, VISA**
No. of Rooms: **7**	
No. of Private Baths: **7**	Pets: **No**
Double/pb: **$50**	Children: **Welcome**
Single/pb: **$40**	Smoking: **No**
Suites: **$50**	Social Drinking: **Permitted**
Open: **All year**	

This gracious home was built in 1864 and is decorated in period style, with four-poster beds and floral bedspreads. For swimming and boating, Pickwick Lake is six miles away; Shiloh National Park, Tishomingo State Park, Coleman State Park, and the Natchez Trace Drive are also nearby.

Oak Square Plantation ✪
1207 CHURCH STREET, PORT GIBSON, MISSISSIPPI 39150

Tel: **(601) 437-4350; (800) 729-0240**
Best Time to Call: **Mornings; evenings**
Hosts: **Mr. and Mrs. William D. Lum**
Location: **On Hwy. 61 between
   Natchez and Vicksburg**
No. of Rooms: **8**
No. of Private Baths: **8**
Double/pb: **$75–$95**

Single/pb: **$65–$70**
Open: **All year**
Breakfast: **Full**
Credit Cards: **AMEX, DISC, MC, VISA**
Pets: **No**
Children: **Welcome**
Smoking: **No**
Social Drinking: **Permitted**

Port Gibson is the town that Union General Ulysses S. Grant said was "too beautiful to burn." Oak Square is the largest and most palatial antebellum mansion, circa 1850, in Port Gibson, and is listed on the National Register of Historic Places. The guest rooms are all furnished with family heirlooms, and most have canopied beds. Guests will enjoy the courtyard, gazebo, and beautiful grounds. A chairlift for upstairs rooms is available. You will enjoy the delightful Southern breakfast and tour of the mansion. Your hosts offer complimentary wine, tea, or coffee, and will enlighten you on the many historic attractions in the area. Oak Square has been awarded a four-star rating by AAA.

MISSOURI

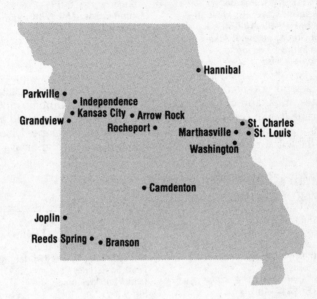

Bed & Breakfast Kansas City—Missouri & Kansas
P.O. BOX 14781, LENEXA, KANSAS 66215

Tel: **(913) 888-3636**
Coordinator: **Edwina Monroe**
States/Regions Covered: **Kansas—
Lenexa, Overland Park, Wichita;
Missouri—Grandview,
Independence, Kansas City, Lee's
Summit, Parkville, St. Joseph,
Springfield, Warrensburg, Weston**

Rates (Single/Double):
  Average: **$35 / $35–$50**
  Luxury: **$55 / $60–$100**
Credit Cards: **No**

You will enjoy visiting such places as the Truman Library and home,
Crown Center, Country Club Plaza, Arrowhead Stadium, Royals Stadium, Kemper Arena, the Missouri Repertory Theatre, and the American Heartland Theater.

Ozark Mountain Country B&B Service ✪
BOX 295, BRANSON, MISSOURI 65616

Tel: (417) 334-4720; (800) 695-1546	Rates (Single/Double):
Best Time to Call: 5–10 PM; 9 AM–	Modest: **$35–$45**
noon	Average: **$50–$65**
Coordinator: **Kay Cameron**	Luxury: **$70–$95**
States/Regions Covered: **Missouri—**	Credit Cards: **AMEX, MC, VISA (5%**
Branson, Hartville, Hollister, Joplin,	**surcharge)**
Marionville, Springfield; Arkansas—	
Eureka Springs, Everton;	
Oklahoma—Tulsa	

Kay will send you a complimentary copy of her descriptive listing of 80 homes, inns, and guest cottages, so you can select the host of your choice; she'll take care of making your reservation. She would appreciate your sending her a self-addressed, stamped envelope. Discounts are available for groups, honeymooners, and several-night stays.

Borgman's Bed & Breakfast ✪
ARROW ROCK, MISSOURI 65320

Tel: (816) 837-3350	Open: **All year**
Best Time to Call: 7–9 AM	Reduced Rates: **10% 3 nights**
Hosts: **Helen and Kathy Borgman**	Breakfast: **Continental**
Location: **100 mi. E of Kansas City**	Other Meals: **Dinner (winter only)**
No. of Rooms: **4**	Pets: **Sometimes**
Max. No. Sharing Bath: **4**	Children: **Welcome**
Double/sb: **$45–$50**	Smoking: **No**
Single/sb: **$40**	Social Drinking: **Permitted**

This 1860 home is spacious and comfortable, and it is furnished with cherished family pieces. Helen is a seamstress, artisan, and baker. Wait till you taste her fresh breads! Daughter Kathy is a town tour guide, so you will get firsthand information on this National Historic Landmark town at the beginning of the Santa Fe Trail. A fine repertory theater, the Lyceum, is open in summer. Craft shops, antique stalls, and the old country store are fun places to browse in. Good restaurants are within walking distance.

Country Gardens B&B ✪
HCR 4 BOX 2202, LAKESHORE DRIVE, BRANSON, MISSOURI 65616

Tel: (417) 334-8564; (800) 727-0723	Single/pb: **$70**
Hosts: **Bob and Pat Cameron**	Guest Cottage: **$75**
Location: **39 mi. from I-44**	Suites: **$100**
No. of Rooms: **3**	Open: **All year**
No. of Private Baths: **3**	Breakfast: **Full**
Double/pb: **$75**	Credit Cards: **MC, VISA**

Pets: **No**
Children: **Welcome, over 12**

Smoking: **Permitted**
Airport/Station Pickup: **Yes**

A parklike setting of gardens and a waterfall surround this wood-frame-and-rock home, located on beautiful Lake Taneycomo. The Camerons have a variety of accommodations with private entrances. The Rose Suite consists of three rooms and features a large bathroom with spa. The Bittersweet Room is decorated with antiques and has a private deck overlooking the water. Dogwood has a single whirlpool tub and kitchen for those who like to prepare light meals. Breakfast specialties such as waffles with strawberries, and hot biscuits with eggs are served in the garden room overlooking the garden. Bob and Pat invite you to swim in the pool and enjoy a picnic under the trees. They say the best trout fishing around is right on the lake, and they have boats and fishing docks for anglers. Music lovers will be glad to know that there are 22 different country music shows in the area.

Lakeside Guest House
RR 2 BOX 41, NORMAC, CAMDENTON, MISSOURI 65020

Tel: **(314) 346-3767**
Best Time to Call: **Evenings**
Host: **Virginia Dyck**
Location: **170 mi. SE of Kansas City**
No. of Rooms: **2**
No. of Private Baths: **2**
Double/pb: **$50**

Single/pb: **$45**
Open: **May 1–Oct. 31**
Breakfast: **Continental**
Pets: **No**
Children: **No**
Smoking: **No**
Social Drinking: **Permitted**

Virginia's lovely home is a bilevel, modified A-frame just 50 feet from the Lake of the Ozarks, with cathedral ceilings and many glass doors opening onto the patio and deck. You will be lulled to sleep by the sound of lapping water. HaHa Tonka Ruins and Trails, Bridal Cave, country music shows, antique shops, and many fine restaurants are all close by.

Ramblewood Bed and Breakfast ✪
402 PANORAMIC DRIVE, CAMDENTON, MISSOURI 65020

Tel: **(314) 346-3410**
Best Time to Call: **After 5 PM**
Host: **Mary Massey**
Location: **90 mi. S of Columbia**
No. of Rooms: **2**
Max. No. Sharing Bath: **4**
Double/sb: **$45**

Single/sb: **$40**
Open: **All year**
Breakfast: **Full**
Pets: **No**
Children: **No**
Smoking: **No**
Social Drinking: **Permitted**

Ramblewood is a Pilgrim-red home with white trim. Set on a quiet, wooded lot, it has the feel of an English country cottage. Spend the

night in an attractive, comfortable room and awaken to breakfast
served on a sunny deck. Ham-and-cheese omelets and homemade
breads are specialties of the house. The inn is minutes from Lake of
the Ozarks, HaHa Tonka State Park and Castle, and antique shops,
malls, and restaurants to suit any taste. After a busy day, enjoy a cool
drink on the porch.

The Fountains ✪
12610 BLUE RIDGE, GRANDVIEW, MISSOURI 64030

Tel: **(816) 763-6260**
Best Time to Call: **9 AM–9 PM**
Host: **Sally J. Stewart**
Location: **1½ mi. W of Rte. 71**
No. of Rooms: **3**
Max. No. Sharing Bath: **4**
Double/sb: **$35**

Single/sb: **$30**
Open: **Jan. 11–Dec. 9**
Breakfast: **Continental**
Pets: **Sometimes**
Children: **Welcome, over 9**
Smoking: **Permitted**
Social Drinking: **Permitted**

Sally's home is convenient to the Truman Library and home, the
Nelson-Atkins Art Gallery, Starlight Theatre, Worlds of Fun park, and
the famous plaza of Kansas City. The guest quarters has its own
private entrance, dining room with fireplace, and kitchen. You are
welcome to use the patio, barbecue, and gazebo. Sally enjoys having
guests, and her good humor and warm hospitality will make you feel
welcome immediately.

Garth Woodside Mansion
NEW LONDON GRAVEL ROAD, RR1, HANNIBAL, MISSOURI 63401

Tel: **(314) 221-2789**
Best Time to Call: **10 AM–7 PM**

Hosts: **Irv and Diane Feinberg**
Location: **99 mi. N of St. Louis**

No. of Rooms: **8**	Credit Cards: **MC, VISA**
No. of Private Baths: **8**	Pets: **No**
Double/pb: **$58–$90**	Children: **Welcome, over 12**
Open: **All year**	Smoking: **No**
Breakfast: **Full**	Social Drinking: **Permitted**

This Second Empire Victorian, built in 1871, has a three-story flying staircase, 14-foot ceilings, and eight handcarved marble fireplaces. Many of the room furnishings date back to the original owners. Stroll the 39 country acres, then sit down for a leisurely afternoon tea. Breakfast, served in the formal dining room, features peach French toast, fluted quiche cups, and eggs picante. This location is ideal for touring Mark Twain country or for a romantic getaway. What's more, your hosts will pamper you with wonderful extras like nightshirts and turndown service.

Visages ✪
327 NORTH JACKSON, JOPLIN, MISSOURI 64801

Tel: **(417) 624-1397**	Double/sb: **$40**
Best Time to Call: **After 4:30 PM**	Single/sb: **$30**
Hosts: **Bill and Marge Meeker**	Open: **All year**
Location: **3 mi. W of Rte. 71**	Breakfast: **Full**
No. of Rooms: **3**	Credit Cards: **MC, VISA**
No. of Private Baths: **2**	Pets: **Yes**
Max. No. Sharing Bath: **4**	Children: **Welcome (crib)**
Double/pb: **$50**	Smoking: **Permitted**
Single/pb: **$45**	Social Drinking: **No**

Visages takes its name from the nineteen sculptured faces imbedded in the masonry walls surrounding the house, a distinctive chocolate-brown Colonial that dates to 1898. The Meekers bought the house as an abandoned wreck in 1977 and spent the next ten years refurbishing it; not surprisingly, Bill lists woodworking as one of his hobbies. The breakfast specialty here is whole-wheat pancakes.

Milford House ✪
3605 GILLHAM ROAD, KANSAS CITY, MISSOURI 64111

Tel: **(816) 753-1269**	Breakfast: **Full**
Hosts: **Ian and Pat Mills**	Credit Cards: **AMEX, MC, VISA**
No. of Rooms: **4**	Pets: **No**
No. of Private Baths: **4**	Children: **No**
Double/pb: **$85**	Smoking: **No**
Single/pb: **$75**	Social Drinking: **Permitted**
Open: **All year**	

A striking architectural hybrid, Milford House is a three-story red-brick mansion combining Queen Anne and Dutch Colonial elements.

Indoors, a dramatic winding staircase leads from the main entrance to a tower on the side; a 70-foot stained-glass window, based on an original Tiffany landscape, dominates the living room. Kansas City's attractions range from museums to theme parks. The athletically inclined can play tennis on courts across the street from Milford House, while more sedentary sorts can exercise their fingers on the Mills's piano. Guests breakfast on dishes like French toast stuffed with cheese, lemon bread, and Southern-style grits.

Pridewell ✪
600 WEST 50TH STREET, KANSAS CITY, MISSOURI 64112

Tel: **(816) 931-1642**	Open: **All year**
Best Time to Call: **4–9 PM**	Breakfast: **Full**
Hosts: **Edwin and Louann White**	Pets: **No**
No. of Rooms: **2**	Children: **Welcome**
No. of Private Baths: **1**	Smoking: **No**
Double/pb: **$70**	Social Drinking: **Permitted**
Single/pb: **$65**	

This fine Tudor residence is situated in a wooded residential area on the battlefield of the Civil War's Battle of Westport. The Nelson Art Gallery, the University of Missouri at Kansas City, and the Missouri Repertory Theatre are close by. It is adjacent to the Country Club Plaza shopping district, which includes several four-star restaurants, tennis courts, and a park.

Gramma's House ✪
1105 HIGHWAY D, MARTHASVILLE, MISSOURI 63357

Tel: **(314) 433-2675**	Single/sb: **$35**
Best Time to Call: **8 AM–5 PM**	Guest Cottage: **$75**
Hosts: **Judy and Jim Jones**	Open: **All year**
Location: **50 mi. W of St. Louis**	Breakfast: **Full**
No. of Rooms: **4**	Credit Cards: **MC, VISA**
No. of Private Baths: **2**	Pets: **Sometimes**
Max. No. Sharing Bath: **4**	Children: **Welcome**
Double/pb: **$60**	Smoking: **No**
Single/pb: **$40**	Social Drinking: **Permitted**
Double/sb: **$55**	

At this romantic 150-year-old farmhouse, morning starts with a full, hearty breakfast like Gramma used to make. You can relax and maybe hear the bobwhite's call, reminding you of special times you spent at your own grandparents' home. Accommodations range from bedrooms to a snug cottage—formerly a smokehouse—with its own fireplace and sleeping loft. There are antique shops in Marthasville and Washington, and wineries in Augusta, Dutzow, and Hermann. Close by is the Missouri River hiking and biking trail. The historic Daniel Boone home and burial site are also in the area.

Bartlett Farm B&B ☉
ROUTE 1 BOX 518, NORWOOD, MISSOURI 65717

Tel: **(417) 746-4161**	Open: **All year**
Hosts: **Burt and Betty Bartlett**	Breakfast: **Full**
Location: **45 mi. E of Springfield**	Pets: **Sometimes**
No. of Rooms: **1**	Children: **Welcome (crib)**
No. of Private Baths: **1**	Smoking: **Permitted**
Double/pb: **$50**	Social Drinking: **Permitted**

Bartlett Farm occupies its own 80-acre valley in the Ozarks, with plenty of farm animals in residence. There are a fishing pond on the property and more fishing sites nearby, plus deer and turkey hunting in season. Burt, a retired real estate broker, and Betty, a registered nurse, like to share their casual, friendly life-style, as well as their screened-in porch, fireplace, and VCR and tape library. The B&B is convenient to such attractions as old mills, float trips, and the Laura Ingalls Wilder Museum and Home in Mansfield.

Down-to-Earth Lifestyles
ROUTE 22, PARKVILLE, MISSOURI 64152

Tel: **(816) 891-1018**	Reduced Rates: **Families**
Hosts: **Lola and Bill Coons**	Breakfast: **Full**
Location: **15 mi. N of downtown Kansas City**	Other Meals: **Available**
	Pets: **No**
No. of Rooms: **4**	Children: **Welcome**
No. of Private Baths: **4**	Smoking: **Permitted**
Double/pb: **$69**	Social Drinking: **Permitted**
Single/pb: **$59**	Airport/Station Pickup: **Yes**
Open: **All year**	

This spacious new earth-integrated home, with its picture windows and skylights, emphasizes close contact with nature. It's located on an 85-acre ranch, where there are horses and cows, a fishing pond, and lots of space for mind and soul. The furnishings complement the country setting, and the heated indoor pool, exercise room, and jogging and walking trails will keep you in shape. Lola and Bill will be pleased to suggest nearby places of interest if you can bear to tear yourself away from this restorative haven.

Journey's End Bed & Breakfast ✪
HCR 6 BOX 4632, REEDS SPRING, MISSOURI 65737

Tel: (417) 338-2685	Open: May 1–Oct. 31
Best Time to Call: 7 AM–10 AM, 7	Reduced Rates: 10% after 3rd night
PM–10 PM	Breakfast: Continental
Host: Liz Bass	Pets: No
Location: 40 mi. S of Springfield	Children: Infants only
No. of Rooms: 1	Smoking: No
No. of Private Baths: 1	Social Drinking: Permitted
Guest Cottage: $60–$80; sleeps 2–4	

Built in the 1920s to house visitors to Marvel Cave—the nation's third-largest commercial cavern—this yellow-and-white clapboard cottage has been recently renovated. The main room contains sleeping, sitting, and dining areas, plus a telephone and a TV. The large bath boasts an old-fashioned pedestal tub, separate shower, and dressing table, while the kitchenette has a refrigerator and microwave. Continental breakfast is brought to the cabin on a tray at a prearranged time; weather permitting, you can dine al fresco on the patio. Because it's surrounded by the Tri-Lakes area of the Ozarks, Journey's End offers both privacy and ready access to country music shows, water sports, crafts and antique shops, factory outlets, and, of course, Silver Dollar City, the 1880s mining-town theme park built around Marvel Cave.

School House Bed & Breakfast ✪
THIRD & CLARK STREETS, ROCHEPORT, MISSOURI 65279

Tel: (314) 698-2022	Open: All year
Hosts: John and Vicki Ott	Breakfast: Full
Location: 10 mi. W of Columbia	Credit Cards: MC, VISA
No. of Rooms: 8	Pets: No
No. of Private Baths: 6	Children: Welcome, over 5
Max. No. Sharing Bath: 4	Smoking: No
Double/pb: $75–$100	Social Drinking: Permitted
Double/sb: $85–$105	Airport/Station Pickup: Yes

Relive those fond school memories as a guest in this former school building offering eight delightfully furnished rooms, each with its own individual charm. All the magical old elements are intact, from the 13-foot ceilings and black slate chalkboards to the cast-iron bell on the front lawn. A delicious breakfast will be prepared before your eyes in one of the turn-of-the-century classrooms. John and Vicki will happily recommend many points of interest in this charming river town, including antique and pottery shops, a local winery, a small bistro, and the romantic river walk.

Caverly Farm and Orchard B&B ○

389 NORTH MOSLEY ROAD, ST. LOUIS, MISSOURI 63141

Tel: (314) 432-5074
Hosts: **David and Nancy Caverly**
Location: **2 mi. from I-270 and I-40-64**
No. of Rooms: **3**
No. of Private Baths: **1**
Max. No. Sharing Bath: **4**
Double/pb: **$55**
Single/pb: **$50**
Double/sb: **$50**

Single/sb: **$45**
Open: **All year**
Reduced Rates: **Weekly; 10% seniors**
Breakfast: **Full**
Pets: **No**
Children: **Welcome (crib)**
Smoking: **No**
Social Drinking: **Permitted**
Airport/Station Pickup: **Yes**

The farm consists of two large vegetable gardens; the orchard has just a few fruit trees, but the farmhouse, built in the 1880s, makes it all seem more rural than suburban. The harvest is often found on the breakfast table in berry dishes and preserves along with delicious omelets and home-baked yeast breads. Victorian and primitive family antiques enhance the charm of the large and airy bedrooms. David and Nancy enjoy families with children, and have an electric stair chair to make the second-floor bedrooms accessible to those who may have difficulty climbing stairs.

Coachlight Bed & Breakfast ○

P.O. BOX 8095, ST. LOUIS, MISSOURI 63156

Tel: (314) 367-5870
Best Time to Call: **8 AM–6 PM**
Hosts: **Susan and Chuck Sundermeyer**
No. of Rooms: **3**
No. of Private Baths: **3**
Double/pb: **$65–$80**
Open: **All year**

Reduced Rates: **Available**
Breakfast: **Full**
Credit Cards: **AMEX, MC, VISA**
Pets: **No**
Children: **Welcome, over 3**
Smoking: **Permitted**
Social Drinking: **Permitted**

This 1904 three-story brick home, with twin dormers and bowed windows, is conveniently located to Forest Park, the St. Louis Zoo, City Art Museum, Powell Symphony Hall, and Washington and St. Louis Universities. Susan and Chuck have deftly combined old-world elegance with modern amenities. Laura Ashley fabrics, fine antique furniture, beautiful woodwork, down comforters, ceiling fans, in-room phone and TV, are accented with dried flower arrangements and stained-glass panels created by Susan. The neighborhood is ideal for browsing, shopping, and fine dining.

Doelling Haus ✪
4817 TOWNE SOUTH, ST. LOUIS, MISSOURI 63128

Tel: **(314) 894-6796**	Single/sb: **$30**
Best Time to Call: **Evenings**	Open: **All year**
Hosts: **David and Carol Doelling**	Reduced Rates: **$5 less Mon.–Thurs.**
Location: **7 mi. S of St. Louis**	Breakfast: **Full**
No. of Rooms: **3**	Pets: **Sometimes**
No. of Private Baths: **1**	Children: **Welcome**
Double/pb: **$55**	Smoking: **Permitted**
Double/sb: **$40**	Social Drinking: **Permitted**

Warmly furnished with European and American antiques and collectibles, Doelling Haus re-creates old-world hospitality. Carol, who lived in Germany, will direct you to wonderful places for antiquing; David will gladly show off his old baseball cards. Enjoy the peaceful patio and swings, or walk around the friendly neighborhood. Many points of interest are nearby, such as the Arch, historic Kimmswick, recreational areas, malls, and fine restaurants. But before you head out, you'll fortify yourself with a full breakfast featuring German, French, and American specialties, fresh-ground coffee, and homemade breads and cakes.

Lafayette House
2156 LAFAYETTE AVENUE, ST. LOUIS, MISSOURI 63104

Tel: **(314) 772-4429**	Open: **All year**
Hosts: **Sarah and Jack Milligan**	Breakfast: **Full**
No. of Rooms: **5**	Pets: **Sometimes**
No. of Private Baths: **2**	Children: **Welcome (crib)**
Max. No. Sharing Bath: **4**	Smoking: **Permitted**
Double/pb: **$60**	Social Drinking: **Permitted**
Double/sb: **$50**	Minimum Stay: **2 nights in suite**
Suite: **$75**	Airport/Station Pickup: **Yes**

This 1876 Queen Anne mansion is located in the historic district overlooking Lafayette Park. The house is furnished comfortably with some antiques and traditional furniture. The suite on the third floor, accommodating six, has a private bath and kitchen. Your hosts serve a special egg dish and homemade breads each morning, and offer wine, cheese, and crackers later. They will gladly take you on tour or can direct you to the Botanical Gardens, Convention Center, and other nearby attractions.

Old Convent Guesthouse
2049 SIDNEY, ST. LOUIS, MISSOURI 63104

Tel: **(314) 772-3531**	Breakfast: **Full**
Best Time to Call: **Before 2 PM**	Other Meals: **Available**
Hosts: **Paul and Mary La Flam**	Pets: **No**
Location: **1 mi. from I-44 and I-55**	Children: **Welcome, over 4**
No. of Rooms: **4**	Smoking: **Yes**
No. of Private Baths: **4**	Social Drinking: **Permitted**
Double/pb: **$55–$85**	Airport/Station Pickup: **Yes**
Open: **All year**	

This three-story brick town house was built in 1881. Its carved marble fireplaces, massive original woodwork, 10-foot pocket doors, and plaster ceiling medallions have all been beautifully restored. The halls have magnificent maple and walnut flooring. This Victorian home is bright and cheery as a result of having 64 windows! Paul is a professional chef, which you'll soon notice from the first breakfast bite, while Mary enjoys collecting art and dictionaries. You are welcome to play their newly acquired baby grand piano. The St. Louis Zoo, the famed Arch, and Busch Stadium are just a 10-minute drive; the Anheuser Busch Brewery is within walking distance.

Stelzer Bed & Breakfast ✪
7106 GENERAL SHERMAN LANE, ST. LOUIS, MISSOURI 63123

Tel: **(314) 843-5757**	Double/sb: **$25**
Best Time to Call: **Mornings; evenings**	Single/sb: **$18**
Hosts: **Pat and Anita Stelzer**	Open: **All year**
Location: **10 mi. W of St. Louis**	Breakfast: **Continental**
No. of Rooms: **2**	Pets: **No**
No. of Private Baths: **1**	Children: **Welcome**
Max. No. Sharing Bath: **4**	Smoking: **No**
Double/pb: **$30**	Social Drinking: **No**
Single/pb: **$20**	Airport/Station Pickup: **Yes**

Pat and Anita Stelzer have a corner house with green siding and window awnings. The lot is quite spacious, with lovely trees and flowers. Inside, you'll find a mixture of Windsor chairs, old-fashioned rockers, books, and family treasures such as the old spoon collection mounted on the wall. Breakfast on fresh fruit, biscuits, cereals, eggs, and bacon. The Stelzers are located 10 miles from the riverfront and within easy reach of the Botanical Garden, fine dining, and shops.

The Winter House ✪
3522 ARSENAL STREET, ST. LOUIS, MISSOURI 63118

Tel: (314) 664-4399	Open: **All year**
Hosts: **Kendall and Sarah Winter**	Reduced Rates: **After 2nd night**
Location: **1 mi. S of I-44; 1 mi. W of I-55**	Breakfast: **Continental, plus**
	Credit Cards: **AMEX, DC, MC, VISA**
No. of Rooms: **3**	Pets: **No**
No. of Private Baths: **3**	Children: **Welcome**
Double/pb: **$55**	Smoking: **No**
Single/pb: **$48**	Social Drinking: **Permitted**
Suites: **$70 for 2**	

This ten-room Victorian, built in 1897, features a first-floor bedroom with a pressed-tin ceiling, and a second-floor suite with a balcony and decorative fireplace. Breakfast, served in the dining room on crystal and antique Wedgwood, always includes fresh-squeezed orange juice. Fruit, candy, and fresh flowers are provided in bedrooms; tea and live piano are available by reservation. Nearby attractions include the Missouri Botanical Garden, which adjoins Tower Grove Park, a Victorian walking park on the National Register of Historic Places. The Arch, Busch Baseball Stadium, the zoo, the symphony, and Union Station are all within four miles, and fine dining is in walking distance.

The Schwegmann House B&B Inn ✪
438 WEST FRONT STREET, WASHINGTON, MISSOURI 63090

Tel: (314) 239-5025	Single/sb: **$40**
Hosts: **Leo and Erin Weyerich**	Open: **All year**
Location: **50 mi. W of St. Louis**	Breakfast: **Continental**
No. of Rooms: **9**	Credit Cards: **MC, VISA**
No. of Private Baths: **7**	Pets: **No**
Max. No. Sharing Bath: **4**	Children: **Welcome**
Double/pb: **$65**	Smoking: **No**
Single/pb: **$55**	Social Drinking: **Permitted**
Double/sb: **$50**	

A three-story 1861 Georgian brick house included on the National Register of Historic Places, it is located on the Missouri River. It is tastefully furnished with antiques; handmade quilts complement the decor of each guest room. It is close to Daniel Boone's home, Meramec Caverns, Missouri's Rhineland wineries, antique shops, and fine restaurants. Relax in the graceful parlor by the fireside or stroll the gardens that overlook the river. The innkeeper serves a bountiful breakfast, including fresh-ground coffee, imported cheeses, croissants, and grape juice from Missouri's vineyards.

Washington House B&B Inn ✪
3 LAFAYETTE STREET, WASHINGTON, MISSOURI 63090

Tel: (314) 239-2417	Breakfast: **Full**
Hosts: **Kathy and Chuck Davis**	Pets: **No**
Location: **50 mi. W of St. Louis**	Children: **Welcome**
No. of Rooms: **3**	Smoking: **No**
No. of Private Baths: **3**	Social Drinking: **Permitted**
Double/pb: **$65–$75**	Minimum Stay: **2 nights weekends**
Single/pb: **$55**	**Oct.**
Open: **All year**	
Reduced Rates: **10% Jan. 2–Mar. 30;**	
10% seniors	

Facing the Missouri River, this two-story brick Federal-style building was built as an inn during the late 1830s. In the heart of the historic district, avid preservationists Kathy and Chuck have painstakingly restored it, using period antiques and decorations of the era. The rooms are air-conditioned and have canopy beds. This is wine country, and many nearby wineries offer tours and tasting.

MONTANA

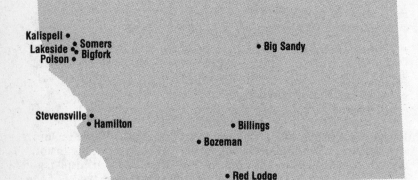

Bed and Breakfast Western Adventure ✪
P.O. BOX 20972, BILLINGS, MONTANA 59104

Tel: **(406) 259-7993**
Best Time to Call: **10 AM**
Coordinator: **Paula Deigert**
States/Regions Covered: **Idaho;**
  Montana; South Dakota—Black
  Hills; Wyoming

Rates (Single/Double):
  Modest: **$35–$49**
  Average: **$50–$64**
  Luxury: **$65–$195**
Credit Cards: **MC, VISA**

These areas—famous for their national parks, fishing streams, ski resorts, and spectacular scenery—are perfect for outdoor enthusiasts. Enjoy the wonders of Glacier Park in Montana, Yellowstone Park in Wyoming, and Mt. Rushmore in South Dakota. Then explore the fascinating past of the Old West with rodeos, Native American powwows, and other attractions that celebrate the history and the natural resources of the four states.

O'Duach'Ain Country Inn ✪
675 FERNDALE DRIVE, BIGFORK, MONTANA 59911

Tel: **(406) 837-6851**	Open: **All year**
Best Time to Call: **Anytime**	Breakfast: **Full**
Hosts: **Margot and Tom Doohan**	Other Meals: **Available**
Location: **17 mi. S of Kalispell**	Credit Cards: **AMEX, DISC, MC, VISA**
No. of Rooms: **5**	Pets: **Sometimes**
Max. No. Sharing Bath: **3**	Children: **Welcome**
Double/sb: **$65**	Smoking: **Restricted**
Single/sb: **$55**	Social Drinking: **Permitted**
Suites: **$85**	Airport/Station Pickup: **Yes**

O'Duach'Ain is a gracious three-level log home set on five beautiful acres. Inside, you'll find a casual atmosphere of open wood logs, stone fireplaces, antiques, and artwork. Guests are welcome to relax on the deck and take in the spectacular view. In the morning, your hosts provide a gourmet breakfast, featuring freshly prepared international dishes. Margot and Tom will direct you to nearby Glacier National Park, Swan Lake, Big Mountain ski area, and Flatland Lake. Walking trails abound.

Sky View
BOX 408, BIG SANDY, MONTANA 59520

Tel: **(406) 378-2549, 386-2464**	Open: **May 1–Dec. 1**
Best Time to Call: **Before 11 AM; after 6 PM**	Reduced Rates: **Families**
	Breakfast: **Continental**
Hosts: **Ron and Gay Pearson and family**	Other Meals: **Available**
	Pets: **Sometimes**
Location: **75 mi. N of Great Falls**	Children: **Welcome**
No. of Rooms: **3**	Smoking: **Permitted**
Double/pb: **$45**	Social Drinking: **Permitted**
Single/pb: **$35**	Airport/Station Pickup: **Yes**
Guest Cottage: **$35–$60**	

Sky View is a working ranch located in an area known for its wild and rugged ambience, sparse population, and spectacular scenery. It's in the heart of Lewis and Clark country, just off a major highway to Glacier National Park. The Pearson family enjoys people of all ages and looks forward to sharing its life-style with guests, keeping you informed of local rodeos, Indian powwows, river float trips, tours, and hunting and fishing opportunities. Children enjoy their playground, and baby-sitters are available. A public swimming pool and tennis courts are nearby.

Torch and Toes B&B
309 SOUTH THIRD AVENUE, BOZEMAN, MONTANA 59715

Tel: **(406) 586-7285; (800) 446-2138**	Single/sb: **$47**
Best Time to Call: **8 AM–noon**	Open: **All year**
Hosts: **Ronald and Judy Hess**	Reduced Rates: **Government**
Location: **100 mi. SE of Helena**	**employees**
No. of Rooms: **4**	Breakfast: **Full**
No. of Private Baths: **2**	Pets: **No**
Max. No. Sharing Bath: **4**	Children: **Welcome**
Double/pb: **$55**	Smoking: **No**
Single/pb: **$50**	Social Drinking: **Permitted**
Double/sb: **$52**	Airport/Station Pickup: **Yes**

Set back from the street, this Colonial Revival house is centrally located in the Bon Ton Historic District. Lace curtains, leaded glass windows, and period pieces remind one that this is a house with a past. Ron is a professor of architecture at nearby Montana State University; Judy is a weaver interested in historic preservation. Their home is furnished in a charming blend of nostalgic antiques, humorous collectibles, and fine furnishings. Breakfast always includes a special egg dish, fresh fruit, and muffins. Afterward, relax on the redwood deck in summer, or by a cozy fire in winter. Nearby attractions include blue-ribbon trout streams, hiking, skiing, and the Museum of the Rockies. Yellowstone National Park is one and a half hours away.

Voss Inn ✪
319 SOUTH WILLSON, BOZEMAN, MONTANA 59715

Tel: **(406) 587-0982**	Reduced Rates: **Business travelers**
Best Time to Call: **10 AM–9 PM**	**Sun.–Thurs.**
Hosts: **Bruce and Frankee Muller**	Breakfast: **Full**
Location: **3 mi. from I-90**	Credit Cards: **MC, VISA**
No. of Rooms: **6**	Pets: **No**
No. of Private Baths: **6**	Children: **Sometimes**
Double/pb: **$60–$70**	Smoking: **Restricted**
Single/pb: **$55–$60**	Social Drinking: **Permitted**
Open: **All year**	

This handsome 100-year-old brick mansion, flanked by Victorian gingerbread porches, is set like a gem on a tree-lined street in historic Bozeman. The bedrooms are elegantly wallpapered and furnished with brass and iron beds, ornate lighting, oriental throw rugs over polished hardwood floors—a perfect spot for a first or second honeymoon. The parlor has a good selection of books, as well as a chess set for your pleasure. It's north of Yellowstone, on the way to Glacier, with trout fishing, mountain lakes, and skiing within easy reach.

Don't miss the Museum of the Rockies on the Montana State University campus ten blocks away.

The Bavarian Farmhouse B&B ✪
163 BOWMAN ROAD, HAMILTON, MONTANA 59840

Tel: **(406) 363-4063**	Double/sb: **$45**
Best Time to Call: **9 AM–noon; 4 PM–**	Single/sb: **$35**
8 PM	Open: **All Year**
Hosts: **Peter and Ann Reuthlinger**	Reduced Rates: **Available**
Location: **44 mi. S of Missoula**	Breakfast: **Full**
No. of Rooms: **5**	Pets: **Sometimes**
No. of Private Baths: **3**	Children: **Welcome**
Max. No. Sharing Bath: **3**	Smoking: **No**
Double/pb: **$50**	Social Drinking: **Permitted**
Single/pb: **$40**	Foreign Languages: **German**

Wilkommen to this 1980s farmhouse on open ranchland just outside the Bitterroot Range of the Rocky Mountains. Peter and Ann are artists and world travelers interested in horses and the human potential movement. They extensively remodeled this home, drawing upon Peter's Bavarian background to create a European-style B&B. With advance notice, your hosts will arrange raft trips, trail rides, and hunting and fishing expeditions. Whatever your plans, you'll begin the day with an ample German farm breakfast of juice, cereal, eggs, cheese, cold cuts, breads, jam, and coffee and tea.

Brick Farmhouse Bed & Breakfast ✪
1946 WHITEFISH STAGE, KALISPELL, MONTANA 59901

Tel: **(406) 756-6230**	Open: **June 1–Oct. 1**
Best Time to Call: **After 4 PM**	Breakfast: **Full**
Hosts: **Don and Carol Young**	Pets: **No**
Location: **2 mi. from Hwy. 93**	Children: **Welcome, over 7**
No. of Rooms: **2**	Smoking: **No**
Max. No. Sharing Bath: **4**	Social Drinking: **Permitted**
Double/sb: **$45–$50**	Airport/Station Pickup: **Yes**
Single/sb: **$35**	

This redbrick two-story home in a country setting comes complete with an early rising rooster, milking cow, and assorted barnyard animals. You are certain to enjoy the farm-fresh breakfast of eggs and home-baked breads. Don and Carol will also cater to special requests and diets. Afterward, walk to the bridge crossing the Whitefish River, or borrow bikes for some cycling. Glacier National Park is 25 miles away, and Flathead Lake offers many recreational activities.

Shoreline Inn
BOX 568, LAKESIDE, MONTANA 59922

Tel: (406) 844-3222
Best Time to Call: 8 AM–6 PM
Hosts: **Bob and Patty Craft**
Location: 13 mi. S of Kalispell
No. of Rooms: 3
No. of Private Baths: 3
Double/pb: $70
Single/pb: $60

Guest Cottage: $80
Open: **All year**
Breakfast: **Continental**
Credit Cards: **AMEX, MC, VISA**
Pets: **Sometimes**
Children: **Welcome**
Smoking: **No**
Social Drinking: **Permitted**

From a beautiful location on Flathead Lake, Shoreline Inn boasts spectacular views of the majestic Mission Mountains. A private beach, boat dock, hot tub, large redwood deck, and lovely garden surroundings are just some of the amenities. This fine B&B features two attractively decorated rooms with private baths and entrances. For couples seeking seclusion, a private cabin equipped with a kitchenette is available. While sitting in the glow of nightly campfires on the beach, you will enjoy getting to know your hosts. If you're interested in relocating, Bob can help you, as he is a licensed realtor. All this lies just minutes from Glacier Park, Big Mountain ski area, and several challenging golf courses. From this location, you can enjoy skiing, golfing, hiking, swimming, canoeing, lake cruises, plays at the Bigfork Playhouse, and much more.

Hidden Pines Bed & Breakfast ✪
792 LOST QUARTZ ROAD, POLSON, MONTANA 59860

Tel: (406) 849-5612
Best Time to Call: 10 AM–10 PM
Hosts: **Earl and Emy Atchley**
Location: 10 mi. NW of Polson Mt.
No. of Rooms: 3
Max. No. Sharing Bath: 4
Double/pb: $60

Double/sb: $40
Open: **All year**
Breakfast: **Full**
Pets: **No**
Children: **Welcome**
Smoking: **No**
Airport/Station Pickup: **Yes**

Stress and tension melt away in the quiet surroundings of Hidden Pines Bed & Breakfast. Relax on the deck of this rustic retreat and watch squirrels and deer graze right in front of you. Bring your canoe and bathing suit for fun in Flathead Lake; pack binoculars for viewing Wild Horse Island. Cross-country skis are useful when the snow flies, and hiking shoes will come in handy year-round. At the end of the day, unwind in the living room and tune in to your favorite TV show or screen a movie on the VCR. Depending on your appetite, Emy will serve you a full country breakfast or lighter Continental fare.

Willows Inn O
224 SOUTH PLATT AVENUE, RED LODGE, MONTANA 59068

Tel: **(406) 446-3913**	Guest Cottages: **$55 for 2**
Best Time to Call: **Mornings, afternoons**	Open: **All year**
Hosts: **Elven, Kerry, and Carolyn Boggio**	Reduced Rates: **10% after 4th night; 10% seniors**
Location: **60 mi. SW of Billings**	Breakfast: **Continental**
No. of Rooms: **5**	Credit Cards: **DISC, MC, VISA**
No. of Private Baths: **3**	Pets: **No**
Max. No. Sharing Bath: **4**	Children: **Welcome**
Double/pb: **$50–$60**	Smoking: **No**
Double/sb: **$50**	Social Drinking: **Permitted**
Single/sb: **$45**	Minimum Stay: **2 nights in cottage**

Tucked beneath the majestic Beartooth Mountains in the northern Rockies, the historic town of Red Lodge provides an ideal setting for this charming three-story Queen Anne. Flanked by giant evergreens and colorful flower beds, the inn is reminiscent of a bygone age, complete with white picket fence, gingerbread trim, and front porch swing. Overstuffed sofas and wicker pieces complement the warm and cheerful decor. Delicious homebaked pastries are Elven's specialty—she uses her own Finnish recipes for these mouthwatering treats. Championship rodeos, excellent cross-country and downhill skiing, opportunities to hike, golf, and fish abound in this special area, still unspoiled by commercial progress. Yellowstone National Park is only 65 miles away.

Osprey Inn Bed & Breakfast O
5557 HIGHWAY 93 SOUTH, SOMERS, MONTANA 59932

Tel: **(406) 857-2042; (800) 258-2042**	Guest Cottage: **$85**
Best Time to Call: **8 AM–9 PM**	Open: **All year**
Hosts: **Sharon and Wayne Finney**	Reduced Rates: **Sept. 15–Dec. 20, Jan. 6–May 15**
Location: **8 mi. S of Kalispell**	Breakfast: **Full**
No. of Rooms: **5**	Credit Cards: **AMEX, MC, VISA**
No. of Private Baths: **3**	Pets: **No**
Max. No. Sharing Bath: **4**	Children: **Welcome, over 9**
Double/pb: **$85**	Smoking: **No**
Single/pb: **$80**	Social Drinking: **Permitted**
Double/sb: **$75**	Airport/Station Pickup: **Yes**
Single/sb: **$70**	

Yes, you can see osprey—as well as geese, loons, and grebes—from the deck of this rustic lakeshore retreat. In the summer, guests are welcome to bring along a boat or canoe; in the winter, pack your skis. Cameras and binoculars come in handy throughout the year. You'll start the day with fresh seasonal fruit, home-baked cinnamon rolls, and pancakes with homemade fruit syrups.

Country Caboose ✪
852 WILLOUGHBY ROAD, STEVENSVILLE, MONTANA 59870

Tel: (406) 777-3145	Open: May–Sept.
Host: Lisa Thompson	Breakfast: Full
Location: 35 mi. S of Missoula	Other Meals: Available
No. of Rooms: 1	Pets: No
No. of Private Baths: 1	Children: Welcome
Double/pb: $50	Smoking: No
Single/pb: $50	Social Drinking: Permitted

If you enjoy romantic train rides, why not spend the night in an authentic caboose? This one dates back to 1923, is made of wood, and is painted red, of course. It is set on real rails in the middle of the countryside. The caboose sleeps two and offers a spectacular view of the Bitterroot Mountains, right from your pillow. In the morning, breakfast is served at a table for two. Specialties include huckleberry pancakes, quiche, and strawberries in season. Local activities include touring St. Mary's Mission, hiking the mountain trails, fishing, and hunting.

NEBRASKA

Osmond •   • Dixon

Neligh •

• Omaha

Gretna •

• Chappell

• Lincoln

Crete •

Bed & Breakfast of the Great Plains ✪
P.O. BOX 2333, LINCOLN, NEBRASKA 68502

Tel: **(402) 423-3480**
Coordinator: **Rose Ann Foster**
States/Regions Covered: **Nebraska—**
statewide; Iowa; Kansas; Western
Missouri

Rates (Single/Double):
  Modest: **$20–$25 / $30**
  Average: **$25–$30 / $35–$45**
  Luxury: **$40–$50 / $55–$80**
Credit Cards: **MC, VISA**

Rose Ann's ever-growing roster includes a modest home within blocks of Interstate-80, an air-conditioned farmhouse where the alarm clock is a rooster, and a mansion on the National Register of Historic Places. The friendly hosts will be delighted to direct guests to rodeos, ethnic festivals, museums, state or county fairs, lakeside recreation areas, Indian powwows, concerts, Cornhusker football, and Boys' Town. Tell them your interests and they will custom-tailor an itinerary to suit you.

The Cottonwood Inn ✪

802 SECOND STREET, CHAPPELL, NEBRASKA 69129

Tel: **(308) 874-3250**
Best Time to Call: **8 AM–9 PM**
Hosts: **Barb and Bruce Freeman**
Location: **130 mi. E of Cheyenne**
No. of Rooms: **6**
Max. No. Sharing Bath: **4**
Double/sb: **$35**
Single/sb: **$30**
Open: **All year**

Reduced Rates: **10% seniors**
Breakfast: **Full**
Other Meals: **Available**
Credit Cards: **MC, VISA**
Pets: **Sometimes**
Children: **Welcome (crib)**
Smoking: **No**
Social Drinking: **Permitted**

Built as a rooming house in 1917, the Cottonwood Inn still has its original floors, light fixtures, and dumbwaiter. The balconies and the large front porch are perfect places to enjoy a summer evening. In cooler months, you can sit around the living room fireplace. Signs of the Old West abound in Chappell—the Oregon and Mormon trails, the Pony Express, and the first transcontinental railroad and highway all went through this town, which boasts a restored period home and an art museum. Other amenities include the public golf course, tennis courts, and swimming pool.

The Parson's House ✪

638 FOREST AVENUE, CRETE, NEBRASKA 68333

Tel: **(402) 826-2634**
Host: **Harold and Sandy Richardson**
Location: **25 mi. SW of Lincoln**
No. of Rooms: **2**
Max. No. Sharing Bath: **4**
Double/sb: **$35**
Single/sb: **$30**

Open: **All year**
Breakfast: **Full**
Pets: **No**
Children: **No**
Smoking: **No**
Social Drinking: **No**
Airport/Station Pickup: **Yes**

Enjoy warm hospitality in this newly refinished, turn-of-the-century home tastefully decorated with antiques. Doane College lies one block away; the beautiful campus is just the place for a leisurely afternoon stroll. It's just a short drive to Lincoln, the state's capital and home of the University of Nebraska. Harold, a Baptist minister with the local U.C.C. church, runs a remodeling business while Sandy runs the bed and breakfast. After a day's activity, they invite you to relax in their modern whirlpool tub and make their home yours for the duration of your stay.

The Georges ✪
ROUTE 1, BOX 50, DIXON, NEBRASKA 68732

Tel: (402) 584-2625
Best Time to Call: 6:30 AM–6 PM
Hosts: Harold and Marie George
Location: 35 mi. W of Sioux City,
  Iowa
No. of Rooms: 3
Max. No. Sharing Bath: 4
Double/sb: $35
Single/sb: $25

Open: All year
Breakfast: Full
Other Meals: Available
Pets: Sometimes
Children: Welcome
Smoking: No
Social Drinking: Permitted
Airport/Station Pickup: Yes
Foreign Languages: Swedish

The Georges have a large, remodeled farmhouse with a spacious backyard. They offer the opportunity to see a farming operation at firsthand, right down to the roosters crowing and the birds singing in the morning. Harold and Marie are now full-time farmers after careers in social work and engineering. They prepare a hearty country breakfast featuring homemade jellies and jams. The Georges are close to Wayne State College and Ponca State Park.

Bundy's Bed and Breakfast ✪
16906 SOUTH 255, GRETNA, NEBRASKA 68028

Tel: (402) 332-3616
Best Time to Call: 7 AM–9 PM
Hosts: Bob and Dee Bundy
Location: 30 mi. S of Omaha
No. of Rooms: 4
Max. No. Sharing Bath: 4
Double/sb: $35

Single/sb: $20
Open: All year
Breakfast: Full
Pets: Sometimes
Children: No
Smoking: No
Social Drinking: No

The Bundys have a pretty farmhouse painted white with black trim. Here you can enjoy country living just 30 minutes from downtown Lincoln and Omaha. The rooms are decorated with antiques, attractive wallpapers, and collectibles. In the morning, wake up to farm-fresh eggs and homemade breads. The house is just a short walk from a swimming lake, and is three miles from a ski lodge.

The Rogers House ✪
2145 B STREET, LINCOLN, NEBRASKA 68502

Tel: (402) 476-6961
Best Time to Call: 10 AM–9 PM
Host: Nora Houtsma
No. of Rooms: 8
No. of Private Baths: 8
Double/pb: $45–$63
Single/pb: $40–$54

Open: All year
Breakfast: Full
Credit Cards: AMEX, MC, VISA
Pets: No
Children: Welcome, over 10
Smoking: Permitted
Social Drinking: Permitted

This Jacobean Revival–style brick mansion was built in 1914 and is a local historic landmark. There are three sun porches, attractively furnished with wicker and plants, and the air-conditioned house is decorated with lovely antiques. Nora will direct you to the diverse cultural attractions available at the nearby University of Nebraska, the surrounding historic district, and antique shops. Don't miss a visit to the Children's Zoo and the beautiful Sunken Gardens. Breakfast is hearty and delicious. A professional staff of five is eager to serve you.

The Offutt House
140 NORTH 39TH STREET, OMAHA, NEBRASKA 68131

Tel: **(402) 553-0951**	Single/sb: **$45**
Host: **Jeannie K. Swoboda**	Suites: **$70–$100**
Location: **1 mi. from I-80**	Open: **All year**
No. of Rooms: **7**	Reduced Rates: **After 5th night**
No. of Private Baths: **5**	Breakfast: **Continental**
Max. No. Sharing Bath: **4**	Pets: **Sometimes**
Double/pb: **$65**	Children: **Welcome**
Single/pb: **$55**	Smoking: **Permitted**
Double/sb: **$55**	Social Drinking: **Permitted**

This comfortable mansion, circa 1894, is part of the city's Historic Gold Coast, a section of handsome homes built by Omaha's wealthiest residents. Offering peace and quiet, the rooms are air-conditioned, spacious, and furnished with antiques; some have fireplaces. Jeannie will direct you to nearby attractions such as the Joslyn Museum or the Old Market area, which abounds with many beautiful shops and fine restaurants. She graciously offers coffee or wine in late afternoon.

Willow Way Bed & Breakfast ✪
ROUTE 2, BOX A20, OSMOND, NEBRASKA 68765

Tel: **(402) 748-3593**	Double/sb: **$45**
Best Time to Call: **After 6 PM**	Single/sb: **$35**
Hosts: **Norman and Jacquie Lorenz**	Open: **All year**
Location: **130 mi. NW of Omaha**	Breakfast: **Full**
No. of Rooms: **4**	Pets: **Yes**
No. of Private Baths: **2**	Children: **Welcome**
Max. No. Sharing Bath: **4**	Smoking: **No**
Double/pb: **$45**	Social Drinking: **Permitted**
Single/pb: **$35**	

Your hosts are retired dairy farmers who run an antiques store and an interior decorating business in addition to this B&B. They make baskets using the local red willow, hence the name Willow Way. Jacquie and Norman built their guest house in 1988 out of lumber from several barns and houses in the area. Osmond is a town of about 800 midway between O'Neal, Nebraska, and Sioux City, Iowa. Ashfall Fossil Beds State Historical Park is thirty miles to the west. Whether you want to inspect fossils or just relax, your hosts promise to give you old-fashioned small-town hospitality.

For key to listings, see inside front or back cover.

○ This star means that rates are guaranteed through December 31, 1993, to any guest making a reservation as a result of reading about the B&B in *Bed & Breakfast U.S.A.*—1993 edition.

Important! To avoid misunderstandings, always ask about cancellation policies when booking.

Please enclose a self-addressed, stamped, business-size envelope when contacting reservation services.

For more details on what you can expect in a B&B, see Chapter 1.

Always mention *Bed & Breakfast U.S.A.* when making reservations!

If no B&B is listed in the area you'll be visiting, use the form on page 733 to order a copy of our "List of New B&Bs."

We want to hear from you! Use the form on page 735.

NEVADA

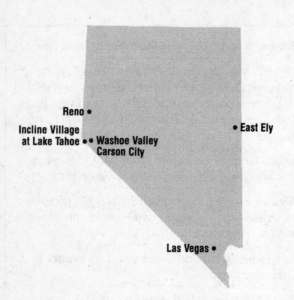

Reno •
Incline Village
at Lake Tahoe • • Washoe Valley
Carson City
• East Ely

Las Vegas •

Steptoe Valley Inn ✪
P.O. BOX 151110, 220 EAST 11TH STREET, EAST ELY, NEVADA 89315-1110

Tel: **(702) 289-8687**
Best Time to Call: **11 AM–3 PM**
Hosts: **Jane and Norman Lindley**
Location: **70 mi. W of Great Basin National Park**
No. of Rooms: **5**
No. of Private Baths: **5**
Double/pb: **$73.15**
Single/pb: **$62.04**

Open: **June–Sept.**
Breakfast: **Full**
Credit Cards: **AMEX, MC, VISA**
Pets: **No**
Children: **Welcome, over 12**
Smoking: **No**
Social Drinking: **Permitted**
Foreign Languages: **Spanish**

This inn opened in July 1991 after major reconstruction. Located near the Nevada Northern Railway Museum, it was originally Ely City Grocery of 1907. The five second-floor rooms have country decor and

private balconies, and the elegant Victorian dining room and library are downstairs. The large yard has mature trees, gazebo, and rose garden. Norman is an airline captain and ex-rancher and Jane is a retired stewardess and local tour guide. Their guests can enjoy cool nights, scenic countryside, the "Ghost Train of Old Ely," the Great Basin National Park, and Cave Lake State Park or just relax on the veranda!

Haus Bavaria ✪

P.O. BOX 3308, 593 NORTH DYER CIRCLE, INCLINE VILLAGE, LAKE TAHOE, NEVADA 89450

Tel: (702) 831-6122; (800) GO-TAHOE [468-2463]
Best Time to Call: Noon–2 PM
Host: Bick Hewitt
Location: 35 mi. SW of Reno
No. of Rooms: 5
No. of Private Baths: 5
Double/pb: $90

Single/pb: $80
Open: All year
Breakfast: Full
Credit Cards: AMEX, MC, VISA
Pets: No
Children: Welcome, over 12
Smoking: No
Social Drinking: Permitted

This Alpine-style residence is framed by the mountains and convenient to the lake. Each guest room opens onto a balcony offering lovely mountain views. It's close to the gambling casinos and shows, all water sports, and, in winter, the challenging slopes of Mount Rose and Heavenly Valley.

Las Vegas B&B ✪

CONTACT: BED AND BREAKFAST INTERNATIONAL, P.O. BOX 282910, SAN FRANCISCO, CALIFORNIA 94128-2910

Tel: (415) 696-1690
Best Time to Call: 8:30 AM–5 PM

Host: Sharene Z. Klein
No. of Rooms: 4

No. of Private Baths: **2**
Max. No. Sharing Bath: **3**
Double/pb: **$65**
Single/pb: **$52**
Double/sb: **$50**
Single/sb: **$45**

Open: **All year**
Breakfast: **Full**
Pets: **No**
Children: **Swimmers only**
Smoking: **Permitted**
Social Drinking: **Permitted**

Located a few minutes from the fabled "Strip" of hotels, casinos, and restaurants is this two-story contemporary home. The quiet, residential neighborhood is a welcome respite from the 24-hour hoopla available nearby. You are welcome to use your host's swimming pool.

Deer Run Ranch Bed and Breakfast ✪
5440 EASTLAKE BOULEVARD, WASHOE VALLEY, NEVADA 89704

Tel: **(702) 882-3643**
Best Time to Call: **6 AM–9 AM, 6 PM–9 PM**
Hosts: **David and Muffy Vhay**
Location: **8 mi. N of Carson City**
No. of Rooms: **2**
No. of Private Baths: **2**
Double/pb: **$85**
Open: **All year**

Reduced Rates: **$10 less Mon.–Thurs.**
Breakfast: **Full**
Credit Cards: **MC, VISA**
Pets: **No**
Children: **Welcome, over 12**
Smoking: **No**
Social Drinking: **Permitted**
Minimum Stay: **2 nights, holidays and special events weekends**

Deer Run Ranch, a working alfalfa farm, overlooks Washoe Lake and the Sierra Nevada Mountains. Navajo rugs, old photographs, and paintings by well-known local artists grace the comfortable guest areas, lending western ambience to this house designed and built by an architect. Your hosts also have a pottery studio, woodshop, and large garden on the premises. Things to do in the area include skiing, biking, hiking, and hang gliding; Washoe Lake State Park is next door. For fine dining, casino hopping, and entertainment, Lake Tahoe, Reno, Virginia City, and Carson City are only minutes away.

NEW HAMPSHIRE

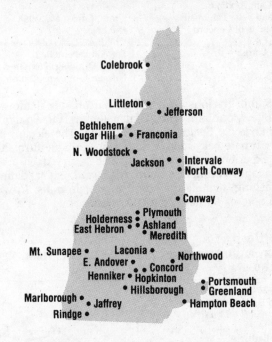

Colebrook •

Littleton •
       • Jefferson

Bethlehem •
Sugar Hill • • Franconia

N. Woodstock •
        Jackson • • Intervale
                • North Conway

               • Conway

         • Plymouth
Holderness • • Ashland
East Hebron •   • Meredith

Mt. Sunapee •   Laconia •   • Northwood
    E. Andover • • Concord
      Henniker • Hopkinton
          • Hillsborough   • Portsmouth
Marlborough •   • Greenland
     • Jaffrey   • Hampton Beach
Rindge •

New Hampshire Bed & Breakfast ✪
329 LAKE DRIVE, GUILFORD, CONNECTICUT 06437

Tel: **(603) 279-8348**
Best Time to Call: **9 AM–8 PM**
Coordinator: **Ernie Taddei**
States/Regions Covered: **Statewide,
  Maine, Massachusetts, New
  Hampshire, Rhode Island, Vermont**

Descriptive Directory: **$2**
Rates (Single/Double):
  Modest: **$35–$50 / $40–$50**
  Average: **$35–$50 / $50–$65**
  Luxury: **$60–$85 / $65–$90**
Credit Cards: **MC, VISA**

Here is New Hampshire travel planning made easy. Just one call puts you in touch with more than 75 locations convenient to the state's breathtaking scenery, four-season recreation, tax-free shopping outlets, and other exciting attractions. Hosts are close to all schools and colleges. Experience 18th-century colonial inns, spacious lakefront homes, large working farms, and ocean and mountainside residences—all with gracious owner hospitality.

Glynn House Victorian Inn ✪

P.O. BOX 719, 43 HIGHLAND STREET, ASHLAND, NEW HAMPSHIRE
03217

Tel: (603) 968-3775
Best Time to Call: **Anytime**
Hosts: **Karol and Betsy Paterman**
Location: **40 mi. N of Concord**
No. of Rooms: **4**
No. of Private Baths: **4**
Double/pb: **$75**
Single/pb: **$75**

Open: **All year**
Breakfast: **Full**
Credit Cards: **MC, VISA**
Pets: **No**
Children: **Welcome, over 5**
Smoking: **Permitted**
Social Drinking: **Permitted**
Foreign Languages: **Polish, Russian**

Built in 1896, this gracious Queen Anne Victorian is shadowed by the majestic White Mountains and nestled among the Squam Lakes—where the movie *On Golden Pond* was filmed. The elegant interior is enhanced by ornate oak woodwork and fine antique furnishings. For a romantic experience, a hearty breakfast is served on a setting of embroidered tapestry and fine china. Afterward, enjoy boating, swimming, and fishing, or hike the scenic mountain trails. In winter, ski Waterville, Loon, or Tenney Mountain, all close by.

The Bells B&B

STRAWBERRY HILL STREET, P.O. BOX 276, BETHLEHEM, NEW
HAMPSHIRE 03574

Tel: (603) 869-2647
Hosts: **Bill and Louise Sims**
Location: **2½ mi. off I-93, Exit 40**
No. of Rooms: **4**
No. of Private Baths: **4**
Double/pb: **$80**
Single/pb: **$50**
Suites: **$70–$80**
Open: **All year**
Breakfast: **Full**
Credit Cards: **AMEX, MC, VISA**
Pets: **No**
Children: **Welcome, over 12**
Smoking: **Restricted**
Social Drinking: **Permitted**

Named for the more than one hundred tin and wooden bells that dangle from its eaves, this four-story 1892 cottage has been cited by *Victorian Homes* magazine for its pagoda-like architecture. The furnishings—an eclectic mixture of antiques and family heirlooms—are also distinctive. Because Bethlehem is in the heart of the White Mountains, Mt. Washington, Franconia State Park, and excellent ski slopes are a 15-minute drive. Tennis courts and two 18-hole golf courses are within walking distance. Substantial full breakfasts may feature a blintz casserole, eggs Benedict, or baked French toast.

The Mulburn Inn ✪
MAIN STREET, BETHLEHEM, NEW HAMPSHIRE 03574

Tel: (603) 869-3389	Reduced Rates: 10% weekly
Best Time to Call: 9 AM–9 PM	Breakfast: Full
Hosts: Bob and Cheryl Burns and Moe and Linda Mulkigian	Other Meals: Available
	Credit Cards: AMEX, DISC, MC, VISA
Location: 20 mi. SE of St. Johnsbury	Pets: No
No. of Rooms: 7	Children: Welcome (crib)
No. of Private Baths: 7	Smoking: No
Double/pb: $55–$85	Social Drinking: Permitted
Single/pb: $40	Airport/Station Pickup: Yes
Open: All year	

Back in the early 1900s, this sprawling Tudor home was known as the Ivie Estate, a family summer retreat. It boasts original oak staircases, stained-glass windows, rounded-corner architecture, three-tile fireplaces, and even has an elevator. There is plenty of room here, with three enclosed wraparound porches for relaxing and a large living room for reading and fireside chats. Breakfast is served by the fire in a sunny dining room. In the afternoon, your hosts offer seasonal snacks such as soup or cider and cheese. If you are visiting in March or April, you'll be treated to fresh syrup right from the family maples. This lively inn is located in the heart of the White Mountains, near Franconia Notch, the Old Man in the Mountain, Mt. Washington, and places to ski, shop, and dine.

Monadnock B&B ✪
1 MONADNOCK STREET, COLEBROOK, NEW HAMPSHIRE 03576

Tel: (603) 237-8216	Open: All year
Best Time to Call: 8 AM–9 PM	Reduced Rates: 15% weekly
Hosts: Barbara and Wendell Woodard	Breakfast: Full
Location: 1 block from the junction of Rtes. 3 and 26	Pets: Sometimes
	Children: Welcome (crib)
No. of Rooms: 7	Smoking: Permitted
Max. No. Sharing Bath: 6	Social Drinking: Permitted
Double/sb: $35	Airport/Station Pickup: Yes
Single/sb: $30	

When Wendell was in the Air Force, the Woodards lived all over the world, and their house is decorated with pieces collected in Europe and Asia. Now they have settled in New Hampshire's North Country, within walking distance of Vermont and only a 15-minute drive from Canada. Wendell cheerfully directs skiers, hunters, fishermen, and golfers to all his favorite haunts. But first, Barbara will ply guests with a hearty breakfast, featuring specialties such as sausage quiche, pancakes, and omelets, accompanied by endless supplies of coffee and tea.

The Foothills Farm ✪
P.O. BOX 1368, CONWAY, NEW HAMPSHIRE 03818

Tel: **(207) 935-3799**	Breakfast: **Full**
Best Time to Call: **Early evenings**	Pets: **Welcome**
Hosts: **Kevin Early and Theresa Rovere**	Children: **Welcome**
Location: **40 mi. W of Portland**	Smoking: **Permitted**
No. of Rooms: **4**	Social Drinking: **Permitted**
Max. No. Sharing Bath: **2**	Minimum Stay: **2 nights weekends,**
Double/sb: **$42–$48**	**during fall foliage, and holidays**
Single/sb: **$32**	Airport/Station Pickup: **Yes**
Open: **All year**	
Reduced Rates: **Available; 10%**	
seniors	

This restored 1850s clapboard farmhouse is located on a quiet back road in the foothills of the White Mountains. The house is surrounded by flowers, a vegetable garden, and asparagus fields. The well-groomed grounds also include a trout stream and plenty of room to bike or cross-country ski. Bedrooms are furnished in period antiques, and one has a fireplace. Guests are welcome to relax in the den, where they'll find books and a crackling fire. In warmer weather, the screened-in porch overlooking the fields and gardens is a favorite spot. Breakfast specialties such as eggs Benedict with home fries, and blueberry pancakes with sausage are served in a country kitchen, which has an antique stove and pine paneling. Kevin and Theresa have bicycles to lend and are glad to direct you to the sights of this scenic region. Scores of restaurants, factory outlets, and canoeing, hiking, and ski areas are also nearby.

Mountain Valley Manner
P.O. BOX 1649, 148 WASHINGTON STREET, CONWAY, NEW HAMPSHIRE 03818

Tel: **(603) 447-3988**	Double/sb: **$45–$78**
Best Time to Call: **9 AM–9 PM**	Single/sb: **$35**
Hosts: **Bob, Lynn, and Amy Lein**	Suites: **$58–$88**
Location: **125 mi. N of Boston, Mass.**	Open: **All year**
No. of Rooms: **4**	Reduced Rates: **10%, after 3 days;**
No. of Private Baths: **2**	**20%, after 4 days**
Max. No. Sharing Bath: **4**	Breakfast: **Full**
Double/pb: **$55–$88**	Credit Cards: **DISC, MC, VISA**
Single/pb: **$45**	Pets: **No**

Children: **Welcome**
Smoking: **No**

Social Drinking: **Permitted**
Station Pickup: **Yes**

This friendly restored country Victorian at the Kancamagus Highway is in sight of two romantic covered Kissing Bridges and Mt. Washington. Elegant, individually decorated, air-conditioned guest rooms are furnished with numerous antiques. Full country breakfast, afternoon tea/beverages, and hot chocolate before bed are all included. Refresh yourself in the pool, swim in the pristine Saco River across the street, stroll through Lynn's Victorian gardens, or mosey over to the shopping outlets. Just minutes to five ski areas, miniature and PGA golf, water slides, hiking, and the health club.

Patchwork Inn ✪

P.O. BOX 107, MAPLE STREET, EAST ANDOVER, NEW HAMPSHIRE 03231

Tel: **(603) 735-6426**
Best Time to Call: **Evenings Mon.–Fri.
10 AM–10 PM Sat., Sun., holidays**
Hosts: **Brad and Ethelyn Sherman**
Location: **23 mi. NW of Concord**
No. of Rooms: **7**
No. of Private Baths: **3**
Max. No. Sharing Bath: **4**
Double/pb: **$60–$65**
Single/pb: **$45–$50**
Double/sb: **$50–$55**
Single/sb: **$40–$45**

Suites: **$85–$95**
Open: **All year**
Reduced Rates: **10% families, seniors;
10% after 3rd night, 20% Nov.–mid-
April**
Breakfast: **Full**
Credit Cards: **MC, VISA**
Pets: **Sometimes**
Children: **Welcome, over 5**
Smoking: **No**
Social Drinking: **Permitted**
Airport/Station Pickup: **Yes**
Minimum Stay: **During special events**

This Colonial inn, built around 1800, has been lovingly restored and furnished with a mixture of antique and country pieces. Guest rooms overlook Highland Lake and Mt. Kearsarge; several other lakes and ski slopes are within an hour's drive. There's cross-country skiing right on the property, and it's an easy walk to the town beach. After the day's adventures, warm up by the living room fireplace, or gather around the piano for an informal singalong. For evening snacking, you'll find fresh fruit and home-baked cookies in your room. House breakfast specialties include cheese strata, baked eggs, French toast, or pancakes bathed in syrup from the Shermans' own maple trees.

Six Chimneys Bed & Breakfast ✪

SR BOX 114, EAST HEBRON, NEW HAMPSHIRE 03232

Tel: **(603) 744-2029**
Best Time to Call: **Evenings**

Hosts: **Peter and Lee Fortescue**
Location: **9 mi. S of Plymouth**

No. of Rooms: **6**
No. of Private Baths: **4**
Max. No. Sharing Bath: **4**
Double/pb: **$60**
Single/pb: **$40**
Double/sb: **$50**
Suites: **$75; sleeps 3**
Open: **Apr.–Feb.**

Reduced Rates: **10% families**
Breakfast: **Full**
Credit Cards: **MC, VISA**
Pets: **No**
Children: **Welcome, over 6**
Smoking: **Restricted**
Social Drinking: **Permitted**
Minimum Stay: **Holiday, weekends**

Located near the shores of Newfound Lake, this 200-year-old former coach stop does indeed have six chimneys. The house is decorated with antiques, family heirlooms, quilts, braided and oriental rugs, and collectibles from England and Spain, where the Fortescues lived when Peter was in the Air Force. Outside, you'll find flower, herb, and vegetable gardens, as well as places to play horseshoes and croquet. A hiking trail starts at the back door and a private beach is close by. Breakfast is served in the dining room, which has exposed beams and an elegant country atmosphere.

Blanche's B&B ○

EASTON VALLEY ROAD, FRANCONIA, NEW HAMPSHIRE 03580

Tel: **(603) 823-7061**
Best Time to Call: **Before 10 PM**
Hosts: **Brenda Shannon and John Vail**
Location: **5 mi. SW of Franconia**
No. of Rooms: **5**
No. of Private Baths: **1**
Max. No. Sharing Bath: **4**
Double/pb: **$75–$85**
Double/sb: **$60**
Single/sb: **$40**
Open: **All year**

Reduced Rates: **Weekly, groups**
Breakfast: **Full**
Credit Cards: **AMEX, MC, VISA**
Other Meals: **Available to groups**
Pets: **No**
Children: **Welcome**
Smoking: **No**
Social Drinking: **Permitted**
Minimum Stay: **2 nights holiday weekends, fall foliage season**
Airport/Station Pickup: **Yes**

Set in a meadow near the Appalachian Trail, this steep-gabled, Victorian farmhouse, circa 1887, is decorated with family pieces and auction finds. Brenda and John provide cotton linens on comfortable beds, a hearty breakfast, and good advice about the nearby hiking and cross-country ski trails. Franconia Notch and Cannon Mountain are a 10-minute drive. Your hosts will be happy to suggest the best spots for antiques, crafts, bird-watching, or help you discover the simple pleasures of life in the White Mountains.

Bungay Jar Bed & Breakfast ✪
EASTON VALLEY ROAD, P.O. BOX 15, FRANCONIA, NEW HAMPSHIRE 03580

Tel: **(603) 823-7775**
Hosts: **Kate Kerivan and Lee Strimbeck**
Location: **6 mi. from Rte. I-93, Exit 38**
No. of Rooms: **6**
No. of Private Baths: **4**
Max. No. Sharing Bath: **4**
Double/pb: **$75–$105**
Double/sb: **$60**
Single/sb: **$50**
Open: **All year**

Breakfast: **Full**
Other Meals: **Available for groups**
Credit Cards: **AMEX, MC, VISA**
Pets: **No**
Children: **Welcome, over 6**
Smoking: **No**
Social Drinking: **Permitted**
Minimum Stay: **2 nights foliage season, holiday weekends**

Built in 1969 from an 18th-century barn, this post-and-beam house is nestled among eight acres of woodland bounded by a river, forest, and spectacular mountain views. In winter, guests are greeted by a crackling fire and the aroma of mulled cider in the two-story living room reminiscent of a hayloft. Antique country furnishings (many for sale) enhance the decor. Apple pancakes served with local maple syrup are a specialty, as are homemade breads, preserves, fruit compotes, granola, and imaginative egg dishes. Refreshments of cider and cheese are served each afternoon. Your hosts are avid hikers and skiers, so you are sure to benefit from their expert knowledge.

Ayers Homestead Bed & Breakfast ✪
47 PARK AVENUE, GREENLAND, NEW HAMPSHIRE 03840

Tel: (603) 436-5992	Single/sb: **$45**
Hosts: **David and Priscilla Engel**	Suites: **$95**
Location: **3 mi. W of Portsmouth**	Open: **All year**
No. of Rooms: **3**	Breakfast: **Full**
No. of Private Baths: **1**	Pets: **Sometimes**
Max. No. Sharing Bath: **4**	Children: **Welcome**
Double/pb: **$55**	Smoking: **No**
Single/pb: **$50**	Social Drinking: **Permitted**
Double/sb: **$50**	

The Thomas Ayers House, begun in 1737 as a two-room post-and-beam structure, has been enlarged and remodeled many times in its 250-year history. Priscilla and Dave will tell you of the famous people, including Paul Revere, George Washington, and John Adams, who passed by its doors. Set on six acres on the historic village green, its nine rooms have wainscoting, exposed beams, and wide board floors; seven have fireplaces. The bedrooms are made cozy with antiques, braided rugs, afghans, and rockers. Breakfast is served in the dining room on an antique table set in front of a brick fireplace with artfully displayed pewterware and ironware.

Roy Family Bed & Breakfast ✪
473 OCEAN BOULEVARD, HAMPTON BEACH, NEW HAMPSHIRE 03842

Tel: (603) 926-7893; (800) 235-2897	Reduced Rates: **Available**
Best Time to Call: **Anytime**	Breakfast: **Continental**
Hosts: **Debbie and Richard Roy**	Credit Cards: **MC, VISA**
Location: **50 mi. N of Boston**	Pets: **No**
No. of Rooms: **6**	Children: **Welcome**
Max. No. Sharing Bath: **4**	Smoking: **Permitted**
Double/sb: **$45–$65**	Social Drinking: **Permitted**
Open: **Jan. 15–Oct. 15**	Foreign Languages: **French**

The Atlantic Ocean is right at your feet when you stay at this comfortable, New England–style home. The house is decorated in a mixture of traditional, Victorian, and casual pieces. Bedrooms are immaculate and furnished Colonial-style. Choose from two spacious decks to enjoy the sun and the ocean view. There is a television room furnished in white wicker for rainy days. The beach is one and a half miles long, and includes boardwalk shops, boutiques, and restaurants. A short drive away are many discount shopping areas, Seabrook Raceway, and Portsmouth Harbor.

Henniker House ✪
BOX 191, 2 RAMSDELL ROAD, HENNIKER, NEW HAMPSHIRE 03242

Tel: **(603) 428-3198**	Single/sb: **$55**
Best Time to Call: **Anytime**	Open: **All year**
Host: **Bertina Williams**	Reduced Rates: **10% after 7th night**
Location: **14 mi. W of Concord**	Breakfast: **Full**
No. of Rooms: **4**	Other Meals: **Available**
No. of Private Baths: **2**	Credit Cards: **MC, VISA**
Max. No. Sharing Bath: **3**	Pets: **Sometimes**
Double/pb: **$65**	Children: **Welcome**
Single/pb: **$60**	Smoking: **Permitted**
Double/sb: **$60**	Social Drinking: **Permitted**

Bertina's very special 19th-century Victorian offers old-world charm with modern amenities. A Jacuzzi and seasonal pool open onto a 50-foot deck that overlooks the Contoocook River. Henniker is the site of New England College and the Fibre Studio of Arts and Crafts. Activities abound, from music festivals and theater to hiking, fishing, and skiing. Best of all is waking to the aroma of Bertina's homemade breakfast served in the bright, airy solarium, with its scenic river view.

Stonewall Farm Bed and Breakfast✪
235 WINDSOR ROAD, HILLSBOROUGH, NEW HAMPSHIRE 03244

Tel: **(603) 478-5424**	Reduced Rates: **10% weekly**
Best Time to Call: **Before 8 AM; after 5 PM**	Breakfast: **Continental**
	Pets: **No**
Hosts: **Anneke and Jaap Rietsema**	Children: **No**
Location: **32 mi. W of Concord**	Smoking: **No**
No. of Rooms: **2**	Minimum Stay: **2 nights weekends, holidays, fall foliage**
No. of Private Baths: **2**	
Double/pb: **$70**	Foreign Languages: **Dutch, French, German, Spanish**
Single/pb: **$60**	
Open: **All year**	

In 1988, Jaap and Anneke took over this 1785 Federal Colonial farmhouse and lovingly restored it. The guest rooms have beamed ceilings and wide floorboards, and there's a deck, accessible via the large country kitchen, for the use of visitors. Full breakfasts are available for skiers, who can warm themselves by the wood-burning stove before heading out to the slopes.

The Inn on Golden Pond ✪
ROUTE 3, BOX 680, HOLDERNESS, NEW HAMPSHIRE 03245

Tel: **(603) 968-7269**	Hosts: **Bill and Bonnie Webb**
Best Time to Call: **Evenings**	Location: **4 mi. from I-93**

No. of Rooms: **9**
No. of Private Baths: **9**
Double/pb: **$95–$135**
Single/pb: **$65**
Open: **All year**
Breakfast: **Full**

Credit Cards: **MC, VISA**
Pets: **No**
Children: **Welcome, over 12**
Smoking: **No**
Social Drinking: **Permitted**

If you saw the film *On Golden Pond*, you are familiar with the beauty of the countryside surrounding this inn. Built in 1879 on 55 acres, the house is across the street from Squam Lake, the setting for the movie. The rooms are bright and airy, decorated in a warm, homey style. Breakfast specialties include apple pancakes with local maple syrup, and a sausage, egg, and cheese casserole. Nearby are two golf courses, Waterville Valley, and Loon Mountain.

Windyledge Bed and Breakfast ✪

RFD 3, HATFIELD ROAD, HOPKINTON, NEW HAMPSHIRE 03229

Tel: **(603) 746-4054**
Best Time to Call: **Anytime**
Hosts: **Dick and Susan Vogt**
Location: **11 mi. W of Concord**
No. of Rooms: **3**
No. of Private Baths: **1**
Max. No. Sharing Bath: **4**
Double/pb: **$75**
Single/pb: **$65**
Double/sb: **$55**

Single/sb: **$45**
Open: **All year**
Reduced Rates: **15% after 7th night**
Breakfast: **Full**
Credit Cards: **MC, VISA**
Pets: **No**
Children: **Welcome**
Smoking: **No**
Social Drinking: **Permitted**
Airport/Station Pickup: **Yes**

This elegant hilltop Colonial is surrounded by nine acres of fields and woods, bordered by picturesque hills and the White Mountains beyond. Susan's delicious apricot glaze French toast or honey-and-spice blueberry pancakes are served at your pleasure on the airy sun porch or outside deck or in the country dining room. Nearby are lakes, a golf course, skiing, craft shops, and numerous restaurants. After a full day's activities, return "home" to an invigorating dip in the pool or to a movie from Dick's vast videocassette collection.

The Forest—A Country Inn

ROUTE 16A, P.O. BOX 37, INTERVALE, NEW HAMPSHIRE 03845

Tel: **(603) 356-9772; (800) 448-3534**
Hosts: **Rae and Ken Wyman**
Location: **50 mi. from Rte. 93**
No. of Rooms: **11**
No. of Private Baths: **9**
Max. No. Sharing Bath: **4**
Double/pb: **$66–$84**

Double/sb: **$56–$82**
Single/sb: **$51–$77**
Guest Cottage: **$80–$102; sleeps 4**
Open: **All year**
Reduced Rates: **May 1–June 30;
  Oct. 20–Dec. 13**
Breakfast: **Full**

Other Meals: **Available**
Credit Cards: **AMEX, MC, VISA**
Pets: **No**

Children: **Welcome**
Smoking: **No**
Social Drinking: **Permitted**

Located three miles from North Conway, and reigning over 25 wooded acres in the White Mountains, this three-story Victorian inn has been in continuous operation since the late 1800s. Inside, the inn has the feel of a big country home—full of oriental rugs, comfortable chairs, antiques, crafts, and country collectibles. The stone cottage has a fireplace and is a favorite of honeymooners. Outside, you're close to all of the wonderful recreational possibilities that the valley has to offer—downhill skiing, hiking, biking, canoeing, kayaking, tennis, golf, and more. In back of the inn is a swimming pool and, in winter, all you have to do is go across the street to the Nordic Center, where the cross-country ski trails begin.

Paisley and Parsley
ROUTE 16B, FIVE MILE CIRCUIT ROAD, BOX 572, JACKSON, NEW HAMPSHIRE 03846

Tel: **(800) 248-0859; (603) 383-0859**
Best Time to Call: **Mornings; evenings**
Hosts: **Bea and Chuck Stone**
Location: **125 mi. NW of Boston**
No. of Rooms: **3**
No. of Private Baths: **3**
Double/pb: **$65–$95**
Single/pb: **$50–$80**
Suites: **$65–$95; sleeps 2–4**
Open: **Jan. 3–Apr. 30; June 20–Nov. 15**

Reduced Rates: **Available**
Breakfast: **Full**
Credit Cards: **MC, VISA**
Pets: **No**
Children: **Welcome, over 10**
Smoking: **No**
Social Drinking: **Permitted**
Minimum Stay: **3 nights holiday weekends**
Airport/Station Pickup: **Yes, fee charged**

From its hillside perch along the road to Black Mountain, Paisley and Parsley enjoys an enviable view of Mt. Washington. As you'd expect, this is a great place for both downhill and cross-country skiers. Jackson also boasts several art galleries. At the end of the day, put away your skis and treat yourself to a moonlight sleigh ride at Nestlenook Farm. Tea is served 4–5 PM.

The Galway House B&B ✪
247 OLD PETERBOROUGH ROAD, JAFFREY, NEW HAMPSHIRE 03452

Tel: **(603) 532-8083**
Best Time to Call: **Evenings**
Hosts: **Joe and Marie Manning**
Location: **1 mi. from US 202**
No. of Rooms: **2**

Max. No. Sharing Bath: **4**
Double/sb: **$50**
Single/sb: **$40**
Open: **Aug. 15–June 30**
Breakfast: **Full**

Pets: **No**
Children: **Welcome (crib)**
Smoking: **Permitted**

Social Drinking: **Permitted**
Airport/Station Pickup: **Yes**

This new, oversize Cape with a spacious yard and sun deck is situated on a rural road surrounded by acres of woodland. It is located at the foot of 3,165-foot Grand Monadnock, in the center of the Monadnock Region, known as the Currier and Ives corner of the state. Picturesque in every season, the area will make sports enthusiasts revel in the choice of activities. Joe and Marie welcome you to a warm hearth, a suitable beverage, and comfortable accommodations! From June through September they offer B&B on board their sailing sloop.

The Jefferson Inn ✪
ROUTE 2, RFD 1, BOX 68A, JEFFERSON, NEW HAMPSHIRE 03583

Tel: **(603) 586-7998; (800) 729-7908**
Hosts: **Greg Brown and Bertie Koelewijn**
Location: **20 mi. from Rte. 93, Exit 35**
No. of Rooms: **10**
No. of Private Baths: **10**
Double/pb: **$50–$80**
Single/pb: **$46–$76**
Suites: **$83–$127**
Open: **Dec.–Mar.; May–Oct.**

Reduced Rates: **Families; winter weekdays**
Breakfast: **Full**
Credit Cards: **AMEX, DISC, MC, VISA**
Pets: **No**
Children: **Welcome**
Smoking: **No**
Social Drinking: **Permitted**
Airport/Station Pickup: **Yes**
Foreign Languages: **Dutch, French, German**

Built in 1896, this B&B is situated in the White Mountain National Forest and boasts beautiful valley and mountain views. Its location is ideal for outdoor activities, including hiking, swimming, canoeing, and golf in summer; downhill and cross-country skiing, skating, and snowshoeing in winter. The village of Jefferson sits within the shadows of Mt. Washington and the Presidential Range, with hiking trails starting near the inn's door. Decorated with period antiques, each impeccably clean room has a distinctive character. Relax on the porch in warm weather and end the day with a soothing cup of tea.

Ferry Point House ✪
R-1, BOX 335, LACONIA, NEW HAMPSHIRE 03246

Tel: **(603) 524-0087**
Best Time to Call: **After 6 PM**
Hosts: **Diane and Joe Damato**
Location: **90 mi. N of Boston**
No. of Rooms: **5**
No. of Private Baths: **5**
Double/pb: **$65–$75**

Single/pb: **$60–$70**
Open: **Memorial Day—Labor Day; weekends during fall foliage**
Reduced Rates: **15% weekly**
Breakfast: **Full**
Pets: **No**
Children: **Welcome**

Social Drinking: **Permitted**　　　　Foreign Languages: **French**
Airport/Station Pickup: **Yes**

New England's past is well preserved in this 150-year-old Victorian located on picturesque Lake Winnisquam. Enjoy breathtaking views of the water and the mountains from a 60-foot veranda. Of course, the view is even more enjoyable when you're sipping lemonade or the house blend of coffee. Guest rooms overlook the lake and are furnished with antiques, collectibles, and fresh flowers. Breakfast is served in a Victorian-style dining room, and your hosts take pride in offering unusual dishes, such as cheese baked apples, crêpes, or Grand Marnier French toast. Ferry Point House is minutes from regional activities such as boating, skiing, dinner cruises, and a large selection of fine restaurants.

The Beal House Inn ✪
247 WEST MAIN STREET, LITTLETON, NEW HAMPSHIRE 03561

Tel: **(603) 444-2661**	Open: **All year**
Best Time to Call: **9 AM–9 PM**	Reduced Rates: **15% groups and**
Hosts: **Catherine and Jean-Marie**	**extended stays**
(John) Fisher-Motheu	Breakfast: **Continental**
Location: **90 mi. N of Concord**	Other Meals: **Available**
No. of Rooms: **13**	Credit Cards: **MC, VISA**
No. of Private Baths: **9**	Pets: **No**
Max. No. Sharing Bath: **4**	Children: **Welcome**
Double/pb: **$50–$75**	Smoking: **No**
Single/pb: **$45**	Social Drinking: **Permitted**
Double/sb: **$45–$60**	Station Pickup: **Yes**
Single/sb: **$40**	Foreign Languages: **French**
Suites: **$85**	

Experience the White Mountains in this 1833 landmark! An inn since 1938, Beal House has charming guest rooms cozy with antiques, canopy beds, down comforters, and special touches. With native artwork and antiques for sale, the inn is a living shop as well. Breakfast gatherings by candlelight feature true Belgian waffles prepared by your Belgian-born host. Dinner in the jazzy little dining room consists of robust European fare. Beal House is located three hours from both Montreal and Boston, close to skiing, hiking, fishing, golf, historic sites, and other attractions.

Peep-Willow Farm ✪
51 BIXBY STREET, MARLBOROUGH, NEW HAMPSHIRE 03455

Tel: **(603) 876-3807**	Host: **Noel Aderer**
Best Time to Call: **Before 8 AM; after**	Location: **7 mi. E of Keene**
8 PM	No. of Rooms: **3**

Max. No. Sharing Bath: **4**	Pets: **No**
Double/sb: **$45**	Children: **Welcome**
Single/sb: **$30**	Smoking: **No**
Open: **All year**	Social Drinking: **Permitted**
Breakfast: **Full**	Airport/Station Pickup: **Yes**

Noel Aderer has a new Colonial farmhouse on a working thorough-bred horse farm. She raises and trains horses for competition, and while there is plenty of room for petting and admiring, guests are not permitted to ride. Peep-Willow is named after horses number one and two, respectively. It is a charming place, with lots of wood accents and antiques. Breakfast specialties include French toast, with local maple syrup, and bacon and eggs. Guests are welcome to watch farm chores, visit the horses, and enjoy a cup of coffee with Noel, who has done everything from working on a kibbutz to training polo ponies for a maharajah.

Blue Goose Inn

ROUTE 103B, P.O. BOX 117, MT. SUNAPEE, NEW HAMPSHIRE 03772

Tel: **(603) 763-5519**	Single/sb: **$40**
Best Time to Call: **Before noon**	Open: **All year**
Hosts: **Meryl and Ronald Caldwell**	Breakfast: **Full**
Location: **10 mi. from I-89**	Credit Cards: **MC, VISA**
No. of Rooms: **5**	Pets: **No**
No. of Private Baths: **4**	Children: **Welcome**
Max. No. Sharing Bath: **3**	Smoking: **Permitted**
Double/pb: **$50**	Social Drinking: **Permitted**
Single/pb: **$45**	Airport/Station Pickup: **Yes**
Double/sb: **$45**	

This cozy, early 19th-century Colonial farmhouse is located at the base of Mt. Sunapee on scenic Lake Sunapee. The guest rooms are quiet and spacious, adorned with handmade quilts and attractive antiques. Whether you're coming here for the greening of spring, the long lush summer, the autumn foliage, or the white-blanketed backdrop for skiing or sleighing, you'll be treated to their breakfast specialty: a combination of bacon, eggs, and cheese, baked in a maple flavored biscuit. It is served on the enclosed porch, which is enhanced by skylights and hanging plants. You're invited to join your hosts and other guests for wine, fruit, and cheese served each evening on the porch or by the fireplace in the common room.

The Buttonwood Inn ☉

P.O. BOX 1817, MT. SURPRISE ROAD, NORTH CONWAY, NEW
HAMPSHIRE 03860

Tel: **(603) 356-2625; (800) 258-2625**	Reduced Rates: **Available; families**
Hosts: **Hugh and Ann Begley**	Breakfast: **Full**
Location: **1½ mi. from Rte. 16**	Other Meals: **Available Jan. and Feb.**
No. of Rooms: **9**	Credit Cards: **AMEX, MC, VISA**
No. of Private Baths: **3**	Pets: **No**
Max. No. Sharing Bath: **4**	Children: **Welcome, over 3**
Double/pb: **$60–$100**	Smoking: **Permitted**
Single/pb: **$50–$80**	Social Drinking: **Permitted**
Double/sb: **$50–$100**	Minimum Stay: **2 nights weekends Jan.**
Single/sb: **$40–$80**	**and Feb.; 3 nights holiday weekends**
Open: **All year**	

The Buttonwood is tucked away on Mt. Surprise, in the heart of the
White Mountains. It is secluded and quiet, yet only two miles from
excellent town restaurants and factory outlet shopping. This New
England–style Cape Cod was built in 1820 and has been enlarged over
the years from four to twenty-four rooms. Most guest bedrooms have
wide-plank floors and are furnished with antique oak and cottage pine
pieces. Hugh loves to fish and ski cross-country; Ann teaches the local
schoolchildren downhill skiing.

Peacock Inn ☉

P.O. BOX 1012, NORTH CONWAY, NEW HAMPSHIRE 03860

Tel: **(603) 356-9041; (800) 328-9041**	Breakfast: **Full**
Best Time to Call: **9 AM–9 PM**	Credit Cards: **AMEX, DISC, MC, VISA**
Hosts: **Claire and Larry Jackson**	Pets: **No**
Location: **60 mi. W of Portland, Maine**	Children: **Welcome**
No. of Rooms: **15**	Smoking: **Restricted**
No. of Private Baths: **15**	Social Drinking: **Permitted**
Double/pb: **$84–$114**	Minimum Stay: **Fall foliage; holiday**
Single/pb: **$74–$94**	**weekends**
Open: **Jan.–Mar.; May–Oct.**	
Reduced Rates: **10% Mar., Apr., Nov.;**	
15% weekly; 10% seniors	

With its intimate atmosphere and comfortable furnishings, the Pea-
cock Inn has all the warmth of a classic country inn. Built in 1773—
with a guest book dating to 1875—the inn stands on a rise overlooking
the beautiful Moat Mountain range, with a river on one side. Claire's
eye for decorating and Larry's skill for remodeling are demonstrated
throughout the handsomely renovated home. Each morning, guests

awake to the aroma of a full country breakfast; in the afternoon, a complimentary beverage is served with cheese and crackers.

Wilderness Inn ✪
ROUTES 3 AND 112, RFD 1, BOX 69, NORTH WOODSTOCK, NEW HAMPSHIRE 03262

Tel: **(603) 745-3890**
Best Time to Call: **10 AM–9 PM**
Hosts: **Michael and Rosanna Yarnell**
Location: **120 mi. N of Boston**
No. of Rooms: **7**
No. of Private Baths: **5**
Max. No. Sharing Bath: **4**
Double/pb: **$50–$75**
Single/pb: **$45–$70**
Double/sb: **$40–$60**
Single/sb: **$35–$55**
Suites: **$60–$85**

Open: **All year**
Reduced Rates: **Midweek; off-season**
Breakfast: **Full**
Credit Cards: **AMEX, MC, VISA**
Pets: **No**
Children: **Welcome**
Smoking: **Permitted**
Social Drinking: **Permitted**
Airport/Station Pickup: **Yes**
Foreign Languages: **French, Italian, Bengali, Amharic**

Escape from it all at this mountainside retreat where, depending on the season, you can ski, swim, ride a bike, and hike to your heart's content. Restaurants, craft shops, and a golf course are all nearby. Fresh fruit, café au lait, and cranberry-walnut pancakes will lure you out of bed in the morning, but if you prefer, the Yarnells will bring a Continental breakfast to your room.

Meadow Farm
JENNESS POND ROAD, NORTHWOOD, NEW HAMPSHIRE 03261

Tel: **(603) 942-8619**
Hosts: **Douglas and Janet Briggs**
Location: **18 mi. E of Concord**
No. of Rooms: **3**
Max. No. Sharing Bath: **4**
Double/sb: **$60**
Single/sb: **$45**
Open: **All year**

Reduced Rates: **Families**
Breakfast: **Full**
Credit Cards: **AMEX**
Pets: **Sometimes**
Children: **Welcome**
Smoking: **No**
Social Drinking: **Permitted**

Meadow Farm is set on 50 acres of quiet woods and horse pastures. The house is an authentic New England Colonial dating back to 1770, with wide-pine floors, beamed ceilings, and old fireplaces. In the morning, a country breakfast of homemade breads, seasonal fruit, and local syrup is served in the keeping room. Guests are invited to relax on the private beach on an adjacent lake. The property also has plenty of wooded trails for long walks or cross-country skiing. Meadow Farm is an ideal location for those en route to Concord, the seacoast, or the mountains.

Crab Apple Inn ☯
ROUTE 25, RR 4, BOX 1955, PLYMOUTH, NEW HAMPSHIRE 03264

Tel: **(603) 536-4476**
Best Time to Call: **Mornings; evenings**
Hosts: **Harry and Maria Dunham**
Location: **4 mi. from Rte. 93**
No. of Rooms: **4**
No. of Private Baths: **4**
Double/pb: **$75–$95**
Suites: **$85–$95**

Open: **All year**
Breakfast: **Full**
Credit Cards: **AMEX, MC, VISA**
Pets: **No**
Children: **Welcome, over 8**
Smoking: **Permitted**
Social Drinking: **Permitted**

Located in the beautiful Baker River Valley at the gateway to the White Mountain region, the inn is an 1835 brick building of Federal design situated beside a small brook at the foot of Tenny Mountain. The bedrooms on the second floor have fireplaces; those on the third floor have a panoramic view of the mountains. All are tastefully furnished. There are several fine restaurants nearby, and the inn is within a 10-minute drive of Plymouth State College. Gift studios and handcraft and antique shops in the area provide treasures for both the discerning and casual buyer.

Grassy Pond House
RINDGE, NEW HAMPSHIRE 03461

Tel: (603) 899-5166, 899-5167	Single/sb: $45
Best Time to Call: Mornings	Open: All year
Hosts: Carmen Linares and Robert Multer	Breakfast: Full
	Pets: No
Location: 60 mi. NW of Boston	Children: Welcome, over 14
No. of Rooms: 3	Smoking: No
No. of Private Baths: 2	Social Drinking: Permitted
Max. No. Sharing Bath: 4	Airport/Station Pickup: Yes
Double/pb: $65	Foreign Languages: Spanish
Double/sb: $55	

This secluded 19th-century farmhouse is set among 150 acres of woods and fields. The house has been restored, enlarged, and decorated in period pieces. Guest quarters, overlooking the gardens and lake, feature a private entrance and a living room with fireplace. Breakfast specialties include pancakes with local maple syrup, fresh eggs and bacon, and plenty of good Colombian coffee. This setting, high in the Monadnock region, is perfect for hiking, skiing, boating, fishing, and swimming.

The Tokfarm ✪
BOX 1124, RR 2, RINDGE, NEW HAMPSHIRE 03461

Tel: (603) 899-6646	Open: Apr. 1–Nov. 29
Best Time to Call: Early mornings; evenings	Breakfast: Continental
	Pets: No
Host: Mrs. W. B. Nottingham	Children: No
Location: 50 mi. NW of Boston	Smoking: No
No. of Rooms: 5	Social Drinking: Permitted
Max. No. Sharing Bath: 4	Airport/Station Pickup: Yes
Double/sb: $35–$45	Foreign Languages: Dutch, French, German
Single/sb: $22	

This 150-year-old farmhouse has a spectacular view of three states from its 1,400-foot hilltop. Mt. Monadnock, the second most climbed peak in the world (Mt. Fuji is first), is practically in its backyard! Mrs. Nottingham raises Christmas trees and is a world traveler. She'll recommend things to keep you busy. Don't miss the lovely Cathedral of the Pines. Franklin Pierce College is nearby.

The Hilltop Inn
SUGAR HILL ROAD, P.O. BOX 9, SUGAR HILL, NEW HAMPSHIRE 03585

Tel: (603) 823-5695	Location: 2½ mi. W of Franconia
Hosts: Mike and Meri Hern	No. of Rooms: 6

No. of Private Baths: **6**
Double/pb: **$60–$85**
Single/pb: **$50–$75**
Suites: **$85–$110**
Open: **All year**
Breakfast: **Full**

Pets: **Welcome**
Children: **Welcome, over 4**
Smoking: **Restricted**
Social Drinking: **Permitted**
Airport/Station Pickup: **Yes**

The Hilltop Inn is a sprawling, 19th-century Victorian located in a small, friendly village. Inside, you'll find a warm, cozy atmosphere, comfortable furnishings, and lots of antiques. The kitchen is the heart of the house in more ways than one. In the morning, homemade muffins are served fresh from the old-fashioned Garland stove. In the evening, the sunsets from the deck are breathtaking. Your hosts are professional caterers and are pleased to cater to you. Fine dining Wed.–Sat. 6–8 PM in the Victorian candlelit dining room. Local attractions include Franconia Notch, White Mountain National Forest, North Conway, great skiing, and spectacular foliage.

NEW JERSEY

Stanhope •
• Glenwood
Denville •
Dover •
• Lyndhurst
Milford •
• Princeton
• Spring Lake
Jobstown •
Alloway •
• Ocean City
• North Wildwood
• Cape May

Bed & Breakfast of Princeton—A Reservation Service
P.O. BOX 571, PRINCETON, NEW JERSEY 08542

Tel: **(609) 924-3189**; fax: **(609) 921-6271**
Coordinator: **John W. Hurley**
States/Regions Covered: **Princeton**

Rates (Single/Double):
  Average: **$40–$55 / $50–$65**
Credit Cards: **No**

Princeton is a lovely town; houses are well set back on carefully tended lawns, screened by towering trees. Some of John's hosts live within walking distance of Princeton University. Nassau Hall, circa 1756, is its oldest building; its chapel is the largest of any at an American university. Nearby corporate parks include national companies, such as RCA, Squibb, and the David Sarnoff Research Center. Restaurants feature every imaginable cuisine, and charming shops offer a wide variety of wares. Personal checks are accepted for deposit or total payment in advance; cash or traveler's checks are required for any balance due.

Josiah Reeve House ✪
P.O. BOX 501, NORTH GREENWICH STREET, ALLOWAY, NEW JERSEY 08001

Tel: **(609) 935-5640**	Suites: **$95**
Best Time to Call: **8 AM–11 AM**	Open: **All year**
Hosts: **Paul and Judith D'Esterre**	Reduced Rates: **Available**
Location: **15 mi. NE of Wilmington, Delaware**	Breakfast: **Full**
	Credit Cards: **MC, VISA**
No. of Rooms: **4**	Pets: **No**
No. of Private Baths: **2**	Children: **Welcome, over 16**
Max. No. Sharing Bath: **4**	Smoking: **No**
Double/pb: **$85**	Social Drinking: **Permitted**
Double/sb: **$80**	

In the early 1700s, shimmering lakes, tall timber stands, fertile fields, and a tidal passage to the Delaware Bay attracted Quaker settlers to what is now Alloway Township (named for a local Indian chief). The lakes supported a variety of water-powered mills, one owned by the family of Josiah Reeve, who built this brick Greek Revival home in 1836. To recreate that era, guest rooms are furnished with four-poster beds, claw-footed tubs, and other period antiques. For more antiques, visit nearby Mullica Hill, with its more than thirty shops. Local activities include golf, fishing, and historic sightseeing—this area has more pre-Revolutionary homes than any county in New Jersey.

Albert G. Stevens Inn ✪
127 MYRTLE AVENUE, CAPE MAY, NEW JERSEY 08204

Tel: (609) 884-4717	Open: All year
Hosts: Diane and Curt Rangen	Breakfast: Full
Location: 40 mi. S of Atlantic City	Credit Cards: DISC, MC, VISA
No. of Rooms: 7	Pets: No
No. of Private Baths: 7	Children: By arrangement
Double/pb: $85–$120	Smoking: No
Suites: $135	Social Drinking: Permitted

Built in 1889, this Queen Anne Victorian boasts an unusual floating staircase and a wraparound veranda where summertime guests can enjoy their two-course breakfasts. Inside, the house is decorated with Victorian treasures, crystal, and porcelain. Dinner is included during two-night visits from November to March. Cape May's better beaches and the Washington Street Mall are a ten-minute walk away. For a superb end to your day, soak in the 350-gallon hot tub.

Barnard-Good House ✪
238 PERRY STREET, CAPE MAY, NEW JERSEY 08204

Tel: (609) 884-5381	Open: Apr.–Nov.
Best Time to Call: 9 AM–9 PM	Breakfast: Full
Hosts: Nan and Tom Hawkins	Pets: No
No. of Rooms: 5	Children: Welcome, over 14
No. of Private Baths: 5	Smoking: No
Double/pb: $86–$110	Social Drinking: Permitted
Single/pb: $77.40–$99	Minimum Stay: 2 nights spring and
Suites: $115	fall; 3 nights summer

Nan and Tom cordially invite you to their Second Empire Victorian cottage, circa 1869, just two blocks from the "swimming" beach. They love antiques and are continually adding to their collection. They use them generously to create the warm and comfortable atmosphere. Nan's breakfast includes homemade exotic juices, delicious home-baked breads, and unusual preserves. In spring and fall, added gourmet entrées and side dishes make for an epicurean feast. Iced tea and snacks are served evenings.

The Mainstay Inn
635 COLUMBIA AVENUE, CAPE MAY, NEW JERSEY 08204

Tel: (609) 884-8690	Double/pb: $95–$180
Best Time to Call: 8 AM–10 PM	Single/pb: $85–$170
Hosts: Tom and Sue Carroll	Suites: $105–$180
No. of Rooms: 12	Open: Mar. 15–Dec. 15
No. of Private Baths: 12	Reduced Rates: Off-season; weekdays

Breakfast: **Full**
Pets: **No**
Children: **Welcome, over 12**

Smoking: **No**
Social Drinking: **Permitted**
Minimum Stay: **3 nights in season**

Located in the heart of the historic district, this 116-year-old mansion was originally built as a private gambling club. Except for a few 20th-century concessions, it still looks much as it did when the gamblers were there, with 14-foot ceilings, elaborate chandeliers, and outstanding Victorian antiques. Tom and Sue serve breakfast either in the formal dining room or on the veranda; afternoon tea and homemade snacks are a ritual. Breakfast often features ham and apple pie, or corn quiche with baked ham. Continental breakfast is served in summer. Rock on the wide veranda, enjoy croquet in the garden, or retreat to the cupola.

Lakeside B&B ✪
11 SUNSET TRAIL, DENVILLE, NEW JERSEY 07834

Tel: **(201) 625-5129**
Hosts: **Annette and Al Bergins**
Location: **35 mi. W of New York City**
No. of Rooms: **1**
No. of Private Baths: **1**
Double/pb: **$50**
Single/pb: **$45**

Open: **All year**
Breakfast: **Full**
Pets: **No**
Children: **No**
Smoking: **No**
Social Drinking: **Permitted**

Just off Route 80, midway between Manhattan and the Pocono Mountains, is this modern, two-story home with private guest quarters on the ground level. There's a lovely view of the bay leading to Indian Lake. Al and Annette will provide you with a rowboat and beach passes, as well as refreshments afterward. Relax on the deck overlooking the bay, or explore the unspoiled towns and points of interest off the tourist trail. Good restaurants of every variety and price range abound.

The Silver Lining Bed & Breakfast ✪
467 ROCKAWAY ROAD, DOVER, NEW JERSEY 07801

Tel: **(201) 361-9245**
Hosts: **Joan and Bill Middleton**
Location: **1 mi. from I-80**
No. of Rooms: **3**
Max. No. Sharing Bath: **4**
Double/sb: **$50**
Single/sb: **$45**
Open: **All year**
Reduced Rates: **Weekly**

Breakfast: **Full**
Credit Cards: **MC, VISA**
Pets: **No**
Children: **Welcome, over 12**
Smoking: **Permitted**
Social Drinking: **Permitted**
Airport/Station Pickup: **Yes**
Foreign Languages: **Spanish**

This 85-year-old Dutch Colonial home is set between stately trees in a suburban area within an hour's drive of the Meadowlands Sports Complex, New York City, Waterloo Village, and Action Park. The newly redecorated guest rooms feature wicker and lacquer furniture, and pretty print accessories. Two bedrooms share a sitting room, private kitchen, and separate entrance, making it ideal for two couples to share as an apartment.

Apple Valley Inn ✪
P.O. BOX 302, CORNER OF ROUTES 517 AND 565, GLENWOOD, NEW JERSEY 07418

Tel: **(201) 764-3735**	Single/sb: **$50**
Best Time to Call: **5–8 PM**	Grist Mill: **$130; sleeps 6 (available**
Hosts: **Mitzi and John Durham**	**June 1–Sept. 15)**
Location: **45 mi. NW of New York City**	Open: **All year**
No. of Rooms: **5**	Reduced Rates: **10% seniors**
No. of Private Baths: **2**	Breakfast: **Full**
Max. No. Sharing Bath: **3**	Pets: **No**
Double/pb: **$60**	Children: **Welcome, over 13**
Single/pb: **$50**	Smoking: **Permitted**
Double/sb: **$60**	Social Drinking: **Permitted**

Apple Valley Inn, a rustic 19th-century mansion with exposed beams, red brick chimneys, and hand-painted fire screens, takes its name from the fruit farms that used to dominate the area. Bedrooms are named for apples—Granny Smith, Jonathan, Yellow Delicious—and are furnished in Colonial style. Guests can stroll in an apple orchard, swim in a pool, and fish for river trout without leaving the property. Local recreational options include skiing and horseback riding. Breakfasts feature ham-cheese dandy or Dutch baby pancakes, accompanied by fresh fruit and homemade breads, muffins, and jams.

Belle Springs Farm ✪
RD 1, BOX 420, JOBSTOWN, NEW JERSEY 08041

Tel: **(609) 723-5364**	Open: **All year**
Host: **Lyd Sudler**	Breakfast: **Full**
Location: **5 miles from N.J. Tpke.,**	Other Meals: **Available**
Exit 7	Pets: **No**
No. of Rooms: **3**	Children: **Welcome**
Max. No. Sharing Bath: **4**	Smoking: **Permitted**
Double/sb: **$50**	Social Drinking: **Permitted**
Suites: **$85**	

This spacious, contemporary farmhouse was built in 1961 and is attractively furnished with family heirlooms. The bedrooms are air-conditioned. From the porch, there's a spectacular view of the pastures with the cows grazing, and the deer that come out of the woods at dusk. It's situated in the heart of Burlington County, where every little town, including Burlington, Bordentown, and Mt. Holly, is a pre-Revolutionary gem. It is a half hour to Philadelphia or Princeton. Lyd enjoys music, gardening, and pampering her guests. If you want to bring your horse, there's a $10 charge for the turnout in the pasture.

Jeremiah J. Yereance House ✪
410 RIVERSIDE AVENUE, LYNDHURST, NEW JERSEY 07071

Tel: **(201) 438-9457**	Suites: **$70–$75**
Best Time to Call: **After 6 PM**	Open: **All year**
Hosts: **Evelyn and Frank Pezzolla**	Reduced Rates: **Weekly; 15% seniors**
Location: **12 mi. W of New York City**	Breakfast: **Continental**
No. of Rooms: **3**	Pets: **No**
No. of Private Baths: **1**	Children: **Welcome, over 12**
Max. No. Sharing Bath: **4**	Smoking: **No**
Double/sb: **$55**	Social Drinking: **Permitted**
Single/sb: **$50**	Airport/Station Pickup: **Yes**

Evelyn and Frank Pezzolla fell in love with this wood-frame Colonial when they first saw it in 1984. After a year of rewiring and replacing the roof and just about everything else, the house began to look like the historical landmark it is. In 1986, the government agreed and placed it on the state and national registers. The house is set in a quiet neighborhood across from a riverside park, with jogging paths, bike trails, and picnic areas. The guest suite occupies the south wing of the house and consists of a small parlor with fireplace and an adjoining bedroom and private bath. In the morning, a help-yourself buffet of hot drinks, homemade breads, muffins, and fresh fruits awaits you. The Jeremiah J. Yereance House is just five minutes from the Meadowlands Sports Complex.

Chestnut Hill on-the-Delaware ✪
63 CHURCH STREET, MILFORD, NEW JERSEY 08848

Tel: **(908) 995-9761**	Single/sb: **$65**
Hosts: **Linda and Rob Castagna**	Open: **All year**
Location: **15 mi. from Rte. 78**	Reduced Rates: **Weekly**
No. of Rooms: **5**	Breakfast: **Full**
No. of Private Baths: **2**	Pets: **No**
Max. No. Sharing Bath: **4**	Children: **Welcome, over 12**
Double/pb: **$85–$95**	Smoking: **No**
Double/sb: **$70**	Social Drinking: **Permitted**

The veranda of this 1860 Neo-Italianate Victorian overlooks the peaceful Delaware River. Linda, Rob, and son Michael have refurbished and restored their home with charm, grace, and beauty. The historic countryside is great for antique hunting, water sports, art shows, and restaurants. It's only minutes to New Hope and Bucks County delights, and to dozens of factory outlets.

Candlelight Inn ✪
2310 CENTRAL AVENUE, NORTH WILDWOOD, NEW JERSEY 08260

Tel: **(609) 522-6200**
Best Time to Call: **8 AM–11 PM**
Hosts: **Paul DiFilippo and Diane Buscham**
Location: **40 mi. S of Atlantic City**
No. of Rooms: **9**
No. of Private Baths: **7**
Max. No. Sharing Bath: **4**
Double/pb: **$80–$110**
Double/sb: **$75–$95**
Open: **Feb.–Dec.**

Reduced Rates: **10% seniors; weekly**
Breakfast: **Full**
Credit Cards: **AMEX, DISC, MC, VISA**
Pets: **No**
Children: **No**
Smoking: **No**
Social Drinking: **Permitted**
Airport/Station Pickup: **Yes**
Foreign Languages: **French**
Minimum Stay: **3 nights July and Aug.**

Leaming Rice, Sr., built this Queen Anne Victorian at the turn of the century. The house remained in the family until Diane and Paul restored it and created a bed and breakfast. Large oak doors with beveled glass invite you into the main vestibule, which has a fireplace nook. A wide variety of original gas lighting fixtures may be found throughout the house. Guest rooms have fresh flowers and are furnished with period pieces and antiques. Breakfast is served in the dining room with a built-in oak breakfront, and chestnut pocket doors. A hot tub and sun deck are special spots for relaxing. In the afternoon, enjoy tea and cookies on the wide veranda. This elegant inn is convenient to the beaches, boardwalk, and historic Cape May.

BarnaGate Bed & Breakfast ✪
637 WESLEY AVENUE, OCEAN CITY, NEW JERSEY 08226

Tel: **(609) 391-9366**
Hosts: **The Barna family**
Location: **10 mi. S of Atlantic City**
No. of Rooms: **5**
No. of Private Baths: **2**
Max. No. Sharing Bath: **4**
Double/pb: **$65–$70**
Double/sb: **$60**
Open: **All year**

Breakfast: **Continental**
Credit Cards: **MC, VISA**
Pets: **No**
Children: **Welcome, over 10**
Smoking: **No**
Social Drinking: **Permitted**
Minimum Stay: **Summer holiday weekends**
Airport/Station Pickup: **Yes**

This 1895 seashore Victorian, painted a soft peach with mauve and burgundy trim, is only three and a half blocks from the ocean. The attractively furnished bedrooms have paddle fans, antique furnish-

ings, pretty quilts, and wicker accessories. You'll enjoy the homey atmosphere and the sensitive hospitality; if you want privacy, it is respected, if you want company, it is offered. Antique shops, great restaurants, the quaint charm of Cape May, and the excitement of Atlantic City are close by.

Northwood Inn Bed & Breakfast
401 WESLEY AVENUE, OCEAN CITY, NEW JERSEY 08226

Tel: **(609) 399-6071**
Hosts: **Marj, John, and Rebecca Loeper**
Location: **8 mi. S of Atlantic City**
No. of Rooms: **9**
No. of Private Baths: **7**
Max. No. Sharing Bath: **4**
Double/pb: **$80–$95**
Single/pb: **$75–$90**
Double/sb: **$75**
Single/sb: **$70**
Suites: **$130; sleeps 4**

Open: **All year**
Breakfast: **Full**
Credit Cards: **MC, VISA**
Pets: **No**
Children: **Welcome, over 10**
Smoking: **No**
Social Drinking: **Permitted**
Minimum Stay: **Holiday weekends only**
Airport/Station Pickup: **Yes**

Antique and wicker furniture sets off the charm of this Queen Anne Victorian, with its sweeping staircase and oak and plank-pine floors. All guest rooms have custom-made bedspreads, ruffles, and window treatments in designer fabrics. Common space on the main floor consists of a parlor, a library and game room, a billiard room with a piano, and a dining room. Guests also have use of two porches and a rooftop deck. The location is ideal, since the beach, the boardwalk, stores, and restaurants are only three blocks away.

Ashling Cottage ✪
106 SUSSEX AVENUE, SPRING LAKE, NEW JERSEY 07762

Tel: (908) 449-3553; (800) 237-1877	Open: Mar.–Dec.
Hosts: Goodi and Jack Stewart	Reduced Rates: Sept. 15–May 15
Location: 6 mi. from Garden State Pkwy., Exit 98	Breakfast: Continental
No. of Rooms: 10	Pets: No
No. of Private Baths: 8	Children: No
Max. No. Sharing Bath: 4	Smoking: No
Double/pb: $70–$120	Social Drinking: Permitted
Single/pb: $65–$115	Airport/Station Pickup: Yes
Double/sb: $65–$90	Minimum Stay: 2–3 nights May–Aug. weekends
Single/sb: $60–$85	

The Jersey shore is a block away from this three-story, mansard-roofed cottage with bay windows, overhangs, nooks, and a small romantic balcony. Each guest room is different, with such features as dormer windows, wainscoting, and individual porches. A buffet breakfast is served in the glass-enclosed solarium with views of the ocean and boardwalk to the east. To the west is the willow-bordered Spring Lake, popular for boaters, with its wooden footbridges, ducks, and geese.

Whistling Swan Inn ✪
BOX 791, 110 MAIN STREET, STANHOPE, NEW JERSEY 07874

Tel: (201) 347-6369	Reduced Rates: Weekly; 10% seniors
Best Time to Call: 9 AM–6 PM	Breakfast: Full
Hosts: Paula Williams and Joe Mulay	Credit Cards: AMEX, DISC, MC, VISA
Location: 45 mi. W of New York City	Pets: No
No. of Rooms: 10	Children: Welcome, over 12
No. of Private Baths: 10	Smoking: No
Double/pb: $65–$95	Social Drinking: Permitted
Open: All year	Airport/Station Pickup: Yes, by arrangement

You'll feel like you're back in grandmother's house when you visit this lovely Queen Anne Victorian located in a small, historic village. The massive limestone wraparound porch leads to comfortable rooms filled with family antiques. Your hosts have labored tirelessly to make the ornate woodwork, large fireplaces, old-fashioned fixtures, and even the banister light look like new. Take a bubble bath in a claw-footed tub and then wrap yourself in a fluffy robe before retiring. Your room will be individually decorated in varying period motifs. Breakfast includes homemade muffins, breads, and fruit, along with a hot egg, cheese, or fruit dish. Special arrangements are easily made for corporate guests who need to eat early or require the use of a private telephone, copy service, or meeting room. The inn is close to the International Trade Zone, Waterloo Village, Lake Musconetcong, restaurants, and state parks and forests.

For key to listings, see inside front or back cover.

✪ This star means that rates are guaranteed through December 31, 1993, to any guest making a reservation as a result of reading about the B&B in *Bed & Breakfast U.S.A.*—1993 edition.

Important! To avoid misunderstandings, always ask about cancellation policies when booking.

Please enclose a self-addressed, stamped, business-size envelope when contacting reservation services.

For more details on what you can expect in a B&B, see Chapter 1.

Always mention *Bed & Breakfast U.S.A.* when making reservations!

If no B&B is listed in the area you'll be visiting, use the form on page 733 to order a copy of our "List of New B&Bs."

We want to hear from you! Use the form on page 735.

NEW MEXICO

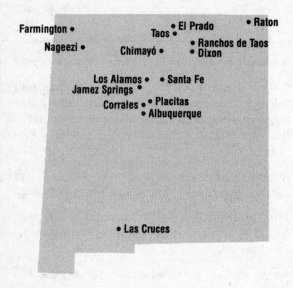

Bed & Breakfast Rocky Mountains—New Mexico
906 SOUTH PEARL STREET, DENVER, COLORADO 80209

Tel: (800) 733-8415	Descriptive Directory of B&Bs: **$4.50**
Best Time to Call: **8:30 AM–5:30 PM**	Rates (Single/Double):
Mon.–Fri.; 9 AM–1 PM Sat. (MST)	Modest: **$35 / $45**
Coordinator: **Cheryl Carroll**	Average: **$60 / $65**
States/Regions Covered: **Colorado,**	Luxury: **$85 / $125**
New Mexico, Utah	Credit Cards: **MC, VISA**

A free reservation service for Colorado, New Mexico and Utah representing over 200 inns and homestays.

Bottger Mansion Bed and Breakfast ✪
110 SAN FELIPE NW, ALBUQUERQUE, NEW MEXICO 87104

Tel: **(505) 243-3639**
Hosts: **Frances Maldonado and Patsy Garcia**
Location: **2 mi. W of I-25, Exit Lomas Blvd.**
No. of Rooms: **3**
No. of Private Baths: **3**
Double/pb: **$79–$99**
Single/pb: **$59–$79**
Suites: **$109; sleeps 4**
Open: **All year**

Reduced Rates: **Available**
Breakfast: **Full**
Other Meals: **Available**
Credit Cards: **AMEX, MC, VISA**
Pets: **Sometimes**
Children: **Welcome**
Smoking: **No**
Social Drinking: **Permitted**
Minimum Stay: **2 nights during holidays and special events**
Foreign Languages: **Spanish**

Included in the National Register of Historic Places, Bottger Mansion is located in Albuquerque's Old Town, within walking distance of the historic old church, museums, and plaza with more than 200 shops and restaurants. Sit in the courtyard of this Victorian B&B, or sample an authentic New Mexican high tea—Frances is sure to bake the official state cookie, the bizcochito, among other local specialties. (Baking and cooking classes available on premises.) At day's end retire to a spacious bedroom and in the morning enjoy more native New Mexican dishes.

The Corner House ✪
9121 JAMES PLACE NORTHEAST, ALBUQUERQUE, NEW MEXICO 87111

Tel: **(505) 298-5800**
Host: **Jean Thompson**

Location: **4 mi. N of I-40**
No. of Rooms: **3**

No. of Private Baths: **1**
Max. No. Sharing Bath: **3**
Double/pb: **$45**
Double/sb: **$35**
Single/sb: **$30**
Open: **All year**
Reduced Rates: **10% families, seniors**

Breakfast: **Full**
Other Meals: **Available**
Pets: **Sometimes**
Children: **Welcome (crib)**
Smoking: **No**
Social Drinking: **Permitted**

Jean welcomes you to her handsome southwestern-style home, decorated in a delightful mix of antiques and collectibles. Breakfast specialties include Jean's homemade muffins. The Corner House is located in a quiet residential neighborhood within view of the magnificent Sandia Mountains. It is convenient to Old Town Albuquerque, Santa Fe, and many Indian pueblos, and the launch site for the International Balloon Festival.

La Posada de Chimayó ✪
P.O. BOX 463, CHIMAYÓ, NEW MEXICO 87522

Tel: **(505) 351-4605**
Host: **Sue Farrington**
Location: **30 mi. N of Santa Fe**
No. of Rooms: **4**
No. of Private Baths: **4**
Double/pb: **$85–$110**
Single/pb: **$75–$85**
Open: **All year**

Reduced Rates: **Weekly in winter**
Breakfast: **Full**
Credit Cards: **MC, VISA (for deposits)**
Pets: **Sometimes**
Children: **Welcome, over 12**
Smoking: **No**
Social Drinking: **Permitted**
Foreign Languages: **Spanish**

Chimayó is known for its historic old church and its tradition of fine Spanish weaving. This is a typical adobe home with brick floors and *viga* ceilings. The suite is composed of a small bedroom and sitting room, and is made cozy with Mexican rugs, handwoven fabrics, comfortable furnishings, and traditional corner fireplaces. Sue's breakfasts are not for the fainthearted, and often feature stuffed French toast or chilies rellenos. Wine or sun tea are graciously offered after you return from exploring Bandelier National Monument Park, the Indian pueblos, cliff dwellings, and the "high road" to Taos.

Sagebrush Circle Bed & Breakfast ✪
23 SAGEBRUSH CIRCLE, CORRALES, NEW MEXICO 87048

Tel: **(505) 898-5393**
Best Time to Call: **8:30 AM–9 PM**
Hosts: **Barbara and Victor Ferkiss**
Location: **10 mi. NW of Oldtown**
No. of Rooms: **2**
No. of Private Baths: **2**
Double/pb: **$58–$65**

Single/pb: **$50–$57**
Open: **All year**
Reduced Rates: **Available**
Breakfast: **Continental**
Other Meals: **Available**
Pets: **No**
Children: **Welcome, 12 and older**

Smoking: **No**   Minimum Stay: **2 nights**
Social Drinking: **Permitted**   Airport/Station Pickup: **Yes**

Sagebrush Circle is a dramatic pueblo-style home nestled in the hills of Corrales, a Spanish village settled in the sixteenth century. All rooms have magnificent views of the Sandia Mountains. During cooler mornings, freshly brewed coffee and homemade breads and muffins are served in the great room, which has a 16-foot beamed ceiling. In warmer weather, guests can eat outdoors. As you dine, you may hear the neighing of horses or see brilliantly colored balloons rise in the turquoise sky—they float over the house during Balloon Fiesta in October. A friendly dog and a shy calico cat share living quarters with Barbara and Victor, who are delighted to give advice and information about the area.

La Casita Guesthouse ✪
P.O. BOX 103, DIXON, NEW MEXICO 87527

Tel: **(505) 579-4297**
Hosts: **Sara Pene and Celeste Miller**
Location: **25 mi. S of Taos**
Guest Cottage: **$60 for 2; $100 for 3; $80 for 4**
Handicapped-Accessible: **Yes**
Open: **All year**

Breakfast: **Continental**
Pets: **No**
Children: **Welcome**
Smoking: **No**
Social Drinking: **Permitted**
Foreign Languages: **Spanish**

The rural mountain village of Dixon is home to many artists and craftspeople. La Casita is a traditional New Mexico adobe with *vigas, latillas,* and Mexican tile floors. Guests enjoy use of the living room, fully equipped kitchen, two bedrooms (each with a double bed), one bath, and a lovely patio. Available only to people traveling together, it is a perfect spot for relaxing and is just minutes from the Rio Grande, river rafting, hiking, and cross-country skiing. Indian pueblos, ancient Anasazi ruins, museums, art galleries, horseback-riding ranches, and alpine skiing are within an hour's drive. Sara is a horticulturist and weaver; Celeste is a teacher and psychotherapist.

Blue Star B&B Retreat ✪
P.O. BOX 800, EL PRADO, NEW MEXICO 87529

Tel: **(505) 758-4634**
Host: **Lee Hester**
Location: **2 mi. N of Taos**
No. of Rooms: **1**
No. of Private Baths: **1**
Guest Studio: **$65**
Open: **All year**
Reduced Rates: **10% weekly**

Breakfast: **Continental**
Pets: **Yes**
Children: **Welcome**
Smoking: **No**
Social Drinking: **Permitted**
Station Pickup: **Yes**
Foreign Languages: **French**

This lovely private studio has a full kitchen, large bath, and king-size bed (or two singles). Its Spanish *viga* trees make for a distinctive ceiling, and the pink flagstone floor is always toasty, thanks to radiant heat. The enclosed porch presents a full view of Taos Sacred Mountain. NordicTrack ski equipment, trampoline, and weights are available to guests; there are juicers for those who want to make their own fruit and vegetable beverages. Outside, a wide variety of adventures await you, such as rafting, skiing, fishing, hot baths, tennis, horseback riding, Indian dances, and arts and crafts.

Silver River Inn ○

3151 WEST MAIN STREET, FARMINGTON, NEW MEXICO 87499

Tel: **(505) 325-8219**	Breakfast: **Continental**
Best Time to Call: **Anytime**	Credit Cards: **MC, VISA**
Hosts: **Diana Ohlson and David Beers**	Wheelchair Accessible: **Yes**
Location: **180 mi. NW of Albuquerque**	Pets: **No**
No. of Rooms: **1**	Children: **Welcome, over 12**
No. of Private Baths: **1**	Smoking: **No**
Suite: **$55–$85**	Social Drinking: **Permitted**
Open: **All year**	Airport/Station Pickup: **Yes**

Silver River Inn is a newly constructed, traditional New Mexican home with massive timber beams and exposed adobe. From its cliffside perch, it overlooks the fork of the San Juan and La Plata rivers. Indian reservations, Aztec ruins, and ski slopes are all within striking distance of this B&B. Private motor tours of the area can be arranged. A highlight of the Continental breakfast is green chili corn bread.

Dancing Bear B&B ○

314 SAN DIEGO LOOP, (MAILING ADDRESS: P.O. 642), JEMEZ SPRINGS, NEW MEXICO 87025

Tel: **(505) 829-3336**	Breakfast: **Full**
Best Time to Call: **8 AM–8 PM**	Other Meals: **Available**
Hosts: **Richard and Carol Crosby**	Credit Cards: **MC, VISA**
Location: **60 mi. S of Santa Fe**	Pets: **No**
No. of Rooms: **2**	Children: **No**
No. of Private Baths: **1**	Smoking: **No**
Max. No. Sharing Bath: **2**	Social Drinking: **Permitted**
Suites: **$90**	Airport/Station Pickup: **Yes**
Open: **All year**	

You are sure to find serenity at this river retreat at the base of a dramatic sandstone mesa, a bit off the beaten path from Santa Fe. During your stay you will have the opportunity to visit the owner's on-site pottery studio. (Workshops and lessons can be arranged.) Local artisans' handcrafted pieces are exhibited throughout the house, and some are for sale. As you get ready for bed, you can anticipate having breakfast by candlelight or by the riverside. The resident chef is sure to whip up homemade muffins and other culinary delights; special dietary needs are never a problem.

Hilltop Hacienda ✪
2520 WESTMORELAND ROAD, LAS CRUCES, NEW MEXICO 88001

Tel: (505) 382-3556
Best Time to Call: 9 AM–9 PM
Hosts: Robert and Teddi Peters
Location: 5 mi. N of Las Cruces
 downtown area
No. of Rooms: 2
Max. No. Sharing Bath: 4
Double/sb: $55

Single/sb: $50
Open: All year
Reduced Rates: 15% weekly
Breakfast: Continental
Pets: Sometimes
Children: Welcome, over 12
Smoking: No
Social Drinking: Permitted

From its spectacular hillside setting, this arched Spanish-Moorish adobe offers stunning views of Las Cruces, the Mesilla Valley, and the Organ and Dona Ana mountains. In summer, sit on the patio with a complimentary beverage and enjoy the sunset; in winter, warm up by one of the two fireplaces and talk with Bob and Teddi. Your hosts will gladly help in planning excursions to the area's many attractions, including White Sands Missile Range, the International Space Museum, Old Mesilla, Fort Seldon, and for unique Mexican shopping, Juárez, Mexico. Morning greetings come from Romeo, Henny, and Denny—the resident rooster and his hens. Breakfast is served in the dining room or, weather permitting, on the patio.

Casa del Rey Bed & Breakfast ✪
305 ROVER, LOS ALAMOS, NEW MEXICO 87544

Tel: (505) 672-9401
Best Time to Call: After 5 PM
Host: Virginia L. King
No. of Rooms: 2
Max. No. Sharing Bath: 4
Double/sb: $30
Single/sb: $25

Open: All year
Reduced Rates: Weekly; families
Breakfast: Continental
Pets: No
Children: Welcome, over 5
Smoking: No
Social Drinking: Permitted

This adobe contemporary home is located in the quiet residential area of White Rock, and is situated in the Jémez mountains with a view of Santa Fe across the valley. The surroundings are rich in Spanish and Indian history. Pueblos, museums, Bandelier National Monument, skiing, hiking trails, tennis, and golf are all within easy reach. Virginia is rightfully proud of her beautifully kept house, with its pretty flower gardens. In summer, her breakfast of granola, home-baked rolls and muffins, along with fruits and beverages, is served on the sun porch, where you can enjoy the lovely scenery.

Chaco Inn at The Post ✪
BOX 40, NAGEEZI, NEW MEXICO 87037

Tel: (505) 632-3646
Hosts: **Don and Carol Batchelor**
Location: **50 mi. S of Farmington,**
    Hwy. 44
No. of Rooms: **3**
No. of Private Baths: **1**
Max. No. Sharing Bath: **4**
Double/pb: **$59**
Single/pb: **$49**
Double/sb: **$49**

Single/sb: **$39**
Open: **All year**
Reduced Rates: **10% seniors**
Breakfast: **Continental**
Credit Cards: **MC, VISA**
Pets: **Yes**
Children: **Welcome**
Smoking: **No**
Social Drinking: **Permitted**
Foreign Languages: **Navajo**

Located in a small New Mexico community, Chaco Inn at The Post offers the accommodations closest to Chaco Canyon Natural Historical Park, 26 miles south. Rooms are decorated with rugs and piñon and juniper trees, with a view of Colorado's mountains in the background. At night, you'll be inspired by the stars as the Anasazi were a thousand years ago.

Casa De Placitas ✪
3 CALLE DEL ARROYO, PLACITAS, NEW MEXICO 87043

Tel: (505) 867-4171
Best Time to Call: **Evenings and**
    weekends
Hosts: **Irving and Rosalie Uffer**
Location: **15 mi. N of Albuquerque**
No. of Rooms: **2**
No. of Private Baths: **2**
Double/pb: **$70**
Single/pb: **$60**

Guest Cottage: **$50**
Open: **Apr. 1–Oct. 31**
Breakfast: **Full**
Credit Cards: **DISC, MC, VISA**
Pets: **Yes**
Children: **Welcome, over 12**
Smoking: **No**
Social Drinking: **Permitted**

This spacious, contemporary adobe, lovingly built by the Uffers, combines all the charm of the fabled haciendas with modern comforts and amenities. Nestled in the foothills of the Sandia Mountains, it is convenient to Albuquerque, Santa Fe, and other sites of interest. Both the spacious guest bedroom and separate guesthouse are tastefully furnished in the southwestern style, with brick and tile floors, beamed ceilings, wood stoves, and a huge Mexican tiled bath in the guest wing. A full Southwestern breakfast is served daily in the sun-filled dining room with its magnificent mountain view.

Two Pipe Bed & Breakfast
BOX 52, TALPA ROUTE, RANCHOS DE TAOS, NEW MEXICO 87557

Tel: **(505) 758-4770**
Hosts: **Dusty and Babs Davis**
Location: **4 mi. SE of Taos**
Guest Cottage: **$75 for 2**
Open: **All year**
Breakfast: **Continental**

Pets: **No**
Children: **Welcome, over 5**
Smoking: **No**
Social Drinking: **Permitted**
Airport/Station Pickup: **Yes**

Beautiful gardens and mountain views surround this 275-year-old adobe hacienda. The house includes many traditional adobe features, such as kiva fireplaces and *viga* ceilings, along with many antiques and family furnishings. Guests are welcome to relax in the hot tub or curl up in front of a cozy fire. Your hosts offer complimentary snacks, wine, and beverages, and will do all they can to make you feel welcome. Five ski areas are located less than an hour from here, and a special hearty skiers' breakfast is served in season. Art galleries, museums, Indian pueblos, and Rio Grande Gorge, as well as great hunting and fishing, can all be enjoyed nearby.

The Red Violet Inn ✪
344 NORTH SECOND STREET, RATON, NEW MEXICO 87740

Tel: **(505) 445-9778**
Best Time to Call: **9 AM–8 PM**
Hosts: **John and Ruth Hanrahan**
Location: **1 mi. from I-25, Exit 455**
No. of Rooms: **4**
No. of Private Baths: **2**
Max. No. Sharing Bath: **4**
Double/pb: **$65**
Single/pb: **$60**
Double/sb: **$55**

Single/sb: **$45**
Open: **Mar. 1–Jan. 30**
Reduced Rates: **10% Oct. 15–Mar.**
Breakfast: **Full**
Other Meals: **Available**
Pets: **No**
Children: **Welcome, over 12**
Smoking: **No**
Social Drinking: **Permitted**
Airport/Station Pickup: **Yes**

Follow the Santa Fe Trail and step back into the past at this appealing 1902 redbrick Victorian home three blocks from Raton's historic downtown. Guests have use of the parlor, dining room, porches, and enclosed flower-filled yard. Repeat visitors arrange to be on hand for the classical music and social hour, from 5 to 6 PM. Late arrivals are welcomed with a glass of sherry. Tea or coffee is delivered to your room when you wake up. Full breakfast is served in the formal dining room, accompanied by friendly conversation. A theater and a gallery are within a few blocks, and hiking and fishing facilities are six miles away. Other area attractions include a golf course, a racetrack, several antique shops; ski slopes are within an hour's drive.

Bed & Breakfast of New Mexico ✪
P.O. BOX 2805, SANTA FE, NEW MEXICO 87504

Tel: **(505) 982-3332**	Rates (Single/Double):
Best Time to Call: **9 AM–9 PM**	Modest: **$55 / $70**
Coordinator: **Rob Bennett**	Average: **$75 / $90**
States/Regions Covered: **Statewide**	Luxury: **$95 / $200**
Descriptive Directory: **Free**	Credit Cards: **AMEX, MC, VISA**

Do come and enjoy the Santa Fe Opera in summer, the vibrant colors of the aspens in autumn, or skiing in winter. Don't miss the Indian pueblos and ancient cliff dwellings, the national forest areas, art colonies, museums, and Taos.

Adobe Abode ✪
202 CHAPELLE, SANTA FE, NEW MEXICO 87501

Tel: **(505) 983-3133**	Open: **All year**
Host: **Pat Harbour**	Breakfast: **Full**
No. of Rooms: 3	Pets: **No**
No. of Private Baths: 3	Children: **Welcome, over 10**
Double/pb: **$85–$110**	Smoking: **Permitted**
Single/pb: **$80–$95**	Social Drinking: **Permitted**

This renovated historic adobe offers all the amenities of a fine country inn just 3 blocks from downtown Santa Fe Plaza. Pat has decorated her house with a discerning eye and a flair for southwestern charm. The bedrooms feature fine linens, private phones, and handsome antiques. Excellent restaurants, museums, and shops are within walking distance.

American Artists Gallery-House ✪
FRONTIER ROAD, P.O. BOX 584, TAOS, NEW MEXICO 87571

Tel: **(505) 758-4446; (800) 532-2041**	Guest Cottage: **$65**
Best Time to Call: **Anytime**	Open: **All year**
Hosts: **Elliot and Judie Framan**	Breakfast: **Full**
Location: **3 blocks from Main St.**	Pets: **No**
No. of Rooms: 6	Children: **Welcome**
No. of Private Baths: 6	Smoking: **No**
Double/pb: **$65–$95**	Social Drinking: **Permitted**
Single/pb: **$60–$90**	Airport/Station Pickup: **Yes**

This charming hacienda is filled with artwork, and has a splendid view of Taos Mountain. Your hosts will gladly advise on local craft shops and boutiques. Their home is close to Rio Grande Gorge State Park, 900-year-old Taos Pueblo, and places to go fishing and rafting. Fireplaces, the outdoor hot tub, gardens, and a sculpture courtyard will delight you.

Harrison's B&B
P.O. BOX 242, TAOS, NEW MEXICO 87571

Tel: **(505) 758-2630**
Hosts: **Jean and Bob Harrison**
Location: **1½ mi. from Rte. 64**
No. of Rooms: **2**
No. of Private Baths: **2**
Double/pb: **$40–$50**
Single/pb: **$30–$40**

Open: **All year**
Reduced Rates: **10% after 4th night**
Breakfast: **Full**
Pets: **No**
Children: **Welcome (crib)**
Smoking: **No**
Social Drinking: **Permitted**

The Harrisons have lived in this large adobe just outside of Taos for 25 years. The house overlooks town from the foot of the western mesa and, framed by trees and bushes, boasts lovely mountain views. Inside, original works of art enhance the southwestern decor. The Harrisons are just over two miles from the Taos plaza, and are conveniently located near many outdoor pursuits, including skiing, hiking, fishing, and river rafting.

NEW YORK

Thousand
Islands Area

Lake Placid/
Adirondacks Area
Saranac Lake

Finger Lakes/
Rochester-Syracuse Area
Fairport-Lima

Niagara/
Buffalo Area
Niagara Falls

Lake George Area
Saratoga Springs

Chautauqua-
Allegheny
Addison

Central New York/
Leatherstocking Area

Hudson Valley/Albany/
Kingston Area

Catskills

Long Island

New York City Area
Bronxville

CATSKILLS

Maplewood ○

PARK ROAD, P.O. BOX 40, CHICHESTER, NEW YORK 12416

Tel: **(914) 688-5433**
Best Time to Call: **After 7 PM**
Hosts: **Nancy and Albert Parsons**
Location: **25 mi. NW of Kingston**
No. of Rooms: **4**
Max. No. Sharing Bath: **4**
Double/sb: **$55**

Single/sb: **$40**
Open: **All year**
Breakfast: **Full**
Pets: **No**
Children: **Welcome**
Smoking: **No**
Social Drinking: **Permitted**

A Colonial manor on a quiet country lane, and nestled among stately
maples, this is a charming B&B. Each spacious bedroom has a view of
the Catskills. In summer, you can swim in the in-ground pool, or play
badminton, croquet, or horseshoes. In winter, ski Belleayre, Hunter,

and Cortina, all only 12 miles away. In any season, enjoy the art galleries, boutiques, great restaurants, and theater at Woodstock, 20 minutes away. After a great day outdoors, come home to a glass of wine and good conversation. After a good night's sleep, you'll enjoy freshly squeezed orange juice, homemade breads and pastries, and freshly ground coffee.

Timberdoodle Inn ✪
MAIN STREET, FLEISCHMANNS, NEW YORK 12430

Tel: **(914) 254-4884**	Open: **All year**
Hosts: **Peggy and Joe Ruff**	Breakfast: **Full**
Location: **39 mi. W of Kingston**	Credit Cards: **MC, VISA**
No. of Rooms: **7**	Pets: **Sometimes**
No. of Private Baths: **5**	Children: **Welcome**
Max. No. Sharing Bath: **4**	Smoking: **Permitted**
Double/pb: **$65–$80**	Social Drinking: **Permitted**
Single/pb: **$60**	Minimum Stay: **2 nights ski season,**
Double/sb: **$60**	**major holidays**

The inn, a sports enthusiast's paradise, is located in the high peaks of the Catskill Mountains. A spacious late Victorian village "cottage" is attractively furnished with select antiques, wicker, brass, and country chintz. Windows framed in stained glass offer views of the ever-changing seasons. Your host, a licensed New York State Guide, can direct you to world-famous trout streams, well-marked hiking trails, and the Forest Preserve. Belleayre, a popular ski center, is five minutes away. Breakfast often features eggs Florentine, Dutch pancakes, or cinnamon muffins.

The Eggery Inn
COUNTY ROAD 16, TANNERSVILLE, NEW YORK 12485

Tel: **(518) 589-5363**	Reduced Rates: **Available**
Best Time to Call: **10 AM–8 PM**	Breakfast: **Full**
Hosts: **Julie and Abe Abramczyk**	Other Meals: **Available**
No. of Rooms: **15**	Credit Cards: **AMEX, MC, VISA**
No. of Private Baths: **13**	Pets: **No**
Max. No. Sharing Bath: **4**	Children: **Welcome**
Double/pb: **$75–$95**	Smoking: Restricted
Single/pb: **$55**	Social Drinking: **Permitted**
Suites: **$170–$190**	Minimum Stay: **2 nights weekends; 3**
Open: **May 16–Sept. 7; Sept. 15–**	**nights holiday weekends**
Apr. 1	

This Dutch Colonial farmhouse, circa 1900, is nestled in the northern Catskills at an elevation of 2,200 feet. The Abramczyks have restored and continually updated their inn. Guest rooms, decorated in a country motif, have carpeting, color TV, and comforters or spreads; queen-size and two-bed accommodations are available. Six first-floor rooms are accessible to wheelchair users. The public rooms' oak balustrade, Franklin stove, player piano, Mission Oak furniture, and panoramic views invite guests to relax. Breakfast selections include omelets, fruit-filled hotcakes, and heart-smart entrées. The inn is ideal for small groups and can be theme catered by prior arrangement. Ski slopes, hiking trails, scenic waterfalls, and the famous Woodstock colony are nearby.

Sunrise Inn ✪
RD 1, BOX 232B, WALTON, NEW YORK 13856

Tel: **(607) 865-7254**	Guest Cottage: **$60 for 2**
Best Time to Call: **9 AM–11 PM**	Open: **All year**
Hosts: **James and Adele Toth**	Reduced Rates: **10% seniors**
Location: **135 mi. NW of New York City; 5 mi. from Rte. 17**	Breakfast: **Continental**
No. of Rooms: **2**	Pets: **No**
Max. No. Sharing Bath: **4**	Children: **Welcome (crib)**
Double/sb: **$45**	Smoking: **No**
Single/sb: **$35**	Social Drinking: **Permitted**

Relax and enjoy the sound of the bubbling brook that borders the landscape of this 19th-century farmhouse. You'll awaken to the aroma of Irish soda bread and other homemade goodies, which you are invited to enjoy in the dining area or, weather permitting, on the wraparound porch. Afterward, browse through the antiques shop adjoining the inn. Area activities include fishing, canoeing, golfing, skiing, country fairs, and fine dining. End the day in quiet and homey comfort around the parlor wood stove.

CENTRAL NEW YORK/LEATHERSTOCKING AREA

Pickle Hill Bed and Breakfast ✪
795 CHENANGO STREET, BINGHAMTON, NEW YORK 13901

Tel: **(607) 723-0259**	Open: **All year**
Best Time to Call: **Anytime**	Reduced Rates: **On long stays**
Hosts: **Leslie and Tom Rossi**	Breakfast: **Full**
Location: **185 mi. NW of New York City**	Credit Cards: **No**
	Pets: **No**
No. of Rooms: **2**	Children: **Welcome**
Max. No. Sharing Bath: **4**	Smoking: **Yes, area available**
Double/sb: **$50**	Social Drinking: **Permitted**
Single/sb: **$40**	Airport/Station Pickup: **Yes**

Make yourself comfortable at Pickle Hill, built more than 100 years ago. Read, listen to music, and play board games in the lounge, then rally around the living room piano for a songfest, or join your hosts in the family room for conversation. Sports lovers can play bocci, basketball, or badminton on the side lawn; baseball fields, tennis courts, golf courses, bike paths, and cross-country ski trails are all nearby. Mark Twain's Elmira home, the Farmer's Museum, and the Baseball Hall of Fame in Cooperstown are all within driving distance. Closer to home, Binghamton's Performing Arts Center supplies top-notch entertainment, and the Tri-Cities Opera Company features some of the nation's most promising young singers.

Creekside Bed & Breakfast ✪
RD 1, BOX 206, COOPERSTOWN, NEW YORK 13326

Tel: **(607) 547-8203**	Breakfast: **Full**
Best Time to Call: **Anytime**	Credit Cards: **AMEX, MC, VISA**
Hosts: **Fred and Gwen Ermlich**	Pets: **No**
Location: **2 mi. S of Cooperstown**	Children: **Welcome (crib)**
No. of Rooms: **4**	Smoking: **No**
No. of Private Baths: **4**	Social Drinking: **Permitted**
Double/pb: **$60–$80**	Minimum Stay: **2 nights seasonal**
Guest Cottage: **$99; sleeps 2**	**weekends; 3 nights holiday**
Suites: **$85**	**weekends**
Open: **All year**	Foreign Languages: **French**
Reduced Rates: **10% after 5th night**	

This nationally renowned B&B offers beautiful furnishings in an elegant atmosphere. All rooms have private baths, queen-size beds, color TV, and HBO. The Bridal Chamber, Penthouse Suite, and Honeymoon Cottage are ideal for newlyweds and other romantics. You can amble through the flower gardens and lawns, and fish or take a dip in the creek. Gwen and Fred, who perform with the Glimmerglass Opera, serve a full breakfast catering to guests who are hankering for something special.

The Inn at Brook Willow Farm ✪
RD 2, BOX 514, COOPERSTOWN, NEW YORK 13326

Tel: **(607) 547-9700**	Open: **All year**
Best Time to Call: **Anytime**	Breakfast: **Full**
Hosts: **Joan and Jack Grimes**	Pets: **No**
No. of Rooms: **4**	Children: **Welcome (crib)**
No. of Private Baths: **4**	Smoking: **No**
Double/pb: **$55–$70**	Social Drinking: **Permitted**

Located on 14 acres of meadow and woods, nestled among the pines and willows, this charming Victorian cottage with its restored barn is furnished with lovely antiques, wicker, and plants. Enjoy homemade blueberry muffins at breakfast, and wine, fresh fruit, and fresh flowers in your room. The world-famous Baseball Hall of Fame is here, as well as countless historic and cultural sites to visit. Recreational activities abound on unspoiled Otsego Lake.

Litco Farms Bed and Breakfast ✪
P.O. BOX 1048, COOPERSTOWN, NEW YORK 13326

Tel: (607) 547-2501	Reduced Rates: **Dec.–Mar.**
Hosts: **Margaret and Jim Wolff**	Breakfast: **Full**
Location: **2 mi. NW of Cooperstown**	Pets: **No**
No. of Rooms: **4**	Children: **Welcome**
Max. No. Sharing Bath: **4**	Smoking: **No**
Double/sb: **$55–$75**	Social Drinking: **Permitted**
Suites: **$95**	Airport/Station Pickup: **Yes**
Open: **All year**	

Seventy acres of unspoiled meadows and woodlands are yours to explore at Litco Farms. The day begins with fresh-baked breads, fresh eggs, milk, and local bacon, served in the dining room–library. Borrow a canoe to fish on Canadarago Lake, which is stocked with freshwater salmon. There are other places to paddle, including Glimmerglass, the lake made famous by James Fenimore Cooper. After spending a day at the Baseball Hall of Fame, guests may relax and unwind around the large in-ground pool. Heartworks, a charming quilt craft shop, is on premises.

Whisperin Pines Chalet ✪
RD 3, BOX 248, COOPERSTOWN, NEW YORK 13326

Tel: (607) 547-5640	Breakfast: **Full**
Best Time to Call: **Anytime**	Pets: **No**
Hosts: **Joyce and Gus Doucas**	Children: **Welcome**
No. of Private Baths: **4**	Smoking: **Permitted**
Max. No. Sharing Bath: **4**	Social Drinking: **Permitted**
Double/sb: **$55–$65**	Airport/Station Pickup: **Yes**
Suites: **$100 for 2**	Foreign Languages: **French, Greek**
Open: **All year**	

Guests may choose from a variety of accommodations, including some with canopy beds, fireplaces, private balconies—even a bubble bath for two. The country setting offers a private walking trail, waterfalls, and a brook from which the lucky can catch a trout for breakfast. The chalet is equipped with a wheelchair ramp. A delicious country breakfast is served in the cozy dining room featuring country-fresh eggs, milk, and butter; homemade sausage and bacon; and Vermont maple syrup.

The White Pillars Inn ✪
82 SECOND STREET, DEPOSIT, NEW YORK 13754

Tel: (607) 467-4191
Best Time to Call: 8–10 AM; 5–10 PM
Host: Najla Aswad
Location: 25 mi. SE of Binghamton
No. of Rooms: 5
No. of Private Baths: 3
Max. No. Sharing Bath: 4
Double/pb: $65–$85
Single/pb: $55
Double/sb: $55
Single/sb: $45

Suites: $85–$110 (sleeps 4)
Open: All year
Reduced Rates: 10% AARP members
Breakfast: Full
Other Meals: Dinner (reservations required)
Credit Cards: AMEX, DC, DISC, MC, VISA
Pets: No
Children: Welcome
Smoking: No
Social Drinking: Permitted
Airport/Station Pickup: Yes

Here's the perfect place to do nothing but eat. With selections like Grand Marnier pecan cream cheese stuffed French toast, fluffy omelets filled with sun-dried tomatoes and fresh mozzarella, New York City bagels, home-baked muffins and coffee cakes, and robust, steaming coffee, five-course gourmet breakfasts are the highlight of your stay. The large guest rooms of this handsome Greek Revival mansion (circa 1820) are magnificently furnished with musuem-quality antiques, inviting beds with fluffy comforters and pillows, concealed televisions and telephones, well-stocked refrigerators, and plenty of reading light. And Najla's cookies are always available in her trademark bottomless cookie jar.

Dorchester Farm Bed & Breakfast ✪
RD 1, BOX 6, KEIBEL ROAD, LISLE, NEW YORK 13797

Tel: (607) 692-4511
Best Time to Call: Anytime
Hosts: Carolan and Scott Mersereau
Location: 15 mi. N of Binghamton
No. of Rooms: 4
No. of Private Baths: 2
Max. No. Sharing Bath: 4
Double/pb: $65
Double/sb: $50

Suites: $75
Open: All year
Breakfast: Full
Credit Cards: MC, VISA
Pets: No
Children: Welcome, over 10
Smoking: Permitted
Social Drinking: Permitted
Airport/Station Pickup: Yes

Enjoy peace and tranquillity at this pre–Civil War farmhouse with a splendid view of rolling hills and a five-mile lake. Carolan and Scott have created a days-gone-by atmosphere with select antiques, lovely accessories, attractively updated bathrooms, all in a light and airy country setting. The area abounds with recreational activities in all seasons. Cornell University and the State University of New York at Binghamton are less than a half hour away.

Country Spread Bed & Breakfast ✪
P.O. BOX 1863, 23 PROSPECT STREET, RICHFIELD SPRINGS, NEW YORK 13439

Tel: **(315) 858-1870**	Single/sb: **$40**
Best Time to Call: **7 AM–8 AM; 4 PM–9 PM**	Suites: **$80**
	Open: **All year**
Hosts: **Karen and Bruce Watson**	Breakfast: **Full**
Location: **20 mi. SE of Utica on Rte. 28**	Credit Cards: **MC, VISA**
	Pets: **No**
No. of Rooms: **2**	Children: **Welcome (crib)**
Max. No. Sharing Bath: **4**	Smoking: **No**
Double/pb: **$60**	Social Drinking: **Permitted**
Single/pb: **$45**	Minimum Stay: **Sometimes**
Double/sb: **$50**	Airport/Station Pickup: **Yes**

Longtime area residents Karen and Bruce have restored their 1893 cozy home into a wonderful retreat, tastefully decorated in country style. Your day will start with warm muffins, homemade preserves, pancakes with pure maple syrup, fresh eggs, granola, and chilled juice. Relax on the deck with the newspaper, and then visit some of the area's attractions, including Cooperstown, museums, summer theater, opera, fine dining, antique and specialty shops, and small-town happenings. Nearby Canadarago and Otsego lakes offer excellent boating, fishing, and swimming.

The Earlington Inn ✪
P.O. BOX 763, 26 EAST MAIN STREET, RICHFIELD SPRINGS, NEW YORK 13439

Tel: **(315) 858-2939**	Reduced Rates: **10% weekly**
Best Time to Call: **3 PM–6 PM**	Breakfast: **Full**
Hosts: **Erich and Kim Boehm**	Credit Cards: **AMEX, DC, MC, VISA**
Location: **14 mi. N of Cooperstown**	Pets: **Sometimes**
No. of Rooms: **4**	Children: **Welcome, over 12**
No. of Private Baths: **4**	Smoking: **No**
Double/pb: **$75–$95**	Social Drinking: **Permitted**
Open: **Apr. 15–Oct. 15**	Foreign Languages: **German**

This gracious Victorian, built in 1877, has been painstakingly restored to its former elegance. The entire house is furnished with period antiques; the guest rooms are beautifully wallpapered and decorated with fine prints and paintings. Designer bedding complements the superb mattresses. Erich, who was trained in the culinary arts in his native Germany, serves his homemade breads, rolls, and pastries along with a full breakfast in the formal dining room. Minutes away is Cooperstown, home of the Baseball Hall of Fame, and Glimmerglass Opera. Otsego and Canandarago lakes are also nearby.

Jonathan House ✪
39 EAST MAIN STREET, P.O. BOX 9, RICHFIELD SPRINGS, NEW YORK 13439

Tel: **(315) 858-2870**	Single/sb: **$55**
Hosts: **Jonathan and Peter Parker**	Suites: **$75**
Location: **14 mi. N of Cooperstown**	Open: **All year**
No. of Rooms: **4**	Breakfast: **Full**
No. of Private Baths: **2**	Credit Cards: **AMEX, MC, VISA**
Max. No. Sharing Bath: **4**	Pets: **Sometimes**
Double/pb: **$65**	Children: **Welcome**
Single/pb: **$65**	Smoking: **No**
Double/sb: **$55**	Social Drinking: **Permitted**

The Parker brothers enjoy cooking and entertaining, so, when they were both widowed, their friends suggested that they open a B&B. Their 1883 house, a hybrid of the Eastlake and Stick styles, has three full floors and a tower room on a fourth level—a total of 17 rooms. The house is elegantly decorated with antiques (some that belonged to the brothers' great-grandparents and grandparents), fine paintings, and oriental rugs. Breakfast is served in the dining room—with bone china, damask linen, and English silver.

CHAUTAUQUA/ALLEGHENY AREA

Rainbow Hospitality, Inc. B&B Reservation Service
466 AMHERST STREET, BUFFALO, NEW YORK 14207

Tel: **(716) 874-8797**	Descriptive Dirctory of B&Bs: **$3**
Best Time to Call: **10 AM–5 PM**	Rates (Single/Double):
Mon.–Fri.	Modest: **$35 / $45**
Coordinator: **Karen Ruckinger**	Average: **$55 / $65**
States/Regions Covered: **Chautauqua,**	Luxury: **$60 / $100**
South Dayton, Little Valley	Credit Cards: **MC, VISA**

This area boasts an infinite variety of cities and farm towns, of colleges and commerce, of skiing and sailing, of attractions both natural and man-made. Chautauqua/Allegheny is famous for the cultural, educational, and religious activities of the summer colony on the lake, as well as for its top-notch recreational diversions.

Spindletop ✪
POLO DRIVE OFF EAST AVENUE, GREENHURST, NEW YORK 14742

Tel: **(716) 484-2070**	No. of Private Baths: **3**
Hosts: **Lee and Don Spindler**	Max. No. Sharing Bath: **4**
Location: **4 mi. W of Jamestown**	Double/pb: **$65**
No. of Rooms: **4**	Double/sb: **$55**

Open: **All year**
Reduced Rates: **Available**
Breakfast: **Continental, plus**
Credit Cards: **AMEX, DISC, MC, VISA**

Pets: **No**
Children: **Welcome (swimmers only)**
Smoking: **Permitted**
Social Drinking: **Permitted**

Casually elegant and elegantly casual, oriental carpets and fine furnishings create a lovely background to this air-conditioned home,
where all guest rooms overlook Chautauqua Lake. You can relax
around the secluded swimming pool, tie your boat at the Spindlers'
dock, or enjoy such distractions as Amish quilt shops, antique stores,
wineries, art galleries, or seasonal sport opportunities. The famed
Chautauqua Institute is nearby.

Plumbush, A Victorian Bed & Breakfast ✪
RD 2, BOX 864, MAYVILLE, NEW YORK 14722

Tel: **(716) 789-5309**
Best Time to Call: **Weekdays**
Hosts: **George and Sandy Green**
Location: **90 mi. SW of Buffalo**
No. of Rooms: **4**
No. of Private Baths: **4**
Double/pb: **$75–$90**
Single/pb: **$65–$80**

Open: **All year**
Breakfast: **Full**
Credit Cards: **MC, VISA**
Pets: **No**
Children: **Welcome, over 12**
Smoking: **No**
Social Drinking: **Permitted**
Minimum Stay: **Peak seasons,
      weekends**

Immerse yourself in a bygone era. The intrinsic beauty of this 1865
Italianate villa is situated on 125 acres of meadow and woods. Painted
in a monochromatic scheme of pink to mauve to burgundy, a tower
offers a commanding view of the countryside. Eleven-foot-high ceilings, arched windows, and ceiling fans assure guests an airy, restful
night's sleep. Savory baked treats, fruit, fresh coffee, a variety of teas,
and homemade granola start the day. Activities run the gamut from

water sports and a musical treat to a visit to the famed Chautauqua Institute, just a mile away.

Scio House

RD 1, BOX 280F, SCIO, NEW YORK 14880

Tel: **(716) 593-1737**	Suites: **$55**
Host: **Mary Ellen Fitzgibbons**	Open: **All year**
Location: **90 mi. S of Buffalo**	Breakfast: **Full or Continental**
No. of Rooms: **4**	Credit Cards: **AMEX**
Max. No. Sharing Bath: **4**	Pets: **No**
Double/pb: **$45**	Children: **Welcome**
Single/pb: **$35**	Smoking: **Permitted**
Double/sb: **$38**	Social Drinking: **Permitted**
Single/sb: **$25**	Airport/Station Pickup: **Yes**

Gracious Victorian atmosphere and old-fashioned hospitality await you at Scio House. Built by a local banker circa 1870, the house retains its original woodwork, pocket doors, and high ceilings. The wraparound porch with its wicker furniture invites you to sit and relax. Stroll the garden or just enjoy the privacy of your room. Have your choice of full or Continental breakfast, served in the formal dining room with heirloom linen, china, and silver.

FINGER LAKES/ROCHESTER AREA

Adventures Bed & Breakfast Reservation Service ✪

BOX 551, LIMA, NEW YORK 14485

Tel: **(716) 582-1040; (800) 724-1932**	Rates (Single/Double):
Best Time to Call: **10 AM–7 PM**	Modest: **$35 / $50**
Coordinator: **Millie Fonda**	Average: **$55 / $75**
States/Regions Covered: **Finger Lakes,**	Luxury: **$80 / $150**
Genesee Valley Area, Rochester	Credit Cards: **MC, VISA**

More than a reservation service representing B&Bs in the Finger Lakes region, Adventures will plan a visit especially for you, whether it be a biking excursion, business meeting, retreat, or wedding. Discover historic villages along the shores of one of the Great Lakes or travel through farmlands and vineyards among the western Finger Lakes. Spend a day in a working Colonial village, take a balloon ride over Letchworth State Park, bicycle along Erie Canal towpaths—the choices are as wide as your imagination. All accommodations are within a few hours of Niagara Falls, Corning, Syracuse, and Toronto by car.

Elaine's Reservation Service for Bed & Breakfasts
4987 KINGSTON ROAD, ELBRIDGE, NEW YORK 13060

Tel: **(315) 689-2082**
Best Time to Call: **After 9:30 AM**
Coordinator: **Elaine Samuels**
States/Regions Covered: **Auburn, Baldwinsville, Cazenovia, Finger Lakes, Oneida Lake, Rome, Saranac Lake, Syracuse and suburbs**

Rates (Single/Double):
Modest: **$35 / $45**
Average: **$45 / $55**
Luxury: **$60 / $85**
Credit Cards: **No**

Elaine has many host homes in the vicinity of Syracuse University, theaters, ski areas, the Finger Lakes, lovely old villages, excellent discount shopping centers, and exclusive boutiques. This is her hometown, and if you tell her your interests, she is certain to find you the perfect home-away-from-home.

Rainbow Hospitality, Inc. B&B Reservation Service
466 AMHERST STREET, BUFFALO, NEW YORK 14207

Tel: **(716) 874-8797**
Best Time to Call: **10 AM–5 PM Mon.–Fri.**
Coordinator: **Karen Ruckinger**
States/Regions Covered: **Berkshire, Canandaigua, Lyons, Naples, Pittsford, Rochester, Syracuse, Webster**

Descriptive Directory of B&Bs: **$3**
Rates (Single/Double):
Modest: **$55**
Average: **$65–$75**
Luxury: **$95+**
Credit Cards: **MC, VISA**

One phone call opens the door to more than seventy select properties. Enjoy the elegance of rural Rochester or the ambience of the beautiful Finger Lakes region. We provide the options—you make the choice.

Addison Rose Bed & Breakfast ✪
37 MAPLE STREET, ADDISON, NEW YORK 14801

Tel: **(607) 359-4650**
Hosts: **Bill and Mary Ann Peters**
No. of Rooms: **3**
No. of Private Baths: **1**
Max. No. Sharing Bath: **4**
Double/pb: **$65**
Single/pb: **$65**
Double/sb: **$55**

Single/sb: **$55**
Open: **All year**
Breakfast: **Full**
Pets: **No**
Children: **No**
Smoking: **No**
Social Drinking: **Permitted**

Warmth, friendliness, and hospitality characterize this bed and breakfast, which combines elegance and country charm. Built in 1892, this magnificent Queen Anne home has been painstakingly restored by the Peters family and furnished with period antiques to recapture the ambience of the Victorian age. Guest rooms, named for the original owners and other local personalities, suggest a bygone era. The city of Corning, museums, and Finger Lake wineries are just minutes away.

Roberts-Cameron House
68 NORTH STREET, CALEDONIA, NEW YORK 14423

Tel: **(716) 538-6316**	Open: **All year**
Best Time to Call: **Evenings**	Reduced Rates: **20% families**
Hosts: **Elizabeth and Robert Wilcox**	Breakfast: **Full**
Location: **12 mi. SW of Rochester**	Pets: **Sometimes**
No. of Rooms: **2**	Children: **Welcome**
Max. No. Sharing Bath: **4**	Smoking: **Permitted (downstairs)**
Double/sb: **$50**	Social Drinking: **Permitted**
Single/sb: **$35**	Airport/Station Pickup: **Yes**

A clapboard farmhouse built in 1886 by William Roberts, a descendant of an early Scottish settler, this B&B is furnished with family antiques and collectibles from western New York. If you want to acquire some antiques of your own, the surrounding countryside is prime browsing territory, and Elizabeth runs her own antiques and crafts shop. Just five minutes from the front door, the Genesee Country Museum lets visitors spend a day strolling through a recreated 19th-century hamlet; costumed villagers and craftspeople go about their daily chores May through October. Your hosts serve a variety of afternoon snacks, as well as a generous country breakfast featuring New York maple syrup.

The Country House ✪
37 MILL STREET, CANASERAGA, NEW YORK 14822

Tel: **(607) 545-6439**	Single/sb: **$30**
Best Time to Call: **11 AM–1 PM; 5–7 PM**	Open: **All year**
	Breakfast: **Full**
Hosts: **Robert and Renée Coombs**	Pets: **Welcome**
Location: **50 mi. S of Rochester**	Children: **Welcome (crib)**
No. of Rooms: **6**	Smoking: **Permitted**
Max. No. Sharing Bath: **4**	Social Drinking: **Permitted**
Double/sb: **$45**	Airport/Station Pickup: **Yes**

This 100-year-old Victorian home stands on a quiet street in a charming rural village. Guest rooms are comfortably furnished with antiques, and all are for sale. Home-baked pastries and fresh fruit are served each morning in the breakfast room or dining room. Your hosts will happily direct you to the many valleys, forests, and streams nearby for hunting, fishing, hiking, and scenic solitude. Swain Ski Center slopes, Corning Glassworks, and Letchworth State Park are minutes away.

1865 White Birch Bed & Breakfast ✪
69 EAST FIRST STREET, CORNING, NEW YORK 14830

Tel: **(607) 962-6355**	Single/sb: **$55**
Hosts: **Kathy and Joe Donahue**	Open: **All year**
Location: **Off Rte. 17**	Breakfast: **Full**
No. of Rooms: **4**	Credit Cards: **AMEX, MC, VISA**
No. of Private Baths: **2**	Pets: **No**
Max. No. Sharing Bath: **4**	Children: **Welcome**
Double/pb: **$75**	Smoking: **Downstairs only**
Single/pb: **$60**	Social Drinking: **Permitted**
Double/sb: **$65**	Airport/Station Pickup: **Yes**

The red-carpet treatment awaits you at this spacious 1865 Victorian home that has been restored to show off the beautifully crafted winding staircase and hardwood floors. Guests are welcome to choose a game or enjoy television by the fire in the common room. After a good night's sleep in a comfortable queen-size bed, you'll wake to the smell of homemade breads, muffins, and plenty of hot coffee. The White Birch is located in a residential area just two blocks from restored downtown Corning, and near such attractions as the Corning Glass Center, Rockwell Museum, and many fine wineries.

Rosewood Inn ✪
134 EAST FIRST STREET, CORNING, NEW YORK 14830

Tel: **(607) 962-3253**	Location: **1 block off Rte. 17**
Hosts: **Winnie and Dick Peer and Stu**	No. of Rooms: **7**
and Suzanne Sanders	No. of Private Baths: **7**

Double/pb: **$88**
Single/pb: **$73**
Suites: **$100**
Open: **All year**
Reduced Rates: **Weekly; families**
Breakfast: **Full**
Credit Cards: **DC, MC, VISA**

Pets: **Sometimes**
Children: **Welcome (crib)**
Smoking: **Permitted**
Social Drinking: **Permitted**
Airport/Station Pickup: **Yes**

This two-story stucco English Tudor is decorated with both antiques and originality. Each guest room is named for a famous person, and the accessories echo the personality of that individual's era. It's within walking distance of the Corning Glass Museum and the Rockwell-Corning Museum of Western Art. Winnie taught school, and Dick was the editor of the daily newspaper. Retired, they look forward to your arrival and greet you with refreshments. Stu and Suzanne are retired printing executives.

Willow Cove ✪

77 SOUTH GLENORA ROAD, RD 1, BOX 87, DUNDEE, NEW YORK 14837

Tel: **(607) 243-8482**
Best Time to Call: **After 4:30 PM**
Hosts: **George and Joan Van Heusen**
Location: **10 mi. N of Watkins Glen**
No. of Rooms: **4**
Max. No. Sharing Bath: **4**
Double/sb: **$45**

Single/sb: **$40**
Open: **Apr.–Nov.**
Breakfast: **Continental**
Pets: **No**
Children: **Welcome (crib)**
Smoking: **Permitted**
Social Drinking: **Permitted**

Located on the western side of Seneca Lake, this 200-year-old inn is a comfortable home base for the many activities the area offers. Wineries, auctions, country fairs, antique shops, music festivals, and art galleries are but a few of the diversions. George and Joan invite you to enjoy their private beach and picnic area.

Woods Edge ✪

151 BLUHM ROAD, FAIRPORT, NEW YORK 14450

Tel: **(716) 223-8877**
Best Time to Call: **8 AM–6 PM**
Hosts: **Betty and Bill Kinsman**
Location: **8 mi. SE of Rochester**
No. of Rooms: **3**
No. of Private Baths: **3**
Double/pb: **$55–$65**
Single/pb: **$50**
Guest cabin: **$75–$90**
Open: **All year**

Reduced Rates: **Long stays; families**
Breakfast: **Full**
Pets: **No**
Children: **Welcome (crib, high chair)**
Smoking: **No**
Social Drinking: **Permitted**
Minimum Stay: **Two nights, weekends during May**
Airport Pickup: **Yes**

Woods Edge is nestled among fragrant pines in a secluded location only 20 minutes from downtown Rochester. The hideaway cabin is a romantically decorated private lodge: a large living room with a fireplace and cathedral ceiling, a bedroom with a queen-size bed, full kitchen, and private bath. The main house has two additional bedrooms, one with king-size or twin beds, the other with a queen-size bed. Both rooms are decorated with white walls, barn beams, and early country pine furnishings. Full breakfasts are served on the screened porch if weather permits. Cabin guests may have the refrigerator stocked or join everyone else in the main house for their morning meal.

The Cobblestones ✪
1160 ROUTES 5 AND 20, GENEVA, NEW YORK 14456

Tel: **(315) 789-1896**	Double/sb: **$15 and up**
Best Time to Call: **7–9:30 PM**	Single/sb: **$10**
Hosts: **The Lawrence Graceys**	Open: **All year**
Location: **3½ mi. W of Geneva on**	Pets: **Sometimes**
Rtes. 5 and 20, on north side of road	Children: **Welcome (crib)**
No. of Rooms: **4**	Smoking: **Permitted**
Max. No. Sharing Bath: **5**	Social Drinking: **Permitted**

Located in the heart of the Finger Lakes area, this inspired example of Greek Revival cobblestone architecture was built in 1848 and listed on the state and national registers of historic places. The four, large, fluted columns crowned by Ionic capitals at the front entrance add to its beauty. There are precious antiques and oriental rugs, which reflect the fine taste of your gracious hosts. Tours are available at nearby wineries. Hobart and William Smith colleges are right in town.

Sandy Creek Manor House ✪
1960 REDMAN ROAD, HAMLIN, NEW YORK 14464

Tel: **(716) 964-7528**
Best Time to Call: **After 5 PM**
Hosts: **Shirley Hollink and James Krempasky**
Location: **20 mi. W of Rochester**
No. of Rooms: **3**
Max. No. Sharing Bath: **4**
Double/sb: **$60**
Single/sb: **$50**

Open: **All year**
Reduced Rates: **Weekly; fisherman's discounts**
Breakfast: **Full**
Pets: **Sometimes**
Children: **Welcome, over 12**
Smoking: **No**
Social Drinking: **Permitted**

Six wooded acres and perennial gardens surround this 1910 English Tudor merely a stroll away from Sandy Creek. Natural woodwork, stained-glass windows, feather pillows, and Amish quilts summon up thoughts of a bygone era, while an antique player piano adds to the nostalgic mood. Full breakfasts include fresh fruit and homemade breads. Hamlin Beach is only 5 minutes away; you can reach Rochester in 30 minutes and Niagara Falls in less than an hour and a half.

Blushing Rose B&B ✪
11 WILLIAM STREET, HAMMONDSPORT, NEW YORK 14840

Tel: **(607) 569-3402**
Best Time to Call: **Anytime**
Hosts: **Ellen and Bucky Laufersweiler**
Location: **20 mi. W of Corning**
No. of Rooms: **4**
No. of Private Baths: **4**
Double/pb: **$65–$90**
Single/pb: **$55**

Open: **All year**
Reduced Rates: **10% seniors, travel agents**
Breakfast: **Full**
Pets: **No**
Smoking: **No**
Social Drinking: **Permitted**
Minimum Stay: **2 nights holiday weekends**

Blushing Rose is like something right out of a country magazine, thanks to the quilts, wall hangings, wreaths, and candles that decorate this B&B. Hammondsport is located at the southern end of the Finger Lakes region, and it's a short walk to Keuka Lake. Watkins Glen, Corning, and the famous Finger Lakes wineries are all a short drive away. You'll look forward to breakfast: baked French toast, lemon poppy-seed waffles, and strawberry bread are among the house specialties.

Hanshaw House ✪
15 SAPSUCKER WOODS ROAD, ITHACA, NEW YORK 14850

Tel: **(607) 273-8034**
Best Time to Call: **7–8 AM; 6–10 PM**

Host: **Helen Scoones**
No. of Rooms: **4**

No. of Private Baths: **4**
Double/pb: **$63–$95**
Single/pb: **$58–$90**
Suites: **$67.50–$135; sleeps 4**
Open: **All year**
Reduced Rates: **10–15% weekly; 10–15% Jan. 15–Apr. 1; corporate/**

educational rate $55–$65 for a single
Breakfast: **Full**
Credit Cards: **AMEX, MC, VISA**
Pets: **No**
Children: **Welcome**
Smoking: **No**
Social Drinking: **Permitted**
Airport/Station Pickup: **Yes**

Not far from downtown Ithaca, this woodframe farmhouse seems light-years away. Built in the 1830s, it has all the comforting country touches, from its white picket fence and dark blue shutters, to the down-filled quilts and pillows in the bedrooms. Bird-lovers should stroll down the road to Cornell's Laboratory of Ornithology and Sapsucker Woods, a bird sanctuary. Breakfasts include fresh fruit, juice, homemade muffins, and a hot entrée such as pancakes or waffles.

Peregrine House
140 COLLEGE AVENUE, ITHACA, NEW YORK 14850

Tel: **(607) 272-0919**
Hosts: **Nancy Falconer and Susan Vance**
No. of Rooms: **8**
No. of Private Baths: **9**
Double/pb: **$69–$99**
Open: **All year**
Reduced Rates: **Nov. 20–Apr. 1; weekly**

Breakfast: **Full**
Credit Cards: **MC, VISA**
Pets: **No**
Children: **Welcome, over 8**
Smoking: **Permitted**
Social Drinking: **Permitted**

This three-story brick home, with mansard roof, dates back to 1874. Its faux-marble fireplaces and carved-wood ceilings have been beautifully preserved and are accented with Victorian oak furnishings. Pick a good book in the library and relax in a wing chair, or watch some television in your air-conditioned bedroom. At five o'clock your hosts have a sherry hour, and they invite you to plan your evening over a drink. Mexican, Italian, Greek, and Indian food can all be enjoyed within a short walk from here. Peregrine House is two blocks from the Cornell campus and only a few blocks from the Ithaca Commons. Cayuga Lake's wonderful boating and swimming, the wine country, biking, hiking, and cross-country skiing are all close by.

Allan's Hill Bed and Breakfast ✪
2446 SAND HILL ROAD, MT. MORRIS, NEW YORK 14510

Tel: **(716) 658-4591**	Open: **All year**
Best Time to Call: **After 5 PM**	Breakfast: **Full**
Hosts: **George and Joyce Swanson**	Pets: **No**
Location: **35 mi. S of Rochester**	Children: **Welcome**
No. of Rooms: **3**	Smoking: **No**
Max. No. Sharing Bath: **4**	Social Drinking: **Permitted**
Double/sb: **$50**	Airport/Station Pickup: **Yes**
Single/sb: **$40**	

Sixteen acres of land surround this restored 1830 country home, giving guests the chance to stroll through stately walnut groves, sit by the pond, picnic, and go bird-watching and cross-country skiing. Nearby Letchworth State Park offers a spectacular, 17-mile drive along the gorge of the Genesee River. The area's wineries will lure you with tours and tastings, and Rochester, with its museums, shops, concerts, and theaters, is within easy driving distance.

Strawberry Castle Bed & Breakfast ✪
1883 PENFIELD ROAD, PENFIELD, NEW YORK 14526

Tel: **(716) 385-3266**	Reduced Rates: **15% weekly**
Best Time to Call: **Evenings**	Breakfast: **Continental**
Hosts: **Charles and Cynthia Whited**	Credit Cards: **AMEX, DISC, MC, VISA**
Location: **8 mi. E of Rochester**	Pets: **No**
No. of Rooms: **3**	Children: **Welcome, over 12**
Double/pb: **$75–$95**	Smoking: **Permitted**
Single/pb: **$60–$80**	Social Drinking: **Permitted**
Suites: **$95**	Airport/Station Pickup: **Yes**
Open: **All year**	

An outstanding example of the Italian villa style of architecture, the Whiteds' home, circa 1878, features columned porches, heavy plaster moldings, high sculptured ceilings, and a white marble fireplace, and is appropriately furnished with antiques and brass beds. Wander the lawns and gardens, sun on the patio, or take a dip in the pool. Charles and Cynthia will direct you to fine restaurants, golf courses, and all of the nearby Rochester attractions.

The Wagener Estate Bed & Breakfast
351 ELM STREET (ROUTE 54-A), PENN YAN, NEW YORK 14527

Tel: **(315) 536-4591**	No. of Rooms: **4**
Hosts: **Norm and Evie Worth**	No. of Private Baths: **2**
Location: **20 mi. from NYS Thruway,**	Max. No. Sharing Bath: **3**
Exit 42, Geneva	Double/pb: **$70**

Single/pb: **$60**
Double/sb: **$60**
Single/sb: **$50**
Open: **All year**
Breakfast: **Full**

Credit Cards: **AMEX, MC, VISA**
Pets: **No**
Children: **Welcome, over 5**
Smoking: **No**
Social Drinking: **Permitted**

The Worths raised their family in this 16-room historic house, furnished with antiques and country charm, located at the edge of the village on four scenic acres with shaded lawns, apple trees, and gentle breezes. The pillared veranda is a perfect spot for quiet reflection, conversation, and refreshments. Once the home of Abraham Wagener, the founder of Penn Yan, this B&B is perfectly situated for visits to wine country, the Corning Glass Museum, Watkins Glen, and beautiful Keuka Lake. The Worths are retired now and "have always loved to travel." They continue, "Now we feel we are still traveling, because people from other states and countries bring the world to our door."

Dartmouth House ✪
215 DARTMOUTH STREET, ROCHESTER, NEW YORK 14607

Tel: **(716) 271-7872, 473-0778**
Best Time to Call: **Anytime**
Hosts: **Ellie and Bill Klein**
Location: **⁴⁄₁₀ mi. from I-490, Exit 18**
No. of Rooms: **3**
No. of Private Baths: **3**
Double/pb: **$65–$75**
Single/pb: **$60–$70**
Open: **All year**

Breakfast: **Full**
Credit Cards: **AMEX**
Pets: **No**
Children: **Welcome, over 10**
Smoking: **No**
Social Drinking: **Permitted**
Minimum Stay: **2 nights some weekends**
Airport/Station Pickup: **Yes**

This 1905 stucco English Tudor is located in the prestigious, quiet, architecturally fascinating Park Avenue neighborhood. A massive fireplace, family antiques, oriental rugs, padded window seats, box-beamed ceilings, leaded-glass windows, and the great oak kitchen create an elegant atmosphere where visitors find friendliness and warmth in abundance. One guest said, "In this Edwardian gem the king himself would feel at home and even commoners are treated royally!" Bill is a retired Kodak engineer now teaching at R.I.T., and Ellie, a former educator, delights in pampering guests with outstanding breakfasts, served by candlelight, that might include eggs Chardonnay or oatmeal-blueberry pancakes. Guests enjoy being able to walk to the George Eastman Mansion and International Museum of Photography, the Rochester Museum and Science Center, the Planetarium, boutiques, restaurants, and antique shops.

Lake View Farm Bed & Breakfast ✪
4761 ROUTE 364, RUSHVILLE, NEW YORK 14544

Tel: **(716) 554-6973**
Hosts: **Betty and Howard Freese**
Location: **15 mi. from NYS Thruway,**
   Exit 44
No. of Rooms: **2**
Max. No. Sharing Bath: **4**
Double/sb: **$50–$55**
Single/sb: **$35–$40**

Reduced Rates: **10% after 2nd night;**
   weekly
Breakfast: **Full**
Credit Cards: **AMEX**
Pets: **No**
Children: **Welcome, over 8**
Smoking: **No**
Social Drinking: **Permitted**

Several rooms have a view of Canandaigua Lake, a Seneca Indian word meaning The Chosen Place. The simple architecture and bright and airy atmosphere create a pleasant background for family antiques and pictures. Stroll the grounds, rest in a hammock, or play horseshoes or badminton. Take the time to explore the 170 acres; in winter, cross-country ski. In summer, restaurants and a public beach are two minutes away.

HUDSON VALLEY/ALBANY/KINGSTON AREA

American Country Collection
4 GREENWOOD LANE, DELMAR, NEW YORK 12054

Tel: **(518) 439-7001**
Best Time to Call: **10 AM–5 PM**
   Mon.–Fri.
Coordinator: **Arthur Copeland**
States/Regions Covered:
   Adirondacks, Albany, Catskill
   Mountains, Schenectady, Troy
   (Capital District), Saratoga,
   Cooperstown, Hudson Valley, Lakes
   George and Champlain

Rates (Single/Double):
   Modest: **$35–$50 / $35–$55**
   Average: **$50–$60 / $55–$85**
   Luxury: **$60–$95 / $85–$135**
Credit Cards: **AMEX, MC, VISA**
Descriptive Directory: **$5**

The American Country Collection offers comfortable lodging in private homes and small inns. Accommodations range from a 1798 farmhouse, where guests are treated to a pancake breakfast with homemade maple syrup, to a stately Georgian home with canopy beds, fireplaces, and oriental rugs. Each host offers distinctive touches, such as fresh flowers in the room or breakfast in bed. Many homes have lakefront property, swimming pools, tennis courts or Jacuzzis. All are in areas of scenic and cultural interest, convenient to such attractions as the Baseball Hall of Fame, Empire State Plaza, Saratoga Racetrack, Lake George and ski areas.

Ananas Hus Bed and Breakfast ✪
ROUTE 3, P.O. BOX 301, AVERILL PARK, NEW YORK 12018

Tel: (518) 766-5035	Breakfast: Full
Hosts: Thelma and Clyde Tomlinson	Pets: No
Location: 6 mi. from Rte. 22	Children: Welcome, over 12
No. of Rooms: 3	Smoking: No
Max. No. Sharing Bath: 4	Social Drinking: Permitted
Double/sb: $55	Foreign Languages: Norwegian
Single/sb: $45	Minimum Stay: 2 nights holiday
Open: All year	weekends

The welcome mat is out at this hillside ranch home on 30 acres, with a panoramic view of the Hudson River Valley. It is informally furnished in the Early American style, accented with mementos from your hosts' international travels and Thelma's lovely needlework. Thelma is a former schoolteacher; Clyde was in the food business. They are serious amateur photographers who compete internationally. It is 15 minutes to Jiminy Peak and Brodie Mountain ski areas; 30 minutes to Tanglewood, Williamstown Theatre Festival, and Clark Art Institute in Massachusetts.

The Gregory House Inn ✪
P.O. BOX 401, ROUTE 43, AVERILL PARK, NEW YORK 12018

Tel: (518) 674-3774	Reduced Rates: Weekly
Best Time to Call: 5 PM	Breakfast: Continental
Hosts: Melissa and Christopher Miller	Other Meals: Available
Location: 10 mi. E of Albany	Credit Cards: AMEX, DC, MC, VISA
No. of Rooms: 12	Pets: No
No. of Private Baths: 12	Children: Welcome, over 6
Double/pb: $70–$90	Smoking: Permitted
Single/pb: $65 and up	Social Drinking: Permitted
Open: All year	

The Gregory House is a clapboard Colonial dating back to 1830. Your hosts purchased the house in 1964 and opened a small restaurant. Recently, the building was expanded to include beautifully appointed guest rooms and a common room, all in keeping with a relaxed, country style. The house is surrounded by the Catskill, Adirondack, Berkshire, and Green mountains, affording year-round beauty and recreation. The inn is also near the Saratoga Performing Arts Center, Tanglewood, Hancock Shaker Village, and Saratoga Springs. Your hosts invite you to explore their beautifully landscaped property and to join them for fine dining in the restaurant. Christopher is a graduate of the Culinary Institute of America and specializes in international cuisine.

Battenkill Bed & Breakfast Barn
ROUTE 313, RD 1, BOX 143, CAMBRIDGE, NEW YORK 12816-9717

Tel: (518) 677-8868; (800) 676-8768
Hosts: **Veronica and Walt Piekarz**
Location: **30 mi. E of Saratoga**
No. of Rooms: **2**
Max. No. Sharing Bath: **4**
Double/sb: **$60**
Single/sb: **$45**
Open: **All year**

Breakfast: **Full**
Other Meals: **Available**
Credit Cards: **AMEX, DISC, MC, VISA**
Pets: **No**
Children: **Welcome**
Smoking: **Permitted**
Social Drinking: **Permitted**

Relax and enjoy yourself at this post-and-beam home nestled in the Annaquassicoke Valley. Veronica delights in creative cooking while Walt, a jazz musician, is always ready to talk shop. Winter activities here include snowshoeing and cross-country skiing, with longer trails nearby. The rest of the year, guests can go fishing, canoeing, kayaking, tubing, and biking; the B&B's property borders the Battenkill River, and equipment may be rented from your hosts.

The Lace House ◐
ROUTE 22, CANAAN, NEW YORK 12029

Tel: **(800) 253-2409**
Host: **David G. Burns**
Location: **9 mi. W of Lenox, Mass.**
No. of Rooms: **7**
Max. No. Sharing Bath: **4**
Double/sb: **$53–$79**
Single/sb: **$38–$64**
Open: **All year**
Reduced Rates: **10% seniors**
Breakfast: **Full**

Other Meals: **Available**
Credit Cards: **AMEX**
Pets: **No**
Children: **Welcome, over 9**
Smoking: **No**
Social Drinking: **Permitted**
Minimum Stay: **2 nights weekends, July–August, fall foliage**
Airport/Station Pickup: **Yes**

Located in the beautiful Berkshire Mountains only minutes from Tanglewood, the Norman Rockwell Museum, and seven major ski areas, this B&B has offered comfort and lodging since it was built in 1806. Totally renovated in 1983, Lace House was placed on the National Register of Historic Places as an outstanding example of Federal architecture. Choose among seven antique-furnished guest rooms and three dining areas. Full country breakfasts are served, and an optional package includes a barbecue or clambake.

One Market Street ◐
COLD SPRING, NEW YORK 10516

Tel: **(914) 265-3912**
Hosts: **Philip and Esther Baumgarten**

Location: **50 mi. N of New York City**
No. of Rooms: **1 suite**

No. of Private Baths: **1**
Suites: **$65**
Open: **All year**
Reduced Rates: **Weekly**
Breakfast: **Continental**

Credit Cards: **VISA**
Pets: **No**
Children: **Welcome, over 10**
Smoking: **Permitted**
Social Drinking: **Permitted**

This beautiful Federal-style building dates back to the 1800s and looks out on the Hudson, surrounding mountains, and the foliage of the valley. The suite's kitchenette is stocked with rolls, juice, tea, and coffee for a make-it-at-your-leisure breakfast. Don't miss nearby West Point, Vassar College, and the Vanderbilt Mansion. Philip and Esther will direct you to the fine restaurants and antique shops in their historic town.

Alexander Hamilton House
49 VAN WYCK STREET, CROTON-ON-HUDSON, NEW YORK 10520

Tel: **(914) 271-6737**
Best Time to Call: **8–9 AM**
Host: **Barbara Notarius**
Location: **30 mi. NW of New York City**
No. of Rooms: **7**
No. of Private Baths: **3**
Max. No. Sharing Bath: **4**
Double/pb: **$75–$125**
Single/pb: **$50–$100**
Double/sb: **$65–$75**
Single/sb: **$50–$60**

Suites: **$150–$250**
Open: **All year**
Breakfast: **Full**
Credit Cards: **AMEX, DISC, MC, VISA**
Pets: **No**
Children: **Welcome**
Smoking: **No**
Social Drinking: **Permitted**
Minimum Stay: **2 nights weekends**
Airport/Station Pickup: **Yes**
Foreign Languages: **French**

No, Hamilton didn't live here; this beautiful Victorian home was built some eight decades after his death, and one suite is named for the victor in the duel between Hamilton and Aaron Burr. The property, with its 35-foot in-ground swimming pool, small apple orchard, and spectacular Hudson River views, would please even the most patrician lodgers. West Point, Van Cortlandt Manor, Boscobel, and Storm King Art Center are all nearby, and New York City is within striking distance. After sightseeing, relax in the large living room complete with fireplace, piano, and numerous antiques. Baby equipment is available for guests with small children.

Sunrise Farm ✪
RD 3, BOX 95, NEW BERLIN, NEW YORK 13411-0003

Tel: **(607) 847-9380**
Hosts: **Janet and Fred Schmelzer**
Location: **70 mi. W of Albany**
No. of Rooms: **1**
No. of Private Baths: **1**

Double/pb: **$45**
Single/pb: **$35**
Open: **All year**
Reduced Rates: **Families; weekly**
Breakfast: **Full**

Other Meals: **Available**
Pets: **No**
Children: **Welcome**

Smoking: **No**
Social Drinking: **Permitted**

Scottish Highland cattle are raised on this 65-acre certified organic farm about 20 miles from both Cooperstown and Oneonta. A restful night is assured in the large, comfortable second-floor guest room where, on clear nights, the stars can be seen through the skylight. Breakfast features home-baked goods, homemade preserves, and honey from the farm's hives. In winter, a wood stove keeps the house cozy. Several state parks lie a short distance away, and the local diversions include cross-country skiing, ice skating, boating, and antiquing.

Maggie Towne's B&B ✪
PHILLIPS ROAD, PITTSTOWN, NEW YORK (MAILING ADDRESS: BOX 82, RD 2, VALLEY FALLS, NEW YORK 12185)

Tel: **(518) 663-8369; 686-7331**
Host: **Maggie Towne**
Location: **14 mi. E of Troy**
No. of Rooms: **3**
Max. No. Sharing Bath: **4**
Double/sb: **$45**
Single/sb: **$25**

Open: **All year**
Breakfast: **Full**
Pets: **Sometimes**
Children: **Welcome (crib)**
Smoking: **No**
Social Drinking: **Permitted**

This lovely old Colonial is located amid beautiful lawns and trees. Enjoy a cup of tea or glass of wine before the huge fireplace in the family room. Use the music room or curl up with a book on the screened-in porch. Mornings, your host serves home-baked goodies. She will gladly prepare a lunch for you to take on tour or enjoy at the house. It's 20 miles to historic Bennington, Vermont, and 30 to Saratoga.

Sharon Fern's Bed & Breakfast ✪
8 ETHIER DRIVE, TROY, NEW YORK 12180

Tel: **(518) 279-1966**
Best Time to Call: **Mornings**
Hosts: **Bill and Sharon Ernst**
Location: **10 mi. from NYS Thruway**
No. of Rooms: **2**
Max. No. Sharing Bath: **3**
Double/sb: **$55**
Single/sb: **$50**

Open: **All year**
Reduced Rates: **10% seniors**
Breakfast: **Continental**
Pets: **No**
Children: **Welcome (crib)**
Smoking: **No**
Social Drinking: **Permitted**

Bill and Sharon's tri-level contemporary home rests on a quiet street in the country just 20 minutes outside of Albany, New York's capital.

Enjoy spacious accommodations plus many extras, including an in-ground pool, a recreation room with a Ping-Pong table, and a beautiful backyard, where badminton and croquet will test your mettle. Skiers and hikers will find mountains in nearly every direction—the Adirondacks, Catskills, and Green Mountains are all a half hour away.

LAKE GEORGE AREA

Hayes's B&B Guest House ✪

P.O. BOX 537, 7161 LAKESHORE DRIVE, BOLTON LANDING, NEW YORK 12814

Tel: **(518) 644-5941**	Suites: **$85–$95**
Best Time to Call: **9 AM–9 PM**	Open: **All year**
Hosts: **Dick Hayes and Mrs. Martha Hayes**	Breakfast: **Continental**
	Children: **Welcome, over 12**
Location: **250 mi. N of New York City**	Pets: **No**
No. of Rooms: **2**	Smoking: **No**
No. of Private Baths: **2**	Social Drinking: **Permitted**
Double/pb: **$75–$80**	Minimum Stay: **2 nights**
Single/pb: **$45**	

Close to the shores of Lake George, this elegantly appointed 1920s Cape Cod estate is located across from the town beach, picnic area, and public docks. A five-minute walk to town brings you to tennis courts, shops, and fine restaurants. The Hayes family will arrange boat tours and a picnic lunch for a nominal fee in summer and fall. Cable TV and HBO are available. It's only 40 minutes to Saratoga and its famous racetrack. There's a private trout stream on the property, so pack your fishing gear.

Hilltop Cottage ✪

P.O. BOX 186, 6883 LAKESHORE DRIVE, BOLTON LANDING, NEW YORK 12814

Tel: **(518) 644-2492**	Guest cabin: **$65**
Best Time to Call: **Anytime**	Open: **All year**
Hosts: **Anita and Charlie Richards**	Breakfast: **Full**
Location: **8 mi. from I-87**	Children: **Welcome, over 4**
No. of Rooms: **4**	Smoking: **Permitted**
Max. No. Sharing Bath: **4**	Social Drinking: **Permitted**
Double/pb: **$55**	Foreign Languages: **German**
Double/sb: **$45**	

Hilltop Cottage is a clean, comfortable, renovated caretaker cottage in the beautiful Lake George–Eastern Adirondack region. You can walk to the beach, marinas, shops, and restaurants. Guests will enjoy the hearty breakfasts, homey atmosphere, helpful hosts, wood-burning stove, and fall foliage. A guest cabin is also available.

Six Sisters Bed and Breakfast
149 UNION AVENUE, SARATOGA SPRINGS, NEW YORK 12866

Tel: **(518) 583-1173**
Best Time to Call: **9 AM–5 PM**
Hosts: **Kate Benton and Steve Ramirez**
Location: **30 mi. N of Albany**
No. of Rooms: **4**
No. of Private Baths: **4**
Double/pb: **$65–$95**
Single/pb: **$60–$90**
Suites: **$75–$130**
Open: **All year**

Reduced Rates: **10%–15% Sun.–
  Thurs. Nov.–Mar.; 10% seniors**
Breakfast: **Full**
Pets: **No**
Children: **Welcome, over 10**
Smoking: **No**
Social Drinking: **Permitted**
Minimum Stay: **Special weekends,
  racing season**
Airport/Station Pickup: **Yes**

Some people visit this town for its naturally carbonated mineral waters, other people for its racetracks. Bathers and railbirds will both be delighted by Kate and Steve's 1890 Victorian, named for the former's sisters. All rooms have air conditioning and either king- or queen-size beds (except for the second floor parlor suite, which has two double beds). After sampling one of Steve's mouth-watering breakfasts, guests are encouraged to take a mug of coffee, tea, or cider out to the veranda overlooking Saratoga's streets and racecourse. Then it's an easy walk to boutiques, antique shops, restaurants, and the National Museum of Racing.

The Westchester House B&B
102 LINCOLN AVENUE, P.O. BOX 944, SARATOGA SPRINGS, NEW YORK 12866

Tel: **(518) 587-7613**
Hosts: **Bob and Stephanie Melvin**
Location: **30 mi. N of Albany**
No. of Rooms: **7**
No. of Private Baths: **7**
Double/pb: **$70–$100**
Sinble/pb: **$70–$100**
Open: **Feb.–Dec.**
Reduced Rates: **10% Feb.–Mar.; 10%
  seniors, midweek**

Breakfast: **Continental**
Credit Cards: **AMEX, MC, VISA**
Pets: **No**
Children: **Welcome, over 10**
Smoking: **No**
Social Drinking: **Permitted**
Minimum Stay: **2 nights June, July,
  Aug.**

This gracious 1885 Queen Anne Victorian boasts handcrafted chestnut moldings and two elaborately carved fireplaces. The whimsical rooftop, complete with cupola and balcony, soars skyward. Comfortable parlors invite you to linger, while elegantly appointed bedrooms combine antique furnishings with up-to-date comforts. Walk to the museums, shops, racetracks, and springs that make Saratoga famous. After a busy day, relax on the porch or in the garden with a refreshing glass of lemonade.

LAKE PLACID/ADIRONDACKS AREA

Highland House ✪

3 HIGHLAND PLACE, LAKE PLACID, NEW YORK 12946

Tel: **(518) 523-2377**
Best Time to Call: **Mornings**
Hosts: **Teddy and Cathy Blazer**
Location: **25 mi. from Rte. 87, Exit 30**
No. of Rooms: **8**
No. of Private Baths: **8**
Double/pb: **$50–$70**
Single/pb: **$50–$65**
Guest Cottage: **$70–$155; sleeps 2–6**

Open: **All year**
Reduced Rates: **Apr.–May, Nov.**
Breakfast: **Full**
Pets: **No**
Children: **Welcome**
Smoking: **Permitted**
Social Drinking: **Permitted**
Airport/Station Pickup: **Yes**

Located on a hill in a lovely section of Lake Placid, Highland House is a five-minute walk from Main Street and the Olympic Center. Cathy and Teddy have created a warm and comfortable atmosphere that guests notice upon entering this 1910 house. Every bedroom is furnished with a large, wooden bunk bed as well as a double bed, each adorned with a bright, fluffy comforter. After a good night's rest, you may look forward to a breakfast of blueberry pancakes or French toast, eggs, and beverages. The cottage is beautifully furnished, and features a fireplace for chilly nights.

Fogarty's Bed and Breakfast ✪

37 RIVERSIDE DRIVE, SARANAC LAKE, NEW YORK 12983

Tel: **(518) 891-3755; (800) 525-3755**
Best Time to Call: **After 3 PM**
Hosts: **Jack and Emily Fogarty**
Location: **150 mi. N of Albany**
No. of Rooms: **5**
Max. No. Sharing Bath: **3**
Double/sb: **$40**
Single/sb: **$25**

Open: **All year**
Breakfast: **Full**
Pets: **No**
Children: **Welcome**
Smoking: **Permitted**
Social Drinking: **Permitted**
Airport Pickup: **Yes**

High on a hill overlooking Lake Flower and Mts. Baker, McKenzie, and Pisgah—but only three minutes from the center of town—you'll find Fogarty's. The B&B porches, wide doors, and call buttons attest to its past as a cure cottage. The living and dining rooms are decorated with handsome woodwork, and the bathrooms have the original 1910 fixtures. Swimmers and boaters can use Fogarty's dock, and cross-country skiers will find trails within a mile. More ambitious athletes should take a brief drive to Lake Placid's Olympic courses or the slopes of Whiteface and Big Tupper. Emily and Jack are Adirondack natives, so feel free to ask them for suggestions.

Moose River House Bed and Breakfast ✪

12 BIRCH STREET, THENDARA, NEW YORK 13472

Tel: (315) 369-3104
Best Time to Call: 8 AM–8 PM
Host: **Frederick J. Fox, Jr.**
Location: **48 mi. N of Utica**
No. of Rooms: 5
No. of Private Baths: 3
Max. No. Sharing Bath: 3
Double/pb: $75–$85
Double/sb: $65
Single/sb: $45

Suites: **$125–$140; sleeps 4**
Open: **May 15–Oct. 20**
Reduced Rates: **10% seniors, families; after 3rd night**
Breakfast: **Full**
Pets: **Sometimes**
Children: **Welcome, over 6**
Smoking: **No**
Social Drinking: **Permitted**
Foreign Languages: **Swedish**

Back in the 19th century, Moose River House was accessible only by the *Fawn*, a tiny side-wheeler that steamed upstream from Minnehaha, where New York's only wooden train rails terminated. Today there are several routes to this northern Adirondack inn. However you get there, you won't want to leave. From cross-country and downhill skiing in the winter to hiking, horseback riding, and waterfront sports in the summer, the recreational options are vast. And the adjacent town of Old Forge has a wealth of shops and restaurants, in addition to the Enchanted Forest amusement park.

LONG ISLAND

A Reasonable Alternative and Hampton B&B ✪

117 SPRING STREET, PORT JEFFERSON, NEW YORK 11777

Tel: (516) 928-4034
Best Time to Call: **11 AM–5 PM Mon.–Fri.**
Rates (Single/Double):
Modest:　$36 / $48
Average:　$44 / $52
Luxury:　$52 / $60–$100+

Coordinator: **Kathleen B. Dexter**
States/Regions Covered:
　Long Island
Credit Cards: **MC, VISA**
Minimum Stay: **2 nights in summer at Hamptons; 3 nights holiday weekends**

Bounded by Long Island Sound and the Atlantic Ocean, from the New York City border to Montauk 100 miles to the east, the cream of host homes has been culled by Kathleen for you. There's much to see and do, including museums, historic homes, theater, horse racing, and the famous beaches, including Jones Beach, Fire Island, Shelter Island, and the exclusive Hamptons. (The Hamptons require a two-day minimum stay in July and August.) Adelphi College, Hofstra University, C. W. Post, Stony Brook, and St. Joseph's are a few of the nearby schools.

Country Life B&B ✪

237 CATHEDRAL AVENUE, HEMPSTEAD, NEW YORK 11550

Tel: **(516) 292-9219**	Suite: **$150; sleeps 4–5**
Best Time to Call: **6–9 PM**	Open: **All year**
Hosts: **Wendy and Richard Duvall**	Breakfast: **Full**
Location: **20 mi. E of New York City,**	Pets: **No**
on the Garden City line	Children: **Welcome (crib)**
No. of Rooms: **4**	Smoking: **No**
No. of Private Baths: **4**	Social Drinking: **Permitted**
Double/pb: **$60–$95**	Foreign Languages: **German, Spanish**

Guests feel right at home in this charming Dutch Colonial, with four-poster beds and antique reproductions. Wine and cheese are served on arrival, and breakfast features puff pancakes and French toast. Guests enjoy the garden or visiting nearby sights. Kennedy International Airport and LaGuardia Airport are less than 40 minutes away; Adelphi and Hofstra universities and the Nassau Coliseum are one mile away.

Compass Rose Bed and Breakfast ✪

415 WEST BROADWAY, PORT JEFFERSON, NEW YORK 11777

Tel: **(516) 474-1111**	Single/sb: **$48–$78**
Best Time to Call: **Anytime**	Open: **All year**
Host: **Kathleen Burk**	Reduced Rates: **10% seniors**
Location: **65 mi. E of New York City**	Breakfast: **Continental**
No. of Rooms: **2**	Credit Cards: **AMEX, MC, VISA**
No. of Private Baths: **2**	Pets: **No**
Max. No. Sharing Bath: **4**	Children: **Welcome**
Double/pb: **$78–$125**	Smoking: **Permitted**
Single:/pb: **$78–$125**	Social Drinking: **Permitted**
Double/sb: **$48–$78**	

A house and barn built for a ship captain in the 1820s, Compass Rose has new baths and central air-conditioning, but the antique and country furnishings gently evoke the past. Drift several centuries backward in Port Jefferson, a restored whaling village on Long Island's picturesque North Shore; you'll find wonderful museums, shops, and restaurants in structures that predate the Revolution. The harbor remains busy, thanks to the ferry to Bridgeport, Connecticut. Because the fresh salt air is sure to whet your appetite, you'll start the day with a Continental breakfast of fresh fruit, cereal, homemade breads, and freshly ground coffee.

Seafield House ✪
2 SEAFIELD LANE, WESTHAMPTON BEACH, NEW YORK 11978

Tel: (800) 346-3290
Best Time to Call: 9 AM–5 PM
Host: Elsie Collins
Location: 90 mi. E of New York City
No. of Rooms: 3 suites
No. of Private Baths: 3
Suites: $175

Open: All year
Reduced Rates: $95, Oct. 15–May 15
Breakfast: Full
Pets: No
Children: No
Smoking: No
Social Drinking: Permitted

This 100-year-old home in posh Westhampton is five blocks from the beach, and boasts its own pool and tennis court. Victorian lounges, a caned rocker, piano, hurricane lamps, Shaker benches, Chinese porcelain all combine to create the casual, country inn atmosphere. When the sea air chills Westhampton Beach, the parlor fire keeps the house toasty warm. The aromas of freshly brewing coffee and Mrs. Collins' breads and rolls baking in the oven are likely to wake you in time for breakfast. You'll leave this hideaway relaxed, carrying one of Mrs. Collins' homemade goodies.

NEW YORK CITY AREA

Abode Bed & Breakfast, Ltd. ✪
P.O. BOX 20022, NEW YORK, NEW YORK 10028

Tel: (212) 472-2000
Best Time to Call: Mon.–Fri., 9 AM–
  5 PM; Sat., 10 AM–2 PM
Coordinator: Shelli Leifer
States/Regions Covered: Manhattan,
  Brooklyn Heights

Rates (Single/Double):
  Average: $60–$70 / $75–$85
  Luxury: $75–$80 / $85–$95
Credit Cards: AMEX
Minimum Stay: 2 nights

Shelli is a friendly, savvy New Yorker with sensitive insight as to which guest would be most comfortable with what host. Her roster grows steadily with accommodations in safe neighborhoods that are "East Side, West Side, and all around the town." Unhosted brownstones boasting a country-inn ambience and unhosted luxury apartments are especially attractive for couples traveling together. Prices range from $85 for a studio to $275 for 3 bedrooms. Reduced rates are available for extended stays. Theaters, museums, galleries, restaurants, and shopping are within easy reach of all accommodations.

Bed & Breakfast (& Books)
35 WEST 92ND STREET, NEW YORK, NEW YORK 10025

Tel: (212) 865-8740
Coordinator: Judith Goldberg Lewis
States/Regions Covered: Manhattan

Rates (Single/Double):
 Average: $60–$75 / $80–$90
Credit Cards: AMEX
Minimum Stay: 2 nights

Accommodations are conveniently located in residential areas near transportation and within walking distance of many cultural attractions. Hosts are photographers, psychologists, lawyers, dancers, teachers, and artists. They are pleased to share their knowledge of fine shops, reasonable restaurants, galleries, theater, and bookstores. There's a $20 surcharge for one-night stays. Unhosted apartments are $90 to $150 for two.

Bed & Breakfast Network of New York ✪
134 WEST 32ND STREET, SUITE 602, NEW YORK, NEW YORK 10001

Tel: (212) 645-8134
Best Time to Call: 8 AM–noon;
 2–6 PM
Coordinator: Mr. Leslie Goldberg
States/Regions Covered: New York
 City

Rates (Single/Double):
 Modest: $50 / $70
 Average: $60 / $80
 Luxury: $70 / $90
Credit Cards: No

Accommodations appropriate to your purpose and purse are available, from the chic East Side to the arty West Side; from SoHo to Greenwich Village. They range from a historic brownstone, where the host is an artist, to a terraced apartment near Lincoln Center. Leslie's hosts are enthusiastic about the Big Apple and happy to share their insider information with you. Unhosted apartments range from $80 to $300 in price.

City Lights B&B, Ltd.
P.O. BOX 20355 CHEROKEE STATION, NEW YORK, NEW YORK 10028

Tel: (212) 737-7049; fax: (212) 535-
 2755
Coordinators: Yedida Mielsen and
 Dee Staff
States/Regions Covered: Brooklyn,
 Long Island, Manhattan, Queens,
 Staten Island

Minimum Stay: 2 nights
Rates (Single/Double):
 Modest: $45–$65
 Average: $60–$80
 Luxury: $75–$95
Credit Cards: AMEX, CB, DC, MC,
 VISA

From the East Side to the West Side; from the downtown New York University and Greenwich Village areas to uptown neighborhoods near Columbia University and the Museum of Natural History, accommodations range from simple to opulent. Many of the hosts are from the theater and the arts; all of them are anxious to make your stay in their town memorable. Unhosted apartments range from $90 to $300 per night, depending upon the location, ambience, and number of people staying. A $10 surcharge is imposed for one-night stays.

Judith Mol Agency ✪
357 WEST 37TH STREET, NEW YORK, NEW YORK 10018

Tel: **(212) 971-9001**
Coordinator: **Judith Mol**
States/Regions Covered: **Manhattan**

Rates (Single/Double):
Average: **$50 / $70**
Luxury: **$75 / $90–$300**
Credit Cards: **No**
Minimum Stay: **2 nights**

Judith's listings are as diverse as the city. An apartment in the old-world area of Gramercy Park has a queen-size bed and antique decor; one that's close to Columbia University has a loft bed, suitable for one, with a great view of the Hudson River. Another, on the chic East Side, is decorated in contemporary style accented with beautiful art. Some have fax machines, some have Jacuzzis; all have cable TV. Unhosted apartments range from $80 to $300, depending upon size and location. There is a 10% surcharge for one-night stays.

Urban Ventures ✪
P.O. BOX 426, NEW YORK, NEW YORK 10024

Tel: **(212) 594-5650**
Best Time to Call: **Mon.–Fri., 9 AM–5 PM**
Coordinator: **Mary McAulay**
States/Regions Covered: **New York— Manhattan; New Jersey**

Rates (Single/Double):
Modest: **$50 / $60**
Average: **$60–$70 / $75–80**
Luxury: **$75–80 / $90–$120**
Credit Cards: **AMEX, CB, DISC, MC, VISA**
Minimum Stay: **2 nights B&Bs; 3 nights unhosted apartments**

Great values are offered by this registry. Mary has bedrooms and complete apartments located throughout New York City, including landmarked historic districts. She'll be happy to help with theater tickets, restaurant information, current museum exhibits, and special tours. Unhosted apartments range from $65 to $140 for two.

The Villa ✪
90 ROCKLEDGE ROAD, BRONXVILLE, NEW YORK 10708

Tel: **(914) 337-7050; messages: (914) 337-5595; fax: (914) 337-5661**

Host: **Helen Zuckermann**
Location: **6 mi. N of New York City**

No. of Rooms: **2**
No. of Private Baths: **2**
Double/pb: **$80**
Single/pb: **$70**
Suites: **$110**
Open: **All year**
Reduced Rates: **Available**
Breakfast: **Continental**

Other Meals: **Available**
Pets: **No**
Children: **Welcome**
Smoking: **Permitted**
Social Drinking: **Permitted**
Airport/Station Pickup: **Yes**
Foreign Languages: **French, German, Italian, Spanish**

A spacious country residence, The Villa was formerly owned by Columbia University—when Dwight Eisenhower was the university's president, he spent weekends here. You'll want to do the same, thanks to the quiet, convenient setting, the large terraces and gardens, and extras like a hot tub and a home office equipped with a personal computer, typewriter, copier, and fax machine (secretarial services can also be arranged). Continental breakfast is set out in a small, sunny dining room, and snacks and beverages are available at other times of the day.

NIAGARA/BUFFALO AREA

Rainbow Hospitality, Inc. B&B Reservation Service
466 AMHERST STREET, BUFFALO, NEW YORK 14207

Tel: **(716) 874-8797**
Best Time to Call: **Mon.–Fri., 10 AM–5 PM**
Coordinator: **Karen Ruckinger**
States/Regions Covered: **Buffalo, Chautauqua, Lewiston, Niagara Falls, Olcott; Youngstown, Ohio**

Descriptive Directory: **$3**
Rates (Single/Double):
Modest: **$35 / $40**
Average: **$45 / $55**
Luxury: **$60 / $90**
Credit Cards: **MC, VISA**

The scenic splendor of Niagara Falls is only the beginning of the attractions in this area. Travelers have a wide variety of activities to keep them interested and busy. Lewiston is the home of Artpark, a 200-acre park and open-air theater featuring productions from May through September. Fishing and antiquing are popular pastimes, too. The best things in the area are the hosts, who open their homes to extend the hand of friendship.

The Eastwood House ✪
45 SOUTH MAIN STREET, ROUTE 39, CASTILE, NEW YORK 14427

Tel: **(716) 493-2335**
Best Time to Call: **Before 8:30 AM; after 6 PM**
Host: **Joan Ballinger**

Location: **63 mi. SE of Buffalo on Rte. 39**
No. of Rooms: **2**
Max. No. Sharing Bath: **4**

Double/sb: **$30**	Pets: **Sometimes**
Single/sb: **$25**	Children: **Welcome, over 5**
Open: **All year**	Smoking: **No**
Breakfast: **Continental**	Social Drinking: **Permitted**

This comfortable older home in a rural area is close to the Genesee Country Museum, Letchworth State Park, which is called the Grand Canyon of the East, Geneseo and Houghton colleges, and Silver Lake, known for fishing and boating. Delicious hot muffins, fresh fruits, and a choice of beverages are typical breakfast fare. Joan will be happy to direct you to local wineries and the Corning Glass factory and museum.

The Teepee ✪
RD 1, BOX 543, ROUTE 438, GOWANDA, NEW YORK 14070

Tel: **(716) 532-2168**	Open: **All year**
Hosts: **Max and Phyllis Lay**	Breakfast: **Full**
Location: **30 mi. S of Buffalo**	Pets: **Sometimes**
No. of Rooms: **3**	Children: **Welcome (crib)**
Max. No. Sharing Bath: **3**	Smoking: **Permitted**
Double/sb: **$45**	Social Drinking: **Permitted**
Single/sb: **$35**	Airport/Station Pickup: **Yes**

Max and Phyllis Lay are Seneca Indians living on the Cattaraugus Indian Reservation. Their airy four-bedroom home is clean, modern, and decorated with family Indian articles, many of them crafted by hand. The reservation offers country living and the opportunity of seeing firsthand the customs of a Native American community. A fall festival with arts, crafts, and exhibition dancing is held in September. Canoeing, fishing, rafting, cross-country and downhill skiing, and a sport called snowsnake are among the local activities. Your hosts will gladly arrange tours of the Amish community, and hot-air balloon rides over the beautiful rolling hills.

The Misserts B&B
66 HIGHLAND AVENUE, HAMBURG, NEW YORK 14075

Tel: **(716) 649-5830**	Open: **All year**
Hosts: **Tom and Betty Missert**	Breakfast: **Full**
Location: **14 mi. S of Buffalo**	Pets: **Sometimes**
No. of Rooms: **3**	Children: **Welcome**
Max. No. Sharing Bath: **6**	Smoking: **Permitted**
Double/sb: **$35**	Social Drinking: **Permitted**
Single/sb: **$30**	Airport/Station Pickup: **Yes**

A three-story wood frame house in a quiet residential neighborhood, The Misserts B&B is designed for company, with its large living room and enclosed front porch. The house is filled with hanging plants and Betty's paintings—she studied art before becoming a professional dressmaker. Lake Erie is 10 minutes away, while Hamburg's large public playground is just around the corner. (Baby-sitting services are available for an extra fee.) Your host enjoys local acclaim as a baker, and her full breakfasts include apricot muffins and mouthwatering coffee cakes fresh from the oven. Weather permitting, meals are served outside on the deck.

The Cameo Inn ✪
4710 LOWER RIVER ROAD, LEWISTON, NEW YORK 14092

Tel: **(716) 754-2075**	Suites: **$95**
Best Time to Call: **9 AM–9 PM**	Open: **All year**
Hosts: **Gregory and Carolyn Fisher**	Reduced Rates: **10% Jan.–Apr.;**
Location: **5 mi. N of Niagara Falls**	**5 nights or more**
No. of Rooms: **4**	Breakfast: **Full**
No. of Private Baths: **2**	Pets: **No**
Max. No. Sharing Bath: **4**	Children: **Welcome**
Double/pb: **$75**	Smoking: **No**
Single/pb: **$70**	Social Drinking: **Permitted**
Double/sb: **$65**	Minimum Stay: **2 nights holiday**
Single/sb: **$60**	**weekends**

Gregory and Carolyn's authentically furnished Queen Anne Victorian home commands a majestic view of the lower Niagara River. Located just 25 miles north of Buffalo and 5 miles north of Niagara Falls, The Cameo is conveniently situated for sightseeing, antiquing, fishing and boating, golfing, bicycling, or shopping at local factory outlets and malls. History buffs will want to travel 5 miles north to Old Fort Niagara, which dates from the American Revolution; the bridge to Canada is minutes away. A full country breakfast is served in the dining room each morning.

Chestnut Ridge Inn
7205 CHESTNUT RIDGE, LOCKPORT, NEW YORK 14094

Tel: **(716) 439-9124**	Breakfast: **Full**
Hosts: **Frank and Lucy Cervoni**	Other Meals: **Available**
Location: **20 mi. E of Niagara Falls**	Credit Cards: **AMEX**
No. of Rooms: **4**	Pets: **No**
No. of Private Baths: **4**	Children: **Welcome, in suite**
Double/pb: **$65–$75**	Smoking: **No**
Single/pb: **$40–$65**	Social Drinking: **Permitted**
Suite: **$75–$95 for 2–6**	Foreign Languages: **Italian**
Open: **All year**	

A white Federal mansion circa 1826, Chestnut Ridge Inn is set on eight acres of lawns and gardens and shaded by century-old trees. The interior is elegant, from the wide central hall with its rose damask wall covering, oriental rug, and curving staircase, to the formal living and dining rooms and cherry-paneled library. The large bedrooms have poster beds and fine linens, and there are fireplaces throughout the house, as well as central air-conditioning. Want to take some of the period furniture home with you? Browse in the carriage-house antiques shop. Lucy and Frank are gracious hosts who will soon make you feel like an honored guest. Afternoon and evening refreshments are served, and holidays are special events.

Manchester House ✪
653 MAIN STREET, NIAGARA FALLS, NEW YORK 14301

Tel: **(716) 285-5717**
Best Time to Call: **9 AM–6 PM**
Hosts: **Lis and Carl Slenk**
No. of Rooms: **4**
Max. No. Sharing Bath: **4**
Double/sb: **$65**
Single/sb: **$50**
Open: **All year**

Reduced Rates: **Available**
Breakfast: **Full**
Credit Cards: **MC, VISA**
Pets: **No**
Children: **Welcome**
Smoking: **No**
Social Drinking: **Permitted**
Foreign Languages: **German**

Before it was incorporated, Niagara Falls was known as Manchester—hence the name for this tastefully renovated B&B, which was a doctor's office for more than sixty years. Lis and Carl collected ideas and furniture for their home during the ten years they spent in England and Germany. Manchester House is conveniently located near the falls, with easy access to Canada. (Spacious off-street parking is provided.) The bright, cheerful guest rooms offer a choice of queen-size or single beds. Breakfast features home-baked specialties.

The William Seward Inn
RD 2, SOUTH PORTAGE ROAD, WESTFIELD, NEW YORK 14787

Tel: (716) 326-4151
Best Time to Call: 8 AM–9 PM
Hosts: Jim and Debbie Dahlberg
Location: 125 mi. E of Cleveland
No. of Rooms: 14
No. of Private Baths: 14
Double/pb: $80–$125
Single/pb: $70–$115
Open: All year
Reduced Rates: Package rates Nov. 1–May 31
Breakfast: Full
Other Meals: Available
Credit Cards: MC, VISA
Pets: No
Children: Welcome, over 12
Smoking: No
Social Drinking: Permitted

Before serving as Abraham Lincoln's secretary of state, William Seward lived in this Greek revival mansion, which echoes the period of Seward's residence with furnishings from the 1840s and '50s. Pieces from all eras are sold in Westfield's 30 antique shops. Five wineries ring the town, and the Chautauqua Institute—an educational and cultural center—is just a few miles away. The schedule of weekend workshops and packages includes ski trips, wine tours, stargazing, maple sugaring, and even a seminar on innkeeping as a career. Full breakfasts feature shirred eggs, Monte Cristos, or pancakes.

THOUSAND ISLANDS AREA

Battle Island Inn ✪
BOX 176, RD 1, FULTON, NEW YORK 13069

Tel: (315) 593-3699
Hosts: Joyce and Richard Rice
Location: 30 mi. N of Syracuse
No. of Rooms: 6
No. of Private Baths: 6
Double/pb: $60–$80
Single/pb: $50–$65
Open: All year
Breakfast: Full
Pets: No
Children: Welcome
Smoking: No
Social Drinking: Permitted

The Rice family welcomes you to their pre–Civil War estate, which they restored themselves with lots of love and hard work. The inn is across the street from a golf course and is surrounded by fields and orchards. The rooms feature Victorian antiques and marble fireplaces. Guest bedrooms are spacious and elegant with imposing high-backed beds. Joyce is a full-time host, who will tempt your palate with homemade rolls, biscuits, and crêpes. Richard is a systems analyst who oversees the challenges of an 1840s house. Whether you're enjoying the privacy of your room or socializing in the formal front parlor, you are sure to appreciate the friendly family atmosphere.

Tug Hill Lodge
8091 SALISBURY STREET, BOX 204, SANDY CREEK, NEW YORK 13145

Tel: **(315) 387-5326**
Best Time to Call: **After 3 PM**
Host: **Margaret Clerkin**
Location: **40 mi. N of Syracuse**
No. of Rooms: **5**
Max. No. Sharing Bath: **3**
Double/sb: **$60**

Single/sb: **$30**
Open: **All year**
Breakfast: **Full**
Pets: **Sometimes**
Children: **Sometimes**
Smoking: **No**
Social Drinking: **Permitted**

Margaret's large Italianate Victorian home, with cupola, was built in 1872. The interior is comfortable, with a two-story sun room and deck. Down quilts on the double or queen-size beds assure a cozy night's sleep. A full English breakfast is the house specialty, but if you prefer vegetarian food or are on a special diet, give Margaret fair notice and she'll accommodate you. Ski, fish, hunt, go to a local concert or theater, shop, or simply curl up with a good book and rest.

NORTH CAROLINA

Sparta • Mt. Airy • Winston-Salem
Boone • • Greensboro • Durham
Spruce Pine • • Banner • Tarboro
Burnsville • Elk Raleigh • • Wilson   Kill Devil Hills
• Black Mountain
Clyde • Asheville • Taylorsville   • Washington
Waynesville • • Hendersonville • Salisbury
Franklin • • Pisgah Forest Statesville   Oriental •
Murphy • Highlands • Tryon   New Bern •   • Beaufort
Saluda • Charlotte   • Swansboro
• Wilmington

Applewood Manor ✪
62 CUMBERLAND CIRCLE, ASHEVILLE, NORTH CAROLINA 28801

Tel: (704) 254-2244
Best Time to Call: **Before 10 PM**
Hosts: **Susan Poole and Maryanne Young**
Location: ¾ mi. from Rte. 240, Exit 4C
No. of Rooms: **4**
No. of Private Baths: **4**
Double/pb: **$75–$85**
Single/pb: **$70–$80**
Guest Cottage: **$100**

Suites: **$95**
Open: **All year**
Reduced Rates: **10% Jan.–Feb.; 10% seniors (Sept. only)**
Breakfast: **Full**
Credit Cards: **DISC, MC, VISA**
Pets: **No**
Children: **Welcome, over 12**
Smoking: **No**
Social Drinking: **Permitted**
Minimum Stay: **2 nights weekends**

Built in 1908, this Colonial Revival home boasts wide porches with rockers and a swing, and two manicured acres perfect for a game of badminton or croquet. Fine lace curtains, antique furnishings, heart-pine floors covered with oriental rugs, and bright and airy rooms,

432

most with fireplaces and balconies, are found throughout. Breakfast always includes something special, such as orange-pecan waffles or apple and brie omelets. It's only a mile away from fine restaurants, antique and craft shops, an art museum, theater, and the Thomas Wolfe Memorial.

Cairn Brae

217 PATTON MOUNTAIN ROAD, ASHEVILLE, NORTH CAROLINA 28804

Tel: **(704) 252-9219**	Breakfast: **Full**
Hosts: **Millicent and Edward Adams**	Credit Cards: **MC, VISA**
Location: **5 mi. NE of Asheville**	Pets: **No**
No. of Rooms: **3**	Children: **Welcome, over 6**
No. of Private Baths: **3**	Smoking: **No**
Double/pb: **$80–$95**	Social Drinking: **Permitted**
Open: **Apr. 1–Nov. 30**	Airport/Station Pickup: **Yes**

Cairn Brae, Scottish for "rocky hillside," is a striking circular contemporary home nestled in the Blue Ridge Mountains. It has lavish wood paneling, a stone fireplace, and a dramatic winding staircase connecting upper and lower levels. This wooded three-and-a-half-acre property invites exploration. For a taste of urban pleasures, downtown Asheville, with its branch of the University of North Carolina, is just 12 minutes away by car.

Carolina Bed & Breakfast ✪

177 CUMBERLAND AVENUE, ASHEVILLE, NORTH CAROLINA 28801

Tel: **(704) 254-3608**	Open: **All year**
Best Time to Call: **7 AM–9 PM**	Breakfast: **Full**
Hosts: **Sam, Karin, and Regina Fain**	Credit Cards: **MC, VISA**
Location: **½ mi. N of Asheville**	Pets: **No**
No. of Rooms: **6**	Children: **Welcome, over 12**
No. of Private Baths: **6**	Smoking: **No**
Double/pb: **$75–$85**	Social Drinking: **Permitted**
Single/pb: **$65**	Airport/Station Pickup: **Yes**
Guest Cottage: **$95**	

This turn-of-the-century Colonial Revival home has been painstakingly restored; feel free to relax on the front and back porches, or just take in the view from the second-floor guest rooms, with their distinctive, twelve-over-one panes. In springtime, the grounds bloom with dogwoods and rhododendrons. On cooler days, you can curl up in front of one of the house's seven fireplaces. Your hosts serve a different full breakfast each day; the usual fare includes eggs or quiche and fresh bread and muffins.

Cedar Crest Victorian Inn ✪
674 BILTMORE AVENUE, ASHEVILLE, NORTH CAROLINA 28803

Tel: **(704) 252-1389; (800) 252-0310**
Best Time to Call: **8 AM–8 PM**
Hosts: **Jack and Barbara McEwan**
Location: **1¼ mi. from I-40**
No. of Rooms: **13**
No. of Private Baths: **9**
Max. No. Sharing Bath: **4**
Double/pb: **$100–$120**
Single/pb: **$95–$115**

Double/sb: **$70–$80**
Single/sb: **$65–$70**
Open: **All year**
Breakfast: **Continental**
Credit Cards: **AMEX, DISC, MC, VISA**
Pets: **No**
Children: **Welcome, over 12**
Smoking: **Permitted**
Social Drinking: **Permitted**

Built in 1891, and listed on the National Register of Historic Places, Cedar Crest is one of the largest and most opulent residences to survive Asheville's boom period. Enter the grand foyer and you'll find the rich warmth of hardwood paneling, lace window treatments, and an intricately carved fireplace. A massive oak staircase leads to the guest rooms, decorated with Victorian antiques and fine linens. Your hosts serve tea or lemonade on the spacious veranda in the summer months. In the cold weather, enjoy hot drinks by the fire. This lovely Queen Anne is located close to the Blue Ridge Parkway, the Biltmore House, and downtown Asheville. Your hosts will be glad to recommend local eateries and invite you back to the inn for hot chocolate and cookies in the evening.

Corner Oak Manor ✪
53 ST. DUNSTANS ROAD, ASHEVILLE, NORTH CAROLINA 28803

Tel: **(704) 253-3525**
Hosts: **Karen and Andy Spradley**
Location: **1¼ mi. from Rte. 40, Exit 50**
No. of Rooms: **4**
No. of Private Baths: **4**
Double/pb: **$80–$95**
Single/pb: **$65**
Open: **All year**
Reduced Rates: **10% Jan.–Mar.**

Breakfast: **Full**
Other Meals: **Available**
Credit Cards: **AMEX, DISC, MC, VISA**
Pets: **No**
Children: **Welcome, over 12 in house, under 12 in cottage**
Smoking: **No**
Social Drinking: **Permitted**

Surrounded by maple, oak, and evergreen trees, this lovely English Tudor home is located minutes away from the famed Biltmore Estate and Gardens. The rooms have queen-size beds beautifully covered in fine linen. The window treatments and coordinated wall coverings could easily grace the pages of a decorating magazine. Handmade wreaths, weavings, and stitchery complement the furnishings. Breakfast specialties include orange French toast, blueberry-ricotta pancakes, or four-cheese-herb quiche. A living room fireplace, baby grand piano, outdoor deck, and Jacuzzi are among the gracious amenities.

Cornerstone Inn ✪
230 PEARSON DRIVE, ASHEVILLE, NORTH CAROLINA 28801

Tel: **(704) 253-5644**
Hosts: **Gary and Nancy Gaither**
No. of Rooms: **4**
No. of Private Baths: **4**
Double/pb: **$65–$85**
Single/pb: **$60–$80**
Open: **All year**

Breakfast: **Full**
Credit Cards: **AMEX, MC, VISA**
Pets: **No**
Children: **Welcome, over 10**
Smoking: **Restricted**
Social Drinking: **Permitted**

The Dutch Tudor home is surrounded by hemlocks and is located in the heart of the historic area. Gary and Nancy have furnished it with family heirlooms, antiques, and treasures. It is a brief walk to the Botanical Garden at the University of North Carolina, and a short distance to shops, restaurants, and cultural events. Depending upon the weather, breakfast may be enjoyed on the covered side porch, in the formal dining room, or in the rock-walled garden amid local wildflowers.

Flint Street Inns ✪
100 & 116 FLINT STREET, ASHEVILLE, NORTH CAROLINA 28801

Tel: **(704) 253-6723**
Hosts: **Rick, Lynne, and Marion Vogel**
Location: **¼ mi. from Rte. 240**
No. of Rooms: **8**
No. of Private Baths: **8**
Double/pb: **$80**
Single/pb: **$65**

Open: **All year**
Breakfast: **Full**
Credit Cards: **AMEX, DISC, MC, VISA**
Pets: **No**
Children: **No**
Smoking: **Permitted**
Social Drinking: **Permitted**

These turn-of-the-century homes on an acre with century-old trees are listed on the National Register of Historic Places. Stained glass, pine floors, and a claw-footed bathtub are part of the Victorian decor. The inns are air-conditioned for summer comfort; some have fireplaces for winter coziness. Guests are served wine, coffee, and soft drinks. The Blue Ridge Parkway is close by.

The Banner Elk Inn Bed & Breakfast ✪
P.O. BOX 1953, ROUTE 3, BOX 1134, HIGHWAY 194 NORTH, BANNER ELK, NORTH CAROLINA 28604

Tel: **(704) 898-6223**
Best Time to Call: **9 AM–10 PM**
Host: **Beverly Lait**
Location: **17 mi. W of Boone**
No. of Rooms: **4**
No. of Private Baths: **2**

Max. No. Sharing Bath: **4**
Double/pb: **$45–$90**
Single/pb: **$45–$90**
Suites: **$90–$120; sleeps 4**
Double/sb: **$60–$75**
Single/sb: **$55–$65**

Open: **All year**
Reduced Rates: **Available**
Breakfast: **Full**
Credit Cards: **MC, VISA**
Pets: **No**
Children: **Welcome**

Smoking: **No**
Social Drinking: **Permitted**
Minimum Stay: **Mid-July; first 2 weeks
of Oct.; 2 nights weekends**
Foreign Languages: **Spanish**

Your host, Beverly, spent years with the Foreign Service, and original tapestries, artwork, and antiques from around the world fill her stunningly renovated historic home. The inn is located halfway between the Sugar Resort and Beech Mountain ski slopes, near such major tourist attractions as Grandfather Mountain and Natural Habitat, Linville Falls, Valle Crucis, and the Blue Ridge Parkway. You'll have energy to visit all these places after Beverly's full breakfasts of homemade breads, eggs, fruit, juice, and coffee or tea.

Delamar Inn ✪
217 TURNER STREET, BEAUFORT, NORTH CAROLINA 28516

Tel: **(919) 728-4300**
Best Time to Call: **Anytime**
Hosts: **Philip and Kay Ross**
Location: **140 mi. SE of Raleigh**
No. of Rooms: **3**
No. of Private Baths: **3**
Double/pb: **$82**
Single/pb: **$82**

Open: **All year**
Breakfast: **Continental**
Credit Cards: **MC, VISA**
Pets: **No**
Children: **Welcome, over 10**
Smoking: **No**
Social Drinking: **Permitted**
Airport/Station Pickup: **Yes**

The Delamar Inn, built in 1866, is located in historic Beaufort, North Carolina's third oldest town. The inn offers three guest rooms furnished with antiques, each room with a private bath. After a delightful breakfast, stroll down to the historic restoration grounds, maritime museum, or the open-air bus, or browse in the waterfront specialty shops. Philip and Kay, your hosts, can offer directions to local beaches for shell collecting, sunbathing, or fishing. Try a short ride to Fort Macon, Tryon Palace, or the ferry to the Outer Banks. A selection of the '91 historic homes tour, the Delamar Inn welcomes you.

Bed and Breakfast Over Yonder ✪
RT 1, BOX 269, NORTH FORK ROAD, BLACK MOUNTAIN, NORTH CAROLINA 28711

Tel: **(704) 669-6762; Nov.–May (919)
945-9958**
Best Time to Call: **11 AM–2 PM**
Host: **Wilhelmina K. Headley**
Location: **2 mi. N of Black Mountain**
No. of Rooms: **5**

No. of Private Baths: **5**
Double/pb: **$40–$65**
Single/pb: **$35–$50**
Open: **June–Oct.**
Reduced Rates: **5% after 3rd night**
Breakfast: **Full**

NORTH CAROLINA • 437

Pets: **No**
Children: **Welcome**

Smoking: **No**
Social Drinking: **Permitted**

Spectacular views of the nearby Black Mountain Range make Bed and Breakfast Over Yonder an ideal place to get away from it all. Hikers, tennis players, golfers, and swimmers will find plenty to do within a mile or two, and white-water rafting, gem mining, and rock climbing are all feasible on day trips. For a change of pace, explore the local craft and antique shops. Weather permitting, full breakfasts of fruit, homemade bread, and mountain trout are served on the deck overlooking the wildflower gardens.

Grandma Jean's Bed and Breakfast ✪
209 MEADOWVIEW DRIVE, BOONE, NORTH CAROLINA 28607

Tel: **(704) 262-3670**
Best Time to Call: **Before 10 AM**
Host: **Dr. Jean Probinsky**
No. of Rooms: **3**
Max. No. Sharing Bath: **4**
Double/sb: **$45–$50**
Single/sb: **$35**
Open: **Apr. 1–Nov. 1**
Breakfast: **Continental**

Pets: **No**
Children: **Welcome, under 2 and
    over 6**
Smoking: **Permitted**
Social Drinking: **Permitted**
Airport/Station Pickup: **Yes**
Minimum Stay: **2 nights**
Foreign Languages: **Spanish**

Wicker furniture and lots of rocking chairs make this a cozy country home. Boone offers easy access to the Blue Ridge Parkway, and Appalachian State University—the summer residence of the North Carolina Symphony—is just one mile away. Grandma Jean prides herself on her southern hospitality. Her Continental breakfast includes coffee, tea, seasonal fruit, and croissants with homemade preserves.

Overlook Lodge ✪
P.O. BOX 1327, BOONE, NORTH CAROLINA 28607

Tel: **(704) 963-5785**
Host: **Nancy Garrett**
Location: **4 mi. from Blue Ridge Pkwy.**
No. of Rooms: **5**
No. of Private Baths: **5**
Double/pb: **$60–$75**
Single/pb: **$50**
Suite: **$90; sleeps 4**
Open: **All year**

Reduced Rates: **15% weekly; Nov. 1–
    Apr. 30**
Breakfast: **Full**
Credit Cards: **MC, VISA**
Pets: **Sometimes**
Children: **Yes (crib)**
Smoking: **Permitted**
Social Drinking: **Permitted**
Airport/Station Pickup: **Yes**

This rustic retreat is perched in the Blue Ridge Mountains and offers intoxicating views from the house's three decks. The secluded setting is ideal for forays into the wilderness. Hikers, canoeists, spelunkers, and fishermen will all find plenty to do here. In cold weather, weary skiers can warm up by the living room's huge stone fireplace. Year round, Nancy serves breakfasts that include home-baked breads and muffins; one of her fortes is cheese soufflé.

Estes Mountain Retreat ✪
ROUTE 1, BOX 1316A (OFF BAKER'S CREEK ROAD), BURNSVILLE, NORTH CAROLINA 28714

Tel: **(704) 682-7264**	Open: **All year**
Best Time to Call: **8 AM–12 noon**	Reduced Rates: **15% weekly; 10% seniors**
Hosts: **Bruce and Maryallen Estes**	
Location: **37 mi. NE of Asheville**	Breakfast: **Full**
No. of Rooms: **2**	Pets: **No**
No. of Private Baths: **1**	Children: **Welcome, over 3**
Max. No. Sharing Bath: **4**	Smoking: **No**
Double/pb: **$60**	Social Drinking: **Permitted**
Double/sb: **$55**	Foreign Languages: **French**

Breathtaking mountain views await you at this three-level cedar log home with a rock chimney, fireplace, and porches. Because Burnsville is in Pisgah National Forest, you won't have to travel far to go rafting, fishing, hiking, and rock and gem hunting, and there's golfing next door at Mountain Air Country Club. Mt. Mitchell, Linville Caverns, outdoor theater, the Biltmore Mansion, and the Carl Sandburg Home are all within an hour's drive.

Hamrick Inn ✪
7787 HIGHWAY 80, BURNSVILLE, NORTH CAROLINA 28714

Tel: **(704) 675-5251**	Single/pb: **$45–$55**
Best Time to Call: **Mornings**	Open: **Apr. 2–Oct. 31**
Hosts: **Neal and June Jerome**	Reduced Rates: **Weekly**
Location: **55 mi. NE of Asheville; 16 mi. from I-40, Exit 72**	Breakfast: **Full**
	Pets: **No**
No. of Rooms: **4**	Children: **Welcome**
No. of Private Baths: **4**	Smoking: **Permitted**
Double/pb: **$50–$60**	Social Drinking: **Permitted**

This charming three-story Colonial-style stone inn is nestled at the foot of Mt. Mitchell, the highest mountain east of the Mississippi River. Much of the lovely furniture was built by Neal and June. The den has a fine selection of books as well as a TV set for your enjoyment. There is a private porch off each bedroom, where you may take in the view and the cool mountain breezes. Golfing, hiking, fishing, rock hounding, craft shopping, and fall foliage wandering are local activities. Pisgah National Park, Linville Caverns, Crabtree Meadows, and the Parkway Playhouse are area diversions.

The Elizabeth ☉
2145 EAST 5TH STREET, CHARLOTTE, NORTH CAROLINA 28204

Tel: (704) 358-1368
Best Time to Call: Evenings
Host: Joan Mastny
Location: 3 mi. from Rte. I-77, Exit 10B
No. of Rooms: 2
No. of Private Baths: 2
Double/pb: $58
Single/pb: $55

Guest Cottage: $70–$78
Suites: $70–$78; sleeps 2
Open: All year
Breakfast: Continental
Credit Cards: MC, VISA
Pets: No
Children: Welcome, over 10
Smoking: No
Social Drinking: No

This 1927 Prairie Style house is located in Elizabeth, Charlotte's second oldest suburb. Wander the old tree-lined streets and discover lovely historic homes. Antique shops, a variety of restaurants, and the Mint Museum of Art are all within walking distance. Guest quarters consist of the Garden Room, featuring Laura Ashley wallpapers and linens, and the Guest Cottage, a decorator's dream in blue and white. Each has a courtyard entrance, private bath, antique brass and iron double bed, central air-conditioning, television, and private telephone. Amenities include complimentary coffee, tea, juice, and hot chocolate. A hearty Continental breakfast-in-a-basket is brought to your room.

The Homeplace
5901 SARDIS ROAD, CHARLOTTE, NORTH CAROLINA 28270

Tel: **(704) 365-1936**
Hosts: **Peggy and Frank Dearien**
Location: **10 mi. from I-77; I-85**
No. of Rooms: **3**
No. of Private Baths: **3**
Double/pb: **$78**
Single/pb: **$68**

Open: **All year**
Breakfast: **Full**
Credit Cards: **AMEX, MC, VISA**
Pets: **No**
Children: **Welcome, over 10**
Smoking: **No**
Social Drinking: **No**

The warm and friendly atmosphere hasn't changed since 1902. The minute you arrive at this country Victorian and walk up to the wraparound porch with its rockers, you'll feel you've "come home." The handcrafted staircase, 10-foot beaded ceilings, and heart-of-pine floors add to the interior's beauty. It's convenient to malls, furniture and textile outlets, and treasure-filled antique shops.

The Inn on Providence
6700 PROVIDENCE ROAD, CHARLOTTE, NORTH CAROLINA 28226

Tel: **(704) 366-6700**
Hosts: **Darlene and Dan McNeill**
No. of Rooms: **5**
No. of Private Baths: **3**
Max. No. Sharing Bath: **4**
Double/pb: **$69–$79**
Double/sb: **$59**
Open: **All year**

Reduced Rates: **Available**
Breakfast: **Full**
Credit Cards: **MC, VISA**
Pets: **No**
Children: **Welcome, over 11**
Smoking: **No**
Social Drinking: **Permitted**

The Inn on Providence is a large, three-story Colonial nestled in South Charlotte, close to many amenities of the Queen City. The walnut-paneled library, sitting room with fireplace, and oak-floored dining room will make both vacationers and business executives feel at home. The bedrooms are decorated with Early American antiques, and each features something special, such as a canopy bed or a sitting room. In warm weather, breakfast is served on the screened veranda, which is decorated with white wicker and paddle fans. The veranda is also a great place to sip afternoon tea while overlooking the gardens and swimming pool.

The Overcarsh House ✪
326 WEST EIGHTH STREET, CHARLOTTE, NORTH CAROLINA 28202

Tel: **(704) 334-8477**
Host: **Dennis Cudd**
Location: **1 mi. from I-77**
No. of Rooms: **1 suite**

No. of Private Baths: **1**
Suites: **$65–$80 for 2–4**
Open: **All year**
Reduced Rates: **10% corporate**

Breakfast: **Continental**
Pets: **No**
Children: **Welcome**

Smoking: **Permitted**
Social Drinking: **Permitted**

The Library Suite is a Victorian-style retreat in the luxurious Overcarsh House. The private entrance into the suite leads to a wraparound gallery overlooking Fourth Ward park. The adjoining sleeping quarters feature a draped Savannah plantation bed. Your host has stocked the floor-to-ceiling bookcases with plenty of books and periodicals. He also provides wine and a wet bar, fresh flowers, cable TV, and coffeemaker. Overcarsh House is listed on the National Register of Historic Places, and is close to the uptown area, the performing arts center, shopping, and restaurants.

Still Waters ✪
6221 AMOS SMITH ROAD, CHARLOTTE, NORTH CAROLINA 28214

Tel: **(704) 399-6299**
Best Time to Call: **Evenings**
Hosts: **Janet and Rob Dyer**
Location: **3 mi. W of Charlotte**
No. of Rooms: **3**
No. of Private Baths: **3**
Double/pb: **$65–$85**
Open: **All year**
Reduced Rates: **Available**

Breakfast: **Full**
Credit Cards: **MC, VISA**
Pets: **No**
Children: **Welcome**
Smoking: **No**
Social Drinking: **Permitted**
Minimum Stay: **2 nights weekends only May 1–Nov. 15**

Relax on the river just outside Charlotte city limits—only minutes away from downtown, the airport, or the interstates, but a world away from the bustle of everyday life. Visit this lakefront log home on two wooded acres. Enjoy the deck, garden, dock, and boat ramp, or play on the sport court. Guests stay in either of two large rooms or in a suite. Full breakfasts always feature homemade sourdough rolls and fresh-ground coffee.

Windsong: A Mountain Inn
120 FERGUSON RIDGE, CLYDE, NORTH CAROLINA 28721

Tel: **(704) 627-6111**	Reduced Rates: **10%, singles and**
Best Time to Call: **8 AM–9 PM**	**weekly bookings**
Hosts: **Donna and Gale Livengood**	Breakfast: **Full**
Location: **36 mi. W of Asheville**	Credit Cards: **MC, VISA**
No. of Rooms: **5**	Pets: **No**
No. of Private Baths: **5**	Children: **Welcome, over 8**
Double/pb: **$90–$95**	Smoking: **No**
Single/pb: **$81–$85.50**	Social Drinking: **Permitted**
Open: **All year**	

From its mountainside perch near Waynesville, this immense contemporary log home affords spectacular views of the surrounding countryside. Inside, the house is bright and airy, thanks to the large windows and skylights and the high exposed-beam ceilings. Each oversized room boasts its own patio, fireplace, and deep tubs for two. There are a tennis court and in-ground pool, plus a billiard table and an extensive video library with in-room VCRs. You'll love their llama herd with group pack trips going into the national forests. Nearby attractions include horseback riding, white-water rafting, Cherokee Indian Reservation, Great Smoky Mountain National Park, Biltmore House, and the Appalachian Trail. You'll relish home-baked breakfast goods. Typical entrées are buckwheat banana pancakes and egg-sausage strata with mushrooms.

Arrowhead Inn
106 MASON ROAD, DURHAM, NORTH CAROLINA 27712

Tel: **(919) 477-8430**; fax: **(919) 477-8430**	Double/sb: **$70**
	Open: **All year**
Hosts: **Jerry and Cathy Ryan**	Reduced Rates: **10% after 3rd night**
Location: **6.8 mi. from I-85, Roxboro, Rd. 501 exit**	Breakfast: **Full**
	Credit Cards: **AMEX, DC, MC, VISA**
No. of Rooms: **8**	Children: **Welcome**
No. of Private Baths: **6**	Smoking: **Permitted**
Max. No. Sharing Bath: **4**	Social Drinking: **Permitted**
Double/pb: **$85–$130**	Foreign Languages: **French**

Arrowhead Inn is a 215-year-old columned manor house in Durham County's tobacco country. Its rooms reflect various moments in the house's history, from Colonial through Tidewater and Victorian. Stroll the nearly four acres, or visit the historic district, the Museum of Life and Science, Duke University, or famous Research Triangle Park. After dinner at one of the area's fine restaurants, join the other guests for VCR, Scrabble, or conversation.

The Blooming Garden Inn ✪
513 HOLLOWAY STREET, DURHAM, NORTH CAROLINA 27701

Tel: **(919) 687-0801**
Best Time to Call: **Evenings**
Hosts: **Frank and Dolly Pokrass**
Location: **Downtown Durham**
No. of Rooms: **5**
No. of Private Baths: **5**
Double/pb: **$75**
Suites: **$125**
Open: **All year**

Reduced Rates: **Available**
Breakfast: **Full**
Other Meals: **Available**
Credit Cards: **AMEX, MC, VISA**
Pets: **No**
Children: **Welcome**
Smoking: **No**
Social Drinking: **Permitted**

If you appreciate flowers—and who doesn't?—you'll love staying at this restored 1892 Victorian with glorious gardens at every turn. The house is handsome, too, with its gabled roof, beveled and stained-glass windows, and wraparound porch supported by Tuscan columns. What's more, you're right in the center of Durham's historic Holloway

District, just moments from shops, galleries, theaters, Duke University, and the University of North Carolina.

Buttonwood Inn ✪

190 GEORGIA ROAD, FRANKLIN, NORTH CAROLINA 28734

Tel: **(704) 369-8985**	Double/sb: **$55**
Best Time to Call: **After 5 PM**	Single/sb: **$45**
Host: **Liz Oehser**	Suites: **$95**
Location: **75 mi. SW of Asheville**	Open: **Apr. 15–Nov. 15**
No. of Rooms: **4**	Breakfast: **Full**
No. of Private Baths: **2**	Pets: **No**
Max. No. Sharing Bath: **4**	Children: **Welcome, over 10**
Double/pb: **$60–$75**	Smoking: **Permitted**
Single/pb: **$50**	Social Drinking: **Permitted**

The Buttonwood is a small country inn surrounded by towering pines, a spacious lawn, and mountain views. The original residence was a small cottage built in the late 1920s adjacent to the greens of the Franklin golf course. Years later, a new wing was added with rustic, charming rooms. Guests may choose from comfortable bedrooms decorated with antiques, cozy quilts, and handcrafts, many of which are offered for sale. Breakfast selections include sausage-apple ring, eggs Benedict, or cheese frittata, with coffee cake and plenty of hot coffee or tea. Golfers will be glad to be so close to the beautiful fairways and Bermuda grass greens right next door. Nearby there are also craft shops, hiking trails, the Blue Ridge Parkway, gem mines, and plenty of places to swim and ride.

Hickory Knoll Lodge

238 EAST HICKORY KNOLL ROAD, FRANKLIN, NORTH CAROLINA 28734

Tel: **(704) 524-9666**	Reduced Rates: **Available**
Host: **Dodie Allen**	Breakfast: **Full, Continental**
Location: **9 mi. SE of Franklin**	Other Meals: **Available**
No. of Rooms: **3**	Pets: **Sometimes**
No. of Private Baths: **3**	Children: **Welcome, over 12**
Double/pb: **$65**	Smoking: **Permitted**
Single/pb: **$55**	Social Drinking: **Permitted**
Open: **All year**	Airport Pickup: **Yes**

Fishing ponds and hiking trails await guests at this lovely vacation spot in the southeastern part of the state. Plus, you'll find all the amenities of home—a TV, a washing machine, and a kitchen where you can prepare yourself a quick bite. (Dodie has complimentary snacks on hand.) Either full or Continental breakfast is available, featuring fresh fruit and homemade jams and breads. All rooms are accessible to disabled visitors.

The Waverly Inn ○
783 NORTH MAIN STREET, HENDERSONVILLE, NORTH CAROLINA
28792

Tel: (800) 537-8195; (704) 693-9193
Best Time to Call: 9:30 AM–10 PM
Hosts: John, Diane, Sheiry, and Darla
  Olmstead
Location: 20 mi. S of Asheville
No. of Rooms: 14
No. of Private Baths: 14
Double/pb: $75–$89
Single/pb: $65
Suites: $145

Open: All year
Reduced Rates: Off-season; 15%
  weekly
Breakfast: Full
Credit Cards: AMEX, DISC, MC, VISA
Pets: No
Children: Welcome
Smoking: Permitted
Social Drinking: Permitted

Built as a boardinghouse in 1898, the Waverly is distinguished by its handsome Eastlake staircase—a factor that earned the inn a listing on the National Register of Historic Places. Furnishings like four-poster canopy beds and claw-footed tubs combine Victorian stateliness and Colonial Revival charm. You'll walk away sated from all-you-can-eat breakfasts of pancakes and French toast. Noteworthy local sites include the Biltmore Estate, the Carl Sandburg house, the Blue Ridge Parkway, and the Flat Rock Playhouse.

Colonial Pines Inn ○
ROUTE 1, BOX 22B, HICKORY STREET, HIGHLANDS, NORTH
CAROLINA 28741

Tel: (704) 526-2060
Best Time to Call: 10 AM–10 PM
Hosts: Chris and Donna Alley
Location: 80 mi. SW of Asheville
No. of Rooms: 7
No. of Private Baths: 7
Double/pb: $70
Single/pb: $60
Suites: $85

Guest Cottage: $75–$85; sleeps 4
Open: All year
Reduced Rates: Weekly
Breakfast: Full
Credit Cards: MC, VISA
Pets: No
Children: Welcome, in cottage only
Smoking: No
Social Drinking: Permitted

Located in a charming, uncommercial mountain resort town, this white Colonial is flanked by tall columns and is surrounded by two acres. The scenic view may be enjoyed from comfortable rocking chairs on the wide veranda. Donna, a former interior decorator, has furnished the inn with antiques, art, and interesting accessories. Chris is a classical guitarist, woodworker, and great cook. The hearty breakfast includes a variety of homemade breads.

Lakeside Lodging ✪
ROUTE 1, BOX 189A, HIGHLANDS, NORTH CAROLINA 28741

Tel: (704) 526-4498
Best Time to Call: 9 AM–9 PM
Hosts: Michael and Eleanor Robel
Location: 100 mi. N of Atlanta,
  Georgia
No. of Rooms: 4
No. of Private Baths: 4
Double/pb: $60–$65
Single/pb: $50–$55
Open: Apr. 1–Dec. 1

Reduced Rates: Sun.–Thurs.
Breakfast: Full
Credit Cards: MC, VISA
Pets: No
Children: Welcome
Smoking: Permitted
Social Drinking: Permitted
Minimum Stay: 2 nights holiday
  weekends

Located in the Smoky Mountains at an elevation of 4,100 feet, this white Colonial-style home with black shutters overlooks Lake Sequoyah and is bordered by the Nantahala National Forest. It combines a peaceful, scenic ambience with the availability of quaint shops, fine restaurants, mountain trails, and dramatic waterfalls. The immaculate interior is warm and inviting and attractively furnished with country charm. Entrées of potato quiche, omelets or soufflés, are breakfast treats. Mike and Eleanor will tell you how to get to the nearby facilities for horseback riding, canoeing, golf, gem mining, and rock rappelling. Asheville is 70 miles away.

Ye Olde Stone House
ROUTE 2, BOX 7, HIGHLANDS, NORTH CAROLINA 28741

Tel: (704) 526-5911
Best Time to Call: Afternoons;
  evenings
Hosts: Jim and Rene Ramsdell
Location: 80 mi. SW of Asheville
No. of Rooms: 4
No. of Private Baths: 3
Max. No. Sharing Bath: 3
Double/pb: $65–$70
Single/pb: $55–$60
Double/sb: $45
Single/sb: $45

Open: All year
Reduced Rates: 10% Sun.–Thurs.;
  weekly
Breakfast: Full
Credit Cards: MC, VISA
Pets: No
Children: Welcome
Smoking: No
Social Drinking: Permitted
Minimum Stay: 2 nights holiday
  weekends

Built of stones taken from a local river by mule and wagon, the house is less than a mile from the center of town, where you will find a nature center, museum, galleries, tennis courts, swimming pool, and shops offering antiques or mountain crafts. The rooms are bright, cheerful, and comfortably furnished. The sun room and porch are perfect spots to catch up on that book you've wanted to read. On cool evenings, the Ramsdells invite you to gather round the fireplace for snacks and conversation.

Ye Olde Cherokee Inn Bed & Breakfast ✪

500 NORTH VIRGINIA DARE TRAIL, KILL DEVIL HILLS, NORTH CAROLINA 27948

Tel: **(919) 441-6127**
Best Time to Call: **Evenings**
Hosts: **Bob and Phyllis Combs**
Location: **75 mi. S of Norfolk**
No. of Rooms: **6**
No. of Private Baths: **6**
Double/pb: **$55–$80**
Open: **Apr. 1–Sept. 30**
Reduced Rates: **$5 less per night, seniors**

Breakfast: **Continental**
Credit Cards: **AMEX, MC, VISA**
Pets: **No**
Children: **No**
Smoking: **No**
Social Drinking: **Permitted**
Minimum Stay: **3 nights July–Aug.; 4 nights holidays**

Only 500 feet from the Atlantic Ocean you'll find this pastel-pink house with wraparound porches, soft cypress interiors, and white ruffled curtains. Cherokee Inn is near the historic Roanoke Island settlement, Cape Hatteras, and the Wright Brothers Memorial at Kitty Hawk. Of course, you may just want to spend the day at the beach. In the evening, curl up with a book or watch TV. You'll start the next day with coffee and pastries.

Pine Ridge B&B Inn ✪

2893 WEST PINE STREET, MT. AIRY, NORTH CAROLINA 27030

Tel: **(919) 789-5034**
Hosts: **Ellen and Manford Haxton**
Location: **2 mi. from I-77**
No. of Rooms: **6**
No. of Private Baths: **6**
Double/pb: **$60–$100**
Open: **All year**
Reduced Rates: **10% Jan.–Mar.**

Breakfast: **Continental**
Other Meals: **Available**
Credit Cards: **AMEX, MC, VISA**
Pets: **No**
Children: **Welcome (crib)**
Smoking: **Permitted**
Social Drinking: **Permitted**
Airport/Station Pickup: **Yes**

Luxury and elegance await you in this 43-year-old mansion set on eight acres in the shadow of the Blue Ridge Mountains. Each guest room is attractively decorated and has a telephone and cable TV. Read in the wood-paneled library, soak in the hot tub, work out on the Nautilus equipment in the exercise room, or swim in the backyard pool. Golf and tennis are available nearby. A few miles away are outlet stores, the world's largest open-face granite quarry, and the famous frescoes of Ashe County.

Huntington Hall Bed and Breakfast ✪
500 VALLEY RIVER AVENUE, MURPHY, NORTH CAROLINA 28906

Tel: (704) 837-9567; (800) 824-6189
Best Time to Call: 8 AM–9 PM
Hosts: **Bob and Kate DeLong**
Location: **100 mi. N. of Atlanta, Georgia**
No. of Rooms: **5**
No. of Private Baths: **5**
Double/pb: **$65**
Single/pb: **$49**
Open: **All year**

Reduced Rates: **10% seniors; 15% Dec.–Feb., based on availability**
Breakfast: **Full**
Credit Cards: **AMEX, DC, DISC, MC, VISA**
Pets: **No**
Children: **Welcome**
Smoking: **Yes**
Social Drinking: **Permitted**
Airport/Station Pickup: **Yes**

Two huge maple trees shade this pleasant clapboard home, circa 1881; tall columns accent the front porch, and English ivy and Virginia creeper climb the low stone wall surrounding the property. Each spacious bedroom blends the old-world charm of tall windows, wooden floors, and Victorian decor with such modern amenities as cable TV and private baths. Wonderful breakfasts served on the sun porch precede the day's explorations of the historical district in nearby Brasstown, or of the Valley River Valley—original home of the Cherokee Indians and site of their "Trail of Tears." Both Bob and Kate are outdoor enthusiasts, eager to help guests plan white-water rafting trips on the Nanathala and Ocoee rivers and hikes in Great Smoky Mountain National Park.

The Aerie ✪
509 POLLOCK STREET, NEW BERN, NORTH CAROLINA 28560

Tel: (919) 636-5553; (800) 849-5553
Hosts: **Rick and Lois Cleveland**
Location: **120 mi. E of Raleigh**
No. of Rooms: **7**
No. of Private Baths: **7**
Double/pb: **$80–$85**
Single/pb: **$60**
Open: **All year**

Breakfast: **Full**
Credit Cards: **AMEX, MC, VISA**
Pets: **No**
Children: **Welcome**
Smoking: **Permitted**
Social Drinking: **Permitted**
Airport/Station Pickup: **Yes**

Just one block from Tryon Palace, the Aerie has the closest accommodations to all of New Bern's historic attractions. This Victorian inn was a private residence for almost a century. Today it is furnished with fine antiques and reproductions. Each of the seven individually decorated rooms has a modern bath, telephone, and cable TV. Complimentary wine, beer, soft drinks, and light refreshments are offered throughout your stay, and a generous country breakfast awaits you each morning in the dining room. Bicycles are available for touring the historic district and airport shuttle service can be arranged.

Harmony House Inn
215 POLLOCK STREET, NEW BERN, NORTH CAROLINA 28560

Tel: (919) 636-3810
Best Time to Call: 9 AM–9 PM
Hosts: A. E. and Diane Hansen
Location: 110 mi. SE of Raleigh
No. of Rooms: 9
No. of Private Baths: 9
Double/pb: $80
Single/pb: $55

Open: All year
Breakfast: Full
Credit Cards: AMEX, MC, VISA
Pets: No
Children: Welcome
Smoking: Permitted
Social Drinking: Permitted

Built in 1850, the inn is located in the historic district just four blocks from Tryon Palace and one block from the confluence of the Trent and Neuse rivers. About 7,000 square feet in area, the house is graced with spacious hallways and an aura of elegance. The air-conditioned guest accommodations are furnished with antiques and fine reproductions. You are welcome to help yourself to soft drinks and ice from the well-stocked guest refrigerator. Relax in the parlor, on the front porch with its rockers and swings, or in the pretty backyard.

New Berne House Bed and Breakfast Inn
709 BROAD STREET, NEW BERN, NORTH CAROLINA 28560

Tel: (919) 636-2250; (800) 842-7688
Hosts: Marcia Drum and Howard
    Bronson
Location: 1 mi. from Hwy. 70
No. of Rooms: 7
No. of Private Baths: 7
Double/pb: $82
Single/pb: $62
Open: All year

Reduced Rates: AAA, AARP
Breakfast: Full
Credit Cards: AMEX, MC, VISA
Pets: No
Children: Welcome, over 12
Smoking: No
Social Drinking: Permitted
Airport/Station Pickup: Yes

Located in the heart of New Bern's historic district, this brick Colonial is furnished in the style of an English country manor with a mixture of antiques, traditional pieces, and attic treasures. Guests are pampered with afternoon tea or coffee served in the parlor. A sweeping stairway leads upstairs to romantic bedchambers, one with a brass bed reportedly rescued in 1897 from a burning brothel. Breakfast specialties such as praline and cream waffles, honey-glazed ham, and homemade breads and muffins are served in the dining room. New Berne House is within walking distance of Tryon Palace, North Carolina's Colonial capitol, and the governor's mansion. Ask about the exciting Mystery Weekends.

The Tar Heel Inn
BOX 176, 205 CHURCH STREET, ORIENTAL, NORTH CAROLINA
28571

Tel: **(919) 249-1078**	Breakfast: **Full**
Best Time to Call: **7 AM–9 PM**	Credit Cards: **MC, VISA**
Hosts: **Patti and David Nelson**	Pets: **No**
Location: **24 mi. E of New Bern**	Children: **Prior arrangements**
No. of Rooms: 7	Smoking: **No**
No. of Private Baths: 7	Social Drinking: **Permitted**
Double/pb: **$65–$75**	Minimum Stay: **2 nights holiday**
Single/pb: **$55–$65**	**weekends**
Open: **Mar.–Nov.**	Airport/Station Pickup: **Yes**

A quiet fishing village on the Neuse River, Oriental is known as the sailing capital of North Carolina. Tar Heel is a spacious country inn with two brick patios and a large grassy lawn. Cheerfully printed wallpapers and upholstery fabrics give the interior an English feeling. Excellent restaurants, shops, tennis courts, and boating, swimming, and fishing areas are within walking distance. A full breakfast will bolster you for all those waterfront activities.

Key Falls Inn ✪
151 EVERETT ROAD, PISGAH FOREST, NORTH CAROLINA 28768

Tel: **(704) 884-7559**	Suites: **$85**
Best Time to Call: **10 AM–10 PM**	Open: **All year**
Hosts: **Clark and Patricia Grosvenor,**	Breakfast: **Full**
and Janet Fogleman	Credit Cards: **AMEX, DC, MC, VISA**
No. of Rooms: 4	Pets: **No**
No. of Private Baths: 4	Children: **Welcome, over 3**
Double/pb: **$55–$65**	Smoking: **No**
Single/pb: **$47.50–$57.50**	Social Drinking: **Permitted**

Visitors to this B&B will be able to make the most of western North Carolina's natural and cultural attractions. Key Falls Inn is situated on a 28-acre estate with its own tennis court, croquet course, pond, and outdoor barbecue. For quieter moments, sit on one of the porches and enjoy the mountain views. Music lovers will want to get tickets to the acclaimed Brevard Festival, an annual summer event.

The Oakwood Inn ✪
411 NORTH BLOODWORTH STREET, RALEIGH, NORTH CAROLINA
27604

Tel: **(919) 832-9712**	Host: **Terri Jones**
Best Time to Call: **9 AM–noon, 3 PM–**	No. of Rooms: 6
9 PM	No. of Private Baths: 6

Double/pb: **$75–$100**
Single/pb: **$65–$90**
Open: **All year**
Breakfast: **Full**
Credit Cards: **AMEX, DISC, MC, VISA**

Pets: **No**
Children: **Welcome, over 12**
Smoking: **Permitted**
Social Drinking: **Permitted**

Built in 1871, the inn is listed on the National Register of Historic Places. Recently restored to their prior elegance, all of the rooms are enhanced by the tasteful use of antique furnishings, appropriate draperies, and accessories. The inn is located within the 20-square-block area of homes built from 1879 to 1920, and visiting it is really like taking a step back in time into an era of horse-drawn carriages and gingerbread architecture. There are six colleges nearby offering cultural opportunities, and a number of museums for history buffs.

The 1868 Stewart-Marsh House ✪
220 SOUTH ELLIS STREET, SALISBURY, NORTH CAROLINA 28144

Tel: **(704) 633-6841**
Host: **Gerry Webster**
Location: **1.5 mi. from I-85, Exit 76B**
No. of Rooms: **2**
No. of Private Baths: **2**
Double/pb: **$50–$55**
Single/pb: **$45–$50**
Open: **All year**

Reduced Rates: **10% after 3rd night**
Breakfast: **Full**
Credit Cards: **MC, VISA**
Pets: **No**
Children: **Sometimes**
Smoking: **No**
Social Drinking: **Permitted**
Airport/Station Pickup: **Yes**

This gracious 1868 Federal-style home is located on a quiet, tree-lined street listed on the National Register of Historic Places. It is furnished with antiques and cherished family pieces reflecting the period immediately following the Civil War. You are welcome to enjoy the cozy library or relax on a wicker chair on the screened-in porch. Gerry is a tour guide and will be happy to conduct a personal tour of interesting local sights and architecture. Shops and restaurants are within walking distance.

Rowan Oak House ✪
208 SOUTH FULTON STREET, SALISBURY, NORTH CAROLINA 28144

Tel: **(704) 633-2086; (800) 786-0437**
Hosts: **Bill and Ruth Ann Coffey**
Location: **1 mi. from I-85**
No. of Rooms: **4**
No. of Private Baths: **2**
Double/pb: **$65–$95**
Single/pb: **$55–$85**
Open: **All year**

Reduced Rates: **10% seniors**
Breakfast: **Full**
Pets: **No**
Children: **Welcome, over 12**
Smoking: **Restricted**
Social Drinking: **Permitted**
Airport/Station Pickup: **Yes**
Foreign Languages: **Spanish**

Milton Brown built the Rowan Oak House for his bride, Fannie, in 1902. Set in the heart of the West Square historic district, this Queen Anne features a cupola, wraparound porch, and carved oak door. Step through the dark wood entry to see the intricate woodwork and stained glass. The original fixtures are well preserved and complemented by period furnishings and reproductions. Ruth Ann and Bill invite you to choose from four lavishly appointed guest rooms, including the master bedroom, which features a double Jacuzzi and a fireplace in the bathroom. Breakfast is served in your private quarters or downstairs in the formal dining room, beneath the painting of Queen Louise of Prussia. In the afternoon, tea or a glass of wine can be enjoyed in the garden, on the porch, or in the sitting room amid the curios and Victorian knickknacks. Your hosts can guide you to Salisbury's antebellum architecture and an abundance of nearby lakes, parks, and golf courses.

The Oaks
P.O. BOX 1008, SALUDA, NORTH CAROLINA 28773

Tel: **(704) 749-9613**	Open: **All year**
Best Time to Call: **Anytime**	Breakfast: **Full**
Hosts: **Ceri and Peggy Dando**	Credit Cards: **MC, VISA**
Location: **12 mi. S of Hendersonville**	Pets: **No**
No. of Rooms: **4**	Children: **No**
No. of Private Baths: **4**	Smoking: **No**
Double/pb: **$55–$58**	Social Drinking: **Permitted**
Guest Cottage: **$85**	

The Saluda mountain breezes benefit this turreted Victorian, built in 1894. Your hosts provide a low-key, welcoming atmosphere. Bedrooms are decorated in period style, with interesting antique "bits and bobs." Your tariff includes a generous breakfast for two. The surrounding porch offers a place for you to relax and mull over plans before you amble down to Main Street's many antique and craft shops. Carl Sandberg's home and Flat Rock Playhouse are nearby.

Turby Villa B&B ✪
STAR ROUTE 1, BOX 48, SPARTA, NORTH CAROLINA 28675

Tel: **(919) 372-8490**	Open: **All year**
Host: **Mrs. R. E. Turbiville**	Breakfast: **Full**
No. of Rooms: **3**	Pets: **No**
No. of Private Baths: **3**	Children: **Welcome**
Double/pb: **$50**	Smoking: **Permitted**
Single/pb: **$35**	Social Drinking: **Permitted**

At an altitude of 3,000 feet, this contemporary two-story brick home is the centerpiece of a 20-acre farm. The house is surrounded by an acre of trees and manicured lawns, and the lovely views are of the scenic Blue Ridge Mountains. Breakfast is served either on the enclosed porch with its white wicker furnishings or in the more formal dining room with its Early American–style furnishings. Mrs. Turbiville takes justifiable pride in her attractive, well-maintained B&B.

The Richmond Inn
101 PINE AVENUE, SPRUCE PINE, NORTH CAROLINA 28777

Tel: **(704) 765-6993**
Best Time to Call: **7 AM–11 PM**
Hosts: **Lenore Boucher and Bill Ansley**
Location: **4 mi. from Blue Ridge
  Pkwy., Exit 331**
No. of Rooms: 7
No. of Private Baths: 7
Double/pb: **$55–$75**

Single/pb: **$45–$65**
Open: **All year**
Breakfast: **Full**
Credit Cards: **MC, VISA**
Pets: **No**
Children: **Welcome**
Smoking: **No**
Social Drinking: **Permitted**

Surrounded by towering pines, this white wooden house trimmed with black window shutters has a stone terrace and rock walls. It is furnished in a comfortable blend of antiques and family treasures. Most mornings, Lenore fixes a Southern repast with bacon, eggs, and grits. Spruce Pine is the mineral capital of the world, and panning for gemstones such as garnets and amethysts is a popular pastime. Hiking the Appalachian Trail, playing golf, or working out at your hosts' community spa will keep you in shape. Internationally known artists schedule shows throughout the year.

Cedar Hill Farm B&B ◯
ROUTE 1, BOX 492, STATESVILLE, NORTH CAROLINA 28677

Tel: **(704) 873-4332**
Best Time to Call: **Before 2 PM; after
  5 PM**
Hosts: **Brenda and Jim Vernon**
Location: **45 mi. N of Charlotte**
No. of Rooms: 2
No. of Private Baths: 2
Double/pb: **$50**
Guest Cottage: **$70**

Open: **All year**
Breakfast: **Full**
Credit Cards: **MC, VISA**
Pets: **Sometimes**
Children: **Welcome**
Smoking: **No**
Social Drinking: **Permitted**

A three-story Federal farmhouse furnished with antique and country pieces, Cedar Hill is surrounded by 32 acres of rolling green, the better to feed the Vernons' sheep. Brenda and Jim sell fleece coverlets and crafts from their own hand-spun wool; they also make furniture and cure turkey and ham in a smokehouse on site. Stay in the farmhouse or in a private cottage. Either way you'll have an air-conditioned room with a telephone and cable TV. The country breakfasts will leave you full, thanks to servings of ham, sausage, fruit, potatoes, and butter-milk biscuits with homemade preserves. You can work off calories swimming in your hosts' pool or playing badminton, but you might want to relax in a porch rocker or hammock first.

Madelyn's Bed & Breakfast ✪
514 CARROLL STREET, STATESVILLE, NORTH CAROLINA 28677

Tel: **(704) 872-3973**	Reduced Rates: **10% seniors**
Best Time to Call: **7 AM–9 PM**	Breakfast: **Full**
Hosts: **John and Madelyn Hill**	Credit Cards: **MC, VISA**
Location: **45 mi. N of Charlotte**	Pets: **No**
No. of Rooms: **3**	Children: **Welcome, over 10**
No. of Private Baths: **3**	Smoking: **No**
Double/pb: **$55–$65**	Social Drinking: **Permitted**
Open: **All year**	Airport/Station Pickup: **Yes**

Madelyn's B&B is nestled in a quiet neighborhood near downtown, historic districts, and a two-mile par course; outlet shopping is nearby. For more fun, Statesville hosts two annual events—the Carolina Dogwood Festival in the spring and the National Balloon Rally in the fall. Madelyn and John try to make each guest feel special. When you arrive, you'll find fresh fruit, candies, and homemade cookies in your room. A sumptuous breakfast is served where you want it: in the formal dining room, before a cozy fire in the breakfast room, on the sun porch, or even in bed. Your hosts are glad to cater to visitors' special dietary needs.

Scott's Keep ✪
308 WALNUT STREET, P.O. BOX 1425, SWANSBORO, NORTH CAROLINA 28584

Tel: **(919) 326-1257; (800) 348-1257**	Open: **All year**
Best Time to Call: **After 3:30 PM**	Reduced Rates: **15% weekly**
Hosts: **Frank and Norma Scott**	Breakfast: **Full**
Location: **150 mi. SE of Raleigh**	Credit Cards: **MC, VISA**
No. of Rooms: **3**	Pets: **No**
Max. No. Sharing Bath: **4**	Children: **Welcome, over 6**
Double/sb: **$40**	Smoking: **Permitted**
Single/sb: **$30**	Social Drinking: **Permitted**

This simple contemporary is located on a quiet street two blocks from the waterfront. Your hosts want you to feel right at home in the bright, spacious living room and comfortable guest rooms. The larger bedroom is decorated with wicker and features an antique trunk, a queen-size bed, and a colorful quilt. The smaller bedroom is furnished in classic maple with a double bed and grandmother's quilt. For breakfast, Norma serves blueberry or apple spice muffins with fruit and homemade jellies. This historic seaside village is filled with inviting shops and waterside seafood restaurants. Your hosts will point the way to beautiful beaches, waterskiing, sailing, and windsurfing.

Little Warren ✪
304 EAST PARK AVENUE, TARBORO, NORTH CAROLINA 27886

Tel: **(919) 823-1314**
Hosts: **Patsy and Tom Miller**
Location: **20 mi. E of Rocky Mount**
No. of Rooms: **3**
No. of Private Baths: **3**
Double/pb: **$65**
Single/pb: **$58**
Open: **All year**

Breakfast: **Full**
Credit Cards: **AMEX, DISC, MC, VISA**
Pets: **No**
Children: **Welcome, over 4**
Smoking: **Permitted**
Social Drinking: **Permitted**
Airport/Station Pickup: **Yes**
Foreign Languages: **Spanish**

Little Warren is actually a large and gracious family home built in 1913. It is located along the Albemarle Trail in Tarboro's historic district. The deeply set, wraparound porch overlooks one of the last originally chartered town commons still in existence. Inside, you'll find rooms of beautiful antiques from England and America, many of which can be purchased. In the morning, choose from a full English, Southern, or Continental breakfast.

Barkley House Bed & Breakfast ✪
ROUTE 6, BOX 12, TAYLORSVILLE, NORTH CAROLINA 28681

Tel: (704) 632-9060
Best Time to Call: Mornings
Host: Phyllis Barkley
Location: 60 mi. NW of Charlotte
No. of Rooms: 2
No. of Private Baths: 2
Double/pb: $49
Single/pb: $38
Open: All year
Reduced Rates: 10% families, seniors; 15% weekly

Breakfast: Full
Credit Cards: AMEX
Wheelchair-Accessible: Yes
Pets: Sometimes
Children: Welcome
Smoking: Permitted
Social Drinking: Permitted
Airport/Station Pickup: Yes

After staying in European B&Bs, Phyllis opened the first one in Taylorsville, a small town surrounded by mountains. Barkley House is a white Colonial with yellow shutters and a gracious front porch with four columns. The furnishings are homey, combining antiques and pieces from the '50s. Haystack eggs and fruity banana splits are two of Phyllis's breakfast specialties; she'll be happy to cater to guests on restricted diets.

Mill Farm Inn ✪
P.O. BOX 1251, TRYON, NORTH CAROLINA 28782

Tel: (704) 859-6992; (800) 545-6992
Best Time to Call: Mornings
Hosts: Chip and Penny Kessler
Location: 45 mi. SE of Asheville
No. of Rooms: 10
No. of Private Baths: 10
Double/pb: $55
Single/pb: $45
Suites: $65–$100

Open: All year
Reduced Rates: 10% seniors
Breakfast: Continental
Wheelchair-Accessible: Yes
Pets: No
Children: Welcome
Smoking: No
Social Drinking: Permitted
Foreign Languages: French

The Pacolet River flows past the edge of this three-and-one-half-acre property in the foothills of the Blue Ridge Mountains. Sitting porches and the living room with fireplace are fine spots to relax. A hearty breakfast of fresh fruit, cereal, English muffins, preserves, and coffee is served. Craft shops, galleries, and antiquing will keep you busy.

Pamlico House ✪
400 EAST MAIN STREET, WASHINGTON, NORTH CAROLINA 27889

Tel: (919) 946-7184
Best Time to Call: 9 AM–8 PM
Hosts: Lawrence and Jeanne Hervey
Location: 20 mi. E of Greenville

No. of Rooms: 4
No. of Private Baths: 4
Double/pb: $55–$65
Single/pb: $45–$55

Open: **All year**
Reduced Rates: **10% weekly**
Breakfast: **Full**
Credit Cards: **MC, VISA**
Pets: **No**

Children: **Welcome**
Smoking: **Permitted**
Social Drinking: **Permitted**
Airport/Station Pickup: **Yes**

Located in the center of a small, historic town, this stately Colonial Revival home's large rooms are a perfect foil for the carefully chosen antique furnishings. Guests are drawn to the classic Victorian parlor or to the spacious wraparound porch for relaxing conversation. Take a self-guided walking tour of the historic district or a stroll along the quaint waterfront. Recreational pleasures abound. Nature enthusiasts enjoy the wildlife and exotic plants in nearby Goose Creek State Park. Should you get homesick for your favorite pet, Lawrence and Jeanne will share theirs.

Belle Meade Inn ○

804 BALSAM ROAD, HAZELWOOD, NORTH CAROLINA 28738 (MAILING ADDRESS: P.O. BOX 1319, WAYNESVILLE, NORTH CAROLINA 28786)

Tel: **(704) 456-3234**
Hosts: **Larry Hanson and William Shaw**
Location: **27 mi. W of Asheville**
No. of Rooms: **4**
No. of Private Baths: **4**
Double/pb: **$50–$55**
Single/pb: **$45–$50**

Open: **Apr.–Jan.**
Reduced Rates: **10% AARP; weekly**
Breakfast: **Full**
Credit Cards: **DISC, MC, VISA**
Pets: **No**
Children: **Welcome, over 6**
Smoking: **No**
Social Drinking: **Permitted**

Nestled in the mountains, and within easy reach of the Great Smoky National Park, this elegant home is a frame dwelling built in the craftsman style popular in the early 1900s. The warm richness of the chestnut woodwork in the formal rooms and the large stone fireplace in the living room complement the appealing blend of antique and traditional furnishings. The friendly attention to guests' needs is exemplified in such thoughtful touches as "early bird" coffee brought to your door, complimentary refreshments on the veranda, and fresh flowers and mints in your room. Nearby attractions include Biltmore House, Catalooche Ski Slope, mountain art and craft festivals, and white-water rafting and tubing.

Anderson Guest House ✪
520 ORANGE STREET, WILMINGTON, NORTH CAROLINA 28401

Tel: **(919) 343-8128**	Open: **All year**
Best Time to Call: **8 AM–5 PM**	Breakfast: **Full**
Hosts: **Landon and Connie Anderson**	Pets: **Sometimes**
No. of Rooms: **2**	Children: **Welcome**
No. of Private Baths: **2**	Smoking: **No**
Double/pb: **$65**	Social Drinking: **Permitted**
Single/pb: **$50**	Airport/Station Pickup: **Yes**

This 19th-century town house has a private guest house overlooking a garden. The bedrooms have ceiling fans, fireplaces, and air-conditioning. Enjoy cool drinks upon arrival and a liqueur before bed. Breakfast specialties are eggs Mornay, blueberry cobbler, and crêpes. Your host can point out the sights of this historic town and direct you to the beaches.

Catherine's Inn on Orange ✪
NO. 410 ORANGE STREET, WILMINGTON, NORTH CAROLINA 28401

Tel: **(919) 251-0863; (800) 476-0723**	Open: **All year**
Best Time to Call: **8 AM–10 PM**	Reduced Rates: **Available**
Hosts: **Catherine and Walter Ackiss**	Breakfast: **Full**
Location: **In Wilmington historical district**	Credit Cards: **AMEX, MC, VISA**
	Pets: **No**
No. of Rooms: **3**	Children: **Welcome, by arrangement**
No. of Private Baths: **3**	Smoking: **Restricted**
Double/pb: **$60**	Social Drinking: **Permitted**
Single/pb: **$55**	Airport/Station Pickup: **Yes**

An Italianate residence built by a merchant and Civil War veteran in 1875, this B&B has blue clapboard, white trim, and a white picket fence. All bedrooms have fireplaces. The grounds include a spacious garden and a small swimming pool. Guests are within walking distance of museums, historic buildings, and antique shops; beaches and golf courses are minutes away by car. Morning coffee is served in the library, followed by breakfast in the dining room.

Murchison House B&B Inn
305 SOUTH 3RD STREET, WILMINGTON, NORTH CAROLINA 28401

Tel: **(919) 343-8580**	Breakfast: **Full**
Best Time to Call: **Before 5 PM**	Credit Cards: **AMEX, MC, VISA**
Host: **Lucy H. Curry**	Pets: **No**
No. of Rooms: **3**	Children: **Welcome**
No. of Private Baths: **3**	Smoking: **Permitted**
Double/pb: **$65**	Social Drinking: **Permitted**
Single/pb: **$55**	Airport/Station Pickup: **Yes**
Open: **All year**	

Built in 1876, Murchison House is an example of modified Victorian Gothic architecture. The back of the house faces a formal garden and courtyard. The Chippendale influence is reflected in all the interior woodwork and trim. Antiques and reproductions, along with the elegant parquet floors and the many unusual fireplaces throughout, lend charm and warmth. Feel welcome to curl up with a book in the Mission oak–paneled library. Located in the heart of the Wilmington historic district, it is within easy walking distance of shops, restaurants, churches, and the Cape Fear River.

The Wine House B&B ✪
311 COLLAGE LANE, WILMINGTON, NORTH CAROLINA 28401

Tel: **(919) 763-0511**	Open: **All year**
Best Time to Call: **8 AM–9 PM**	Reduced Rates: **10% seniors**
Host: **Kathleen Benson**	Breakfast: **Continental**
Location: **10 mi. NW of Raleigh**	Pets: **Sometimes**
No. of Rooms: **2**	Children: **Welcome, downstairs only**
No. of Private Baths: **2**	Smoking: **No**
Double/pb: **$69.70**	Social Drinking: **Permitted**
Single/pb: **$65**	Airport/Station Pickup: **Yes**

Stay in a winery (circa 1863) that has been lovingly restored to accommodate two large guest suites decorated with antiques and oriental rugs. Each room has a private bath, wet bar with refrigerator, fireplace, and ceiling fans. Enjoy the Charlestonian courtyard or walk to nearby restaurants, museums, art galleries, antique shops, and river.

Miss Betty's Bed & Breakfast Inn ✪
600 WEST NASH STREET, WILSON, NORTH CAROLINA 27893

Tel: **(919) 243-4447; (800) 258-2058** (reservations only)	Suites: **$75**
	Open: **All year**
Best Time to Call: **8 AM–10 PM**	Breakfast: **Full**
Hosts: **Elizabeth A. and Fred Spitz**	Credit Cards: **AMEX, DISC, MC, VISA**
Location: **50 mi. E of Raleigh**	Pets: **No**
No. of Rooms: **8**	Children: **No**
No. of Private Baths: **8**	Smoking: **Permitted**
Double/pb: **$60–$75**	Social Drinking: **Permitted**
Single/pb: **$50–$60**	Airport/Station Pickup: **Yes**

Miss Betty's bathes the business traveler and the vacationer in Victorian elegance and beauty, offering peace and tranquillity in a warm, friendly setting. Guests in the Davis-Whitehead-Harris house, circa 1858, which is listed on the National Register of Historic Places, are staying in one of Wilson's oldest homes. The Riley house, circa 1900, also on the premises, offers more lodging, plus a conference room equipped with audio/visual aids. Both homes feature cable TV, phones, and zoned heating and air-conditioning. Nearby are four beautiful golf courses, many tennis courts, and an Olympic-size pool. Collectors take note: Wilson's numerous antique shops earn it the title of "antique capital of North Carolina."

Lady Anne's Victorian Bed & Breakfast
612 SUMMIT STREET, WINSTON-SALEM, NORTH CAROLINA 27101

Tel: **(919) 724-1074**	Open: **All year**
Best Time to Call: **8 AM–9 PM**	Reduced Rates: **$10 less suites, Sun.–Thurs.**
Host: **Shelley Kirley**	
Location: **100 mi. W of Raleigh**	Breakfast: **Full**
No. of Rooms: **4**	Pets: **No**
No. of Private Baths: **4**	Children: **Welcome, over 12, infants under 7 months**
Double/pb: **$55–$85**	
Single/pb: **$40**	Smoking: **Permitted**
Suites: **$85–$95; sleeps 4**	Social Drinking: **Permitted**

Warm southern hospitality surrounds you in this elegant 1890 Victorian. An aura of romance touches each suite or room, all individually decorated with period antiques and treasures and modern luxuries. Some rooms have two-person whirlpool, cable TV, stereo, telephone, and refrigerator. An evening dessert and tea tray served in the privacy of your room helps you relax; a delicious full breakfast is served on fine china and lace in the morning. Lady Anne's is ideally situated near downtown attractions, performances, restaurants, shops and Old Salem historic village. The hostess, previously a recreational therapist, now enjoys innkeeping and antique collecting.

Mickle House ✪

**927 WEST FIFTH STREET, WINSTON-SALEM, NORTH CAROLINA
27101**

Tel: **(919) 722-9045**
Best Time to Call: **9 AM–noon; 6–10
PM**
Host: **Barbara Garrison**
Location: **1 mi. from Rte. 40, Broad St.
exit**
No. of Rooms: **2**
No. of Private Baths: **1**
Max. No. Sharing Bath: **3**
Double/pb: **$65**
Single/pb: **$60**

Double/sb: **$55**
Single/sb: **$50**
Open: **All year**
Reduced Rates: **Available**
Breakfast: **Full**
Credit Cards: **MC, VISA**
Pets: **No**
Children: **No**
Smoking: **No**
Social Drinking: **Permitted**

Step back in time to visit a quaint Victorian cottage painted a soft yellow, with dark green shutters and gingerbread trim. The fully restored home, located in the National Historic District of West End, is furnished with lovely antiques, such as the canopy and poster beds in the guest rooms. Dessert is served in the afternoon or evening, and a full breakfast, with fresh fruit and freshly baked breads and muffins, awaits you in the morning. Old Salem, the Medical Center, and the Convention Center are five minutes away; fine restaurants, parks, shops, and the library are within walking distance.

Wachovia B&B, Inc. ✪

**513 WACHOVIA STREET, WINSTON-SALEM, NORTH CAROLINA
27101**

Tel: **(919) 777-0332**
Best Time to Call: **9 AM–5 PM**
Host: **Carol Royals**
Location: **½ mi. S of Winston-Salem**
No. of Rooms: **5**
No. of Private Baths: **2**
Max. No. Sharing Bath: **4**
Double/pb: **$55**
Single/pb: **$45**

Double/sb: **$45**
Single/sb: **$35**
Open: **All year**
Breakfast: **Continental**
Pets: **No**
Children: **Welcome (crib)**
Smoking: **No**
Social Drinking: **Permitted**

This white and rose Victorian cottage, with its appealing wraparound porch, is just outside the Old Salem historic district, and antique shops, excellent restaurants, and a scenic strollway are within a one-block radius. Noted institutions like North Carolina School of the Arts and Wake Forest University are only a few miles away. This is a good area for cycling, and guests may borrow the house bicycles. Carol serves breakfasts of juice, fruit, yogurt, muesli, and baked goods she learned to make while traveling in Europe. Later in the day, she offers complimentary tea, wine, and cheese.

NORTH DAKOTA

- Stanley

Carrington •

- Scranton

Kirkland Bed and Breakfast
RR 2, BOX 18, CARRINGTON, NORTH DAKOTA 58421

Tel: (701) 652-2775
Hosts: James and Maria Harmon
Location: 3 mi. N of Carrington
No. of Rooms: 3
Max. No. Sharing Bath: 4
Double/sb: $50
Single/sb: $40
Suites: $80

Open: All year
Breakfast: Full
Other Meals: Available
Pets: No
Children: Welcome
Smoking: No
Social Drinking: Permitted

Welcome to the Harmon family's farm, established in 1886 by the
proprietors' great-grandparents. Enrolled on the National Register of
Historic Places, Kirkland remains a working farm, producing wheat,
corn, beans, and sunflowers. The Colonial Plantation–style home,
which dates to 1910, has a wraparound veranda with stately columns,
a large open stairway, oak woodwork, and windows of stained and
leaded glass. In addition to books of collector quality, the library
contains Indian artifacts accumulated by the farm founder, who found
time to serve as a territorial sheriff, Indian agent, and legislator.

Breakfast specialties include blueberry pancakes, deer sausage, and muffins, accompanied by real maple syrup and homemade jams.

Historic Jacobson Mansion ✪
RR 2, BOX 27, SCRANTON, NORTH DAKOTA 58653

Tel: **(701) 275-8291**
Best Time to Call: **Evenings**
Hosts: **Melvin and Charlene Pierce**
Location: **15 mi. N of Scranton**
No. of Rooms: **2**
Max. No. Sharing Bath: **4**
Double/sb: **$50**
Single/sb: **$40**
Open: **All year**

Reduced Rates: **10% after 2nd night; 10% seniors**
Breakfast: **Full**
Other Meals: **Available**
Pets: **Yes**
Children: **Welcome**
Smoking: **No**
Social Drinking: **Permitted**

This three-story Queen Anne Victorian mansion was built in 1895 by a gentleman farmer and merchant. In 1988 it was rescued from the wrecking ball and moved 450 miles to its present location on a working farm and ranch. Melvin and Charlene have painstakingly restored their home to its former elegance, filling it with antiques and modern conveniences. They invite you and your family to experience their rural activities, from raising cattle and sheep to seeding and farming their lush pastures.

The Triple T Ranch ✪
RR 1, BOX 93, STANLEY, NORTH DAKOTA 58784

Tel: **(701) 628-2418**
Best Time to Call: **8 AM–noon**
Hosts: **Joyce and Fred Evans**
Location: **60 mi. W of Minot**
No. of Rooms: **2**
Max. No. Sharing Bath: **4**
Double/sb: **$30**
Single/sb: **$25**

Open: **All year**
Reduced Rates: **Available**
Breakfast: **Full**
Pets: **Sometimes**
Children: **Welcome (crib)**
Smoking: **No**
Social Drinking: **No**

You're warmly invited to come to Joyce and Fred's rustic ranch home, where you're welcome to take a seat in front of the stone fireplace, put your feet up, and relax. There's a lovely view of the hills and the valley, and their herd of cattle is an impressive sight. Lake Sakakawea, for seasonal recreation such as fishing and swimming, is 11 miles away. Indian powwows, area rodeos, and hunting for Indian artifacts are fun. The State Fair is held every July.

OHIO

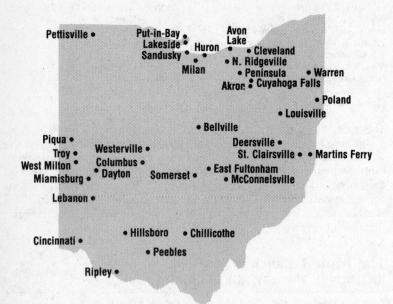

Pettisville •
Put-in-Bay •
Avon Lake •
Lakeside •
Huron •
Sandusky •
• Cleveland
• N. Ridgeville
Milan •
• Peninsula
• Warren
Akron •
Cuyahoga Falls
• Poland
• Louisville
• Bellville
Piqua •
Deersville •
Troy •
Westerville •
St. Clairsville •
• Martins Ferry
West Milton •
Columbus •
Miamisburg •
Dayton •
Somerset •
• East Fultonham
• McConnelsville
Lebanon •
Cincinnati •
• Hillsboro
• Chillicothe
• Peebles
Ripley •

Helen's Hospitality House
1096 PALMETTO, AKRON, OHIO 44306

Tel: **(216) 724-7151; 724-3034**
Best Time to Call: **8 AM–11 PM**
Host: **Helen Claytor**
Location: **1 mi. from I-77 S, Exit 123B**
No. of Rooms: **2**
No. of Private Baths: **1**
Max. No. Sharing Bath: **4**
Double/pb: **$30**
Single/pb: **$25**
Double/sb: **$30**

Single/sb: **$25**
Open: **All year**
Reduced Rates: **Weekly**
Breakfast: **Full**
Pets: **No**
Children: **Welcome, over 10**
Smoking: **No**
Social Drinking: **Permitted**
Airport/Station Pickup: **Yes**

Located in a quiet neighborhood on a dead-end street, Helen's centrally air-conditioned house is a bit of country in the city. It is a renovated old farmhouse furnished with antiques and reproductions. On warm days, breakfast is served on the screened, glass-enclosed porch. Quaker Square, Akron University, the Firestone PGA, and Portage Lakes are just a few of the local attractions. Helen is a retired teacher who enjoys being a B&B hostess.

Portage House ✪

601 COPLEY ROAD, STATE ROUTE 162, AKRON, OHIO 44320

Tel: (216) 535-1952
Best Time to Call: 8 AM–11 PM
Host: Jeanne Pinnick
Location: 2 mi. from I-77
No. of Rooms: 5
No. of Private Baths: 1
Max. No. Sharing Bath: 4
Double/pb: $35
Double/sb: $35

Single/sb: $30
Open: Feb. 1–Nov. 30
Reduced Rates: $3 less after 1st night
Breakfast: Full
Pets: Restricted
Children: Welcome (crib)
Smoking: No
Social Drinking: Permitted
Foreign Languages: French, Spanish

Steeped in history, this gracious Tudor home, nestled in a parklike setting, dates back to 1917. A stone wall down the street served as the western boundary of the United States in 1785. Jeanne and her late husband Harry, a physics professor at the nearby University of Akron, opened their B&B in 1982. Jeanne manages the B&B and has the coffeepot on with refreshments available for arriving guests. If bread is being baked, you'll be offered some hot out of the oven.

Williams House ✪

249 VINEWOOD, AVON LAKE, OHIO 44012

Tel: (216) 933-5089
Best Time to Call: 9 AM–9 PM
Host: Margaret Williams
Location: 20 mi. W of Cleveland
No. of Rooms: 1
No. of Private Baths: 1
Double/pb: $40
Single/pb: $25

Open: Closed Christmas
Reduced Rates: 20% seniors
Breakfast: Full
Pets: No
Children: No
Smoking: No
Social Drinking: Permitted
Airport/Station Pickup: Yes

Located a mile from the Lake Erie public beach, Margaret lives in a quiet residential neighborhood. The house is comfortably decorated in a harmonious blend of styles. She serves beverages and snacks upon your arrival, and will help you plan a pleasant visit. Breakfast is a dandy, from juice to cereal to eggs to bacon to coffee or tea.

The Frederick Fitting House ✪
72 FITTING AVENUE, BELLVILLE, OHIO 44813

Tel: **(419) 886-2863**
Hosts: **Ramon and Suzanne Wilson**
Location: **50 mi. N of Columbus**
No. of Rooms: **3**
No. of Private Baths: **3**
Double/pb: **$54–$66**
Single/pb: **$44–$56**
Open: **All year**

Breakfast: **Full**
Other Meals: **Available**
Pets: **No**
Children: **Welcome, over 8**
Smoking: **Permitted**
Social Drinking: **Permitted**
Airport/Station Pickup: **Yes**

Named for the prominent Bellville citizen who built it in 1863, the Frederick Fitting House is a restored Italianate home with a hand-stenciled dining room and a garden gazebo. Ramon and Suzanne are avid music buffs; you are welcome to play selections from their jazz and classical collection as you lounge by the sitting-room fire. Nearby, Mohican and Malabar Farm State Parks offer a variety of activities, from cross-country skiing to canoeing. Kingwood Garden, Amish country, and Kenyon, Wooster, and Ashland colleges are a short drive away.

The Old McDill-Anderson Place ✪
3656 POLK HOLLOW ROAD, CHILLICOTHE, OHIO 45601

Tel: **(614) 774-1770**
Hosts: **Ruth and Del Meyer**
Location: **45 mi. S of Columbus**
No. of Rooms: **4**
No. of Private Baths: **3**
Max. No. Sharing Bath: **4**
Double/pb: **$65**
Single/pb: **$50**
Double/sb: **$55**

Single/sb: **$40**
Open: **All year**
Reduced Rates: **20% weekly; 10%
 after 3rd night**
Breakfast: **Full**
Pets: **No**
Children: **Sometimes**
Smoking: **No**
Social Drinking: **No**

This two-story 1864 brick Italianate residence was homesteaded in 1798. Your hosts pursue a variety of interests, including fine wood-working and historic preservation. They cater to their guests' needs by combining some of the bedrooms to make suites—a boon to families. Some rooms have working fireplaces or wood stoves, down comforters and feather beds, especially nice on chilly nights. Breakfast and snacks feature seasonal food and "from scratch" preparation. Chillicothe was Ohio's first capital. You will enjoy the early architecture and fine museums.

Auburn Suite Bed & Breakfast
312 MILTON STREET, CINCINNATI, OHIO 45210

Tel: (513) 651-4220
Best Time to Call: **Anytime**
Hosts: **Mr. and Mrs. Jill Kartisek and Kris Carmichael**
Location: **1½ mi. N of downtown Cincinnati**
Suites: **$69**
Open: **All year**

Reduced Rates: **10% seniors; extended stays**
Breakfast: **Continental**
Pets: **By arrangement**
Children: **Welcome**
Smoking: **Permitted**
Social Drinking: **Permitted**
Airport/Station Pickup: **Yes**

Stay in a spacious suite in the Prospect Hill historic district, within walking distance of downtown Cincinnati and the riverwalk, and accessible by public transportation to most area hospitals, universities, playhouses, and museums. Ask your hosts for directions. The suite's decor is warm and inviting, with polished hardwood floors and the original Greek Revival fireplace; depending on the season, you may see the Reds' fireworks from the living room window. A well-stocked, fully equipped kitchen allows you to make your own meals, but the home-baked breakfast treats, presented at your leisure, are on your hosts.

Berry Hill House ○
9694 BERRY HILL DRIVE, CINCINNATI, OHIO 45241

Tel: (513) 777-4613, 753-1600
Best Time to Call: **9 AM–5 PM**
Hosts: **Ed and Inge Roll**
Location: **3 mi. from I-75 or I-71**
No. of Rooms: **1**
No. of Private Baths: **1**
Double/pb: **$45**
Single/pb: **$40**

Open: **All year**
Breakfast: **Full**
Pets: **Sometimes**
Children: **Welcome**
Smoking: **Permitted**
Social Drinking: **Permitted**
Airport/Station Pickup: **Yes**
Foreign Languages: **German**

When you arrive at this lovely brick house, be prepared for an abundance of hospitality. Ed and Inge have traveled extensively and know exactly how to make a guest's stay special. It is a short drive to the city's historic areas, cultural activities, sports attractions, and excellent dining possibilities. Kings Island, a famous golf center, is nearby.

Prospect Hill Bed and Breakfast ○
408 BOAL STREET, CINCINNATI, OHIO 45210

Tel: (513) 421-4408
Best Time to Call: **Anytime**
Host: **Gary Hackney**

Location: **½ mi. from I-71**
No. of Rooms: **3**
No. of Private Baths: **1**

Max. No. Sharing Bath: **4**
Double/pb: **$89**
Single/pb: **$89**
Double/sb: **$69**
Single/sb: **$69**
Open: **All year**
Reduced Rates: **10% weekly**

Breakfast: **Full**
Credit Cards: **MC, VISA**
Pets: **No**
Children: **Welcome, over 10**
Smoking: **No**
Social Drinking: **Permitted**

This restored Italianate Victorian town house was built in 1867 on Prospect Hill, Cincinnati's first suburb, now a national historic district. The original woodwork, doors, hardware, and light fixtures remain intact—your host is interested in historic preservation. All the rooms have spectacular views, fireplaces, and period antique furniture. It's only a fifteen-minute walk from here to Fountain Square or the Ohio River. Mt. Adams, the University of Cincinnati, Playhouse in the Park, the Music Hall, Eden Park, the William Howard Taft Historic Site, and most area museums and hospitals are within a mile.

Private Lodgings, Inc. ✪
P.O. BOX 18590, CLEVELAND, OHIO 44118

Tel: **(216) 249-0400**
Best Time to Call: **Weekdays 9 AM–noon; 3–5 PM**
Coordinators: **Elaine Phillips and Roberta Cahen**
States/Regions Covered: **Cleveland**

Rates (Single/Double):
Modest: **$32 / $40**
Average: **$45 / $60**
Luxury: **$65 / $90**
Credit Cards: **No**

This is a city with world-renowned cultural and biomedical resources, as well as major corporations and recreational areas. Special attention is given to the needs of relocating and visiting professionals, out-patients, and relatives of hospital inpatients, as well as vacationers. Every effort is made to accommodate persons with physical handicaps. Discounted rates are provided for extended stays. Case Western Reserve, John Carroll, and Cleveland State universities are convenient to the B&Bs. A $5 surcharge is made for one-night stays. Office is closed on Wednesday and Saturday.

Harrison House ✪
313 WEST 5TH AVENUE, COLUMBUS, OHIO 43201

Tel: **(614) 421-2202; (800) 827-4203**
Best Time to Call: **Anytime**
Hosts: **Maryanne and Dick Olson**
No. of Rooms: **4**
No. of Private Baths: **4**
Double/pb: **$84**
Single/pb: **$74**
Open: **All year**

Breakfast: **Full**
Credit Cards: **MC, VISA**
Pets: **No**
Children: **Welcome**
Smoking: **No**
Social Drinking: **Permitted**
Airport Pickup: **Yes**

At Harrison House, original cut-glass windows, magnificent wood-work, elegant lace curtains, and picturesque landscaping encourage you to escape back to the past. This Queen Anne Victorian, built in 1890, is listed on the National Register of Historic Places. The B&B is located within walking distance of Battelle Institute and Ohio State University, while downtown Columbus, City Center, and the airport are only minutes away. Breakfast specialties include cinnamon grape-fruit, lemon puff crêpes, and Swedish pancakes.

Studio 12 Bed and Breakfast ✪
2850 BAILEY ROAD, CUYAHOGA FALLS, OHIO 44221

Tel: **(216) 928-5843**	Open: **All year**
Host: **Edith L. Stinaff**	Reduced Rates: **10% seniors; after 1st**
Location: **6 mi. N of Akron; 7 mi.**	**night**
from I-80	Breakfast: **Full**
No. of Rooms: **2**	Children: **Welcome (crib)**
Max. No. Sharing Bath: **4**	Smoking: **No**
Double/sb: **$35**	Social Drinking: **Permitted**
Single/sb: **$25**	

Edith Stinaff offers attractive accommodations for guests in the new addition to her home, a 1930s brick bungalow. Guest quarters consist of two bedrooms on the second floor with a studio living room and bath. In the morning your host serves a hearty breakfast of scrambled eggs, fresh fruit, bacon, and warm muffins or toast. Studio 12 is convenient to the University of Akron, Kent State University, Blossom Music Center, and Hale Farm.

Candlewick Bed & Breakfast ✪
4991 BATH ROAD, DAYTON, OHIO 45424

Tel: **(513) 233-9297**	Open: **All year**
Hosts: **George and Nancy Thompson**	Breakfast: **Continental**
Location: **10 mi. NE of Dayton**	Pets: **No**
No. of Rooms: **2**	Children: **No**
Max. No. Sharing Bath: **4**	Smoking: **No**
Double/sb: **$45–$50**	Social Drinking: **No**
Single/sb: **$35**	Airport Pickup: **Yes**

This tranquil Dutch Colonial home sits atop a hill on five rolling acres. George, a retired engineer, and Nancy, a retired teacher, invite you to spend a quiet, restful night in comfortable rooms containing a charm-ing blend of antiques and Colonial and country furnishings. Continen-tal breakfast includes fresh fruit and juice, choice homemade pastries, and freshly brewed coffee. Weather permitting, enjoy breakfast on the screened porch overlooking a large pond often visited by wild ducks and geese. Convenient to Wright-Patterson Air Force Base and Museum and two major universities, Candlewick is a peaceful retreat, perfect for either business or pleasure.

Prices' Steamboat House B&B ✪
6 JOSIE STREET, DAYTON, OHIO 45403

Tel: **(513) 223-2444**	Open: **All year**
Best Time to Call: **4–12 PM**	Reduced Rates: **10% after 5th night**
Hosts: **Ron and Ruth Price**	Breakfast: **Full**
Location: **On edge of downtown**	Pets: **No**
Dayton	Children: **Welcome, over 12**
No. of Rooms: 3	Smoking: **No**
No. of Private Baths: 3	Social Drinking: **Permitted**
Double/pb: **$69**	Airport/Station Pickup: **Yes**
Single/pb: **$59**	

Built in 1852, this grand 22-room mansion is listed on the National Register of Historic Places. The house is furnished with period antiques and oriental rugs. Guests can play the piano, browse in the library, or survey Dayton's skyline from rocking chairs on the first- and second-floor porches. Tours, by reservation only, cover the entire residence, ending in a formal tea. The Dayton Art Institute, the U.S. Air Force Museum, and two universities are a few minutes away. Full breakfasts feature home-baked sourdough bread or sour cream coffee cake.

Mulberry Lane ✪
224 WEST MAIN STREET, P.O. BOX 61, DEERSVILLE, OHIO 44693

Tel: **(614) 922-0425**	Single/sb: **$45**
Best Time to Call: **9 AM–4 PM**	Open: **All year**
Hosts: **Dick and Ferrel Zeimer**	Breakfast: **Full**
Location: **90 mi. S of Cleveland**	Pets: **No**
No. of Rooms: 2	Children: **No**
Max. No. Sharing Bath: 4	Smoking: **No**
Double/sb: **$50**	Social Drinking: **Permitted**

Built in 1830, restored in 1989, and tastefully furnished with antiques and period pieces, Mulberry Lane is a great getaway place. Peaceful little Deersville lies between two large lakes where guests can go fishing and boating. Country auctions, antique shops, glass factories, the birthplaces of Clark Gable and General Armstrong Custer, early Moravian settlements, and Amish country are all within reach. If you don't feel like touring, you're welcome to relax on the porch swing with a good book. Freshly baked muffins are always served at Dick and Ferrel's breakfasts in their country kitchen.

Hill View Acres ✪
7320 OLD TOWN ROAD, EAST FULTONHAM, OHIO 43735

Tel: **(614) 849-2728**
Hosts: **Jim and Dawn Graham**
Location: **10 mi. SW of Zanesville**
No. of Rooms: **2**
Max. No. Sharing Bath: **4**
Double/sb: **$40**
Single/sb: **$35**
Open: **All year**

Breakfast: **Full**
Other Meals: **Available**
Credit Cards: **MC, VISA**
Pets: **No**
Children: **Welcome**
Smoking: **Permitted**
Social Drinking: **Permitted**

Hill View is a comfortable, large white house situated on 21 acres with a fishing pond. Homemade breads and delicious gourmet specialties are breakfast fare. You are welcome to relax on the deck, play the piano, or watch TV. Antique shops, potteries, the famous Y Bridge, and the *Lorena* stern-wheeler are some of the area's attractions. An on-premises pool and year-round spa add to your summer enjoyment.

Candle Wick ✪
245 E. MAIN STREET, HILLSBORO, OHIO 45133

Tel: **(513) 393-2743**
Best Time to Call: **After 6 PM**
Hosts: **Mark and Melody Johnson**
Location: **50 mi. E of Cincinnati**
No. of Rooms: **2**
Max. No. Sharing Bath: **4**
Double/sb: **$47.50**
Single/sb: **$42**

Open: **All year**
Reduced Rates: **5% seniors**
Breakfast: **Full**
Pets: **No**
Children: **Welcome**
Smoking: **Permitted**
Social Drinking: **Permitted**

Melody and Mark Johnson make this bed and breakfast a treat you won't want to miss. Candle Wick is a lovely Victorian home built in the Eastlake style of the 1880s. It boasts a magnificent walnut stairway and stained-glass windows. Fireplaces and functional antiques make each room cozy. Breakfast is your choice of full or Continental, served with homemade breads and spreads, muffins, and fresh (seasonal) fruit. Located in the heart of historic Hillsboro, Candle Wick is within an hour's drive of Cincinnati, Columbus, Dayton, and the scenic Ohio River. You can explore quaint antique shops, play at the lakes, enjoy a quiet drive in the country, or a hike through one of the three state parks nearby.

Captain Montague's Guest House ✪
229 CENTER STREET, HURON, OHIO 44839

Tel: **(419) 433-4756**
Hosts: **Shirley and Bob Reynolds**

Location: **54 mi. W of Cleveland**
No. of Rooms: **6**

No. of Private Baths: **6**
Double/pb: **$68–$85**
Open: **April 1–Dec. 15**
Reduced Rates: **Oct. 1–May 14**
Breakfast: **Continental, plus**
Pets: **No**

Children: **No**
Smoking: **No**
Social Drinking: **Permitted**
Minimum Stay: **2 nights weekends**
   Memorial Day–Labor Day

Just two blocks from the beach at Lake Erie, Shirley and Bob have turned their 1876 Southern Colonial into a lavishly appointed accommodation for travelers. The beautiful grounds boast a lattice enclosed garden with a fountain, a gazebo furnished with wicker, and an in-ground swimming pool. The interior has been comfortably furnished and decorated with Victorian accents. A vintage player piano sets the tone for relaxation while you visit in front of the living room fireplace. Take a walk on the mile-long pier, dine at a nearby restaurant, browse in local shops, or enjoy a play at Ohio's oldest summer theater.

Idlewyld Bed & Breakfast ✪
350 WALNUT STREET, LAKESIDE, OHIO 43440

Tel: **(419) 798-4198**
Hosts: **Dan and Joan Barris**
Location: **70 mi. W of Cleveland**
No. of Rooms: **14**
No. of Private Baths: **5**
Max. No. Sharing Bath: **3**
Double/pb: **$42**
Double/sb: **$37**

Open: **Mid-May–Oct.**
Reduced Rates: **Available**
Breakfast: **Continental, plus**
Pets: **No**
Children: **Welcome**
Smoking: **No**
Social Drinking: **No**

A stay at Idlewyld is like visiting an era when life was uncomplicated by high tech. Nestled in a quaint Victorian community on the shore of Lake Erie, the house is newly decorated in a country antique style. Many rooms feature stenciling. Guests gather in the large dining room for a Continental buffet breakfast, which includes an uncommon assortment of fresh fruit and homemade breads and muffins. Afterward, you can relax on one of the two spacious porches or participate in a myriad of family-oriented activities offered in the Lakeside community.

White Tor ✪
1620 OREGONIA ROAD, LEBANON, OHIO 45036

Tel: **(513) 932-5892**
Best Time to Call: **Before 9 AM; after 6 PM**
Hosts: **Eric and Margaret Johnson**
Location: **25 mi. N of Cincinnati**

No. of Rooms: **1 suite**
No. of Private Baths: **1**
Suite: **$60**
Open: **All year**
Breakfast: **Full**

Pets: **No**
Children: **Welcome (crib)**
Smoking: **No**

Social Drinking: **Permitted**
Foreign Languages: **French**

Just a half hour's drive from both Cincinnati and Dayton, this hand-some farmhouse, built in 1862, crowns a hilltop on seven wooded acres. Margaret's full English breakfast will give you stamina for a day of antique shopping or viewing artful stitchery at local quilt shows. Area attractions range from Kings Island and the Beach Waterpark to the Honey and Sauerkraut festivals. Or, simply relax on the porch in view of the pretty Miami Valley, with a good book and cold drink.

The Mainstay ✪
1320 EAST MAIN STREET, LOUISVILLE, OHIO 44641

Tel: **(216) 875-1021**
Hosts: **Mary and Joe Shurilla**
Location: **7 mi. E of Canton**
No. of Rooms: **3**
Max. No. Sharing Bath: **4**
Double/sb: **$45**
Single/sb: **$35**
Suite: **$50; sleeps 3**

Open: **All year**
Reduced Rates: **15% weekly**
Breakfast: **Full**
Pets: **No**
Children: **Welcome, over 3**
Smoking: **No**
Social Drinking: **Permitted**
Airport/Station Pickup: **Yes**

Enjoy a step backward in time at this century-old Queen Anne Victorian with its richly carved oak woodwork, spacious rooms, original tin ceilings, and numerous antiques. Louisville was the home of Charles Juilliard, founder of the famous New York City music school that bears his name; his house, listed on the National Register of Historic Places, may be toured by arrangement. If you prefer halftime shows to string quartets, you'll probably want to visit the Pro Football Hall of Fame in nearby Canton. Mary and Joe, both educators, greet newly arrived guests with fruit, cheese, and a sparkling beverage. In the morning, have your choice of full or Continental breakfast, with specialties like quiche and home-baked bread.

Mulberry Inn ✪
53 NORTH FOURTH STREET, MARTINS FERRY, OHIO 43935

Tel: **(614) 633-6058**
Host: **Shirley Probst**
Location: **5 mi. W of Wheeling, W. Va.**
No. of Rooms: **4**
Max. No. Sharing Bath: **4**
Double/sb: **$40**
Single/sb: **$35**
Open: **All year**

Reduced Rates: **Jan.–Feb.; after 3rd
 night; 5% seniors**
Breakfast: **Continental**
Credit Cards: **DISC**
Pets: **No**
Children: **Welcome, over 12**
Smoking: **Permitted**
Social Drinking: **Permitted**

Built in 1868, this frame Victorian is on a tree-lined street within walking distance of a Civil War cemetery and the Sedgwick Museum. (Martins Ferry is the oldest settlement in Ohio.) Beautiful woodwork, antiques, and mantels grace the large rooms, and air-conditioning cools the house in summer. A retired medical secretary, Shirley devotes her time to making her guests feel comfortable and welcome, tempting them with her unusual French toast recipe. Dog races, recreational activities, the Fostoria Glass Outlet, the Jamboree-in-the-Hills, Ohio University, and Bethany College are less than 10 miles away.

The Outback Inn ✪
171 EAST UNION AVENUE, McCONNELLSVILLE, OHIO 43756

Tel: **(614) 962-2158**	Breakfast: **Continental**
Best Time to Call: **5 PM**	Credit Cards: **AMEX, MC, VISA**
Host: **Emily Matusek**	Pets: **Sometimes**
No. of Rooms: **3**	Children: **No**
No. of Private Baths: **3**	Smoking: **No**
Double/pb: **$55**	Social Drinking: **Permitted**
Open: **All year**	

The Outback Inn is a restored 1880s home located in a tiny historic village midway between Zanesville and Marietta. In addition to the three bedrooms, guests have use of the living room, dining room, kitchen, front porch, and private fenced-in backyard with a pool. Emily is a schoolteacher and weaver, her husband a stained-glass artist; their inn displays his own work as well as pieces by contemporary local artists. You'll discover excellent restaurants within three blocks. Animal lovers will want to travel the eight miles to the New Wildlife Preserve, where rare and vanishing species are bred.

English Manor ✪
505 EAST LINDEN AVENUE, MIAMISBURG, OHIO 45342

Tel: **(513) 866-2288**	Suites: **$140–$150; sleeps 4**
Best Time to Call: **9 AM–8 PM**	Open: **All year**
Hosts: **Marilyn and Jack Didrichsen**	Reduced Rates: **10% after 3 nights**
Location: **9 mi. SW of Dayton**	Breakfast: **Full**
No. of Rooms: **4**	Other Meals: **Available**
No. of Private Baths: **3**	Credit Cards: **DC**
Max. No. Sharing Bath: **2**	Pets: **No**
Double/pb: **$80**	Children: **Welcome**
Single/pb: **$75**	Smoking: **No**
Double/sb: **$70**	Social Drinking: **Permitted**
Single/sb: **$65**	Airport Pickup: **Yes**

Marilyn, a retired real estate investor, and Jack, a retired executive, welcome you to their antique-filled 1920s home in historic Miamisburg. Read by the fireplace, lounge in the hammock, sip lemonade on the wicker porch. Then wander past charming neighborhood homes, or head toward the Great Miami River walking and bike trail. Antique shops, ancient Indian mounds, golf courses, tennis courts, and fine restaurants are all nearby. To start your day, a sumptuous breakfast is served on antique china, silver, and linens.

Gastier Farm Bed & Breakfast ✪
1902 STRECKER ROAD, MILAN, OHIO 44846

Tel: **(419) 499-2985**
Best Time to Call: **After 4 PM**
Hosts: **Ted and Donna Gastier**
Location: **60 mi. W of Cleveland**
No. of Rooms: **3**
Max. No. Sharing Bath: **3**
Double/sb: **$50**
Single/sb: **$35**

Open: **All year**
Breakfast: **Continental**
Credit Cards: **MC, VISA**
Pets: **No**
Children: **Welcome**
Smoking: **No**
Social Drinking: **No**
Aiport/Station Pickup: **Yes**

Ted and Donna's working farm has been a family tradition for more than one hundred years, providing the local community with grain, fresh produce, cattle, and a variety of house plants. Now the farm-house has become a bed and breakfast. The rooms have all been decorated in a homey country atmosphere. Nearby attractions include Edison Birthplace, Milan Museum, Lake Erie, Cedar Point Amusement Park, and antique shops.

St. George House
33941 LORAIN ROAD, NORTH RIDGEVILLE, OHIO 44039

Tel: **(216) 327-9354**	Double/sb: **$40**
Best Time to Call: **Early mornings; evenings until 9 PM**	Single/sb: **$35**
	Open: **All year**
Hosts: **Helen Bernardine and Muriel Dodd**	Reduced Rates: **Weekly**
	Breakfast: **Continental**
Location: **30 mi. W of Cleveland**	Pets: **Sometimes**
No. of Rooms: **4**	Children: **Welcome, over 12**
No. of Private Baths: **1**	Smoking: **Permitted**
Max. No. Sharing Bath: **4**	Social Drinking: **Permitted**
Double/pb: **$50**	Airport/Station Pickup: **Yes**
Single/pb: **$45**	Minimum stay: **2 nights**

This Colonial gray house, with its bright red shutters, is decorated with furnishings artfully restored by Helen and Muriel. The surrounding property includes barns, a bird sanctuary, and a pond that is home to a variety of wild ducks and frogs. The game room is the evening gathering place and your hosts will gladly join in the fun. Within 35 miles are Case Western Reserve and John Carroll universities, and the famed Cleveland Clinic. Oberlin College is ten miles away. Closer by are the clean beaches of Lake Erie, a zoo, and a variety of theaters.

The Bayberry Inn
25675 STATE ROUTE 41 NORTH, PEEBLES, OHIO 45660

Tel: **(513) 587-2221**	Open: **May 15–Oct. 15**
Hosts: **Marilyn and Larry Bagford**	Breakfast: **Full**
Location: **75 mi. E of Cincinnati**	Pets: **No**
No. of Rooms: **3**	Children: **Welcome**
Max. No. Sharing Bath: **4**	Smoking: **No**
Double/sb: **$45**	Social Drinking: **No**
Single/sb: **$35**	

If you expect to find warm hospitality, cozy accommodations with comfortable appointments, and a front porch on which to relax after a hearty old-fashioned breakfast, you won't be disappointed in Marilyn and Larry's Victorian farmhouse. It's located in Adams County, the hub for those with geological, historical, recreational, and agricultural interests. You are certain to enjoy visiting Serpent Mound, museums, natural wildlife areas, and herb gardens.

Tudor Country Inn ○
BOX 113, PETTISVILLE, OHIO 43553

Tel: **(419) 445-2531**
Best Time to Call: **8:30 AM–9 PM**
Hosts: **LeAnna and Dale Gautsche**
Location: **30 mi. W of Toledo; 5 mi. from Ohio Tpke.**
No. of Rooms: **2**
Max. No. Sharing Bath: **4**
Double/sb: **$45**

Single/sb: **$40**
Open: **All year**
Breakfast: **Full**
Pets: **No**
Children: **Welcome**
Smoking: **No**
Social Drinking: **No**

LeAnna and Dale were restaurant owners until they opened this English Tudor inn. It is set on the edge of a small village, surrounded by farmland in the heart of the Mennonite community. Besides soaking in the hot tub, you may lounge in the great room, where snacks are served in the evenings and a fire burns in winter. Breakfast often includes "Belly Stickers," a creamy-bottom tart, and homemade raised donuts. Local attractions include a farm and craft village, a country store, and an ice-cream parlor and restaurant, all in the Pennsylvania Dutch style.

The Pickwinn ○
707 NORTH DOWNING STREET, PIQUA, OHIO 45356

Tel: **(513) 773-8877**
Hosts: **Rosemary and Paul Gutmann**
Location: **25 mi. N of Dayton**
No. of Rooms: **4**
No. of Private Baths: **1**
Max. No. Sharing Bath: **4**
Double/pb: **$60**
Single/pb: **$50**
Double/sb: **$50**

Single/sb: **$40**
Open: **Mar. 1–Oct. 31; other times by arrangement**
Breakfast: **Full**
Pets: **Sometimes**
Children: **Welcome**
Smoking: **Permitted**
Social Drinking: **Permitted**

A brick Second Empire house built in 1883 and lovingly restored 105 years later, this B&B is listed on the National Register of Historic Places. The Pickwinn is beautifully furnished with antique English pine and wicker, and oriental rugs. North Downing Street is in the middle of the Caldwell Historic District; another local landmark is the Johnston Farm and Indian Museum, which operates a canal boat along part of the Miami and Erie Canal route. You'll have plenty of energy

for sightseeing. Your hosts, who live in the house next door, prepare full breakfasts of juice, fruit, eggs, meat, toast, pastry, and coffee.

Inn at the Green ✪
500 SOUTH MAIN STREET, POLAND, OHIO 44514

Tel: **(216) 757-4688**
Best Time to Call: **After 12 PM**
Hosts: **Ginny and Steve Meloy**
Location: **7 mi. SE of Youngstown**
No. of Rooms: **4**
No. of Private Baths: **4**
Double/pb: **$60**
Single/pb: **$55**

Open: **All year**
Breakfast: **Continental**
Other Meals: **No**
Credit Cards: **MC, VISA**
Pets: **No**
Children: **Welcome, over 10**
Smoking: **Permitted**
Social Drinking: **Permitted**

The Inn at the Green is an 1876 Victorian town house located on the south end of the village green. The rooms have the grandeur of bygone days, with original moldings, 12-foot-high ceilings, and original poplar floors. There are five Italian marble fireplaces and extensive public rooms furnished with gracious antiques. Guests are welcome to relax in the parlor, sitting room, and library. Sleeping quarters are air-conditioned, and are furnished with poster beds, Sealy Posturepedic mattresses, and antiques. Coffee, croissants, muffins, and French jam are served in the greeting room in winter and on the wicker-furnished porch during moderate weather. Enjoy a glass of sherry on the porch overlooking the garden before dinner. Your hosts will gladly direct you to gourmet dining as well as cross-country ski trails, golf, tennis, and the Butler Institute, home of one of the nation's finest American art collections.

The Vineyard ○
BOX 283, PUT-IN-BAY, OHIO 43456

Tel: (419) 285-6181	Single/sb: $70
Hosts: Barbi and Mark Barnhill	Open: All year
Location: An island 35 mi. E of Toledo	Breakfast: Full
No. of Rooms: 3	Pets: Sometimes
No. of Private Baths: 1	Children: No
Max. No. Sharing Bath: 4	Smoking: No
Double/pb: $85	Social Drinking: Permitted
Double/sb: $70	Airport/Station Pickup: Yes

This 130-year-old wood frame house is set on 20 acres of island seclusion. Your hosts grow Catawba grapes for the local winery, which is part of the region's famous wine industry. Guests are greeted with wine and cheese and shown to newly renovated bedrooms furnished with family antiques. You are invited to sun and swim on a private beach after a day of touring. Local attractions include a picturesque harbor, a monument offering a view of Lake Erie's islands, and a unique Victorian village featuring excellent restaurants.

The Signal House ○
234 NORTH FRONT STREET, RIPLEY, OHIO 45167

Tel: (513) 392-1640; reservations:	Double/sb: $58–$68
(800) 742-3471	Open: All year
Best Time to Call: Mornings	Breakfast: Full
Hosts: Vic and Betsy Billingsley	Pets: No
Location: 55 mi. E of Cincinnati	Children: No
No. of Rooms: 2	Smoking: Permitted
Max. No. Sharing Bath: 4	Social Drinking: Permitted

Before the Civil War, the abolitionist who lived in Signal House hung a lantern from an attic window to tell runaway slaves that the coast was clear. Today this Greek Italianate house is one of the notable sights in Ripley's 55-acre historical district. From the building's three porches, you can watch paddle-wheel boats steam up the Ohio River. Ripley boasts several excellent antique shops; in August, the town holds an old-fashioned tobacco festival complete with beauty pageants, a husband-calling competition, and an ugliest-dog contest. Thirteen miles east, Moyer's Winery pleases palates with inexpensive vintages and excellent meals. You'll also savor Betsy's breakfasts of egg-and-cheese strata and homemade breads and jams.

My Father's House Bed and Breakfast ✪
173 SOUTH MARIETTA STREET, ST. CLAIRSVILLE, OHIO 43950

Tel: (614) 695-5440	Reduced Rates: 10% after 4 nights
Best time to Call: 9 AM–9 PM	Breakfast: Continental
Hosts: Mark and Polly Loy	Credit Cards: MC, VISA
Location: 9 mi. W of Wheeling, W.Va.	Pets: No
No. of Rooms: 3	Children: Welcome
No. of Private Baths: 3	Smoking: No
Double/pb: $45–$55	Social Drinking: No
Single/pb: $40–$55	Station Pickup: Yes
Open: All year	

This stately Federal home was built in 1810 by Benjamin Ruggles, one of Ohio's first U.S. senators. Today, antique and modern furnishings combine to create a quaint yet comfortable overnight experience. The living room features a romantic open fireplace, while the parlor affords guests the opportunity to watch television. There are many opportunities for shopping and sightseeing in the area. Historic Wheeling, West Virginia, just 15 minutes away, features a variety of attractions, including the spectacular Festival of Lights (November–February).

The Red Gables B&B
421 WAYNE STREET, SANDUSKY, OHIO 44870

Tel: (419) 625-1189	Reduced Rates: Oct. 1–May 1 all
Best Time to Call: 8 AM–10 PM	rooms are $50
Host: Jo Ellen Cuthbertson	Breakfast: Continental, plus
Location: 60 mi. W of Cleveland	Credit Cards: MC, VISA
No. of Rooms: 4	Pets: No
No. of Private Baths: 2	Children: Welcome
Max. No. Sharing Bath: 4	Smoking: No
Double/pb: $70–$75	Social Drinking: Permitted
Double/sb: $60–$65	Station Pickup: Yes
Open: Feb.–Dec.	

A lovely old Tudor Revival home finished in 1907, The Red Gables is located in the historic Old Plat District. Guests are welcomed into the great room, which features a massive fireplace and large bay window where breakfast is served. The home's many interesting architectural details include lots of oak woodwork. The Red Gables is decorated in a very eclectic style, from Asian artifacts in the great room to flowered chintz in the bedrooms. The innkeeper, a semi-retired costume maker, has filled the rooms with handmade slipcovers, curtains, and comforters. Guest rooms are light and airy, with easy access to a wicker-filled sitting room, a refrigerator, and coffeemaker or teakettle. Guests have said, "It's like going to Grandma's house!"

Wagner's 1844 Inn ✪
230 EAST WASHINGTON STREET, SANDUSKY, OHIO 44870

Tel: **(419) 626-1726**	Reduced Rates: **Oct.–Apr.**
Hosts: **Walt and Barb Wagner**	Breakfast: **Continental**
Location: **8 mi. from Ohio Tpke., Exit 7**	Credit Cards: **DISC, MC, VISA**
	Pets: **Sometimes**
No. of Rooms: **3**	Children: **No**
No. of Private Baths: **3**	Smoking: **No**
Double/pb: **$75**	Social Drinking: **Permitted**
Single/pb: **$65**	Airport/Station Pickup: **Yes**
Open: **All year**	

This elegantly restored Italianate home, built in 1844, is listed on the National Register of Historic Places. The warm interior features old-fashioned amenities like a billiard room, an antique piano, and a wood-burning fireplace. The screened porch and enclosed courtyard provide tranquil settings for conversation with your hosts Walt, an attorney, and Barb, a registered nurse. Within easy walking distance are parks, tennis courts, antique shops, art galleries, and ferries to Cedar Point Amusement Park and the Lake Erie Islands.

Somer Tea B&B ✪
200 SOUTH COLUMBUS STREET, BOX 308, SOMERSET, OHIO 43783

Tel: **(614) 743-2909**	Open: **All year**
Hosts: **Richard and Mary Lou Murray**	Breakfast: **Full**
Location: **40 mi. SE of Columbus**	Pets: **Welcome**
No. of Rooms: **2**	Children: **Welcome**
Max. No. Sharing Bath: **4**	Smoking: **Permitted**
Double/sb: **$45**	Social Drinking: **Permitted**
Single/sb: **$35**	

Somerset was the boyhood home of the Civil War general Phil Sheridan. Two of his nieces lived in the Somer Tea, a stately brick residence listed on the National Register of Historic Places. And yes, tea is always available here; guests are encouraged to sit with a cup on the porch swing. Ask Mary Lou to show you her collection of more than 225 teapots. If you'd like to do some collecting yourself, she'll direct you to the region's numerous antique shops and craft stores. Full country breakfasts, with an egg casserole, a fruit dish, home fries, and raisin bran muffins, are served in the elegant dining room.

Allen Villa B&B ✪
434 SOUTH MARKET STREET, TROY, OHIO 45373

Tel: (513) 335-1181
Best Time to Call: 9 AM–9 PM
Hosts: Robert and June Smith
Location: 20 mi. N of Dayton
No. of Rooms: 4
No. of Private Baths: 4
Double/pb: $65
Single/pb: $45
Open: All year

Reduced Rates: 10% seniors
Breakfast: Full
Credit Cards: AMEX, MC, VISA
Pets: No
Children: Welcome, over 12
Smoking: Permitted
Social Drinking: Permitted
Airport/Station Pickup: Yes

After painstakingly restoring this Victorian mansion, built in 1874, the Smiths furnished it with the antiques they collect as a hobby. The wooden Venetian blinds, walnut trim, and decorative stencils are all original to the house. This is a good neighborhood for strolling. Other local attractions include a public golf course, Stillwater Vineyards, and Brukner Nature Center. Full breakfasts feature such specialties as vegetable omelets and French toast. You are welcome to use the snack bar with its refrigerator, ice maker, and microwave.

Shirlee's Chambers ✪
535 ADELAIDE NORTH EAST, WARREN, OHIO 44483

Tel: (216) 372-1118
Hosts: Shirlee and Wayne Chambers
Location: 7 mi. from I-80
No. of Rooms: 3
Max. No. Sharing Bath: 3
Double/sb: $40
Single/sb: $35

Open: All year
Breakfast: Full
Pets: No
Children: Welcome, over 10
Smoking: Permitted
Social Drinking: Permitted
Airport/Station Pickup: Yes

Shirlee welcomes you to her Colonial home with wine, cheese, or tea and cookies. Her guest rooms are comfortably furnished. Start the day with a French mushroom omelet, the specialty of the house. Your hosts can direct you to the many nearby antique shops. Local attractions include summer theater and fine dining. Lake Erie is an hour's drive.

Locust Lane Farm ✪
5590 KESSLER COWLESVILLE ROAD, WEST MILTON, OHIO 45383

Tel: **(513) 698-4743**
Best Time to Call: **Early mornings; late evenings**
Host: **Ruth Shoup**
Location: **7 mi. SW of Troy**
No. of Rooms: **3**
No. of Private Baths: **1**
Max. No. Sharing Bath: **4**
Double/pb: **$50**

Single/pb: **$45**
Double/sb: **$45**
Single/sb: **$35**
Open: **All year**
Breakfast: **Full**
Pets: **No**
Children: **Welcome (high chair)**
Smoking: **No**
Social Drinking: **Permitted**

Enjoy a peaceful night in a big old farmhouse, tucked away in a locust grove, set on 58 acres in the country. This air-conditioned house is tastefully decorated with family antiques. Your host offers fluffy bath towels, extra pillows, and goodies such as hot spiced cider, quick breads, and iced tea in the afternoon. Ruth loves entertaining and serves a farm-style breakfast of fresh fruit, muffins, eggs, homemade breads, and sweet rolls. In the warmer weather, breakfast is served on a lovely screened-in porch. Locust Lane is convenient to Milton and Troy, and four restaurants are located within two miles.

Priscilla's Bed & Breakfast ✪
5 SOUTH WEST STREET, WESTERVILLE, OHIO 43081

Tel: **(614) 882-3910**
Best Time to Call: **10 AM–5 PM**
Host: **Priscilla H. Curtis**
Location: **2 mi. N of Columbus**
No. of Rooms: **2**
Max. No. Sharing Bath: **4**
Double/sb: **$40–$50**
Single/sb: **$35**

Open: **All year**
Breakfast: **Continental**
Pets: **No**
Children: **Welcome**
Smoking: **Permitted**
Social Drinking: **Permitted**
Airport/Station Pickup: **Yes**

Located in a historic area adjacent to Otterbein campus, this 1854 home, surrounded by a white picket fence, abounds with antiques and collectibles. Guests are welcome to borrow bicycles, use the patio, enjoy concerts in the adjoining park, walk to the Benjamin Hanby Museum or the quaint shops, or just stay "home" and relax. Priscilla is an authority on miniatures and dollhouse construction. Everyone enjoys browsing through her on-premises shop.

OKLAHOMA

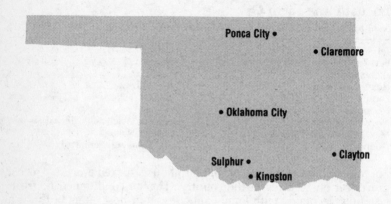

Country Inn
ROUTE 3, BOX 1925, CLAREMORE, OKLAHOMA 74017

Tel: **(918) 342-1894**
Best Time to Call: **8 AM–8 PM**
Hosts: **Leland and Kay Jenkins**
Location: **25 mi. NE of Tulsa**
No. of Rooms: **3**
No. of Private Baths: **3**
Double/pb: **$47**
Single/pb: **$35**

Suite: **$59**
Open: **All year**
Reduced Rates: **10% seniors**
Breakfast: **Full**
Children: **No**
Smoking: **No**
Social Drinking: **Permitted**

Leland and Kay look forward to making you feel right at home in the charming barn-style guest quarters, separate from the main house. They invite you to enjoy the swimming pool, improve your suntan, or just sit back in the shade and enjoy a cool drink. A gift shop featuring handcrafted quilts is on premises. The Will Rogers Memorial, the J. M. Davis Gun Museum, the 29,500-acre Oologah Lake, and Oral Roberts

University are close by. Horse racing buffs will enjoy pari-mutuel betting at Will Rogers Downs during August and September.

Clayton Country Inn ✪
ROUTE 1, BOX 8, HIGHWAY 271, CLAYTON, OKLAHOMA 74536

Tel: (918) 569-4165, 627-1956
Best Time to Call: 7 AM–10 PM
Host: Betty Lundgren
Location: 140 mi. SE of Tulsa
No. of Rooms: 11
No. of Private Baths: 11
Double/pb: $35
Single/pb: $29

Guest Cottage: $37–$50; sleeps 5
Open: All year
Breakfast: Continental
Other Meals: Available
Credit Cards: MC, VISA
Pets: No
Children: Welcome
Smoking: Permitted
Social Drinking: Permitted

Perched on a hill amid 140 acres and surrounded by the Kiamichi Mountains is this 50-year-old, two-story, stone and wood inn. It's furnished in a simple, traditional style with a beamed ceiling and fireplace. The on-premises restaurant is noted for its fine cooking. Bass fishing at Lake Sardis is two miles away, and an 18,000-acre game preserve is just across the highway. Feel free to bring your horse and enjoy trail rides under the vast western skies.

The Sun Ray Ranch Bed & Breakfast
P.O. BOX 491, 999 NORTH MARSHALL, KINGSTON , OKLAHOMA 73439

Tel: (405) 564-3602
Best Time to Call: After 7 PM
Hosts: L. V. and Bobbie Little
Location: 29 mi. E of Ardmore
Double/pb: $45
Suites: $65
Open: All year
Reduced Rates: Available

Breakfast: Full
Credit Cards: MC, VISA
Pets: Sometimes
Children: Welcome
Smoking: Permitted
Social Drinking: Permitted
Airport Pickup: Yes

The Southwest comes alive at Sun Ray, a working ranch that offers guests a taste of life that is hard to find in the fast-paced world of today. Guests can not only experience an age gone by, but become a part of it. Enjoy the many antiques, some dating back to when Oklahoma was known as OK I.T. (for Indian Territory), or help with ranch chores. Lake Texoma, a fishing hole known for its stripers and bass, is four miles away. So come to the country, fish in the morning, and become a ranch hand in the afternoon at this B&B.

Country House ✪
10101 OAKVIEW ROAD, OKLAHOMA CITY, OKLAHOMA 73165

Tel: **(405) 794-4008**	Reduced Rates: **10% seniors**
Best Time to Call: **8 AM–9 PM**	Breakfast: **Full**
Hosts: **Dee and Nancy Ann Curnutt**	Other Meals: **Available**
Location: **10 mi. SE of Oklahoma City**	Pets: **Sometimes**
No. of Rooms: **3**	Children: **Welcome**
No. of Private Baths: **2**	Smoking: **Permitted**
Double/pb: **$45**	Social Drinking: **Permitted**
Single/pb: **$35**	Airport/Station Pickup: **Yes**
Open: **All year**	

At Country House you will find genuine, old-fashioned hospitality in a warm romantic setting. The house rests on five beautiful acres; the interior is tastefully furnished with 19th-century antiques and country collectibles. Nancy offers in-room color TV on request, as well as a scrumptious breakfast served on the balcony if you wish. For fishing and water sports, go to nearby Lake Draper, where Captain Dee, Nancy's husband, runs a charter boat service. For a fee he will happily take you on a four- or eight-hour fishing excursion in search of the elusive black bass.

The Grandison ✪
1841 NORTHWEST FIFTEENTH STREET, OKLAHOMA CITY, OKLAHOMA 73106

Tel: **(405) 521-0011**	Breakfast: **Continental**
Hosts: **Claudia and Bob Wright**	Other Meals: **Available**
Location: **2 mi. off I-44, Tenth St. exit**	Credit Cards: **AMEX, MC, VISA**
No. of Rooms: **5**	Pets: **Sometimes**
No. of Private Baths: **5**	Children: **Welcome, over 12**
Double/pb: **$40–$85**	Smoking: **Permitted**
Suites: **$90–$125**	Social Drinking: **Permitted**
Open: **All year**	Airport/Station Pickup: **Yes**

Named for its first owner and resident, Grandison Crawford, this turn-of-the-century brick Colonial was expanded in 1919, and again in the 1930s. It is furnished with antiques from many eras, so each bedroom has a distinctive look. The closest attractions—Civic Center Music Hall, the Convention Center, and Oklahoma City's fairgrounds—are just five minutes away. Breakfast consists of a meat or egg dish, fresh fruit, home-baked pastries, and beverage. For snacking, you'll find fruit, nuts, cookies, and mints in your bedroom.

Davarnathey Inn ✪
1001 WEST GRAND, PONCA CITY, OKLAHOMA 74601

Tel: (405) 765-9922	Breakfast: Full
Hosts: David and Shirley Zimmerman	Credit Cards: MC, VISA
Location: 80 mi. S of Witchita, Kans.	Pets: No
No. of Rooms: 3	Children: Welcome
No. of Private Baths: 3	Smoking: No
Double/pb: $65	Social Drinking: Permitted
Single/pb: $55	Airport/Station Pickup: Yes
Open: All year	

Built in 1906 by an Oklahoma oilman, Davarnathey Inn has its original fretwork stairway, ornate mirrored mantel, and stained-glass windows. Period furnishings and floral wallpapers sustain the Victorian mood. Guests are encouraged to browse in the library; the musically inclined have both a piano and an organ to play. Other amenities include a hot tub and a pool. Snacks are served, but after a full breakfast of fresh baked Scandinavian breads, fruit crêpes, soufflés, and quiche, it may be awhile before you're hungry again.

Shepherd Rest ✪
1103 SOUTH 7TH, PONCA CITY, OKLAHOMA 74601

Tel: (405) 762-0850	Reduced Rates: Available
Host: Donna Shepherd	Breakfast: Full
Location: 85 mi. N of Oklahoma City	Credit Cards: MC, VISA
No. of Rooms: 3	Pets: No
No. of Private Baths: 3	Children: No
Double/pb: $65	Smoking: No
Single/pb: $55	Social Drinking: Permitted
Open: All year	Airport Pickup: Yes

Shepherd Rest, a brick Colonial built in 1926, is a quiet place to stay. The bedrooms are large, and each has a TV and a private bath. Your hostess is interested in arts and crafts and interior decorating—the bedrooms have lovely window treatments and homemade quilts. Full breakfasts are served in a formal setting.

Artesian Bed and Breakfast ✪
1022 WEST 12TH STREET, SULPHUR, OKLAHOMA 73086

Tel: **(405) 622-5254**
Hosts: **Karen and Tom Byrd**
Location: **71 mi. S of Oklahoma City**
No. of Rooms: **2**
No. of Private Baths: **2**
Double/pb: **$60**
Single/pb: **$50**
Suites: **$70**

Open: **All year**
Reduced Rates: **15% Dec.–Mar.**
Breakfast: **Full**
Pets: **No**
Children: **Welcome, over 10**
Smoking: **No**
Social Drinking: **No**

A quiet, homey atmosphere prevails at this 1904 Sears, Roebuck Victorian, where the L-shaped front porch is furnished with swing and willow chairs. Inside, you'll admire the wooden staircase, the tiled parlor fireplace, and the bay windows overlooking the backyard. There's natural beauty at every turn. For hiking, swimming, or just picnicking, Chickasaw Recreation Area is only half a mile away. For fishing, boating, and waterskiing, take the ten-mile drive to Arbuckle Lake. Your hosts, a retired veterinarian and a homemaker, can help you make the most of your stay.

OREGON

Seaside •

Portland •
Newberg • • Oregon
Woodburn • City • Welches

• Stayton

Corvallis •
Junction City •
Elmira • • Eugene • Leaburg
• North Bend • Bend

Coos Bay •

Bandon •

Grants Pass •

• Ashland

Northwest Bed and Breakfast Travel Unlimited
610 SW BROADWAY, SUITE 606, PORTLAND, OREGON 97205

Tel: (503) 243-7616
Coordinator: **LaVonne Miller**
States/Regions Covered: **California,
Hawaii, Idaho, Oregon, Washington;
Canada—British Columbia**

Rates (Single/Double):
Modest: **$30–$40 / $40–$45**
Average: **$40–$50 / $45–$55**
Luxury: **$50–$100 / $60–$150**
Credit Cards: **MC, VISA**
Descriptive Directory: **$7.95**

Northwest Bed and Breakfast is a network established in 1979 of hundreds of host homes throughout the Pacific Northwest and Canada. They charge an annual membership fee of $25. Upon joining, you will receive a directory of all the lodgings, which range from city to suburban to rural to coast, mountains, and desert. There is just a $10 processing fee for those who will only use the service once; no fee to members.

Mt. Ashland Inn ✪
550 MT. ASHLAND ROAD, P.O. BOX 944, ASHLAND, OREGON 97520

Tel: (503) 482-8707
Best Time to Call: 11 AM–7 PM
Hosts: Elaine and Jerry Shanafelt
Location: 6 mi. from I-5, Exit 6
No. of Rooms: 5
No. of Private Baths: 5
Double/pb: $80–$130
Single/pb: $75–$125

Open: All year
Breakfast: Full
Other Meals: Dinner available Nov.–
  Apr. only by arrangement
Pets: No
Children: Welcome, over 10
Smoking: No
Social Drinking: Permitted

Nestled among tall evergreens, this beautifully handcrafted log structure is situated on a mountain ridge with views of the Cascade Mountains, including majestic Mt. Shasta. Inside, handcarvings, oriental rugs, homemade quilts, antiques, and finely crafted furniture provide an atmosphere of comfort and elegance. Breakfasts are hearty to satisfy the appetites of skiers and hikers who take advantage of nearby trails. For quiet relaxation, you are welcome to enjoy the sunny deck or curl up with a book by the large stone fireplace.

Royal Carter House ✪
514 SISKIYOU BOULEVARD, ASHLAND, OREGON 97520

Tel: (503) 482-5623
Best Time to Call: Mornings

Hosts: Alyce and Roy Levy
No. of Rooms: 4

No. of Private Baths: **4**
Double/pb: **$55–$75**
Suites: **$75**
Open: **All year**
Breakfast: **Full**

Pets: **No**
Children: **Welcome, over 7**
Smoking: **No**
Social Drinking: **Permitted**
Airport/Station Pickup: **Yes**

This beautiful 1909 Craftsman home is listed on the National Historic Register. Located four blocks from Ashland's famous Shakespeare Theatre, it is surrounded by lovely old trees in a parklike setting. It is suitably modernized but retains the original room structure. Alyce has added decorator touches of vintage hats and old periodicals to the antique furnishings. The Levys have traveled extensively abroad and will share stories of their experiences with you. Southern Oregon State College is six blocks away.

The Woods House Bed & Breakfast Inn
333 NORTH MAIN STREET, ASHLAND, OREGON 97520

Tel: **(503) 488-1598**
Best Time to Call: **After 10 AM**
Hosts: **Françoise and Lester Roddy**
Location: **½ mi. N of Ashland**
No. of Rooms: **6**
No. of Private Baths: **6**
Double/pb: **$90–$105**
Single/pb: **$85–$100**

Open: **All year**
Reduced Rates: **Available**
Breakfast: **Full**
Credit Cards: **MC, VISA**
Pets: **No**
Children: **Welcome, over 12**
Smoking: **No**
Social Drinking: **Permitted**
Minimum Stay: **2 days June–Oct.;
    weekends Nov.–May**
Station Pickup: **Yes**

The Woods House is located in Ashland's historic district four blocks from the Shakespearean theaters, shops, restaurants, and 100-acre Lithia Park. The inn, a 1908 Craftsman home renovated in 1984, has six sunny and spacious guest rooms. Simple furnishings, comprising warm woods, antique furniture and linens, watercolors, oriental carpets and leather books, combine with high-quality amenities to create a sophisticated comfortable atmosphere. The terraced English gardens provide many areas for guests to relax and socialize. Françoise previously worked in human resources and event planning and is skilled in calligraphy, cooking, and needle crafts. Lester has spent the past 25 years in business management and consulting. Their aim is to make each guest feel like a special friend, not just a paying customer. They strive to anticipate guests' needs and cheerfully accommodate the unexpected, always maintaining the highest standards of cleanliness, cordiality, and fine food.

Lighthouse Bed & Breakfast ✪
650 JETTY ROAD, P.O. BOX 24, BANDON, OREGON 97411

Tel: **(503) 347-9316**
Best Time to Call: **3–6 PM**
Hosts: **Bruce and Linda Sisson**
Location: **26 mi. S of Coos Bay**
No. of Rooms: **4**
No. of Private Baths: **4**
Double/pb: **$85–$125**
Open: **All year**

Breakfast: **Continental, plus**
Credit Cards: **MC, VISA**
Pets: **No**
Children: **Welcome, over 12**
Smoking: **No**
Social Drinking: **Permitted**
Airport/Station Pickup: **Yes**

Located on the beach across from the historic Bandon Lighthouse, Bruce and Linda's contemporary home is light and airy, with an ocean-view deck. The guest rooms are bright and comfortable and have pretty plants. All have river or ocean views. "Old Town" and many of Bandon's finest seafood restaurants are within easy walking distance. A short stroll along the beach will give you a glimpse of the ancient sea stacks jutting from the water just offshore. This is a wonderful environment for those who like to beachcomb, bird-watch, or photograph spectacular sunsets.

Farewell Bend Bed & Breakfast ✪
29 NW GREELEY, BEND, OREGON 97701

Tel: **(503) 382-4374**
Best Time to Call: **Anytime**
Host: **Lorene Bateman**
Location: **160 mi. SE of Portland**
No. of Rooms: **3**
No. of Private Baths: **3**
Double/pb: **$65**
Suites: **$75 for 2; $90 for 3**
Open: **All year**

Reduced Rates: **10% weekly**
Breakfast: **Full**
Credit Cards: **AMEX, MC, VISA**
Pets: **No**
Children: **Welcome, over 12**
Smoking: **No**
Social Drinking: **Permitted**
Airport/Station Pickup: **Yes**

Farewell Bend is a recently renovated 1920s Dutch Colonial just minutes from shops, restaurants, and Drake Park—where the town music festival takes place every June and hungry ducks and geese demand bread crumbs year-round. It's only 17 miles to Mt. Bachelor for skiing, and white-water rafting on the Deschutes is a special warm-weather treat. Afterward, settle in the living room with sherry or tea, read a book, or watch a movie on the VCR. All bedrooms have king-size beds, down comforters, and hand-stitched quilts, and bathrooms are supplied with terry robes. Full breakfasts are served in the sunny dining room.

This Olde House B&B ✪

202 ALDER AVENUE, CORNER NORTH 2ND STREET, COOS BAY, OREGON 97420

Tel: **(503) 267-5224**	Open: **All year**
Hosts: **Ed and Jean Mosieur**	Reduced Rates: **10% seniors**
Location: **½ block from Hwy. 101**	Breakfast: **Full**
No. of Rooms: **4**	Pets: **No**
No. of Private Baths: **1**	Children: **Welcome, over 12**
Max. No. Sharing Bath: **4**	Smoking: **No**
Double/sb: **$55**	Social Drinking: **Permitted**
Single/sb: **$50**	Airport/Station Pickup: **Yes**
Suite: **$65**	

Situated with a view of the bay, this stately Victorian beauty is located only one half block from Highway 101. Guests can catch a glimpse of ships on the bay just before they head downstairs to a breakfast of fresh fruit, eggs, muffins, coffee or tea, served in the dining room. Downtown Coos Bay is only two blocks away from the house, and after a short drive, guests will find a lovely state park, a small boat basin, beaches, South Slough Sanctuary, and the beautiful gardens of Shore Acres.

Huntington Manor

3555 N.W. HARRISON BOULEVARD, CORVALLIS, OREGON 97330

Tel: **(503) 753-3735**	Open: **All year**
Best Time to Call: **8 AM–8 PM**	Reduced Rates: **10% weekly**
Host: **Ann Sink**	Breakfast: **Full**
Location: **84 mi. S of Portland**	Pets: **No**
No. of Rooms: **3**	Children: **Welcome, over 12**
No. of Private Baths: **3**	Smoking: **No**
Double/pb: **$53**	Social Drinking: **Permitted**
Single/pb: **$48**	

Huntington Manor is a 64-year-old Williamsburg-style Colonial, set beneath towering trees and surrounded by gardens. The house has been completely refurbished and furnished with a mixture of American and European antiques. Guest rooms feature queen-size or double beds, phones, color TV, down comforters, fine imported linens, and special touches such as a decanter of wine and fresh fruit. Your host has 20 years of experience in interior design, and she loves caring for her home and catering to guests. Breakfast specialties include ham-and-cheese-filled crêpes, egg strata, and homemade muffins; tea and scones are served in the afternoon. Huntington Manor is four blocks from Oregon State University and within walking distance of parks, churches, and the countryside.

Shady Maple Farm Bed & Breakfast ✪
27183 BUNDY ROAD, CORVALLIS, OREGON 97333

Tel: **(503) 847-5992; (800) 821-4129**	Open: **All year**
Best Time to Call: **8 AM–7 PM**	Reduced Rates: **Available**
Host: **Carol May**	Breakfast: **Full**
Location: **80 mi. N of Eugene**	Credit Cards: **MC, VISA**
No. of Rooms: **3**	Pets: **Sometimes**
No. of Private Baths: **1**	Children: **Welcome, over 10**
Max. No. Sharing Bath: **4**	Smoking: **No**
Double/pb: **$65–$75**	Social Drinking: **Permitted**
Double/sb: **$55**	Minimum Stay: **On holidays and special weekends**
	Airport Pickup: **Yes**

At Shady Maple Farm guests will enjoy privacy, relaxation, and seclusion. This small working farm sits on 48 acres along the banks of the Willamette River. The tastefully decorated farmhouse, nestled beneath a towering maple tree and surrounded by flower gardens, radiates warmth and welcome. A hearty breakfast of farm-fresh eggs and favorite homemade specialties is served in the dining room overlooking the pasture where cattle and sheep graze. In wet weather, curl up by a crackling fire in the living or dining room and enjoy a good book, games, stereo, VCR, or the piano. In summer guests can swim, fish, and picnic on the wooded riverbank or play tennis on the outdoor court.

McGillivray's Log Home and Bed and Breakfast
88680 EVERS ROAD, ELMIRA, OREGON 97437

Tel: **(503) 935-3564**	Open: **All year**
Best Time to Call: **8 AM–8 PM**	Breakfast: **Full**
Host: **Evelyn McGillivray**	Credit Cards: **MC, VISA**
Location: **14 mi. W of Eugene**	Pets: **No**
No. of Rooms: **2**	Children: **Welcome**
No. of Private Baths: **2**	Smoking: **No**
Double/pb: **$50–$70**	Social Drinking: **Permitted**
Single/pb: **$40–$60**	Airport/Station Pickup: **Yes**

This massive home is situated on five acres covered with pines and firs. The air-conditioned structure is designed with six types of wood, and features a split-log staircase. Guests may choose from a spacious, wheelchair-accessible bedroom, or an upstairs room that can accommodate a family. All are beautifully decorated in a classic Americana motif. Evelyn usually prepares buttermilk pancakes using an antique griddle her mother used to use. She also offers fresh-squeezed juice from farm-grown apples and grapes, fresh bread, eggs, and all the trimmings. It's just three miles to a local vineyard; country roads for bicycling and a reservoir for fishing and boating are close by.

Aristea's Guest House ✪
1546 CHARNELTON STREET, EUGENE, OREGON 97401

Tel: **(503) 683-2062**
Best Time to Call: **Afternoons**
Host: **Arie Hupp**
Location: **75 mi. S of Portland**
No. of Rooms: **2**
Max. No. Sharing Baths: **4**
Double/sb: **$50–$60**
Single/sb: **$45–$55**
Open: **All year**

Reduced Rates: **Available**
Breakfast: **Full**
Pets: **Sometimes**
Children: **Welcome**
Smoking: **No**
Social Drinking: **Permitted**
Minimum Stay: **2 nights during log
  conference or conventions**

Handmade moldings and lavish wainscoting make this B&B, built in 1928, a splendid example of Craftsman style. Arie is equally proud of her flower and fruit and vegetable gardens; she raises much of the fresh produce served at her gourmet breakfasts. From this central Eugene address, the University of Oregon, Hult Center for the Performing Arts, the Fifth Street Public Market, and the Willamette River are within walking distance, as are many shops and restaurants. Or get behind the wheel—you can reach the Oregon Coast or the Mc-Kenzie River within an hour.

Getty's Emerald Garden B&B ✪
640 AUDEL, EUGENE, OREGON 97404

Tel: **(503) 688-6344**
Best Time to Call: **Before 8 AM; after
  6 PM**
Hosts: **Bob and Jackie Getty**
Location: **3 mi. N of Eugene**
No. of Rooms: **1 suite**
Suite: **$50–$55**
Open: **All year**
Reduced Rates: **10% weekly**

Breakfast: **Full**
Credit Cards: **AMEX, MC, VISA**
Pets: **No**
Children: **Welcome**
Smoking: **No**
Social Drinking: **Permitted**
Airport/Station Pickup: **Yes**

Bob and Jackie have lived in Eugene for more than thirty years and can help you plan a wonderful vacation. Their contemporary home has vaulted ceilings, large windows, and a cozy living room with a fireplace. Full breakfasts feature specialties from your hosts' garden. Guests have use of the family room and its piano, TV, and VCR; less sedentary types will want to borrow bicycles and head out for the area's scenic trails. For more activity, visit the local park, which has a heated swimming pool, sauna, hot tubs, jogging trails, and playground. Hult Center for the Performing Arts, Lane County Fairgrounds, the University of Oregon, golf courses, Valley River Shopping Center, and City Center are all within a ten-minute drive.

The House in the Woods ⊘
814 LORANE HIGHWAY, EUGENE, OREGON 97405

Tel: **(503) 343-3234**
Best Time to Call: **Mornings; evenings**
Hosts: **Eunice and George Kjaer**
Location: **3 mi. from I-5**
No. of Rooms: **2**
No. of Private Baths: **1**
Max. No. Sharing Bath: **2**
Double/pb: **$65**
Single/pb: **$42**
Double/sb: **$55**
Single/sb: **$40**

Open: **All year**
Reduced Rates: **Available**
Breakfast: **Full**
Pets: **No**
Children: **Welcome, under 1 and over 14**
Smoking: **No**
Social Drinking: **Permitted**
Airport/Station Pickup: **Yes**
Foreign Languages: **German**

This turn-of-the-century home is situated in a wooded glen sur-rounded by fir trees, rhododendrons, and azaleas. Inside, you'll find oriental rugs on the original hardwood floors, a cozy fireplace, an-tiques, and a square grand piano. Guest rooms always have fresh flowers. Breakfast is served in the formal dining room or beside the warmth of the Franklin stove. Specialties of the house include breads, fruit soups, and a variety of egg dishes. The neighborhood is full of wildlife and bicycle and jogging trails, yet is close to shops, art galleries, museums, wineries, and restaurants.

The Lyon & The Lambe Inn ⊘
988 LAWRENCE AT TENTH, EUGENE, OREGON 97401

Tel: **(503) 683-3160**
Best Time to Call: **Anytime**
Hosts: **Barbara and Henri Brod**
No. of Rooms: **4**
No. of Private Baths: **4**
Double/pb: **$65–$80**
Single/pb: **$60–$75**
Open: **All year**
Breakfast: **Full**
Other Meals: **Available**

Credit Cards: **MC, VISA**
Pets: **Welcome**
Children: **Welcome, over 12**
Smoking: **Permitted**
Social Drinking: **Permitted**
Minimum Stay: **2 nights major holiday weekends**
Airport/Station Pickup: **Yes**
Foreign Languages: **French, German, Spanish, Portuguese**

This elegant, charm-filled home rests on a quiet residential street in the very heart of downtown Eugene. Barbara's mouth-watering break-fasts always include freshly baked croissants, breads, or muffins, and one truly special entrée such as eggs Florentine, David Eyre pancakes, or French Toast Aphrodisia. End a vigorous day with a luxurious whirlpool bath complete with lotions and potions. Afterward, enjoy a complimentary glass of sherry and relax in the library, where a VCR, a CD collection, and numerous books await you.

Maryellen's Guest House
1583 FIRCREST, EUGENE, OREGON 97403

Tel: **(503) 342-7375**	Reduced Rates: **10% weekly**
Best Time to Call: **9 AM–9 PM**	Breakfast: **Full**
Hosts: **Maryellen and Bob Larson**	Other Meals: **Available**
Location: **1 mi. off I-5, Exit 191**	Credit Cards: **MC, VISA**
No. of Rooms: **2**	Pets: **No**
No. of Private Baths: **2**	Children: **Welcome, over 12**
Double/pb: **$72**	Smoking: **No**
Single/pb: **$62**	Social Drinking: **Permitted**
Open: **All year**	Airport/Station Pickup: **Yes**

Maryellen's Guest House is one and a half blocks from beautiful Hendricks Park, and just a few minutes away from the University of Oregon campus. In Maryellen's own backyard you'll find a swimming pool and a hot tub. You can also luxuriate in the master suite bathroom, with its double shower and deep Roman tub. In the morning, enjoy Continental breakfast in your room, or come to the dining room for fresh fruit followed by your choice of eggs, cereal, waffles, and muffins. When weather permits, meals can be served on the deck overlooking the pool.

Pookie's Bed 'n' Breakfast on College Hill ✪
2013 CHARNELTON STREET, EUGENE, OREGON 97405

Tel: **(503) 343-0383**	Single/sb: **$55**
Hosts: **Pookie and Doug Walling**	Open: **All year**
Location: **110 mi. S of Portland**	Reduced Rates: **20% families**
No. of Rooms: **2**	Breakfast: **Full**
No. of Private Baths: **1**	Pets: **No**
Max. No. Sharing Bath: **4**	Children: **Welcome, over 6**
Double/pb: **$80**	Smoking: **No**
Single/pb: **$70**	Social Drinking: **Permitted**
Double/sb: **$65**	

Although it has been remodeled on the outside, this Craftsman-style house, built in 1918, retains much of its original interior charm. One room has antique mahogany furniture and a queen-size bed; the other has oak furnishings and either a single or twin beds. Pookie's is in a quiet older neighborhood just south of downtown, where you'll find great shopping, excellent dining, and access to the Hult Performing Arts Center. The University of Oregon campus is all of a mile away. Early morning coffee is served in the small sitting room upstairs. A full breakfast, with specialties like quiche and orange custard baked French toast, follows.

Ahlf House Bed & Breakfast ✪

762 N.W. 6TH STREET, GRANTS PASS, OREGON 97526

Tel: (503) 474-1374	Single/sb: $55
Hosts: Herbert and Betty Buskirk, and	Open: All year
Rosemary Althaus	Breakfast: Full
Location: 2 blocks from downtown	Pets: No
Grants Pass	Children: No
No. of Rooms: 2	Smoking: No
Max. No. Sharing Bath: 4	Social Drinking: Permitted
Double/sb: $65	Airport/Station Pickup: Yes

Ahlf House is located on a main street on a hill overlooking the surrounding mountains. The house dates back to 1902, and is listed on the National Register of Historic Places. The rooms are beautifully appointed and furnished in fine antiques. Guest rooms feature fluffy comforters, down pillows, fresh flowers, and candles. Enjoy a cup of fresh coffee first thing in the morning in the quiet of your room or on the sunny front porch. Your coffee is followed by a full gourmet breakfast including fruit, fresh-baked muffins, and homemade jams and jellies. There is much to explore in Grants Pass, which is set on the Rogue River and is surrounded by the beautiful Cascade Mountains. Your hosts can direct you to guided fishing, raft trips, and jet boats. In the evening, return to this lovely Victorian for parlor music, complimentary wine, and a light snack.

The Washington Inn Bed & Breakfast ✪

1002 NORTHWEST WASHINGTON BOULEVARD, GRANTS PASS, OREGON 97526

Tel: (503) 476-1131	Open: All year
Hosts: Maryan and Bill Thompson	Reduced Rates: Available
Location: ½ mi. from I-5	Breakfast: Full
No. of Rooms: 3	Credit Cards: MC, VISA
No. of Private Baths: 2	Pets: No
Max. No. Sharing Bath: 2	Children: Welcome, over 14
Double/pb: $50–$65	Smoking: No
Single/pb: $40–$55	Social Drinking: Permitted
Double/sb: $40–$55	Airport/Station Pickup: Yes
Single/sb: $30–$45	

The Washington Inn is a charming Victorian listed on the National Register of Historic Places. Each guest room is named for one of the Thompsons' three children and offers individual charms. Linda's is a large suite with fireplace, queen-size bed, private bath, and balcony overlooking the mountains; Pattie's Parlor is a spacious red room with fireplace and large private bath with claw-footed tub; Sally's Sunny View overlooks the mountains, has a canopied bed, and is decorated in delicate pink. Your hosts offer bicycles for exploring the area, and many interesting shops and restaurants are within easy walking distance. Fishing, rafting, and jet-boat rides can be enjoyed on the Rogue River. If you prefer, spend the afternoon relaxing on the porch swing, taking in the view.

Black Bart Bed & Breakfast ✪
94125 LOVE LAKE ROAD, JUNCTION CITY, OREGON 97448

Tel: **(503) 998-1904**
Hosts: **Don and Irma Mode**
Location: **14 mi. N of Eugene**
No. of Rooms: **2**
No. of Private Baths: **2**
Double/pb: **$50–$60**
Single/pb: **$45–$55**
Open: **All year**

Breakfast: **Full**
Credit Cards: **MC, VISA**
Pets: **No**
Children: **No**
Smoking: **No**
Social Drinking: **Permitted**
Airport/Station Pickup: **Yes**

Don and Irma named this B&B for their National Grand Champion mammoth donkey, who strutted his stuff in a parade of equines at the 1984 Olympics; time and weather permitting, Black Bart will oblige guests by pulling them around in an antique shay. The other resident equines, the Belgian mules Nip and Tuck, can be called on for wagon rides. The B&B itself is a remodeled 1880s farmhouse, filled with antiques and—surprise!—lots of donkey collectibles. Nearby, you'll find lots of wineries and farmers' markets, plus golf courses and antique shops. Ableskivers, eggs, bacon or sausage, fruit, and juice constitute the hearty farm breakfasts.

Marjon Bed and Breakfast Inn ✪
44975 LEABURG DAM ROAD, LEABURG, OREGON 97489

Tel: **(503) 896-3145**
Host: **Marguerite Haas**
Location: **24 mi. E of Eugene**
No. of Rooms: **2**
No. of Private Baths: **2**
Double/pb: **$80**
Suites: **$100**
Open: **All year**

Breakfast: **Full**
Credit Cards: **MC, VISA**
Pets: **No**
Children: **No**
Smoking: **Permitted**
Social Drinking: **Permitted**
Airport/Station Pickup: **Yes**

This cedar chalet is located on the banks of the McKenzie River. The suite overlooks the river and a secluded Japanese garden, and features a sunken bath. The other has a fishbowl shower and a view of a 100-year-old apple tree. Relax in the living room with its wraparound seating and massive stone fireplace. One of the walls is made entirely of glass with sliding doors that lead to a terrace that faces the river. A multicourse breakfast is served there on balmy days. Waterfalls, trout fishing, white-water rafting, and skiing are all nearby.

Secluded B&B ☉

19719 NORTHEAST WILLIAMSON ROAD, NEWBERG, OREGON 97132

Tel: **(503) 538-2635**
Best Time to Call: **8 AM**
Hosts: **Del and Durell Belanger**
Location: **27 mi. SW of Portland**
No. of Rooms: **2**
No. of Private Baths: **1**
Max. No. Sharing Bath: **4**
Double/pb: **$50**
Double/sb: **$40**

Single/sb: **$40**
Open: **All year**
Breakfast: **Full**
Pets: **No**
Children: **Welcome, under 1 and over 6**
Smoking: **No**
Social Drinking: **No**

A rustic home with a gambrel roof and sunny decks, this B&B is secluded, but not isolated. Set on 10 wooded acres, it is near several notable wineries. George Fox College is also in the area. Your hosts' hobbies include gardening, cooking, and carpentry; Durell made the stained-glass windows that accent the house. The mouth-watering breakfasts might include fresh shrimp omelets, Grand Marnier French toast, or Dutch babies swathed in apple-huckleberry sauce and whipped cream, accompanied by juice, fruit, and coffee or tea.

The Highlands Bed and Breakfast ☉

608 RIDGE ROAD, NORTH BEND, OREGON 97459

Tel: **(503) 756-0300**
Hosts: **Jim and Marilyn Dow**
Location: **4 mi. from Hwy. 101**
No. of Rooms: **2**

No. of Private Baths: **2**
Double/pb: **$65–$70**
Single/pb: **$60–$65**
Open: **All year**

Breakfast: **Full**
Credit Cards: **MC, VISA**
Pets: **No**
Children: **Welcome, over 10**

Smoking: **No**
Social Drinking: **Permitted**
Airport/Station Pickup: **Yes**

This uniquely designed contemporary cedar home, with its wide expanses of glass and wraparound deck, has a spectacular view of the valley, inlet, and bay. From the floor-to-ceiling windows of the family room you'll be able to watch unforgettable sunrises and sunsets. Dark oak-pegged flooring, beamed vaulted ceilings, and cedar paneling make a perfect setting for the Dows' antiques. A separate entrance for guests assures privacy, and separate heat controls assure comfort. Breakfast includes fresh-squeezed juice, fruit compote with special sauce, baked eggs on rice with cheese, ham or bacon, and freshly baked muffins or popovers. A short drive away are Oregon's beaches, sand dunes, and many fine restaurants. The Dows are retired and like to fly, sail, and garden.

Inn of the Oregon Trail ✪
416 SOUTH MCLOUGHLIN, OREGON CITY, OREGON 97045

Tel: **(503) 656-2089**
Best Time to Call: **7 AM–5 PM**
Hosts: **Mary and Tom DeHaven**
Location: **13 mi. SE of Portland**
No. of Rooms: **4**
No. of Private Baths: **4**
Double/pb: **$47.50–$57.50**
Suites: **$77.50**

Open: **All year**
Breakfast: **Full**
Credit Cards: **MC, VISA**
Pets: **No**
Children: **Welcome, over 12**
Smoking: **No**
Social Drinking: **Permitted**

A superb Gothic Revival home built in 1867 by a Willamette River captain, Inn of the Oregon Trail is listed on the National Register of Historic Places. In fact, this Oregon City neighborhood is filled with distinctive buildings and museums—ask your hosts to recommend walking and driving tours. You'll have plenty of energy for sightseeing after one of Tom's ample breakfasts of juice, coffee, eggs, pancakes, and French toast.

John Palmer House ✪
4314 NORTH MISSISSIPPI AVENUE, PORTLAND, OREGON 97217

Tel: **(503) 284-5893**
Best Time to Call: **7 AM–8 PM**
Hosts: **Mary and Richard Sauter**
Location: **3½ mi. N of Portland**
No. of Rooms: **7**
No. of Private Baths: **3**
Max. No. Sharing Bath: **4**
Double/sb: **$40–$60**

Single/sb: **$30**
Guest Cottage: **$135; sleeps 6**
Suites: **$85–$120**
Open: **All year**
Reduced Rates: **$10 less Sun.–Thurs., Jan.–Apr.**
Breakfast: **Full**
Other Meals: **Available**

Credit Cards: **AMEX, DISC, MC, VISA**
Pets: **No**
Children: **Welcome, in cottage**

Smoking: **No**
Social Drinking: **Permitted**
Airport/Station Pickup: **Yes**

John Palmer built this ornate Victorian in 1890, and today it is a nationally registered landmark home. Hundred-year-old gaslight fixtures, gleaming woodwork, and hand-screened wallpapers have been beautifully preserved and are complemented by plush carpets, lace, and velvet accents. Your hosts cater to the romantic in everyone with afternoon tea, chilled champagne, and an occasional recital from the resident pianist. Guest quarters range from the main house's bridal suite with canopy bed and balcony to one of grandma's cottage rooms with its pretty wallpapers and brass beds. Breakfast choices such as blueberry crêpes and mushroom omelets are served in the formal dining room and enhanced by fresh roses and candlelight. This sprawling house has two parlors, a veranda, and a Jacuzzi on the porch. The Sauters will arrange a horse-and-carriage ride to your favorite restaurant or, if you like, can prepare a gourmet dinner at the house.

Trinity House Bed and Breakfast ✪
1956 NORTH WEST EVERETT STREET, PORTLAND, OREGON 97209

Tel: **(503) 294-0753**
Hosts: **Wayne and Jan Case**
Location: **Northwest Portland**
No. of Rooms: **4**
Max. No. Sharing Bath: **4**
Double/sb: **$65**
Open: **All year**

Reduced Rates: **$10 less after third night**
Breakfast: **Full**
Pets: **No**
Children: **Welcome, over 12**
Smoking: **No**
Social Drinking: **Permitted**
Airport/Station Pickup: **Yes**
Foreign Languages: **French**

In 1906, when Trinity House was built, the surrounding Nob Hill district was one of Portland's most fashionable neighborhoods, and it

remains so to this day. You'll discover boutiques, antique shops, cafés, and galleries in beautifully restored buildings. This three-story Victorian has been lovingly renovated and elegantly furnished. Rooms have queen- or king-size beds. Guests may avail themselves of off-street parking and the washer and dryer. Full breakfasts include freshly squeezed orange juice, fruit, and hot entrées like gingerbread pancakes.

The Boarding House Bed & Breakfast
208 NORTH HOLLADAY DRIVE, SEASIDE, OREGON 97138

Tel: (503) 738-9055	Open: All year
Hosts: Dick and Barb Edwards	Reduced Rates: Available
Location: ½ mi. from Rte. 101	Breakfast: Full
No. of Rooms: 6	Credit Cards: MC, VISA
No. of Private Baths: 6	Pets: No
Double/pb: $60–$75	Children: Welcome
Single/pb: $55–$70	Smoking: No
Guest Cottage: $95; sleeps 6, $600 weekly	Social Drinking: Permitted
	Airport/Station Pickup: Yes

Located on the banks of the Necanicum River, this rustic Victorian was built as a private residence in 1898. During World War I, the house became a boarding home. After an extensive renovation, the wood walls and beamed ceilings have been restored to their original charm. Guest rooms feature brass or white iron beds, down quilts, family heirlooms, wicker, and wood. Claw-footed tubs, window seats, antiques, and a picture of grandma make you feel as if this house is your own. A fire is often burning in the fir-paneled parlor, and an old melody sounds just right on the old-fashioned Victrola. A 100-year-old guest cottage with wood paneling, country furnishings, bedroom, loft, and river view is also available. Breakfast specialties such as cheese-and-egg strata, orange French toast, and blueberry scones are served in the dining room or outside on the wraparound porch. The house is just four blocks from the ocean and two blocks from downtown.

Horncroft ✪
42156 KINGSTON LYONS DRIVE, STAYTON, OREGON 97383

Tel: (503) 769-6287	Double/sb: $35
Hosts: Dorothea and Kenneth Horn	Single/sb: $30
Location: 17 mi. E of Salem	Open: All year
No. of Rooms: 3	Breakfast: Full
No. of Private Baths: 1	Pets: No
Max. No. Sharing Bath: 4	Children: Sometimes
Double/pb: $45	Smoking: No
Single/pb: $40	Social Drinking: Permitted

This lovely home is situated in the foothills of the Cascade Mountains on the edge of Willamette Valley. In summer, swim in the heated pool or hike on one of the scenic nature paths. The area is dotted with farms, and the valley is abundant in fruits, berries, and vegetables. Willamette and Oregon State universities are nearby. The Mount Jefferson Wilderness hiking area is an hour away. A guest comments, "The hospitality and breakfasts were topnotch!"

Old Welches Inn ○
26401 EAST WELCHES ROAD, WELCHES, OREGON 97067

Tel: **(503) 622-3754**	Breakfast: **Full**
Best Time to Call: **After 6 PM**	Credit Cards: **AMEX, MC, VISA**
Hosts: **Judith and Ted Mondun**	Pets: **Dogs welcome**
Location: **50 mi. E of Portland**	Children: **Welcome, over 12**
No. of Rooms: **3**	Smoking: **No**
Max. No. Sharing Bath: **3**	Social Drinking: **Permitted**
Double/sb: **$55–$65**	Minimum Stay: **2 nights holidays**
Open: **All year**	

Built as a resort in the late 19th century, the Old Welches Inn is a large white Colonial with blue shutters. The house stands on the edge of the Mt. Hood wilderness area, crisscrossed by miles of hiking and ski trails. Fishermen may carry poles to the back of the B&B property, where they can drop lines in the Salmon River. And just across the road, golfers will find that 27 holes await. You'll be ready for action after a full, Southern-style breakfast, highlighted by home-baked muffins, biscuits, and breads.

The Carriage House ○
515 SOUTH PACIFIC HIGHWAY, WOODBURN, OREGON 97071

Tel: **(503) 982-6321**	Open: **All year**
Best Time to Call: **Before 9 AM; after 6 PM**	Breakfast: **Full**
	Credit Cards: **MC, VISA**
Hosts: **Lawrence and Marilyn Paradis**	Pets: **Sometimes**
Location: **30 mi. S of Portland**	Children: **Welcome**
No. of Rooms: **2**	Smoking: **No**
Max. No. Sharing Bath: **4**	Social Drinking: **Permitted**
Double/sb: **$50**	Airport/Station Pickup: **Yes**
Single/sb: **$45**	Foreign Languages: **French**

The Carriage House is a 1906 Victorian known for its peaceful country elegance. Completely restored, it is furnished with family treasures and heirloom quilts. Lawrence and Marilyn keep horses and an antique buggy in a carriage house next to the inn. This is an excellent location for visiting the Enchanted Forest, the Oregon State Fair, the Octoberfest in Mt. Angel, the Bach Festival, historic Champoeg, and numerous antique shops and wineries.

PENNSYLVANIA

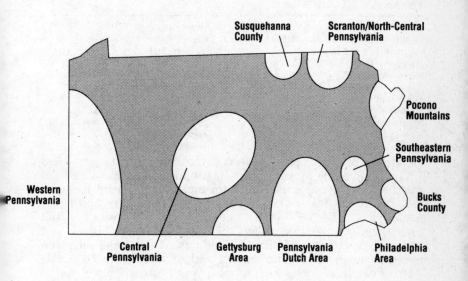

Susquehanna County — Scranton/North-Central Pennsylvania — Pocono Mountains — Southeastern Pennsylvania — Bucks County — Western Pennsylvania — Central Pennsylvania — Gettysburg Area — Pennsylvania Dutch Area — Philadelphia Area

Bed & Breakfast in Pennsylvania ✪
P.O. BOX 169, PINE GROVE MILLS, PENNSYLVANIA 16868

Tel: **(814) 238-1484**
Best Time to Call: **9 AM–noon**
Coordinator: **Linda Feltman**
States/Regions Covered: **Statewide**

Rates (Single/Double):
    Average: **$30–$80 / $40–$200**
Credit Cards: **Varies with each B&B**

Call Linda for the name and phone number of a B&B in the area you want to visit anywhere in the state. You can then call the host directly. Accommodations range from a clean, simple mountain lodge to a comfortable suburban split-level to a pre-Revolutionary manor house. There is no charge for this service. If you haven't decided where in the state you'd like to go, Linda's quarterly newsletter includes up-to-the-minute information on Pennsylvania's more than 500 inns.

BUCKS COUNTY

Maplewood Farm Bed & Breakfast ✪
5090 DURHAM ROAD, P.O. BOX 239, GARDENVILLE,
PENNSYLVANIA 18926

Tel: **(215) 766-0477**	Open: **All year**
Best Time to Call: **10 AM–10 PM**	Reduced Rates: **Mon.–Thurs.**
Hosts: **Cindy and Dennis Marquis**	Breakfast: **Full**
Location: **45 mi. NW of Philadelphia**	Credit Cards: **AMEX, DISC, MC, VISA**
No. of Rooms: **7**	Pets: **No**
No. of Private Baths: **5**	Children: **Sometimes**
Double/pb: **$85–$100**	Smoking: **No**
Double/sb: **$65–$80**	Social Drinking: **Permitted**
Single/pb: **$80–$95**	Minimum Stay: **2 nights weekends, 3**
Suites: **$135**	**nights holidays**

Hundred-year-old maples shelter this fieldstone farmhouse, dated 1792. The five-acre property includes a tranquil stream, sheep-filled pastures, and a two-story bank barn that houses playful barnyard cats. Inn rooms feature local antiques, cozy comforters, and hand-made quilts. Choose Victoria's Room, with a four-poster bed and ceiling fan, or the two-story loft suite, with its exposed beams and sitting room. Upon your arrival, Cindy and Dennis will offer you refreshments in the antique summer kitchen, which boasts a double walk-in fireplace. For year-round fun, your hosts will direct you to Peddler's Village, New Hope, and lots of charming river towns. In the morning, gather eggs fresh from the source and have them turned into fluffy omelets, crisp waffles, fruit-filled pancakes, or Dennis' famous French toast. Breakfast is served in the country dining room with random-width floors, beamed ceilings, and an exposed stone wall. After dinner, return to the inn to enjoy conversation and a nightcap with your hosts, and exchange tales of your day with the other guests.

Aaron Burr House ✪
80 WEST BRIDGE STREET, NEW HOPE, PENNSYLVANIA 18938

Tel: **(215) 862-2343**	Single/pb: **$70**
Best Time to Call: **12–10 PM**	Suites: **$95–$145; sleeps 3**
Host: **Carl Glassman**	Open: **All year**
Location: **20 mi. N of Philadelphia**	Reduced Rates: **Mon.–Thurs.,**
No. of Rooms: **6**	**corporate guests**
No. of Private Baths: **6**	Breakfast: **Continental**
Double/pb: **$75**	Pets: **Sometimes**

Children: **Welcome**
Smoking: **No**
Social Drinking: **Permitted**

Minimum Stay: **2 nights on weekends,
3 nights holidays**
Station Pickup: **Yes**

This 1854 Victorian is tucked onto a tree-lined street in the town's historic district, just steps from the village center. New Hope was founded in 1681, so visitors can absorb three centuries of architecture and American history, plus fine antique shops, excellent restaurants, and art galleries and crafts shops. At the end of the day, join your hosts in the parlor for reading, games, refreshments, and friendly conversation. After a peaceful night's rest in a canopy bed, you'll wake up to the aroma of fresh coffee and home-baked muffins.

Wedgwood Inn of New Hope ✪
111 WEST BRIDGE STREET, NEW HOPE, PENNSYLVANIA 18938

Tel: **(215) 862-2520**
Best Time to Call: **10 AM–10 PM**
Hosts: **Carl Glassman and Nadine
Silnutzer**
Location: **62 mi. SW of New York City**
No. of Rooms: **12**
No. of Private Baths: **10**
Max. No. Sharing Bath: **4**

Double/pb: **$70–$125**
Single/pb: **$65–$115**
Double/sb: **$65–$85**
Single/sb: **$60–$80**
Suites: **$90–$155**
Open: **All year**
Reduced Rates: **Available**
Breakfast: **Continental**

Credit Cards: **AMEX**
Pets: **Sometimes**
Children: **Welcome**
Smoking: **No**
Social Drinking: **Permitted**

Minimum Stay: **3 holiday weekends, 2 nights if stay includes Saturday**
Station Pickup: **Yes**
Foreign Languages: **French, Hebrew, Spanish**

Wedgwood pottery is displayed throughout this aptly named two-and-a-half-story home with lots of nineteenth-century details: a gabled roof, veranda, porte cochere, and gazebo. Rooms are decorated with antiques, original art, handmade quilts, and fresh flowers. You can breakfast on house specialties like lemon yogurt poppyseed bread and ricotta pineapple muffins on the sun porch, in the gazebo, or in the privacy of your room. Carl and Nadine are such accomplished hosts that they conduct workshops and seminars on innkeeping, and Carl has taught courses on buying and operating country inns.

CENTRAL PENNSYLVANIA

Rest & Repast Bed & Breakfast Service ✪
P.O. BOX 126, PINE GROVE MILLS, PENNSYLVANIA 16868

Tel: **(814) 238-1484**
Coordinators: **Linda and Brent Peters**
States/Regions Covered: **Aaronsburg, Bellefonte, Boalsburg, Huntingdon, Phillipsburg, Potters Mills, Spruce Creek, State College, Tyrone**

Rates (Single/Double):
  Average: **$35–$40 / $40–$50**
  Luxury: **— / $50–$70**
Credit Cards: **No**

You will enjoy touring historic mansions, Penns Cave, Woodward Cave, and several Civil War museums in this lovely area. A two-day minimum stay is required for the second week in July, the time of the annual Central Pennsylvania Festival of the Arts, and for the Penn State University Homecoming Football game in autumn. Rates are increased during peak weekends to a maximum of $70 per night double. (No single rates on football weekends.) Pennsylvania State University is close by.

Bedford House ✪
203 W. PITT STREET, BEDFORD, PENNSYLVANIA 15522

Tel: **(814) 623-7171**
Best Time to Call: **10 AM–10 PM**
Hosts: **Lyn and Linda Lyon**
Location: **107 mi. E of Pittsburgh**
No. of Rooms: **6**
No. of Private Baths: **6**
Double/pb: **$45–$75**
Single/pb: **$35–$65**

Open: **All year**
Reduced Rates: **Available**
Breakfast: **Full**
Credit Cards: **AMEX, DISC, MC, VISA**
Pets: **No**
Children: **Welcome, over 12**
Smoking: **No**
Social Drinking: **Permitted**

Minimum Stay: **2 nights first 2 weekends Oct.**

Airport/Station Pickup: **Yes**

Situated halfway between Pittsburgh and Harrisburg, Bedford is a lovely little town that sprang up around Fort Bedford, built in 1758. Bedford House, constructed some forty years later, is a large brick village home on one of the National Historic District's original town lots. Guest rooms are furnished with a mixture of antiques, reproductions, and family heirlooms. This B&B is a five-minute stroll from Fort Bedford Museum and Park, shops, restaurants, and churches. Other area attractions include Old Bedford Village, Shawnee State Park, Coral Caverns, and Blue Knob Ski Area.

Highland House ✪
108 BUCHER HILL, BOILING SPRINGS, PENNSYLVANIA 17007

Tel: **(717) 258-3744**	Double/sb: **$75**
Best Time to Call: **3 PM–10 PM**	Single/sb: **$65**
Host: **Barry Buchter**	Open: **All year**
Location: **17 mi. N of Harrisburg**	Breakfast: **Full**
No. of Rooms: **3**	Pets: **No**
No. of Private Baths: **1**	Children: **No**
Max. No. Sharing Bath: **4**	Smoking: **Permitted**
Double/pb: **$75**	Social Drinking: **Permitted**
Single/pb: **$65**	Airport Pickup: **Yes**

Local ironmaster Michael Ege, who supplied cannons and cannonballs to George Washington at Valley Forge, built this Federal brick house sometime around 1776. Robert Morris and John Hancock are said to have been among Ege's overnight guests. In the next century, Highland House allegedly served as a stop for escaped slaves traveling the Underground Railroad. Your host, a retired TV executive who bought the property in 1990, can show you the secret third-floor compartment where slaves are thought to have been concealed. He also promises that the best trout fishing in the eastern seaboard is in the area. If you don't get any bites, you can always take a short drive to Harrisburg, Gettysburg Battlefield, or Hershey Theme Park.

Yoders ✪
RD 1, BOX 312, HUNTINGDON, PENNSYLVANIA 16652

Tel: **(814) 643-3221**	Single/pb: **$30**
Best Time to Call: **After 4 PM**	Open: **All year**
Hosts: **Randy and Peggy Yoder**	Reduced Rates: **10% seniors**
Location: **On Rte. 22**	Breakfast: **Continental**
No. of Rooms: **3**	Other Meals: **Available**
No. of Private Baths: **2**	Pets: **Sometimes**
Double/pb: **$40**	Children: **No**

Smoking: **No**   Airport/Station Pickup: **Yes**
Social Drinking: **No**

After you've visited the Swigart Museum of antique American auto-
mobiles, explored the caves of Lincoln Caverns, or taken advantage of
Lake Raystown with its recreational diversions, come home to Randy
and Peggy's. The house, fronted with a huge picture window and
native stone, is located at the edge of a 200-acre forest where you may
feel free to hike. Breakfast often features croissants, waffles, pancakes,
or special omelets. Fresh fruit and cheese snacks are complimentary.

Bedford's Covered Bridge Inn ✪
RD 1, BOX 196, SCHELLSBURG, PENNSYLVANIA 15559

Tel: **(814) 733-4093**	Reduced Rates: **Available**
Best Time to Call: **10 AM–10 PM**	Breakfast: **Full**
Hosts: **Greg and Martha Lau**	Credit Cards: **DISC, MC, VISA**
Location: **97 mi E of Pittsburgh**	Pets: **No**
No. of Rooms: **6**	Children: **Welcome, over 12**
No. of Private Baths: **6**	Smoking: **No**
Double/pb: **$55–$65**	Social Drinking: **Permitted**
Suites: **$75**	Minimum Stay: **Holidays, fall**
Open: **All year**	**weekends**

Just minutes from Bedford's historic district, this turn-of-the-century
farmhouse and covered bridge adjoin 4,000-acre Shawnee State Park.
Biking, hiking, birding, trout fishing, and cross-country skiing are
available right at the B&B door. Shawnee Lake is nearby, for swimming
and boating, while the less athletically inclined can explore Old
Bedford Village, Fort Bedford Museum, the Pennsylvania Transportation Museum, and Coral Caverns. The area is also rich in antique
shops and covered bridges. Mention your interests and Greg and
Martha will help you plan an itinerary.

Mrs. G's Bed & Breakfast ✪
256 WEST RIDGE AVENUE, STATE COLLEGE, PENNSYLVANIA 16803

Tel: **(814) 238-0733**	Reduced Rates: **Weekly**
Best Time to Call: **Evenings**	Breakfast: **Continental**
Host: **Ursula A. Gusse**	Pets: **No**
Location: **140 mi. NE of Pittsburgh**	Children: **Welcome, over 6**
No. of Rooms: **2**	Smoking: **Permitted**
Max. No. Sharing Bath: **4**	Social Drinking: **Permitted**
Double/sb: **$40–$60**	Airport/Station Pickup: **Yes**
Single/sb: **$30–$45**	Foreign Languages: **German, some**
Open: **All year**	**French**

Simply but comfortably furnished, Mrs. G's B&B offers visitors the
best of both worlds: the college town pleasures of Penn State University and the rural charm of the surrounding communities. Attend

performances by internationally celebrated musicians and actors on the Penn State campus, then go hiking or skiing in the area's many parks. Continental breakfasts feature fresh fruit, sweet rolls and Danish, specialty breads, and muesli.

GETTYSBURG AREA

Valentine Flohrs House ✪
616 FLOHRS CHURCH ROAD, BIGLERVILLE, PENNSYLVANIA 17307

Tel: **(717) 334-5827**	Open: **All year**
Best Time to Call: **Evening**	Breakfast: **Full**
Hosts: **Tom and Camila Baumgartner**	Credit Cards: **MC, VISA**
Location: **6½ mi. W of Gettysburg**	Pets: **No**
No. of Rooms: **1**	Children: **No**
No. of Private Baths: **1**	Smoking: **No**
Suite: **$75**	Social Drinking: **Permitted**

Escape the hectic pace of your life at the Valentine Flohrs House, where the soothing atmosphere and the beauty of the surrounding countryside will rejuvenate your spirits. This early nineteenth-century Georgian Colonial has been beautifully restored and decorated with antiques and early hooked rugs. The private suite—including bedroom, bath, and sitting room with fireplace—is equipped with a TV, VCR, and complimentary classic movies. The full breakfasts feature gourmet entrées and home-baked items. Gettysburg Battlefield, the Eisenhower farm, Ski Liberty, and the Appalachian Trail are always worth a visit. Tom and Cam look forward to welcoming you.

Goose Chase ✪
200 BLUEBERRY ROAD, GARDNERS, PENNSYLVANIA 17324

Tel: **(717) 528-8877**	Open: **All year**
Best Time to Call: **Evenings**	Breakfast: **Full**
Hosts: **Marsha and Rich Lucidi**	Credit Cards: **MC, VISA**
Location: **12 mi. N of Gettysburg**	Pets: **No**
No. of Rooms: **5**	Children: **Welcome, over 12**
No. of Private Baths: **3**	Smoking: **No**
Max. No. Sharing Bath: **4**	Social Drinking: **Permitted**
Double/pb: **$79–$89**	Airport/Station Pickup: **Yes**
Double/sb: **$69**	

This restored 18th-century stone house on a 25-acre farm is located in apple orchard country. Air-conditioned for summer comfort, it is handsomely furnished with handmade quilts, folk art, and carefully chosen American antiques. Wide-plank floors, oriental rugs, stenciled walls, and deep-silled windows add to the charming atmosphere. Breakfast always features a delicious main dish and is served by

Marsha in authentic Colonial garb. Fresh flowers, terry cloth robes, and beds turned down with chocolate treats on the pillow are a few of the Lucidis' thoughtful touches. Wine or tea is graciously offered and, in winter, hot mulled cider is served by a crackling fire. Gettysburg Battlefield is within easy reach. Summer swimming pool and walking trails are on the property. Inquire about the package featuring weekday cooking school classes. Antiquing, skiing, fishing, and golf are nearby.

The Brafferton Inn ✪
44–46 YORK STREET, GETTYSBURG, PENNSYLVANIA 17325

Tel: **(717) 337-3423**	Double/sb: **$70**
Hosts: **Mimi and Jim Agard**	Open: **All year**
Location: **90 mi. N of D.C.; 2 mi. from**	Breakfast: **Full**
Rte. 15, York exit	Credit Cards: **MC, VISA**
No. of Rooms: **10**	Pets: **No**
No. of Private Baths: **6**	Children: **Welcome, over 7**
Max. No. Sharing Bath: **4**	Smoking: **No**
Double/pb: **$90**	Social Drinking: **Permitted**

This Early American stone structure is listed on the National Register of Historic Places. The clapboard addition dates back to pre–Civil War days. Six of the guest rooms, decorated with hand-painted stencils, are separated from the main house by an atrium where one may sit and enjoy the pretty plantings during the warm months. The sumptuous breakfast is served in the dining room on antique tables. There are hosts of activities to whet the appetite of the history buff, sportsman, antique collector, or nature lover.

Keystone Inn ✪
231 HANOVER STREET, GETTYSBURG, PENNSYLVANIA 17325

Tel: **(717) 337-3888**	Open: **All year**
Best Time to Call: **7 AM–10 PM**	Reduced Rates: **Available**
Hosts: **Wilmer and Doris Martin**	Breakfast: **Full**
Location: **35 mi. S of Harrisburg**	Other Meals: **Available**
No. of Rooms: **4**	Credit Cards: **MC, VISA**
No. of Private Baths: **2**	Pets: **No**
Max. No. Sharing Bath: **4**	Children: **Welcome**
Double/pb: **$75**	Smoking: **No**
Double/sb: **$59**	Social Drinking: **No**

Keystone Inn is a large Victorian built in 1913 by Clayton Reaser, a local furniture maker. His talents as a craftsman are evident in the natural oak and chestnut found throughout the house. The beautiful woodwork is complemented with lace, ruffles, and floral designs favored by the Martin family. The guest rooms are decorated with brass or antique wood beds and soft pastel wallpapers, and each bedroom has a reading nook and windowside writing table overlooking historic Gettysburg. A full breakfast features such specialties as cinnamon-apple or blueberry pancakes, waffles, eggs, and fruits. Afternoon lemonade is served on the front porch in summer; in winter guests can enjoy a hot drink by the fireplace. The inn is close to historic sites and Civil War battlefields, antique shops, state parks, and is nine miles from the Liberty ski area.

The Old Appleford Inn
218 CARLISLE STREET, GETTYSBURG, PENNSYLVANIA 17325

Tel: (717) 337-1711;	Open: All year
fax: (717) 334-6228	Breakfast: Full
Hosts: Frank and Maribeth Skradski	Credit Cards: AMEX, MC, VISA
No. of Rooms: 12	Pets: No
No. of Private Baths: 12	Children: Welcome, over 14
Double/pb: $83–$93	Smoking: No
Suite: $133; sleeps 4	Social Drinking: Permitted

This is a beautiful brick mansion built in 1867 and decorated with Victorian antique furnishings dating back to the Civil War. After your tour of the battlefield, Frank and Maribeth invite you to enjoy the warmth of several fireplaces, sip a complimentary sherry, and bask in the mellifluous strains of the baby grand piano in the parlor. There are ski slopes nearby for winter sports enthusiasts, spring apple blossoms, and fall foliage to enjoy. All rooms are air-conditioned for summer comfort. You are certain to awaken each morning to the scent of homemade breads, muffins, or to other olfactory indications of the gourmet breakfast to come.

The Tannery B&B ○
449 BALTIMORE STREET, GETTYSBURG, PENNSYLVANIA 17325

Tel: (717) 334-2454	Breakfast: Continental
Best Time to Call: 9 AM–9 PM	Credit Cards: MC, VISA
Hosts: Charlotte and Jule Swope	Pets: No
No. of Rooms: 5	Children: Welcome, over 12
No. of Private Baths: 5	Smoking: No
Double/pb: $75–$95	Social Drinking: Permitted
Open: All year	

To stay in this large Gothic home is to rub shoulders with history. During the third day of the Battle of Gettysburg, Union soldiers took over the front porch, Rebels occupied the building's rear, and the owner—a tanner named John Rupp—dodged bullets by hiding in the cellar. Civil War buffs can walk to most of Gettysburg's museums and landmarks. Those who would rather dwell in the present can take advantage of several local golf courses. At the end of the day you can relax with complimentary wine and cheese, or a glass of iced tea. Continental breakfast consists of juice, fresh fruit, cereal, baked goods, and coffee.

The Doubleday Inn ✪
104 DOUBLEDAY AVENUE, GETTYSBURG BATTLEFIELD, PENNSYLVANIA 17325

Tel: **(717) 334-9119**	Open: **All year**
Hosts: **Joan and Sal Chandon, and Olga Krossick**	Breakfast: **Full**
	Credit Cards: **MC, VISA**
No. of Rooms: **9**	Pets: **No**
No. of Private Baths: **5**	Children: **Welcome, over 10**
Max. No. Sharing Bath: **4**	Smoking: **No**
Double/pb: **$84–$100**	Social Drinking: **Permitted**
Double/sb: **$74**	

The only B&B located on the battlefield, this beautifully restored Colonial recalls past-century charms with Civil War furnishings and antique accessories. Afternoon tea is served with country-style drinks and hors d'oeuvres on the outdoor patio, or by the fireplace in the main parlor. One of the largest known library collections devoted exclusively to the Battle of Gettysburg is available to you. On selected evenings, you are welcome to participate in a discussion with a Civil War historian who brings the battle alive with accurate accounts and displays of authentic memorabilia and weaponry.

Beechmont Inn ✪
315 BROADWAY, HANOVER, PENNSYLVANIA 17331

Tel: **(717) 632-3013; (800) 553-7009**	Suites: **$105–$125**
Best Time to Call: **9 AM–9 PM**	Open: **All year**
Hosts: **Terry and Monna Hormel, and Glenn and Maggie Hormel**	Breakfast: **Full**
	Credit Cards: **AMEX, MC, VISA**
Location: **13 mi. E of Gettysburg**	Pets: **No**
No. of Rooms: **7**	Children: **Welcome, over 12**
No. of Private Baths: **7**	Smoking: **Permitted**
Double/pb: **$70–$85**	Social Drinking: **Permitted**
Single/pb: **$64–$69**	

This Georgian house, restored to its Federal-period elegance, offers the visitor a bridge across time. Climb the winding staircase to freshly decorated rooms named in honor of the gallant heroes of the Civil War. At breakfast time, enjoy homemade granola, baked goods, a hot entrée, and fruit. Join the other guests in the dining room, or take a tray to your room for breakfast in bed. Visit nearby Gettysburg, the Eisenhower Farm, Hanover Shoe Farms, Codorus State Park for boating and fishing, or go antique hunting in New Oxford. Upon your return, you may relax in the quiet comfort of the parlor. The Hormels look forward to pampering you.

PENNSYLVANIA DUTCH AREA

Adamstown Inn ✪
62 WEST MAIN STREET, ADAMSTOWN, PENNSYLVANIA 19501

Tel: **(215) 484-0800; (800) 594-4800**	Reduced Rates: **10% after 4th night**
Hosts: **Tom and Wanda Berman**	Breakfast: **Continental, plus**
Location: **10 mi. SW of Reading**	Credit Cards: **MC, VISA**
No. of Rooms: **4**	Pets: **No**
No. of Private Baths: **4**	Children: **Welcome, over 12**
Double/pb: **$70–$100**	Smoking: **Restricted**
Open: **All year**	Social Drinking: **Permitted**

In the heart of Adamstown's antique district, and just a short drive from Pennsylvania Dutch Country and Reading's factory outlets, you'll find this handsome brick Victorian. Inside, lace and balloon curtains and oriental rugs complement the chestnut woodwork and leaded-glass windows. Two rooms feature two-person Jacuzzis. Your hosts are avid antiquers and will gladly direct you to their favorite haunts. Coffee or tea will be brought to your door in the morning; refills, as well as juice, fresh fruit, cheese, and home-baked goodies are served during a Continental breakfast.

Umble Rest ✪
RD 1, BOX 79, ATGLEN, PENNSYLVANIA 19310

Tel: **(215) 593-2274**	Open: **May 15–Oct. 15**
Best Time to Call: **7–10 AM; 3–7 PM**	Breakfast: **No**
Hosts: **Ken and Marilyn Umble**	Pets: **No**
Location: **15 mi. E of Lancaster**	Children: **Welcome**
No. of Rooms: **3**	Smoking: **No**
Max. No. Sharing Bath: **6**	Social Drinking: **No**
Double/sb: **$25–$30**	Minimum Stay: **Holiday weekends**

Ken and Marilyn are busy Mennonite farmers with interests in crafts, quilting, and restoring their 1800 farmhouse. You are invited to watch the milking of their 50 cows, stroll a country lane to their pond, and to participate in the simple life-style. Bring your children to play with their boys, ages three, seven, and ten. All the popular tourist attractions are nearby.

Sunday's Mill Farm B&B
RD 2, BOX 419, BERNVILLE, PENNSYLVANIA 19506

Tel: **(215) 488-7821**	Max. No. Sharing Bath: **4**
Hosts: **Sally and Len Blumberg**	Double/sb: **$45–$60**
Location: **11 mi. N of Reading**	Single/sb: **$35–$45**
No. of Rooms: **5**	Suite: **$140–$155; sleeps 6**

Open: **All year**
Reduced Rates: **10% after 1st night;
    families**
Breakfast: **Full**
Pets: **Horses welcome**

Children: **Welcome**
Smoking: **No**
Social Drinking: **Permitted**
Airport/Station Pickup: **Yes**

With a grist mill dating to 1820 and main buildings that are thirty years younger, this pastoral property is part of a National Historic District. Sunday's Mill Farm looks like a farmhouse should: exposed beams, rich woodwork, a brick dining room fireplace, quilts on the beds. Bring your fishing pole—Len stocks the pond. This is the rare B&B that accommodates both horseback riders and their mounts. Guests who prefer to use their own legs can explore the area's antique shops and factory outlets; Sally is active in historic preservation and can tell you a lot about the region over a breakfast of deep dish apple pancakes and sausage.

Greystone Manor B&B ✪
2658 OLD PHILADELPHIA PIKE, P. O. BOX 270, BIRD-IN-HAND, PENNSYLVANIA 17505

Tel: **(717) 393-4233**
Hosts: **Sally and Ed Davis**
No. of Rooms: **13**
No. of Private Baths: **13**
Double/pb: **$55–$75**
Single/pb: **$55–$75**
Suites: **$70–$90**
Open: **All year**

Reduced Rates: **Available**
Breakfast: **Continental**
Credit Cards: **MC, VISA**
Pets: **No**
Children: **Welcome**
Smoking: **Permitted in carriage house**
Social Drinking: **Permitted**

Situated on two acres of lush lawn and trees, the lodge was built in 1883. Back then, this French Victorian mansion and carriage house did not boast of air-conditioning, TV, and suites as it does today. Though a great deal of renovation has taken place, the antique features and charm of the mansion are intact. Good restaurants are nearby.

The Enchanted Cottage ✪
(formerly Cottage at the Quiltery)
RD 4, BOX 337, BENFIELD ROAD, BOYERTOWN, PENNSYLVANIA 19512

Tel: **(215) 845-8845**
Hosts: **Peg and Richard Groff**
Location: **16 mi. S of Allentown**
No. of Private Baths: **1**
Guest Cottage: **$70–$80**
Open: **All year**

Reduced Rates: **$5 less after 2nd night**
Breakfast: **Full**
Pets: **No**
Children: **Welcome, over 12**
Smoking: **Permitted**
Social Drinking: **Permitted**

Complete privacy awaits you in this cozy cottage nestled in a clearing in the woods. Downstairs, the exposed beams, wood-burning fireplace, quilts, and antique furniture lend themselves to quiet, romantic evenings. On the second floor you'll find an air-conditioned double bedroom and a Laura Ashley bathroom. Gourmet breakfasts are served in the main house in front of either the garden or a cheerful fire, depending on the season. While the cottage is a destination in itself, you'll have easy access to the Pennsylvania Dutch area, the Reading factory outlets, antique shops, historic sites, and country auctions. An excellent restaurant is within walking distance.

Twin Turrets Inn ✪
11 EAST PHILADELPHIA AVENUE, BOYERTOWN, PENNSYLVANIA 19512

Tel: **(215) 367-4513**	Reduced Rates: **Corp. rate $60 single;**
Best Time to Call: **9 AM–5 PM**	**10% seniors**
Host: **Gary Slade**	Breakfast: **Continental**
Location: **40 mi. NW of Philadelphia**	Credit Cards: **AMEX, DISC, MC, VISA**
No. of Rooms: **10**	Pets: **No**
No. of Private Baths: **10**	Children: **Welcome, over 12**
Double/pb: **$80**	Smoking: **No**
Single/pb: **$70**	Social Drinking: **Permitted**
Open: **All year**	Airport/Station Pickup: **Yes**

The Twin Turrets is a wonderful Victorian mansion in all its restored glory: stained-glass windows, chandeliers, elegant wallpaper, period furniture, and drapery. If this whets your appetite, an antiques shop on the first floor sells sterling silver, glass, china, and furniture. Guests have use of the parlor piano. Each bedroom has a newfangled amenity—remote-controlled TV.

Churchtown Inn B&B ✪
ROUTE 23 W, CHURCHTOWN, PENNSYLVANIA 17555

Tel: **(215) 445-7794**	Double/sb: **$49–$55**
Best Time to Call: **9 AM–9 PM**	Open: **All year**
Hosts: **Jim Kent Hermine and Stuart Smith**	Reduced Rates: **Weekly**
	Breakfast: **Full**
Location: **4 mi. off Pennsylvania Turnpike, Exit 22**	Other Meals: **Available**
	Credit Cards: **MC, VISA**
No. of Rooms: **8**	Pets: **No**
No. of Private Baths: **6**	Children: **Welcome, over 12**
Max. No. Sharing Bath: **4**	Smoking: **No**
Double/pb: **$75–$95**	Social Drinking: **Permitted**
Single/pb: **$65–$85**	Foreign Languages: **German**

Churchtown Inn is a lovely fieldstone Federal Colonial mansion built in 1735. Located in the heart of Pennsylvania Dutch country, this B&B

is close to Amish attractions, antique markets, and manufacturers' outlets. Rooms are decorated with the hosts' personal treasures: antique furniture, original art, and music boxes. Stuart (a former music director) and Jim (a former accountant who moonlighted as a ballroom dance instructor) stage events throughout the year. The schedule includes concerts, costume balls, carriage rides, walks, and holiday celebrations. Every Saturday, guests have the opportunity of joining Amish or Mennonite families for dinner at an additional fee. Of course, after a Churchtown Inn breakfast, you may not have room for any more meals; the table groans with English oatmeal custard, apple pancakes, Grand Marnier French toast, homemade coffee cake, and other delectables.

The Foreman House B&B ✪
2129 MAIN STREET, CHURCHTOWN, PENNSYLVANIA 17555

Tel: **(215) 445-6713**
Best Time to Call: **Mornings; evenings**
Hosts: **Stephen and Jacqueline Mitrani**
Location: **19 mi. E of Lancaster**
No. of Rooms: **2**
Max. No. Sharing Bath: **4**
Double/sb: **$55–$65**
Single/sb: **$40**
Open: **All year**

Breakfast: **Full (weekends);**
  Continental (weekdays)
Pets: **No**
Children: **Welcome, over 10**
Smoking: **No**
Social Drinking: **Permitted**
Minimum Stay: **Holiday weekends**
Foreign Languages: **Spanish**

An elaborate leaded-glass front door adorns the entrance to the Foreman House, a Georgian Revival building constructed in 1919. The interior is decorated with family heirlooms, oriental rugs, and locally handmade quilts, some of which are for sale. Crafts made by local artisans are displayed in the dining room and may be purchased by guests. Churchtown, founded in 1722, is a residential area surrounded by Amish farmland. From the porch and guest-room windows, you can watch the Amish and Mennonite horse-drawn carriages pass by. Outlet shopping and a variety of entertainment are within reasonable driving distances.

The Columbian
360 CHESTNUT STREET, COLUMBIA, PENNSYLVANIA 17512

Tel: **(717) 684-5869; (800) 422-5869**
Hosts: **Linda and John Straitiff**
Location: **8 mi. W of Lancaster**
No. of Rooms: **5**
No. of Private Baths: **5**
Double/pb: **$60–$65**
Suites: **$75**

Open: **All year**
Reduced Rates: **10% less after 3rd**
  night
Breakfast: **Full**
Credit Cards: **MC, VISA**
Pets: **No**
Children: **Welcome, over 12**

Smoking: **No**   Airport/Station Pickup: **Yes**
Social Drinking: **Permitted**

The Columbian is a restored turn-of-the-century brick mansion, a fine example of Colonial Revival architecture with unique wraparound porches, stained-glass windows, and a majestic tiered staircase. The air-conditioned rooms are decorated with antiques in Victorian and simple country style. Breakfast is a hearty buffet offering a chef's choice of such morsels as Quiche Lorraine, Peaches and Cream French Toast, or Belgian Waffles along with fresh fruit and homemade breads. A brief stroll takes you to antique shops, art galleries, the Wright's Ferry Mansion, the Bank Museum, the National Watch and Clock Museum, and the Susquehanna Glass Factory.

Danmar House ✪
RD 21, BOX 107, DOVER, PENNSYLVANIA 17315

Tel: **(717) 292-5128**	Open: **All year**
Best Time to Call: **8 AM–10 PM**	Breakfast: **Full**
Hosts: **Marilyn and Danny Muir**	Pets: **No**
Location: **8 mi. W of York**	Children: **Welcome, over 12**
No. of Rooms: **3**	Smoking: **Permitted**
Max. No. Sharing Bath: **3**	Social Drinking: **Permitted**
Double/sb: **$55**	Airport/Station Pickup: **Yes**
Suites: **$85**	

This twelve-room country house, built in three stages from the mid-1700s, was completely overhauled in 1988: the interior and exterior were restored, and modern plumbing and electrical systems were installed. Guest quarters are air-conditioned and comfortably furnished with antiques. After breakfasting on entrées such as cheese and bacon soufflé or apple sausage ring, you can head out for ski slopes, golf courses, parks, antique shops, or York and Gettysburg—all less than a half hour away.

Detters Acres Bed and Breakfast ✪
6631 OLD CARLISLE ROAD, DOVER, PENNSYLVANIA 17315

Tel: **(717) 292-3172**	Single/sb: **$45**
Best Time to Call: **Anytime**	Open: **All year**
Hosts: **Lorné and Ailean Detter**	Breakfast: **Full**
Location: **7 mi. N of York**	Other Meals: **Available**
No. of Rooms: **3**	Pets: **No**
No. of Private Baths: **1**	Children: **Welcome**
Max. No. Sharing Bath: **4**	Smoking: **No**
Double/pb: **$65**	Social Drinking: **Permitted**
Single/pb: **$55**	Airport/Station Pickup: **Yes**
Double/sb: **$55**	

Visit a 76-acre working beef cattle farm in northern York County. For a nominal fee, your hosts will take you for a ride in one of their three Amish buggies. Or get behind the wheel of a more modern vehicle for

the short drive to Gettysburg, Hershey Amusement Park and Zoo, Amish country, Hanover Shoe Farms Standardbred Stables, Roundtop's ski slopes, and innumerable farmers' markets and shopping malls. On a chilly evening, gather around the fireplace in the recreation room, where you can play games or the piano. Weather permitting, full breakfasts, including fruit and homemade breads, are served in the gazebo.

Bechtel Mansion Inn ✪
400 WEST KING STREET, EAST BERLIN, PENNSYLVANIA 17316

Tel: **(717) 259-7760**
Hosts: **Mariam and Charles Bechtel, and Ruth Spangler**
Location: **18 mi. E of Gettysburg**
No. of Rooms: **8**
No. of Private Baths: **8**
Double/pb: **$70–$110**
Single/pb: **$65–$90**
Suites: **$120–$135**

Open: **All year**
Reduced Rates: **10% seniors; 10% Dec. 1–Mar. 31**
Breakfast: **Continental**
Credit Cards: **AMEX, DISC, MC, VISA**
Pets: **No**
Children: **Welcome**
Smoking: **No**
Social Drinking: **Permitted**

A romantic getaway, this sprawling mansion was designed for the William Leas family in 1897. It is listed on the National Register of Historic Places, and located in the historic district. The rooms have been beautifully restored and feature original brass chandeliers. Air-conditioned sleeping quarters are elegantly appointed with handmade

quilts and antique furnishings. Choose from the Sara Leas Room, with its turret-shaped bay window, or the Downstairs Suite, with its hand-made walnut furniture and folding oak interior shutters. Guests are welcome to relax in the living room with an oak-and-mahogany secretary and red Bokhara rug. Fresh muffins, juice, fruit ambrosia, coffee cake, and coffee are served in the dining room, which has a large window seat, etched-glass windows, and antique rug. There is a large front-and-side porch for sipping a glass of wine or just relaxing and watching the village activity.

Red Door Studio B&B ✪
6485 LEMON STREET, EAST PETERSBURG, PENNSYLVANIA 17520

Tel: **(717) 569-2909**
Best Time to Call: **8–9 AM**
Host: **Mary Elizabeth Patton**
Location: **1½ mi. N of Lancaster**
No. of Rooms: **3**

Max. No. Sharing Bath: **5**
Double/sb: **$30–$40**
Single/sb: **$20**
Open: **All year**
Breakfast: **Continental**

Pets: **Sometimes**
Children: **Welcome (crib)**
Smoking: **No**

Social Drinking: **Permitted**
Airport/Station Pickup: **Yes**

Open the red door and you instantly know you're in an artist's home. A former teacher of art history, Mary Elizabeth is now a full-time artist and portrait painter. Her B&B is warm, bright, and inviting, with many souvenirs and paintings of her world travels. Of special interest is her collection of Indian and African works. Breakfast is an inviting spread of fresh fruit, yogurt, granola, Danish pastry, coffee, or herb tea. You are welcome to relax in the backyard, use the barbecue, or watch TV.

Elm Country Inn Bed & Breakfast ✪
P.O. BOX 37, ELM AND NEWPORT ROADS, ELM, PENNSYLVANIA 17521

Tel: **(717) 664-3623; (800) 245-0532**
Best Time to Call: **After 4:30 PM**
Hosts: **Betty and Melvin Meck**
Location: **12 mi. N of Lancaster**
No. of Rooms: **2**
Max. No. Sharing Bath: **4**
Double/sb: **$40–$45**
Single/sb: **$25–$30**
Open: **All year**

Reduced Rates: **10% Jan. 2–Mar. 31;
    10% seniors, Sun.–Thurs.**
Breakfast: **Full**
Credit Cards: **MC, VISA**
Pets: **No**
Children: **Welcome**
Smoking: **No**
Social Drinking: **Permitted**
Airport/Station Pickup: **Yes**

Located in a small country village, this 1860 brick farmhouse overlooks beautiful farmland. The large, sunny rooms feature original wood trim and are furnished with a pleasing blend of antiques and collectibles. Antique shops, craft shops, and opportunities to fish or canoe are available. Betty and Melvin thoroughly enjoy having visitors and do their best to have them feel instantly at home.

Rocky-Side Farm ✪
RD 1, ELVERSON, PENNSYLVANIA 19520

Tel: **(215) 286-5362**
Best Time to Call: **After 5 PM**
Host: **Reba Yoder**
Location: **18 mi. S of Reading**
No. of Rooms: **2**
Max. No. Sharing Bath: **4**
Double/sb: **$35**
Single/sb: **$25**

Open: **All year**
Breakfast: **Full**
Other Meals: **Available**
Pets: **No**
Children: **Welcome (crib)**
Smoking: **No**
Social Drinking: **No**

You will be warmly welcomed by the Yoders to their farm, where they raise beef cows, corn, wheat, soybeans, and hay. The stone farmhouse dates back to 1919 and has a wraparound columned porch for lazying away an afternoon. The rooms are furnished country style, complemented by handmade braided-wool rugs and pretty quilts. Light breakfasts are Reba's style. Hopewell Village and the Amish countryside are pleasant destinations.

Clearview Farm Bed & Breakfast ✪
355 CLEARVIEW ROAD, EPHRATA, PENNSYLVANIA 17522

Tel: **(717) 733-6333**	Double/sb: **$59**
Best Time to Call: **Evenings**	Open: **All year**
Hosts: **Glenn and Mildred Wissler**	Breakfast: **Full**
Location: **9 mi. N of Lancaster**	Credit Cards: **MC, VISA**
No. of Rooms: **5**	Pets: **No**
No. of Private Baths: **3**	Children: **No**
Max. No. Sharing Bath: **4**	Smoking: **No**
Double/pb: **$79**	Social Drinking: **Permitted**

A lovely rural retreat, this limestone farmhouse surveys a 200-acre working farm. As you watch swans drift around the pond, you'll find it hard to believe that major highways are only a mile away. The antique beds, graceful chandeliers, and elegant wallpapers allow guests to relax in style. The convenient location offers easy access to five antique malls, Hershey Park, and other area attractions. Ham-and-cheese soufflés, French cinnamon toast, eggs Benedict, and waffles are a few of the highlights of the Wisslers' breakfasts.

Historic Smithton Country Inn ✪
900 WEST MAIN STREET, EPHRATA, PENNSYLVANIA 17522

Tel: **(717) 733-6094**	Host: **Dorothy Graybill**
Best Time to Call: **9 AM–10 PM**	Location: **12 mi. NE of Lancaster**

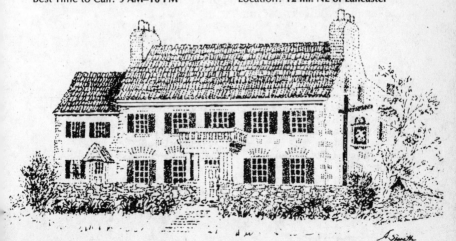

No. of Rooms: **8**
No. of Private Baths: **8**
Double/pb: **$65–$115**
Single/pb: **$55–$105**
Suites: **$140–$170**
Open: **All year**
Breakfast: **Full**

Credit Cards: **AMEX, MC, VISA**
Pets: **By arrangement**
Children: **By arrangement**
Smoking: **No**
Social Drinking: **Permitted**
Minimum Stay: **2 nights weekends**
Airport/Station Pickup: **Yes**

The inn has been serving guests since 1763. Picture yourself returning "home" after seeing the Pennsylvania Dutch sights and trudging wearily to your bedroom. Waiting for you are candle sconces, canopy beds, Amish quilts, down pillows, and on cool nights, a cozy fire. There's even a flannel nightshirt to snuggle in. And after a restful sleep, come down to an all-you-can-eat breakfast that often features blueberry waffles.

Hershey Bed & Breakfast Reservation Service
P.O. BOX 208, HERSHEY, PENNSYLVANIA 17033

Tel: **(717) 533-2928**
Best Time to Call: **10 AM–4 PM**
Coordinator: **Renee Deutel**
States/Regions Covered: **Hanover, Harrisburg, Hershey, Lancaster, Palmyra**

Rates (Single/Double):
  Modest: **$50 / $55**
  Average: **$60 / $65**
  Luxury: **$70 / $75**
Credit Cards: **MC, VISA**

Renee has a small roster of lovely homes close to main thoroughfares. Hosts come from a variety of interesting backgrounds, and all share a common enthusiasm to share their homes and communities. You may choose a cozy farmhouse, a large older home with beautiful furnishings, or a country inn. Whatever your wishes, the town that chocolate made famous will welcome you.

The Forge Bed & Breakfast Inn ✪
RD 1, BOX 438, PINE GROVE, PENNSYLVANIA 17963

Tel: **(717) 345-8349**
Best Time to Call: **AM**
Owners: **Margo and Dick Ward**
Host: **Lucille Valibus**
Location: **34 mi. NE of Harrisburg**
No. of Rooms: **6**
No. of Private Baths: **2**
Max. No. Sharing Bath: **4**
Double/pb: **$70–$75**
Single/pb: **$65**

Double/sb: **$60–$65**
Single/sb: **$55**
Open: **All year**
Breakfast: **Full**
Credit Cards: **MC, VISA**
Pets: **No**
Children: **Welcome, over 14**
Smoking: **No**
Social Drinking: **Permitted**
Airport/Station Pickup: **Yes**

This magnificent three-story fieldstone mansion dates to 1830, and has been in Margo's family since 1860. Many of the antique furnishings are treasured heirlooms. Picturesque hiking paths crisscross the 250-acre property, and fishermen are welcome to try their luck in the stream in front of the house. Visitors can also avail themselves of the swimming pool and the library. Home-baked goods, like sticky buns and blueberry muffins, highlight breakfast.

Gibson's Bed & Breakfast ✪
141 WEST CARACAS AVENUE, HERSHEY, PENNSYLVANIA 17033

Tel: **(717) 534-1305**
Hosts: **Frances and Bob Gibson**
Location: **One block off Rte. 422**
No. of Rooms: **3**
Max. No. Sharing Bath: **3**
Double/sb: **$45**
Single/sb: **$35**
Open: **All year**

Breakfast: **Full**
Pets: **No**
Children: **Welcome, over 5**
Smoking: **No**
Social Drinking: **Permitted**
Airport/Station Pickup: **Yes**
Foreign Languages: **Italian**

Bob and Frances Gibson have a 50-year-old Cape Cod, located in the center of Hershey, walking distance from many local attractions. The house has been recently renovated to enhance the charm of the hardwood floors, wood trim, and original windows. The atmosphere is friendly and informal, and your hosts are glad to offer complimentary nibbles. The Gibsons will gladly help you find local sights such as Hershey Park, Chocolate World, Founders Hall, and the Amish country.

Bed & Breakfast—The Manor ✪
830 VILLAGE ROAD, P.O. BOX 416, LAMPETER, PENNSYLVANIA 17537

Tel: **(717) 464-9564**
Best Time to Call: **9 AM–9 PM**
Hosts: **Mary Lou Paolini and Jackie Curtis**
Location: **3 mi. SE of Lancaster**
No. of Rooms: **3**
No. of Private Baths: **1**
Max. No. Sharing Bath: **4**
Double/pb: **$60**
Single/pb: **$55**
Double/sb: **$55**

Single/sb: **$50**
Open: **All year**
Reduced Rates: **25% seniors Oct.– Mar.**
Breakfast: **Full**
Credit Cards: **MC, VISA**
Pets: **No**
Children: **Welcome**
Smoking: **No**
Social Drinking: **No**
Airport/Station Pickup: **Yes**

Set on four and a half acres of lush Amish farmland, this cozy farmhouse is just minutes away from Lancaster's historical sights and attractions. Dutch Wonderland, the Strasburg Railroad, Amish farms, and Hershey are but a few of the don't-miss sights nearby. Guests delight in Mary Lou's delicious breakfasts, which often feature gourmet treats such as Eggs Mornay, crêpes or strata, apple cobbler, and her homemade jams and breads. In summer, a swim in the pool or a nap under one of the many shade trees is the perfect way to cap a day of touring.

Walkabout Inn ✪
837 VILLAGE ROAD, LAMPETER, PENNSYLVANIA 17537

Tel: **(717) 464-0707**
Hosts: **Richard and Maggie Mason**
Location: **3 mi. S of Lancaster**
No. of Rooms: **5**
No. of Private Baths: **5**
Double/pb: **$69**
Single/pb: **$59**
Suites: **$149; sleeps 5**
Open: **All year**

Reduced Rates: **Available**
Breakfast: **Full**
Other Meals: **Available**
Credit Cards: **AMEX, MC, VISA**
Pets: **No**
Children: **Welcome (crib)**
Smoking: **No**
Social Drinking: **Permitted**
Airport/Station Pickup: **Yes**

The Walkabout Inn takes its name from the Australian word, which means to go out and discover new places. Australian-born host Richard Mason and his wife, Maggie, will help you explore the Amish country that surrounds their brick Mennonite farmhouse. The twenty-two-room house was built in 1925 and features wraparound porches, balconies, and chestnut woodwork. Guest rooms feature Maggie's hand stenciling and are decorated with antiques, oriental rugs, and Pennsylvania Dutch quilts. When it's time to say "good day," a candlelight gourmet breakfast is served on silver and crystal in the dining room. Homemade Australian bread, pastries, and tea imported from down under are always on the menu. You can choose a romantic honeymoon or anniversary suite that comes with a gift. Special packages include dinner with the Amish, 3-hour scenic bus tour, and free maps and information. The inn is AAA rated.

Buona Notte B&B ✪
2020 MARIETTA AVENUE, LANCASTER, PENNSYLVANIA 17603

Tel: **(717) 295-2597**
Best Time to Call: **Evenings**
Hosts: **Joe and Anna Kuhns Predoti**
Location: **1 mi. off Route 30,**
  Rohrerstown exit
No. of Rooms: **3**
No. of Private Baths: **1**
Max. No. Sharing Bath: **4**
Double/pb: **$50**
Double/sb: **$45**

Open: **All year**
Breakfast: **Continental**
Pets: **No**
Children: **Welcome, over 2**
Smoking: **No**
Social Drinking: **No**
Minimum Stay: **2 nights holiday**
  weekends
Foreign Languages: **French, Italian**

This spacious, turn-of-the-century home is within striking distance of Hershey Park and Gettysburg, while Pennsylvania Dutch country is only 10 minutes away. Franklin and Marshall College and Millersville University are also in the area. For breakfast, you'll enjoy a variety of homemade muffins, breads, and jams, accompanied by all the coffee or tea you can drink.

Hollinger House
2336 HOLLINGER ROAD, LANCASTER, PENNSYLVANIA 17602

Tel: **(717) 464-3050**	Reduced Rates: **Dec.–May; families**
Best Time to Call: **Mornings**	Breakfast: **Full**
Host: **Jean Thomas**	Pets: **No**
No. of Rooms: **4**	Children: **Welcome**
Max. No. Sharing Bath: **4**	Smoking: **No**
Double/sb: **$45–$55**	Social Drinking: **Permitted**
Single/sb: **$35–$40**	Airport/Station Pickup: **Yes**
Open: **All year**	Foreign Languages: **German**

While this house, built in 1870, is undeniably grand in style, it is also homey. Jean invites you to relax on the wide porch, or stroll about the five acres of land crossed by a woodland stream. Although it is convenient to all the area's attractions, it is peacefully away from the tourist traffic. Jean has led tours throughout the Lancaster area and will be happy to answer your questions and give expert advice.

Lincoln Haus Inn Bed & Breakfast ✹
1687 LINCOLN HIGHWAY EAST, LANCASTER, PENNSYLVANIA 17602

Tel: **(717) 392-9412**	Open: **All year**
Best Time to Call: **Before 11 PM**	Reduced Rates: **Available**
Host: **Mary K. Zook**	Breakfast: **Full**
Location: **2 mi. E of Lancaster**	Other Meals: **Available**
No. of Rooms: **5**	Pets: **No**
No. of Private Baths: **5**	Children: **Welcome**
Double/pb: **$45–$55**	Smoking: **No**
Single/pb: **$43–$53**	Social Drinking: **No**
Suites: **$50–$90**	Station Pickup: **Yes**

Ten minutes east of historic Lancaster and five minutes from Route 30 and the Pennsylvania Dutch Visitors Bureau in Lancaster County, you'll find this 1915 stucco home with distinctive hip roofs and black trim. Above the living room door, your host has hung a "Welcome" sign. Mary prides herself on giving guests a glimpse of the Amish lifestyle; the farmers' market, horse auctions, buggy rides, quilt sales, and traditional Amish farmlands are all within ten to twenty minutes by car. But before you set out, you'll have a hearty family-style breakfast including juice, fruit, quiche, sausage, and different kinds of muffins.

Meadowview Guest House ✪
2169 NEW HOLLAND PIKE, LANCASTER, PENNSYLVANIA 17601

Tel: **(717) 299-4017**
Best Time to Call: **Before 10:30 PM**
Hosts: **Edward and Sheila Christie**
No. of Rooms: **3**
No. of Private Baths: **1**
Max. No. Sharing Bath: **4**
Double/pb: **$40**
Single/pb: **$40**
Double/sb: **$25–$30**

Reduced Rates: **$3 less 3rd night; off-season**
Open: **Mar. 1–Nov. 30**
Breakfast: **Continental**
Pets: **No**
Children: **Welcome, over 7**
Smoking: **No**
Social Drinking: **Permitted**
Airport/Station Pickup: **Yes**

Situated in the heart of Pennsylvania Dutch country, the house has a pleasant blend of modern and traditional furnishings. Your hosts offer a fully equipped guest kitchen where you can store and prepare your own light meals. Ed and Sheila supply coffee and tea. The area is known for great farmers' markets, antique shops, craft shops, country auctions, and wonderful restaurants.

Patchwork Inn Bed & Breakfast ✪
2319 OLD PHILADELPHIA PIKE, LANCASTER, PENNSYLVANIA 17602

Tel: **(717) 293-9078**
Best Time to Call: **Mornings**

Hosts: **Lee and Anne Martin**
No. of Rooms: **4**

No. of Private Baths: **2**
Max. No. Sharing Bath: **4**
Double/pb: **$65**
Double/sb: **$55**
Suites: **$75**
Open: **All year**
Breakfast: **Full**

Credit Cards: **DISC, MC, VISA**
Pets: **No**
Children: **Welcome, over 10**
Smoking: **No**
Social Drinking: **Permitted**
Airport/Station Pickup: **Yes**

Upon entering this lovely 19th-century farmhouse, you won't be surprised to discover that quilts are the innkeeper's hobby. Gorgeous quilts cover the queen-size beds, art and posters feature quilts, and several adorn the walls as hangings. Lee and Anne will be happy to direct you to special shops where quilting material or completed quilts are sold. The inn features a handsome collection of fine oak furniture including an oak phone booth where Lee displays a collection of interesting antique telephones. Breakfast, served in the dining room decorated with Holland Delft, is a generous repast.

The Loom Room
RD 1, BOX 1420, LEESPORT, PENNSYLVANIA 19533

Tel: **(215) 926-3217**
Hosts: **Mary and Gene Smith**
Location: **4 mi. N of Reading**
No. of Rooms: **3**
No. of Private Baths: **1**
Max. No. Sharing Bath: **4**
Double/pb: **$50**
Single/pb: **$50**
Double/sb: **$45**

Single/sb: **$45**
Open: **All year**
Breakfast: **Full**
Reduced Rates: **Weekly**
Pets: **No**
Children: **Welcome (crib)**
Smoking: **No**
Social Drinking: **Permitted**
Airport/Station Pickup: **Yes**

The Loom Room is a stucco-covered stone farmhouse dating back more than 175 years. It is located in the countryside surrounded by shade trees, flowers, and herb gardens. Inside, the spacious rooms feature country antiques, open beams, fireplaces, and handwoven accessories. Mary invites you to her studio, where her work is on display. Her talents also extend to the kitchen, where she helps Gene cook up eggnog French toast, homemade jams, muffins, and chipped beef. Breakfast may be served in the sunny kitchen or outside in the gazebo. This lovely farm is near Reading's outlet complexes, Blue Marsh Lake Recreation Area, antique shops, and many historic sights.

The Sleepy Fir Bed & Breakfast ✪

RD 2, BOX 2802, ZIEGLER NURSERY ROAD, LEESPORT,
PENNSYLVANIA 19533

Tel: (215) 926-1014	Single/sb: $35–$45
Best Time to Call: 3–9 PM	Open: All year
Hosts: Phil and Judy Whitmoyer	Reduced Rates: After 2nd night
Location: 7 mi. NW of Reading	Breakfast: Full
No. of Rooms: 2	Pets: No
No. of Private Baths: 1	Children: Welcome, over 12
Max. No. Sharing Bath: 4	Smoking: No
Double/pb: $50–$60	Social Drinking: Permitted
Single/pb: $45–$55	Airport/Station Pickup: Yes
Double/sb: $40–$50	

A brick Cape Cod with black shutters, this house offers rural privacy on three and a half acres of landscaped and wooded countryside. The guest rooms have double beds and share a luxury bath with a sauna. Your hosts, Phil and Judy Whitmoyer, tour guides at the Berks County Heritage Center, are natives of the area, and they will be happy to direct you to outlet shopping, public golf courses, and the sights of Pennsylvania Dutch country. The Whitmoyers have bicycles and a 17-foot canoe to lend for exploring the nearby Blue Marsh Lake Recreation Area. After a busy day they invite you to unwind with a game of pool or a stroll through the wooded property.

Alden House ✪

62 EAST MAIN STREET, LITITZ, PENNSYLVANIA 17545

Tel: (717) 627-3363; (800) 584-0753	Open: All year
Best Time to Call: 1–9 PM	Reduced Rates: 10% after 2nd night
Host: Gloria Adams	Nov. 1–Apr. 30
Location: 7 mi. N of Lancaster	Breakfast: Continental
No. of Rooms: 7	Credit Cards: MC, VISA
No. of Private Baths: 5	Pets: No
Max. No. Sharing Bath: 4	Children: Welcome, over 6
Double/pb: $75	Smoking: Permitted
Double/sb: $65–$70	Social Drinking: Permitted
Suites: $85–$95	

Built in 1850 and fully restored, this brick town house has lots of old-fashioned appeal. At the end of the day, grab a chair on one of the three porches and savor the chocolate aroma wafting over from the local candy factory. The farmers' markets and craft shops of Amish country are a short drive away, and numerous restaurants are within walking distance. Breakfast includes juice, coffee or tea, cereal, fresh seasonal fruit, and baked goods.

Dot's Bed & Breakfast ✪
435 WOODCREST AVENUE, LITITZ, PENNSYLVANIA 17543

Tel: **(717) 627-0483**
Best Time to Call: **7–9 AM; 6–11 PM**
Hosts: **Dorothy and Erwin Boettcher**
Location: **7 mi. N of Lancaster**
No. of Rooms: **2**
Max. No. Sharing Bath: **4**
Double/sb: **$40**
Single/sb: **$30**

Open: **All year**
Breakfast: **Continental**
Pets: **Sometimes**
Children: **Welcome (crib)**
Smoking: **No**
Social Drinking: **Permitted**
Foreign Languages: **German**

Dot's is located in a quiet residential suburb of Lititz, home of the country's first pretzel bakery. Much of this quaint little town has stayed the way it was in 1756, the year it was founded. You are sure to enjoy an easy stroll past Lititz Springs Park, the historic buildings on Main Street, and the Linden Hall Girl's School. After a busy day, you'll be glad to return to Dot's, where you'll find a quiet guest room furnished with a cozy bed, lounge chair, rocker, and plenty of books. Awake to the birds singing and join your hosts for some of Dot's homemade muffins or shoofly pie. Your hosts will gladly direct you to the nearby sights, including the Wilbur Chocolate Factory.

Market Sleigh Bed & Breakfast ✪
BOX 99, WALNUT VALLEY FARM, LOGANVILLE, PENNSYLVANIA 17342-0099

Tel: **(717) 428-1440**
Best Time to Call: **3–6 PM**
Hosts: **Judy and Jerry Dietz**
Location: **7 mi. S of York**
No. of Rooms: **1**
No. of Private Baths: **1**
Suite: **$55–$100**
Open: **All year**
Reduced Rates: **Corporate travelers Mon.–Thurs.**

Breakfast: **Full**
Wheelchair-Accessible: **Yes**
Credit Cards: **MC, VISA**
Pets: **No**
Children: **Welcome, over 12**
Smoking: **No**
Social Drinking: **Permitted**
Minimum Stay: **2 nights convention weekends**

This bed and breakfast takes its name from the large 19th-century sleigh parked by the main entrance, as if stranded when the snow melted. Guests are encouraged to wander around the 22-acre property, or just sit with a book in the back porch swing. The many local attractions range from parks and wineries to museums and malls. Judy dishes out a hearty farmer's breakfast of fruit, homemade breads, eggs, cheese, bacon, and French toast or pancakes.

Herr Farmhouse Inn ✪
2256 HUBER DRIVE, MANHEIM, PENNSYLVANIA 17545

Tel: (717) 653-9852
Best Time to Call: After 4 PM
Host: Barry A. Herr
Location: 9 mi. W of Lancaster; ¼ mi. from Rte. 283
No. of Rooms: 4
No. of Private Baths: 2
Max. No. Sharing Bath: 4
Double/pb: $85

Double/sb: $70
Suites: $95
Open: All year
Breakfast: Continental
Credit Cards: MC, VISA
Pets: No
Children: Welcome, over 6
Smoking: Permitted
Social Drinking: Permitted

Nestled on more than 11 acres of rolling farmland, this farmhouse, dating back to 1738, has been restored with the greatest of care and attention to detail. Fanlights adorn the main entrance, there are six working fireplaces, and it has the original pine floors. Whether spending a winter's night by a cozy fire, or a bright summer morning sipping tea in the sun room, it is the perfect retreat. It is less than 20 minutes to the sights, shops, and restaurants of Amish country.

Cedar Hill Farm ✪
305 LONGENECKER ROAD, MOUNT JOY, PENNSYLVANIA 17552

Tel: (717) 653-4655
Best Time to Call: Anytime
Hosts: Russel and Gladys Swarr
Location: 10 mi. W of Lancaster
No. of Rooms: 4
No. of Private Baths: 4
Double/pb: $55–$60
Single/pb: $45–$50
Open: All year

Reduced Rates: Weekly
Breakfast: Continental
Credit Cards: AMEX, MC, VISA
Pets: No
Children: Welcome (crib)
Smoking: No
Social Drinking: Permitted
Airport/Station Pickup: Yes

Russel was born in this restored 1817 farmhouse and can tell you all about its history. It has an open, winding staircase, original pine floors, and an Indian door; breakfast is served beside a walk-in fireplace. Stroll the acreage or relax on the large porch overlooking a peaceful stream. Beautiful wallpapers and family heirlooms enhance the comfortable, air-conditioned bedrooms; the honeymoon suite has a private balcony. Quilt auctions and other attractions for collectors are plentiful year-round. Every Tuesday a farmers' market and antiques auction take place just minutes away. Amish country, Hershey Park, and Chocolate World are nearby attractions.

The "Hen-Apple" Bed and Breakfast ✪
409 SOUTH LINGLE AVENUE, PALMYRA, PENNSYLVANIA 17078

Tel: **(717) 838-8282**	Reduced Rates: **Available**
Best Time to Call: **10 AM–11 PM**	Breakfast: **Full**
Hosts: **Flo and Harold Eckert**	Credit Cards: **MC, VISA**
Location: **E of Hershey**	Pets: **No**
No. of Rooms: **6**	Children: **No**
No. of Private Baths: **6**	Smoking: **No**
Double/pb: **$65**	Social Drinking: **Permitted**
Single/pb: **$55**	Airport/Station Pickup: **Yes**
Open: **All year**	

Wood floors, stenciling, antiques, and candlelit windows create a cozy country atmosphere at this 1825 farmhouse five minutes from Hershey. Flo will offer you complimentary snacks upon your arrival or later in the afternoon. Home-baked breads and muffins, served on old china, make breakfast a treat, whether you enjoy it on the screened porch or in the dining room. In warm weather, if you feel inclined to cook, there are a grill and a picnic area for guests' use. The local attractions are many and varied: antique and crafts shops, horse racing and ice hockey, theaters and museums, even a winery and a bologna factory that welcome visitors.

Frogtown Acres Bed and Breakfast Inn ✪
44 FROGTOWN ROAD, PARADISE, PENNSYLVANIA 17562

Tel: **(717) 768-7684**	Open: **All year**
Best Time to Call: **Anytime**	Breakfast: **Full**
Hosts: **Patrick and Phyllis**	Pets: **No**
Location: **10 mi. E of Lancaster**	Children: **Welcome, over 10**
No. of Rooms: **5**	Smoking: **No**
Max. No. Sharing Bath: **4**	Social Drinking: **Permitted**
Double/sb: **$60–$70**	

Set amid the rolling pastures of the Pennsylvania Dutch farmlands, Frogtown Acres was once a country gentleman's estate, circa 1810. Each of the four rooms is individually decorated and filled with furnishings from days gone by. Slate floors, stone walls, and four-poster beds adorn the ground floor. Upstairs, a fireplace and a sitting balcony distinguish the rooms, which have lustrous hardwood floors. A full breakfast is served each morning in the main house, from where you are likely to see the Amish already at work in the fields. This B&B is perfect for bicycle groups, for visiting the Amish, or for a quiet country weekend.

Maple Lane Guest House ✪
505 PARADISE LANE, PARADISE, PENNSYLVANIA 17562

Tel: **(717) 687-7479**
Best Time to Call: **Anytime**
Hosts: **Edwin and Marion Rohrer**
Location: **10 mi. E of Lancaster**
No. of Rooms: **4**
No. of Private Baths: **1**
Max. No. Sharing Bath: **4**
Double/pb: **$40–$60**
Single/pb: **$40–$48**

Double/sb: **$40–$55**
Single/sb: **$40–$45**
Open: **All year**
Breakfast: **Continental, plus**
Pets: **No**
Children: **Welcome (crib)**
Smoking: **No**
Social Drinking: **Permitted**

For an unusual experience, travel along a back country road to this 200-acre dairy farm with woodland and a winding stream. Relax, watch the dairy in operation, or hike up the hill for a 40-mile panoramic view. Nearby are excellent restaurants, farmers' markets, Amish craft and quilt shops, historic sites, and the Strasburg train museum. Air-conditioned rooms are pleasantly furnished with poster and canopy beds, quilts, crafts, and wall stenciling. Breakfast includes fresh fruit, cheese, coffee, tea, cereal, and homemade breads.

The House on the Canal ✪
1200 WHITNER ROAD, READING, PENNSYLVANIA 19605

Tel: **(215) 921-3015**
Best Time to Call: **After 5:30 PM**
Host: **Wanda Edye**
No. of Rooms: **2**
Max. No. Sharing Bath: **4**
Double/sb: **$60**
Suites: **$60**

Open: **All year**
Breakfast: **Full**
Other Meals: **Available**
Pets: **Sometimes**
Children: **Welcome, over 5**
Smoking: **No**
Social Drinking: **Permitted**

This secluded old lockkeeper's house was built back in the late 1700s and recently restored. The property's two-foot stone walls and 200-year-old trees are nestled along the banks of the Schuylkill River, and fishing, hiking, and biking are literally at your doorstep. Depending on the season, you might even catch a glimpse of the Canadian wild geese who have made their home by the old wooden dam nearby. Whatever your interests, you'll find something to do here. It's 5 minutes to Reading Airport and the Reading outlets; 10 minutes to the campuses of Albright, Alvernia, and Penn State; and 30 minutes to Redners Antique Market and Black Angus Beer Fest.

PJ's Guest Home ✪
101 WEST MAIN STREET, STRASBURG, PENNSYLVANIA 17579

Tel: (717) 687-8800
Best Time to Call: Anytime
Hosts: Pat and John Settle
Location: 5 mi. E of Lancaster, Route 741
No. of Rooms: 3
No. of Private Baths: 2
Max. No. Sharing Bath: 4
Double/pb: $48
Double/sb: $38

Open: Feb. 15–Dec. 31
Reduced Rates: $10 less Sept. 4–May 24
Breakfast: Continental
Credit Cards: MC, VISA
Pets: No
Children: Welcome
Smoking: No
Social Drinking: Permitted
Airport/Station Pickup: Yes

The serene Amish countryside of Lancaster County surrounds this lovely guest home, built in 1824. Your hosts, Pat and John, are longtime residents whose knowledge of this special area can help you plan a fun-filled vacation. Attractions include the Strasburg Railroad Museum, Amish craft shops, antique shops, and numerous historic sites.

The Inn at Mundis Mills ✪
586 MUNDIS RACE ROAD, YORK, PENNSYLVANIA 17402

Tel: (717) 755-2002
Best Time to Call: Afternoons
Hosts: Joseph and Marilyn Korsak
Location: 2½ mi. from Rte. 30
No. of Rooms: 2
No. of Private Baths: 2
Double/pb: $60

Single/pb: $45
Open: All year
Breakfast: Full
Pets: No
Children: Welcome
Smoking: No
Social Drinking: Permitted

This quiet country inn is surrounded by York County farmland. The wide front porch welcomes guests to sit and spend some time listening to the chatter of the birds. The pre–Civil War Dutch farmhouse is restored and warmly furnished with antiques. Homemade muffins and jams, fruits, cereals, eggs, and meats will start your day. And, you can walk off the calories as you tour the nearby museums, battlegrounds, and wineries.

PHILADELPHIA AREA

Bed and Breakfast Connections
P.O. BOX 21, DEVON, PENNSYLVANIA 19333

Tel: (215) 687-3565; (800) 448-3619
Best Time to Call: 9 AM–9 PM Mon.–Sat.

Coordinators: Peggy Gregg and Lucy Scribner
States/Regions Covered: Amish

country, Philadelphia and Main Line
suburbs; Reading, Valley Forge, York
County

Rates (Single/Double):
Modest: $30 / $40
Average: $45 / $85
Luxury: $75 / $175
Credit Cards: AMEX, MC, VISA

Bed and Breakfast Connections invites you to select a personally inspected host home in the greater Philadelphia area, from historic Center City to revolutionary Valley Forge. It also serves the scenic Brandywine Valley and Pennsylvania Dutch country. While the locations range from country farmhouses to downtown high-rises, they all offer an inviting atmosphere and dedicated, attentive hosts.

Bed & Breakfast of Chester County
P.O. BOX 825, KENNETT SQUARE, PENNSYLVANIA 19348

Tel: (215) 444-1367
Coordinator: Doris Passante
States/Regions Covered: Chester
  County, Chadds Ford, Valley Forge

Rates (Single/Double):
Modest: $40 / $45–$55
Average: $45 / $55–$65
Luxury: $50 / $70 and up
Credit Cards: No

Doris has a wide selection of homes located in the beautiful and historic Brandywine Valley, which is known for the River Museum, Longwood Gardens, Winterthur, Brandywine Battlefield, and Valley Forge. The area is convenient to the Pennsylvania Dutch country. Send for her brochure, which fully describes each B&B. The University of Delaware, Lincoln University, and West Chester University are close by. There's a $5 surcharge for one-night stays.

Bed & Breakfast of Philadelphia ✪
1616 WALNUT STREET, SUITE 1102, PHILADELPHIA, PENNSYLVANIA 19103

Tel: (215) 735-1917; (800) 220-1917
Best Time to Call: 9 AM–7 PM
Coordinator: John A. Miller
States/Regions Covered: Philadelphia
  and suburbs, Amish country,
  Brandywine Valley, Bucks County;
  New Hope, Valley Forge

Descriptive Directory: Free
Rates (Single/Double):
Modest: $25–$35 / $35–$45
Average: $45–$55 / $55–$65
Luxury: $65–$75 / $75–$150
Credit Cards: AMEX, MC, VISA

John represents over 40 host homes in Center City, the Main Line suburbs, Valley Forge, Chester County, the Brandywine Valley, and New Hope. The accommodations vary from city town houses to country manors or farms to suburban mansions. Several historic properties are available, including several listed on the National Register of Historic Places.

Bed & Breakfast of Valley Forge and Subsidiaries ✪
All About Town—B&B in Philadelphia
All About the Brandywine Valley B&B
P.O. BOX 562, VALLEY FORGE, PENNSYLVANIA 19481

Tel: **(215) 783-7838; (800) 344-0123;**
  fax: **(215) 933-4986**
Best Time to Call: **9 AM–9 PM**
Coordinator: **Eileen M. Luck**
States/Regions Covered: **Brandywine**
  Valley, Bucks County, Lancaster
  County, Philadelphia, Poconos,
  Reading, Valley Forge

Descriptive Directory: **$3**
Rates (Single/Double):
  Modest: **$25–$35 / $45–$55**
  Average: **$40–$55 / $60–$75**
  Luxury: **$60–$75 / $80–up**
Credit Cards: **AMEX, DC, MC, VISA**

Even George Washington would applaud the manner in which Eileen has brought the British tradition of bed and breakfast to his former headquarters. Choose from more than 120 location selections in southeast Pennsylvania. Whether you are on vacation, business, personal getaway, or using up a gift certificate, Eileen says, "There is a B&B for you!" Her roster includes city/country inns, historic and farm homes, ski locations, guest cottages, carriage houses, and elegant and grand estates close to where you need to be. Featured in *Philadelphia Magazine*.

Guesthouses ✪
BOX 2137, WEST CHESTER, PENNSYLVANIA 19380

Tel: **(215) 692-4575;**
  fax: **(215) 692-4451**
Best Time to Call: **noon–4 PM Mon.–**
  Fri.
Coordinator: **Janice K. Archbold**
States/Regions Covered:
  Pennsylvania—Amish country,
  Brandywine Valley, Bucks County,
  Carlisle, Chesapeake Bay,
  Gettysburg, Harrisburg, Main Line
  Philadelphia, Poconos; Delaware;
  Maryland; New Jersey

Rates (Single/Double):
  Modest: **$40–$65**
  Average: **$70–$95**
  Luxury: **$100–$200**
Credit Cards: **AMEX, MC, VISA**

With more than 200 locations in the mid-Atlantic region, Guesthouses provides a choice among various accommodations even during the busiest seasons. Guesthouses specializes in historic National Register or landmark sites, with four categories of offerings: separate guesthouses for two on private estates; private one-to-three-guest-room homes; private manor houses with four to twelve guest rooms and suites; and small, owner-occupied bed-and-breakfast inns and hotels with up to 40 rooms. Guest stays can last from one night to one year. Packages are available, including tickets to an area's museums, gardens, and historic sites.

Bed & Breakfast at Walnut Hill
214 CHANDLER'S MILL ROAD, AVONDALE, PENNSYLVANIA 19311

Tel: (215) 444-3703	Single/sb: $60
Best Time to Call: Anytime	Open: All year
Hosts: Sandy and Tom Mills	Breakfast: Full
Location: 2 mi. S of Kennett Square	Pets: No
No. of Rooms: 2	Children: Welcome, over 8
Max. No. Sharing Bath: 4	Smoking: Permitted
Double/sb: $75	Social Drinking: Permitted

Sandy and Tom's 1844 mill house is in Kennett Square (despite the mailing address above) in the heart of the Brandywine Valley, midway between Philadelphia and Amish country. Longwood Gardens, Chadds Ford Winery, Winterthur, and other museums are all within an eight-mile radius. But nature lovers may want to stay on the B&B grounds, where horses graze in the meadow and a great blue heron fishes in the stream. Deer, Canada geese, and the occasional red fox also put in appearances. However you plan to spend your day, you'll begin it with breakfast specialties like cottage cheese pancakes with blueberry sauce, fresh mushroom omelets, and French toast.

Meadow Spring Farm ◐
201 EAST STREET ROAD, KENNETT SQUARE, PENNSYLVANIA 19348

Tel: (215) 444-3903	Double/sb: $55
Best Time to Call: 8 AM	Open: All year
Hosts: Anne Hicks and Debbie	Breakfast: Full
Axelrod	Other Meals: Available
Location: 2 mi. from Rte. 1	Pets: No
No. of Rooms: 7	Children: Welcome (crib)
No. of Private Baths: 5	Smoking: Permitted
Max. No. Sharing Bath: 4	Social Drinking: Permitted
Double/pb: $65	Airport/Station Pickup: Yes

Meadow Spring Farm is in the heart of the Brandywine Valley, close to Brandywine River Museum, Longwood Gardens, and Winterthur. This 1836 farmhouse is filled with family antiques, Amish quilts, and doll, cow, and Santa Claus collections that delight visitors of all ages. All rooms have air-conditioning, TVs, and desks; the queen-size bedroom has its own fireplace. One first-floor room is accessible to wheelchair users. The swimming pool, surrounded by perennial gardens, and the hot tub are favorite spots among guests, as are the paths that lead around the farm. Anne welcomes you with tea, wine, hot cider, and goodies. Breakfast, served on the screened porch or in the spacious dining room, features fruit pancakes, mushroom omelets, and homemade breads and jams.

The Log House Bed and Breakfast ✪
RD #1, BOX 365A, RED LION, PENNSYLVANIA 17356

Tel: **(717) 927-6854**	Open: **Jan.–Nov.**
Best Time to Call: **6–8 AM; 4–9 PM**	Reduced Rates: **7th night free**
Hosts: **William and Mary McCue**	Breakfast: **Full**
Location: **15 mi. S of York**	Other Meals: **Available**
No. of Rooms: **2**	Pets: **No**
Max. No. Sharing Bath: **4**	Children: **Welcome, over 10**
Double/sb: **$55**	Smoking: **No**
Single/sb: **$45**	Social Drinking: **Permitted**

Relax and enjoy William and Mary's warm hospitality at their eclectically furnished, comfortable log home surrounded by rolling hills. The Log House's charming homey atmosphere puts guests at ease instantly. Bright, cheerful guest rooms are air-conditioned for summer comfort, and the hearty breakfasts include eggs right from the henhouse. Within an easy scenic drive are Gettysburg, Hershey, Amish country, and Baltimore.

POCONO MOUNTAINS

La Anna Guest House ✪
RD 2, BOX 1051, CRESCO, PENNSYLVANIA 18326

Tel: **(717) 676-4225**	Location: **9 mi. from I-80 and I-84**
Hosts: **Kay Swingle and Julie Wilson**	No. of Rooms: **2**

Max. No. Sharing Bath: **4**
Double/sb: **$30**
Single/sb: **$25**
Open: **All year**
Breakfast: **Continental**

Pets: **No**
Children: **Welcome (crib)**
Smoking: **Permitted**
Social Drinking: **Permitted**

This Victorian home has large rooms furnished with antiques; it is nestled on 25 acres of lush, wooded land, and has its own pond. Kay will happily direct you to fine dining spots that are kind to your wallet. Enjoy scenic walks, waterfalls, mountain vistas, Tobyhanna and Promised Land state parks; there's cross-country skiing right on the property. Lake Wallenpaupack is only 15 minutes away.

Academy Street Bed & Breakfast ✪
528 ACADEMY STREET, HAWLEY, PENNSYLVANIA 18428

Tel: **(717) 226-3430**
Hosts: **Judith and Sheldon Lazan**
Location: **100 mi. NW of New York City**
No. of Rooms: **7**
No. of Private Baths: **4**
Max. No. Sharing Bath: **3**
Double/pb: **$75**
Single/pb: **$40**

Double/sb: **$65**
Single/sb: **$35**
Open: **May–Oct.**
Breakfast: **Full**
Credit Cards: **MC, VISA**
Pets: **No**
Children: **Welcome, over 12**
Smoking: **Permitted**
Social Drinking: **Permitted**

This Italian-style Victorian, circa 1865, is situated on a rise near the Lackawaxen River. Judith and Sheldon have done a marvelous job of restoring the rare and beautiful woodwork, paneling, and inlay to make a fitting background for their lovely antiques and furnishings. You'd better diet before you arrive because you won't be able to resist the culinary delights at breakfast or the complimentary high tea. It's only minutes away from famed Lake Wallenpaupack.

Morning Glories ✪
204 BELLEMONTE AVENUE, HAWLEY, PENNSYLVANIA 18428

Tel: **(717) 226-0347**
Best Time to Call: **6 AM–noon; 5 PM–10 PM**
Hosts: **Becky and Roberta Holcomb**
Location: **35 mi. E of Scranton**
No. of Rooms: **2**
No. of Private Baths: **1**
Max. No. Sharing Bath: **4**
Double/pb: **$50**
Single/pb: **$50**

Double/sb: **$45**
Single/sb: **$45**
Open: **All year**
Reduced Rates: **Weekly**
Breakfast: **Full**
Pets: **No**
Children: **No**
Smoking: **Permitted**
Social Drinking: **Permitted**

From this B&B's location in the small town of Hawley, you can walk to the downtown shopping area, summer theater, and several fine restaurants. Your own transportation will allow you to enjoy the area's attractions, such as Lake Wallenpaupack, the Delaware River, train rides, canoeing, rafting, skiing, horseback riding, antiquing, hunting, and fishing. The house has a front porch and a deck in the rear for relaxation, and the living room makes a nice gathering place. The oak staircase leads to the guest rooms on the second floor.

Bonny Bank ✪
P.O. BOX 481, MILLRIFT, PENNSYLVANIA 18340

Tel: **(717) 491-2250**	Open: **May 15–Sept. 15**
Best Time to Call: **9 AM–9 PM**	Reduced Rates: **10% weekly**
Hosts: **Doug and Linda Hay**	Breakfast: **Full**
Location: **5 mi. from I-84**	Pets: **No**
No. of Rooms: **1**	Children: **No**
No. of Private Baths: **1**	Smoking: **No**
Double/pb: **$35**	Social Drinking: **Permitted**
Single/pb: **$30**	

Stay in a picture-book small town on a dead-end road. The sound of the rapids will lull you to sleep in this charming bungalow perched on the banks of the Delaware River. Doug and Linda invite you to use their private swimming area and will lend you inner tubes for float trips. Nearby attractions include the Zane Grey house, Minisink Battlefield, Grey Towers Historical Site, the Victorian village of Milford, and all the sports and variety of restaurants the Poconos are known for.

Elvern Country Lodge ✪
RR 2, BOX 2099A, STONE CHURCH–FIVE POINTS ROAD, MOUNT BETHEL, PENNSYLVANIA 18343-9998

Tel: **(215) 588-7922**	Double/sb: **$50**
Best Time to Call: **After 4 PM**	Single/sb: **$30**
Host: **Doris Deen**	Open: **All year**
Location: **16 mi. N of Easton; 7 mi. S of Delaware Water Gap**	Reduced Rates: **10% seniors; weekly; former guests**
No. of Rooms: **4**	Breakfast: **Full**
No. of Private Baths: **2**	Pets: **No**
Max. No. Sharing Bath: **4**	Children: **Welcome**
Double/pb: **$60**	Smoking: **Permitted downstairs only**
Single/pb: **$35**	

Enjoy the country atmosphere of a working farm in the foothills of the Pocono Mountains. The house, which dates to the early 1800s, includes a shaded second-floor deck where guests can relax in the summer months. Your hostess's breakfasts typically include country bacon or sausage, fresh eggs, and a variety of homemade breads and jams. You are invited to visit the farm animals, stroll through the fruit orchards, and fish on the property's two-acre lake. In the autumn, visitors have the opportunity to watch apple cider being pressed. The Delaware Water Gap Recreation Area, Appalachian Trail, and Pocono Recreation Area are a short drive away.

The Lampost Bed & Breakfast
HC BOX 154, ROUTE 507, PAUPACK, PENNSYLVANIA 18451

Tel: **(717) 857-1738**	Single/sb: **$50**
Best Time to Call: **9 AM–6 PM**	Open: **Apr.–Oct.**
Hosts: **Lily, Karen, and David Seagaard**	Reduced Rates: **10% Mon.–Thurs.**
Location: **9 mi. S of Hawley**	Breakfast: **Continental**
No. of Rooms: **3**	Credit Cards: **MC, VISA**
No. of Private Baths: **2**	Pets: **Sometimes**
Max. No. Sharing Bath: **4**	Children: **Welcome, over 10**
Double/pb: **$70**	Smoking: **No**
Double/sb: **$60**	Social Drinking: **Permitted**

An assortment of lampposts line the driveway leading to this white Colonial home on two acres overlooking Lake Wallenpaupack. This is an ideal stopover for those who love waterfront activities—swimming, boating, fishing, and waterskiing. If you'd rather stay high and dry, there are facilities for golfing, tennis, and horseback riding nearby. Other recreational options include scenic train excursions and balloon rides.

High Hollow ☸
STAR ROUTE, BOX 9-A1, SOUTH STERLING, PENNSYLVANIA 18460

Tel: **(717) 676-4275**	Open: **All year**
Best Time to Call: **10 AM–10 PM**	Reduced Rates: **Available**
Hosts: **Tex and Robbie Taylor**	Breakfast: **Continental**
Location: **From I-80, 12 mi. N of**	Pets: **Sometimes**
Mount Pocono; from I-84, 5.4 mi.	Children: **Sometimes**
No. of Rooms: **1 Suite**	Smoking: **No**
No. of Private Baths: **1**	Social Drinking: **Permitted**
Suite: **$40–$50**	

This tranquil rustic home overlooks a pond and mountain stream. Walk into the guest suite by its separate entrance and inside you'll find a decorative fireplace, TV, kitchenette with refrigerator and micro-wave, and private bath. There are woodlands for strolling, with a BBQ grill and picnic tables, and a secluded streamside area where guests can relax to the sounds of rippling water. Lakes, state parks, nighttime entertainment, and fine dining are all nearby.

The Redwood House ✪
BOX 9B, EAST SIDE BORO, WHITE HAVEN, PENNSYLVANIA 18661

Tel: **(717) 443-7186; (215) 355-1754**
Hosts: **John and Emma Moore**
No. of Rooms: **4**
No. of Private Baths: **2**
Max. No. Sharing Bath: **4**
Double/pb: **$35**
Single/pb: **$25**
Double/sb: **$30**
Single/sb: **$20**

Suites: **$60**
Open: **All year**
Reduced Rates: **5% seniors**
Breakfast: **Continental**
Pets: **No**
Children: **Welcome**
Smoking: **Permitted**
Social Drinking: **Permitted**

This frame chalet is minutes from the slopes at Big Boulder and Jack Frost. In summer enjoy sunning and swimming at Hickory Run State Park. Nearby Lehigh River offers fishing and rafting. Your hosts recommend a visit to Eckley, where the movie *The Molly Maguires* was filmed—a true example of what life was like in a 19th-century mining community. After a day of touring, come and relax on the large, comfortable porch.

SCRANTON/NORTH-CENTRAL PENNSYLVANIA

Irondale Inn Bed & Breakfast ✪
100 IRONDALE AVENUE, BLOOMSBURG, PENNSYLVANIA 17815

Tel: **(717) 784-1977**
Best Time to Call: **After 4 PM**
Hosts: **Robert and Linda Wink**
Location: **100 mi. S of New York City;
   135 mi. N of Philadelphia**
No. of Rooms: **4**
Max. No. Sharing Bath: **4**
Double/sb: **$75**
Single/sb: **$60**
Open: **All year**

Breakfast: **Full**
Other Meals: **Available**
Pets: **No**
Children: **Welcome, over 10**
Smoking: **Permitted**
Social Drinking: **Permitted**
Minimum Stay: **2 nights special
   college weekends**
Airport/Station Pickup: **Yes**

Relax and let the world go by in Robert and Linda's charming home, built in 1838. Gracious extras include a sun porch for reading or watching TV, a billiard room with a regulation-size table, and two living rooms where you can sit around a hearth and enjoy a rousing fire and conversation. In each guest room, "terrific mattresses" and fine bedding ensure a restful night's sleep. The carefully groomed grounds offer leisurely strolls amid several gardens, while the covered patio beckons you to sit down with a cool drink at sunset. Within walking distance lie Bloomsburg University, unique shops, and fine restaurants. An added attraction is the annual Bloomsburg Fair, which runs during the last week of September.

Ponda-Rowland Bed & Breakfast Inn ☉
RR 1, BOX 349, DALLAS, PENNSYLVANIA 18612

Tel: **(717) 639-3245; (800) 950-9130**	Reduced Rates: **$15, after 3 days**
Best Time to Call: **12–4 PM; 8–11 PM**	Breakfast: **Full**
Hosts: **Jennette and Cliff Rowland**	Credit Cards: **MC, VISA**
Location: **7 mi. N of Wilkes-Barre**	Pets: **Yes (outside)**
No. of Rooms: **3**	Children: **Welcome**
No. of Private Baths: **3**	Smoking: **No**
Double/pb: **$50–$70**	Social Drinking: **Permitted**
Single/sb: **$50–$70**	Airpot Pickup: **Yes**
Open: **All year**	

You'll have a memorable stay at this large scenic farm in the Endless Mountains region of northeast Pennsylvania. The farmhouse (circa 1850) features a big stone fireplace, beamed ceilings, and museum quality antiques. Outside you'll see farm animals as well as the less domesticated kind—the property includes a private 34-acre wildlife refuge with six ponds and walking and skiing trails. Athletic types can go canoeing, swimming, ice skating and ice fishing, or play horseshoes, volleyball, and badminton. Over a full breakfast, your hosts can tell you about local horse rentals, air tours, state parks, hunting and trout fishing sites, restaurants, country fairs, and ski slopes.

Sommerville Farms ☉
R.R. 4, BOX 22, JERSEY SHORE, PENNSYLVANIA 17740

Tel: **(717) 398-2368**	Reduced Rates: **Available**
Best Time to Call: **Noon–11 PM**	Breakfast: **Continental**
Hosts: **Bill and Jane Willams**	Credit Cards: **MC, VISA**
Location: **12 mi. W of Williamsport**	Pets: **No**
No. of Rooms: **4**	Children: **Welcome, over 6**
Max. No. Sharing Bath: **4**	Smoking: **No**
Double/sb: **$45**	Social Drinking: **Permitted**
Single/sb: **$35**	Minimum Stay: **Holidays and October**
Open: **Apr.–Dec.**	

As part of a 200-acre working farm, this large white nineteenth-century farmhouse looks the way it's supposed to, from the gabled roof to the side porch. The living room fireplace has an imposing hand-rubbed cherry mantel, and hand-painted scenes decorate the ceiling. Jane, a former antiques dealer, has furnished the house in period style. This area draws hunters, fishermen, skiers, canoeists, and shoppers—Woolrich Woolen Mills Outlet Store is a notable attraction. You'll be ready for any activity after breakfasting on a variety of muffins, breads, and coffee cake.

The Carriage House at Stonegate ○
RD 1, BOX 23, MONTOURSVILLE, PENNSYLVANIA 17754

Tel: **(717) 433-4340**
Best Time to Call: **5:30–9:30 PM**
Hosts: **Harold and Dena Mesaris**
Location: **6 mi. E of Williamsport**
No. of Rooms: **2**
No. of Private Baths: **1**
Guest Cottage: **$50 for 2; $70 for 4**

Open: **All year**
Breakfast: **Continental**
Pets: **Welcome**
Children: **Welcome**
Smoking: **Permitted**
Social Drinking: **Permitted**
Airport/Station Pickup: **Yes**

This self-contained facility was converted from the original carriage house of an 1830 farmhouse. Perfect for a family, there are two bedrooms, a bathroom, a living room with cable television, a dining area, and a kitchen stocked with all your breakfast needs. Decorated in country fashion, with some antiques, it offers complete privacy just 30 yards from your hosts' home. You'll have access to a creek, a barn complete with a variety of animals, and 30 acres on which to roam. It's close to the Little League Museum and Loyalsock Creek for swimming, canoeing, tubing, and fishing.

The Bodine House ○
307 SOUTH MAIN STREET, MUNCY, PENNSYLVANIA 17756

Tel: **(717) 546-8949**
Best Time to Call: **Evenings**
Hosts: **David and Marie Louise Smith**
Location: **15 mi. S of Williamsport; 10 mi. from I-80, Exit 31B**
No. of Rooms: **4**
No. of Private Baths: **3**
Max. No. Sharing Bath: **3**
Double/pb: **$55–$65**
Single/pb: **$50–$60**

Double/sb: **$45**
Single/sb: **$35**
Open: **All year**
Credit Cards: **AMEX, MC, VISA**
Breakfast: **Full**
Pets: **No**
Children: **Welcome, over 6**
Smoking: **No**
Social Drinking: **Permitted**

This restored town house dates back to 1805. A baby grand piano, four fireplaces, and a candlelit living room add to its old-fashioned appeal. A full country breakfast and wine and cheese are on the house. Local attractions include the Susquehanna River, the Endless Mountains, and the fall foliage.

Blackberry Inn Bed & Breakfast
820 WEST MAIN STREET, SMETHPORT, PENNSYLVANIA 16749

Tel: **(814) 887-7777**
Hosts: **Marilyn and Arnie Bolin**

Location: **100 mi. E of Erie**
No. of Rooms: **5**

Max. No. Sharing Bath: **4**	Pets: **No**
Double/sb: **$42–$47**	Children: **Welcome**
Single/sb: **$38–$43**	Smoking: **No**
Open: **All year**	Social Drinking: **No**
Breakfast: **Full**	Airport Pickup: **Yes**

Built in 1881 and completely restored in 1988–89, Blackberry Inn is a Victorian home set in a friendly little borough in the Allegheny Mountains. Marilyn and Arnie are retired professionals devoting all their time to providing warm hospitality to visitors. Nearby attractions include the Kinzua Bridge State Park, the Allegheny National Forest, America's First Christmas Store, and miles of country roads winding through forested mountains. Outdoor activities include hiking, fishing, biking, hunting, cross-country skiing, picnicking and swimming. Or relax in the guest parlor or on one of the large front porches. Breakfast is served at the time chosen by the guest.

Collomsville Inn ✪
RD #3, WILLIAMSPORT, PENNSYLVANIA 17701

Tel: **(717) 745-3608**	Open: **All year**
Best Time to Call: **9 AM–5 PM**	Breakfast: **Continental**
Host: **Betty Callahan**	Credit Cards: **MC, VISA**
Location: **13 mi. W of Williamsport**	Pets: **Sometimes**
No. of Rooms: **5**	Children: **Welcome, over 12**
Max. No. Sharing Bath: **5**	Smoking: **No**
Double/sb: **$40**	Social Drinking: **Permitted**
Single/sb: **$35**	Airport/Station Pickup: **Yes**

A distinctive four-story wooden building with many balconies, this B&B is located on Route 44 in the lush green countryside just west of Williamsport. During the early 19th century, Collomsville served as a stagecoach stop. Today, the five guest rooms retain a rustic charm, and the dining and kitchen areas are filled with antiques suggestive of the inn's rich heritage. Williamsport, the county seat, is best known as the home of the Little League Hall of Fame and Museum. Bargain hunters are sure to score a hit with accessories from Woolrich Woolen Mills, just a short drive away. And sport of another kind waits nearby at Pine Creek, a paradise for anglers, hunters, hikers, cross-country skiers, and snowmobilers.

SOUTHEASTERN PENNSYLVANIA

Brennans B&B ✪
3827 LINDEN STREET, ALLENTOWN, PENNSYLVANIA 18104

Tel: (215) 395-0869
Best Time to Call: 11:30 AM–
  11:30 PM
Hosts: Lois and Edward Brennan
Location: 1 mi. from 78 and 22
No. of Rooms: 2
No. of Private Baths: 1
Max. No. Sharing Bath: 2
Double/pb: $40
Single/pb: $35

Double/sb: $30
Single/sb: $25
Open: Apr.–Dec.
Breakfast: Full
Pets: Sometimes
Children: Welcome
Smoking: Permitted
Social Drinking: Permitted
Airport/Station Pickup: Yes

Furnished in Early American fashion, accented with lush plants and family treasures, this comfortable brick ranch-style house can be your home away from home. The Brennans are history buffs who, now that they're retired, enjoy traveling and entertaining travelers. Breakfast features bacon and eggs with home fries, or sausages and pancakes, or delicious muffins to go with the homemade jam. You can walk off the calories on your way to the Haines Mill, Dorney Park, or one of the area's many museums.

Longswamp Bed and Breakfast ✪
RD 2, BOX 26, MERTZTOWN, PENNSYLVANIA 19539

Tel: (215) 682-6197
Hosts: Elsa Dimick and Dr. Dean
  Dimick
Location: 12 mi. SW of Allentown
No. of Rooms: 10
No. of Private Baths: 6
Max. No. Sharing Bath: 4
Double/pb: $75–$78
Single/pb: $60
Double/sb: $75–$78

Single/sb: $60
Open: All year
Breakfast: Full
Credit Cards: MC, VISA
Pets: No
Children: Welcome
Smoking: No
Social Drinking: Permitted
Airport/Station Pickup: Yes
Foreign Languages: French

This guest house was originally built around 1750 and served as the first post office in town. The main house, completed in 1863, was a stop on the Underground Railroad. Today, Longswamp is a comfortable place with high ceilings, antiques, large fireplaces, plants, and bookcases full of reading pleasure. Breakfast specialties include home-dried fruits, *pain perdu*, quiche, and homemade breads. Elsa offers wine, cheese, and coffee anytime. She will gladly direct you to antique shops, auction houses, Reading, and the Amish country.

SUSQUEHANNA COUNTY

1889 House ☉
114 WEST MAIN STREET, TROY, PENNSYLVANIA 16947

Tel: (717) 297-3771
Best Time to Call: Anytime
Host: Vivian Armstrong
Location: 25 mi. S of Elmira, New York
No. of Rooms: 5
Max. No. Sharing Bath: 3
Double/sb: $40

Single/sb: $30
Open: All year
Breakfast: Full
Pets: No
Children: Welcome
Smoking: No
Social Drinking: Permitted

The 1889 House stands in the center of the charming town of Troy, the gateway to the Endless Mountains. This area is famous for hunting and fishing, as well as for winter sports like snowmobiling and cross-country skiing. Weekday breakfast is Continental, consisting of fruits, juices, cheeses, and breads; on Sundays, breakfast is prepared to your order.

WESTERN PENNSYLVANIA

Bluebird Hollow Bed & Breakfast
BLUEBIRD HOLLOW, R.R. 1, BOX 56, BROOKVILLE, PENNSYLVANIA 15825-8105

Tel: (814) 856-2858
Best Time to Call: Before 8 AM; after 6 PM
Hosts: Ned and Joan Swigart
Location: 4 mi. S of I-80, Exit 13, Brookville
No. of Rooms: 4
No. of Private Baths: 1
Max. No. Sharing Bath: 4
Double/pb: $53–$59

Single/pb: $48–$54
Double/sb: $46–$52
Single/sb: $41–$47
Open: All year
Reduced Rates: 15% weekly
Breakfast: Full
Children: Welcome, infants free (crib)
Smoking: Permitted
Social Drinking: Permitted
Airport/Station Pickup: Yes

A white farmhouse built in 1894, Bluebird Hollow is filled with cherished family antiques, restored "finds," and lovely old quilts. There's something for everyone here, from trout fishing in nearby Redbank Creek to workshops and demonstrations at Cook Forest Sawmill Center for the Arts. It's always fun to stroll the Swigarts' 17-acre property, where you're likely to see deer and other wildlife. To start you off properly, Joan serves up a big country breakfast of berries from her own garden, homemade muffins, blueberry French toast casserole, and locally cured ham.

Mountain View Bed and Breakfast and Antiques ✪
MOUNTAIN VIEW ROAD, DONEGAL, PENNSYLVANIA 15628

Tel: **(412) 593-6349**
Hosts: **Lesley and Jerry O'Leary**
Location: **1 mi. E of Pa. Tpke. Exit 9**
No. of Rooms: **6**
No. of Private Baths: **3**
Max. No. Sharing Bath: **4**
Double/pb: **$90–$125**
Double/sb: **$75–$95**

Open: **All year**
Breakfast: **Full**
Credit Cards: **AMEX, DC, DISC, MC, VISA**
Pets: **No**
Children: **Welcome, over 10**
Smoking: **No**
Social Drinking: **Permitted**

In a quiet pastoral setting in the heart of the Laurel Highlands, you can enjoy lodging and breakfast in a restored 1850s farmhouse and barn furnished with period American furniture. Mountain View is a Westmoreland County historic landmark which affords a magnificent view of the Laurel Ridge. This location is convenient to several mountain resorts, state parks, white-water rafting, and Frank Lloyd Wright's Fallingwater.

Blueberry Acres ✪
3925 McCREARY ROAD, ERIE, PENNSYLVANIA 16506

Tel: **(814) 833-6833**
Hosts: **Nan and Don Fabian**
Location: **100 mi. W of Buffalo**
No. of Rooms: **1 suite**
No. of Private Baths: **1**
Suite: **$50**

Open: **All year**
Breakfast: **Full**
Pets: **No**
Children: **Welcome**
Smoking: **No**
Social Drinking: **Permitted**

This quaint red house is set on a country lane, surrounded by nine acres of wooded land and blueberry bushes. The house was originally built as a summer retreat and has been remodeled for year-round use. The Fabians offer a second-floor suite with private entrance and separate patio for guests. The suite includes a living room, small kitchen, and a bedroom decorated with maple furnishings and ruffled curtains. Breakfast is served in the downstairs dining room and features homemade blueberry muffins and blueberry pancakes served with plenty of bacon or sausage. In summer, when the bushes are bearing luscious fruit, the grounds are perfect for hiking and picnicking. Presque Isle State Park on the shores of Lake Erie offers year-round recreational activities and is located just two miles away.

The Lamberton House ✪
1331 OTTER STREET, FRANKLIN, PENNSYLVANIA 16323-1530

Tel: **(814) 432-7908**
Hosts: **Jack and Sally Clawson**
Location: **80 mi. N of Pittsburgh**

No. of Rooms: **2**
No. of Private Baths: **2**
Max. No. Sharing Bath: **4**

Double/pb: **$65**
Single/pb: **$55**
Double/sb: **$55**
Single/sb: **$40**
Open: **All year**
Reduced Rates: **Available**

Breakfast: **Full**
Pets: **Sometimes**
Children: **Welcome**
Smoking: **Restricted**
Social Drinking: **Permitted**

Named for its original occupant, this Queen Anne Victorian was built in 1874 and is listed in the National Register of Historic Places. The rooms feature beautiful glass, original brass chandeliers, and wood-work of old-world craftsmanship. When they aren't exploring nearby recreational and historic sites, guests can relax in the drawing room, watch TV, play the piano, read in the library, swing on the front porch, or walk in the flower garden. A full country breakfast is served in the elegant dining room each morning.

The Reese House ✪

8311 AVONIA ROAD, GIRARD, PENNSYLVANIA 16417

Tel: **(814) 474-3342**
Best Time to Call: **Before 9:00 AM**
Hosts: **Bill and Carol Reese**
Location: **12 mi. W of Erie, 1 mi. from Rte. 90, Exit 4**
No. of Rooms: **2**
Max. No. Sharing Bath: **4**
Double/sb: **$40**

Single/sb: **$35**
Open: **All year**
Breakfast: **Continental**
Pets: **Sometimes**
Children: **Welcome**
Smoking: **No**
Social Drinking: **No**
Airport/Station Pickup: **Yes**

Just one mile off I-90 on Route 98, this comfortable restored farmhouse oversees eight acres of meadow, woods, orchard, and lawn. A walking track skirts the woods, where you can watch bluebirds and sample raspberries and blackberries in season. Carol's breakfast specialties include rhubarb bread and blueberry muffins, accompanied by fruit, juice, coffee, and tea. (Check out her gift nook for her homemade jellies and craft items.) A short drive brings you to a covered bridge, golf course, or cross-country skiing. Presque Isle's beaches and the Lake Erie waterfront are only fifteen minutes away.

Snow Goose Inn ✪
112 EAST MAIN STREET, GROVE CITY, PENNSYLVANIA 16127

Tel: **(412) 458-4644**	Open: **All year**
Best Time to Call: **10 AM–10 PM**	Breakfast: **Full**
Hosts: **Orvil and Dorothy McMillen**	Credit Cards: **MC, VISA**
Location: **60 mi. N of Pittsburgh**	Pets: **Sometimes**
No. of Rooms: **4**	Children: **Welcome**
Max. No. Sharing Bath: **4**	Smoking: **No**
Double/sb: **$55**	Social Drinking: **Permitted**
Single/sb: **$55**	Airport/Station Pickup: **Yes**

Formerly a country doctor's home and office, the Snow Goose Inn, built around 1895, has a large porch with an old-fashioned swing. Inside, you'll find tastefully furnished bedrooms with a cozy, warm atmosphere. Each morning, freshly brewed coffee and a complete breakfast, including homemade muffins and nut breads, await guests in the dining room. The inn is conveniently located across from Grove City College, next door to a restaurant, and two blocks from the business district. Orvil and Dorothy will be glad to direct you to all the local points of interest.

Neff House ✪
P.O. BOX 67, 552 MAIN STREET, HARMONY, PENNSYLVANIA 16037

Tel: **(412) 452-7512**	Reduced Rates: **Available**
Host: **Sally Jones**	Breakfast: **Full**
Location: **N of Pittsburgh**	Pets: **No**
No. of Rooms: **2**	Children: **Welcome, under 1½ or over 12**
Max. No. Sharing Bath: **4**	Smoking: **No**
Double/sb: **$45–$50**	Social Drinking: **Permitted**
Single/sb: **$30–$35**	Airport Pickup: **Yes**
Open: **All year**	

You will find a cozy atmosphere in this 1808 home located in the national historic district of Harmony, founded as a religious commune in 1805. Museums, antique shops, and fine restaurants are within walking distance. For Amish country, state parks, universities, and the hustle and bustle of Pittsburgh, you will have only a thirty-minute drive. Upon your arrival, Sally, owner and restorer of Neff House, will greet you with cold drinks, wine, and cheese. Good weather may find you savoring her special breakfast on her garden patio.

Gillray Bed and Breakfast ✪

215 N. MAIN STREET, P.O. BOX 493, HARRISVILLE, PENNSYLVANIA 16038

Tel: **(412) 735-2274**	Reduced Rates: **10% seniors, families;**
Best Time to Call: **Anytime**	**weekly**
Hosts: **Dick and Wendy Christner**	Breakfast: **Full**
Location: **5 mi. S of Exit 3 on I-80**	Pets: **No**
No. of Rooms: **3**	Children: **Welcome, over 12**
No. of Private Baths: **3**	Smoking: **Permitted**
Double/pb: **$45**	Social Drinking: **Permitted**
Single/pb: **$35**	Airport/Station Pickup: **Yes**
Open: **All year**	

Old-fashioned hospitality is the hallmark of this restored mid-nineteenth-century home, which is furnished with antiques. The gracious decor is enhanced by the tall arched windows and the original staircase. You can relax with a book in the formal parlor or watch television in the Sherlockian Parlor. A tempting country breakfast is served by candlelight. Slippery Rock University and Grove City College are nearby.

Eagle's Mere ✪

1199 EAST LAKE ROAD, JAMESTOWN, PENNSYLVANIA 16134

Tel: **(412) 932-3572**	Open: **Spring–Fall**
Best Time to Call: **8 AM–9 PM**	Reduced Rates: **10% seniors**
Hosts: **Richard and Doris Ostermeyer**	Breakfast: **Full**
No. of Rooms: **1**	Pets: **Sometimes**
No. of Private Baths: **1**	Children: **Welcome**
Double/pb: **$45**	Smoking: **No**
Single/pb: **$35**	Social Drinking: **Permitted**

From the wraparound porch of this rustic home, you can look down on gardens, trees, and Pymatuning State Park Lake—the view is especially picturesque in autumn. Inside, the decor is primitive, with country motifs. Since the guest room is detached from the main house, you'll have complete privacy, but you can join your hosts for conversation and breakfast. Gardeners take note: both Dick and Doris love cultivating dahlias. For athletic sorts, fishing and nature trails are within walking distance, and five golf courses are nearby.

Beighley Flower Cottage ✪

515 WEST SIXTH STREET, OIL CITY, PENNSYLVANIA 16301

Tel: **(814) 677-3786**	No. of Rooms: **2**
Hosts: **Martha and Jack Beighley**	Max. No. Sharing Bath: **4**
Location: **60 mi. S of Erie**	Double/sb: **$45**

Open: **All year**
Reduced Rates: **Long stays; families
with children**
Breakfast: **Full**
Pets: **No**

Children: **Welcome, over 10**
Smoking: **No**
Social Drinking: **Permitted**
Airport/Station Pickup: **Yes**

Welcome to Pennsylvania's oil country, where you can see some of
the world's oldest producing oil wells. The Beighleys are avid gardeners, which accounts for the name of this B&B. For the best view of the
flowers, your hosts will pour you a beverage and settle you on the
back porch of their white ranch house. Full breakfasts are served in
the country-style kitchen, with its exposed beams and hanging wicker
baskets. While the menu varies, you can expect to sample homemade
bran-raisin muffins and peach honey.

La-Fleur Bed & Breakfast ✪
1830 CRAFTON BOULEVARD, PITTSBURGH, PENNSYLVANIA 15205

Tel: **(412) 921-8588**
Best Time to Call: **10 AM**
Host: **Robert R. Vales**
Location: **4 mi. W of Pittsburgh**
No. of Rooms: **4**
No. of Private Baths: **4**
Double/pb: **$74.50**
Single/pb: **$44.50**
Open: **All year**

Reduced Rates: **Weekly; 10% seniors,
10% families**
Breakfast: **Full**
Credit Cards: **MC, VISA**
Pets: **No**
Children: **Welcome, over 16**
Smoking: **Permitted**
Social Drinking: **Permitted**
Airport/Station Pickup: **Yes**

La-Fleur is a handsome three-story Victorian with porches that let you
enjoy the sun, and cheerful red awnings that prevent you from getting
too warm. Guests have access to a TV, piano, rental bikes, and in the
summer, a swimming pool. If you're not sure how to spend your
time, your host can offer suggestions.

Applebutter Inn ✪
152 APPLEWOOD LANE, SLIPPERY ROCK, PENNSYLVANIA 16057

Tel: **(412) 794-1844**
Best Time to Call: **9 AM–9 PM**
Hosts: **Gary and Sandra McKnight**
Location: **60 mi. N of Pittsburgh**
No. of Rooms: **11**
No. of Private Baths: **11**
Double/pb: **$69–$115**
Single/pb: **$55–$81**
Handicapped-Accessible: **Yes**

Open: **All year**
Reduced Rates: **10% seniors; 15%
weekly**
Breakfast: **Full**
Credit Cards: **MC, VISA**
Pets: **No**
Children: **Welcome**
Smoking: **No**
Social Drinking: **Permitted**

Applebutter Inn offers a window to the past. A six-room farmhouse
built in 1844, it has been expanded, retaining the fine original mill-

work, flooring, and brick fireplaces. It is furnished with antiques and canopied beds, combining today's comforts and yesterday's charm. Slippery Rock University, Grove City College, two state parks, Amish country, and Wendall August Forge are local points of interest. A variety of sporting activities abound close by. Full country breakfasts feature rolled omelets, specialty pancakes, and home-baked muffins and breads. Evening refreshments are served in the keeping room. Guests celebrating a special occasion receive complimentary champagne or wine or a pint of homemade apple butter. Lunch and dinner available in the Wolf Creek School Café next door to the Inn.

Heart of Somerset ✪
130 WEST UNION STREET, SOMERSET, PENNSYLVANIA 15501

Tel: **(814) 445-6782**
Best Time to Call: **8 AM–10 PM**
Hosts: **Ken and Rita Halverson**
Location: **67 mi. SE of Pittsburgh**
No. of Rooms: **4**
No. of Private Baths: **2**
Max. No. Sharing Bath: **4**
Double/pb: **$60–$85**
Single/pb: **$45–$75**
Double/sb: **$50–$75**

Single/sb: **$40–$65**
Open: **All year**
Reduced Rates: **$10 less Sun.–Thurs.**
Breakfast: **Continental**
Credit Cards: **AMEX, MC, VISA**
Pets: **No**
Children: **Sometimes**
Smoking: **No**
Social Drinking: **Permitted**
Airport/Station Pickup: **Yes**

Located in the historic section of town, one can see the ridges of the Laurel Highlands from the front porch. This 1839 Federal-style clapboard home has been restored and furnished with suitable antiques and collectibles. Guests comment on the comfortable beds, original pine floorboards, and the freshly baked muffins at breakfast. You can take a walking tour, climb mountains, ski at Seven Springs or Hidden Valley, hunt, fish, golf, or shoot the rapids. Some folk just enjoy relaxing at this quiet, spacious house.

Saint's Rest ✪
MAIN STREET, P.O. BOX 15, WEST ALEXANDER, PENNSYLVANIA 15376

Tel: **(412) 484-7950**
Best Time to Call: **8 AM–9 PM**
Hosts: **Myrna and Earl Lewis**
Location: **45 mi. W of Pittsburgh; 1 minute from I-70 E or W**
No. of Rooms: **2**
No. of Private Baths: **2**
Double/pb: **$60**

Single/pb: **$40**
Open: **All year**
Breakfast: **Continental, plus**
Credit Cards: **No**
Pets: **No**
Children: **Welcome**
Smoking: **No**
Social Drinking: **Permitted**

Earl and Myrna invite you to visit their beautiful gingerbread-style Victorian home located just minutes from Oglebay Park, Jamboree

U.S.A., and Wheeling Downs Dog Track. Fresh flowers and livable antiques decorate the Federal-style interior, while breakfasts are served on collectible linens and fine china. Earl and Myrna cater to special diets. Saint's Rest stands on Old National Road—the former route of the Underground Railroad, and is within an easy stroll of many fine shops in the West Alexander historical district.

For key to listings, see inside front or back cover.

○ This star means that rates are guaranteed through December 31, 1993, to any guest making a reservation as a result of reading about the B&B in *Bed & Breakfast U.S.A.—1993* edition.

Important! To avoid misunderstandings, always ask about cancellation policies when booking.

Please enclose a self-addressed, stamped, business-size envelope when contacting reservation services.

For more details on what you can expect in a B&B, see Chapter 1.

Always mention *Bed & Breakfast U.S.A.* when making reservations!

If no B&B is listed in the area you'll be visiting, use the form on page 733 to order a copy of our "List of New B&Bs."

We want to hear from you! Use the form on page 735.

RHODE ISLAND

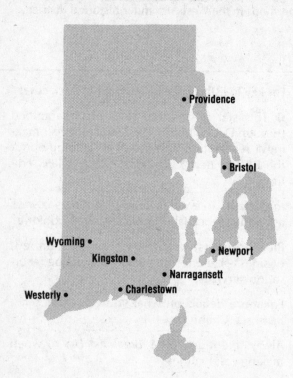

- Providence
- Bristol
- Wyoming
- Kingston
- Newport
- Narragansett
- Westerly
- Charlestown

Rockwell House Inn ✪
610 HOPE STREET, BRISTOL, RHODE ISLAND 02809

Tel: **(401) 253-0040**
Hosts: **Debra and Steve Krohn**
Location: **15 mi. SE of Providence**
No. of Rooms: **4**
No. of Private Baths: **2**
Max. No. Sharing Bath: **4**
Double/pb: **$75–$90**
Double/sb: **$60–$80**
Open: **All year**

Reduced Rates: **Weekly; off-season**
Breakfast: **Continental**
Credit Cards: **AMEX, MC, VISA**
Pets: **Welcome**
Children: **Welcome, over 12**
Smoking: **No**
Social Drinking: **Permitted**
Minimum Stay: **Only major holidays**
Foreign Languages: **Spanish**

This beautifully restored Federal-style home, built in 1809 and listed in the National Register of Historic Places, is located in the heart of Bristol's historic waterfront district, 20 minutes from Newport and within walking distance of museums and antique shops. Rooms feature fireplaces, king-size beds, and a casual elegance that will immediately put you at ease. Enjoy afternoon tea in the garden, read in one of the parlors, and meet new friends over evening sherry. Your hosts Steve and Debra will share their passion for wines, cooking, and entertaining.

Inn the Meadow ✪
1045 SHANNOCK ROAD, CHARLESTOWN, RHODE ISLAND 02813

Tel: **(401) 789-1473**	Breakfast: **Full**
Best Time to Call: **7–9 AM**	Credit Cards: **DISC, MC, VISA**
Hosts: **Yolanda and Michael Day**	Pets: **No**
Location: **30 mi. S of Providence**	Children: **Welcome, over 14**
No. of Rooms: **4**	Smoking: **No**
Max. No. Sharing Bath: **4**	Social Drinking: **Permitted**
Double/sb: **$50–$60**	Minimum Stay: **2 nights Memorial**
Single/sb: **$40**	**Day, Labor Day, 4th of July**
Open: **All year**	Airport/Station Pickup: **Yes**
Reduced Rates: **20% Nov.–Apr.**	Foreign Languages: **German**

Inn the Meadow is on a five-acre former horse farm in southern Rhode Island, an area known for beaches, seafood, and summer theater. In this tranquil setting, guests can explore the woods, listening for whippoorwills and katydids. Then there's still time to enjoy the common room, with its library, games, fireplace, and piano. If you're up for a brief excursion, take a trip to the mansions of Newport or the seaport of Mystic, Connecticut. Your hosts will provide free Newport Bridge tokens, bicycles, and your choice of breakfast from their menu.

The House of Snee
191 OCEAN ROAD, NARRAGANSETT, RHODE ISLAND 02882

Tel: **(401) 783-9494**	Location: **15 mi. SW of Newport**
Best Time to Call: **Anytime**	No. of Rooms: **3**
Host: **Mildred Snee**	Max. No. Sharing Bath: **4**

Double/sb: **$65**
Single/sb: **$40**
Open: **All year**
Breakfast: **Full**
Pets: **No**

Children: **Welcome, over 2**
Smoking: **Permitted**
Social Drinking: **Permitted**
Airport/Station Pickup: **Yes**

This century-old Dutch Colonial overlooks the waters of Rhode Island Sound. It's just across the street from the fishing pier where you can buy tackle and everything you need to hook a big one. It's a mile to the beach and just minutes from the Block Island ferry. Mildred's kitchen is her kingdom and her breakfast often features delicious specialties such as crêpes, egg and meat combinations, homemade scones, and plenty of freshly brewed coffee. Winery tours are a fun diversion in the area. The University of Rhode Island is nearby.

The Richards ✪
144 GIBSON AVENUE, NARRAGANSETT, RHODE ISLAND 02882

Tel: **(401) 789-7746**
Hosts: **Steven and Nancy Richards**
Location: **1 mi. from Rte. 1, Narra**
No. of Rooms: **4**
No. of Private Baths: **2**
Max. No. Sharing Bath: **4**
Double/pb: **$75–$80**
Double/sb: **$60–$65**

Single/sb:: **$50–$55**
Open: **All year**
Breakfast: **Full**
Pets: **No**
Children: **Welcome, over 12**
Smoking: **No**
Social Drinking: **Permitted**

Built by a prominent Rhode Island family in 1884, this massive English-style granite house is listed on the National Register. The B&B, surrounded by tall trees, is located only one mile from the beach and the center of town. Guest rooms are on the second floor, with working fireplaces, canopy and sleigh beds covered with down comforters, oriental rugs, antiques, wicker, and lace. Leave your alarm clock at home; the delightful aromas of johnnycakes, cheese blintzes, strudels, fresh-baked muffins, and gourmet coffees and teas will get you out of bed. Steve works in real estate and is involved in politics; Nancy enjoys restoration, decorating, gardening, and tennis.

The Melville House ✪
39 CLARKE STREET, NEWPORT, RHODE ISLAND 02840

Tel: **(401) 847-0640**
Hosts: **Rita and Sam Rogers**
Location: **35 mi. from I-95, Exit 3**
No. of Rooms: **7**
No. of Private Baths: **5**
Max. No. Sharing Bath: **4**
Double/pb: **$45–$100**
Double/sb: **$40–$85**

Open: **Mar. 1–Jan. 1**
Breakfast: **Continental, plus**
Credit Cards: **AMEX, MC, VISA**
Pets: **No**
Children: **Welcome, over 12**
Smoking: **Permitted**
Social Drinking: **Permitted**
Minimum Stay: **2 nights weekends**

The Melville House is a 1750s shingled home set in Newport's historic Hill section. This quiet street is just one block from the Brick Market and wharfs, and around the corner from Touro Synagogue and Trinity Church. Rita and Sam welcome you to guest rooms decorated with oak furnishings, braided rugs, and lace curtains, with special touches such as fresh flowers and a bowl of fruit. Rita will start your day off with homemade muffins and granola served at polished wood tables in her sunny breakfast room. When you want to relax, the country parlor with its collection of old grinders and gadgets and comfortable wing chairs awaits. Rita will be glad to provide sightseeing advice, and when the day is at a close, enjoy a 5 o'clock sherry at the house.

The Pilgrim House ✺

123 SPRING STREET, NEWPORT, RHODE ISLAND 02840

Tel: **(401) 846-0040; (800) 525-8373**	Double/sb: **$45–$115**
Best Time to Call: **8 AM–9 PM**	Open: **Feb. 1–Dec. 31**
Host: **Mary Rose**	Breakfast: **Continental**
Location: **10 mi. from I-95, Exit 3**	Credit Cards: **MC, VISA**
No. of Rooms: **10**	Pets: **No**
No. of Private Baths: **8**	Children: **Welcome, over 12**
Max. No. Sharing Bath: **2**	Smoking: **No**
Double/pb: **$55–$130**	Social Drinking: **Permitted**

Steal away to this elegant Victorian inn located in the heart of Newport's Historic Hill. Generous rooms with private baths are furnished with beautiful antiques, a diary to record the events of your stay, and countless other thoughtful details. Homemade English Continental breakfast is served each morning. Enjoy sherry and shortbread in the parlor each afternoon. Watch the sunset over the harbor from the rooftop deck. Unique village shops, superb restaurants, theater, mansions, and wharf are all a stroll away.

Cady House ✺

127 POWER STREET, PROVIDENCE, RHODE ISLAND 02906

Tel: **(401) 273-5398**	Open: **All year**
Hosts: **Anna and Bill Colaiace**	Breakfast: **Continental**
Location: **1 mi. from Rte. 95, Exit 2**	Other Meals: **Available**
No. of Rooms: **3**	Pets: **Sometimes**
No. of Private Baths: **2**	Children: **No**
Max. No. Sharing Bath: **3**	Smoking: **No**
Double/pb: **$65**	Social Drinking: **Permitted**
Single/pb: **$60**	Airport/Station Pickup: **Yes**
Suites: **$75; sleeps 4**	

Cady House is a beautiful Classical Revival house (circa 1839) on College Hill, in the heart of the Brown University campus and within walking distance of the Rhode Island School of Design and Johnson and Wales University. The interior is decorated with antique furnishings, oriental carpets, and the owners' extensive collection of American and international folk art. A screened veranda overlooks a large landscaped garden and patio for warm weather relaxation. The hosts are health professionals, cooks, and musicians. They enjoy helping guests discover the attractions of Providence and Rhode Island.

Woody Hill B&B ✪
330 WOODY HILL ROAD, WESTERLY, RHODE ISLAND 02891

Tel: **(401) 322-0452**	Single/sb: **$50**
Best Time to Call: **After 5 PM during**	Open: **All year**
school year	Reduced Rates: **Off-season**
Host: **Ellen L. Madison**	Breakfast: **Full**
Location: **¾ mi. from Rte. 1**	Pets: **No**
No. of Rooms: **3**	Children: **Welcome**
Max. No. Sharing Bath: **4**	Smoking: **No**
Double/sb: **$65**	Social Drinking: **Permitted**

This Colonial reproduction is set on a hilltop among informal gardens and fields. Antiques, wide-board floors, and handmade quilts create an Early American atmosphere. Your hostess may serve homemade jams, muffins, and fresh raspberries in the morning. She can direct you to Mystic Seaport, Block Island, and historic areas. Watch Hill and Westerly beaches are two miles away.

The Cookie Jar B&B ✪
64 KINGSTOWN ROAD, ROUTE 138, WYOMING, RHODE ISLAND 02898

Tel: **(401) 539-2680**	Single/sb: **$49.50**
Best Time to Call: **After 5 PM**	Open: **All year**
Hosts: **Dick and Madelein Sohl**	Reduced Rates: **20% Nov. 15–Apr. 15**
Location: **25 mi. SW of Providence**	Breakfast: **Full**
No. of Rooms: **3**	Credit Cards: **MC, VISA**
No. of Private Baths: **1**	Pets: **No**
Max. No. Sharing Bath: **4**	Children: **Welcome**
Double/pb: **$55**	Smoking: **No**
Double/sb: **$55**	Social Drinking: **Permitted**

The heart of this house, the living room, was a blacksmith's shop built in 1732; the original ceiling, hand-hewn beams, and granite walls are still in use. Fittingly, Dick and Madelein have furnished their home with a mixture of antique, country, and contemporary pieces. You'll enjoy strolling around their property, which includes a barn, swimming pool, flower garden, and lots of fruit trees, berry bushes, and grapevines. Despite the rural setting, you'll have only a short drive to the University of Rhode Island, the beaches, and cities like Mystic and Providence. Golfing, horseback riding, bicycling, and waterfront sports are all close at hand.

SOUTH CAROLINA

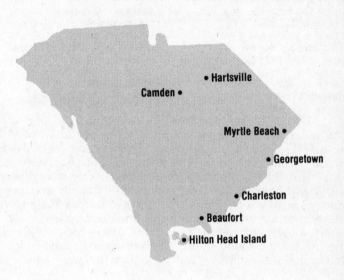

The Rhett House Inn
1009 CRAVEN STREET, BEAUFORT, SOUTH CAROLINA 29902

Tel: **(803) 524-9030**
Hosts: **Steve and Marianne Harrison**
Location: **28 mi. E of I-95**
No. of Rooms: **10**
No. of Private Baths: **10**
Double/pb: **$80–$150**
Single/pb: **$70–$140**
Open: **All year**
Breakfast: **Full**

Other Meals: **Available weekends by**
  reservation
Wheelchair-Accessible: **Yes**
Credit Cards: **MC, VISA**
Pets: **No**
Children: **Welcome, over 5**
Smoking: **No**
Social Drinking: **Permitted**

If you ever wondered what the South was like before the Civil War, come visit this inn located in the historic district. Two of the bedrooms have fireplaces; all have homespun quilts and pretty touches such as freshly cut flowers. After breakfast, stroll in the lovely gardens or take a bicycle ride around town. The restored waterfront on the Intracoastal

Waterway, with its shops and restaurants, is within walking distance. If you ask, your hosts will pack a picnic lunch and direct you to the beach. Hilton Head Island is 35 miles away.

TwoSuns Inn Bed & Breakfast
1705 BAY STREET, BEAUFORT, SOUTH CAROLINA 29902

Tel: **(803) 522-1122; fax: (803) 522-1122, (800) 532-4244**
Best Time to Call: **9 AM–9 PM**
Hosts: **Carrol and Ron Kay**
Location: **28 mi. E of I-95**
No. of Rooms: **5**
No. of Private Baths: **5**
Double/pb: **$89–$99**
Single/pb: **$79–$89**

Suites: **$178; sleeps 4**
Open: **All year**
Breakfast: **Full**
Credit Cards: **AMEX, MC, VISA**
Pets: **No**
Children: **Welcome, over 12**
Smoking: **No**
Social Drinking: **Permitted**

Warm, informal hospitality is the order of the day at TwoSuns Inn. Built in 1917, this restored Neoclassic Revival home looks down on beautiful Beaufort Bay, with its picturesque marina and surrounding islands. Throughout the home, a comfortable blend of Victorian, country, and Oriental themes are accented by family antiques and heirlooms. Breakfast features Carrol's special recipes and always includes homemade muffins and breads. Stroll or bicycle ride through Beaufort, a charming historic community dating back to 1711. Then return to "Tea and Toddy Hour," sit on the veranda, and be soothed by the fresh southern breezes wafting in from the bay.

The Carriage House ✪
1413 LYTTLETON STREET, CAMDEN, SOUTH CAROLINA 29020

Tel: **(803) 432-2430**
Best Time to Call: **After 10 AM**

Hosts: **Appie and Bob Watkins**
Location: **30 mi. N of Columbia**

No. of Rooms: **2**	Pets: **No**
No. of Private Baths: **1½**	Children: **Welcome, over 6**
Double/pb: **$50**	Smoking: **Permitted**
Open: **All year**	Social Drinking: **Permitted**
Breakfast: **Full**	

The Carriage House is an antebellum cottage with window boxes and a picket fence. Located in the center of historic Camden, it is within walking distance of tennis, parks, and shops. The guest rooms have twin or queen-size beds and are decorated with colorful fabrics and lovely antiques. Visitors are welcomed to their quarters with complimentary sherry and fruit. Your hosts serve a Southern-style breakfast.

Almost Home ✪
1236 OCEAN VIEW ROAD, CHARLESTON, SOUTH CAROLINA 29412

Tel: **(803) 795-8705**	Reduced Rates: **Weekly**
Hosts: **Randy and Leita Harrison**	Breakfast: **Continental**
Location: **7 mi. SW of Charleston**	Pets: **No**
No. of Rooms: **2**	Children: **Welcome**
Max. No. Sharing Bath: **4**	Smoking: **Permitted**
Double/sb: **$50**	Social Drinking: **Permitted**
Open: **All year**	

You'll wish this big white house with its red shutters and roof were your home. The location is ideal, seven miles from downtown Charleston and five miles to the nearest beach. The city's charms include landmark buildings and excellent restaurants. Each room at Almost Home has its own TV. In the morning, a light breakfast of fresh fruit and home-baked breads is served.

Ann Harper's Bed & Breakfast
56 SMITH STREET, CHARLESTON, SOUTH CAROLINA 29401

Tel: **(803) 723-3947**	Single/sb: **$50**
Best Time to Call: **Before 10 AM;**	Open: **All year**
after 6 PM	Breakfast: **Full**
Host: **Ann D. Harper**	Pets: **No**
Location: **1 mi. from I-26**	Children: **Welcome, over 10**
No. of Rooms: **2**	Smoking: **Permitted**
Max. No. Sharing Bath: **3**	Social Drinking: **Permitted**
Double/sb: **$55–$60**	

This attractive home, circa 1870, is located in Charleston's historic district. The rooms, ideally suited for two friends traveling together, are decorated with wicker pieces and family treasures. Take a moment to relax on the porch or in the intimate walled garden out back. Ann serves a hot, Southern-style breakfast each morning featuring homemade bread and hominy grits. She will gladly direct you to the interesting sights of this historic area. There is a $5 surcharge for one-night stays; no single rates March 15 to June 15.

Cannonboro Inn
184 ASHLEY AVENUE, CHARLESTON, SOUTH CAROLINA 29403

Tel: **(803) 723-8572**	Open: **All year**
Best Time to Call: **9 AM–9 PM**	Breakfast: **Full**
Hosts: **Bud and Sally Allen**	Credit Cards: **MC, VISA**
Location: **Downtown Charleston**	Pets: **No**
No. of Rooms: **6**	Children: **Welcome, over 12**
No. of Private Baths: **6**	Smoking: **No**
Double/pb: **$59–$89**	Social Drinking: **Permitted**

This gracious restored house, dating to the mid–1800s, is located in the historic district. Each bedroom has original heart pine floors, tiled fireplaces with Victorian mantels, oriental rugs, and four-poster nice beds. For guests, Sally and Bud pour sherry in the formal room, in front of the fireplace. For breakfast, they prepare gourmet fare such as ginger apple crêpes with cinnamon cider sauce, orange waffles with honey orange syrup, quiche, and homemade breads and scones; you can eat in the formal dining room or on the piazza overlooking a low country garden with a fountain and goldfish pond.

Charleston East Bed & Breakfast
1031 TALL PINE ROAD, MOUNT PLEASANT, SOUTH CAROLINA 29464

Tel: **(803) 884-8208**	Rates (Single/Double):
Best Time to Call: **9 AM–6 PM**	Modest: **$20 / $40**
Coordinator: **Bobbie Auld**	Average: **$35 / $50**
States/Regions Covered: **East Cooper,**	Luxury: **$50 / $60**
Isle of Palms, McClellanville, Mount	
Pleasant, Sullivans Island	

East Cooper is a historic area dating back to 1767. Fort Moultrie, on Sullivans Island, stands guard over quiet beaches. Bobbie's hosts are convenient to the historic district of Charleston and close to the sights that have made this city famous. The B&Bs range from quiet village homes near the harbor to modern suburban homes.

Country Victorian Bed and Breakfast ✪
105 TRADD STREET, CHARLESTON, SOUTH CAROLINA 29401

Tel: **(803) 577-0682**	No. of Private Baths: **2**
Host: **Diane Deardurff Weed**	Double/pb: **$65–$90**
Location: **96 mi. S of Myrtle Beach**	Single/pb: **$65–$90**
No. of Rooms: **2**	Suites: **$100–$115**

Open: **All year**
Breakfast: **Continental**
Pets: **No**

Children: **Welcome**
Smoking: **No**
Social Drinking: **Permitted**

As tourists pass in horse-drawn carriages, their eyes are drawn to the beautiful screen doors of this Victorianized house, built in 1820. Rooms have private entrances and are comfortably decorated with antique iron and brass beds, old quilts, and antique oak and wicker furniture. You'll find homemade cookies waiting for you when you arrive. Coffee and tea can be prepared in your room at any time, and snacks are served in the afternoon. Restaurants, churches, antique shops, museums, and art galleries are all within walking distance.

Historic Charleston Bed & Breakfast ✪
43 LEGARE STREET, CHARLESTON, SOUTH CAROLINA 29401

Tel: **(803) 722-6606**
Best Time to Call: **9:30 AM–6 PM Mon.–Fri.**
Coordinator: **Charlotte Fairey**
States/Regions Covered: **South Carolina—Georgia—Savannah**
Descriptive Directory: **Free**

Rates (Single/Double):
Modest: **$65 / $75**
Average: **$80 / $95**
Luxury: **$100 / $135**
Credit Cards: **AMEX, MC, VISA**
Minimum Stay: **2 nights Mar. 15–June 15, Oct.**

This port city is one of the most historic in the United States. Through the auspices of Charlotte, you will enjoy your stay in a private home, carriage house, or mansion in a neighborhood of enchanting walled gardens, cobblestoned streets, and moss-draped oak trees. Each home is unique, yet each has a warm and friendly atmosphere provided by a host who sincerely enjoys making guests welcome. All are historic properties dating from 1720 to 1890, yet all are up to date with air-conditioning, phones, and television. Reduced rates are available for weekly stays, but there is a $5 surcharge for one-night stays.

Johnson's Six Orange Street B&B
6 ORANGE STREET, CHARLESTON, SOUTH CAROLINA 29401

Tel: **(803) 722-6122**
Hosts: **Becky and Bill Johnson**
Location: **Located in historic district of Charleston**
No. of Rooms: **1**
No. of Private Baths: **1**
Double/pb: **$90**
Open: **All year**

Breakfast: **Continental**
Credit Cards: **No**
Pets: **No**
Children: **Welcome (crib)**
Smoking: **No**
Social Drinking: **Permitted**
Foreign Languages: **French, German**

Within Charleston's historical district, Becky and Bill maintain an attached guest house complete with sitting room, efficiency kitchen, upstairs bedroom, and private bath and entrance. The bedroom sleeps three and features an antique sleigh bed plus an iron and brass single bed. A crib is also available for families with an infant. Enjoy scrumptious home-baked coffee cakes, pastries, and breads before you explore the numerous sights and attractions this city has to offer.

Villa de la Fontaine
138 WENTWORTH STREET, CHARLESTON, SOUTH CAROLINA 29401

Tel: **(803) 577-7709**
Best Time to Call: **8 AM–6 PM**
Hosts: **Aubrey W. Hancock and Bill Fontaine**
No. of Rooms: **4**
No. of Private Baths: **4**
Double/pb: **$85–$100**
Single/pb: **$85–$100**
Suites: **$135–$165**

Open: **All year**
Reduced Rates: **Available**
Breakfast: **Full**
Credit Cards: **AMEX, MC, VISA**
Pets: **No**
Children: **No**
Smoking: **No**
Social Drinking: **Permitted**

Villa de la Fontaine is an enormous four-columned Greek Revival home in the heart of the historic district. The house was built in 1838, and boasts a half-acre garden complete with fountain and terraces. Inside, the rooms have been restored to mint condition, and Aubrey, a retired interior designer, has decorated them with 18th-century American antiques and reproductions. Several of the guest rooms feature canopy beds. Breakfast is prepared by a master chef who prides himself on serving something different every day. Guests staying in the cottage gazebo are provided with Continental fare.

Shaw House ✪
8 CYPRESS COURT, GEORGETOWN, SOUTH CAROLINA 29440

Tel: **(803) 546-9663**
Best Time to Call: **Early mornings**
Host: **Mary Shaw**
Location: **1 block off Hwy. 17**
No. of Rooms: **3**
No. of Private Baths: **3**
Double/pb: **$45–$50**
Single/pb: **$45**

Open: **All year**
Reduced Rates: **10% after 4th night**
Breakfast: **Full**
Pets: **No**
Children: **Welcome**
Smoking: **Permitted**
Social Drinking: **Permitted**
Airport/Station Pickup: **Yes**

Shaw House is a two-story Colonial with a beautiful view of the Willowbank Marsh. Your host is knowledgeable about antiques and has filled the rooms with them. The rocking chairs and cool breeze will tempt you to the porch. Each morning a pot of coffee and Southern-style casserole await you. Fresh fruit and homemade snacks are available all day. The house is within walking distance of the historic district and is near Myrtle Beach, Pawleys Island, golf, tennis, and restaurants.

Missouri Inn B&B ✪

314 EAST HOME AVENUE, HARTSVILLE, SOUTH CAROLINA 29550

Tel: (803) 383-9553
Best Time to Call: Noon–9 PM
Hosts: Kyle and Kenny Segars, and Lucy Brown
Location: 28 mi. NW of Florence
No. of Rooms: 5
No. of Private Baths: 5
Double/pb: $85
Single/pb: $75

Open: All year
Reduced Rates: Corporate
Breakfast: Full
Credit Cards: AMEX, MC, VISA
Pets: No
Children: No
Smoking: Permitted
Social Drinking: Permitted

An elegant Southern mansion built around the turn of the century and completely renovated in 1990, the Missouri Inn offers discriminating guests exceptional peace, quiet, and privacy in a small, luxurious setting. Located in Hartsville's official historic district, the inn stands opposite the lovely Coker College campus, on about five acres landscaped with stately trees and flowering shrubs. The distinctively furnished rooms not only have telephones and TVs, but terry robes, bath sheets, towel warmers, hair dryers, and fresh floral arrangements. Amenities include afternoon tea and complimentary beverages at all times.

Ambiance Bed & Breakfast

8 WREN DRIVE, HILTON HEAD ISLAND, SOUTH CAROLINA 29928

Tel: (803) 671-4981
Best Time to Call: Evenings
Host: Marny Kridel Daubenspeck
Location: 40 mi. from I-95, Exit 28
No. of Rooms: 2
No. of Private Baths: 2
Double/pb: $65–$75

Single/pb: $60–$70
Open: All year
Breakfast: Continental
Pets: No
Children: Welcome, over 12
Smoking: Permitted
Social Drinking: Permitted

This contemporary cypress home is located in the area of Sea Pines Plantation. Floor-length windows afford beautiful views of the subtropical surroundings. Marny runs an interior decorating firm, so it's no surprise that everything is in excellent taste. The beach and the Atlantic Ocean are immediately accessible, and sports facilities are readily available.

Brustman House ✪

400 25TH AVENUE SOUTH, MYRTLE BEACH, SOUTH CAROLINA 29577

Tel: (803) 448-7699
Best Time to Call: AM
Hosts: Mina and Wendell Brustman

Location: 90 mi. N of Charleston
No. of Rooms: 4
No. of Private Baths: 3

Max. No. Sharing Bath: **4**
Double/pb: **$50–$60**
Single/pb: **$50**
Double/sb: **$40**
Single/sb: **$40**
Open: **Feb.–Nov.**
Reduced Rates: **10% after 3rd night;**
    10% Nov.–Mar.

Breakfast: **Continental**
Pets: **No**
Children: **Welcome, over 10**
Smoking: **No**
Social Drinking: **Permitted**
Airport/Station Pickup: **Yes**

Brustman House, a Georgian-style home on a one-acre estate, is located two short blocks from the beach. Golf courses, seafront restaurants, and the Carolina Opry are in the immediate area, and Brookgreen Gardens and historic Georgetown are also close at hand. Of course, you may not want to leave the property at all; Mina will supply picnic lunches, lawn games, bicycles, and indoor diversions like Ping-Pong and piano. Healthful breakfast entrées, such as nine-grain sourdough pancakes, are her specialty. Her daughters can direct you to factory outlets and the local amusement park as they pour you afternoon tea.

Serendipity, an Inn ✪

407 71ST AVENUE NORTH, MYRTLE BEACH, SOUTH CAROLINA 29577

Tel: **(803) 449-5268**
Best Time to Call: **8 AM–11 PM**
Hosts: **Cos and Ellen Ficarra**
Location: **60 mi. from Rte. 95**
No. of Rooms: **15**
No. of Private Baths: **15**
Double/pb: **$65–$85**
Suites: **$72–$85**

Open: **Feb.–Nov.**
Breakfast: **Continental**
Credit Cards: **AMEX, MC, VISA**
Pets: **No**
Children: **Welcome**
Smoking: **Permitted**
Social Drinking: **Permitted**
Foreign Languages: **Italian, Spanish**

Serendipity is a Spanish Mission-style inn surrounded by lush tropical plants and flowers. The setting is peaceful, the street is quiet, and the ocean is less than 300 yards away. Bedrooms are highlighted with antiques drawing from Art Deco, Oriental, wicker, and pine motifs. The Garden Room is the place for a generous breakfast of homemade breads, fresh fruit, eggs, and cereal. Guests also gather here for afternoon drinks and conversation. Your hosts invite you to use the heated pool and spa, play shuffleboard, Ping-Pong, or just share a quiet moment beside the patio fountain. Myrtle Beach is known for its fine restaurants, but the Ficarras have a gas grill if you want to do your own cooking. Cos and Ellen will gladly direct you to nearby shops, fishing villages, golf courses, and miles of beaches.

SOUTH DAKOTA

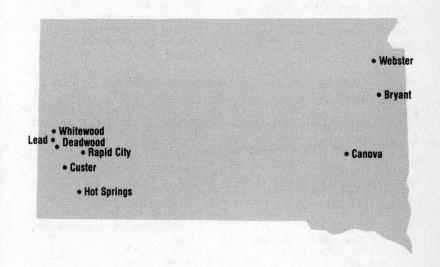

The Big Brown Country Inn
ROUTE 1, BOX 186, BRYANT, SOUTH DAKOTA 57221

Tel: **(605) 628-2049**
Best Time to Call: **Early mornings;
    evenings**
Hosts: **Floyd and Myrta Rossel**
Location: **38 mi. SW of Watertown**
No. of Rooms: **3**
Max. No. Sharing Bath: **6**
Double/sb: **$25**

Single/sb: **$15**
Open: **All year**
Breakfast: **Full**
Pets: **Sometimes**
Children: **Welcome**
Smoking: **Permitted**
Social Drinking: **Permitted**

The Rossels' 100-year-old Victorian home lies on a quiet tree-lined street in this small country town where friendliness and hospitality have blossomed for generations. Guest rooms are cheerfully decorated in a homey mix of Early American and country styles, while Myrta's antiques and homemade crafts supply an air of yesteryear. Begin the day with a hearty breakfast featuring farm-fresh specialties, jams, and breads. Afterward, enjoy the nearby parks and lakes, or visit the Laura Ingalls Wilder Museum in DeSmet, just a short drive away. Floyd, an avid collectible-car enthusiast, is eager to show you his latest pride and joy.

Skoglund Farm ✪
CANOVA, SOUTH DAKOTA 57321

Tel: **(605) 247-3445**	Open: **All year**
Best Time to Call: **Early mornings;**	Reduced Rates: **Under 18**
evenings	Breakfast: **Full**
Hosts: **Alden and Delores Skoglund**	Other Meals: **Dinner included**
Location: **12 miles from I-90**	Pets: **Welcome**
No. of Rooms: **5**	Children: **Welcome (crib)**
Max. No. Sharing Bath: **3**	Smoking: **Permitted**
Double/sb: **$50**	Social Drinking: **Permitted**
Single/sb: **$30**	Airport/Station Pickup: **Yes**

This is a working farm where the emphasis is on the simple, good life. It is a welcome escape from urban living. You may, if you wish, help with the farm chores, or just watch everyone else work; the family raises cattle, fowl, and peacocks. You may ride the horses over the wide, open spaces. You are welcome to use the laundry facilities or play the piano. The coffeepot is always on.

Custer Mansion Bed & Breakfast
35 CENTENNIAL DRIVE, CUSTER, SOUTH DAKOTA 57730

Tel: **(605) 673-3333**	Reduced Rates: **Off-season, extended**
Hosts: **Millard and Carole Seaman**	**stays**
Location: **42 mi. W of Rapid City**	Breakfast: **Full**
No. of Rooms: **6**	Pets: **No**
No. of Private Baths: **2**	Children: **Welcome**
Max. No. Sharing Bath: **4**	Smoking: **No**
Double/pb: **$60–$75**	Social Drinking: **No**
Double/sb: **$45–$60**	Foreign Languages: **Spanish**
Open: **All year**	

Soon after it was built in 1891, this Victorian Gothic house became the center of many community activities. Today, antique light fixtures, ceiling fans, and the transoms and stained glass above the doors preserve the turn-of-the-century mood. There is a guest lounge in the front parlor, a tree-shaded patio, and a spacious yard. Located near Mt. Rushmore, Crazy Horse, Custer State Park, and many other attractions, the area offers swimming, fishing, hiking, golf, biking, and skiing. Mill, a retired school administrator, and Carole, mother of six and grandmother of ten, specialize in friendly hospitality and delicious home-cooked breakfasts.

Adams House ✪
22 VAN BUREN, DEADWOOD, SOUTH DAKOTA 57732

Tel: **(605) 578-3877**	Host: **Lynda Clark, Director**
Best Time to Call: **10 AM–6 PM**	Location: **40 mi. NW of Rapid City**

No. of Rooms: **4**
No. of Private Baths: **4**
Double/pb: **$65–$90**
Single/pb: **$55–$80**
Open: **All year**
Breakfast: **Full**

Credit Cards: **MC, VISA**
Pets: **No**
Children: **Welcome, over 12**
Smoking: **No**
Social Drinking: **Permitted**

Deadwood has retained the flavor of the old frontier and the gold strikes of the 1870s. Listed on the National Register of Historic Places, this 1892 Queen Anne Victorian mansion was unoccupied for more than 50 years. Periodic, careful maintenance preserved the elegant furnishings, and they are today still in their original condition. Three presidents—Taft, Teddy Roosevelt, and Coolidge—were once house-guests here. You'll awaken to the fragrance of freshly ground coffee and homemade specialties. It's a short walk to Mt. Moriah, the burial place of Wild Bill Hickock and Calamity Jane. Back ''home'' you are welcome to play the parlor piano or play tennis not two blocks away. Your host invites you to afternoon tea.

Villa Theresa Guest House B&B ✪
801 ALMOND STREET, HOT SPRINGS, SOUTH DAKOTA 57747

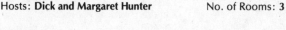

Tel: **(605) 745-4633**
Hosts: **Dick and Margaret Hunter**

Location: **60 mi. S of Rapid City**
No. of Rooms: **3**

Double/pb: **$65**
Double/sb: **$60**
Open: **All year**
Breakfast: **Full**
Credit Cards: **MC, VISA**

Pets: **No**
Children: **Welcome**
Smoking: **No**
Social Drinking: **No**
Airport/Station Pickup: **Yes, fee**

The Villa Theresa Guest House was built in 1891 as a "pleasure and gaming house" for a group of Sioux City vacationers. The rear veranda overlooks the town of Hot Springs, which boasts the world's largest natural warm-water indoor swimming pool. The town also contains the western hemisphere's largest repository of mammoth bones. If living mammals are more your speed, visit the Hot Springs wild mustang ranch. Deer and antelope—not to mention buffalo, prairie dogs, and wild burros—play nearby, in Wind Cave National Park and Custer State Park.

Cheyenne Crossing B&B ✪
HC 37, BOX 1220, LEAD, SOUTH DAKOTA 57754

Tel: **(605) 584-3510, 584-2636**
Hosts: **Jim and Bonnie LeMar**
Location: **Junction Hwys. 85 and 14A**
No. of Rooms: **3**
Max. No. Sharing Bath: **4**
Double/sb: **$59**
Single/sb: **$45**
Open: **All year**

Reduced Rates: **Families; groups**
Breakfast: **Full**
Other Meals: **Available**
Credit Cards: **DISC, MC, VISA**
Pets: **No**
Children: **Welcome, over 6**
Smoking: **No**
Social Drinking: **Permitted**

This two-story frame building with its facade of rough-sawed pine is situated in the heart of Spearfish Canyon. The main floor houses a typical country general store and café; the guest quarters are upstairs. From 1876 to 1885 the original building was a stop for the Deadwood–Cheyenne stagecoach. After it burned down in 1960, the present building was built to replace it. Jim and Bonnie will be delighted to map out special trips tailored to your interests. Spend the day visiting Mt. Rushmore and Crazy Horse Monument, pan for gold, hike, or fish for trout on Spearfish Creek, which flows behind the store. It's also close to the Black Hills Passion Play. Sourdough pancakes are a frequent breakfast treat.

Abend Haus Cottage & Audrie's Cranbury Corner Bed & Breakfast ✪
RR 8, BOX 2400, RAPID CITY, SOUTH DAKOTA 57702

Tel: **(605) 342-7788**
Best Time to Call: **Anytime**
Hosts: **Hank and Audry Kuhnhauser**
Location: **¼ mi. from Hwy. 44**
No. of Rooms: **6**

No. of Private Baths: **6**
Double/pb: **$78**
Single/pb: **$70**
Guest Cottage: **$75–$85**
Suites: **$75–$85**

Open: **All year**
Breakfast: **Full**
Pets: **No**

Children: **No**
Smoking: **No**
Social Drinking: **Permitted**

At this country home and five-acre estate in a secluded Black Hills setting just 30 miles from Mt. Rushmore and 7 miles from Rapid City, you can experience charm and old-world hospitality. There are free trout fishing, biking, and hiking on the property, which is surrounded by thousands of acres of national forest land. Each room, suite, and cottage has a private entrance, bath, hot tub, patio, cable TV, and refrigerator. Full breakfasts are served.

Abigail's Garden ✪
ROUTE 8, BOX 2670, RAPID CITY, SOUTH DAKOTA 57702

Tel: **(605) 343-6530**
Best Time to Call: **Before 10 AM;**
  after 4 PM
Hosts: **Dee and Wally Gunderson**
Location: **8 mi. W of Rapid City**
No. of Rooms: **2**
No. of Private Baths: **2**
Double/pb: **$95–$100**
Single/pb: **$90–$95**

Open: **May 1–Oct. 1**
Reduced Rates: **10% weekly**
Breakfast: **Full**
Credit Cards: **MC, VISA**
Pets: **No**
Children: **No**
Smoking: **No**
Social Drinking: **Permitted**

Leave your worries behind as you motor down the birch canopied lane into peace and tranquillity. Survey the romantically landscaped grounds and flower gardens, or listen to the clear stream bubble by your bedroom deck. Rare botanical prints, antiques, ethnic collectibles, and cheerful fabrics give this B&B a charming atmosphere. Guests can expect to be pampered here. Upon arrival, you'll restore yourself with a complimentary English tea or an array of Sandinavian open sandwiches, served brookside or in the garden gazebo. Breakfast gives Dee another opportunity to showcase her culinary talents.

Bed and Breakfast Domivara ✪
HC 33, BOX 3004, RAPID CITY, SOUTH DAKOTA 57702

Tel: **(605) 574-4207**
Best Time to Call: **Mornings; 6–8 PM**
Host: **Betty Blount**
Location: **26 mi. SW of Rapid City**
No. of Rooms: **2**
No. of Private Baths: **2**
Double/pb: **$65–$70**
Single/pb: **$55**

Open: **All year**
Breakfast: **Full**
Other Meals: **Available**
Pets: **Sometimes**
Children: **Welcome**
Smoking: **Permitted**
Social Drinking: **Permitted**
Minimum Stay: **2 nights**

Enjoy Western hospitality in a unique log home located in the picturesque Black Hills of South Dakota. The homey wood interior is decorated with comfortable antiques and accents of stained glass. A large picture window overlooks the countryside where you may see an occasional wild turkey or deer. Betty Blount offers complimentary snacks served with wine or coffee. She prepares a variety of special breakfast dishes including sourdough pancakes, egg soufflés, fresh trout, and homemade blueberry muffins. There are good restaurants nearby, or if you prefer home cooking, your host will be glad to prepare dinner for you. Domivara is conveniently located just 20 minutes from Mt. Rushmore and the Crazy Horse memorial.

Willow Springs Cabins ✪
HC 39, BOX 108, RAPID CITY, SOUTH DAKOTA 57702

Tel: **(605) 342-3665**	Breakfast: **Full**
Hosts: **Joyce and Russell Payton**	Pets: **No**
Location: **15 mi. off I-90, Exit 57**	Children: **Welcome (crib)**
Guest Cottage: **$70–$87 for 2**	Smoking: **No**
Open: **All year**	Social Drinking: **Permitted**

Willow Springs is a one-room rustic log cabin nestled in the native pines just inside the Black Hills National Forest. The cabin is cozily decorated with family heirlooms. Guests begin each day with freshly ground coffee, seasonal fruits, and warm-from-the-oven breads. Afterward, diversions include hiking, swimming or fishing in a private mountain stream, or just relaxing on the front porch while admiring the breathtaking view. In winter, ice skating and cross-country skiing are popular. Centrally located in the Black Hills, it's just minutes away from the Mt. Rushmore National Monument.

Lakeside Farm ✪
RR 2, BOX 52, WEBSTER, SOUTH DAKOTA 57274

Tel: **(605) 486-4430**	Single/sb: **$25**
Hosts: **Joy and Glenn Hagen**	Open: **All year**
Location: **60 mi. E of Aberdeen on Hwy. 12**	Breakfast: **Full**
	Pets: **No**
No. of Rooms: **2**	Children: **Welcome**
Maximum No. Sharing Bath: **4**	Smoking: **No**
Double/sb: **$40**	Social Drinking: **No**

This 750-acre farm where Joy and Glenn raise oats, corn, and Holstein dairy cows, is located in the Lake Region where recreational activities abound. You are certain to be comfortable in their farmhouse, built in 1970 and furnished in a simple, informal style. You will awaken to the delicious aroma of Joy's heavenly cinnamon rolls or bread and enjoy breakfast served on the enclosed porch. Nearby attractions include Fort Sisseton and the June festival that recounts Sam Brown's historic ride. You will also enjoy the Blue Dog fish hatchery, and the Game

Reserve. Dakotah, Inc., manufacturers of linens and wall hangings, is located in Webster. They have an outlet shop where great buys may be found.

Rockinghorse Bed & Breakfast ✪
RR 1, BOX 133, WHITEWOOD, SOUTH DAKOTA 57793

Tel: (605) 269-2625
Hosts: Jerry and Sharleen Bergum
Location: 35 mi. N of Rapid City
No. of Rooms: 3
No. of Private Baths: 1
Max. No. Sharing Bath: 4
Double/pb: $45
Single/pb: $40

Double/sb: $35
Single/sb: $30
Open: All year
Reduced Rates: 10% seniors, families
Breakfast: Full
Pets: Sometimes
Children: Welcome
Smoking: No

A cedar clapboard–sided house, built in 1914 to accommodate local timber teams, Rockinghorse was moved one and a half miles from its first site by Jerry and Sharleen, who have lovingly restored much of the interior. Handsome wood floors, columns, and trims grace the living and dining areas, and the original stairway is still usable. This B&B is situated at the base of the rustic Black Hills; deer graze in nearby fields and wild turkeys strut across the valley below the house. Domestic animals abound, too: after a rooster's crow awakens you, you may pet a bunny in your hosts' petting zoo or visit their horses.

TENNESSEE

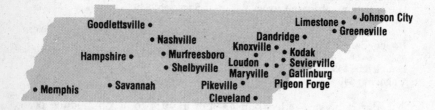

Bed & Breakfast—About Tennessee
P.O. BOX 110227, NASHVILLE, TENNESSEE 37222-0227

Tel: (615) 331-5244 for information;
  fax: (615) 833-7701; (800) 458-2421
  for reservations
Coordinator: **Fredda Odom**
States/Regions Covered: **Statewide**

Rates (Single/Double):
  Average: **$40–$50 / $65**
  Luxury: **$80–$100 / $80–$150**
Credit Cards: **AMEX, DISC, MC, VISA**
Descriptive Directory: **$5**

From the Great Smoky Mountains to the Mississippi, here is a diversity of attractions that includes fabulous scenery, Tennessee's Grand Ole Opry and Opryland, universities, Civil War sites, horse farms, and much more. Fredda will arrange sightseeing tours, car rentals, tickets to events, and everything she can to assure you a pleasant stay. There is a $5 booking fee.

Chadwick House ✪
2766 MICHIGAN AVENUE RD NORTH EAST, CLEVELAND, TENNESSEE 37312

Tel: (615) 339-2407
Host: **Winnie A. Chadwick**
Location: **35 mi. N of Chattanooga**
No. of Rooms: **3**
No. of Private Baths: **1**
Max. No. Sharing Bath: **4**
Double/pb: **$47**
Double/sb: **$38**

Single/sb: **$30**
Open: **All year**
Reduced Rates: **10% seniors**
Breakfast: **Full**
Other Meals: **Available**
Credit Cards: **MC, VISA**
Pets: **No**
Children: **Welcome**

Smoking: **Permitted**
Social Drinking: **Permitted**

Airport/Station Pickup: **Yes**

White shutters and trim accent the multicolored bricks of this handsome ranch home just a half hour from Chattanooga. White water rafting, Red Clay's historic Indian meeting grounds, and Cherokee National Forest are close by, and golfing and tennis are available right in Cleveland. In their spare moments B&B guests can watch the squirrels and birds in the back garden or relax by the fireplace with a glass of locally made wine. Winnie's full country breakfasts include homemade rolls and muffins.

Sugarfork Bed & Breakfast
743 GARRETT ROAD, DANDRIDGE, TENNESSEE 37725

Tel: **(615) 397-7327; (800) 487-5634**
Hosts: **Mary and Sam Price**
Location: **30 mi. E of Knoxville**
No. of Rooms: **3**
No. of Private Baths: **1**
Max. No. Sharing Bath: **4**
Double/pb: **$65**
Single/pb: **$55**
Double/sb: **$55**

Single/sb: **$45**
Open: **All year**
Reduced Rates: **Available**
Breakfast: **Full**
Credit Cards: **MC, VISA**
Pets: **No**
Children: **Welcome, over 6**
Smoking: **Permitted**
Social Drinking: **Permitted**

Guests will appreciate the tranquil setting of Sugarfork Bed & Breakfast, located on Douglas Lake in the foothills of the Great Smoky Mountains. Your hosts have private lake access and their own floating dock. Swimming, waterskiing, and boating are the main warm-weather activities here, while fishing is a year-round sport. On chilly mornings sit by the stone fireplace in the downstairs common room, or study the lake and mountains from the wall of windows upstairs. A hearty breakfast featuring homemade biscuits, country ham, and Mary's own special egg casseroles is served in the spacious dining room or, weather permitting, on the deck.

Eight Gables Inn ✪
219 NORTH MOUNTAIN TRAIL, GATLINBURG, TENNESSEE 37738

Tel: **(615) 430-3344**
Best Time to Call: **11 AM–2 PM**
Host: **Helen Smith**
Location: **30 mi. NE of Knoxville**
No. of Rooms: **10**
No. of Private Baths: **10**
Double/pb: **$89**
Suites: **$110**
Open: **All year**

Breakfast: **Full**
Other Meals: **Available**
Credit Cards: **AMEX, DISC, MC, VISA**
Pets: **No**
Children: **Welcome, over 12**
Smoking: **No**
Social Drinking: **Permitted**
Minimum Stay: **2 nights**

This B&B is nestled in the shadows of Great Smoky Mountains, with its scores of trails for hikers, motor tourists, and horseback riders. Beyond the woods, you'll find craft shops and outlets galore. Back at Eight Gables Inn, you can socialize in the first floor's Gathering Place, watch TV in Shelboby's Lounge, or retire to your own room for peace and quiet. A full breakfast buffet is set out in the Temptations Room, while early risers can get their morning meal at 7 AM. If you're around between 3 and 5 PM, it's time to join your host and fellow guests for tea.

Woodshire B&B ✪
600 WOODSHIRE DRIVE, GOODLETTSVILLE, TENNESSEE 37072

Tel: (615) 859-7369	Guest Cabin: $60–$70
Best Time to Call: Before 9 AM; after 9 PM	Open: All year
	Breakfast: Continental
Hosts: Beverly and John Grayson	Pets: No
Location: 11 mi. N of Nashville	Children: Welcome
No. of Rooms: 2	Smoking: No
No. of Private Baths: 2	Social Drinking: No
Double/pb: $50	Airport/Station Pickup: Yes
Single/pb: $40	

A blue clapboard house inspired by New England saltboxes, Woodshire B&B is 20 minutes from downtown Nashville and its attractions—Opryland Park, Andrew Jackson's Hermitage, and the homes and museums of country music stars. Beverly will gladly tell you the stories behind the antique family furniture. She's a retired art teacher, and as you look around you'll see her paintings and weavings, and John's woodcrafts. Continental breakfast features homemade preserves. In the afternoon, the Graysons like to serve tea in their Japanese garden.

Big Spring Inn ✪
315 NORTH MAIN STREET, GREENEVILLE, TENNESSEE 37743

Tel: (615) 638-2917	Open: All year
Hosts: Jeanne Driese and Cheryl Van Dyck	Reduced Rates: Available
	Breakfast: Full
Location: 70 mi. NE of Knoxville	Other Meals: Available
No. of Rooms: 6	Credit Cards: AMEX, MC, VISA
No. of Private Baths: 5	Pets: Sometimes
Max. No. Sharing Bath: 2	Children: Welcome, over 12
Double/pb: $78	Smoking: Permitted
Single/pb: $70	Social Drinking: Permitted
Double/sb: $60	Airport/Station Pickup: Yes
Single/sb: $52	

Big Spring Inn is a three-story manor house located in Greeneville's historic district, an area that includes President Andrew Johnson's home and tailor shop. The inn has a grand entrance hall, leaded and stained-glass windows, and many fireplaces. The rooms are spacious, with high ceilings, and are decorated with a comfortable mix of antiques and reproductions. The bedrooms have special touches, such as fresh flowers, snacks, baskets of toiletries, and even terry cloth robes. Jeanne and Cheryl serve homemade breads and pastries, with a variety of egg dishes for breakfast; gourmet dinners are also available. Big Spring is within an hour of Great Smoky Mountains National Park and the Blue Ridge Parkway.

Hilltop House Bed and Breakfast Inn ✪
ROUTE 7, BOX 180, GREENEVILLE, TENNESSEE 37743

Tel: **(615) 639-8202**
Best Time to Call: **8 AM–7 PM**
Host: **Denise M. Ashworth**
Location: **7 mi. S of Greeneville**
No. of Rooms: **3**
No. of Private Baths: **3**
Double/pb: **$70**
Single/pb: **$65**
Open: **All year**
Reduced Rates: **Available**

Breakfast: **Full**
Other Meals: **Available**
Credit Cards: **AMEX, MC, VISA**
Pets: **No**
Children: **Welcome, over 3 years**
Smoking: **No**
Social Drinking: **Permitted**
Minimum Stay: **Weekends, 2 nights**
Airport/Station Pickup: **Yes**

Hilltop House is a 1920s Victorian manor on a hillside above the Nolichucky River Valley, with the Appalachian Mountains in the background. All the guest rooms, which are furnished in eighteenth-century English antiques and period reproductions, have mountain views; two have verandas. In keeping with her British birth, the innkeeper sets out a proper English tea every afternoon. The family-style breakfast consists of fruit, cereal, egg dishes, and homemade biscuits or muffins. Then it's time to explore the great outdoors: white-water rafting, hiking, biking, trout fishing, golfing, hunting, and bird-watching are among your options. Cherokee National Forest is within striking distance, as are the Great Smoky Mountains and the Blue Ridge Parkway.

Natchez Trace B&B Reservation Service ✪
P.O. BOX 193, HAMPSHIRE, TENNESSEE 38461

Tel: **(800) 377-2770**
Best Time to Call: **Evening; weekends**
Coordinator: **Kay Jones**
States/Regions Covered:
  Mississippi—Corinth, Kosciusko,
  Lorman, Natchez, Vicksburg;
  Tennessee—Hampshire
Descriptive Directory of B&Bs: **Free**

Rates (Single/Double):
  Modest: **$40 / $45**
  Average: **$60 / $75**
  Luxury: **$75 / $100**
Credit Cards: **MC, VISA**

Kay's reservation service is unique in that the homes are all convenient to the Natchez Trace National Parkway, the historic Nashville-to-Natchez route that was first designated by President Thomas Jefferson. The parkway is known for both its natural beauty and the charming southern towns along the way. Kay can help you plan your trip and give you access to homes ranging from rustic, woodsy sites to fine antebellum mansions. Call her for a free list of homes, as well as literature about the Natchez Trace.

Hart House Bed and Breakfast ✪
207 EAST HOLSTON AVENUE, JOHNSON CITY, TENNESSEE 37601

Tel: **(615) 926-3147**
Hosts: **Francis and Vanessa Gingras**
Location: **90 mi. NE of Knoxville**
No. of Rooms: **3**
No. of Private Baths: **3**
Double/pb: **$60**
Single/pb: **$50**
Open: **All year**

Reduced Rates: **10% seniors**
Breakfast: **Full**
Credit Cards: **MC, VISA**
Pets: **Sometimes**
Children: **Welcome**
Smoking: **No**
Social Drinking: **Permitted**

Hart House is named after the original owner of this 1910 Dutch Colonial, which Francis and Vanessa have filled with antiques and collectibles. Johnson City is located in the heart of upper northeast

Tennessee, an area brimming with both notable sites and scenic beauty. For history buffs, Jonesborough, the oldest town in the state, is five miles away, and those who love the great outdoors—camping, hiking, fishing, white-water rafting—will find plenty to do here. Each morning, guests wake up to an elegant breakfast of fresh fruit, homemade muffins, eggs, and fresh brewed coffee.

Windy Hill B&B ✪
1031 WEST PARK DRIVE, KNOXVILLE, TENNESSEE 37909

Tel: **(615) 690-1488**
Host: **Mary M. Mitchell**
Location: **1.6 mi. from I-75-40,**
  Exit 380
No. of Rooms: **1**
No. of Private Baths: **1**
Double/pb: **$40**
Single/pb: **$35**

Open: **All year**
Breakfast: **Continental**
Pets: **Sometimes**
Children: **Welcome**
Smoking: **Permitted**
Social Drinking: **Permitted**
Airport/Station Pickup: **Yes**

Located in a pleasant, quiet neighborhood with numerous shade trees, Mary's B&B is air-conditioned and has a private entrance with no steps to climb. There's a double bed and a rollaway is available. Breakfast features homemade muffins or cinnamon rolls with coffee. Windy Hill is convenient to the University of Tennessee; Oakridge is only a 15-minute drive while Great Smoky Mountains National Park is an hour away.

Grandma's House ✪
734 POLLARD ROAD, KODAK, TENNESSEE 37764

Tel: (615) 933-3512; reservations: (800) 676-3512
Best Time to Call: 8 AM–5 PM
Hosts: Charlie and Hilda Hickman
Location: 8 mi. N of Sevierville; 2 mi. from I-40, Exit 407
No. of Rooms: 3
No. of Private Baths: 3
Double/pb: $65
Suites: $75

Open: All year
Breakfast: Full
Credit Cards: MC, VISA
Pets: No
Children: Sometimes
Smoking: No
Social Drinking: No
Airport/Station Pickup: Yes

Grandma's House is located on a quiet country lane in Dumplin Valley at the base of the Great Smoky Mountains. Nearby attractions include: Great Smoky Mountains National Park, Dollywood in Pigeon Forge, Museum of Science and Energy in Oak Ridge, and much more. The farm-style house is furnished with country antiques, handmade quilts, and interesting family heirlooms. The hearty farm breakfast features buttermilk biscuits, Hilda's own homemade jams and jellies, and the house specialty, Apple Stack Cake. Both hosts are native East Tennesseans with lots of down-home friendliness to share with their guests.

Snapp Inn B&B
1990 DAVY CROCKETT ROAD, LIMESTONE, TENNESSEE 37681

Tel: (615) 257-2482; (800) 524-0595
Best Time to Call: Before 10 AM; after 7 PM
Hosts: Dan and Ruth Dorgan
Location: 4 mi. from Rte. 11 E
No. of Rooms: 2
No. of Private Baths: 2
Double/pb: $50

Single/sb: $40
Open: All year
Breakfast: Full
Pets: Welcome
Children: Welcome (one at a time)
Smoking: No
Social Drinking: Permitted
Airport/Station Pickup: Yes

Built in 1815 and situated in farm country, this Federal brick home has lovely mountain views. The house is decorated with antiques, including a Victorian reed organ. Now retired, Ruth and Dan have the time to pursue their interests in antiques restoration, history, needlework, and bluegrass music. It is an easy walk to Davy Crockett Birthplace State Park, and 15 minutes to historic Jonesboro or the Andrew Johnson Home in Greeneville. A swimming pool, golf, and fishing are close by. You are welcome to use the laundry facilities, television, and pool table.

Sports Haven Bed & Breakfast ✪
845 BINFIELD ROAD, MARYVILLE, TENNESSEE 37801

Tel: **(615) 982-8382**
Best Time to Call: **Morning or evening**
Host: **Flo Shirley**
Location: **6 mi. W of Maryville**
No. of Rooms: **3**
No. of Private Baths: **3**
Double/pb: **$65**
Single/pb: **$60**
Suites: **$75**

Open: **All year**
Reduced Rates: **15% weekly**
Breakfast: **Continental**
Credit Cards: **MC, VISA**
Pets: **Sometimes**
Children: **Welcome, over 6**
Smoking: **No**
Social Drinking: **Permitted**
Airport Pickup: **Yes**

A contemporary home with lots of woods and glass, this bed and breakfast is justly named: your host has her own racquetball court, fitness room, and game room, not to mention a small private lake stocked with bass, bluegill, brim, and catfish. If you wish to venture farther afield, it's fifteen miles to Knoxville and thirty miles to Gatlinburg, home of the Smokies. Flo, whose interests include racquetball, skiing, biking, and hiking, can suggest likely destinations.

Lowenstein-Long House ✪
217 NORTH WALDRAN, MEMPHIS, TENNESSEE 38105

Tel: **(901) 527-7174**
Host: **Samantha Long**
No. of Rooms: **4**
No. of Private Baths: **4**
Double/pb: **$60–$65**
Open: **All year**

Breakfast: **Full**
Pets: **Sometimes**
Children: **Welcome**
Smoking: **Permitted**
Social Drinking: **Permitted**

Listed on the National Register of Historic Places, Lowenstein-Long House has been fully restored to its original grandeur. It is located half a mile from a Victorian village, and close to Mud Island, the DeSoto Bridge, and Beale Street. Elvis fans will note that the route to Graceland is nearby.

Clardy's Guest House ✪
435 EAST MAIN STREET, MURFREESBORO, TENNESSEE 37130

Tel: **(615) 893-6030**	Double/sb: **$30**
Best Time to Call: **After 4 PM**	Single/sb: **$25**
Hosts: **Robert and Barbara Deaton**	Open: **All year**
Location: **2 mi. from I-24**	Breakfast: **Continental**
No. of Rooms: **4**	Pets: **Sometimes**
No. of Private Baths: **2**	Children: **Welcome (crib)**
Max. No. Sharing Bath: **4**	Smoking: **Permitted**
Double/pb: **$40**	Social Drinking: **Permitted**
Single/pb: **$32**	

This Romanesque-style Victorian dates back to 1898. The 20 rooms are filled with antiques; with 40 antiques dealers in town, you can guess what Murfreesboro is best known for. The world championship horse show at Shelbyville is 30 minutes away. Your hosts will be glad to advise on local tours and can direct you to the home of Grand Ole Opry, one hour away in Nashville, and fine eating places. Middle Tennessee State University is close by.

Quilts and Croissants
2231 RILEY ROAD, MURFREESBORO, TENNESSEE 37130

Tel: **(615) 893-2933**	Open: **All year**
Hosts: **Robert and Mary Jane Roose**	Reduced Rates: **Seniors**
Location: **28 mi. S of Nashville**	Breakfast: **Continental**
No. of Rooms: **1**	Pets: **No**
No. of Private Baths: **1**	Smoking: **No**
Double/pb: **$35**	Social Drinking: **Permitted**
Single/pb: **$30**	

This unusual home, constructed out of logs hewn in 1834, combines old-fashioned country charm and modern efficiency. Stencils and folk art ornament the walls of the guest room, and patchwork quilts drape the twin beds. Don't be fooled by the kitchenette's quaint icebox appearance—it's really a refrigerator stocked with juice, breakfast foods, and soda. Quilts and Croissants is less than an hour's drive from Nashville, but your hosts can steer you to the notable sights of Murfreesboro, such as Oaklands Mansion (a mid-19th-century landmark) and Canonsburgh (a restored Civil War–era village). Breakfast here is a do-it-yourself affair; take whatever you want from the refrigerator.

Day Dreams Country Inn ✪
2720 COLONIAL DRIVE, PIGEON FORGE, TENNESSEE 37863

Tel: **(615) 428-0370**
Best Time to Call: **Mornings; evenings**
Hosts: **Yvonne and Mark Trombley**
Location: **35 mi. S of Knoxville**
No. of Rooms: **6**
No. of Private Baths: **6**
Double/pb: **$89–$120**
Single/pb: **$69–$100**
Open: **All year**

Reduced Rates: **10% after 3rd night;
10% Jan.–Feb.**
Breakfast: **Full**
Credit Cards: **MC, VISA**
Pets: **No**
Children: **Welcome**
Smoking: **No**
Social Drinking: **Permitted**
Minimum Stay: **2 nights Oct.**

Relax in the warm country atmosphere of this B&B, protected from the hustle and bustle of Pigeon Forge's many tourist attractions and outlet malls. Day Dreams Country Inn is nestled among willow, hemlock, and redbud trees; a stream runs on two sides of the property. If you are a hiker, a horseback rider, or just a nature lover, you'll appreciate the fact that the Great Smoky Mountains are only seven miles away. An old-fashioned country breakfast is served daily at 9:00 AM, and your hosts promise you won't leave the table hungry.

Fall Creek Falls Bed & Breakfast ✪
ROUTE 3, P.O. BOX 309, PIKEVILLE, TENNESSEE 37367

Tel: **(615) 881-5494**
Hosts: **Doug and Rita Pruett**
Location: **50 mi. N of Chattanooga**
No. of Rooms: **3**
No. of Private Baths: **1**
Max. No. Sharing Bath: **4**
Double/pb: **$60**
Single/pb: **$55**
Double/sb: **$50**

Open: **All year**
Reduced Rates: **$10 less per night,
Dec. 1–Mar. 1**
Breakfast: **Full**
Pets: **No**
Children: **Welcome, over 11**
Smoking: **No**
Social Drinking: **No**
Minimum Stay: **2 nights, weekends**

Enjoy the country atmosphere of an English manor on forty acres of rolling hillside one mile from the nationally acclaimed Fall Creek Falls State Resort Park in Pikeville. Beautiful upstairs accommodations have pickled oak floors and antique furniture with a common sitting area. Lodging includes a full breakfast served in a cozy country kitchen, an elegant dining room, or a sunny Florida room with a magnificent view of Tennessee farmland. Doug, a retired building contractor, enjoys grouse hunting and trout fishing. Rita, a semiretired insurance executive, likes antique auctions and bargain hunting. Touring, dining, and shopping information is always available.

Ross House Bed and Breakfast ✪

504 MAIN STREET, P.O. BOX 398, SAVANNAH, TENNESSEE 38372

Tel: **(901) 925-3974**
Best Time to Call: **9 AM–5 PM**
Hosts: **John and Harriet Ross**
Location: **110 mi. E of Memphis**
No. of Rooms: **4**
No. of Private Baths: **1**
Max. No. Sharing Bath: **4**
Double/pb: **$75**
Single/pb: **$55**
Double/sb: **$55**

Single/sb: **$45**
Suites: **$100**
Open: **All year**
Breakfast: **Continental**
Credit Cards: **MC, VISA**
Pets: **No**
Children: **Welcome, over 10**
Smoking: **No**
Social Drinking: **Permitted**
Foreign Languages: **French, Spanish**

Part of Savannah's National Register Historic District, which contains residences from the late 1860s to the 1920s, this B&B is a Neoclassical brick house built in 1908 by John's grandparents. Inside you'll see the original owners' furniture, books, paintings, and photographs. An earlier Ross home serves as the city's Chamber of Commerce. It is a short walk to the Cherry Mansion and Tennessee River and a short drive to Shiloh National Military Park and Pickwick Lake, for fishing and boating. If you'd rather paddle your canoe, take the 45-minute drive to the Buffalo River. John practices law next door where his grandfather once did, but when time permits, he accompanies guests on bicycle tours. Harriet is a full-time hostess.

Blue Mountain Mist Country Inn ✪

1811 PULLEN ROAD, SEVIERVILLE, TENNESSEE 37862

Tel: **(800) 497-2335**
Best Time to Call: **10 AM–4 PM**
Hosts: **Norman and Sarah Ball**
Location: **4 mi. E of Pigeon Forge**
No. of Rooms: **12**
No. of Private Baths: **12**
Double/pb: **$79**
Guest Cottage: **$125**
Suites: **$95–$115**

Open: **All year**
Breakfast: **Full**
Pets: **No**
Children: **Welcome (2 rooms)**
Smoking: **No**
Social Drinking: **Permitted**
Minimum Stay: **2–3 nights holiday
    weekends and Oct.**

This Victorian-style inn is remote from congestion and noise, yet has easy access to Pigeon Forge, Dollywood, factory outlets, and the crafts community. A view of rolling meadows framed by the Great Smoky Mountains can be enjoyed from rocking chairs on the huge front porch or from the backyard hot tub and patio. Country antiques, claw-foot tubs, handmade quilts and accessories, all make for a homey atmosphere. Two suites have in-room Jacuzzis. The large, fireplaced living room is the gathering spot on cool evenings. The Southern breakfast often features fresh fruit, sausages and eggs, grits and gravy, and homemade biscuits.

Milk & Honey Country Hideaway ✪
2803 OLD COUNTRY WAY, SEVIERVILLE, TENNESSEE 37862

Tel: **(615) 428-4858**
Best Time to Call: **8 AM–noon**
Hosts: **Fern Miller, and Ray and Linda Barnhart**
Location: **5 mi. W of Pigeon Forge**
No. of Rooms: **6**
No. of Private Baths: **2**
Max. No. Sharing Bath: **4**
Double/pb: **$70–$110**
Single/pb: **$60–$100**
Double/sb: **$54–$70**

Single/sb: **$44–$60**
Open: **All year**
Reduced Rates: **After 3rd night**
Breakfast: **Full**
Credit Cards: **MC, VISA**
Pets: **No**
Children: **Welcome, over 14**
Smoking: **No**
Social Drinking: **No**
Minimum Stay: **2 nights Oct., holiday weekends**

Rustic charm awaits you at this peaceful mountain retreat with its large wraparound front porch. Guest rooms are furnished with antiques and quilts in a decor that combines Victorian, Amish, and country styles. Often the aroma of sumptuous home-baked goodies will draw you into the parlor. Ray is responsible for much of the woodwork in the house, and Linda and Fern are accomplished cooks. To test their talents, sample the full breakfasts, which consist of seasonal fruit, biscuits and gravy, fried apples, and surprise oven omelets. If you care to venture out into civilization, Pigeon Forge, Gatlinburg, and Dollywood are nearby.

Seaton Springs Inn ✪
2345 SEATON SPRINGS ROAD, SEVIERVILLE, TENNESSEE 37862

Tel: **(615) 453-1583**
Hosts: **Bob and Barbara Kacin**
Location: **6 mi. SW of Pigeon Forge**
No. of Rooms: **3**
No. of Private Baths: **1**
Max. No. Sharing Bath: **4**
Double/pb: **$65–$85**
Double/sb: **$55–$75**
Open: **All year**

Reduced Rates: **10% after 3rd night**
Breakfast: **Full**
Other Meals: **Available**
Credit Cards: **MC, VISA**
Pets: **No**
Children: **Welcome**
Smoking: **No**
Social Drinking: **Permitted**
Airport/Station Pickup: **Yes**

Rich in history, this restored 1880 farmhouse lies in the valley surrounded by Tennessee's renowned Smoky Mountains. Step into the past as you explore eleven acres of streams and trails, and a cantilevered barn and corncrib. The tiger-oak floors, 10-foot ceilings, and queen-size beds are enhanced by the fireplaces in each room. Bob and Barbara, drawing on thirteen years of restaurant experience, try to make every meal memorable. Breakfasts include cream cheese crêpes with fruit, fresh cinnamon rolls, and omelets made to order. When the weather's right, homemade ice cream is served on the front porch. Adjacent attractions are Great Smoky Mountains National Park, Dollywood, and Pigeon Forge.

County Line Bed and Breakfast
ROUTE 6, BOX 126, SHELBYVILLE, TENNESSEE 37160

Tel: **(615) 759-4639**
Best Time to Call: **7 AM–9 PM**
Hosts: **Harriet and Jim Rothfeldt**
No. of Rooms: **3**
No. of Private Baths: **2**
Max. No. Sharing Bath: **5**
Double/pb: **$38**
Single/pb: **$32**
Double/sb: **$38**

Single/sb: **$32**
Open: **All year**
Breakfast: **Continental**
Credit Cards: **MC, VISA**
Pets: **No**
Children: **Welcome, over 5**
Smoking: **Permitted**
Social Drinking: **Permitted**

Enjoy the relaxed atmosphere of a 230-acre horse farm just four miles from the Jack Daniel's Distillery and Lynchburg Square. Three spacious bedrooms, all on the second floor, have country furnishings, air conditioners, and ceiling fans. If you're trailering a horse, ask your hosts about stall space. Continental breakfast, featuring home-baked muffins, is served by the dining area fireplace. Weather permitting, you can take your meal onto the back porch and watch the horses canter around the pasture.

TEXAS

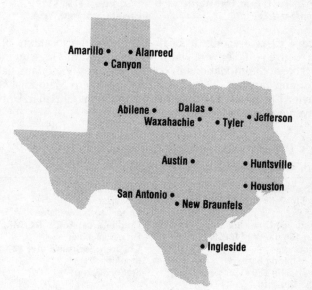

Amarillo •   • Alanreed
• Canyon

Abilene •   Dallas •
Waxahachie •   • Tyler   • Jefferson

Austin •   • Huntsville

• Houston

San Antonio •
• New Braunfels

• Ingleside

The Bed & Breakfast Society of Texas ✪
1200 SOUTHMORE AVENUE, HOUSTON, TEXAS 77004

Tel: **(713) 523-1114**	Rates (Single/Double):
Best Time to Call: **9 AM–5 PM**	Modest: **$40 / $45**
Coordinator: **Pat Thomas**	Average: **$45 / $60**
States/Regions Covered: **Statewide**	Luxury: **$65 / $85**

Whether you're traveling for business or pleasure, Pat's hosts offer the kind of friendliness and individualized care that will make your stay pleasant. The area is known for the Astrodome, Galveston Bay, NASA, and the Texas Medical Center. There are wonderful restaurants, shops, museums, and historic sights, and Baylor, Rice, and the University of Houston are nearby. Many are conveniently located urban homes, serene country houses, historic inns, waterfront cottages, and one is a 42-foot yacht.

Bed & Breakfast Texas Style ✪
4224 WEST RED BIRD LANE, DALLAS, TEXAS 75237

Tel: **(214) 298-8586**	Descriptive Directory: **$5**
Best Time to Call: **9 AM–5 PM**	Rates (Single/Double):
Coordinator: **Ruth Wilson**	Modest: **$40 / $45**
States/Regions Covered: **Arlington,**	Average: **$45 / $60**
Austin, Dallas, El Paso, Fort Worth,	Luxury: **$75 / $125**
Houston, Santa Fe	Credit Cards: **MC, VISA**

The above cities are only a small sample of the locations of hosts waiting to give you plenty of warm hospitality. Ruth's register includes comfortable accommodations in condos, restored Victorians, lakeside cottages, and ranches. Texas University, Southern Methodist University, Baylor University, Rice University, and Texas Christian University are convenient to many B&Bs.

Bolin's Prairie House Bed & Breakfast ✪
508 MULBERRY, ABILENE, TEXAS 79601

Tel: **(915) 675-5855**	Open: **All year**
Best Time to Call: **8AM–8 PM**	Breakfast: **Full**
Mon.–Sat.	Other Meals: **Available**
Hosts: **Sam and Ginny Bolin**	Credit Cards: **AMEX, DC, MC, VISA**
Location: **180 mi. W of Dallas**	Pets: **Sometimes**
No. of Rooms: **4**	Children: **Welcome, over 12**
Max. No. Sharing Bath: **4**	Smoking: **No**
Double/sb: **$40–$50**	Station Pickup: **Yes**
Single/sb: **$30–$40**	

Tucked into the heart of this famous frontier town is Bolin's Prairie House, a 1902 house furnished with antiques and modern luxuries. The warm, homey atmosphere puts guests at their ease. Relax in the living room with its wood-burning stove, or settle in the den for a little TV. Each of the four bedrooms—named Love, Joy, Peace, and Patience—has its own special charm. Breakfast features Ginny's delicious baked egg dishes, fresh fruit, and homemade bread, all lovingly served in the dining room, where fine china and cobalt Depression glass are displayed.

Whitefish Creek Ranch B&B ✪
BOX 123, ALANREED, TEXAS 79002

Tel: **(806) 779-3205**	No. of Private Baths: **3**
Best Time to Call: **10 AM–noon; 3–6**	Max. No. Sharing Bath: **4**
PM	Double/pb: **$40**
Hosts: **Kittie and Ray Harris**	Single/pb: **$30**
Location: **70 mi. E of Amarillo**	Double/sb: **$40**
No. of Rooms: **5**	Single/sb: **$25**

Open: **All year**	Children: **No**
Breakfast: **Full**	Smoking: **Permitted, 1st floor**
Other Meals: **Available**	Social Drinking: **Permitted**
Pets: **Sometimes**	

The two-story house on this working ranch is set among black walnut and cottonwood trees on Whitefish Creek. Massive cedar beams and redwood ceilings give the downstairs a rustic country air. Upstairs, comfort is the rule in the five antique-furnished bedrooms. After a hearty breakfast, including many homebaked treats, hike over the ranch, watch for wild turkey and a host of other animals, or read and relax on the porch. If you are interested, Ray will fill you in on some of the more colorful tidbits of Panhandle history.

Parkview House
1311 SOUTH JEFFERSON, AMARILLO, TEXAS 79101

Tel: **(806) 373-9464**	Suite: **$75**
Best Time to Call: **Before 10 AM; after 5 PM**	Open: **All year**
Hosts: **Nabil and Carol Dia**	Breakfast: **Continental**
Location: **½ mi. from I-40**	Credit Cards: **MC, VISA**
No. of Rooms: **5**	Pets: **No**
No. of Private Baths: **1**	Children: **No**
Max. No. Sharing Bath: **4**	Smoking: **No**
Double/pb: **$60**	Social Drinking: **Permitted**
Double/sb: **$50**	Foreign Languages: **Arabic**
	Airport/Station Pickup: **Yes**

Carol is a full-time host; Nabil a civil engineer. Both share interests in restoration and antiques, which is evident in their charming Prairie Victorian located in the historic district. The guest rooms are furnished with selected antiques, lace, and luxurious linens. The large columned porch is a fine place to start the day with breakfast or to relax. Carol will lend you a bike and be glad to prepare a picnic basket to take to nearby Palo Duro Canyon State Park or Lake Meredith. West Texas State University is nearby. They enjoy having guests join them for a "social hour" before dinner.

Carrington's Bluff B&B ✪
1900 DAVID STREET, AUSTIN, TEXAS 78705

Tel: **(512) 479-0638**	Double/sb: **$55–$60**
Best Time to Call: **8 AM–9 PM**	Single/sb: **$45–$55**
Hosts: **Gwen and David Fullbrook**	Suites: **$75–$105**
No. of Rooms: **5**	Open: **All year**
No. of Private Baths: **3**	Reduced Rates: **Midweek business rate $10 less**
Max. No. Sharing Bath: **4**	Breakfast: **Full**
Double/pb: **$65–$75**	Credit Cards: **AMEX, DC, MC, VISA**
Single/pb: **$60–$70**	

Pets: **No**
Children: **Welcome, over 10**

Smoking: **No**
Social Drinking: **Permitted**

After operating other B&Bs in Vermont and Texas, Gwen and David are experienced innkeepers who know how to pamper their guests. Their 1877 farmhouse has an enviable downtown Austin location seven blocks from the University of Texas and nine blocks from the State Capitol. Still, you'll feel like you're in the country, since the 35-foot front porch faces a tree-covered bluff. The interior is decorated in an English country style, with English and American antiques. Full breakfasts feature homemade muffins or breads, egg dishes, and homemade granola.

The McCallum House ✪

613 WEST 32ND, AUSTIN, TEXAS 78705

Tel: **(512) 451-6744**
Hosts: **Roger and Nancy Danley**
Location: **2 mi. from I-35**
No. of Rooms: **5**
No. of Private Baths: **5**
Double/pb: **$75**
Single/pb: **$65**
Suites: **$90**
Open: **All year**

Reduced Rates: **$10 off, 4 nights or more**
Breakfast: **Full**
Credit Cards: **MC, VISA (reservations only)**
Pets: **No**
Children: **Welcome, over 8**
Smoking: **No**
Social Drinking: **Permitted**

This late Victorian home is just 10 blocks north of the University of Texas and 20 blocks from the capitol and downtown. Air-conditioned and furnished with antiques, the house has one guest room with a large screened-in porch with wicker furniture; all have kitchen facilities ideal for longer stays. Roger and Nancy will be happy to share the interesting history of their house, built by a former Texas secretary of state and her husband. Fruit cups, quiches, and muffins are breakfast delights.

Peaceful Hill Bed & Breakfast ✪
10817 RANCH ROAD 2222, AUSTIN, TEXAS 78730-1102

Tel: **(512) 338-1817**	Open: **All year**
Best Time to Call: **Anytime**	Reduced Rates: **$10 weekly**
Host: **Peninnah Thurmond**	Breakfast: **Full**
Location: **15 min. W of Austin**	Credit Cards: **MC, VISA**
No. of Rooms: **2**	Children: **Welcome**
No. of Private Baths: **2**	Smoking: **Permitted**
Double/pb: **$60**	Social Drinking: **Permitted**
Single/pb: **$60**	

Deer watch you come to a small country inn located on ranchland high in the beautiful rolling hills fifteen minutes from Austin and ten minutes from Lake Travis and the Oasis. In springtime, settle on the porch with a cup of coffee and admire the countryside and the city below. Laze away the summer in a hammock built for two, or hike and bicycle; golf, swimming, and tennis are only two miles away. In the winter, warm up by a crackling fire in the grand stone fireplace in the living room, where a glass wall looks over both the country and the city. All this and a home-cooked breakfast. Peaceful is the name and peaceful is the game. Deer watch you go.

The Wild Flower Inn ✪
1200 WEST 22½ STREET, AUSTIN, TEXAS 78705

Tel: **(512) 477-9639**	Double/sb: **$59**
Best Time to Call: **Anytime**	Single/sb: **$50**
Hosts: **Kay Jackson and Claudean Schultz**	Open: **All year**
	Reduced Rates: **10% seniors**
Location: **2 mi. from Rte. IH35, Exit MLK**	Breakfast: **Full**
	Credit Cards: **AMEX, MC, VISA**
No. of Rooms: **4**	Pets: **No**
No. of Private Baths: **2**	Smoking: **No**
Max. No. Sharing Bath: **4**	Social Drinking: **Permitted**
Double/pb: **$69**	Airport/Station Pickup: **Yes**
Single/pb: **$60**	

Nestled on a quiet, tree-lined street, this fifty-year-old central Austin home is within a few blocks of the University of Texas and within minutes of the State Capitol complex. Outdoor enthusiasts will love the hike and bike trails at Shoal Creek or tennis at Caswell Courts. Kay and Claudean pride themselves on their warm Texas hospitality and delight in serving you their hearty gourmet specialties each morning.

Hudspeth House ✪
1905 4TH AVENUE, CANYON, TEXAS 79015

Tel: **(806) 655-9800**
Hosts: **Sally and David Haynie**
Location: **14 mi. S of Amarillo**
No. of Rooms: **8**
No. of Private Baths: **4**
Max. No. Sharing Bath: **4**
Double/pb: **$50–$75**
Double/sb: **$45–$50**
Suites: **$90–$110**
Open: **All year**

Reduced Rates: **15% Jan. 1–Apr. 30; 20% weekly**
Breakfast: **Full**
Other Meals: **Available**
Credit Cards: **MC, VISA**
Pets: **No**
Children: **Welcome (crib)**
Smoking: **Restricted**
Social Drinking: **Permitted**
Airport/Station Pickup: **Yes**

Named for Mary E. Hudspeth, a leading Texas educator, this landmark home is rich in local history. Restored several times, the house was bought by Sally and Dave in 1987, and they have again refurbished it while retaining much of the original stained glass and chandeliers. In keeping with the elegant tone, breakfast features such delights as eggs Benedict. Sally, a former manager of the chic Zodiac Dining Room at Neiman-Marcus in Dallas, knows all about elegance with comfort. Within walking distance are Canyon Square, West Texas State University, and the Panhandle Plains Museum.

Durham House Bed & Breakfast ✪
921 HEIGHTS BOULEVARD, HOUSTON, TEXAS 77008

Tel: **(713) 868-4654**
Best Time to Call: **Anytime**
Host: **Marguerite Swanson**
No. of Rooms: **5**
No. of Private Baths: **4**
Max. No. Sharing Baths: **3**
Double/pb: **$65–$75**
Single/pb: **$50–$60**
Double/sb: **$50**
Single/sb: **$45**
Suites: **$85–$95; sleeps 4**

Open: **All year**
Reduced Rates: **10% seniors; 10% weekly**
Breakfast: **Full**
Credit Cards: **AMEX, MC, VISA**
Pets: **No**
Children: **Welcome, infants and over 12**
Smoking: **No**
Social Drinking: **Permitted**

A Queen Anne Victorian listed on the National Register of Historic Places, Durham House is conveniently located just five minutes from downtown Houston. Antique-filled rooms, a player piano, a screened porch, and a gazebo make this the perfect setting for both business travelers and weekend visitors in search of a romantic getaway. The amenities include a bicycle built for two. Memorable full breakfasts are served at the time and location requested. Marguerite, a former school counselor, now devotes all her time to her guests and her murder-mystery dinner parties.

The Lovett Inn ✪
501 LOVETT BOULEVARD, HOUSTON, TEXAS 77006

Tel: (713) 522-5224; fax: (713) 528-6708
Best Time to Call: 9 AM–5 PM
Host: Tom Fricke
Location: In Houston
No. of Rooms: 6
No. of Private Baths: 4
Max. No. Sharing Bath: 2
Double/pb: $55–$75
Single/pb: $55–$70
Double/sb: $45–$65

Single/sb: $45–$60
Suites: $50–$100
Open: All year
Reduced Rates: Weekly
Breakfast: Continental
Credit Cards: AMEX, MC, VISA
Pets: Sometimes
Children: No
Smoking: No
Social Drinking: Permitted

It's easy to be fooled by the Lovett Inn: although it looks far older, this stately Federalist-style mansion, attractively furnished with 19th-century reproductions, was actually built in 1924. Its convenient museum-district location puts visitors within easy striking distance of downtown Houston, the Galleria, and the Houston Medical Center. After spending the day in the city, guests are sure to appreciate a dip in the pool. Each room has a color TV.

Sara's Bed & Breakfast Inn ✪
941 HEIGHTS BOULEVARD, HOUSTON, TEXAS 77008

Tel: (713) 868-1130; (800) 593-1130
Best Time to Call: Anytime
Hosts: Donna and Tillman Arledge
Location: 6 blocks from I-10
No. of Rooms: 11
No. of Private Baths: 6
Max. No. Sharing Bath: 4
Double/pb: $60
Double/sb: $50–$57

Suites: $120 for 4
Open: All year
Breakfast: Continental
Credit Cards: AMEX, CB, DC, MC, VISA
Pets: No
Children: Welcome
Smoking: Restricted
Social Drinking: Permitted

This Queen Anne Victorian, with its turret and widow's walk, is located in Houston Heights, a neighborhood of historic homes, many of which are on the National Historic Register. Each bedroom is uniquely furnished, having either single, double, queen- or king-size beds. The Balcony Suite consists of two bedrooms, two baths, full kitchen, living area, and a fine view overlooking the deck and spa. Cool drinks or hot coffee are graciously offered in the afternoon. The sights and sounds of downtown Houston are four miles away.

Blue Bonnet Bed & Breakfast ✪
1215 AVENUE G #4, HUNTSVILLE, TEXAS 77340

Tel: (409) 295-2072	Suites: $48
Hosts: John and Bette Nelson	Open: All year
Location: 70 mi. N of Houston	Breakfast: Continental
No. of Rooms: 4	Pets: Sometimes
No. of Private Baths: 3	Children: Welcome
Max. No. Sharing Bath: 4	Smoking: No
Double/sb: $38	Social Drinking: Permitted
Single/sb: $35	

Seven tree-shaded acres frame this appealing blue Victorian-style house, with its white trim and wraparound porch. Try your luck fishing in the pond, sit on the porch, or play horseshoes and croquet on the lawn. The house is less than five minutes from Sam Houston State University and the adjacent Sam Houston Grave and Museum complex. Antique lovers will find plenty of shops in the neighborhood; Bette, who manages two antique malls, can give you some good suggestions. Continental breakfast may include apple fritters, poppy seed muffins, filled croissants, and fruit compote.

Sunset Retreat Bed & Breakfast ✪
ROUTE 1, BOX 282, 38 BAYSHORE DRIVE, INGLESIDE, TEXAS 78362

Tel: (512) 776-2534	Reduced Rates: 1 free night for a 7-night stay
Hosts: Betty and Jim Barnes	Breakfast: Continental, Full
Location: 15 mi. NE of Corpus Christi	Wheelchair-Accessible: Yes
No. of Rooms: 3	Pets: No
No. of Private Baths: 2	Children: Welcome, over 12
Max. No. Sharing Bath: 4	Smoking: Permitted
Double/sb: $60	Social Drinking: Permitted
Suites: $75	Airport/Station Pickup: Yes
Open: All year	

Located on the Texas Coast, with beautiful views of Ingleside Cove and Corpus Christi Bay, Sunset Retreat lives up to its name. The house commands 135 feet of waterfront; guests can fish from the Barneses' dock, watch porpoises, and swim to their hearts' content. Boats can be chartered for voyages to nearby islands. Enjoy a breakfast of fresh fruit, homemade breads, cinnamon rolls, and quiche in your room, on the patio, or in the sun room.

McKay House ✪
306 EAST DELTA, JEFFERSON, TEXAS 75657

Tel: (903) 665-7322	No. of Private Baths: 4
Hosts: Peggy and Tom Taylor	Double/pb: $70–$95
No. of Rooms: 4	Suites: $115–$145

Guest Cottage: **$80–$85**
Open: **All year**
Breakfast: **Full**
Credit Cards: **MC, VISA**

Pets: **No**
Children: **Welcome**
Smoking: **No**
Social Drinking: **Permitted**

The McKay House is listed on the National Register of Historic Places. It dates back to 1851 and is within walking distance of more than 200 homes and commercial buildings in the historic district. This Greek Revival house has 14-foot-high ceilings and nine-foot windows. Each room has been restored and features a fireplace and antique furnishings. Peggy wears a long period dress when she serves breakfast. Enjoy country ham and biscuits with the sun streaming through the lace curtains of the garden conservatory. After you've had a "gentleman's breakfast," you're ready to explore the delights of this riverboat town. Guests are provided with Victorian gowns and sleepshirts to better enjoy an old-fashioned night's sleep.

River Haus Bed & Breakfast ✪
817 EAST ZIPP ROAD, NEW BRAUNFELS, TEXAS 78130

Tel: **(512) 625-6411**
Hosts: **Dick and Arlene Buhl**
Location: **25 mi. NE of San Antonio**
No. of Rooms: **1**
No. of Private Baths: **1**
Double/pb: **$65**
Single/pb: **$60**
Open: **All year**

Reduced Rates: **10% Sun.–Thurs.**
Breakfast: **Full**
Pets: **Sometimes**
Children: **No**
Smoking: **No**
Social Drinking: **No**
Foreign Languages: **German**

Historic New Braunfels, a major tourist destination, offers museums, antique shopping, and unparalleled canoeing and river sports, all in the charming setting of the German Hill Country. River Haus is a delightful hill country–style home located on the Guadalupe River at Lake Dunlap. Watch the sun set over the lake from your spacious bedroom or sitting room. On the enclosed porch, with its deck overlooking the lake, you can sip a cool drink or enjoy the warmth of a wood stove fire. The complete gourmet breakfasts include local specialties and homemade bread and preserves.

The White House ✪
217 MITTMAN CIRCLE, NEW BRAUNFELS, TEXAS 78130

Tel: **(210) 629-9354**
Best Time to Call: **9 AM–9 PM**
Hosts: **Beverly and Jerry White**
Location: **25 mi. N of San Antonio**
No. of Rooms: **2**
Max. No. Sharing Bath: **4**
Double/sb: **$40–$45**
Single/sb: **$35–$40**

Open: **All year**
Breakfast: **Full**
Other Meals: **Available**
Pets: **Sometimes**
Children: **Welcome (crib)**
Smoking: **No**
Social Drinking: **Permitted**

This Spanish-style white-brick ranch home is nestled among cedar and oaks in Texas hill country. Guests are welcomed here with tea and pastries and shown to comfortable rooms with antique iron beds and oak dressers. A large fishing pond is located on the premises, and a few miles away you may enjoy a refreshing tube or raft ride down the Guadalupe River. Your hosts have giant inner tubes to lend. Other attractions include the Alamo, the Riverwalk, and the many old missions located in nearby San Antonio.

Bed & Breakfast Hosts of San Antonio ✪
166 ROCKHILL, SAN ANTONIO, TEXAS 78209

Tel: **(512) 824-8036; (800) 356-1605**
Best Time to Call: **9 AM–5 PM**
 weekdays; 9 AM–noon Sat.
Coordinator: **Lavern Campbell**
States/Regions Covered: **Bandera,**
 Boerne, Comfort, New Braunfels,
 San Antonio, Schertz

Descriptive Directory: **Free**
Rates (Single/Double):
 Modest: **$47.50 / $60**
 Average: **$60 / $80**
 Luxury: **$80 / $113**
Credit Cards: **AMEX, DISC, MC, VISA**

You'll find hospitable hosts waiting to welcome you and to suggest how best to enjoy this beautiful and historic city. Don't miss the Paseo del Rio (a bustling river walk), the Alamo, the Arneson River Theatre showplace, El Mercado (which is a restored Mexican and Farmers Market), the Southwest Craft Center, wonderful restaurants, marvelous shops, and delightful, friendly folks. The University of Texas, Trinity University, and St. Mary's University are nearby.

The Belle of Monte Vista ✪
505 BELKNAP PLACE, SAN ANTONIO, TEXAS 78212

Tel: **(512) 732-4006**
Hosts: **Mary Lou and Jim Davis**
No. of Rooms: **5**
No. of Private Baths: **3**
Max. No. Sharing Bath: **4**
Double/pb: **$50**
Single/pb: **$40**
Double/sb: **$50**

Single/sb: **$40**
Open: **All year**
Breakfast: **Full**
Pets: **No**
Children: **Welcome**
Smoking: **No**
Social Drinking: **Permitted**
Airport/Station Pickup: **Yes**

J. Riely Gordon designed this Queen Anne Victorian as a model house for a local developer. Built in 1890 with limestone that was quarried less than half a mile away, the house has been beautifully restored and is located in the elegant Monte Vista historic district. Inside, you'll find eight fireplaces, stained-glass windows, a hand-carved oak staircase, and Victorian furnishings. Mary Lou and Jim serve a Southern breakfast with homemade muffins and jellies each morning. They are happy to help you plan your day and will direct you to nearby attractions such as Alamo Plaza, the River Walk, and El Mercado Market Place.

Falling Pines B&B ✪
300 WEST FRENCH PLACE, SAN ANTONIO, TEXAS 78212

Tel: **(512) 733-1998; (800) 880-4580**	Reduced Rates: **15% families; weekly**
Best Time to Call: **9 AM–noon**	Breakfast: **Full**
Hosts: **Grace and Bob Daubert**	Pets: **No**
No. of Rooms: **5**	Children: **Welcome, over 10**
No. of Private Baths: **5**	Smoking: **No**
Double/pb: **$67.37**	Social Drinking: **Permitted**
Single/pb: **$65**	Minimum Stay: **2 nights**
Open: **All year**	

When you enter Falling Pines through the magnificent front archway, you realize that they don't make estates like this anymore. Pines, oaks, and pecan trees shade the one-acre property. Inside, the brick-and-limestone mansion is sumptuously decorated with oak paneling, oriental rugs, and antique furnishings. Tennis courts, a swimming pool, and a zoo are all a short walk away, or you can ride over on the bikes Grace and Bob will lend you. A breakfast of fresh fruit, pastries, and hot and cold cereals is served in the tiled solarium.

Rosevine Inn ✪
415 SOUTH VINE AVENUE, TYLER, TEXAS 75702

Tel: **(903) 592-2221**	Breakfast: **Full**
Hosts: **Bert and Rebecca Powell**	Pets: **No**
Location: **10 mi. from I-20**	Children: **Welcome, over 12**
No. of Rooms: **5**	Smoking: **No**
No. of Private Baths: **5**	Social Drinking: **Permitted**
Double/pb: **$65–$75**	Airport/Station Pickup: **Yes**
Open: **All year**	

Dr. Irwin Pope, Jr., made his home here on a quaint brick street back in the 1930s. Years later a devastating fire burned all but the foundation and beautiful grounds. Your hosts bought the property in 1986 and built the Rosevine Inn, a Federal-style redbrick home. They have furnished the house with antiques and country collectibles. In the morning, wake-up coffee is provided in the central hallway. When you come downstairs, hot muffins, baked breads, fresh fruit, and quiches are served. Your hosts will help you discover the charms of Tyler, known as the Rose Capital of the World. Antique shops are nearby, and the Rosevine makes an excellent base for discovering the many parks and lakes in the area. After a busy day, return to the inn, where you can sip a hot chocolate by the fire or relax in a quiet courtyard.

UTAH

Salt Lake City • • Farmington
• Sandy

• Nephi

Saint George • • Springdale   • Bluff

Bed and Breakfast Rocky Mountains—Utah
906 SOUTH PEARL STREET, DENVER, COLORADO 80209

Tel: **(800) 733-8415**
Best Time to Call: **8:30 AM–5:30 PM**
 Mon.–Fri.; 9 AM–1 PM Sat. (MST)
Coordinator: **Cheryl Carroll**
States/Regions Covered: **Colorado,**
 New Mexico, Utah
Descriptive Directory of B&Bs: **$4.50**

Rates (Single/Double):
 Modest: **$25 / $35**
 Average: **$30 / $45**
 Luxury: **$65 / $95–140**
Credit Cards: **MC, VISA**

A free reservation service for Colorado, New Mexico, and Utah representing over 200 inns and homestays.

Bluff Bed and Breakfast ✪
BOX 158, BLUFF, UTAH 84512

Tel: **(801) 672-2220**	Breakfast: **Full**
Host: **Rosalie Goldman**	Other Meals: **Available**
Location: **On Rtes. 163 and 191**	Pets: **No**
No. of Rooms: **2**	Children: **Welcome**
No. of Private Baths: **2**	Smoking: **No**
Double/pb: **$59**	Social Drinking: **Permitted**
Single/pb: **$64.80**	Airport/Station Pickup: **Yes**
Open: **All year**	Foreign Languages: **French**

Close to the Four Corners (the junction of Colorado, New Mexico, Arizona, and Utah), this Frank Lloyd Wright–style home is nestled among huge boulders at the foot of redrock cliffs, beside the San Juan River. On the main highway between Grand Canyon and Mesa Verde, it is secluded on seventeen desert acres. Across the river is the Navajo Reservation, and prehistoric ruins have been discovered nearby. Simply furnished, it is bright and tidy; large picture windows frame four different spectacular views. Rosalie prepares your breakfast of choice, from oatmeal to steak.

Annie's B&B ✪
1642 SOUTH 200 EAST, FARMINGTON, UTAH 84025

Tel: **(801) 451-7561**	Breakfast: **Full**
Hosts: **Ann and Charles Murphy**	Other Meals: **Available**
Location: **10 mi. N of Salt Lake City**	Pets: **Sometimes**
No. of Rooms: **1**	Children: **No**
No. of Private Baths: **1**	Smoking: **No**
Double/pb: **$50**	Social Drinking: **Permitted**
Open: **All year**	Airport/Station Pickup: **Yes**

A brick and stone home set in a small country-style community, Annie's B&B is 12 miles north of downtown Salt Lake City. Tourist attractions include Great Salt Lake and the Mormon Temple, plus hiking, biking, and horse trails. Ten excellent ski resorts, which have plenty of summertime entertainment, are within one hour's drive. Your hostess, an avid horsewoman and fitness instructor, provides full country breakfasts with fruit muffins and other healthful entrées. Guests have access to a local health club.

The Whitmore Mansion ✪
110 SOUTH MAIN STREET, NEPHI, UTAH 84648

Tel: **(801) 623-2047**	No. of Rooms: **6**
Best Time to Call: **Evenings**	No. of Private Baths: **6**
Hosts: **Bob and Dorothy Gliske**	Double/pb: **$45–$65**
Location: **85 mi. S of Salt Lake City**	Suites: **$75**

Open: **All year**	Pets: **No**
Breakfast: **Full**	Children: **Sometimes**
Other Meals: **Available**	Smoking: **No**
Credit Cards: **MC, VISA**	Social Drinking: **Permitted**

Located in a small farming community, this 1898 Victorian brick and sandstone mansion, listed on the National Register of Historic Places, has leaded glass windows, a huge front porch, and is topped by a turret that encases a sitting room of the third-floor suite. The interior has imported oak woodwork, a magnificent staircase, and high ceilings. Hand-crocheted afghans and handcrafted rugs complement the antique furnishings. The hearty breakfast often includes such delights as fresh apple muffins or German pancakes. In warm weather, lemonade is graciously served; during the cooler months, hot cider.

Seven Wives Inn ✪
217 NORTH 100 WEST, ST. GEORGE, UTAH 84770

Tel: **(801) 628-3737; (800) 484-1084, Code, 0165**	Single/pb: **$25–$70**
	Open: **All year**
Best Time to Call: **After 9 AM**	Breakfast: **Full**
Hosts: **Jay and Donna Curtis, and Alison and Jon Bowcutt**	Credit Cards: **AMEX, DC, MC, VISA**
	Children: **Welcome (crib)**
Location: **125 mi. NE of Las Vegas**	Smoking: **No**
No. of Rooms: **13**	Social Drinking: **Permitted**
No. of Private Baths: **13**	Airport/Station Pickup: **Yes**
Double/pb: **$35–$70**	

This delightful inn is featured on the walking tour of St. George; it is just across from the Brigham Young home and two blocks from the historic Washington County Court House. Your hosts offer traditional Western hospitality. Their home is decorated with antiques collected in America and Europe. Some bedrooms are named after one of the seven wives of Donna's polygamous great-grandfather. A gourmet breakfast is served in the elegant dining room that will give you a hint of the past. St. George is located near Zion and Bryce national parks, boasts eight golf courses, and is noted for its mild winters. Dixie College is nearby. There's a swimming pool for your pleasure.

Anton Boxrud House ✪
57 SOUTH 600 EAST, SALT LAKE CITY, UTAH, 84102

Tel: **(801) 363-8035; (800) 524-5511**	Double/pb: **$59**
Best Time to Call: **9 AM–9 PM**	Single/pb: **$55**
Hosts: **Ray and Margaret Fuller**	Double/sb: **$49**
Location: **5 blocks from downtown**	Single/sb: **$35**
No. of Rooms: **5**	Open: **All year**
No. of Private Baths: **2**	Reduced Rates: **10% weekly**
Max. No. Sharing Bath: **4**	Breakfast: **Full**

Credit Cards: **MC, VISA**	Smoking: **No**
Pets: **No**	Social Drinking: **Permitted**
Children: **Welcome (crib)**	Airport/Station Pickup: **Yes ($5 fee)**

Located in the downtown historic district, the Anton Boxrud House is one of Salt Lake City's grand old homes. The beveled-glass windows and beautiful woodwork have been carefully restored according to the original 1899 plans. Rooms are furnished with antiques, including a hand-carved German dining room table where breakfast is served. Guests are invited to meet one another in the parlor and sitting rooms and enjoy the tunes of the old player piano. This Victorian inn is close to the governor's mansion, Temple Square, and two major shopping malls. Ray and Margaret can guide you to the sights and can arrange to have a horse-drawn carriage take you on a tour.

Dave's Cozy Cabin Inn B&B ✪
2293 EAST 6200 SOUTH, SALT LAKE CITY, UTAH 84121

Tel: **(801) 278-6136**	Open: **All year**
Best Time to Call: **10 AM–6 PM**	Reduced Rates: **5% seniors, families,**
Hosts: **David and Dorothy Moore**	**after 5th night**
No. of Rooms: **3**	Breakfast: **Full**
No. of Private Baths: **1**	Pets: **No**
Max. No. Sharing Bath: **4**	Children: **Welcome, over 12**
Double/pb: **$45**	Smoking: **No**
Single/pb: **$35**	Social Drinking: **Permitted**
Double/sb: **$40**	Minimum Stay: **2 nights**
Single/sb: **$30**	

This log cabin at the base of the Wasatch Mountains is a handsome retreat, with its knotty pine paneling, large fireplace, and lovely garden patio. For that extra bit of relaxation, hop into the redwood hot tub. Between the nearby ski slopes and the sights of Salt Lake City, visitors will find plenty to do. You'll start the day off right with a full breakfast highlighted by oven-fresh muffins with homemade jams and jellies.

Alta Hills Farm ✪

10852 SOUTH 20TH EAST SANDY, SANDY, UTAH 84092

Tel: **(801) 571-1712**	Reduced Rates: **10% weekly, seniors**
Hosts: **Blaine and Diane Knight**	Breakfast: **Continental**
Location: **15 mi. S of Salt Lake**	Credit Cards: **DISC, MC, VISA**
No. of Rooms: **4**	Pets: **Yes**
No. of Private Baths: **2**	Children: **Welcome**
Max. No. Sharing Bath: **4**	Smoking: **No**
Double/pb: **$65**	Social Drinking: **No**
Double/sb: **$45**	Airport/Station Pickup: **Yes**
Open: **Sept. 1–May 31**	

This B&B is nestled at the base of the Rocky Mountains fifteen minutes from the Alta and Snow Bird ski resorts. Alta Hills Farm has been an English Huntseat Equestrian Center for the past twenty years. In the summer the Knights run a riding camp for children of all ages. Their home has a warm, spacious English country style. Every evening, guests can relax with hot apple cider in a private living room with a fireplace. You are also invited to join the Knights downstairs. Blaine and Diane love kids and welcome families who come to ski or to enjoy beautiful Salt Lake.

Under the Eaves Guest House ✪

P.O. BOX 29, 980 ZION PARK BOULEVARD, SPRINGDALE, UTAH 84767

Tel: **(801) 772-3457**	Single/sb: **$35**
Hosts: **Kathleen Brown-Wilkerson,**	Suites: **$75**
John O'Shea, Dale Wilkerson	Open: **All year**
Location: **45 mi. E of St. George**	Reduced Rates: **Available**
No. of Rooms: **5**	Breakfast: **Full**
No. of Private Baths: **3**	Credit Cards: **MC, VISA**
Max. No. Sharing Bath: **4**	Pets: **Sometimes**
Double/pb: **$55–$75**	Children: **Welcome**
Single/pb: **$40–$55**	Smoking: **No**
Double/sb: **$45**	Social Drinking: **Permitted**

Under the Eaves is a historic stone-and-stucco cottage located at the gate of Zion National Park. Constructed of massive sandstone blocks from the canyon, the guest house has served as a landmark for visitors to Zion for more than 50 years. Choose from two antique-filled bedrooms or a luxurious suite. The garden cottage dates from the 1920s and has two nonconnecting private bedrooms and baths.

VERMONT

Montgomery   North Troy   Derby Line
North Hero •   •   • Morgan
  Swanton
Jeffersonville •   Craftsbury •   • East Haven
  Common   • East Burke
Jericho •   • Stowe
Waterbury •   • Cabot
Waitsfield •   • Northfield
Warren •
Middlebury •   • Fairlee
  Brookfield •   • Chelsea
  Bethel •
  • Gaysville
Brandon •
Cuttingsville • Rutland
Fair Haven •   • Wallingford
Danby •   • Belmont
East Dorset •
Manchester •   • Chester
Manchester Center •
  • Townsend
  • West Dover

American Country Collection–Bed & Breakfast Vermont
4 GREENWOOD LANE, DELMAR, NEW YORK 12054

Tel: (518) 439-7001
Best Time to Call: 10 AM–5 PM
  Mon.–Fri.
Coordinator: **Arthur Copeland**
States/Regions Covered: **Bennington,
Burlington, Fairfax, Ludlow,
Manchester, Newport, North Hero,
Stowe, Waterbury, West Rutland**
Descriptive Directory of B&Bs: **$4.95**

Rates (Single/Double):
  Modest: **$35–$50 / $35–$55**
  Average: **$50–$60 / $55–$85**
  Luxury: **$60–$95 / $85–$135**
Credit Cards: **AMEX, MC, VISA**

The American Country Collection offers comfortable lodging in private homes and country inns throughout northern, central, and southern Vermont. Accommodations include an 1850 Colonial on eight acres in South Stratford with full breakfast, a luxurious inn (with all meals provided) in West Rutland, a tranquil home bordered by a brook in Manchester, and a farmhouse inn with solarium, pool, farm animals, and complete play area for children in Fairfax. Many locations are also equipped to serve the needs of small business meetings. In addition, reservations through the American Country Collection are handled for the Massachusetts Berkshire area, as well as eastern New York.

The Parmenter House ☉
BOX 106, BELMONT, VERMONT 05730

Tel: (802) 259-2009
Best Time to Call: 7:30 AM–noon; evenings
Hosts: Lois and Jeff Predom
Location: 25 mi. SE of Rutland; 2 mi. from Rte. 155
No. of Rooms: 4
No. of Private Baths: 4
Double/pb: $55–$90
Single/pb: $45

Open: All year
Reduced Rates: Available
Breakfast: Continental
Credit Cards: MC, VISA
Pets: No
Children: Welcome
Smoking: No
Social Drinking: Permitted

You are certain to benefit from the clear mountain air of this idyllic lakeside village. In summer, swim or canoe on Star Lake by day, stargaze from the large deck by night. Explore a country lane on a crisp autumn morning or rent an all-terrain bike for an excursion followed with mulled cider from the wood stove. Lois and Jeff invite you to relax in the serene atmosphere of their parlor. Retire to your bedroom furnished with Victorian antiques, handmade quilts, and herbal wreaths. The bountiful breakfast buffet of fruit, local cheeses, homemade granola, and freshly baked breads is a gastronomic treat.

Greenhurst Inn
RIVER STREET, BETHEL, VERMONT 05032

Tel: (802) 234-9474
Hosts: Lyle and Claire Wolf
Location: 30 mi. E of Rutland
No. of Rooms: 13
No. of Private Baths: 7
Max. No. Sharing Bath: 4
Double/pb: $75–$95
Single/pb: $65–$85
Double/sb: $50–$65

Single/sb: $40–$55
Open: All year
Breakfast: Continental
Credit Cards: DISC, MC, VISA
Pets: Welcome (no cats)
Children: Welcome (crib)
Smoking: Permitted
Social Drinking: Permitted

Located 100 yards from the White River, this elegant Queen Anne mansion, built in 1890, is listed on the National Register of Historic

Places. The heavy brass hinges, embossed floral brass doorknobs, and etched windows at the entry have withstood the test of time. The cut-crystal collection is magnificent, and the stereoscope and old Victrola add to the old-fashioned atmosphere. The mansion is close to many points of historic interest, and seasonal recreational activities are abundant. Vermont Law School is close by.

Rosebelle's Victorian Inn ✪
31 FRANKLIN STREET, ROUTE 7, BRANDON, VERMONT 05733 .

Tel: **(802) 427-0098**	Breakfast: **Full**
Best Time to Call: **9 AM–9 PM**	Other Meals: **Available**
Hosts: **Ginette and Norman Milot**	Credit Cards: **MC, VISA**
Location: **14 mi. N of Rutland**	Pets: **No**
No. of Rooms: **6**	Children: **Welcome, over 16**
No. of Private Baths: **3**	Smoking: **No**
Max. No. Sharing Bath: **4**	Social Drinking: **Permitted**
Double/pb: **$85**	Minimum Stay: **During foliage**
Double/sb: **$65–$75**	Airport/Station Pickup: **Yes**
Single/sb: **$50**	Foreign Languages: **French**
Open: **All year**	
Reduced Rates: **10% Mar., Apr., Nov.; 10% seniors**	

In a village known for beautiful antique homes, this French Second Empire–style manor stands out with its stunning mansard roof, Italianate porch, and artistic exterior filigree. Inside you'll find folding doors, high ceilings, large windows, wide soft pine floors, and a sitting room with a fireplace. The furniture, wallpaper, and drapes enhance the nineteenth-century atmosphere. Visit your hosts' gift shop with Victorian and country crafts, read a book in the flower garden, or play croquet on the lawn. The village center is within walking distance; hiking, biking, cross-country and downhill skiing, museums, and antique shops are only minutes away.

Green Trails Country Inn ✪
POND VILLAGE, BROOKFIELD, VERMONT 05036

Tel: **(802) 276-3412; (800) 243-3412**	Open: **May–Mar.**
Hosts: **Peter and Pat Simpson**	Reduced Rates: **Groups, AARP**
Location: **8 mi. from I-89, Exit 4**	Breakfast: **Full**
No. of Rooms: **15**	Other Meals: **Available**
No. of Private Baths: **9**	Pets: **No**
Max. No. Sharing Bath: **4**	Children: **Welcome (crib)**
Double/pb: **$77–$90**	Smoking: **No**
Single/pb: **$56–$66**	Social Drinking: **Permitted**
Double/sb: **$69–$80**	Airport/Station Pickup: **Yes**
Single/sb: **$50–$56**	

The inn consists of two buildings. One is an 1840 farmhouse; the other was built in the late 1700s and has pumpkin pine floorboards. They are located across from the famous Floating Bridge and Sunset Lake. Furnished in antiques and "early nostalgia," the rooms have stenciling, circa 1800, handmade quilts, and fresh flowers. The historic village is a perfect base for seasonal excursions to the Shelburne Museum or Woodstock. Cross-country skiers can start at the doorstep, while downhill enthusiasts can try Sugarbush and Killington.

Creamery Inn Bed & Breakfast ✪
P.O. BOX 187, CABOT, VERMONT 05647

Tel: **(802) 563-2819**	Suites: **$60**
Hosts: **Dan and Judy Lloyd**	Open: **All year**
Location: **18 mi. NE of Montpelier**	Reduced Rates: **Families, Nov.–July**
No. of Rooms: **3**	Breakfast: **Full**
No. of Private Baths: **1**	Other Meals: **Available**
Max. No. Sharing Bath: **4**	Pets: **Sometimes**
Double/pb: **$60**	Children: **Welcome**
Single/pb: **$35**	Smoking: **No**
Double/sb: **$55**	Social Drinking: **Permitted**
Single/sb: **$35**	

Enjoy lovely year-round accommodations in this Federal-style home, circa 1835. Guest rooms are tastefully decorated, with stenciling, old-fashioned wallpaper, a canopy bed, and old trunks. Located one mile from Cabot Creamery, the inn is on two acres in a country setting beautiful in any season. New lambs each spring attract many visitors. It's a great area for joggers, hikers, bicyclists, and nature lovers—walk up the road and delight in ponds and waterfalls along the way. Full breakfasts include Finnish pancakes and other homemade fare.

Shire Inn
MAIN STREET, CHELSEA, VERMONT 05038

Tel: **(802) 685-3031; (800) 441-6908**	Breakfast: **Full**
Hosts: **James and Mary Lee Papa**	Other Meals: **Available**
Location: **20 mi. from I-89**	Credit Cards: **MC, VISA**
No. of Rooms: **6**	Pets: **No**
No. of Private Baths: **6**	Children: **Welcome, over 6**
Double/pb: **$80–$95**	Smoking: **No**
Open: **All year**	Social Drinking: **Permitted**

In 1832 a successful Chelsea businessman built this stately home entirely of Vermont brick. The Federal-style house was made to last, from the unusually high ceilings above to the pine floors below, now carefully restored and gleaming under coats of varnish. Enter through the granite front archway and step into the parlor, where a crackling fire and a warm welcome await. Your hosts are transplanted New York professionals who have left the city life for a white picket fence and a river flowing out back. They invite you to antique-filled bedrooms, several with fireplaces, and modern baths with fluffy, oversize towels. A typical Shire breakfast features German pancakes served with apricot sauce. Home cooking can also be enjoyed in the evening, when a five-course meal is served in the dining room. The inn is set on 17 acres in a quiet country village that is said to have the state's oldest general store.

Stone Hearth Inn ✪
ROUTE 11, CHESTER, VERMONT 05143

Tel: **(802) 875-2525**	Breakfast: **Full**
Hosts: **Janet and Don Strohmeyer**	Pets: **No**
Location: **10 mi. from I-91, Exit 6**	Children: **Welcome (crib)**
No. of Rooms: **10**	Smoking: **Permitted**
No. of Private Baths: **10**	Social Drinking: **Licensed pub**
Double/pb: **$60–$95**	Airport/Station Pickup: **Yes**
Single/pb: **$40–$65**	Foreign Languages: **Dutch, French,**
Open: **All year**	**German**
Reduced Rates: **Available**	

This white 19th-century Colonial is set on seven acres of fields and wooded land. The rooms have been lovingly restored and feature wide-board pine floors and open beams, floral wallpapers, antiques, quilts, and a player piano. A fire-warmed living room and library are available. After a busy day, relax in the licensed pub and recreation room, or enjoy the whirlpool spa. Horseback riding, downhill and cross-country skiing, and swimming in the river across the road are but a handful of the local pleasures. Your hosts offer fresh-baked breads, pancakes, and French toast for breakfast. The dining room and licensed pub are open to the public.

Craftsbury Bed & Breakfast on Wylie Hill ✪
CRAFTSBURY COMMON, VERMONT 05827

Tel: **(802) 586-2206**	Open: **All year**
Best Time to Call: **Mornings; evenings**	Breakfast: **Full**
Host: **Margaret Ramsdell**	Pets: **No**
Location: **40 mi. N of Montpelier**	Children: **Welcome (crib)**
No. of Rooms: **4**	Smoking: **No**
Max. No. Sharing Bath: **4**	Social Drinking: **Permitted**
Double/sb: **$55–$65**	Foreign Languages: **French**
Single/sb: **$40**	

This 1860 Georgian hilltop farmhouse has beautiful views. The homey guest rooms adjoin the living room with its wood stove, where you are welcome to relax and visit. You may use Margaret's kitchen, barbecue, and picnic table should the crisp mountain air stoke your appetite. You're sure to enjoy the bountiful breakfast that often features cinnamon apple pancakes with fresh maple syrup. Dinner is served only by prior arrangement. The ski slopes of Stowe are 30 miles away, and lakes and rivers are within a two-mile radius. Cross-country skiing starts at the door.

Buckmaster Inn ✪
LINCOLN HILL ROAD, CUTTINGSVILLE, VERMONT 05738

Tel: **(802) 492-3485**	Single/sb: **$40–$50**
Best Time to Call: **8 AM–8 PM**	Open: **All year**
Hosts: **Sam and Grace Husselman**	Reduced Rates: **Weekly**
Location: **8 mi. SE of Rutland**	Breakfast: **Full**
No. of Rooms: **3**	Pets: **No**
No. of Private Baths: **2**	Children: **Welcome, over 8**
Max. No. Sharing Bath: **4**	Smoking: **No**
Double/pb: **$60–$65**	Social Drinking: **Permitted**
Single/pb: **$50–$65**	Airport/Station Pickup: **Yes**
Double/sb: **$50**	Foreign Languages: **Dutch**

The Buckmaster Inn, located near Cuttingsville in the Green Mountains, is a Federal clapboard Colonial overlooking a picturesque valley. Its center hall, grand staircase, and wide pine floors are typical of 19th-century style. This is New England relaxation at its best: fireplaces, wood-burning stove, library, and two porches. Homemade muffins, casseroles, and jams are among the specialties served in the country kitchen each morning. A pond for skating and fishing is within walking distance, and ski slopes, hiking trails, and craft shops are nearby.

The Quail's Nest Bed and Breakfast ✪
P.O. BOX 221, MAIN STREET, DANBY, VERMONT 05739

Tel: **(802) 293-5099**	Open: **All year**
Hosts: **Chip and Anharad Edson**	Breakfast: **Full**
Location: **13 mi. N of Manchester**	Credit Cards: **MC, VISA**
No. of Rooms: **4**	Pets: **No**
No. of Private Baths: **4**	Children: **Welcome, over 2**
Double/pb: **$75**	Smoking: **Restricted**
Single/pb: **$50**	Social Drinking: **Permitted**
Reduced Rates: **$10 less Apr., May, and Nov.**	

The Quail's Nest is a Greek Revival–style inn circa 1835. The guest rooms are furnished with antiques and handmade country quilts. Your host loves entertaining and offers such homemade breakfast specialties as apple-puff pancakes, muffins, and quiches. Danby is a quiet village close to five major ski areas. The Green Mountains are just east of here, offering some of the finest swimming, fishing, hiking, and downhill and cross-country skiing in the state.

Derby Village Inn ✪
46 MAIN STREET, DERBY LINE, VERMONT 05830

Tel: (802) 873-3604	Open: **All year**
Hosts: **Tom and Phyllis Moreau**	Breakfast: **Full**
Location: **45 mi. N of St. Johnsbury**	Credit Cards: **MC, VISA**
No. of Rooms: **5**	Pets: **No**
No. of Private Baths: **5**	Children: **Welcome**
Double/pb: **$50–$60**	Smoking: **No**
Single/pb: **$40–$60**	Social Drinking: **Permitted**

The village of Derby Line straddles the U.S.–Canadian border. Phyllis and Tom's home is a rambling Victorian mansion boasting beautiful wood wainscoting. The immaculate, airy bedrooms are furnished with select antiques, braided rugs, charming wallpaper and tieback curtains. Breakfast menus may feature cheddar cheese strata apple pancakes with cider syrup. It's an easy walk to the town's unique international library and opera house. Downhill or cross-country skiing, water sports, golf, fishing, and antiquing are just some of the seasonal activities.

Lanier's Hilltop Bed and Breakfast ✪
P.O. BOX 103, HIGHWAY 19, EAST BURKE, VERMONT 05832

Tel: (802) 626-9637	Open: **All year**
Hosts: **Marilyn and Lionel Lanier**	Reduced Rates: **10% Mar. and Apr.**
Location: **10 mi. N of St. Johnsbury**	Breakfast: **Full**
No. of Rooms: **3**	Credit Cards: **MC, VISA**
No. of Private Baths: **1**	Pets: **No**
Max. No. Sharing Bath: **4**	Children: **Welcome (crib, high chair)**
Double/pb: **$55**	Smoking: **No**
Double/sb: **$50**	Social Drinking: **Permitted**
Single/sb: **$40**	Station Pickup: **Yes**

Marilyn and Lionel's contemporary split-level home is set high on a hill, with a brook and spectacular views. To name a few activities, guests can swim in the Laniers' pool, explore the snowmobile trails that branch out from the driveway, ski nearby Burke Mountain, or play golf at any of the three local courses. For boating and fishing, there are two lakes in the area. Animal lovers of all ages will want to visit the fallow deer farm ten minutes away or admire the cows, horses, ducks, and chickens at the working farm down the road.

Christmas Tree Bed & Breakfast
BENEDICT ROAD, EAST DORSET, VERMONT 05253

Tel: (802) 362-4889	No. of Rooms: **4**
Hosts: **Dennis and Catherine Conroy**	Max. No. Sharing Bath: **4**
Location: **4.5 mi. N of Manchester**	Double/pb: **$50–$55**

Single/pb: **$30–$35**
Double/sb: **$45**
Single/sb: **$25**
Open: **All year**
Breakfast: **Continental**

Pets: **Sometimes**
Children: **Welcome**
Smoking: **No**
Social Drinking: **Permitted**

Dennis and Catherine invite you to share their contemporary wood-paneled home where you are welcome to relax on the deck or in front of the wood stove, depending upon the season. There's a pond and a stream for fishing, and it is located close to Emerald Lake State Park. It is 15 minutes from the slopes at Bromley; 30 minutes from Stratton. The coffeepot is always on, and pretzels and chips are complimentary. The generous breakfast may let you skip lunch.

Hansel & Gretel Haus ✪
BOX 95, TOWN HIGHWAY 34, EAST HAVEN, VERMONT 05837

Tel: **(802) 467-8884**
Hosts: **Eileen and John Hombach**
Location: **20 mi. N of St. Johnsbury**
No. of Rooms: **3**
Max. No. Sharing Bath: **4**
Double/sb: **$45**
Single/sb: **$35**
Open: **Jan.–Nov.**
Reduced Rates: **10% seniors; 10% after 3 nights**

Breakfast: **Full**
Other Meals: **Available**
Credit Cards: **MC, VISA**
Pets: **No**
Children: **Welcome, over 10**
Smoking: **No**
Social Drinking: **Permitted**

Appropriately enough, Hansel & Gretel Haus is located in the forest of Vermont's Northeast Kingdom. Your hosts strive for coziness in their rooms and decor; they also operate a small gift and craft shop on the premises. For downhill and cross-country skiers, nearby Burke Mountain Ski Area is a promising destination. Numerous lakes will appeal to swimmers and fishermen. Other outdoor types, from golfers and bicyclists to hikers and snowmobilers, will find plenty to do here.

Maplewood Inn
ROUTE 22A SOUTH, FAIR HAVEN, VERMONT 05743

Tel: **(802) 265-8039; (800) 253-7729**
Best Time to Call: **2–9 PM**
Hosts: **Cindy and Doug Baird**
Location: **18 mi. W of Rutland**
No. of Rooms: **5**
No. of Private Baths: **5**
Double/pb: **$65–$70**
Suites: **$95**
Open: **All year**
Reduced Rates: **After 5th night**

Breakfast: **Continental, plus**
Credit Cards: **AMEX, MC, VISA**
Pets: **No**
Children: **Welcome, over 5**
Smoking: **Permitted**
Social Drinking: **Permitted**
Minimum Stay: **Parents college weekends, holidays**
Airport/Station Pickup: **No**

The inn is a beautifully restored Greek Revival–style home, built in 1850, with lovely country views from every window. Chippendale furnishings, original pine floors polished to a warm glow, four-poster or brass beds, wingback chairs, and carefully chosen accessories provide a soothing backdrop for a relaxing visit. After a multicourse breakfast, enjoy a walk in the historic village or participate in the recreational activities at nearby Lakes Bomoseen and St. Catherine, or take a short drive to ski the slopes of Killington or Pico. Linger on the porch, play croquet on the lawn, enjoy a board game or a book in the parlor. The gourmet restaurants and shops of Rutland are close by. Reserve early for the fall foliage season. Don't forget to visit their shops in the Red Barn behind Maplewood Inn!

Our Home Bed & Breakfast ✪
36 WEST STREET, FAIR HAVEN, VERMONT 05743

Tel: **(802) 265-3245**
Best Time to Call: **After 4 PM**
Hosts: **Carol and Dick Adams**
Location: **15 mi. W of Rutland**
No. of Rooms: **3**
No. of Private Baths: **2**
Max. No. Sharing Bath: **3**
Double/pb: **$65**
Suites: **$75; sleeps 3**

Open: **All year**
Reduced Rates: **10% Mar., May, June, Nov.**
Breakfast: **Continental**
Pets: **No**
Children: **Welcome, over 12**
Smoking: **No**
Social Drinking: **Permitted**

This 1890 Queen Anne Victorian stands on a quiet, tree-lined street in a peaceful village in the heart of Vermont's lake region. Both Castleton State College and Green Mountain College are nearby, as are the Killington and Pico ski resorts. Listed on the Vermont Register of Historic Places, Our Home is decorated with period furniture. But there are plenty of modern amenities, such as the in-ground swimming pool, where guests tend to gather on warm afternoons.

Silver Maple Lodge and Cottages ✪
SOUTH MAIN STREET, RR1, BOX 8, FAIRLEE, VERMONT 05045

Tel: (802) 333-4326; (800) 666-1946	Single/sb: $40
Hosts: Scott and Sharon Wright	Open: All year
Location: 20 mi. N of White River	Reduced Rates: 10% seniors, AAA
Junction	Breakfast: Continental
No. of Rooms: 14	Credit Cards: AMEX, MC, VISA
No. of Private Baths: 12	Pets: Sometimes
Max. No. Sharing Bath: 4	Children: Welcome
Double/pb: $48–$68	Smoking: Permitted
Single/pb: $46–$66	Social Drinking: Permitted
Double/sb: $44	Airport/Station Pickup: Yes

Built as a farmhouse in 1855, Silver Maple Lodge became an inn some seventy years later. To accommodate extra guests, several cottages were added, constructed from lumber cut on the property. It's easy to see why this B&B remains popular. There's swimming, boating, and fishing at two local lakes. Other outdoor activities in the area include golf, tennis, horseback riding, canoeing, hiking, and skiing. If you're tired of feeling earthbound, Post Mills Airport, seven miles away, offers flights in a hot-air balloon and gliding rides. (Special packages, combining a flight in a hot-air balloon and other activities of your choice, can be arranged.) And for concerts, theater, and art exhibits, it's an easy drive to Dartmouth College, in Hanover, New Hampshire.

Cobble House Inn
P.O. BOX 49, GAYSVILLE, VERMONT 05746

Tel: (802) 234-5458	Breakfast: Full
Best Time to Call: 8 AM–9 PM	Other Meals: Available
Hosts: Philip and Beau Benson	Credit Cards: AMEX, MC, VISA
Location: Off Rte. 107	Pets: No
No. of Rooms: 6	Children: Welcome, over 6
No. of Private Baths: 6	Smoking: No
Double/pb: $80–$100	Social Drinking: Permitted
Open: All year	

A grand 1860s mansion awaits you on a hilltop overlooking the beautiful Green Mountains. Each guest room is decorated with antiques and accented with country furnishings. Ornate carved beds, colorful quilts, and flannel sheets are sure to offer a peaceful night's rest. Breakfast specialties such as French apple pancakes, homemade coffee cakes, peach fritters, or eggs Benedict are served each morning. Just outside the door is the White River, with its clear waters for fishing, canoeing, tubing, and swimming. Skiing, golf, tennis, and horseback riding are all within easy reach. In the evening, the inn offers Italian and French cuisine served in the country dining room.

Kelldarra, a Vermont Bed and Breakfast ✪
P.O. BOX 197, JEFFERSONVILLE, VERMONT 05464

Tel: **(802) 644-6575**
Host: **Darra Kell**
Location: **25 mi. NE of Burlington**
No. of Rooms: **4**
No. of Private Baths: **1**
Max. No. Sharing Bath: **4**
Double/pb: **$70**
Single/pb: **$60**
Double/sb: **$50–$60**

Single/sb: **$40–$50**
Open: **All year**
Breakfast: **Full**
Pets: **No**
Children: **Welcome, over 10**
Smoking: **No**
Social Drinking: **Permitted**
Minimum Stay: **2 nights**

Nestled on a wooded hillside, with its own pond and brook, this brick gabled farmhouse (circa 1826) evokes the bucolic traditions of early America. The spacious stenciled rooms feature quilts and English country antiques. Darra serves candlelight breakfasts made with local cheeses, maple products, numerous varieties of apples, and wild berries and herbs. The easy access to downhill and cross-country skiing, hiking, cycling, and fine dining guarantees guests' year-round pleasure.

Henry M. Field House Bed & Breakfast
ROUTE 15, RR2, BOX 395, JERICHO, VERMONT 05452

Tel: **(802) 899-3984**
Best Time to Call: **After 5 PM**
Hosts: **Mary Beth Perilli and Terrence L. Horan**
Location: **12 mi. E of Burlington**
No. of Rooms: **3**
No. of Private Baths: **1**
Max. No. Sharing Bath: **4**
Double/pb: **$60–$70**

Double/sb: **$50–$60**
Open: **All year**
Breakfast: **Full**
Credit Cards: **MC, VISA**
Pets: **No**
Children: **Welcome, over 8**
Smoking: **No**
Social Drinking: **Permitted**

This is an opulent, Italian-style Victorian with all the trimmings: high ceilings, ornamental plaster, etched glass, and butternut and walnut woodwork. Guests may relax on one of three porches or stroll along the Browns River, which borders the lovely three-and-a-half-acre property. Jericho is convenient to skiing at Bolton Valley or Smuggler's Notch; hiking, biking, golf, and water sports are all within a 30-minute drive. The Henry M. Field House also offers easy access to Burlington, home of the University of Vermont, and many fine shops and restaurants.

Milliken's ✪
RD 2, BOX 397, JERICHO, VERMONT 05465

Tel: **(802) 899-3993**	Suites: **$60**
Best Time to Call: **Mornings; evenings**	Open: **All year**
Hosts: **Rick and Jean Milliken**	Breakfast: **Full**
Location: **12 mi. E of Burlington**	Pets: **No**
No. of Rooms: **3**	Children: **Welcome**
Max. No. Sharing Bath: **4**	Smoking: **No**
Double/sb: **$40**	Social Drinking: **Permitted**
Single/sb: **$30**	Airport/Station Pickup: **Yes**

This Second Empire early Victorian was built in 1867 by a lumber magnate. The house has a graceful mansard roof, original woodwork, and floors of alternating cherry and white maple. The spaciousness of the rooms is enhanced by high ceilings, large windows, and gracious decor. Rick is a hotel manager and Jean is a choreographer and host. She prepares such breakfast specialties as French toast with maple syrup and hot mulled cider. In the evening, a good-night brandy and snack are offered. Your family is sure to enjoy its stay with the Millikens, their two children, and a friendly dog named Bailey. Nearby attractions are hiking trails on Mt. Mansfield, skiing, and fabulous fall foliage.

Minterhaus Bed & Breakfast ✪
P.O. BOX 226, JERICHO, VERMONT 05465

Tel: **(802) 899-3900**	No. of Rooms: **3**
Best Time to Call: **9 AM–9 PM**	Max. No. Sharing Bath: **4**
Host: **Ruth Minter**	Double/sb: **$45**
Location: **12 mi. NE of Burlington**	Single/sb: **$40**

Open: **Aug. 1–June 30**	Children: **Welcome**
Breakfast: **Continental**	Smoking: **No**
Pets: **No**	Social Drinking: **Permitted**

Minterhaus is located on two riverfront acres in the historic village of Jericho, within walking distance of Old Red Mill Museum and Craft Shop and Old Mill Park. It is also near Mt. Mansfield, a source of year-round recreation with its hiking paths and ski areas. Lake Champlain and Burlington are a half hour away by car. This home was built in the mid–1800s, and guests appreciate the warmth of its butternut wood-work, pine floors and many antique furnishings. A generous Continental breakfast of juice, fruits, cereals, home-baked breads, and other specialties is served.

Brook 'n' Hearth ○
STATE ROAD 11/30, BOX 508, MANCHESTER CENTER, VERMONT 05255

Tel: **(802) 362-3604**	Open: **May 22–Oct. 30; Nov. 20–**
Best Time to Call: **2–10 PM**	**Apr. 17**
Hosts: **Larry and Terry Greene**	Reduced Rates: **Available**
Location: **1 mi. E of US 7**	Breakfast: **Full**
No. of Rooms: **3**	Credit Cards: **AMEX, DISC, MC, VISA**
No. of Private Baths: **3**	Pets: **No**
Double/pb: **$70**	Children: **Welcome (crib)**
Single/pb: **$46**	Smoking: **Permitted**
Suites: **$80 for 2**	Social Drinking: **Permitted**

True to its name, a brook runs through the property and a fire warms the living room of this country home. Terry and Larry offer setups and happy-hour snacks for your self-supplied cocktails. You're within five miles of the ski slopes at Bromley and Stratton; it is also convenient to art centers, summer theater, restaurants, and a score of sports that include hiking on the Long Trail. Air-conditioned in summer, enjoy the pool, lawn games, and barbecue. The game room, with its VCR, pocket billiards, and Ping-Pong, is always available.

Brookside Meadows Country Bed & Breakfast
RD 3, BOX 2460, MIDDLEBURY, VERMONT 05753-8751

Tel: **(802) 388-6429;**	Breakfast: **Full**
reservations only **(800) 442-9887**	Credit Cards: **MC, VISA**
Hosts: **Linda and Roger Cole**	Pets: **No**
Location: **2½ mi. from Rte. 7**	Children: **Welcome, over 5**
No. of Rooms: **5**	Smoking: **No**
No. of Private Baths: **5**	Social Drinking: **Permitted**
Double/pb: **$70–$90**	Minimum Stay: **2 nights weekends and**
Suites: **$85–$130**	**peak times**
Open: **All year**	Airport/Station Pickup: **Yes**

This handsome farmhouse was built in 1979, based on a nineteenth-century design. Located on a country road, on twenty acres of meadowland, the property borders a brook. The two-bedroom suite has a living room with wood stove, dining area, and kitchen as well as a private entrance and bath. Relax and enjoy spacious lawns, perennial gardens, a spectacular view of the Green Mountains, and only country sounds. Area attractions include excellent downhill and cross-country skiing, hiking, swimming, Lake Champlain ferryboat trips, maple syrup operations, Middlebury College, the University of Vermont, Morgan Horse Farm, Fort Ticonderoga, and Shelburne Museum.

Phineas Swann ✪
P.O. BOX 344, MONTGOMERY, VERMONT 05471

Tel: **(802) 326-4306**	Single/sb: **$45**
Best Time to Call: **9 AM–9 PM**	Open: **All year**
Hosts: **Frank and Maureen Kane**	Reduced Rates: **15% weekly**
Location: **56 mi. NE of Burlington**	Breakfast: **Full**
No. of Rooms: **4**	Credit Cards: **MC, VISA**
No. of Private Baths: **2**	Pets: **No**
Max. No. Sharing Bath: **4**	Children: **Welcome, over 6**
Double/pb: **$70**	Smoking: **No**
Single/pb: **$50**	Social Drinking: **Permitted**
Double/sb: **$60**	Airport/Station Pickup: **Yes**

A Victorian house with a country flavor, Phineas Swann has an enclosed porch and lots of gingerbread trim. Inside, the house is decorated in pastels, with overstuffed chairs and sofas and period-style furniture. Because of its Green Mountain setting, this B&B draws hikers, skiers, and cyclists. If you didn't bring your own bicycle, you can rent both road and mountain bikes from your hosts, who also can arrange tours. More sedentary types will want to visit the many area antique shops and restaurants. Full breakfasts, served by candlelight, consist of home-baked breads and muffins and an entrée like French toast or apple pancakes.

Hunt's Hideaway
RR 1, BOX 570, WEST CHARLESTON, MORGAN, VERMONT 05872

Tel: **(802) 895-4432, 334-8322**	Open: **All year**
Best Time to Call: **7 AM–11 PM**	Reduced Rates: **Available**
Host: **Pat Hunt**	Breakfast: **Full**
Location: **6 mi. from I-91**	Pets: **Sometimes**
No. of Rooms: **3**	Children: **Welcome**
Max. No. Sharing Bath: **4**	Smoking: **Permitted**
Double/sb: **$35**	Social Drinking: **Permitted**
Single/sb: **$25**	

This modern, split-level home is located on 100 acres of woods and fields, with a brook, pond, and large swimming pool. Pancakes with

Vermont maple syrup are featured at breakfast. Ski Jay Peak and Burke, or fish and boat on Lake Seymour, two miles away. Visiting antique shops or taking a trip to nearby Canada are other local possibilities.

Charlie's Northland Lodge
BOX 88, NORTH HERO, VERMONT 05474

Tel: **(802) 372-8822**	Guest Cottage: **$350–$550 weekly;**
Best Time to Call: **Before 8 PM**	**sleeps 6**
Hosts: **Charles and Dorice Clark**	Open: **All year**
Location: **60 mi. S of Montreal,**	Breakfast: **Continental**
Canada	Pets: **No**
No. of Rooms: 3	Children: **Welcome, over 5**
Max. No. Sharing Bath: 5	Smoking: **Permitted**
Double/sb: **$40–$50**	Social Drinking: **Permitted**

The lodge is a restored Colonial, circa 1850, located on Lake Champlain, where bass and walleye abound. A sport and tackle shop is on the premises. Fall and winter fishing should appeal to all anglers. In summer, tennis, hiking, or relaxing in the reading room are pleasant activities.

Rose Apple Acres Farm ✪
RR 2, BOX 300, EAST HILL ROAD, NORTH TROY, VERMONT 05859

Tel: **(802) 988-4300**	Single/sb: **$32**
Best Time to Call: **Evenings**	Open: **All year**
Hosts: **Jay and Camilla Mead**	Breakfast: **Full**
Location: **60 mi. N of St. Johnsbury**	Pets: **No**
No. of Rooms: 3	Children: **Welcome, over 6**
No. of Private Baths: 1	Smoking: **No**
Max. No. Sharing Bath: 4	Social Drinking: **Permitted**
Double/pb: **$52**	Airport/Station Pickup: **Yes**
Double/sb: **$42**	

Located 2 miles from the Canadian border and 2 hours from Montreal or Burlington, the farm is situated on 52 acres of fields, woods, and streams. The farmhouse has a bright and friendly atmosphere, enhanced by panoramic mountain views. Hiking, cross-country skiing, and snowshoeing may be enjoyed on-premises. Horse-drawn carriage and sleigh rides are offered. It is only 10 miles to Jay Peak for skiing. Camilla and Jay are interested in classical music and gardening.

Northfield Inn
27 HIGHLAND AVENUE, NORTHFIELD, VERMONT 05663

Tel: **(802) 485-8558**	Hosts: **Aglaia and Alan Stalb**
Best Time to Call: **Day**	Location: **9 mi. S of Montpelier**

No. of Rooms: **8**
No. of Private Baths: **8**
Double/pb: **$85**
Single/pb: **$75**
Double/sb: **$75**
Single/sb: **$55**
Suites: **$115–$135; sleeps 2–3**
Open: **All year**
Breakfast: **Full**

Other Meals: **Available**
Pets: **No**
Children: **Welcome, over 16**
Smoking: **No**
Social Drinking: **No**
Minimum Stay: **During special events**
Airport/Station Pickup: **Yes, fee**
Foreign Languages: **Greek**

This fully restored Victorian mansion is nestled on a sun-bathed hillside with a magnificent view of the Green Mountains and the valley below. A visit here provides a romantic interlude that refreshes and rejuvenates your spirit. The luxurious furnishings include antiques, brass and carved wooden beds, European feather beds, and oriental rugs. A hearty breakfast, afternoon tea, snacks, and beverages are yours to enjoy.

Hillcrest Guest House
RR 1, BOX 4459, RUTLAND, VERMONT 05701

Tel: **(802) 775-1670**
Hosts: **Bob and Peg Dombro**
Location: **3/10 mi. from Rte. 7**
No. of Rooms: **3**
Max. No. Sharing Bath: **5**
Double/sb: **$45**
Single/sb: **$40**

Open: **All year**
Breakfast: **Continental**
Pets: **No**
Children: **Welcome (crib)**
Smoking: **No**
Social Drinking: **Permitted**
Airport/Station Pickup: **Yes**

This 150-year-old farmhouse, with a comfortable screened porch for warm-weather relaxing, is furnished with country antiques. Pico and Killington ski areas are 7 and 16 miles away, respectively. Summer brings the opportunity to explore charming villages, covered bridges, and antiques and craft centers. Country auctions, marble quarries, trout streams, and Sunday-evening band concerts are pleasant pastimes. Bob and Peg always offer something in the way of between-meal refreshments.

Bittersweet Inn
692 SOUTH MAIN STREET, STOWE, VERMONT 05672

Tel: **(802) 253-7787**
Best Time to Call: **7 AM–11 PM**
Hosts: **Barbara and Paul Hansel**
Location: **36 mi. E of Burlington**
No. of Rooms: **8**
No. of Private Baths: **5**
Max. No. Sharing Bath: **4**
Double/pb: **$60–$76**
Double/sb: **$54–$68**

Suites: **$125–$157**
Open: **All year**
Reduced Rates: **5-night stays**
Breakfast: **Continental**
Credit Cards: **AMEX, MC, VISA**
Children: **Welcome (play area)**
Smoking: **Permitted**
Social Drinking: **Permitted**

Bittersweet Inn is a brick Cape with converted clapboard carriage house, dating back to 1835. The house is set on nine and a half acres, overlooking Camel's Hump Mountain. Inside you'll find comfortable rooms decorated with a combination of antiques and family pieces. It's just a half mile to the center of town and minutes to ski lifts and a cross-country touring center. A good-size swimming pool is located out back with plenty of room for laps or just taking it easy. In the winter season, hot soup and the indoor hydro-spa will be waiting after your last ski run. Your hosts, Barbara and Paul, invite you to relax in the game room with BYOB bar and will help you plan your evening.

The Inn at the Brass Lantern ☉
717 MAPLE STREET, STOWE, VERMONT 05672

Tel: **(802) 253-2229; (800) 729-2980**	Reduced Rates: **Available**
Best Time to Call: **9 AM–9 PM**	Breakfast: **Full**
Hosts: **Mindy and Andy Aldrich**	Credit Cards: **AMEX, MC, VISA**
Location: **10 mi. from I-89, Exit 10**	Pets: **No**
No. of Rooms: **9**	Children: **Welcome**
No. of Private Baths: **9**	Smoking: **No**
Double/pb: **$70–$130**	Social Drinking: **Permitted**
Single/pb: **$60–$120**	Minimum Stay: **ski season, foliage,**
Open: **All year**	**and holidays**

The inn was originally built as a farmhouse and carriage barn around 1800. Andy and Mindy won an award for their efforts in its restoration by maintaining its character with the artful use of period antiques, handmade quilts, and handmade accessories. Its setting provides panoramic views of Mt. Mansfield and the valley. A 10-percent gratuity is added to all rates. You are invited to join your hosts for wine, tea, and dessert while watching the sun set over the Green Mountains.

Ski Inn
ROUTE 108, STOWE, VERMONT 05672

Tel: **(802) 253-4050**	Open: **All year**
Best Time to Call: **9–11 AM; evenings**	Reduced Rates: **Off-season**
Hosts: **The Heyer Family**	Breakfast: **Continental**
Location: **47 mi. NE of Burlington**	Other Meals: **In winter, full breakfast**
No. of Rooms: **10**	**and dinner (additional fee)**
No. of Private Baths: **5**	Pets: **Sometimes**
Max. No. Sharing Bath: **5**	Children: **Welcome**
Double/pb: **$40–$55**	Smoking: **Permitted**
Double/sb: **$35–$45**	Social Drinking: **Permitted**
Single/sb: **$30–$40**	

This traditional New England inn, set back from the highway among evergreens on a gentle sloping hillside, is a quiet place to relax and sleep soundly. In winter, it's a skier's delight, close to Mt. Mansfield's downhill and cross-country trails. In summer, the rates drop and include just Continental breakfast. The Heyer Family offers warm hospitality in all seasons.

Heron House Bed & Breakfast
HIGHGATE SPRINGS, VERMONT (MAILING ADDRESS: RR 2, BOX 174-2, SWANTON, VERMONT 05488)

Tel: (802) 868-7433	Single/pb: $45
Best Time to Call: **Anytime before 10 PM**	Open: **All year**
	Reduced Rates: **10% seniors**
Hosts: **Shirley and Ray Henderson**	Breakfast: **Full**
Location: **42 mi. N of Burlington**	Pets: **No**
No. of Rooms: **1**	Children: **No**
No. of Private Baths: **1**	Smoking: **No**
Double/pb: **$50**	Social Drinking: **Permitted**

It's a short stroll to Lake Champlain from Shirley and Ray's recently built country home, which lies off a secluded private road, surrounded by trees and wildlife. The pleasant mauve-and-lavender color scheme lends a fresh, airy feeling to the carpeted bedroom, which has a four-poster bed and an indoor balcony overlooking the cathedral-style living room (a favorite place for their fluffy orange cat, Fritz). Shirley's generous breakfast features freshly baked muffins, bacon, and oat pancakes served with Vermont's celebrated maple syrup. The Canadian border is a short drive away, while Montreal and Jay and Smuggler's ski areas are within one hour by car.

Boardman House Bed & Breakfast ✪
P.O. BOX 112, TOWNSEND, VERMONT 05353

Tel: (802) 365-4086	Suites: **$90–$100**
Hosts: **Sarah Messenger and Paul Weber**	Open: **All year**
	Reduced Rates: **10–15% seniors; off-season; weekly**
Location: **125 mi. N of Boston**	
No. of Rooms: **6**	Breakfast: **Full**
No. of Private Baths: **5**	Pets: **Sometimes**
Max. No. Sharing Bath: **4**	Children: **Welcome**
Double/pb: **$70–$80**	Smoking: **Permitted**
Single/pb: **$65–$75**	Social Drinking: **Permitted**

If you tried to imagine an idealized New England home, it would resemble this white 19th-century farmhouse set on Townsend's Village Green. This is a prime foliage and antiquing area. Direct access to State Routes 30 and 35 allows you to pursue other interests, from skiing at Stratton to canoeing on the West River. Gourmet breakfasts feature pear pancakes, individual soufflés, hot fruit compotes, and more.

Newton's 1824 House Inn
ROUTE 100, BOX 159, WAITSFIELD, VERMONT 05673

Tel: **(802) 496-7555**
Best Time to Call: **9:30 AM**
Hosts: **Nick and Joyce Newton**
Location: **18 mi. SE of Montpelier**
No. of Rooms: **6**
No. of Private Baths: **6**
Double/pb: **$75–$105**
Single/pb: **$65–$95**
Guest Cottage: **$135; sleeps 4**
Open: **All year**

Breakfast: **Full**
Credit Cards: **AMEX, MC, VISA**
Pets: **No**
Children: **By arrangement**
Smoking: **No**
Social Drinking: **Permitted**
Minimum Stay: **2 nights Sept. 18–
  Oct. 18**
Airport/Station Pickup: **Yes**
Foreign Languages: **Spanish**

Surrounded by original art, oriental rugs, select antiques, and period furniture, guests enjoy a relaxed elegance at this two-story clapboard farmhouse crowned with ten gables. Built in 1824, it was recently recommended for National Register status. The farm's 52 acres include scenic hills, pastures, stands of pines and sugarbush. The Mad River runs through the property and feeds a great private swimming hole. It's only minutes from Sugarbush Resort and Mad River Glen ski areas. After a good night's sleep in one of the cozy bedrooms, one can look forward to such breakfast treats as baked stuffed pears with nuts and currants, oatmeal soufflé, or apple muffins.

White Rocks Inn ✪
RR 1, BOX 297, ROUTE 7, WALLINGFORD, VERMONT 05773

Tel: **(802) 446-2077**
Best Time to Call: **Mornings; evenings**
Hosts: **June and Alfred Matthews**
Location: **20 mi. N of Manchester**
No. of Rooms: **5**
No. of Private Baths: **5**
Double/pb: **$65–$95**
Single/pb: **$60–$90**
Guest Cottage: **$130–$140**
Open: **Dec. 1–Oct. 31**

Breakfast: **Full**
Credit Cards: **MC, VISA**
Pets: **No**
Children: **Welcome, over 10**
Smoking: **No**
Social Drinking: **Permitted**
Minimum Stay: **2 nights holidays, fall
  foliage season**
Foreign Languages: **French, Spanish**

If your idea of paradise is a pasture, a creek stocked with trout, an old-fashioned swimming hole, and a peaceful valley surrounded by mountains, then reserve a room here. June and Alfred have renovated their vintage 1800 farmhouse with care, preserving the charm of wide-board floors, wainscoting, ornate moldings, and high ceilings, while enhancing it with antiques, oriental rugs, and canopied beds. In summer, such breakfast delights as banana pancakes or raisin bread French toast is served on the large veranda overlooking the meadows. In cooler weather, this feast is presented in the dining room. Five downhill ski areas are a short drive away, and miles of cross-country ski trails are adjacent to the inn.

West Hill House ☉

RR 1, BOX 292, WEST HILL ROAD, WARREN, VERMONT 05674

Tel: (802) 496-7162
Best Time to Call: 2–9 PM
Hosts: Nina and Bob Heyd
Location: 25 mi. SW of Montpelier
No. of Rooms: 4
No. of Private Baths: 2
Max. No. Sharing Bath: 4
Double/pb: $75–$80
Single/pb: $65–$70
Double/sb: $65–$70
Single/sb: $55–$60

Open: All year
Reduced Rates: 10% seniors; 5-night
  midweek discount
Breakfast: Full
Credit Cards: MC, VISA
Pets: No
Children: Welcome, over 10
Smoking: No
Social Drinking: Permitted
Minimum Stay: 2 nights weekends in
  ski season

Enjoy casual country lodging at Bob and Nina's charming Vermont farmhouse located a mile from the famed Sugarbush Ski Resort and adjacent to its golf course. Each guest room is attractively decorated with handmade quilts and curtains, and country crafts accented with lovely antiques. Begin your day with homemade treats such as crêpes, quiche, muffins, or coffee cake and burn off the calories by skiing, horseback riding, canoeing, river bathing, soaring, or golfing. In winter, après-ski treats are served near the fireplace in the living room; on summer afternoons, tea and pastries are proffered on the porch.

Grünberg Haus ☉

RR2, BOX 1595, WATERBURY, VERMONT 05676

Tel: (802) 244-7726; (800) 800-7760
Hosts: Christopher Sellers and Mark
  Frohman
Location: 25 mi. E of Burlington
No. of Rooms: 10
Max. No. Sharing Bath: 4
Double/sb: $55–$70
Single/sb: $40–$50
Open: All year

Reduced Rates: 10% after 3rd night
Breakfast: Full
Other Meals: Available
Credit Cards: AMEX, DISC, MC, VISA
Pets: No
Children: Welcome
Smoking: No
Social Drinking: Permitted
Airport/Station Pickup: Yes

You'll think you're in the Alps when you see this hand-built Tyrolean chalet perched on a secluded hillside. The living room features an eight-foot grand piano, a massive fieldstone fireplace, and a long breakfast table overlooking the valley and distant forest. All ten guest rooms open onto the quaint balcony that surrounds the chalet. The BYOB rathskeller features hand-stenciled booths; the formal dining room is furnished with antiques. Outside, cleared logging trails provide cross-country skiing and hiking access to hundreds of acres of meadows and woodlands. And Waterbury's central location makes it easy to get to ski resorts like Stowe and Sugarbush. Whatever you plan to do, bring an appetite; Grünberg Haus serves memorable gourmet breakfasts, and other meals can be arranged.

Inn at Blush Hill ✪

BOX 1266, BLUSH HILL ROAD, WATERBURY, VERMONT 05676

Tel: **(802) 244-7529; (800) 736-7522**
Hosts: **Gary and Pam Gosselin**
Location: **22 mi. E. of Burlington**
No. of Rooms: **6**
No. of Private Baths: **2**
Max. No. Sharing Bath: **4**
Double/pb: **$75–$110**
Double/sb: **$55–$90**
Open: **All year**

Reduced Rates: **Available**
Breakfast: **Full**
Credit Cards: **AMEX, DISC, MC, VISA**
Pets: **No**
Children: **Welcome, over 6**
Smoking: **Permitted**
Social Drinking: **Permitted**
Airport/Station Pickup: **Yes**

This 1790 brick farmhouse is located halfway between the Stowe and Sugarbush ski areas. The atmosphere is warm and homey, with antiques, old-time rockers, books, and lots of fireplaces. Your host is a gourmet cook and enjoys making her own bread and muffins each morning. A huge lake with boating, swimming, and fishing is located just one and a half miles from the house, and a nine-hole golf course is located directly across the street. At the end of the day, sit back and enjoy the surroundings, relaxing on the large, old-fashioned porch. Afternoon and evening refreshments are served.

The Weathervane Lodge B&B ✪

BOX 57, DORR FITCH ROAD, WEST DOVER, VERMONT 05356

Tel: **(802) 464-5426**
Hosts: **Liz and Ernie Cabot**
Location: **1 mi. from Rte. 100**
No. of Rooms: **10**
No. of Private Baths: **3**
Max. No. Sharing Bath: **4**
Double/pb: **$64–$72**
Single/pb: **$42–$56**
Double/sb: **$42–$56**
Single/sb: **$39–$42**

Suites: **$88–$160; sleeps 2–4**
Open: **All year**
Breakfast: **Full**
Pets: **Sometimes**
Children: **Welcome**
Smoking: **Permitted**
Social Drinking: **Permitted**
Minimum Stay: **2 nights weekends; ski and foliage seasons**

Only four miles from Haystack, Mount Snow, and Corinthia, this Tyrolean-style ski lodge is decorated with authentic antiques and Colonial charm. The lounge and recreation room have fireplaces and a bring-your-own bar. Winter rates include cross-country ski equipment, sleds, and snowshoes, so that you may explore the lovely marked trails. Summer brings lakeshore swimming, boating, fishing, tennis, riding, museums, and the Marlboro Music Festival.

Golden Maple Inn ✪
ROUTE 15, WOLCOTT VILLAGE, VERMONT 05680

Tel: **(802) 888-6614**
Hosts: **Dick and Jo Wall**
Location: **45 mi. NE of Burlington**
No. of Rooms: **3**
No. of Private Baths: **1**
Max. No. Sharing Bath: **4**
Double/pb: **$69**
Single/pb: **$53**
Double/sb: **$61**
Single/sb: **$47**

Suites: **$69**
Open: **All year**
Reduced Rates: **10% Apr. and Nov.;
10% seniors**
Breakfast: **Full**
Credit Cards: **AMEX, MC, VISA**
Pets: **No**
Children: **Welcome, over 12**
Smoking: **No**
Social Drinking: **Permitted**

Originally the home of mill owner William Bundy, this 1865 Greek Revival inn has been designated one of Vermont's historically significant structures. The large common rooms and spacious bedchambers are furnished with antiques and cozy comforters. Dick and Jo serve a scrumptious breakfast on a table set with linen tablecloths and sterling silverware; entrées include oven-baked French toast and baked holiday eggs, accompanied by juice, fruit, cereal, tea, hot chocolate, or freshly ground coffee. Guests canoe, fish, hike, bike, and cross-country ski right from the inn or simply enjoy the gardens and lawns which roll down to the river's edge. Stowe, Craftsbury, Bread & Puppet, and Ben & Jerry's are all in the area.

VIRGINIA

- Gore
- Woodstock
- Flint Hill
- New Market
- Washington
- Alexandria
- Manassas
- Gordonsville
- Fredericksburg
- Montross
- Chincoteague Island
- Staunton
- Charlottesville
- Mollusk
- New Church
- Scottsville
- Richmond
- Morattico
- Lexington
- Lynchburg
- Urbanna
- Buchanan
- Amherst
- Williamsburg
- Cape Charles
- Roanoke
- Smith Mountain Lake
- Smithfield
- Christiansburg
- Abingdon
- Chilhowie
- Cluster Springs
- Capron
- Virginia Beach

Summerfield Inn ✪
101 WEST VALLEY STREET, ABINGDON, VIRGINIA 24210

Tel: **(703) 628-5905**
Best Time to Call: **Mornings; after 3 PM**
Hosts: **Champe and Don Hyatt**
Location: **15 mi. NE of Bristol**
No. of Rooms: **4**
No. of Private Baths: **4**
Double/pb: **$65–$75**
Single/pb: **$55**

Open: **Apr. 1–Nov. 1**
Breakfast: **Continental**
Credit Cards: **AMEX, MC, VISA**
Pets: **No**
Children: **Welcome, over 12**
Smoking: **Permitted**
Social Drinking: **Permitted**
Airport/Station Pickup: **Yes**

A large covered porch with comfortable rockers graces the front and side of this meticulously restored Victorian residence. Guests are welcome to share the large living room, handsomely appointed morning room, and refreshing sun room. A guest pantry is also available for the preparation of light snacks. Summerfield Inn is but a short

walk from Barter Theatre, Abingdon's historic district, the Virginia
Creeper Trail, and excellent dining. Set at 2,300 feet above sea level
and surrounded by mountains, Abingdon, chartered in 1778, is the
jumping-off point to the Mt. Rogers National Recreational Area and
the Appalachian Trail.

Princely B&B Ltd. ✪
819 PRINCE STREET, ALEXANDRIA, VIRGINIA 22314

Tel: (703) 683-2159	States/Regions Covered: **Alexandria**
Best Time to Call: **10 AM–6 PM**	Rates (Single/Double):
Mon.–Fri.	Modest: **$75–$90**
Coordinator: **E. J. Mansmann**	Minimum Stay: **2 nights**

This reservation service lists more than thirty privately owned historic
homes, circa 1750 to 1890, many furnished with fine antiques, located
in the heart of the Old Town area of Alexandria. All are within eight
miles of the White House or Mount Vernon and afford easy access to
shopping, dining, and monuments in and around Washington, D.C.

Dulwich Manor B&B Inn ✪
ROUTE 5, BOX 173A, AMHERST, VIRGINIA 24521

Tel: (804) 946-7207	Open: **All year**
Hosts: **Robert and Judith Reilly**	Reduced Rates: **Weekly; 10% after**
Location: **14 mi. N of Lynchburg**	**5th night**
No. of Rooms: **6**	Breakfast: **Full**
No. of Private Baths: **4**	Pets: **No**
Max. No. Sharing Bath: **4**	Children: **Welcome**
Double/pb: **$75–$85**	Smoking: **Restricted**
Single/pb: **$70–$80**	Social Drinking: **Permitted**
Double/sb: **$65**	Airport/Station Pickup: **Yes**
Single/sb: **$60**	

A stately English country house built at the turn of the century,
Dulwich Manor sits on five secluded acres surrounded by the Blue
Ridge Mountains. The scenic Blue Ridge Parkway and the Washington
and Jefferson national forests are among the area's major attractions.
Points of historic interest include Appomattox Courthouse and Monticello. Guests start off the day with a full country breakfast either in
the formal dining room or on the veranda. In the evening, your hosts
will offer you wine and cheese. Outdoor hot tub for guest enjoyment.
Guest rooms have fireplaces or whirlpool baths.

The Berkley House ✪
ROUTE 2, BOX 220A, BUCHANAN, VIRGINIA 24066

Tel: **(703) 254-2548**
Hosts: **John and Sue Shotwell**
Location: **13 mi. N of Roanoke**
No. of Rooms: **4**
No. of Private Baths: **1**
Max. No. Sharing Bath: **4**
Double/pb: **$65**
Single/pb: **$55**
Double/sb: **$55–$65**
Single/sb: **$45–$55**

Suites: **$95–$125**
Open: **All year**
Reduced Rates: **Available**
Breakfast: **Full**
Credit Cards: **AMEX, MC, VISA**
Pets: **No**
Children: **Welcome, over 8**
Smoking: **No**
Social Drinking: **Permitted**
Airport/Station Pickup: **Yes**

Farmland surrounds this 1887 Victorian country home, located within minutes of the Peaks of Otter on the Blue Ridge Parkway. Three porches, a guest kitchen, and a TV/VCR room are at your disposal. Golfers have a choice of several excellent courses in the immediate area. Sue's breakfast menu features homemade pancakes, waffles, and breads; complimentary refreshments, served from 4 to 5 PM, will tide visitors over until dinnertime.

Nottingham Ridge
P.O. BOX 97-B, CAPE CHARLES, VIRGINIA 23310

Tel: **(804) 331-1010**
Best Time to Call: **Evenings**
Host: **Bonnie Nottingham**
Location: **20 mi. N of Norfolk**
No. of Rooms: **3**
No. of Private Baths: **2**
Max. No. Sharing Bath: **3**
Double/pb: **$75**
Double/sb: **$65**

Single/sb: **$50**
Open: **All year**
Breakfast: **Full**
Other Meals: **Available**
Pets: **No**
Children: **Welcome, over 8**
Smoking: **Restricted**
Social Drinking: **Permitted**
Airport/Station Pickup: **Available**

Nottingham Ridge is a picturesque country retreat high atop the sand dunes of Virginia's Eastern Shore. Guests can spend hours on a private beach, or charter a fishing boat for the day. Bonnie offers comfortable rooms furnished with antiques and reproductions. She loves entertaining and offers homemade biscuits, Virginia ham, and quiche for breakfast. Later in the day, enjoy wine, cheese, and a breathtaking view of the sun setting over the water. This lovely home is just three and a half miles north of the Chesapeake Bay Bridge Tunnel, and 25 minutes from the Norfolk and Virginia Beach areas. Bonnie will gladly direct you to historic sights, the Nature Conservancy, and the U.S. Fish and Wildlife Refuge.

Picketts Harbor
BOX 97AA, CAPE CHARLES, VIRGINIA 23310

Tel: **(804) 331-2212**
Best Time to Call: **5–7:30 AM; after 5 PM**
Hosts: **Sara and Cooke Goffigon**
Location: **21 mi. N of Norfolk**
No. of Rooms: **6**
Max. No. Sharing Bath: **4**
Double/pb: **$75**
Single/pb: **$60**
Double/sb: **$65**

Single/sb: **$50**
Open: **All year**
Breakfast: **Full**
Other Meals: **Available**
Pets: **No**
Children: **Welcome**
Smoking: **No**
Social Drinking: **Permitted**
Airport/Station Pickup: **Yes**

Picketts Harbor is set in a rural, wooded section of Virginia's Eastern Shore. The house is decorated country-style, with antiques, reproductions, plants, and collectibles. Outside, the property spans 17 acres including a large private beach. Breakfast is served overlooking Chesapeake Bay. There are many local opportunities for fishermen and birdwatchers, and your hosts will gladly provide a picnic lunch. Williamsburg, Yorktown, and many historic sights are within an hour's drive.

Sandy Hill Farm B&B ✪
11307 RIVERS MILL ROAD, CAPRON, VIRGINIA 23829

Tel: **(804) 658-4381**
Best Time to Call: **6:30–8 AM; 7:30–11:30 PM**
Host: **Anne Kitchen**
Location: **11 mi. from I-95**
No. of Rooms: **2**
Max. No. Sharing Bath: **3**
Double/sb: **$30**
Single/sb: **$25**

Open: **Mar. 20–Dec. 5**
Reduced Rates: **Families; 5 nights**
Breakfast: **Continental**
Other Meals: **Available**
Pets: **Welcome**
Children: **Welcome**
Smoking: **Permitted**
Social Drinking: **Permitted**

Experience the pleasures of an unspoiled rural setting at this ranch-style farmhouse. There are animals to visit, quiet places to stroll, and a lighted tennis court on the grounds. This is an ideal hub from which to tour southeastern and central Virginia. Day trips to Williamsburg, Norfolk, and Richmond are possibilities. Fresh fruits and homemade breads are served at breakfast.

Guesthouses Reservation Service ✪
P.O. BOX 5737, CHARLOTTESVILLE, VIRGINIA 22905

Tel: **(804) 979-7264**	Rates (Single/Double):
Best Time to Call: **12–5 PM Mon.–Fri.**	Modest: **$48 / $56**
Coordinator: **Mary Hill Caperton**	Average: **$60 / $68**
States/Regions Covered: **Albemarle**	Luxury: **$72 / $160**
County, Charlottesville, Luray	Estate Cottages: **$100 up**
Descriptive Directory: **$1**	Credit Cards: **AMEX, MC, VISA**

Charlottesville is a gracious town. The hosts in Mary's hospitality file offer you a genuine taste of Southern hospitality. All places are close to Thomas Jefferson's Monticello and James Madison's Ash Lawn, as well as the University of Virginia. Unusual local activities include ballooning, steeplechasing, and wine festivals. Please note that the office is closed from Christmas through New Year's Day. Reduced rates are available for extended stays, and most hosts offer a full breakfast.

Clarkcrest Bed and Breakfast
STAR ROUTE BOX 60, CHILHOWIE, VIRGINIA 24319

Tel: **(703) 646-3707**	Location: **35 mi. E of Bristol, Virginia-**
Hosts: **Doug and Mary Clark**	**Tennessee**

No of Rooms: **4**
No. of Private Baths: **2**
Max. No. Sharing Bath: **4**
Double/pb: **$60–$70**
Single/pb: **$55**
Double/sb: **$50**
Single/sb: **$45**
Open: **Apr. 15–Nov. 15**

Reduced Rates: **$5 off 2nd night**
Breakfast: **Continental**
Credit Cards: **MC, VISA**
Pets: **No**
Children: **Welcome, over 12**
Smoking: **Permitted**
Social Drinking: **No**

Doug and Mary invite you to their brick farmhouse in one of western Virginia's oldest communities. Hikers, bikers, and horseback riders will find several likely destinations within a twenty- to thirty-minute drive: Mount Rogers National Recreation Area, Hungry Mother State Park, the Appalachian Trail, and the Virginia Creeper Trail. For dining and entertainment, try the nearby town of Abingdon. Continental breakfast is served from 7 to 9 each morning.

Miss Molly's Inn
113 NORTH MAIN STREET, CHINCOTEAGUE ISLAND, VIRGINIA 23336

Tel: **(804) 336-6686**
Hosts: **Barbara and David Wiedenheft**
Location: **50 mi. S of Salisbury, Md.**
No. of Rooms: **7**
No. of Private Baths: **5**
Max. No. Sharing Bath: **4**
Double/pb: **$59–$115**
Single/pb: **$59–$115**
Single/sb: **$59–$99**

Open: **Valentine's Day–New Year's Eve**
Reduced Rates: **Before Memorial Day; after Labor Day**
Breakfast: **Full**
Pets: **No**
Children: **Welcome, over 12**
Smoking: **Restricted**
Social Drinking: **Permitted**
Minimum Stay: **2 nights weekends**

The 22 rooms of this seaside Victorian have been lovingly restored to their 19th-century charm. Relax in an ambience of lace curtains, stained-glass windows, and period pieces. While writing her book *Misty*, Marguerite Henry stayed here. The ponies made famous by that story roam wild at the nearby National Wildlife Refuge. You too may find "Miss Molly's" cool breezes, five porches, and afternoon teas worth writing about. Chincoteague has beaches, gourmet restaurants, and the NASA museum. Your hosts will gladly direct you to these sights, beginning with the bay, which is 150 feet from the front door.

The Oaks Bed & Breakfast Country Inn
311 EAST MAIN STREET, CHRISTIANSBURG, VIRGINIA 24073

Tel: (703) 381-1500	Breakfast: Full
Best Time to Call: 11 AM–7 PM	Credit Cards: AMEX, MC, VISA
Hosts: Margaret and Tom Ray	Pets: No
Location: 22 mi. S of Roanoke	Children: Welcome, over 12
No. of Rooms: 5	Smoking: No
No. of Private Baths: 5	Social Drinking: Permitted
Double/pb: $75–$105	Airport/Station Pickup: Yes
Open: All year	

Step into the wide entry hall of this Queen Anne/Victorian and you'll experience the graciousness of the 19th century. With its grand staircase, stained-glass windows, turrets, window nooks, and elaborate fireplaces, The Oaks delights the eye and the spirit. Visitors are pampered with lavish breakfasts, complimentary fresh fruit, fluffy terry robes, and luxurious linens. A spa, sauna, and small kitchen are at your disposal. Assuming you can tear yourself away, the Blue Ridge Parkway, Virginia Tech, Radford University, and the Shenandoah Valley are within an easy drive.

Oak Grove Plantation ☉
P.O. BOX 45, CLUSTER SPRINGS, VIRGINIA 24535

Tel: (804) 575-7137	Breakfast: Full
Host: Mary Pickett Craddock	Other Meals: Available
Location: 60 mi. N of Durham	Pets: No
No. of Rooms: 2	Children: Welcome
Max. No. Sharing Bath: 4	Smoking: Permitted
Double/sb: $50	Social Drinking: Permitted
Single/sb: $45	Airport/Station Pickup: Yes
Open: May–Sept.	Foreign Languages: Spanish
Reduced Rates: Available	

Prominent Virginia legislator Thomas Easley built this estate in 1820, and it has remained in the family ever since—Mary, a Washington,

D.C., preschool teacher, is his fifth-generation descendant. She encourages visitors to hike, bike, and look at wildlife on the 400-acre grounds. The two bedrooms have fireplaces and are furnished with comfortable period pieces and family heirlooms. Guests enjoy reading or chatting in the elegant parlor and cheerful sun porch. Full country breakfasts are served in the Victorian dining room. Buggs Island Lake, for water sports, and historic Danville, the last capital of the Confederacy, are within a half-hour drive.

Caledonia Farm
ROUTE 1, BOX 2080, FLINT HILL, VIRGINIA 22627

Tel: **(703) 675-3693**	Suite: **$100**
Best Time to Call: **Weekdays**	Open: **All year**
Host: **Phil Irwin**	Breakfast: **Full**
Location: **68 mi. SW of Washington,**	Credit Cards: **MC, VISA**
D.C.; 4 mi. N of Washington, Va.	Pets: **No**
No. of Rooms: **3**	Children: **Welcome, over 12**
Max. No. Sharing Bath: **4**	Smoking: **No**
Double/sb: **$70**	Social Drinking: **Permitted**

This charming 1812 stone manor house and its companion "summer kitchen" are located on a working beef cattle farm adjacent to Shenandoah National Park. Each accommodation has a fireplace, period furnishings, individual temperature controls for heat or air-conditioning, and spectacular views of the Blue Ridge Mountains. A candlelight breakfast is served from a menu that offers a choice of omelet, smoked salmon, or eggs Benedict. The Skyline Drive, fine dining, caves, wineries, hayrides, antiquing, historic sites, and sporting activities are a few of the possible diversions. Caledonia Farm is now a Virginia Historic Landmark and on the National Register of Historic Places.

La Vista Plantation ○

4420 GUINEA STATION ROAD, FREDERICKSBURG, VIRGINIA 22408

Tel: **(703) 898-8444**
Best Time to Call: **Before 9:30 PM**
Hosts: **Michele and Edward Schiesser**
Location: **60 mi. S of D.C.; 4.5 mi. from I-95**
No. of Rooms: **2**
No. of Private Baths: **2**
Double/pb: **$85**
Single/pb: **$65**
Suite: **$80; sleeps 6**

Open: **All year**
Reduced Rates: **7th night free; families**
Breakfast: **Full**
Credit Cards: **MC, VISA**
Pets: **No**
Children: **Welcome**
Smoking: **No**
Social Drinking: **Permitted**

One of the guest lodgings at La Vista is located in an English basement blessed with a sunny exposure and featuring a private entrance. The spacious, air-conditioned suite has a large living room with fireplace, full kitchen, sitting room, and bath. Ten acres surround the manor house, circa 1838, and you are welcome to stroll, bird-watch, or fish in a pond stocked with bass and sunfish.

The Spooner House Bed and Breakfast ○

1300 CAROLINE STREET, FREDERICKSBURG, VIRGINIA 22401

Tel: **(703) 371-1267**
Best Time to Call: **After 6 PM**
Hosts: **Peggy and John Roethel**
Location: **54 mi. S of Washington, D.C.**
Suites: **$60–$70; sleeps 2, $15 each additional person**
Open: **All year**
Reduced Rates: **10% weekly**

Breakfast: **Continental**
Pets: **No**
Children: **Welcome**
Smoking: **No**
Social Drinking: **Permitted**
Station Pickup: **Yes**
Foreign Languages: **German**

Built in 1793 on land once owned by George Washington's youngest brother, Charles, the Spooner House operated as a general store and later a tavern. Located in Fredericksburg's historic district, it is within walking distance of museums, restaurants, shops, and the Amtrak station. The lovely two-room suite has its own private entrance. Breakfast, along with the morning paper, is delivered to guests at their convenience. A complimentary guided tour of the Rising Sun Tavern, the National Historic Landmark that is adjacent to the Spooner House, is available to guests.

Sleepy Hollow Farm Bed & Breakfast ○

16280 BLUE RIDGE TURNPIKE, ROUTE 231 N, GORDONSVILLE, VIRGINIA 22942

Tel: **(703) 832-5555**	Suites: **$95–$125**
Best Time to Call: **8 AM–noon;**	Open: **All year**
5–10 PM	Reduced Rates: **Weekly**
Host: **Beverley Allison**	Breakfast: **Full**
Location: **25 mi. N of Charlottesville**	Credit Cards: **MC, VISA**
No. of Rooms: **6**	Pets: **Sometimes**
No. of Private Baths: **6**	Children: **Welcome**
Double/pb: **$60–$125**	Smoking: **Permitted**
Single/pb: **$50–$75**	Social Drinking: **Permitted**
Guest Cottage: **$100–$210; sleeps**	Minimum Stay: **2 nights weekends**
4–8	**Sept.–Nov. and May–June**

Sleepy Hollow Farm lies in the heartland of American history, where evidence of Indians and the Revolutionary and Civil War periods still exists. The air-conditioned brick farmhouse evolved from an 18th-century structure, and today boasts terraces, porches, gazebo, pond, a croquet lawn, and rooms with fireplaces. Furnished with antiques and carefully chosen accessories, the decor is picture pretty. Beverley, a retired missionary and journalist, is a fine cook as evidenced by breakfast treats such as sausage pie, fried apples, apple cake, and fruit compote. While in the area, you may want to visit Montpelier, home of James and Dolley Madison, local wineries, a church dating back to 1769, or fish at Lake Orange.

Rainbow's End B&B

ROUTE 1, BOX 335, GORE, VIRGINIA 22637

Tel: **(703) 858-2808**	Single/sb: **$40**
Best Time to Call: **10 AM–8 PM**	Open: **All year**
Hosts: **Eleanor and Thom McKay**	Breakfast: **Continental**
Location: **20 mi. W of Winchester**	Pets: **No**
No. of Rooms: **2**	Children: **No**
Max. No. Sharing Bath: **3**	Smoking: **No**
Double/sb: **$45**	Social Drinking: **Permitted**

Rainbow's End is a brick and wood ranch situated on Timber Ridge in the Blue Ridge Mountains. The McKays offer cozy rooms filled with comfortable family furnishings. Eleanor serves a tasty breakfast of homemade breads, muffins, cakes, and coffee. Later in the day, join your hosts for wine and cheese. Guests can experience rural life in the heart of apple country. You may see a deer, a fox, or any one of a number of colorful birds that frequent the pond nestled among the pines. Nearby attractions include George Washington's Office, Ole Towne Winchester with its quaint stores, several famous caverns, and Civil War battlefields.

Holly Point ○
ROUTE 3, BOX 410, LANCASTER, VIRGINIA 22503

Tel: **(804) 462-7759**	Single/sb: **$30**
Host: **Mary Chilton Graham**	Wheelchair-Accessible: **Yes**
Location: **60 mi. N of Williamsburg**	Open: **May 1–Nov. 1**
No. of Rooms: **3**	Breakfast: **Continental**
No. of Private Baths: **1**	Pets: **Welcome**
Max. No. Sharing Bath: **5**	Children: **Welcome**
Double/pb: **$40**	Smoking: **Permitted**
Single/pb: **$35**	Social Drinking: **Permitted**
Double/sb: **$35**	Airport/Station Pickup: **Yes**

George Washington never slept here, but his aunt was Mary Graham's direct ancestor. Situated halfway between Williamsburg and Fredericksburg, her immaculate farmhouse offers breathtaking views of the Rappahannock River and the surrounding countryside. There are plenty of opportunities for land or water sports, including hiking, boating, and swimming. Weather permitting, breakfast is served on the wraparound porch featuring jams made from property trees and home-baked bread from George's favorite recipe.

Asherowe ○
314 SOUTH JEFFERSON STREET, LEXINGTON, VIRGINIA 24450

Tel: **(703) 463-4219**	Open: **Closed July**
Best Time to Call: **Early mornings**	Breakfast: **Continental**
Host: **Yvonne Emerson**	Pets: **Sometimes**
Location: **45 mi. N of Roanoke**	Children: **Welcome, over 15**
No. of Rooms: **2**	Smoking: **No**
Max. No. Sharing Bath: **4**	Social Drinking: **Permitted**
Double/sb: **$53.75**	Foreign Languages: **French, German**
Single/sb: **$30**	

This comfortable 1904 wooden home lies only minutes from downtown, in the Golden Triangle section of Lexington's historic district. Sights include the Marshall Library, Washington and Lee University, the Virginia Horse Center, and the Virginia Military Institute, formerly the home of Stonewall Jackson. Guests from both sides of the Atlantic will feel right at home here, since Yvonne speaks fluent French and German as well as English. With the Blue Ridge Parkway to the east, and the Allegheny Mountains to the west, the breathtaking scenery is sure to entice any outdoor enthusiast. Lady Calypso, the resident cat, greets all guests on arrival as any good Southern hostess would.

Llewellyn Lodge at Lexington ✪

603 SOUTH MAIN STREET, LEXINGTON, VIRGINIA 24450

Tel: **(703) 463-3235; (800) 882-1145**
Best Time to Call: **9:30 AM–7:30 PM**
Hosts: **Ellen and John Roberts**
Location: **50 mi. N of Roanoke**
No. of Rooms: **6**
No. of Private Baths: **6**
Double/pb: **$65–$80**
Single/pb: **$55–$70**

Open: **All year**
Breakfast: **Full**
Credit Cards: **AMEX, MC, VISA**
Pets: **No**
Children: **Welcome, over 10**
Smoking: **Restricted**
Social Drinking: **Permitted**
Airport/Station Pickup: **Yes**

A warm and friendly atmosphere, combining country charm with a touch of class, awaits you at this lovely brick Colonial furnished in traditional and antique pieces. Guests are welcomed with a cool drink on the deck in warm months, or with a refreshment by the fire in the winter. Ellen spent twenty years in the airline, travel, and hospitality business before moving to Lexington in 1985 to start her B&B. John, a native Lexingtonian, is acquainted with the hiking and biking trails and knows where the fish are hiding. A hearty gourmet breakfast is offered each morning, including omelets, Belgian waffles, Virginia maple syrup, sausage, bacon, and Ellen's famous blueberry muffins. The lodge is an easy walk to the Robert E. Lee Chapel, the Stonewall Jackson House, Washington and Lee University, and the Virginia Military Institute.

Lynchburg Mansion Inn B&B ✪

405 MADISON STREET, LYNCHBURG, VIRGINIA 24504

Tel: **(804) 528-5400; (800) 352-1199**
Hosts: **Bob and Mauranna Sherman**

Location: **65 mi. S of Charlottesville**
No. of Rooms: **3**

No. of Private Baths: **3**
Double/pb: **$89**
Suites: **$109**
Open: **All year**
Reduced Rates: **Available**
Breakfast: **Full**

Credit Cards: **AMEX, MC, VISA**
Pets: **No**
Children: **Welcome**
Smoking: **No**
Social Drinking: **No**

Restored with your every comfort in mind, this Spanish Georgian mansion has pretty gardens, a spacious veranda, oak floors, tall ceilings, pocket doors, and cherry woodwork. Bedrooms are lavish, with either king- or queen-size beds, luxurious linens, fireplaces, TVs, and turndown service. Fine china, silver, and crystal complement the sumptuous full breakfasts. The mansion surveys a half-acre in downtown Lynchburg's Garland Hill Historic District, which is listed on the National Register of Historic Places; impressive Federal and Victorian homes line Madison Street, still paved in its turn-of-the-century brick. Plus there are Civil War sites, antique shops, art galleries, and countless programs offered by the city's colleges and universities.

Winridge Bed & Breakfast ✪
ROUTE 1, BOX 362, MADISON HEIGHTS, VIRGINIA 24572

Tel: **(804) 384-7220**
Best Time to Call: **8 AM–9 PM**
Hosts: **Lois Ann and Ed Pfister**
Location: **6 mi. N of Lynchburg**
No. of Rooms: **3**
No. of Private Baths: **1**
Max. No. Sharing Bath: **4**
Double/pb: **$69**
Double/sb: **$49–$59**

Open: **All year**
Reduced Rates: **Available**
Breakfast: **Full**
Pets: **No**
Children: **Welcome**
Smoking: **No**
Social Drinking: **No**
Airport/Station Pickup: **Yes**

Enjoy wonderful mountain views while relaxing on the large porches of this grand Colonial southern home. Swing under the shade trees and stroll through the gardens, where you'll admire the beauty of flowers, birds, and butterflies. Spacious rooms with high ceilings, large sunny windows, and a delightful mix of modern and antique furniture await you. Breakfasts are tempting, with offerings like oven baked pecan French toast and blueberry patch muffins. The Blue Ridge Parkway, Appomattox Courthouse, Poplar Forest, and much more are close by for your diversion.

Sunrise Hill Farm ✪
5513 SUDLEY ROAD, MANASSAS, VIRGINIA 22110

Tel: **(703) 754-8309**
Best Time to Call: **Anytime**
Hosts: **Frank and Sue Boberek**
Location: **35 minutes W of Washington, D.C.**
No. of Rooms: **2**
No. of Private Baths: **2**
Double/pb: **$68**
Double/sb: **$68**

Open: **All year**
Reduced Rates: **15% families using both rooms**
Breakfast: **Full**
Credit Cards: **MC, VISA**
Pets: **Horses boarded**
Children: **Welcome, over 10**
Smoking: **No**
Social Drinking: **Permitted**

Standing in the heart of the 6,000-acre Manassas National Battlefields, this Civil War treasure overlooks Bull Run Creek. Sunrise Hill Farm is an uncommonly charming, Federal-era country home furnished in period style. This B&B is a haven for Civil War buffs and guests visiting northern Virginia and the nation's capital. Situated within the renowned Virginia hunt country, it is just 35 minutes from Washington, D.C., and close to Harpers Ferry, Antietam, Skyline Drive, Luray Caverns, and numerous historic sites and antique-filled towns.

Greenvale Manor Waterfront Inn
ROUTE 354, P.O. BOX 70, MOLLUSK, VIRGINIA 22517

Tel: **(804) 462-5995**
Hosts: **Pam and Walt Smith**
Location: **70 mi. NE of Richmond**
No. of Rooms: **6**
No. of Private Baths: **6**
Double/pb: **$70–$85**
Single/pb: **$65**
Suites: **$105**

Open: **All year**
Breakfast: **Full**
Pets: **No**
Children: **Welcome, over 14**
Smoking: **Permitted**
Social Drinking: **Permitted**
Minimum Stay: **Holiday weekends**

Greenvale Manor is an 1840 Colonial set on the Rappahannock River and Greenvale Creek. It is located in an area known for its historic waterfront homes. The house has been owned by several prominent Virginia families and has been beautifully restored and maintained.

The 13-acre estate includes a sandy beach, pool, and private dock. The house is furnished in period antiques and reproductions and its large windows make the most of its best feature—the waterfront. Breakfast is served on a large screened veranda in summer, and in winter the day begins beside a crackling fire in the Federal Room. The manor offers many diversions, such as croquet, badminton, rental boats, fishing, and crabbing right off the dock. Pam and Walt will gladly suggest nearby restaurants and historic sites.

The Inn at Montross
COURTHOUSE SQUARE, MONTROSS, VIRGINIA 22520

Tel: (804) 493-9097; (800) 321-0979
Hosts: Eileen and Michael Longman
Location: 46 mi. E of Fredericksburg
No. of Rooms: 6
No. of Private Baths: 6
Double/pb: $65–$125
Single/pb: $65–$100
Open: All year

Reduced Rates: Available
Breakfast: Continental
Other Meals: Available
Credit Cards: AMEX, DISC, MC, VISA
Pets: Sometimes
Children: Welcome
Smoking: Permitted
Social Drinking: Permitted

The original sections of the Inn at Montross date back over 300 years. Your hosts have decorated the rooms with a mixture of primitive and modern art, porcelains, antiques, and reproductions. Each guest room is furnished with four-poster beds, with extras such as bedside brandy and chocolates. The main floor boasts a magnificent grand piano, which guests are welcome to use. A small lounge with television and a spacious living room are available for relaxing. Your hosts serve home-baked croissants, fresh fruit, muffins, or Danish for breakfast. Bountiful meals at affordable prices are served in the Colonial dining rooms, which are open to the public. The Longmans will be glad to direct you to Stratford Hall, Ingleside Winery, and Westmoreland State Park. Golf and fishing can be enjoyed nearby, and there are tennis courts on the grounds.

The Garden and the Sea Inn ✪
P.O. BOX 275, NEW CHURCH, VIRGINIA 23415

Tel: (804) 824-0672
Best Time to Call: 10 AM–3 PM
Hosts: Victoria Olian and Jack Betz
Location: 10 mi. W of Chincoteague
No. of Rooms: 2
No. of Private Baths: 2
Double/pb: $85–$105
Open: Apr. 1–Oct. 31
Reduced Rates: Available
Breakfast: Continental

Other Meals: Available
Credit Cards: AMEX, DC, DISC, MC, VISA
Pets: No
Children: Welcome
Smoking: Permitted
Social Drinking: Permitted
Minimum Stay: 2 nights holiday weekends
Airport/Station Pickup: Yes

Known as Bloxom's Tavern when it was built in 1802, this historic building eventually served as New Church's first voting precinct. With the addition of porches at the turn of the century, the tavern became a picturesque Victorian country home. Today this B&B offers fine dining and elegant lodging in the tradition of a small French inn. You'll be offered snacks upon arrival, afternoon tea, and Continental breakfast. But save room for dinner: using local produce and fresh seafood, Victoria and Jack prepare a carefully selected menu. To gratify your other senses, your hosts sponsor art shows and chamber music concerts.

A Touch of Country Bed & Breakfast ✪
9329 CONGRESS STREET, NEW MARKET, VIRGINIA 22844

Tel: (703) 740-8030	Open: **All year**
Hosts: **Jean Schoellig and Dawn Kasow**	Breakfast: **Full**
Location: **18 mi. N of Harrisonburg**	Credit Cards: **MC, VISA**
No. of Rooms: **6**	Pets: **No**
No. of Private Baths: **6**	Children: **Welcome, over 12**
Double/pb: **$65**	Smoking: **No**
Single/pb: **$55**	Social Drinking: **Permitted**

This restored 1870s home is located in a historic town in the beautiful Shenandoah Valley. It displays the original hardwood floors and is decorated with antiques and collectibles in a country motif. You'll start your day with a hearty breakfast of pancakes, meats, gravy, and biscuits. Daydream on the porch swings or stroll through town with its charming shops, dine at a variety of restaurants or visit the legendary New Market Battlefield and Park. Close by are Skyline Drive, George Washington National Forest, caverns, and vineyards.

Oak Spring Farm and Vineyard ✪
ROUTE 1, BOX 356, RAPHINE, VIRGINIA 24472

Tel: (703) 377-2398	Breakfast: **Continental**
Best Time to Call: **9 AM–5 PM**	Credit Cards: **MC, VISA**
Hosts: **Jim and Pat Tichenor**	Pets: **No**
Location: **55 mi. S of Charlottesville**	Children: **Welcome, over 16**
No. of Rooms: **3**	Smoking: **No**
No. of Private Baths: **3**	Minimum Stay: **Parents weekends**
Double/pb: **$55–$65**	**(September–October), graduation**
Single/pb: **$45–$55**	**(May–June)**
Open: **All year**	Airport/Station Pickup: **Yes**

This is a 40-acre working farm and vineyard. There are wonderful views of the Blue Ridge Mountains, an orchard, gardens, lawns, and a pasture with a herd of friendly burros. Located halfway between historic Lexington and Staunton, this B&B offers historical sites and antique shops to visit and opportunities to ski or swim. The plantation house was built in 1826 and has been completely restored and renovated—including air-conditioning. It is filled with family heirlooms and treasures collected during Jim's 26 years of worldwide military service. Virginia Military Institute and Washington and Lee University are nearby.

Bensonhouse of Richmond and Williamsburg ✪
2036 MONUMENT AVENUE, RICHMOND, VIRGINIA 23220

Tel: (804) 353-6900
Best Time to Call: 9–11 AM; 2–6 PM
Coordinator: **Lyn Benson**
States/Regions Covered:
  **Fredericksburg, Northern Neck,
  Petersburg, Richmond, Williamsburg**
Descriptive Directory: **$3**

Rates (Single/Double):
  Modest: **$60 / $65**
  Average: **$68 / $72**
  Luxury: **$75–$105 / $85–$125**
Credit Cards: **MC, VISA**
Minimum Stay: **Williamsburg: 2 nights weekends**

Houses and inns on Lyn's list are of architectural or historic interest, offering charm in the relaxed comfort of a home. Most have private bath accommodations, and some have fireplaces and/or Jacuzzis. The hosts delight in guiding you to the best sights and advising you on how to get the most out of your visit.

The Emmanuel Hutzler House ✪
2036 MONUMENT AVENUE, RICHMOND, VIRGINIA 23220

Tel: (804) 353-6900
Best Time to Call: 11AM–6 PM
Host: **John E. Richardson**
Location: **1½ mi. from Rte. I-95/64**
No. of Rooms: **4**
No. of Private Baths: **4**
Double/pb: **$89–$135**
Open: **All year**

Reduced Rates: **Corporate, 5%, seniors**
Breakfast: **Full**
Credit Cards: **AMEX, MC, VISA**
Pets: **No**
Children: **Welcome, over 12**
Smoking: **No**
Social Drinking: **Permitted**

This spacious Italian Renaissance inn, built in 1914, recently received a total renovation. The classical interior has raised mahogany paneling, lavish wainscoting, leaded glass windows, and, on the first floor, coffered ceilings with dropped beams. Mahogany bookcases flank the marble fireplace in the living room, where guests can relax and converse. The generously sized guest rooms, all on the second floor, are furnished with antiques and handsome draperies; two rooms have fireplaces. The central location makes this an ideal location for either a midweek business trip or a weekend getaway.

The Mary Bladon House ✪

381 WASHINGTON AVENUE SOUTH WEST, ROANOKE, VIRGINIA 24016

Tel: (703) 344-5361
Hosts: **Mr. and Mrs W. D. Bestpitch**
Location: **220 mi. S of Washington, D.C.**
No. of Rooms: **3**
No. of Private Baths: **3**
Double/pb: **$75**
Single/pb: **$60**
Suites: **$110**
Open: **All year**

Reduced Rates: **Available**
Breakfast: **Full**
Credit Cards: **MC, VISA**
Pets: **No**
Children: **Welcome**
Smoking: **No**
Social Drinking: **Permitted**
Airport/Station Pickup: **Yes**
Foreign Languages: **German**

The Mary Bladon House is located in the old southwest neighborhood, just five minutes away from the Blue Ridge Parkway. This Victorian dates back to the late 1800s and has four porches. Although the original brass light fixtures are still in place, the decor in the public rooms is constantly changing, with works by local artists and craftsmen. All the rooms are elegantly appointed with antiques, and guest rooms feature fresh flowers in season.

High Meadows—Virginia's Vineyard Inn ✪

ROUTE 4, BOX 6, ROUTE 20 SOUTH, SCOTTSVILLE, VIRGINIA 24590

Tel: (804) 286-2218
Hosts: **Peter Sushka and Jae Abbitt**
Location: **17 mi. S of Charlottesville**
No. of Rooms: **12**
No. of Private Baths: **12**
Double/pb: **$85–$105**
Single/pb: **$85**
Suites: **$110–$140**
Open: **All year**

Breakfast: **Full**
Other Meals: **Available**
Pets: **Sometimes**
Children: **Welcome, over 8**
Smoking: **No**
Social Drinking: **Permitted**
Foreign Languages: **French**
Minimum Stay: **2 nights weekends Apr., May, Sept., Nov., and all holidays**

This Virginia Historic Landmark is situated on 23 acres, and comprises dwellings built in 1832 and 1882 that are joined by a longitudinal "grand" hall. Recently restored, it is furnished with carefully chosen period antiques. You will enjoy the many fireplaces and whirlpool bath, the lovely flower gardens, the Pinot Noir vineyard, the ponds, and the gazebo. Bicycles are available for local touring. Jefferson's Monticello, Monroe's Ash Lawn, the University of Virginia, and James River tubing, fishing, and canoeing are nearby. Peter is a retired naval submariner; Jae's a financial analyst with the Securities Exchange Commission; son Peter plays classical guitar. Virginia wine with hors d'oeuvres is an evening tradition.

Isle of Wight Inn ✪
1607 SOUTH CHURCH STREET, SMITHFIELD, VIRGINIA 23430

Tel: **(804) 357-3176**
Best Time to Call: **10 AM–9 PM**
Hosts: **Bob Hart, Sam Earl, and Sharon
  Blackwell**
Location: **27 mi. W of Norfolk**
No. of Rooms: **10**
No. of Private Baths: **10**
Double/pb: **$59**
Single/pb: **$49**

Suites: **$79–$99**
Open: **All year**
Breakfast: **Full**
Credit Cards: **AMEX, MC, VISA**
Pets: **No**
Children: **Welcome**
Smoking: **No**
Social Drinking: **Permitted**

The Isle of Wight Inn is a sprawling brick Colonial, one mile from downtown Smithfield. Inside you will find antiques, reproductions, and motifs of glass, wood, and wicker. Wake up to fresh coffee and Smithfield's own ham rolls. This riverport town has numerous historic homes that will surely delight you. Williamsburg, Norfolk, and Virginia Beach are less than an hour's drive from the house. An antiques shop is on the premises.

The Manor at Taylor's Store ✪
ROUTE 1, BOX 533, SMITH MOUNTAIN LAKE, VIRGINIA 24184

Tel: **(703) 721-3951**
Hosts: **Lee and Mary Lynn Tucker**
Location: **20 mi. E of Roanoke**
No. of Rooms: **6**
No. of Private Baths: **4**
Double/pb: **$65–$100**
Guest Cottage: **$85–$175; sleeps 2–8**
Open: **All year**
Reduced Rates: **$340–$700 weekly
  for cottage**

Breakfast: **Full**
Credit Cards: **MC, VISA**
Pets: **No**
Children: **Welcome in cottage**
Smoking: **Cottage only**
Social Drinking: **Permitted**
Airport/Station Pickup: **Yes**

Situated on 100 acres in the foothills of the Blue Ridge Mountains, this elegant manor house, circa 1799, was the focus of a prosperous tobacco plantation. It has been restored and refurbished, and you'll experience the elegance of the past combined with the comfort of tasteful modernization. The estate invites hiking, swimming, and fishing. The sun room, parlor, and hot tub are special spots for relaxing. Smith Mountain Lake, with its seasonal sporting activity, is five miles away. Breakfast, designed for the health-conscious, features a variety of fresh gourmet selections.

Kenwood ✪

235 EAST BEVERLEY STREET, STAUNTON, VIRGINIA 24401

Tel: **(703) 886-0524**
Hosts: **Liz and Ed Kennedy**
Location: **30 mi. W of Charlottesville**
No. of Rooms: **4**
No. of Private Baths: **2**
Max. No. Sharing Bath: **4**
Double/pb: **$70**
Single/pb: **$60**
Double/sb: **$60**

Single/sb: **$50**
Open: **All year**
Breakfast: **Full**
Credit Cards: **MC, VISA**
Pets: **No**
Children: **Welcome**
Smoking: **Permitted**
Social Drinking: **Permitted**
Airport/Station Pickup: **Yes**

Kenwood, a stately brick Colonial revival home built in 1910, has been restored and decorated with floral wallpapers and antique furniture. The Woodrow Wilson Birthplace—and its museum and research library—are next door. Staunton boasts several other museums and numerous antique shops, and it's only a half-hour drive to attractions like Monticello and the Virginia Horse Center. Select your destinations over such breakfast fare as fresh seasonal fruit and homemade baked goods.

The Sampson Eagon Inn ✪

238 EAST BEVERLEY STREET, STAUNTON, VIRGINIA 24401

Tel: **(703) 886-8200**
Best Time to Call: **10 AM–10 PM**
Hosts: **Laura and Frank Mattingly**
Location: **35 mi. W of Charlottesville**
No. of Rooms: **4**
No. of Private Baths: **4**
Double/pb: **$75**
Single/pb: **$65**
Suites: **$80–$85**
Open: **All year**
Reduced Rates: **10% seniors; $10 less December–February; 20% corporate weekdays**

Breakfast: **Full**
Pets: **No**
Children: **Welcome, over 12**
Smoking: **No**
Social Drinking: **Permitted**
Minimum Stay: **Weekends in Oct.; 4th weekend in May**
Station Pickup: **Yes**

Located in Staunton's historic Gospel Hill District, this recently restored Greek Revival mansion (circa 1840) provides affordable luxury accommodations. The canopied beds and other antique furnishings reflect the various periods of the building's past. Woodrow Wilson Birthplace and Museum and Mary Baldwin Cottage are adjacent to the inn, and a variety of restaurants, antique shops, and gift shops are within walking distance. Nearby, guests can enjoy the Museum of American Frontier Culture, Statler Brother Complex and Museum, and many other natural and historic attractions in the central Shenandoah Valley. If you're interested, your hosts will be glad to discuss old house restoration, Frank's part-time occupation.

Thornrose House at Gypsy Hill ✪
531 THORNROSE AVENUE, STAUNTON, VIRGINIA 24401

Tel: **(703) 885-7026**
Best Time to Call: **Anytime**
Hosts: **Suzanne and Otis Huston**
Location: **3½ mi. from Rte. I-81, Exit 222**
No. of Rooms: **5**
No. of Private Baths: **5**
Double/pb: **$50–$65**
Single/pb: **$40–$55**
Open: **All year**

Reduced Rates: **Available**
Breakfast: **Full**
Pets: **No**
Children: **Welcome**
Smoking: **No**
Social Drinking: **Permitted**
Minimum Stay: **3 days over July 4th; 2 days October weekends**
Airport/Station Pickup: **Yes**

This 1912 Georgian Revival home is six blocks from the center of Victorian Staunton and adjacent to 300-acre Gypsy Hill Park, which has facilities for golf, tennis, swimming, and summer concerts. A wraparound veranda and Greek colonnades grace the exterior of the house. Inside, there's a cozy parlor with a fireplace and a grand piano. A relaxed, leisurely breakfast is set out in the dining room, which offers the comfort of a fireplace on chilly mornings. Local attractions include Blue Ridge National Park, Natural Chimneys, Skyline Drive, Woodrow Wilson's birthplace, and the Museum of American Frontier Culture.

The Duck Farm Inn
P.O. BOX 787, RTES. 227 AND 639, URBANNA, VIRGINIA 23175

Tel: **(804) 758-5685**
Host: **Fleming Godden**
Location: **55 mi. E of Richmond**
No. of Rooms: **6**
No. of Private Baths: **2**
Max. No. Sharing Bath: **4**
Double/pb: **$75**
Single/pb: **$60**
Double/sb: **$65**
Single/sb: **$50**

Guest Cottage: **$150; sleeps 6**
Open: **All year**
Reduced Rates: **After first visit**
Breakfast: **Full**
Pets: **No**
Children: **Welcome**
Smoking: **No**
Social Drinking: **Permitted**
Airport/Station Pickup: **Yes**

This elegant, contemporary inn is situated on Virginia's middle peninsula, surrounded by 800 secluded acres and bordered by the Rappahannock River. Guests are welcome to hike along the shore or through the woods, fish in the river, sunbathe on the private beach, lounge on the deck, or retire to the cozy library with a good book. Fleming has traveled all over the world and thoroughly enjoys her role as full-time innkeeper. One of her breakfast menus consists of seasonal fresh fruit, jumbo blueberry muffins, cheese-and-egg scramble served with spiced sausage, and a variety of hot beverages.

Angie's Bed & Breakfast ✪
3023 LITTLE ISLAND ROAD, VIRGINIA BEACH, VIRGINIA 23456

Tel: **(804) 426-7824**
Best Time to Call: **After 6 PM**
Host: **Angie Cross**
Location: **12 mi. S of Virginia Beach**
No. of Rooms: **3**
Max. No. Sharing Bath: **4**
Double/sb: **$85**
Single/sb: **$85**

Open: **All year**
Reduced Rates: **Oct.–Apr.; 10%, seniors**
Breakfast: **Continental**
Pets: **No**
Children: **Welcome, under 2**
Smoking: **No**
Social Drinking: **Permitted**
Minimum Stay: **2 nights**

Spend a couple of days, or even a week, at this quiet haven at Sandbridge, a family-type beach along the canal between the bay and the ocean. There are a golf course and a marine science museum in the area, but you may never want to leave the premises. Angie provides guests with bikes, beach gear, a fishing dock, a hot tub, and comfortable air-conditioned rooms equipped with cable TV. Twin, double, and queen-size beds are available. The Continental breakfast buffet consists of fresh seasonal fruit, yummy baked goods, cereal, juice, coffee, and tea.

Angie's Guest Cottage ✪
302 24TH STREET, VIRGINIA BEACH, VIRGINIA 23451

Tel: **(804) 428-4690**
Best Time to Call: **10 AM–10 PM**
Host: **Barbara G. Yates**
Location: **20 mi. E of Norfolk**
No. of Rooms: **6**
No. of Private Baths: **1**
Max. No. Sharing Bath: **4**
Double/pb: **$64**
Single/pb: **$54**
Double/sb: **$44–$60**
Single/sb: **$36–$50**

Guest Cottage: **$375–$500 weekly; sleeps 2–6**
Open: **Apr. 1–Oct. 1**
Reduced Rates: **Off-season**
Breakfast: **Continental**
Pets: **Sometimes**
Children: **Welcome (crib)**
Smoking: **No**
Social Drinking: **Permitted**
Minimum Stay: **2 nights**

Just a block from the beach, shops, and restaurants is this bright and comfortable beach house. Former guests describe it as: "cozy, cute, and clean." Deep-sea fishing, nature trails, and harbor tours are but a few things to keep you busy. Freshly baked croissants in various flavors are a breakfast delight. You are welcome to use the sundeck, barbecue, and picnic tables.

The Foster-Harris House ✪
P.O. BOX 333, WASHINGTON, VIRGINIA 22747

Tel: **(703) 675-3757; (800) 666-0153**
Hosts: **Patrick Foster and Camille
  Harris**
Location: **65 mi. W of Washington,
  D.C.**
No. of Rooms: **4**
No. of Private Baths: **3**
Double/pb: **$85**
Single/pb: **$75**
Double/sb: **$70**

Single/sb: **$60**
Suites: **$105**
Open: **All year**
Reduced Rates: **3 nights or more**
Breakfast: **Full**
Pets: **Sometimes**
Children: **Welcome**
Smoking: **Permitted**
Social Drinking: **Permitted**

Located on the edge of the historic village of Washington, Virginia, this Victorian home offers marvelous views of the Blue Ridge Mountains and country estates. Rooms are furnished with antiques, down comforters, queen-size beds, plush bathrobes, and fresh flowers. One room has a fireplace stove and whirlpool bath. A full gourmet breakfast is served in the formal dining room. For other meals, try five-star dining at a world-famous inn just three blocks away. Your hosts also recommend hiking, antiquing, and visiting wineries, the Skyline Drive, Luray Caverns, Civil War battlefields, and numerous other area attractions.

Sycamore Hill House & Gardens
ROUTE 1, BOX 978, WASHINGTON, VIRGINIA 22747

Tel: **(703) 675-3046**
Best Time to Call: **9 AM–9 PM**
Hosts: **Kerri and Stephen Wagner**
Location: **66 mi. SW of Washington,
  D.C.**
No. of Rooms: **3**
No. of Private Baths: **3**
Double/pb: **$90–$120**
Open: **All year**
Reduced Rates: **10% 4-night stay
  Mon.–Fri. only**

Breakfast: **Full**
Credit Cards: **MC, VISA**
Pets: **No**
Children: **Welcome, over 14**
Smoking: **No**
Social Drinking: **Permitted**
Minimum Stay: **2-day minimum on
  3-day holiday weekends**
Airport/Station Pickup: **Yes**

Atop Menefee Mountain in the foothills of the Blue Ridge Mountains lies this contemporary stone manor home. The National Wildlife Federation has designated the property—52 rolling acres of flowering gardens and natural woodlands—a wildlife habitat. One sixty-five-foot veranda presents breathtaking views, while the elegant modern interior offers gracious accommodations. Stephen is an internationally published free-lance illustrator whose artworks adorn the walls of every room. Kerri, a former agricultural lobbyist, enjoys Asian needlework and can direct you to nearby vineyards, canoeing sites, hiking areas, and antique shops.

The Iris Inn ✪

191 CHINQUAPIN DRIVE, WAYNESBORO, VIRGINIA 22980

Tel: **(703) 943-1991**
Best Time to Call: **10 AM–8 PM**
Hosts: **Wayne and Iris Karl**
Location: **25 mi. W of Charlottesville**
No. of Rooms: **7**
No. of Private Baths: **7**
Double/pb: **$75–$85**
Single/pb: **$65**
Open: **All year**
Reduced Rates: **10% seniors, Sun.–
   Thurs.; corporate, Sun.–Thurs.**

Breakfast: **Full**
Credit Cards: **MC, VISA**
Pets: **No**
Children: **Welcome, by arrangement**
Smoking: **No**
Social Drinking: **Permitted**
Minimum Stay: **2 nights weekends**
Airport: **Yes**

The charm and grace of southern living in a totally modern facility, nestled in a wooded tract on the western slope of the Blue Ridge overlooking the historic Shenandoah Valley—that's what awaits you at the Iris Inn in Waynesboro. It's ideal for a weekend retreat, a refreshing change for the business traveler, and a tranquil spot for the tourist to spend a night or a week. Guest rooms are spacious, comfortably furnished, and delightfully decorated in nature and wildlife motifs. Each room has private bath and individual temperature control.

The Travel Tree ✪

P.O. BOX 838, WILLIAMSBURG, VIRGINIA 23187

Tel: **(804) 253-1571; (800) 989-1571**
Best Time to Call: **6–9 PM, weekdays**
Coordinators: **Joann Proper and
   Sheila Zubkoff**
States/Regions Covered:
   Williamsburg, Jamestown, Yorktown

Rates (Single/Double):
   Modest: **$50–$65**
   Average: **$70–$90**
   Luxury: **$95–$110**
Credit Cards: **No**

You will thoroughly enjoy Colonial Williamsburg, historic Jamestown and Yorktown, Busch Gardens, and Carter's Grove Plantation. Your bedroom might be furnished with four-poster beds and antiques, or be tucked under the eaves in a wooded setting, or be a two-room suite with a private entrance. Other choices are, of course, available.

Blue Bird Haven B&B ✪

8691 BARHAMSVILLE ROAD, WILLIAMSBURG-TOANO, VIRGINIA 23168

Tel: **(804) 566-0177**
Best Time to Call: **Early mornings**
Hosts: **June and Ed Cottle**
Location: **9 mi. N of Williamsburg**

No. of Rooms: **3**
No. of Private Baths: **2**
Max. No. Sharing Bath: **4**
Double/pb: **$48**

Double/sb: **$38**
Suites: **$58**
Open: **All year**
Breakfast: **Full**
Other Meals: **Available**

Pets: **Sometimes**
Children: **Welcome**
Smoking: **Permitted**
Social Drinking: **Permitted**

June and Ed welcome you to their ranch-style home, located 20 minutes from Colonial Williamsburg. Guest accommodations, located in a private wing, feature traditional furnishings. June is interested in many kinds of handcrafts and has decorated the rooms with one-of-a-kind quilts, spreads, rugs, and pictures. Breakfast includes a southern-style assortment of Virginia ham, spoon bread, red-eye gravy, blueberry pancakes, fresh fruits, home-baked biscuits, and granola. Blue Bird Haven is convenient to Busch Gardens, James River Plantations, and Civil War battlefields. After a full day of seeing the sights, you are welcome to enjoy some of June's evening desserts.

Colonial Capital Bed & Breakfast ✪
501 RICHMOND ROAD, WILLIAMSBURG, VIRGINIA 23185

Tel: **(800) 776-0570**
Hosts: **Barbara and Phil Craig**
Location: **2.5 mi. from I-64, Exit 238**
No. of Rooms: **5**
No. of Private Baths: **5**
Double/pb: **$90**
Single/pb: **$70**
Suites: **$145; sleeps 4**
Open: **All year**

Reduced Rates: **15% Jan. 1–Mar. 31**
Breakfast: **Full**
Credit Cards: **MC, VISA**
Pets: **No**
Children: **Welcome, over 6**
Smoking: **Permitted**
Social Drinking: **Permitted**
Airport/Station Pickup: **Yes**

Three blocks from the historic area, Barbara and Phil offer a warm welcome to guests in their Colonial Revival, circa 1926, three-story home. Decorated with period antiques, oriental rugs, and most of the original lighting and plumbing fixtures, rooms are furnished with four-poster beds, many crowned with charming canopies. In the morning you can look forward to such treats as a soufflé, French toast, or fluffy omelet, served either in the sunny solarium or in the formal dining room. After a full day that might include a visit to Jamestown, Yorktown, and some of the state's finest plantations, you can enjoy complimentary snacks and visit in the parlor. Games, books, and puzzles are provided for your pleasure.

For Cant Hill Guest Home
4 CANTERBURY LANE, WILLIAMSBURG, VIRGINIA 23185

Tel: **(804) 229-6623**
Best Time to Call: **After 5 PM; weekends**

Hosts: **Martha and Hugh Easler**
No. of Rooms: **2**
No. of Private Baths: **2**

Double/pb: **$55**
Open: **All year**
Breakfast: **Continental**
Pets: **No**

Children: **Welcome, over 10**
Smoking: **No**
Social Drinking: **Permitted**

Martha and Hugh's home is in a secluded, wooded setting overlooking a lake, which is part of the campus of William and Mary. It is a short walk to the restored district. The guest rooms are attractively decorated, accented with homemade quilts in winter. Restaurants to suit every budget are nearby. Your hosts will be happy to make dinner reservations for you and provide helpful information on the area's attractions.

Fox Grape Bed & Breakfast ✪
701 MONUMENTAL AVENUE, WILLIAMSBURG, VIRGINIA 23185

Tel: **(804) 229-6914; (800) 292-3699**
Best Time to Call: **9 AM–9 PM**
Hosts: **Bob and Pat Orendorff**
Location: **2 mi. from I-64, Exit 238**
No. of Rooms: **4**
No. of Private Baths: **4**
Double/pb: **$78**
Single/pb: **$78**

Open: **All year**
Reduced Rates: **10% seniors**
Breakfast: **Continental**
Pets: **No**
Children: **Welcome**
Smoking: **Permitted**
Social Drinking: **Permitted**
Station Pickup: **Yes**

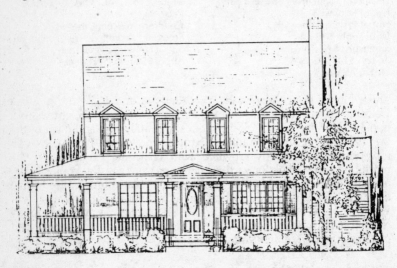

Warm hospitality awaits you just a seven-minute walk north of Virginia's restored Colonial capital. Furnishings include counted cross-stitch pieces, antiques, stained glass, stenciled walls, duck decoys, and a cup-plate collection. Pat enjoys doing counted cross-stitch. Bob carves walking sticks and makes stained-glass windows.

Governor's Trace ✪
303 CAPITOL LANDING ROAD, WILLIAMSBURG, VIRGINIA 23185

Tel: **(804) 229-7552**
Best Time to Call: **9 AM–10 PM**
Hosts: **Sue and Dick Lake**
Location: **2 mi. from I-64**
No. of Rooms: **2**
No. of Private Baths: **2**
Double/pb: **$85–$115**
Single/pb: **$85–$115**
Open: **All year**

Breakfast: **Continental**
Credit Cards: **MC, VISA**
Pets: **No**
Children: **No**
Smoking: **No**
Social Drinking: **Permitted**
Minimum Stay: **2 nights Apr.–Dec.**
  weekends only

This Georgian brick home, built on the site of a former peanut plantation, lets you step back into history—Colonial Williamsburg—just one door away. Choose a room with a waist-high, king-size four-poster bed and a working fireplace, or a room with a Colonial canopy bed and private screened-in porch. Featured on the back cover of the 1992 edition of *Bed & Breakfast U.S.A.* A delightful breakfast will be served by candlelight in the privacy of your antique-filled room. Your hosts, Sue and Dick, will help you forget the modern world's hectic pace and relax in an 18th-century atmosphere.

Legacy of Williamsburg Tavern
930 JAMESTOWN ROAD, WILLIAMSBURG, VIRGINIA 23185-3917

Tel: **(804) 220-0524; (800) 962-4722**
Hosts: **Ed and Mary Ann Lucas**
Location: **2 mi. from Rte. 64, Exit 59**
No. of Rooms: **4**
No. of Private Baths: **4**
Double/pb: **$75**
Suite: **$130**

Open: **All year**
Breakfast: **Full**
Credit Cards: **MC, VISA**
Pets: **No**
Children: **No**
Smoking: **No**
Social Drinking: **Permitted**
Airport/Station Pickup: **Yes**

Ed and Mary Ann have furnished their 18th-century-style home with lovely antiques from that era. The suite is the ultimate in privacy, and features a canopy bed in the bedroom and a comfortable sofa facing a fireplace in the living room. Flowers, fruit, wine, and candy will make you feel welcome. You'll awaken to the aroma of freshly baked breads, just the beginning of a hearty breakfast. Afterward, stroll across the street to the campus of William and Mary College, walk to the restored area, or drive to Busch Gardens nearby.

Liberty Rose B&B ✪
1022 JAMESTOWN ROAD, WILLIAMSBURG, VIRGINIA 23185

Tel: **(800) 545-1825**
Best Time to Call: **9 AM–9 PM**

Hosts: **Brad and Sandi Hirz**
No. of Rooms: **4**

No. of Private Baths: **4**
Double/pb: **$90–$145**
Suites: **$125–$155**
Open: **All year**
Breakfast: **Full**
Credit Cards: **MC, VISA**

Pets: **No**
Children: **Welcome, over 7**
Smoking: **No**
Social Drinking: **Permitted**
Minimum Stay: **Weekends**
Airport/Station Pickup: **Yes**

This enchanting old home is one of Williamsburg's most romantic—Brad and Sandi created their B&B as a honeymoon project! Antiques from all periods fill the Liberty Rose. In the guest rooms, comfortable queen-size poster beds are draped with fringed reproduction damasks and topped with silk-covered goose-down duvets. Alongside the bed, in an old-fashioned armoire, you'll find a TV-VCR. The luxurious baths have claw-footed tubs, marble showers, and ample supplies of robes, towels, and bubble bath. And everywhere you'll notice little extras, such as a dish full of chocolates, complimentary soft drinks, freshly baked chocolate chip cookies, and a long-stemmed silk rose that's yours to keep.

Newport House ✪
710 SOUTH HENRY STREET, WILLIAMSBURG, VIRGINIA 23185

Tel: **(804) 229-1775**
Best Time to Call: **8–10 AM**
Hosts: **John and Cathy Millar**
No. of Rooms: **2**
No. of Private Baths: **2**
Double/pb: **$90–$120**
Open: **All year**

Breakfast: **Full**
Pets: **No**
Children: **Welcome**
Smoking: **No**
Social Drinking: **Permitted**
Airport/Station Pickup: **Yes**
Foreign Languages: **French**

Constructed in 1988, this house is based on blueprints drawn in 1756. In an unusual touch, the wood siding is cut to resemble stone. John, a former museum director, has furnished the house with period antiques and top-quality reproductions; many of the pieces are for sale. On Tuesday nights, the past really comes alive, as your hosts sponsor Colonial-style country dancing. Guests are welcome to participate, and no experience is necessary. Waffles, eggs, baked apples, and other breakfast favorites are served in the morning.

War Hill ✪
4560 LONG HILL ROAD, WILLIAMSBURG, VIRGINIA 23188

Tel: **(804) 565-0248**
Best Time to Call: **9 AM–9 PM**
Hosts: **Shirley, Bill, and Will Lee**
Location: **2 mi. from Williamsburg**
No. of Rooms: **5**
No. of Private Baths: **5**
Double/pb: **$65–$80**
Suite: **$85; sleeps 2**

Cottage: **$100; sleeps 2**
Open: **All year**
Breakfast: **Full**
Credit Cards: **MC, VISA**
Pets: **No**
Children: **Welcome**
Smoking: **No**
Social Drinking: **Permitted**

War Hill is situated in the center of a 32-acre working farm, just three miles from the tourist attractions. Built in 1968, this Colonial replica couples the charm of yesteryear with today's contemporary conveniences. The suite is composed of two bedrooms and a bath. The wide heart-pine floors came from an old school, the stairs from a church, the overhead beams from a barn; the oak mantel is over 200 years old. Fruits from a variety of trees in the orchard are yours to pick in season. In autumn, Shirley and Bill serve delicious homemade applesauce and cider. Angus show cattle graze in the pasture, and the sounds you'll hear are crickets, frogs, owls, and the morning crowing of the rooster.

Azalea House ✪
551 SOUTH MAIN STREET, WOODSTOCK, VIRGINIA 22664

Tel: (703) 459-3500
Hosts: Margaret and Price McDonald
Location: 35 mi. N of Harrisonburg
No. of Rooms: 3
Max. No. Sharing Bath: 3
Double/sb: $45–$65
Open: All year

Breakfast: Full
Credit Cards: AMEX, MC, VISA
Pets: No
Children: Welcome
Smoking: No
Social Drinking: Permitted

This spacious home, built in the early 1890s, served as a parsonage for 70 years. It has been restored following its Victorian tradition and has porches, bay windows, and a white picket fence—in spring, one hundred blooming azaleas enhance its beauty. The interior is made particularly lovely with family heirlooms and pretty color schemes. Azalea House is within walking distance of fine restaurants, antique shops, and an art gallery. It is convenient to wineries, orchards, trails, horseback riding, and fishing. Air-conditioning assures your summer comfort.

The Country Fare
402 NORTH MAIN STREET, WOODSTOCK, VIRGINIA 22664

Tel: (703) 459-4828
Best Time to Call: 7–11 AM; 6–10 PM
Host: Bette Hallgren
Location: 35 mi. S of Winchester
No. of Rooms: 3
No. of Private Baths: 1
Max. No. Sharing Bath: 3
Double/pb: $65

Double/sb: $45–$55
Single/sb: $35
Open: All year
Breakfast: Continental
Pets: No
Children: Welcome, by arrangement
Smoking: No
Social Drinking: Permitted

A small cozy inn, circa 1772, The Country Fare is one of Shenandoah County's oldest homes. It is restored and carefully preserved and has wide pine floorboards upstairs, original doors and hardware, and walls hand-stenciled with original designs. Nana's Room boasts hand-painted furniture and a private bath. Two other bedrooms—one with a queen-size, the other with a full-size bed—share an old-fashioned bathroom with a claw-footed tub. Expanded Continental breakfast, served before the dining room's wood-burning stove, consists of seasonal fruits, juices, home-baked breads and muffins, and some of Nana's surprises. Your host will share information on the interesting sights and attractions of the valley.

For key to listings, see inside front or back cover.

✪ This star means that rates are guaranteed through December 31, 1993, to any guest making a reservation as a result of reading about the B&B in *Bed & Breakfast U.S.A.*—1993 edition.

Important! To avoid misunderstandings, always ask about cancellation policies when booking.

Please enclose a self-addressed, stamped, business-size envelope when contacting reservation services.

For more details on what you can expect in a B&B, see Chapter 1.

Always mention *Bed & Breakfast U.S.A.* when making reservations!

If no B&B is listed in the area you'll be visiting, use the form on page 733 to order a copy of our "List of New B&Bs."

We want to hear from you! Use the form on page 735.

WASHINGTON

Eastsound •   • Ferndale
Deer Harbor •   • Anacortes

      • Mt. Vernon

Port Townsend •   • Langley
    Sequim •   • Edmonds

Port Orchard •   • Seattle/Kirkland   • Leavenworth   Spokane •

    Tacoma •   • Ritzville

     • Olympia

                                      Clarkston •

• Cathlamet

       • White Salmon

Pacific Bed & Breakfast Agency ✪
701 NORTHWEST 60TH STREET, SEATTLE, WASHINGTON 98107

Tel: **(206) 784-0539**; fax **(206) 782-4036**
Best Time to Call: **9 AM–5 PM**
Coordinator: **Irmgard Castleberry**
States/Regions Covered: **Statewide; Canada—Vancouver, Victoria, British Columbia**

Rates (Single/Double):
  Modest: **$35 / $45**
  Average: **$45 / $55**
  Luxury: **$85 / $145**
Credit Cards: **AMEX, MC, VISA**
Minimum Stay: **2 nights in Seattle**
Descriptive Directory: **$5**

Victorians, contemporaries, island cottages, waterfront houses, and private suites with full kitchens are available. Most are close to downtown areas, near bus lines, in fine residential neighborhoods, or within walking distance of a beach. Many extras are included, such as pickup service, free use of laundry facilities, guided tours and more. The University of Washington and the University of Puget Sound are nearby. There is a $5 surcharge for one-night stays.

A Burrow's Bay B&B
4911 MACBETH DRIVE, ANACORTES, WASHINGTON 98221

Tel: **(206) 293-4792**
Hosts: **Beverly and Winfred Stocker**
Location: **92 mi. N of Seattle**
Suite: **$85; sleeps 2–6**
Open: **All year**
Breakfast: **Full**

Credit Cards: **MC, VISA**
Pets: **Sometimes**
Children: **Welcome**
Smoking: **No**
Social Drinking: **Permitted**
Airport/Station Pickup: **Yes**

Enjoy sweeping views of the San Juan Islands from this lovely contemporary Northwest home. The guest suite consists of a large sitting room with a view and a comfortable bedroom with a blue-and-tan motif and wall-to-wall carpeting. You are sure to enjoy the privacy and relaxation of having your own private deck, fireplace, TV, and a separate entrance. Beverly and Winfred offer an extensive menu from which you may select breakfast. They are located within walking distance of Washington Park, restaurants, and ferry rides to the nearby islands. Your hosts will be glad to provide touring advice for day trips to Victoria, B.C., Deception Pass, and Port Townsend.

The Channel House
2902 OAKES AVENUE, ANACORTES, WASHINGTON 98221

Tel: **(206) 293-9382**
Hosts: **Dennis and Patricia McIntyre**

Location: **65 mi. N of Seattle; 18 mi. W of I-5, Exit 230**

No. of Rooms: **6**
No. of Private Baths: **4**
Max. No. Sharing Bath: **4**
Double/pb: **$69–$89**
Double/sb: **$69**
Single/sb: **$59**
Open: **All year**

Breakfast: **Full**
Credit Cards: **DISC, MC, VISA**
Pets: **No**
Children: **Welcome, over 12**
Smoking: **No**
Social Drinking: **Permitted**

Built in 1902 by an Italian count, this three-story Victorian house has stained-glass windows, rare antiques, gracious ambience, and is in mint condition. The guest rooms have beautiful views of Puget Sound and the San Juan Islands. It's an ideal getaway for relaxing in the "cleanest corner of the country." Your hosts serve gourmet breakfasts in front of the fireplace. The communal hot tub is a treat after salmon fishing, tennis, or golf. And it's only minutes from the ferry for visiting Victoria, British Columbia.

The Country Keeper Bed & Breakfast Inn
61 MAIN STREET, CATHLAMET, WASHINGTON 98612

Tel: **(206) 795-3030**
Hosts: **Barbara and Tony West**
Location: **70 mi. NW of Portland, Ore.**
No. of Rooms: **4**
No. of Private Baths: **2**
Max. No. Sharing Bath: **3**
Double/pb: **$70–$75**
Single/pb: **$60–$65**
Double/sb: **$55–$65**
Single/sb: **$45–$65**

Open: **All year**
Reduced Rates: **Weekly; Sun.–Thurs. Nov.–Mar.**
Breakfast: **Full**
Credit Cards: **MC, VISA**
Pets: **No**
Children: **Welcome, over 10**
Smoking: **No**
Social Drinking: **Permitted**

Cathlamet is a scenic, quiet place on the Columbia River, within an easy drive of the Mount St. Helens National Monument. It is a fishing and farming community with a strong sense of history. The inn was built in 1907 from local timber; the fine work of craftsmen is seen in the inlaid floors and stained-glass windows. Breakfast is a romantic affair served by candlelight in the handsome dining room. Afterward, cycle the game refuge, play a round of golf or a set of tennis, fish, sail, or windsurf.

The Cliff House ✪
2000 WESTLAKE DRIVE, CLARKSTON, WASHINGTON 99403

Tel: **(509) 758-1267**
Best Time to Call: **8 AM–8 PM**
Hosts: **Doug and Sonia Smith**
Location: **8 mi. W of Clarkston**
No. of Rooms: **2**
No. of Private Baths: **2**

Double/pb: **$65–$75**
Single/pb: **$60–$70**
Open: **All year**
Reduced Rates: **10% seniors; weekly**
Breakfast: **Full**
Other Meals: **Available**

Credit Cards: **MC, VISA**
Pets: **No**
Children: **Welcome, over 10**
Smoking: **No**

Social Drinking: **Permitted**
Minimum Stay: **2 nights on weekends
   and holidays**
Airport/Station Pickup: **Yes**

Breathtaking is one of the best ways to describe The Cliff House's view of the Snake River, 500 feet below. Chief Timothy State Park, named for the Nez Percé Indian leader, lies along the river. Depending on the season, you may see geese, ducks, pheasant, deer, even an occasional bald eagle in the area. White-water rafting and jet boat trips along North America's deepest gorge, Hells Canyon, can be arranged. Your hosts set out different breakfasts each day; apple pancakes, waffles, and stratas are among the typical offerings.

Palmer's Chart House ✪
P.O. BOX 51, ORCAS ISLAND, DEER HARBOR, WASHINGTON 98243

Tel: **(206) 376-4231**
Hosts: **Majean and Don Palmer**
Location: **50 mi. N of Seattle**
No. of Rooms: **2**
No. of Private Baths: **2**
Double/pb: **$60–$70**
Single/pb: **$45**
Open: **All year**

Breakfast: **Full**
Other Meals: **Dinner: $7.50**
Pets: **No**
Children: **Welcome, over 10**
Smoking: **No**
Social Drinking: **Permitted**
Foreign Languages: **Spanish**

It's just an hour's ride on the Washington State ferry from Anacortes to Orcas Island. Seasoned travelers, Majean and Don know how to make your stay special. Each guest room has a private deck from which to view the harbor scene. Blueberry pancakes are a breakfast specialty. *Amante*, the 33-foot sloop, is available for sailing with Don, the skipper.

Turtleback Farm Inn
ROUTE 1, BOX 650, EASTSOUND, ORCAS ISLAND, WASHINGTON 98245

Tel: **(206) 376-4914**
Best Time to Call: **9 AM–9 PM**
Hosts: **William and Susan Fletcher**
Location: **60 mi. NW of Seattle**
No. of Rooms: **7**
No. of Private Baths: **7**
Double/pb: **$65–$155**
Single/pb: **$55–$145**
Open: **All year**

Reduced Rates: **Off-season**
Breakfast: **Full**
Credit Cards: **MC, VISA**
Pets: **No**
Children: **Welcome, over 8**
Smoking: **No**
Social Drinking: **Permitted**
Minimum Stay: **2 nights weekends,
   holidays, summer season**

This peaceful retreat is situated on 80 acres of meadow, pasture, ponds, and woods overlooking lovely Crow Valley. The farmhouse dates back to the early 1900s. Each bedroom is furnished with antiques and each bed boasts an unusual cotton-covered wool comforter. Breakfast might consist of strawberry crêpes, corn waffles, or a delectable quiche, served on Aynsley china with pretty crystal. Guests enjoy leisurely walks, bird-watching, the music of Mozart, relaxing on the expansive deck, and the pleasant peace of being pampered.

Aardvark House ☉
7219 LAKE BALLINGER WAY, EDMONDS, WASHINGTON 98026

Tel: (206) 778-7866
Best Time to Call: Anytime
Hosts: Jim and Arline Fahey
Location: 13 mi. N of Seattle
No. of Rooms: 3
Max. No. Sharing Bath: 4
Double/sb: $45

Single/sb: $38
Open: All year
Breakfast: Full
Pets: No
Children: Welcome (crib, high chair)
Smoking: No
Social Drinking: Permitted

This lovely lakefront home is within walking distance of a four-star restaurant and a city bus. Your hosts, a well-traveled retired Air Force couple, enjoy square dancing, outdoor living, gardening, and swimming. They'll be glad to take you on a cruise around Lake Ballinger on their barge. Breakfasts are varied, with home-grown raspberries, blueberries, and plums, and entrées like coddled eggs, omelets, and the house specialty, sourdough waffles cooked outdoors over a wood fire.

Driftwood Lane Bed and Breakfast ☉
724 DRIFTWOOD LANE, EDMONDS, WASHINGTON 98020

Tel: (206) 776-2686
Best Time to Call: 8–10 AM; 6–9 PM
Hosts: Ed and Lois Schaeffer
Location: 15 mi. N of Seattle
No. of Rooms: 1
No. of Private Baths: 1
Double/pb: $45

Single/pb: $40
Open: All year
Breakfast: Continental
Pets: No
Children: No
Smoking: No
Social Drinking: Permitted

This contemporary home in the heart of Edmonds reflects the relaxed life-style of the town, where you can take in Puget Sound and the snowcapped Olympic Mountains. Listen to the cry of sea gulls and watch nearby ferryboats as you walk along the beach or savor the excellent cuisine in town. Or catch a lingering sunset from the Schaeffers' deck. Their newly decorated guest room has a queen-size bed and an adjoining private bath. Continental breakfast is highlighted by fresh fruits, applesauce, and preserves from your hosts' own trees.

The Harrison House ✪
210 SUNSET AVENUE, EDMONDS, WASHINGTON 98020

Tel: **(206) 776-4748**
Hosts: **Jody and Harve Harrison**
Location: **15 mi. N of Seattle**
No. of Rooms: **2**
No. of Private Baths: **2**
Double/pb: **$45–$55**
Single/pb: **$35–$45**

Open: **All year**
Breakfast: **Continental**
Pets: **No**
Children: **No**
Smoking: **No**
Social Drinking: **Permitted**

This new, informal, waterfront home has a sweeping view of Puget Sound and the Olympic Mountains. It is a block north of the ferry dock and two blocks from the center of this historic town. Many fine restaurants are within walking distance. Your spacious room has a private deck, TV, wet bar, telephone, and king-size bed. The University of Washington is nearby.

Heather House ✪
1011 "B" AVENUE, EDMONDS, WASHINGTON 98020

Tel: **(206) 778-7233**
Best Time to Call: **5–6:30 PM**
Hosts: **Harry and Joy Whitcutt**
Location: **15 mi. N of Seattle**
No. of Rooms: **1**
No. of Private Baths: **1**
Double/pb: **$48.50**

Single/pb: **$38**
Open: **All year**
Breakfast: **Continental**
Pets: **No**
Children: **No**
Smoking: **No**
Social Drinking: **Permitted**

This contemporary home has a spectacular view of Puget Sound and the Olympic Mountains. The guest room has a comfortable king-size bed and opens onto a private deck. Joy and Harry are world travelers and enjoy their guests. The homemade jams, jellies, and marmalades are delicious. You can work off breakfast by walking a mile to the shops, beaches, and fishing pier.

Hudgens Haven ✪
9313 190 SOUTH WEST, EDMONDS, WASHINGTON 98020

Tel: **(206) 776-2202**
Best Time to Call: **4–8 PM**
Hosts: **Lorna and Edward Hudgens**
Location: **20 min. from downtown Seattle**
No. of Rooms: **1**
No. of Private Baths: **1**
Double/pb: **$45**

Single/pb: **$40**
Open: **Mar. 1–Nov. 30**
Breakfast: **Continental**
Pets: **No**
Children: **Welcome, over 10**
Smoking: **No**
Social Drinking: **Permitted**

Hudgens Haven is located in a picture postcard town on Puget Sound. Windows on the west side boast a lovely view of the waterfront. The guest room is furnished with antiques as well as a queen-size bed, rocker, and plenty of drawer space. Edmonds, located 20 minutes from downtown Seattle, is a former lumber town with interesting old houses and an abundance of small shops and excellent restaurants. Continental breakfast is included in the room rate, but for an additional $3.50 per person, Lorna will gladly prepare her hearty woodsman's breakfast.

The Maple Tree ✪
18313 OLYMPIC VIEW DRIVE, EDMONDS, WASHINGTON 98020

Tel: **(206) 774-8420**
Hosts: **Marion and Hellon Wilkerson**
Location: **15 mi. N of Seattle**
No. of Rooms: **1**
No. of Private Baths: **1**
Double/pb: **$45**
Single/pb: **$40**

Open: **All year**
Breakfast: **Continental**
Pets: **No**
Children: **Welcome, over 5**
Smoking: **No**
Social Drinking: **Permitted**

The Maple Tree is a beautifully restored older home with landscaped grounds. Located across the street from Puget Sound, it commands a stunning view of the Olympic Mountains. You're welcome to watch the activity on Puget Sound through the telescope in the solarium. Lounge on the brick patio or watch the sun set over the snowcapped mountains as you sip a glass of Washington State wine. Hellon and Marion enjoy having guests and exchanging travel experiences with them. Hellon loves to cook; both like to work in their rose garden.

Hill Top Bed and Breakfast
5832 CHURCH STREET, FERNDALE, WASHINGTON 98248

Tel: **(206) 384-3619**
Best Time to Call: **Mornings; evenings**
Hosts: **Paul and Doris Matz**
Location: **12 mi. S of Canadian border**
No. of Rooms: **3**
No. of Private Baths: **3**
Double/pb: **$44–$54**
Single/pb: **$39–$49**
Open: **All year**

Reduced Rates: **Available**
Breakfast: **Full**
Credit Cards: **MC, VISA**
Pets: **No**
Children: **Welcome (crib)**
Smoking: **No**
Social Drinking: **Permitted**
Airport/Station Pickup: **Yes**

Hill Top Bed and Breakfast is located in the Puget Sound area close to several beautiful state and local parks. The house overlooks Mt. Baker and the Cascade Mountain Range, and the view is especially nice from the patio. The house is decorated with Early American charm and the rooms have four-poster beds and homemade quilts to snuggle up in. The suite has a fireplace and kitchenette. Homemade breakfast specialties include coffee cakes, muffins, jams, applesauce and rhubarb.

This is a perfect spot for families and is convenient to Birch Bay, local islands, and Vancouver, Canada.

Shumway Mansion ☺
11410-99 PLACE NORTH EAST, KIRKLAND, WASHINGTON 98033

Tel: **(206) 823-2303**
Best Time to Call: **9 AM–7 PM**
Hosts: **Richard and Sallie Haris, and Julie Blakemore**
Location: **5 mi. NE of Seattle**
No. of Rooms: **8**
No. of Private Baths: **8**
Double/pb: **$65–$82**

Suites: **$95; sleeps 4**
Open: **All year**
Breakfast: **Full**
Credit Cards: **AMEX, MC, VISA**
Pets: **No**
Children: **Welcome, over 12**
Smoking: **No**
Social Drinking: **Permitted**

This stately 24-room mansion, built in 1909, has a regal presence overlooking Lake Washington. The eight antique-filled guest rooms, including a charming corner suite, pair today's comforts with intricately carved pieces from yesteryear. Richard and Sallie will indulge your palate with variety-filled breakfasts that always feature homemade scones and jams. Within a short distance are water and snow recreation, an athletic club, downtown Seattle, and lots of shopping. After a busy day, return "home" and relax in front of the fire with a seasonal treat.

Log Castle Bed & Breakfast ☺
3273 EAST SARATOGA ROAD, LANGLEY, WASHINGTON 98260

Tel: **(206) 321-5483**
Best Time to Call: **8 AM–9 PM**
Hosts: **Jack and Norma Metcalf**
Location: **40 mi. N of Seattle**
No. of Rooms: **4**
No. of Private Baths: **4**
Double/pb: **$80–$100**
Open: **All year**

Breakfast: **Full**
Credit Cards: **MC, VISA**
Pets: **No**
Children: **Welcome, over 11**
Smoking: **No**
Social Drinking: **No**
Airport/Station Pickup: **Yes**

You don't have to build your castle on the sand on Whidbey Island, because one already awaits you. The imaginative design of this log lodge includes an eight-sided tower where any modern-day princess would feel at home. Taredo wood stairways, leaded and stained-glass motifs, and comfortable furnishings create a rustic yet sophisticated atmosphere. The four guest rooms all offer beautiful views of the surrounding mountains and water. Relax beside a large stone fireplace, take a rowboat ride, or a long walk on the beach. Your hosts offer breads and cinnamon rolls right from the oven as part of a hearty breakfast served on a big, round, log table. Host Jack Metcalf is a state senator and also loves to entertain when he is not working at the legislature.

Run of the River ☉

P.O. BOX 448, 9308 EAST LEAVENWORTH ROAD, LEAVENWORTH, WASHINGTON 98826

Tel: **(509) 548-7171; (800) 288-6491**
Hosts: **Monty and Karen Turner**
Location: **110 mi. E of Seattle**
No. of Rooms: **5**
No. of Private Baths: **5**
Double/pb: **$90**
Suites: **$110–$140**

Open: **All year**
Breakfast: **Full**
Pets: **No**
Children: **No**
Smoking: **No**
Social Drinking: **Permitted**
Foreign Languages: **Spanish**

As its name suggests, this large log inn is set in splendid seclusion. While you soak in the hot tub on the deck, watch ducks, geese, eagles, herons, and pheasant from the area's bird refuge flock to the Icicle River. Wood-burning stoves add to the rustic ambience. Nonetheless, the shops of downtown Leavenworth are merely a mile away. The Turners pamper guests with enormous breakfasts that start with juice, fruit, muffins, yogurt, and freshly ground coffee, followed by platters of French toast and ham and eggs.

The White Swan Guest House

1388 MOORE ROAD, MT. VERNON, WASHINGTON 98273

Tel: **(206) 445-6805**
Best Time to Call: **Mornings; evenings**
Host: **Peter Goldfarb**
Location: **60 mi. N of Seattle**
No. of Rooms: **4**
Max. No. Sharing Bath: **3**
Double/sb: **$70**
Single/sb: **$60**
Guest Cottage: **$100–$150; sleeps 4**

Open: **All year**
Reduced Rates: **Weekly in cottage**
Breakfast: **Continental**
Credit Cards: **MC, VISA**
Pets: **Sometimes**
Children: **Welcome (in cottage)**
Smoking: **No**
Social Drinking: **Permitted**

Surrounded by farmland and country roads, this storybook Victorian farmhouse, built in 1898, is painted crayon yellow and framed by English-style gardens. There's a wood stove in the parlor, wicker chairs on the porch, books for browsing, and a unique collection of old samplers. A platter of homemade chocolate chip cookies is waiting for you on the sideboard. It's only 6 miles to LaConner, a delightful fishing village brimful of interesting art galleries, shops, waterfront restaurants, and antique stores. The San Juan ferries are a half hour away.

Puget View Guesthouse ✪
7924 61ST NORTHEAST, OLYMPIA, WASHINGTON 98506

Tel: **(206) 459-1676**
Best Time to Call: **Evenings**
Hosts: **Dick and Barbara Yunker**
Location: **4½ mi. from I-5, Exit 111**
No. of Rooms: **1 cottage**
No. of Private Baths: **1**
Guest Cottage: **$72–$102; sleeps 4**
Open: **All year**
Reduced Rates: **Families; weekly; off-season**
Breakfast: **Continental**
Credit Cards: **MC, VISA**
Pets: **Sometimes**
Children: **Welcome**
Smoking: **Permitted**
Social Drinking: **Permitted**

This charming waterfront guest cottage is located next to Tolmie State Park and adjacent to Dick and Barbara's log home. The panoramic Puget Sound setting makes it a popular, romantic getaway. You are apt to discover simple pleasures such as beachcombing or bird-watching and activities such as kayaking or scuba diving. Barbara and Dick are likely to invite you on a boat picnic or an oystering excursion. Your breakfast tray, a lavish and elegant repast, is brought to the cottage. You are welcome to use the beachside campfire for an evening cookout or to barbecue on your deck.

"Reflections"—A Bed and Breakfast Inn ✪
3878 REFLECTION LANE EAST, PORT ORCHARD, WASHINGTON 98366

Tel: **(206) 871-5582**
Best Time to Call: **Anytime**
Hosts: **Jime and Cathy Hall**
Location: **15 mi. W of Seattle**
No. of Rooms: **4**
No. of Private Baths: **2**
Max. No. Sharing Bath: **4**
Double/pb: **$65**
Single/pb: **$65**
Double/sb: **$55**
Single/sb: **$55**
Suites: **$90**
Open: **All year**
Breakfast: **Full**
Credit Cards: **MC, VISA**
Pets: **No**
Children: **Welcome, over 15**
Smoking: **Permitted**
Social Drinking: **Permitted**

This sprawling Colonial home stands majestically on a bluff overlooking Puget Sound and Bainbridge Island. Each cheerful guest room, furnished with New England antiques, affords superb views of the water and ever-changing scenery. Port Orchard offers a variety of diversions, from small shops filled with antiques and crafts, to marinas, parks, and boat excursions around the peninsula.

Holly Hill House ✪
611 POLK, PORT TOWNSEND, WASHINGTON 98368

Tel: **(206) 385-5619**	Breakfast: **Full**
Best Time to Call: **12–3 PM**	Credit Cards: **AMEX, MC, VISA**
Hosts: **Bill and Laurie Medlicott**	Pets: **No**
Location: **60 mi. NW of Seattle**	Children: **Welcome, over 12**
No. of Rooms: **4**	Smoking: **No**
No. of Private Baths: **4**	Social Drinking: **Permitted**
Double/pb: **$76–$130**	Minimum Stay: **2 nights festival**
Single/pb: **$71–$125**	**weekends**
Suite: **$125**	Airport/Station Pickup: **Yes**
Open: **All year**	
Reduced Rates: **10% Sun.–Thurs.**	
Nov. 1–Apr. 15	

Built in 1872, Holly Hill House is the former residence of R. C. Hill, who served variously as mayor, state representative, and the first banker of Port Townsend. Each room, lavishly furnished with Victorian antiques, is lovingly maintained down to the stippled woodwork. The grounds feature distinctive plantings, including holly trees and two unusual Camperdown elms known as upside-down trees. Nearby are marinas, golf courses, fishing sites, beaches, and many fine restaurants for your dining pleasure.

The Portico ✪
502 SOUTH ADAMS STREET, RITZVILLE, WASHINGTON 99169

Tel: **(509) 659-0800**	Reduced Rates: **10% Mar.–Apr.; 10%**
Best Time to Call: **Days; evenings**	**seniors; 20% after 5th night**
Hosts: **Mary Anne and Bill Phipps**	Breakfast: **Full**
Location: **60 mi. SW of Spokane**	Other Meals: **Available**
No. of Rooms: **2**	Credit Cards: **AMEX, DISC, MC, VISA**
No. of Private Baths: **2**	Pets: **No**
Double/pb: **$56–$68**	Children: **Welcome**
Single/pb: **$50–$62**	Smoking: **No**
Open: **All year**	Social Drinking: **Permitted**

This stately 1902 mansion, listed on the National Historic Register, combines Queen Anne and Classical Revival architecture. The interior is distinguished by gleaming oak woodwork, wood-spindled screens and columns, a grand entry staircase, and antique furnishings. In season, the grounds are resplendent with flowers, wild berries, fruit trees, and a vegetable garden, making for some tasty treats. Bill, a retired air force officer, and his wife, Mary Anne, provide a romantic setting that lets guests experience the serenity of this rural eastern Washington community.

Chelsea Station B&B Inn ○
4915 LINDEN AVENUE NORTH, SEATTLE, WASHINGTON 98103

Tel: **(206) 547-6077**
Best Time to Call: **10 AM–1 PM**
Hosts: **Dick and Marylou Jones**
Location: **2 mi. N of downtown Seattle**
No. of Rooms: **5**
No. of Private Baths: **5**
Double/pb: **$79**
Suites: **$94**
Open: **All year**

Reduced Rates: **Available**
Breakfast: **Full**
Credit Cards: **AMEX, DC, DISC, MC, VISA**
Pets: **No**
Children: **Welcome, over 12**
Smoking: **No**
Social Drinking: **Permitted**

Just five minutes from Seattle's downtown bustle, Chelsea Station consistently provides the peaceful surroundings travelers appreciate. Lace curtains, ample breakfasts, comfy king-size beds, and antique furnishings recreate the warmth of Grandma's time. This 1920 Federal Colonial is an outstanding example of the bricklayer's art. The nearby Seattle Rose Gardens contribute beauty to the surroundings. With a cup of tea in the afternoon, you will find Chelsea Station is a perfect place for relaxation and renewal. Full-time innkeepers Dick and Marylou bring their backgrounds in health care to the nurturing spirit of their B&B. Early reservations are recommended.

Mildred's Bed & Breakfast ○
1202 15TH AVENUE EAST, SEATTLE, WASHINGTON 98112

Tel: **(206) 325-6072**
Best Time to Call: **Mornings, before 9:30 PM**
Hosts: **Mildred and Melodee Sarver**
Location: **2 mi. NE of Seattle**
No. of Rooms: **2**
Max. No. Sharing Bath: **4**
Double/sb: **$65**
Single/sb: **$55**

Open: **All year**
Breakfast: **Full**
Credit Cards: **AMEX, DC, MC, VISA**
Pets: **No**
Children: **Welcome**
Smoking: **No**
Social Drinking: **No**
Airport/Station Pickup: **Yes**

Mildred's is the ultimate trip-to-Grandmother's fantasy come true. A large white 1890 Victorian, it's the perfect setting for traditional, caring B&B hospitality. Guest rooms on the second floor have sitting alcoves, lace curtains, and antiques. Off the hallway are a half-bath and a full bath with a six-foot skylight view. Mildred's special touches, like coffee and juice delivered to your room one half hour before breakfast, and tea and cookies on arrival, make her guests feel truly pampered. Across the street is historic 44-acre Volunteer Park with its art museum, flower conservatory, and tennis courts. An electric trolley stops at the front door and there is ample street parking. It is just minutes to the city center, freeways, and all points of interest.

Prince of Wales ⊙
133 THIRTEENTH AVENUE EAST, SEATTLE, WASHINGTON 98102

Tel: **(206) 325-9692**
Best Time to Call: **10 AM–9 PM**
Hosts: **Naomi Reed and Bert Brun**
Location: **In heart of Seattle**
No. of Rooms: **4**
No. of Private Baths: **2**
Max. No. Sharing Bath: **4**
Double/sb: **$55–60**
Suites: **$70–$80**
Open: **All year**

Reduced Rates: **10% weekly**
Breakfast: **Full**
Credit Cards: **MC, VISA**
Pets: **No**
Children: **Welcome**
Smoking: **No**
Social Drinking: **Permitted**
Foreign Languages: **French, Norwegian, Spanish**

From this convenient address, it's just a brief walk to the Convention Center and a short bus ride to the Space Needle, Pikes Place Market, and downtown Seattle's many other attractions. In the evening, you're sure to be tempted by the menus of neighborhood restaurants. Wake up to coffee in your bedroom, then come down to the dining room for a delicious breakfast. The guest rooms have great views; the suite has a queen-size bed, sitting room, and private bath.

Roberta's Bed and Breakfast
1147 SIXTEENTH AVENUE EAST, SEATTLE, WASHINGTON 98112

Tel: **(206) 329-3326**
Host: **Roberta Barry**
No. of Rooms: **5**
No. of Private Baths: **4**
Max. No. Sharing Bath: **3**
Double/pb: **$82–$95**
Single/pb: **$75–$87**
Double/sb: **$76**

Single/sb: **$69**
Open: **All year**
Breakfast: **Full**
Credit Cards: **AMEX, DC, MC, VISA**
Pets: **No**
Children: **Sometimes**
Smoking: **No**
Social Drinking: **Permitted**

Roberta's is a 1900 frame Victorian with a large, old-fashioned front porch. The house is located in a quiet, historic neighborhood near the heart of the city. The cheerful rooms all boast queen-size beds. The Peach Room has bay windows, oak furniture, and Grandma's fancy desk; the Rosewood Room has a window seat and built-in oak shelves; all five rooms are filled with books. In the morning you'll smell a pot of coffee right beside your door. That's just a warm-up for the large breakfast to come. The specialty of the house is Dutch Babies, a local dish, served with powdered sugar or fresh berries. For your convenience the *New York Times* and local newspapers are available every morning.

Salisbury House ✪

750 16TH AVENUE EAST, SEATTLE, WASHINGTON 98112

Tel: **(206) 328-8682**
Hosts: **Mary and Cathryn Wiese**
Location: **1 mi. from I-5**
No. of Rooms: **4**
No. of Private Baths: **4**
Double/pb: **$75–$90**
Single/pb: **$65–$80**
Open: **All year**

Reduced Rates: **10% weekly Oct.–Apr.**
Breakfast: **Full**
Credit Cards: **DC, MC, VISA**
Pets: **No**
Children: **Welcome, over 12**
Smoking: **No**
Social Drinking: **Permitted**

This elegant urban B&B, built in 1904, has been lovingly restored by your hosts, a mother-daughter team. It is located on a quiet tree-lined street just minutes from city center, within walking distance of parks, restaurants, and shops. Guest rooms have private baths; some rooms have window seats or a canopy bed. A full gourmet breakfast is served in the sunny dining room. Salisbury House is the most convenient location for your vacation or business travels.

Seattle Bed & Breakfast ✪

2442 N.W. MARKET # 300, SEATTLE, WASHINGTON 98107

Tel: **(206) 783-2169**
Host: **Inge Pokrandt**
Location: **1 mi. from I-5**
No. of Rooms: **4**
No. of Private Baths: **2**
Suite: **$40–$45**
Guest Cottage: **$75 for 2**
Open: **All year**

Breakfast: **Continental**
Credit Cards: **AMEX, MC, VISA**
Pets: **No**
Children: **Welcome (crib)**
Smoking: **No**
Social Drinking: **Permitted**
Foreign Languages: **German**

Built in 1925, this charming two-bedroom cottage is close to downtown, the University of Washington, fine beaches and all sightseeing. Enjoy the privacy, the fine oak furniture, the fireplace, and all the little touches that make you feel welcome. The private suite in Inge's home has a full kitchen, and some breakfast food is provided. Fresh flowers, fruits, and candy all spell out a warm welcome. The cedar deck in the sunny backyard is most enjoyable.

Greywolf Inn ✪

177 KEELER ROAD, SEQUIM, WASHINGTON 98382

Tel: **(206) 683-5889**
Hosts: **Peggy and Bill Melang**
Location: **N of Seattle**
No. of Rooms: **6**
No. of Private Baths: **6**
Double/pb: **$49–$95**
Suites: **$125; sleeps 4**
Open: **All year**

Reduced Rates: **Off-season**
Breakfast: **Full**
Credit Cards: **AMEX, MC, VISA**
Pets: **No**
Children: **Welcome, over 12**
Smoking: **No**
Social Drinking: **Permitted**

Take the scenic two-hour drive to this northwestern contemporary tucked between field and forest, in the rainshadow of the Olympic Mountains. The guest rooms, decorated in themes like French Country and Oriental, have panoramic views. Follow your full breakfast by ambling through five acres of meadows, gardens, woods, and streams. Then sun yourself on the broad decks or relax by the fire with a book from the inn's well-stocked library. Enjoy nearby fishing, boating, or golf. Or head for the woods; your choices include Olympic National Park, Hurricane Ridge, and the Hoh Rain Forest.

Spokane Bed & Breakfast Reservation Service
627 EAST 25TH, SPOKANE, WASHINGTON 99203

Tel: (509) 624-3776
Best Time to Call: 8 AM–7 PM
Coordinator: Pat Conley
States/Regions Covered: Canada—
British Columbia, Vancouver,
Victoria; Idaho—Coeur d'Alene,
LaClede, Sandpoint; Washington—
Seattle, Spokane, Yakima

Descriptive Directory: Free
Rates (Single/Double):
Modest: $40 / $45
Average: $45 / $50
Luxury: $62 / $68
Credit Cards: AMEX, MC, VISA
Minimum Stay: Only on 3 weekends

You can't beat the attractions of the Spokane area: excellent skiing and snowmobiling, perfect lakes for waterfront sports, large family-oriented parks, museums, symphonies, opera, and theater. This service will put you in touch with all manner of guest houses, from charming riverfront contemporaries to elegant, turn-of-the-century homes.

Hillside House ○
1729 EAST 18TH AVENUE, SPOKANE, WASHINGTON 99203

Tel: (509) 534-1426, 7 AM–9 PM;
(509) 535-1893, evenings, weekends
Best Time to Call: 7 AM–9 PM
Hosts: Jo Ann and Bud
Location: 2 mi. from US 90
No. of Rooms: 2
Max. No. Sharing Bath: 4
Double/sb: $50
Single/sb: $45
Open: All year

Reduced Rates: Weekly
Breakfast: Full
Credit Cards: MC, VISA
Pets: Sometimes
Children: Sometimes
Smoking: No
Social Drinking: Permitted
Minimum Stay: 2 nights
Airport/Station Pickup: Yes

Hillside House has a spectacular view of Spokane and the nearby mountains. A cozy home, furnished in the country manner with antiques, its quiet, residential setting is within walking distance of lovely parks. Jo Ann is a third generation B&B hostess—her mother helped Grandma Jenny host guests in Minnesota over 70 years ago. Exotic egg dishes, unusual breakfast meats, and crêpes are often choices at breakfast. Pampering guests and guiding them to exciting events, places, and personalities are your hosts' pleasures.

Marianna Stoltz House ✪
427 EAST INDIANA, SPOKANE, WASHINGTON 99207

Tel: **(509) 483-4316**	Breakfast: **Full**
Hosts: **James and Phyllis Maguire**	Credit Cards: **AMEX, MC, VISA**
No. of Rooms: **4**	Pets: **No**
No. of Private Baths: **3**	Children: **Welcome, over 12**
Max. No. Sharing Bath: **4**	Smoking: **No**
Double/pb: **$59**	Social Drinking: **Permitted**
Single/pb: **$49**	Airport/Station Pickup: **Yes**
Open: **All year**	

The Marianna Stoltz House, a Spokane landmark, is a classic American foursquare home built in 1908. Period furnishings complement the house's woodwork, tile fireplace, and leaded glass bookshelves and cupboards. The bedroom quilts are heirlooms from Phyllis' mother, the B&B's namesake. The Maguires are Spokane natives—Phyllis grew up in this very house—and can tell you about local theaters, museums, and parks. Full breakfasts consist of juice, fruit, muffins, and main dishes such as sausage-cheese strata and puffy Dutch pancakes with homemade syrup.

Shakespeare Inn ✪
3227 EAST 22ND AVENUE, SPOKANE, WASHINGTON 99223

Tel: **(509) 534-0935**	Reduced Rates: **10% seniors, families**
Best Time to Call: **Anytime**	Breakfast: **Full**
Hosts: **Ron and Mary McDaniels**	Other Meals: **Available**
Location: **1 mi. from Hwy. I-90, Exit**	Pets: **No**
Thor-Freya	Children: **Welcome, over 2**
No. of Rooms: **2**	Smoking: **No**
No. of Private Baths: **2**	Social Drinking: **Permitted**
Double/pb: **$32–$48**	Airport/Station Pickup: **Yes**
Single/pb: **$28–$43**	
Open: **All year**	

Whether you're looking for a romantic retreat or for the fun and excitement of the city, you'll love this rustic, half-timbered Olde English mini-inn set in the heart of Spokane's historic South Hill. Sit down to a Shakespearean feast of Hamlet (omelet with ham and exotic delights), Canterbury Compote, and Romeo and Juliet Sweet Hearts, served by your hostess in Shakespearean costume, accompanied by the enchanting sound of Scottish bagpipes. Ron and Mary extend a hearty welcome, and will be glad to show you around the beautiful Pacific Northwest inland.

Inge's Place ✪
6809 LAKE GROVE SW, TACOMA, WASHINGTON 98499

Tel: **(206) 584-4514**
Host: **Ingeborg Deatherage**
Location: **3 mi. from I-5**
No. of Rooms: **3**
No. of Private Baths: **1**
Max. No. Sharing Bath: **4**
Double/pb: **$45**
Single/pb: **$35**
Double/sb: **$40**
Single/sb: **$30**

Suites: **$60**
Open: **All year**
Reduced Rates: **Available**
Breakfast: **Full**
Pets: **No**
Children: **Welcome**
Smoking: **Permitted**
Social Drinking: **Permitted**
Airport/Station Pickup: **Yes**
Foreign Languages: **German**

This spic-and-span home is in a lovely Tacoma suburb called Lakewood. Feel welcome to use the hot tub, large backyard, and patio. There are many restaurants and shopping centers within walking distance, and several nearby lakes where fishing is excellent. Tacoma is the gateway to Mount Rainier. Inge is a world traveler, teacher, and enthusiast about B&Bs.

Keenan House ✪
2610 NORTH WARNER, TACOMA, WASHINGTON 98407

Tel: **(206) 752-0702**
Best Time to Call: **Evenings**
Host: **Lenore Keenan**
Location: **2½ mi. from I-5**
No. of Rooms: **8**
No. of Private Baths: **2**
Max. No. Sharing Bath: **4**
Double/pb: **$60**
Single/pb: **$50**

Double/sb: **$50**
Single/sb: **$45**
Open: **All year**
Reduced Rates: **Weekly; 15% families**
Breakfast: **Full**
Pets: **No**
Children: **Welcome**
Smoking: **No**
Social Drinking: **Permitted**

This spacious Victorian house is located in the historic district near Puget Sound. It is furnished in antiques and period pieces. Afternoon tea is served, and ice is available for cocktails; fruit and croissants are served with breakfast. Local possibilities include Puget Sound, Vashon Island, the state park, zoo, and ferry. It's only five blocks to the University of Puget Sound.

Traudel's Haus ✪
15313 17TH AVENUE COURT EAST, TACOMA, WASHINGTON 98445

Tel: **(206) 535-4422**
Host: **Gertraude M. Taut**
Location: **5 mi. from I-5**
No. of Rooms: **3**
No. of Private Baths: **2**
Max. No. Sharing Bath: **4**

Double/pb: **$50**
Single/pb: **$45**
Double/sb: **$40**
Single/sb: **$35**
Suites: **$55–$60**
Open: **All year**

Reduced Rates: **Available**	Smoking: **No**
Breakfast: **Continental**	Social Drinking: **Permitted**
Pets: **No**	Airport/Station Pickup: **Yes**
Children: **Welcome**	Foreign Languages: **German**

Mrs. Taut offers a guest-oriented haven located in a quiet neighborhood only minutes from Pacific Lutheran University, Spanaway Park, and Sprinker Recreation Center. It is an easy springboard to other explorations, including the Tacoma Dome, Mt. Rainier National Park and Mount St. Helens. The German-born Mrs. Taut collects antiques and clocks and enjoys making lace.

Llama Ranch Bed & Breakfast ✪
1980 HIGHWAY 141, WHITE SALMON, WASHINGTON 98672

Tel: **(509) 395-2786; (800) 800-LAMA [5262]**	Reduced Rates: **$5 less Dec.–Mar.; 15% weekly**
Hosts: **Jerry and Rebeka Stone**	Breakfast: **Full**
Location: **50 mi. E of Portland, Oreg.**	Credit Cards: **DISC, MC, VISA**
No. of Rooms: **5**	Pets: **Sometimes**
Max. No. Sharing Bath: **4**	Children: **Welcome**
Double/sb: **$55**	Smoking: **No**
Single/sb: **$45**	Social Drinking: **Permitted**
Open: **All year**	

Jerry and Rebeka enjoy sharing their love of llamas with their guests, and it is a rare person who can resist a llama's charm. Their B&B commands stunning views of Mt. Adams and Mt. Hood. The guest rooms are unpretentious and comfortable. Llama Ranch is located on 97 acres at the base of the Mt. Adams Wilderness Area. Nearby activities include horseback riding, white-water rafting, plane trips over Mount Saint Helens, water sports, and cave exploration. The less adventurous are certain to enjoy learning about the ranch's serene animals.

WEST VIRGINIA

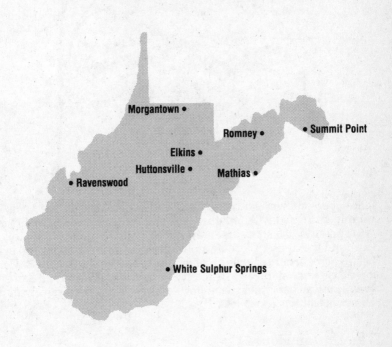

- Morgantown •
- Romney •
- • Summit Point
- Elkins •
- Huttonsville •
- Mathias •
- • Ravenswood
- • White Sulphur Springs

The Retreat at Buffalo Run ✪
214 HARPERTOWN ROAD, ELKINS, WEST VIRGINIA 26241

Tel: **(304) 636-2960**
Best Time to Call: **8 AM–9 PM**
Hosts: **Kathleen, Bertha, and Earl Rhoad**
Location: **160 mi. S of Pittsburgh**
No. of Rooms: **6**
Max. No. Sharing Bath: **4**
Double/sb: **$44**
Single/sb: **$34**

Open: **All year**
Reduced Rates: **Weekly**
Breakfast: **Full**
Pets: **Sometimes**
Children: **Welcome**
Smoking: **No**
Social Drinking: **Permitted**
Airport Pickup: **Yes**

This gracious turn-of-the-century home is located at the gateway to the 840,000-acre Monongahela National Forest, within walking dis-

tance of downtown Elkins and Davis and Elkins College. The home is warmly decorated with antiques, art, and contemporary furnishings. Wide porches, tall shade trees, evergreens, and rhododendron groves surround the house. Close by are wilderness areas for hiking, biking, fishing, cross-country skiing; country auctions; and the Augusta Heritage Arts Festival. Breakfasts receive rave reviews. Bertha and Earl are avid bird-watchers; their daughter Kathleen is a college career counselor who collects cookbooks.

The Hutton House ✪
ROUTES 219 AND 250, HUTTONSVILLE, WEST VIRGINIA 26273

Tel: **(800) 234-6701**
Best Time to Call: **Anytime**
Hosts: **Dean and Loretta Murray**
Location: **17 mi. S of Elkins**
No. of Rooms: **7**
No. of Private Baths: **3**
Max. No. Sharing Bath: **4**
Double/pb: **$65**
Single/pb: **$58**
Double/sb: **$55**
Single/sb: **$48**

Suites: **$85**
Open: **All year**
Reduced Rates: **Available**
Breakfast: **Full**
Other Meals: **Available**
Credit Cards: **MC, VISA**
Pets: **No**
Children: **Welcome**
Smoking: **No**
Social Drinking: **Permitted**
Airport/Station Pickup: **Yes**

Built in 1899 by a scion of Huttonsville's founder, Hutton House commands a broad view of the Tygart Valley and Laurel Mountain ridges. This ornate Queen Anne mansion, with its extraordinary woodwork and windows, is listed on the National Register of Historic Places. Travelers come here to ski at Snowshoe, visit Cass Railroad, and hike in the Monongahela National Forest. Civil War buffs will find plenty of battle sites to study, and the Augusta Heritage Arts Festival, in nearby Elkins, also merits a detour. For breakfast, your hosts dish out cantaloupe sorbet and whole wheat pancakes drizzled with maple syrup made from their own trees.

Valley View Farm ✪
ROUTE 1, BOX 467, MATHIAS, WEST VIRGINIA 26812

Tel: (304) 897-5229
Best Time to Call: Evenings after 7 PM
Host: Edna Shipe
Location: 130 mi. SW of D.C.
No. of Rooms: 4
Max. No. Sharing Bath: 6
Double/sb: $30
Single/sb: $15
Open: All year

Reduced Rates: Weekly
Breakfast: Full
Other Meals: Available
Pets: Welcome
Children: Welcome (crib)
Smoking: Permitted
Social Drinking: Permitted
Airport/Station Pickup: Yes

This 1920s farmhouse is decorated with comfortable Early American–style furniture and family mementos, and there's a nice porch for relaxed visiting. This is no place to diet because Edna is a good cook. Seasonal recreational activities are available in nearby Lost River State Park and on Rock Cliff Lake. You are certain to enjoy the local festivals, house tours, and interesting craft shops. Bryces Ski Resort is less than an hour away.

Chestnut Ridge School ✪
1000 STEWARTSTOWN ROAD, MORGANTOWN, WEST VIRGINIA 26505

Tel: (304) 598-2262
Hosts: Sam and Nancy Bonasso
Location: 70 mi. S of Pittsburgh, Pa.
No. of Rooms: 4
No. of Private Baths: 4
Double/pb: $54
Single/pb: $48

Open: All year
Breakfast: Continental
Pets: No
Children: Welcome (crib)
Smoking: No
Social Drinking: Permitted

A yellow brick and stucco building erected in the 1920s, Chestnut Ridge retains the oversize windows, beadboard trim, and broad staircase that mark its past as an elementary school. Situated on the outskirts of Morgantown, this B&B is just minutes from the West Virginia University campus and medical center. A state park, a large lake, a golf course and tennis courts are all within easy reach. Continental breakfast features fresh, multigrain muffins. Guests can take this morning meal in their rooms, in the kitchen, in the parlor, or on the deck.

Hemlock Farm ✪
ROUTE 1, BOX 121, RAVENSWOOD, WEST VIRGINIA 26164

Tel: **(304) 273-5572**
Host: **Jeannette Morton**
No. of Rooms: **1**
No. of Private Baths: **1**
Suite: **$65 for 2, $10 for each extra person**
Open: **May–Oct.**

Breakfast: **Full**
Other Meals: **Available**
Pets: **Welcome**
Children: **Welcome, over 10**
Smoking: **No**
Social Drinking: **Permitted**
Airport/Station Pickup: **Yes**

There's room for you and your horse at this small thoroughbred farm—a good thing to remember should you want to use the bridle paths at the nearest state parks, about 50 miles away. Those who prefer water travel should drive the 44 miles into Charleston and book seats on a stern-wheeler cruise. Hemlock Farm's guest studio has a cathedral ceiling, stone hearth, and private entrance. Breakfast is served in the room, and a microwave and small refrigerator are provided for snacking purposes. Your host acquired a flair for international cooking on her many overseas travels, and by advance arrangement she'll prepare foreign-flavored meals.

Hampshire House 1884 ✪
165 NORTH GRAFTON STREET, ROMNEY, WEST VIRGINIA 26757

Tel: **(304) 822-7171**
Hosts: **Jane and Scott Simmons**
Location: **35 mi. W of Winchester, Va.**
No. of Rooms: **4**
No. of Private Baths: **4**
Double/pb: **$60–$70**
Single/pb: **$50–$60**
Open: **All year**
Reduced Rates: **Available**

Breakfast: **Full**
Other Meals: **Available**
Credit Cards: **AMEX, DC, MC, VISA**
Pets: **No**
Children: **Welcome**
Smoking: **No**
Social Drinking: **Permitted**
Airport/Station Pickup: **Yes**

Only two and one half hours west of Washington, D.C., via Route 50 lies Romney, the oldest town in West Virginia. Surrounded by beautiful rolling hills, Hampshire House is conveniently located to the downtown area. Bicycles are ready for touring the town, with its quaint shops and historic buildings. Trail rides and hayrides are available at the local equestrian center, and winery tours are nearby. The bedrooms are attractively furnished with old-fashioned furniture and wallpapers and kept comfortable with central heating and air-conditioning. Jane and Scott graciously offer complimentary snacks and invite you to enjoy the old pump organ, television, VCR, or a variety of games.

Countryside ✪
P.O. BOX 57, SUMMIT POINT, WEST VIRGINIA 25446

Tel: **(304) 725-2614**
Best Time to Call: **8–10 AM; 8–10 PM**
Hosts: **Lisa and Daniel Hileman**
Location: **6 mi. from Rtes. 7 and 340**
No. of Rooms: **2**
No. of Private Baths: **2**
Double/pb: **$50–$70**
Single/pb: **$50–$70**
Open: **All year**

Breakfast: **Continental**
Credit Cards: **MC, VISA**
Pets: **Sometimes**
Children: **Welcome, over 10**
Smoking: **No**
Social Drinking: **Permitted**
Minimum Stay: **2 nights Oct. and holiday weekends**
Station Pickup: **Yes**

In the Shenandoah Valley of the Eastern Panhandle, only 20 minutes from Harpers Ferry, this cheerful country home with white shutters, large yard, and patio is on a quiet street in a charming old village. It is attractively furnished with country oak furniture, antique quilts, original art, pretty baskets, and collectibles. Breakfast trays are brought to each guest room. Afternoon tea is served; snacks and beverages are always available. Guests always remark on the cleanliness and hospitality Lisa and Daniel provide.

The James Wylie House ✪
208 EAST MAIN STREET, WHITE SULPHUR SPRINGS, WEST VIRGINIA 24986

Tel: **(304) 536-9444**
Hosts: **Cheryl and Joe Griffith**

Location: **100 mi. SE of Charleston**
No. of Rooms: **3**

No. of Private Baths: **3**
Double/pb: **$55–$65**
Single/pb: **$50–$55**
Open: **All year**
Reduced Rates: **10% after 3rd night**
Breakfast: **Full or Continental**

Credit Cards: **AMEX, MC, VISA**
Pets: **No**
Children: **Welcome**
Smoking: **No**
Social Drinking: **Permitted**
Airport/Station Pickup: **Yes**

This three-story Georgian Colonial-style dwelling dating back to 1819 features large, airy rooms that are comfortably furnished and accented with antiques. Pretty quilts, iron beds, old toys, and select period pieces enhance the bedrooms' decor. Specialties such as apple pudding, homemade coffee cake, and a delicious egg-and-sausage casserole are often part of the breakfast fare. The world-famous Greenbrier Resort is less than one mile away and historic Lewisburg is less than nine miles away. Recreational opportunities abound in the nearby state parks and ski resorts.

WISCONSIN

Lac Du Flambeau •
Eagle River • • Phelps
• Fish Creek
• Sturgeon Bay
Strum •
Stevens Point •
• Newton
Elroy •
La Farge • Baraboo • • Portage
• Cedarburg
Madison •
• Milwaukee
Belleville • • Eagle
Mineral Point • • Burlington
Janesville •

Bed & Breakfast Guest-Homes
698 COUNTY U, ALGOMA, WISCONSIN 54201

Tel: **(414) 743-9742**
Best Time to Call: **7 AM–9 PM**
Coordinator: **Eileen Wood**
States/Regions Covered: **Statewide**
Descriptive Directory: **$6.95**

Rates (Single/Double):
  Average: **$45–$75 / $55–$85**
  Luxury: **$100–$145**
Credit Cards: **MC, VISA**

This reservation service offers you local color and relaxing surroundings, with many accommodations in popular Door County. Eileen carefully selects the accommodations to assure each guest of a hospitable host in clean, comfortable homes. Most serve full breakfasts. Homes on the waterfront are slightly more expensive from July to early September. There is a 10-percent discount for week-long stays.

Baraboo's Gollmar Guest House ✪
422 3RD STREET, BARABOO, WISCONSIN 53913

Tel: **(608) 356-9432**
Best Time to Call: **10 AM–10 PM**
Hosts: **Tom and Linda Luck**
Location: **200 mi. NW of Chicago**
No. of Rooms: **4**
No. of Private Baths: **3**
Max. No. Sharing Bath: **4**
Double/pb: **$65**
Double/sb: **$50–$60**

Open: **All year**
Breakfast: **Full**
Credit Cards: **MC, VISA**
Pets: **No**
Children: **Welcome, over 7**
Smoking: **No**
Social Drinking: **Permitted**
Station Pickup: **Yes**

Built in 1889 by the Gollmars, a renowned Victorian circus family, this handsome home contains its original chandeliers, beveled glass windows, oak woodwork, hardwood floors, and beautiful hand-painted murals. All bedrooms have queen-size beds. A special guest parlor leads to an outdoor patio, and the grounds include flower gardens and a picnic area. Before heading out for the local sights, which range from Circus World Museum to the world famous Crane Foundation, you'll dine on breakfast dishes like decadent French toast and turkey bacon and sausage.

Pinehaven
E13083 STATE HIGHWAY 33, BARABOO, WISCONSIN 53913

Tel: **(608) 356-3489**
Best Time to Call: **8 AM–10 AM**
Hosts: **Lyle and Marge Getschman**
Location: **10 mi. from I-90**
No. of Rooms: **4**
No. of Private Baths: **4**
Double/pb: **$55–$70**
Single/pb: **$50–$65**

Open: **All year**
Breakfast: **Full**
Credit Cards: **MC, VISA**
Pets: **No**
Children: **Welcome, over 5**
Smoking: **No**
Social Drinking: **Permitted**

Lyle and Marge's home is nestled in a pine grove with a beautiful view of the Baraboo Bluffs and a small private lake. Guest rooms are all new, with air-conditioning. The full breakfast may include fresh-baked muffins, coffee cakes, egg dishes, meat, fruit, and juice. Eat in the dining room, on the deck, or on the screened-in porch. Play the baby grand piano. Feel free to take a leisurely stroll in these inviting surroundings. A tour to see your hosts' Belgian draft horses and antique wagons and sleighs on the farm side of the highway, and wagon or sleigh rides pulled by the Belgians, may be arranged. Fine restaurants and numerous activities abound in the area.

Abendruh Bed and Breakfast Swiss Style ✪
7019 GEHIN ROAD, BELLEVILLE, WISCONSIN 53508

Tel: **(608) 424-3808**	Open: **All year**
Best Time to Call: **7 AM–9 PM**	Reduced Rates: **Available**
Hosts: **Mathilde and Franz Jaggi**	Breakfast: **Full**
Location: **13 mi. SW of Madison**	Wheelchair-Accessible: **Yes**
No. of Rooms: **3**	Pets: **No**
No. of Private Baths: **2**	Children: **No**
Max. No. Sharing Bath: **3**	Smoking: **No**
Double/pb: **$55**	Social Drinking: **Permitted**
Single/pb: **$45**	Foreign Languages: **French, German,**
Double/sb: **$45**	**Swiss**
Single/sb: **$40**	

Abendruh is a stucco-and-stone ranch designed and built by the Jaggi family. The house is filled with homemade items ranging from the furniture to the afghans. Your host, Franz, is a master brick-and-stone mason. Mathilde is certified as a French chef, and in hotel and restaurant management. Together they provide a Swiss atmosphere and the utmost in international service. The breakfast menu changes daily according to guest preference. Specialties include homemade muffins, croissants, and a variety of egg dishes. Guests are welcome to explore the spacious grounds or relax in front of a crackling fire at one of the four fireplaces. Abendruh is 30 minutes from downtown Madison, and is close to such attractions as New Glarus, America's Little Switzerland, Mt. Horeb, Cave of the Mounds, skiing, and biking.

Hillcrest ✪
540 STORLE AVENUE, BURLINGTON, WISCONSIN 53105

Tel: **(414) 763-4706**	Double/sb: **$60**
Best Time to Call: **Anytime**	Open: **All year**
Hosts: **Dick and Karen Granholm**	Breakfast: **Full**
Location: **30 mi. SW of Milwaukee**	Credit Cards: **MC, VISA**
No. of Rooms: **3**	Pets: **No**
No. of Private Baths: **1**	Children: **Welcome, over 12**
Max. No. Sharing Bath: **4**	Smoking: **No**
Double/pb: **$75**	Social Drinking: **Permitted**

The Granholms welcome you to their 100-year-old home with a snack of locally prepared cheese and sausage. Hillcrest is a historic estate set on four wooded acres, just a short walk from downtown. The house is peaceful and quiet, with a spectacular view of Echo Lake. It has several leaded and beveled-glass windows and doors, mahogany woodwork, beamed ceilings, and a huge staircase dominating the first and second floors. Each guest room is decorated with antiques, lace curtains, and brass accents. Two large porches furnished with wicker chairs, love seats, and rockers will tempt you to doze away the afternoon. Breakfast dishes include fresh fruit and homemade muffins served with omelets and plenty of hot coffee. Your hosts will gladly direct you to nearby craft and antique shops, golf courses, and lakes.

Stagecoach Inn Bed & Breakfast ✪
W61 N520 WASHINGTON AVENUE, CEDARBURG, WISCONSIN 53012

Tel: (414) 375-0208	Open: All year
Hosts: Brook and Liz Brown	Breakfast: Continental
Location: 17 mi. N of Milwaukee	Credit Cards: AMEX, MC, VISA
No. of Rooms: 13	Pets: No
No. of Private Baths: 13	Children: Welcome, over 12
Double/pb: $65	Smoking: No
Single/pb: $55	Social Drinking: Permitted
Suites: $95	

The inn, listed on the National Register of Historic Places, is housed in a completely restored 1853 stone building in downtown, historic Cedarburg. The rooms, air-conditioned for summer comfort, combine antique charm with modern conveniences. Each bedroom is decorated with Laura Ashley linens and trimmed with wall stenciling. A candy shop and a pub that is a popular gathering place for guests occupy the first floor. Specialty stores, antique shops, a winery, a woolen mill, and a variety of fine restaurants are within walking distance.

Eagle Centre House B&B ✪
W370 S9590 HIGHWAY 67, EAGLE, WISCONSIN 53119

Tel: (414) 363-4700	Open: All year; closed Christmas Eve and Christmas Day
Best Time to Call: 7 AM–10 PM	Reduced Rates: Available
Hosts: Riene Wells Herriges and Dean Herriges	Breakfast: Full
Location: 30 mi. SW of Milwaukee	Credit Cards: AMEX, MC, VISA
No. of Rooms: 5	Pets: No
No. of Private Baths: 5	Children: Welcome, over 12
Double/pb: $79	Smoking: No
Single/pb: $69	Social Drinking: Permitted
Suites: $115	

Eagle Centre House is an authentic replica of an 1846 Greek Revival stagecoach inn built on 16 secluded acres. From the front parlor to the third-floor bedrooms, you will admire the splendid collection of antiques. Take a seat on the porch or in the parlor and browse through period publications. Even the breakfast specialties are inspired by the 19th century. There are hiking and cross-country ski trails in both Kettle Moraine State Forest and Old World Wisconsin, an unusual outdoor museum. Other athletic options include downhill skiing, sledding, biking, golfing, horseback riding, and waterfront sports.

Brennan Manor, Old World Bed and Breakfast ✪
1079 EVERETT ROAD, EAGLE RIVER, WISCONSIN 54521

Tel: **(715) 479-7353**	Reduced Rates: **10% seniors; 15%**
Best Time to Call: **Days**	**weekly**
Hosts: **Connie and Bob Lawton**	Breakfast: **Full**
Location: **3 mi. E of Eagle River**	Credit Cards: **MC, VISA**
No. of Rooms: **4**	Pets: **No**
No. of Private Baths: **4**	Children: **No**
Double/pb: **$69–$89**	Smoking: **No**
Single/pb: **$59–$79**	Social Drinking: **Permitted**
Guest Cottage: **$650 weekly; sleeps 6**	Airport/Station Pickup: **Yes**
Open: **All year**	

Built in the 1920s, the era of the great lumber barons, this lakeside country estate combines a relaxed atmosphere and old-world charm. With its 30-foot timbered ceiling, large arched windows, massive stone fireplace, and hand-hewn woodwork, the great room may conjure up King Arthur's Camelot. For summer fun, there's boating, golfing, biking, water skiing, canoeing, fishing, and more. Winter sports enthusiasts will enjoy cross-country and downhill skiing, as well as the 500 miles of marked snowmobile trails that begin at the B&B's front door.

Thorp House Inn
4135 BLUFF ROAD, P.O. BOX 490, FISH CREEK, WISCONSIN 54212

Tel: **(414) 868-2444**	Reduced Rates: **Weekly**
Best Time to Call: **8 AM–10 PM**	Breakfast: **Continental**
Hosts: **Christine and Sverre Falck-**	Pets: **No**
Pedersen	Children: **Welcome, in cottages**
No. of Rooms: **4**	Smoking: **Yes, in cottages**
No. of Private Baths: **4**	Social Drinking: **Permitted**
Double/pb: **$70–$115**	Minimum Stay: **2 nights weekends; 3**
Single/pb: **$65–$110**	**nights holiday weekends**
Open: **All year**	Foreign Languages: **Norwegian**

Thorp House is a turn-of-the-century country Victorian inn perched on a wooded hill overlooking Green Bay. The beach, shops, restaurants, and Peninsula State Park are just a stroll away. Four elegant guest rooms recreate romantic periods of the past with fine antiques and accessories, documentary wall coverings, and European lace. Each room has a private bath (one with a whirlpool), central air-conditioning, and ceiling fans. Guests have their own parlor with its original granite fireplace. A delicious home-baked breakfast is included. Also

The Thorp House – Fish Creek, WI

available: country cottages with wood-burning fireplaces, full kitchens and baths (one with a whirlpool), decks, and views of the bay.

Jackson Street Inn ✪
210 SOUTH JACKSON STREET, JANESVILLE, WISCONSIN 53545

Tel: **(608) 754-7250**
Hosts: **Ilah and Bob Sessler**
Location: **1.9 mi. from I-90, on Hwy. 11**
No. of Rooms: **4**
No. of Private Baths: **2**
Max. No. Sharing Bath: **4**
Double/pb: **$65**
Single/pb: **$55**
Double/sb: **$55**
Single/sb: **$45**
Open: **All year**
Reduced Rates: **Available**
Breakfast: **Full**
Credit Cards: **AMEX, MC, VISA**
Pets: **No**
Children: **Welcome**
Smoking: **Restricted**
Social Drinking: **Permitted**
Airport/Station Pickup: **Yes**

This turn-of-the-century home is finely appointed, with brass fixtures, leaded beveled-glass windows, and Italian fireplace mantels. The air-conditioned rooms are in soft colors with Colonial-period English wallpaper, fancy pillows, dust ruffles, and cozy quilts. The guest sitting room has books and a refrigerator with ice. Your hosts serve breakfast on the screened-in porch or by the fireplace in the dining room overlooking the grounds. A four-hole putting green, shuffleboard, and a horseshoe court are part of their landscaping. Local attractions include the beach, Old Town restorations, hiking trails, golf, and museums.

Trillium ✪
ROUTE 2, BOX 121, LA FARGE, WISCONSIN 54639

Tel: (608) 625-4492
Best Time to Call: Mornings; evenings
Hosts: Joe Swanson and Rosanne
  Boyett
Location: 40 mi. SE of La Crosse
Guest Cottage: $65 for 2
Open: All year
Breakfast: Full

Reduced Rates: Single guest; weekly;
  winter
Pets: No
Children: Welcome (crib)
Smoking: Permitted
Social Drinking: Permitted
Airport/Station Pickup: Yes

This private cottage is on a working farm located in the heart of a thriving Amish community. It has a large porch and is surrounded by an orchard, garden, and a lovely tree-shaded yard. There's a path beside the stream that winds through woods and fields. The cottage is light and airy, with comfortable wicker furniture. Nearby attractions include the Elroy-Sparta Bike Trail, Mississippi River, trout streams, and cheese factories.

Ty Bach B&B ✪
3104 SIMPSON LANE, LAC DU FLAMBEAU, WISCONSIN 54538

Tel: (715) 588-7851
Best Time to Call: 8 AM–10 PM
Hosts: Janet and Kermit Bekkum
Location: 70 mi. N of Wausau
No. of Rooms: 2
No. of Private Baths: 2
Double/pb: $50–$60

Single/pb: $45–$55
Open: All year
Breakfast: Full
Pets: Sometimes
Children: No
Smoking: No
Social Drinking: Permitted

In Welsh, *ty-bach* means "little house." Located on an Indian reservation in Lac du Flambeau, this modern little house overlooks a small, picturesque Northwoods lake. Sit back on the deck and enjoy the beautiful fall colors, the call of the loons, and the tranquillity of this out-of-the-way spot. Choose from two comfortable rooms: one features a brass bed, the other opens onto a private deck. Your hosts offer oven-fresh coffee cakes, homemade jams, and plenty of fresh coffee along with hearty main entrées.

Annie's Hill House
2117 SHERIDAN DRIVE, MADISON, WISCONSIN 53704

Tel: **(608) 244-2224**
Hosts: **Anne and Larry Stuart**
No. of Rooms: **2 suites**
No. of Private Baths: **2**
Suites: **$75–$85 for 2; $125–$135 for 4**
Open: **All year**
Reduced Rates: **Business accounts**

Breakfast: **Full**
Credit Cards: **AMEX, MC, VISA**
Pets: **No**
Children: **No**
Smoking: **No**
Social Drinking: **Permitted**
Airport/Station Pickup: **Yes**

When you want the world to go away, come to Annie's, a quiet inn with a beautiful view of meadows, water, and woods. This charming, fully air-conditioned cedar shake home has been a getaway for travelers since 1985. The house is a block from a large lake and directly adjoining Warner Park, allowing guests a broad selection of activities, including swimming, boating, tennis, hiking, and biking during summer, and cross-country skiing and skating in winter. The four antique-filled guest rooms are full of surprises and unusual amenities. There is a great-hall dining room, pine-paneled library with a well-stocked wood stove, and a soothing double whirlpool surrounded by plants. The unusually lovely gardens, with romantic gazebo and pond, have been selected for the annual Madison Garden Tours.

Marie's Bed & Breakfast ✪
346 EAST WILSON STREET, MILWAUKEE, WISCONSIN 53207

Tel: **(414) 483-1512**
Best Time to Call: **8 AM–8 PM**
Host: **Marie M. Mahan**
No. of Rooms: **4**
Max. No. Sharing Bath: **4**
Double/sb: **$55–$65**
Open: **All year**

Breakfast: **Full**
Pets: **No**
Children: **Welcome**
Smoking: **No**
Social Drinking: **Permitted**
Airport/Station Pickup: **Yes**

Your hostess has decorated this turn-of-the-century Victorian with an eclectic mixture of antiques, collectibles, and her own original artwork. Give yourself time to walk around the historic Bay View neighborhood, with its many architectural styles. Downtown Milwaukee is just six minutes away. Breakfast, served in the garden when weather permits, is highlighted by homemade breads, pastries, and a variety of locally prepared sausages.

Ogden House ✪
2237 NORTH LAKE DRIVE, MILWAUKEE, WISCONSIN 53202

Tel: **(414) 272-2740**
Hosts: **Mary Jane and John Moss**

No. of Rooms: **2**
No. of Private Baths: **2**

Double/pb: **$75**
Single/pb: **$75**
Suites: **$85**
Open: **All year**
Breakfast: **Continental**

Pets: **No**
Children: **Welcome**
Smoking: **Permitted**
Social Drinking: **Permitted**

The Ogden House is a white-brick Federal-style home listed on the National Register of Historic Places. It is located in the North Point–South historic district, a neighborhood shared by venerable mansions overlooking Lake Michigan. Miss Ogden herself would feel at home here having homemade butterhorns for breakfast. You are sure to feel at home, too, whether you're relaxing on the sun deck, sitting by the fire, or retiring to your four-poster bed. Ogden House is convenient to theaters, the botanical garden, the Brewers' Stadium, the breweries, and many fine restaurants.

The Wilson House Inn ✪
110 DODGE STREET, MINERAL POINT, WISCONSIN 53565

Tel: **(608) 987-3600**
Best Time to Call: **Evenings**
Hosts: **Bev and Jim Harris**
Location: **50 mi. SW of Madison**
No. of Rooms: **4**
No. of Private Baths: **2**
Max. No. Sharing Bath: **4**
Double/pb: **$55–$60**
Single/pb: **$50–$55**

Double/sb: **$45–$55**
Single/sb: **$40–$50**
Open: **All year**
Breakfast: **Full**
Credit Cards: **MC, VISA**
Pets: **Sometimes**
Children: **Welcome (crib)**
Smoking: **No**
Social Drinking: **Permitted**

The Wilson House Inn is located in the heart of the beautiful uplands area. This redbrick Federal mansion was built in 1853 by Alexander Wilson, who became one of the state's first attorneys general. A veranda was added later, and it is where guests are welcomed with lemonade. The rooms are airy, comfortable, and furnished in antiques. Mineral Point was a mining and political center in the 1880s, and it is filled with many historic sites. Fishing, golfing, swimming, skiing, and the House on the Rock are all nearby.

Rambling Hills Tree Farm ✪
8825 WILLEVER LANE, NEWTON, WISCONSIN 53063

Tel: **(414) 726-4388**
Best Time to Call: **Evenings**
Hosts: **Pete and Judie Stuntz**
Location: **18 mi. N of Sheboygan**
No. of Rooms: **4**
No. of Private Baths: **2**
Max. No. Sharing Bath: **5**
Double/pb: **$40**
Single/pb: **$30**

Double/sb: **$40**
Single/sb: **$30**
Open: **All year**
Breakfast: **Full**
Pets: **No**
Children: **Welcome**
Smoking: **Permitted**
Social Drinking: **Permitted**
Airport/Station Pickup: **Yes**

Enjoy the serenity of country living in a comfortable modern home set on 50 acres. The house overlooks the beautiful hills and a private fishing lake. Guests are welcome to make themselves at home, enjoy the screened-in porch, or curl up with a book before the fire. Outside there are hiking trails, boats, a swimming pond with a beach, and a play area for the children. When the snow falls, the trails are suitable for cross-country skiing and the pond freezes for skating. Your hosts recommend several nearby supper clubs, and can direct you to the attractions of Lake Michigan and the city of Manitowoc.

The Limberlost Inn
HIGHWAY 17, #2483, PHELPS, WISCONSIN 54554

Tel: **(715) 545-2685**	Reduced Rates: **10% weekly**
Hosts: **Bill and Phoebe McElroy**	Breakfast: **Full**
No. of Rooms: **2**	Pets: **No**
Max. No. Sharing Bath: **4**	Children: **Welcome, over 10**
Double/sb: **$47**	Smoking: **No**
Open: **All year**	Social Drinking: **Permitted**

The inn was designed and constructed by Bill and Phoebe McElroy. They picked a fine spot for their log home, just a minute from one of the best fishing lakes and largest national forests in the state. Each guest room is decorated with antiques, and the beds all have cozy down pillows and hand-stitched coverlets. Breakfast is served on the screened porch, by the fieldstone fireplace, in the dining room, or in your room. Stroll through the garden, rock on the porch swing, or take a picnic lunch and explore the streams and hiking trails. When you return, a Finnish sauna and a glass of wine or a mug of beer await.

Country Aire
N4452 COUNTY U, BOX 175, PORTAGE, WISCONSIN 53901

Tel: **(608) 742-5716**	Suites: **$60**
Best Time to Call: **Evenings**	Open: **All year**
Hosts: **Bob and Rita Reif**	Breakfast: **Continental**
Location: **37 mi. N of Madison**	Pets: **No**
No. of Rooms: **3**	Children: **Welcome**
No. of Private Baths: **2**	Smoking: **No**
Double/pb: **$45**	Social Drinking: **Permitted**
Single/pb: **$35**	

Forty acres of woods and meadows surround this spacious country home, built into a hillside overlooking the Wisconsin River. The house has open cathedral ceilings and a beautiful view from every room. Choose from comfortable bedrooms with queen-size or twin beds; the kids will enjoy the room with bunk beds. Guests are welcome to use the tennis court or go canoeing on the river. In the winter, skating can be enjoyed on the pond, and the area is perfect for cross-country skiing. Devil's Head and Cascade Mountain are close by for downhill skiing. Bob and Rita are minutes away from the Wisconsin Dells, Baraboo, and Devil's Lake State Park. At the end of the day, relax with wine and cheese, and enjoy a beautiful sunset.

Bed and Breakfast of Milwaukee, Inc.
727 HAWTHORNE AVENUE, SOUTH MILWAUKEE, WISCONSIN 53172

Tel: **(414) 571-0780**
Best Time to Call: **9 AM–7 PM Mon.– Fri.**
Coordinator: **Mark Tyborski**
States/Regions Covered: **Milwaukee and southeastern Wisconsin**

Rates (Single/Double):
  Modest: **$35 / $40**
  Average: **$55 / $60**
  Luxury: **$75 / $120**
Credit Cards: **AMEX, MC, VISA**

Choose from a variety of inns and homes throughout the state. Accommodations range from modest to luxurious and in everything from farm areas to cities, near all types of activity, whether rural or urban. Corporate rates and group facilities are available. All establishments are inspected. Mark will match your needs to appropriate facilities for a grand experience.

Dreams of Yesteryear Bed & Breakfast ✪
1100 BRAWLEY STREET, STEVENS POINT, WISCONSIN 54481

Tel: **(715) 341-4525**
Best Time to Call: **After 4 PM**
Hosts: **Bonnie and Bill Maher**
Location: **30 mi. S of Wausau**
No. of Rooms: **4**
No. of Private Baths: **2**
Double/pb: **$55–$75**
Single/pb: **$50–$70**

Open: **All year**
Breakfast: **Full**
Credit Cards: **MC, VISA**
Pets: **No**
Children: **Welcome, over 12**
Smoking: **No**
Social Drinking: **Permitted**
Airport/Station Pickup: **Yes**

Dreams, listed on the National Register of Historic Places and featured in *Victorian Homes* magazine, was designed by architect J. H. Jeffers, who also designed the Wisconsin Building at the St. Louis World's Fair of 1904. Lavish in Victorian detail, the home is handsomely decorated, with floral wallpapers and period furniture. One bathroom has a claw-footed tub and a pedestal sink. Bonnie, a University of Wisconsin secretary and square dance caller, and Bill, owner of a water-conditioning business, love to talk about the house and its furnishings. Skiing, canoeing, shopping, and university theater, among other activities, are in close proximity.

The Lake House ✪
515 ELM STREET, STRUM, WISCONSIN 54770

Tel: **(715) 695-3223**
Host: **Florence Gullicksrud**
Location: **20 mi. S of Eau Claire**
No. of Rooms: **2**
No. of Private Baths: **1**
Double/pb: **$50**
Single/pb: **$45**
Suites: **$45–$55**

Open: **June–Oct.**
Reduced Rates: **20% weekly; 10% seniors**
Breakfast: **Continental**
Pets: **Sometimes**
Children: **Welcome**
Smoking: **No**
Social Drinking: **Permitted**

This lovely lakeside home sits on the edge of a small village, surrounded by parks and hills. There are miles of hiking trails through scenic farm country, as well as a nine-hole golf course and free tennis. Or, you can just stay "home" and use the canoe and rowboat. A public swimming beach is a few blocks away. There are an antique store, crafts shop, restaurant, and other amenities in the village. The two-bedroom suite is suitable for a couple, a couple with children, friends traveling together, or a single person. It's a half hour to the University of Wisconsin, theater, concerts, and movies. Florence is a retired nurse interested in art and books, who devotes herself to making her guests feel at home.

White Lace Inn—A Victorian Guest House
16 NORTH FIFTH AVENUE, STURGEON BAY, WISCONSIN 54235

Tel: **(414) 743-1105**
Best Time to Call: **8 AM–10 PM**
Hosts: **Dennis and Bonnie Statz**
Location: **150 mi. N of Milwaukee**
No. of Rooms: **15**
No. of Private Baths: **15**
Double/pb: **$64–$98**
Single/pb: **$47–$91**
Suites: **$120–$140**

Open: **All year**
Reduced Rates: **Nov.–May**
Breakfast: **Continental**
Credit Cards: **MC, VISA**
Pets: **No**
Children: **Welcome, over 12**
Smoking: **Permitted**
Social Drinking: **Permitted**
Airport/Station Pickup: **Yes**

This elegant Victorian inn is composed of three lovingly restored turn-of-the-century homes linked by a winding garden path. Guest rooms are furnished with Victorian and Empire antiques, down comforters, lace curtains, floral wallpapers, and coordinating chintz fabrics. Some rooms have a wood-burning fireplace, an oversized whirlpool tub, or both. Located in a residential area close to the bay, White Lace Inn is near shops and historic sites. In winter, guests enjoy snow sports and relaxing in front of the fireplace with hot chocolate. Summer activities include boating, tennis, and swimming, with iced tea served on the front porch.

WYOMING

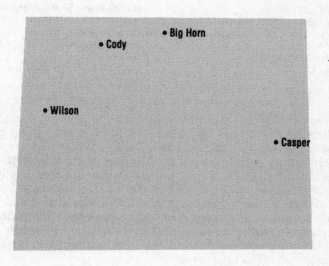

• Big Horn

• Cody

• Wilson

• Casper

Spahn's Big Horn Mountain Bed and Breakfast
P.O. BOX 579, BIG HORN, WYOMING 82833

Tel: **(307) 674-8150**
Hosts: **Ron and Bobbie Spahn**
Location: **15 mi. SW of Sheridan**
No. of Rooms: **2**
No. of Private Baths: **2**
Double/pb: **$60–$75**
Open: **All year**

Cabins: **$70–$90**
Breakfast: **Full**
Pets: **No**
Children: **Welcome (baby-sitter)**
Smoking: **No**
Social Drinking: **Permitted**
Airport/Station Pickup: **Yes**

Ron and Bobbie Spahn and their two children built their home and this authentic log cabin. The house is set on 40 acres of whispering pines, and borders the Big Horn Mountain forestland, which stretches for over a million acres. The main house has two guest bedrooms with private baths, a three-story living room, and an outside deck. The cabin is secluded from the main house and features a queen-size bed, a shower bath, and an old-fashioned front porch. You are invited to relax in the hot tub, sip a drink beside the wood stove, or take in the 100-mile view from an old porch rocker. Ron Spahn is a geologist and former Yellowstone Ranger. He can direct you to nearby fishing and hunting and can also tell you where to find the best walking and cross-country skiing trails.

Bessemer Bend Bed & Breakfast ✪
5120 ALCOVA ROUTE, BOX 40, CASPER, WYOMING 82604

Tel: **(307) 265-6819**
Hosts: **Opal and Stan McInroy**
Location: **10 mi. SW of Casper**
No. of Rooms: **3**
Max. No. Sharing Bath: **4**
Double/sb: **$45**
Single/sb: **$35**
Open: **All year**

Reduced Rates: **$5 less after 1st night**
Breakfast: **Full**
Pets: **Sometimes**
Children: **Welcome**
Smoking: **No**
Social Drinking: **Permitted**
Airport/Station Pickup: **Yes**

This two-level ranch house offers great views of the North Platte River and Bessemer Mountain; the McInroys' property was once part of the Goose Egg Ranch, as commemorated in Owen Wister's *The Virginian*. Western history buffs will want to visit other points of interest, such as the site of the Red Butte Pony Express Station. In Casper you'll find a wealth of museums, parks, and restaurants. The sports-minded will be challenged by local options ranging from rock climbing and hang gliding to fishing and skiing. For indoor diversions, the McInroys' recreation room is equipped with a Ping-Pong table, an exercise bike, and plenty of books and games. Breakfasts feature coffee, fresh fruit or juice, toast, and an egg casserole.

Durbin St. Inn Bed & Breakfast
843 SOUTH DURBIN, CASPER, WYOMING 82601

Tel: **(307) 577-5774**
Best Time to Call: **9 AM–9 PM**
Hosts: **Don and Sherry Frigon**
No. of Rooms: **4**
Max. No. Sharing Bath: **4**
Double/sb: **$45–$60**
Single/sb: **$35–$50**
Open: **All year**
Reduced Rates: **Available**

Breakfast: **Full**
Other Meals: **Available**
Credit Cards: **AMEX, DC, DISC, MC, VISA**
Pets: **No**
Children: **No**
Smoking: **Restricted**
Social Drinking: **Permitted**
Airport Pickup: **Yes**

The Frigons' 75-year-old home has been lovingly refurbished and decorated. Soft colors, warm woods, antique and contemporary furniture, and romantic furnishings create a quiet, relaxed atmosphere. All the rooms are sunny and cheerful. The fireplaces are cozy on cold winter nights and the side deck is delightful on warm summer nights. Sherry enjoys cooking for you and making you feel at home. Don would love to take you to visit a secluded waterfall and hand-feed

deer at the foot of Casper Mountain. Books, games, or conversation are all available, as well as advice on all the things to see and do in Casper.

The Lockhart Inn
109 WEST YELLOWSTONE AVENUE, CODY, WYOMING 82414

Tel: **(307) 587-6074**
Best Time to Call: **After noon**
Host: **Cindy Baldwin**
No. of Rooms: 7
No. of Private Baths: 7
Double/pb: **$50–$75**
Open: **All year**
Breakfast: **Full**

Other Meals: **Available**
Credit Cards: **CB, DISC, MC, VISA**
Pets: **No**
Children: **Welcome, over 4**
Smoking: **Restricted**
Social Drinking: **Permitted**
Airport/Station Pickup: **Yes**

Once the home of Cody's famous turn-of-the-century novelist, Caroline Lockhart, Cindy's historic frontier home has been beautifully restored while retaining the flavor of the Old West. The old-fashioned decor is combined with such modern amenities as cable TV, phones, and individually controlled heat. Breakfast is graciously served on fine china in the dining room. The house is located 50 miles from the eastern entrance to Yellowstone National Park, and there's plenty to do in addition to relaxing on the front porch. The Trail Town Museum, Buffalo Bill Historical Center, and the Cody Nightly Rodeo are just some of the attractions.

Fish Creek Bed & Breakfast
2455 FISH CREEK ROAD, P.O. BOX 366, WILSON, WYOMING 83014

Tel: **(307) 733-2586**
Best Time to Call: **Early mornings;**
  evenings
Hosts: **Putzi and John Harrington**
Location: **6 mi. W of Jackson**
No. of Rooms: **3**
No. of Private Baths: **3**
Double/pb: **$85–$95**
Open: **All year**

Breakfast: **Full**
Credit Cards: **MC, VISA**
Pets: **No**
Children: **Welcome, over 8**
Smoking: **No**
Social Drinking: **Permitted**
Minimum Stay: **2 nights**
Foreign Languages: **German, French**

From the doorsteps of Putzi and John's rustic log cabin home, summertime guests can go fly fishing in complete privacy. Other warm-weather activities include bird-watching, exploring Yellowstone and Grand Teton national parks, and relaxing in the hot tub. In the winter, the Harringtons will be glad to guide you to both downhill and cross-country skiing. Whatever the season, you'll savor homemade breakfast specialties like fruit, quiche, egg-and-vegetable ramekins, and coffee cakes, breads, and muffins.

Teton Tree House ☻
P.O. BOX 550, WILSON, WYOMING 83014

Tel: **(307) 733-3233**
Hosts: **Chris and Denny Becker**
Location: **8 mi. W of Jackson**
No. of Rooms: **5**
No. of Private Baths: **5**
Double/pb: **$85–$115**
Single/pb: **$80–$110**
Open: **All year**

Reduced Rates: **Available**
Breakfast: **Full**
Credit Cards: **MC, VISA**
Pets: **No**
Children: **Welcome**
Smoking: **No**
Social Drinking: **Permitted**

This is an impressive house of rustic open-beam construction, where guests are entertained in the large living room. The bedroom windows and decks overlook a private, forested mountainside. Wildflowers and berry bushes cover the land in summer; in winter it's a pristine, snowy wonderland. Breakfast is a low-cholesterol feast featuring huckleberry pancakes, zucchini breads, and other homemade treats. It is only eight miles from Grand Teton National Park, ski areas, a mountain climbing school, and a rodeo.

5

Canada

ALBERTA

Note: All prices listed in this section are quoted in Canadian dollars.

Alberta Bed & Breakfast ✪
P.O. BOX 15477, M.P.O., VANCOUVER, BRITISH COLUMBIA, CANADA V6B 5B2 (FORMERLY EDMONTON, ALBERTA)

Tel: **(604) 944-1793**
Best Time to Call: **8 AM–2 PM**
Coordinator: **June Brown**
States/Regions Covered: **Alberta—Banff, Calgary, Canmore, Edmonton, Jasper; British Columbia—Kamloops, Vancouver, Victoria, Whistler**

Rates (Single/Double):
  Modest: **$30 / $40**
  Average: **$35 / $45**
  Luxury: **$45–$90 / $50–$95**
Credit Cards: **No**

Try a bit of Canadian western hospitality by choosing from June's variety of lovely homes in Alberta and British Columbia. Make a circle tour of Calgary, Banff, Lake Louise, the Columbia Icefields, Jasper, and Edmonton, and stay in B&Bs all the way. Send two dollars for a descriptive list of the cordial hosts on her roster, make your selections, and June will do the rest. The agency is closed on Canadian holidays and October through March. There's a $5 surcharge for each Banff, Jasper, and Victoria reservation.

Harrison's B&B Home ✪
6016 THORNBURN DRIVE NORTHWEST, CALGARY, ALBERTA, CANADA T2K 3P7

Tel: **(403) 274-7281**
Best Time to Call: **7–8 AM; 4–7 PM**

Host: **Susan Harrison**
Location: **¼ mi. from Rte. 2**

No. of Rooms: **2**
Max. No. Sharing Bath: **4**
Double/sb: **$50**
Single/sb: **$30**
Open: **All year**

Breakfast: **Full**
Pets: **Sometimes**
Children: **Welcome, over 10**
Smoking: **Permitted**
Social Drinking: **Permitted**

Sound environmental practices are followed at this cozy bungalow in a well-treed, quiet residential neighborhood where birds and squirrels are regular visitors. Your host's interests are gardening to attract birds, walking Calgary's extensive pathway and park system, hiking and cross-country skiing in Kananaskis Country and Banff (in the Canadian Rockies, one-hour drive west), art exhibitions, and secondhand shopping. The B&B is within ten miles of Calgary Exhibition and Stampede, the Calgary Zoo and Prehistoric Park, and the University of Calgary. Nose Hill Park, shopping, restaurants in walking distance.

BRITISH COLUMBIA

Note: All prices listed in this section are quoted in Canadian dollars.

Canada-West Accommodations ✪
P.O. BOX 86607, NORTH VANCOUVER, BRITISH COLUMBIA, CANADA V7L 4L2

Tel: **(604) 929-1424; (800) 873-7976;**
  fax: **(604) 685-3400**
Best Time to Call: **Daily to 10 PM**
Coordinator: **Ellison Massey**
States/Regions Covered: **Greater**
  Vancouver, Victoria, Kelowna,
  Whistler

Rates (Single/Double):
  Average: **$40–$50 / $60–$81**
Credit Cards: **AMEX, MC, VISA**

This registry has over 100 hosts with comfortable bed-and-breakfast accommodations. All serve a full breakfast, and most have a private bath for guest use. When traveling through British Columbia, visitors should note that B&Bs are available within a day's drive of one another. Canada-West features friendly host families eager to share their knowledge of cultural and scenic attractions.

Weston Lake Inn ✪
813 BEAVER POINT ROAD RR 1, FULFORD HARBOUR, BRITISH COLUMBIA, CANADA V0S 1C0

Tel: **(604) 653-4311**
Hosts: **Susan Evans and Ted Harrison**
Location: **30 mi. N of Victoria**
No. of Rooms: **3**
No. of Private Baths: **3**
Double/pb: **$80–$95**
Single/pb: **$65–$85**
Open: **All year**
Reduced Rates: **10% weekly; winter**
  rates Nov.–Mar.

Breakfast: **Full**
Credit Cards: **MC, VISA**
Pets: **Sometimes**
Children: **Welcome, over 14**
Smoking: **No**
Social Drinking: **Permitted**
Foreign Languages: **French**

Nestled on a knoll of flowering trees and shrubs overlooking Weston Lake, the inn offers old-world charm in a comfortable new home. The house is on a 10-acre farm on Salt Spring Island, the largest of British Columbia's Gulf Islands. Each guest room overlooks the countryside and has a down comforter. The rooms all have different finishing touches such as a brass bed, Chilean folk art, or Eskimo prints. Throughout the house there are a number of original Canadian art pieces and intricate petit point needlework crafted by your host, Ted. Breakfast is a full-course meal served to the sounds of classical music in the antique-filled dining room. Eggs Benedict, quiche, homemade muffins, and jams are specialties of the house. Guests can relax in the hot tub, on the garden terrace, or enjoy a book in the lounge beside a wood-burning stove. It's just a few steps to swimming, boating, and fishing. You can also follow forest trails or take to a bicycle and explore this quaint country island with its country roads, pastoral beauty, and talented artisans.

Cassidy's Bed & Breakfast ✪
2010 CASSIDY ROAD, S43 C23 RR2, GIBSON, BRITISH COLUMBIA, CANADA V0N 1V0

Tel: (604) 886-7222	Reduced Rates: 10% Feb., Mar., Nov., Dec.
Best Time to Call: 6–8 PM	
Hosts: Bill and Rita Clark	Breakfast: Full
Location: 10 mi. NW of Vancouver	Pets: Sometimes
No. of Rooms: 2	Children: No
Max. No. Sharing Bath: 4	Smoking: Permitted
Double/sb: $55	Social Drinking: Permitted
Single/sb: $40	Airport/Station Pickup: Yes
Open: Feb.–Dec.	Foreign Languages: German

If you need to get away from it all, this is the place. Cassidy's B&B is on the Sunshine Coast, a 52-mile Pacific peninsula accessible only by the ferry that sails from Vancouver eight times daily. Bill and Rita will be happy to meet you at the dock and show you around. As you relax on the sun deck of their ranch house, you can watch Alaska Cruise ships pass by on their way up north. Fishing charters are a big attraction here, but there are also golf and tennis facilities nearby. Afternoon tea and hors d'oeuvres are served, as well as full breakfasts that have gotten rave reviews from past guests.

Kamloops Hospice B&B Registry ✪
311 COLUMBIA STREET, KAMLOOPS, BRITISH COLUMBIA, CANADA V2C 2T1

Tel: (604) 374-0668	Rates: (Single/Double):
Best time to Call: 8:30 AM–4:30 PM	Modest: $35 / $40
Coordinator: Fern Niblock	Average: $40 / $65
States/Regions Covered: Kamloops	Luxury: $45 / $65

Stay in semidesert cowboy country, the site of the 1993 Canada Summer Games. The area isn't entirely dry; numerous fishing lakes are tucked into the hills. Funds raised by the registry support the Kamloops Hospice Association.

Deep Cove Bed & Breakfast ☉
2590 SHELLEY ROAD, NORTH VANCOUVER, BRITISH COLUMBIA, CANADA V7H 1J9

Tel: **(604) 929-3932; fax: (604) 929-9330**	Open: **All year**
Hosts: **Diane and Wayne Moore**	Reduced Rates: **Available**
Location: **8 mi. NE of Vancouver**	Breakfast: **Full**
No. of Rooms: **2**	Credit Cards: **MC**
No. of Private Baths: **2**	Pets: **No**
Double/pb: **$75**	Smoking: **No**
Single/pb: **$65**	Social Drinking: **Permitted**

Only 15 minutes from downtown Vancouver, Deep Cove Bed & Breakfast combines the privacy of a large secluded property and easy access to all points of interest. A separate guest cottage offers the visitor a choice of a twin or queen bedroom with a private bath. Guests are invited to relax in the red cedar hot tub on the terrace or in the lounge room with its billiard table, wood-burning fireplace, TV, and VCR. Hearty breakfasts—served either in the morning room or on the patio—feature French toast, freshly baked breads, and muffins topped with homemade jams and jellies or Quebec maple syrup. Diane will be happy to direct you to all the special places that make this city so exiting.

Grouse Mountain Bed and Breakfast ☉
900 CLEMENTS AVENUE, NORTH VANCOUVER, BRITISH COLUMBIA, CANADA V7R 2K7

Tel: **(604) 986-9630**	Double/pb: **$65**
Best Time to Call: **Early mornings; evenings**	Double/sb: **$65**
Hosts: **Lyne and John Armstrong**	Open: **All year**
Location: **10 min. from city core**	Breakfast: **Full**
No. of Rooms: **2**	Pets: **Welcome**
No. of Private Baths: **1**	Children: **Welcome (crib)**
Max. No. Sharing Bath: **2**	Smoking: **No**
	Social Drinking: **Permitted**

Your hosts welcome you to a comfortable, clean, modern home in the foothills of Grouse Mountain. Enjoy views of Vancouver Island from two sun decks overlooking the secluded grounds, with close proximity to Stanley Park, the beaches, and downtown. Large rooms await you, one with cedar-paneled bath, the other with flagstone fireplace. Both have ample sitting room. Breakfast features something different each day, such as berry pancakes, waffles, and scones with homemade jam. Skiing is only five minutes away.

The Grahams Cedar House B&B ✪

1825 LANDSEND ROAD, RR3, SIDNEY, BRITISH COLUMBIA, CANADA V8L 3X9

Tel: **(604) 655-3699; fax: (604) 655-1422**
Best Time to Call: **Anytime**
Hosts: **Kay and Dennis Graham**
Location: **15 mi. N of Victoria**
No. of Rooms: **3**
No. of Private Baths: **2**
Max. No. Sharing Bath: **4**
Double/pb: **$75**
Double/sb: **$60**

Suites: **$95; sleeps 6**
Open: **All year**
Reduced Rates: **Weekly**
Breakfast: **Full**
Pets: **No**
Children: **Welcome, over 10**
Smoking: **No**
Social Drinking: **Permitted**
Airport Pickup: **Yes**

This modern chalet rests in a woodsy setting of tall pines and green ferns, minutes from the Swartz Bay and Anacortes ferries. Parks, marinas, and the beach are all nearby. A spacious guest room with two double beds, a private entrance, a deck, and a full kitchen/family room can be rented on its own, or as part of a suite with an adjoining bedroom sleeping an additional two people. Between June 1 and September 30, a master bedroom that opens onto a private deck and patio is also available.

Johnson House Bed & Breakfast

2278 WEST 34TH AVENUE, VANCOUVER, BRITISH COLUMBIA, CANADA V6M 1G6

Tel: **(604) 266-4175**
Best Time to Call: **10 AM–noon**
Hosts: **Sandy and Ron Johnson**
Location: **1½ mi. from Rte. 99, Oak St. Exit**
No. of Rooms: **3**
No. of Private Baths: **1**
Max. No. Sharing Bath: **4**
Double/pb: **$75–$90**
Single/pb: **$65–$80**

Double/sb: **$55–$70**
Single/sb: **$45–$50**
Open: **All year**
Reduced Rates: **Long stays, winter**
Breakfast: **Full**
Pets: **No**
Children: **Welcome, over 8**
Smoking: **No**
Social Drinking: **Permitted**

Sandy and Ron invite you to their charming home on a quiet tree-lined avenue in Vancouver's lovely Kerrisdale district. Outside, a rock garden and sculpture catch the visitor's eye; inside, wooden carousel animals add to the homey decor. After a good night's rest on brass beds, you'll be treated to homemade muffins, breads, and jams. Then it's time to explore downtown Vancouver—a good selection of shops, restaurants, and city bus stops are only a few blocks away.

Kenya Court Guest House At-the-Beach ✪
2230 CORNWALL AVENUE, VANCOUVER, BRITISH COLUMBIA, CANADA V6K 1B5

Tel: **(604) 738-7085**
Host: **Dorothy-Mae Williams**
Location: **20 mi. from the U.S. border**
Suites: **$85 up**
Open: **All year**
Breakfast: **Full**

Pets: **No**
Children: **Welcome, over 8**
Smoking: **No**
Social Drinking: **Permitted**
Foreign Languages: **French, German, Italian**

There is an unobstructed view of the park, ocean, mountains, and downtown Vancouver from this heritage building on the waterfront. Across the street are tennis courts, a large heated outdoor saltwater pool, and walking and jogging paths along the water's edge. Just minutes from downtown, it's an easy walk to Granville Market, the Planetarium, and interesting shops and restaurants. All the rooms are large and tastefully furnished. Breakfast is served in a glass solarium with a spectacular view of English Bay.

Town & Country Bed & Breakfast in B.C. ✪
P.O. BOX 74542, 2803 WEST 4TH AVENUE, VANCOUVER, BRITISH COLUMBIA V6K 1K2

Tel: **(604) 731-5942**
Coordinator: **Helen Burich**
States/Regions Covered: **Vancouver, Vancouver Island, Victoria**

Rates (Single/Double):
Modest: **$35–$45 / $45–$55**
Average: **$40–$50 / $55–$65**
Luxury: **$55–$90 / $65–$160**
Minimum Stay: **2 nights**

Helen has the oldest reservation service in British Columbia. She has dozens of host homes, many of which have been accommodating guests for eight years. Ranging from a simple bungalow to a grand waterfront home, they are located near Stanley Park, excellent beaches, convenient to the ferry to Vancouver Island, the Grouse Mountain Sky Ride, Capilano Canyon, museums, art galleries, and restaurants. There is a $5 surcharge for Victoria and Vancouver Island reservations. In addition to normal business hours, Helen is often available evenings and weekends.

Bayridge Guest Lodge ✪
5175 BECKTON ROAD, VICTORIA, BRITISH COLUMBIA, CANADA V8Y 2C2

Tel: **(604) 658-8592; fax: (604) 658-5109**
Best Time to Call: **After 6 PM**
Hosts: **Ernst and Lydia Kaufmann**

No. of Rooms: **6**
No. of Private Baths: **6**
Double/pb: **$55–$75**
Single/pb: **$50–$70**

Suites: **$82.50**
Open: **All year**
Reduced Rates: **10% seniors; off-season**
Breakfast: **Full**
Credit Cards: **AMEX, MC, VISA**

Pets: **No**
Children: **Welcome, over 12**
Smoking: **No**
Social Drinking: **Permitted**
Airport/Station Pickup: **Yes**
Foreign Languages: **German, Spanish**

Bayridge Guest Lodge stands on a slope facing east, with a view of the ocean, just a short ride from downtown Victoria. Within five or ten minutes walking distance are sandy beaches with parks, an eighteen-hole golf course with a driving range, miniature golf, tennis courts, and restaurants and shops. Other local diversions include fishing, boating, hiking, and whale and wildlife watching. All bedrooms have TVs and refrigerators, and some have kitchenettes. Full breakfasts, served in the lounge, feature homemade jams.

Sonia's Bed & Breakfast ○
175 BUSHBY STREET, VICTORIA, B.C., CANADA V8S 1B5

Tel: **(604) 385-2700**
Best Time to Call: **8–10 AM or 5 PM**
Host: **Sonia McMillan**
Location: **1½ mi. E of Victoria**
No. of Rooms: **3**
No. of Private Baths: **3**
Double/pb: **$60**
Single/pb: **$65**

Open: **Mar. 1–Sept. 30**
Reduced Rates: **$10 Mar. 1–Apr.**
Breakfast: **Full**
Pets: **Yes**
Children: **Welcome, over 13**
Smoking: **No**
Social Drinking: **Permitted**

After visiting Victoria's world famous Butchart Gardens and the Royal British Columbia Museum, treasure hunting in the city's numerous antique shops, or experiencing the West Coast wilderness nearby, relax in this centrally located B&B. Just a stone's throw from the Pacific Ocean and a city bus route, Sonia's offers immaculate, spacious accommodations. Queen- and king-size beds with private baths are available in this adult-oriented home. Your congenial host serves a three-course hot breakfast and gladly shares her extensive knowledge of her native city.

Sunnymeade House Inn
1002 FENN AVENUE, VICTORIA, BRITISH COLUMBIA, CANADA V8Y 1P3

Tel: **(604) 658-1414**
Best Time to Call: **Mid-mornings; evenings**
Hosts: **Jack and Nancy Thompson**
Location: **1½ mi. from Rte. 17**
No. of Rooms: **5**
Max. No. Sharing Bath: **4**
Double/pb: **$79–$110**

Double/sb: **$69–$79**
Open: **All year**
Breakfast: **Full**
Pets: **No**
Children: **No**
Smoking: **No**
Social Drinking: **Permitted**

Take the scenic route into Victoria and discover this inn on a winding country road by the sea. The Thompsons designed, built, decorated, and custom furnished the English-style house. Nancy, a former professional cook, will prepare your breakfast from a choice of seven. You'll be steps away from the beach and within walking distance of tennis courts and restaurants. All bedrooms have vanity sinks and mirrors for makeup and shaving.

Viewfield Inn ✪

1024 MUNRO STREET, VICTORIA, BRITISH COLUMBIA, CANADA V9A 5N9

Tel: **(604) 389-1190**	Reduced Rates: **50% 2nd night Oct.**
Best Time to Call: **Mornings**	**1–Mar. 31,**
Hosts: **Larry and Valarie Terry**	Breakfast: **Full**
Location: **2 mi. W of downtown**	Credit Cards: **MC, VISA**
Victoria	Pets: **No**
No. of Rooms: **2**	Children: **No**
No. of Private Baths: **2**	Smoking: **No**
Double/pb: **$80–$95**	Social Drinking: **Permitted**
Open: **All year**	

Named for its sweeping vistas of both the Olympic Mountains and the Straits of Juan de Fuca, this 1895 country home is just 10 minutes from downtown Victoria. Larry and Valarie's bed-and-breakfast wing, a recent addition, beautifully complements the rest of their house. For a quiet evening, there are Victorian parlor games, puzzles, old books and magazines, and romantic promenades to the nearby parks and beaches. Your hosts promise that you will always have pleasant memories of your stay at Viewfield Inn.

Weathervane ✪

1633 ROCKLAND AVENUE, VICTORIA, BRITISH COLUMBIA, CANADA V8S 1W6

Tel: **(604) 592-0493**	Breakfast: **Full**
Best Time to Call: **Anytime**	Credit Cards: **MC, VISA**
Hosts: **John and Susan Cabeldu**	Pets: **No**
No. of Rooms: **4**	Children: **Welcome, over 10**
No. of Private Baths: **4**	Smoking: **No**
Double/pb: **$90–$130**	Social Drinking: **Permitted**
Single/pb: **$80**	Station Pickup: **Yes**
Open: **All year**	Foreign Languages: **French, German**
Reduced Rates: **Nov.–Mar.**	

The Weathervane is located in the historic Rockland area, three blocks from Government House Mansion. Craigdarroch Castle and the Victoria Art Gallery are also nearby, and so are tennis courts, beaches, marinas, and the inner harbor. A 5-minute drive or 15-minute walk leads to town through tree-lined residential streets. At this B&B, you can choose among king-size and queen-size beds—one of the rooms is wheelchair-accessible—decorated with chintz, down quilts, antiques, and original art. Scrumptious full breakfasts are served, with complimentary tea and coffee available at other times.

Beachside Bed and Breakfast ✪
4208 EVERGREEN AVENUE, WEST VANCOUVER, BRITISH COLUMBIA, CANADA V7V 1H1

Tel: **(604) 922-7773; fax: (604) 926-8073**	Open: **All year**
Hosts: **Gordon and Joan Gibbs**	Breakfast: **Full**
Location: **4 mi. NW of Vancouver**	Credit Cards: **MC, VISA**
No. of Rooms: **3**	Pets: **No**
No. of Private Baths: **3**	Children: **Welcome**
Double/pb: **$95–$150**	Smoking: **No**
	Social Drinking: **Permitted**

Guests are welcomed to this beautiful waterfront home with a fruit basket and fresh flowers. The house is a Spanish-style structure, with stained-glass windows, located at the end of a quiet cul-de-sac. Its southern exposure affords a panoramic view of Vancouver. A sandy beach is just steps from the door. You can watch the waves from the patio or spend the afternoon fishing or sailing. The hearty breakfast features homemade muffins, French toast, and Canadian maple syrup. Gordon and Joan are knowledgeable about local history, and can gladly direct you to Stanley Park, hiking, skiing, and much more.

De Gruchy Bed and Breakfast
4710 WILLOW PLACE, WEST VANCOUVER, BRITISH COLUMBIA, CANADA V7W 1C5

Tel: **(604) 926-4267**	Pets: **No**
Host: **Shena**	Children: **Welcome**
Location: **6 mi. W of Vancouver**	Smoking: **No**
Suite: **$150–$170; sleeps 4**	Social Drinking: **Permitted**
Open: **May–Sept.**	Minimum Stay: **$5 extra for 1 night**
Breakfast: **Full**	

Shena's home has a comfortable two-bedroom suite. One bedroom has a queen-size bed and the other has a double. The living room features a fireplace and a color TV. From your suite, you have private access to the swimming pool and deck area. Guests also enjoy the beautifully landscaped garden and the quiet relaxed atmosphere of this West Vancouver neighborhood, 20 minutes by bus from the heart of Vancouver and a 10-minute stroll to the beach.

ONTARIO

Note: All prices listed in this section are quoted in Canadian dollars.

Bed & Breakfast—Kingston ⊘
P.O. BOX 37, KINGSTON, ONTARIO, CANADA K7L 4V6

Tel: **(613) 542-0214**
Coordinator: **Janet Borlase**
Best Time to Call: **Anytime**
States/Regions Covered: **Ontario—
Bath, Gananoque, Harrowsmith,
Kingston, Morrisburg, Napanee,
Seeley's Bay, Sydenham, Westport**

Descriptive Directory: **$1**
Rates (Single/Double):
  Average: **$38 / $49–$54**
  Luxury: **$43 / $54–$60**
Credit Cards: **No**

Situated at the eastern end of Lake Ontario, at the head of the St. Lawrence River, Kingston has much to offer besides gorgeous scenery. There's Old Fort Henry, boat cruises through the Thousand Islands, historic sites, museums, and sports activities of every sort; the Rideau Nature Trail starts here and heads northeast toward Ottawa.

Bed and Breakfast Homes of Toronto ⊘
P.O. BOX 46093, COLLEGE PARK POST OFFICE, 444 YONGE STREET, TORONTO, ONTARIO, CANADA M5B 2L8

Tel: **(416) 363-6362**
Coordinator: **John Kolkman**
States/Regions Covered: **Toronto,
Mississauga**

Rates (Single/Double):
  Modest: **$30–$40**
  Average: **$45–$55**
  Luxury: **$70–$85**

Bed and Breakfast Homes of Toronto is a group of independent, quality B&Bs located in many prime locations spread over the city, near Toronto's excellent public transit. Accommodations range from downtown locations to suburban settings.

Windmere Bed & Breakfast ⊘
SELWYN, RR 3, LAKEFIELD, ONTARIO, CANADA K0L 2H0

Tel: **(705) 652-6290; fax: (705) 652-
6949**
Hosts: **Joan and Wally Wilkins**
Location: **12 mi. NE of Peterborough**

No. of Rooms: **3**
No. of Private Baths: **2**
Max. No. Sharing Bath: **4**
Double/pb: **$60**

Double/sb: **$50**
Single/sb: **$40**
Guest Apt: **$70–$90; sleeps 2–4**
Open: **All year**
Reduced Rates: **Available**
Breakfast: **Full**

Pets: **No**
Children: **Welcome**
Smoking: **No**
Social Drinking: **Permitted**
Airport/Station Pickup: **Yes**
Foreign Languages: **French**

Windmere is located in the heart of the Kawartha Lakes, a water-skiers' and fishermen's paradise. Joan and Wally have an 1839 stone farmhouse, set amid shaded lawns and a large spring-fed swimming pond. The older part of the house has high-ceilinged rooms decorated with fine art and Victorian antiques. In the new wing, the accent is on wood, warmth, and informality. Freshly baked bran muffins and homemade jams are served each morning; in the evening, tea and a snack are offered in the family room. Your hosts can direct you to walking trails, art galleries, golf courses, and Petroglyphs Provincial Park, known for its Indian rock carvings.

Glen Mhor Guesthouse ✪
5381 RIVER ROAD, NIAGARA FALLS, ONTARIO, CANADA L2E 3H1

Tel: **(416) 354-2600**
Host: **Vi Moncur**
Location: **2 mi. from Rte. I-190, Exit 62 north**
No. of Rooms: **4**
No. of Private Baths: **2**
Max. No. Sharing Bath: **5**
Double/pb: **$65**
Single/pb: **$55**
Double/sb: **$55**

Single/sb: **$40**
Open: **All year**
Reduced Rates: **10% Mar., Apr., Nov.**
Breakfast: **Full**
Credit Cards: **VISA**
Pets: **No**
Children: **Welcome, infants and over 7**
Smoking: **Restricted**
Social Drinking: **Permitted**
Station Pickup: **Yes**

A warm welcome awaits you at this turn-of-the-century home overlooking the awesome Niagara River Gorge. Leave your car while you take a leisurely walk to Horseshoe Falls and numerous other attractions. A short drive or bicycle ride along the Scenic Niagara River Parkway takes you to the quaint historic town of Niagara-on-the-Lake, home of the Shaw Festival Theatre. Free bicycles are available. Full breakfasts, including fresh fruit and home-baked bread, are served in the antique-furnished dining room or in the sun room overlooking the garden.

Gretna Green ✪
5077 RIVER ROAD, NIAGARA FALLS, ONTARIO, CANADA L2E 3G7

Tel: **(416) 357-2081**
Hosts: **Stan and Marg Gardiner**
Location: **25 mi. NE of Buffalo, N.Y.**
No. of Rooms: **4**

No. of Private Baths: **4**
Double/pb: **$55**
Single/pb: **$45**
Open: **All year**

Reduced Rates: **10% Oct. 1–Apr. 30**
Breakfast: **Full**
Pets: **No**

Children: **Welcome**
Smoking: **Restricted**
Social Drinking: **No**

Gretna Green is an easy stroll from the falls—the front porch of this 90-year-old brick home overlooks Niagara Gorge. With Marineland, the Imax Theatre, the local museums, and year-round festivals, this area is rich in diversions. But you won't miss out on your favorite shows because each bedroom has a TV. Marg loves to bake, and prides herself on the homemade muffins and scones she serves at breakfast.

Hiebert's Guest House ✪
BOX 1371, 275 JOHN STREET, NIAGARA-ON-THE-LAKE, ONTARIO, CANADA L0S 1J0

Tel: **(416) 468-3687**
Hosts: **Otto and Marlene Hiebert**
Location: **10 mi. N of Niagara Falls**
No. of Rooms: **3**
No. of Private Baths: **3**
Double/pb: **$75–$85**
Double/sb: **$60–$65**
Single/sb: **$55–$60**

Open: **All year**
Reduced Rates: **10% Dec.–Mar.**
Breakfast: **Full**
Pets: **No**
Children: **Welcome**
Smoking: **No**
Social Drinking: **No**

We wish we could share with you the many letters of reference attesting to "the cleanliness," "the warm Mennonite hospitality," "the delicious food," "the friendliness of the Hieberts." Their air-conditioned home is 10 miles from Niagara Falls, Ontario, and the U.S. border. The Shaw Festival Theatre and all of the area's points of interest are within walking distance. The breakfast muffins, served with homemade jams, are a special treat.

Ottawa Bed & Breakfast ✪
488 COOPER STREET, OTTAWA, ONTARIO, CANADA K1R 5H9

Tel: **(613) 563-0161**
Best Time to Call: **10 AM–10 PM**
Coordinators: **Robert Rivoire and
R. G. Simmens**
States/Regions Covered: **Ontario,
Ottawa**

Rates (Single/Double):
Average: **$40 / $50**
Credit Cards: **No**

If you are seeking an interesting but inexpensive holiday, then Canada's capital, Ottawa, is the place for you. The city is packed with free activities including museums, the House of Parliament, art galleries, and historic sites. You can skate on the Rideau Canal or bike on miles of parkways and trails.

Australis Guest House ✪

35 MARLBOROUGH AVENUE, OTTAWA, ONTARIO, CANADA K1N 8E6

Tel: **(613) 235-8461**
Best Time to Call: **After 4 PM**
Hosts: **Brian, Carol, and Olivia Waters**
Location: **1 mi. E of Ottawa**
No. of Rooms: **3**
No. of Private Baths: **1**
Max. No. Sharing Bath: **4**
Double/pb: **$58**
Single/pb: **$48**
Double/sb: **$50**
Single/sb: **$35**

Open: **All year**
Reduced Rates: **10% seniors; 10% less Nov.–Mar.**
Breakfast: **Full**
Pets: **No**
Children: **Welcome, over 6**
Smoking: **Yes**
Social Drinking: **No**
Station Pickup: **Yes**
Foreign Languages: **French**

Located on a quiet tree-lined street in Sandy Hill, one of Ottawa's first residential areas, Australis House is next to the Rideau River and Strathcona Park. It is but a twenty-minute walk to the Parliament buildings, museums, and the art gallery. This handsome brick house boasts leaded windows, fireplaces, oak floors, and eight-foot stained-glass windows overlooking the hall. Your hosts have lived in Africa, Asia, and Latin America, and mementos from their travels are displayed throughout. Hearty, delicious breakfasts, with fruit salads and home-baked breads and pastries, ensure that guests start the day in the right way.

The Downtown Toronto Association of B&B Guest Houses ✪

P.O. BOX 190, STATION B, TORONTO, ONTARIO, CANADA M5T 2W1

Tel: **(416) 690-1724; fax: (416) 690-5730**
Best Time to Call: **9 AM–2 PM**
Coordinator: **Niloufer Gray**
States/Regions Covered: **Toronto**

Rates (Single/Double):
  Modest: **$45–$55**
  Average: **$50–$60**
  Luxury: **$60–$70**
Credit Cards: **VISA**
Minimum Stay: **2 nights**

Quality, charm, and safety are the three main elements of the roster, which includes accommodations in more than twenty-five restored older homes throughout Toronto. A free brochure contains a map listing each neighborhood where the homes are located. All provide ample parking and are within 30 minutes of Eaton Centre, theaters, fine restaurants, and 24-hour public transit lines.

Toronto Bed & Breakfast (1987) Inc. ✪
BOX 269, 253 COLLEGE STREET, TORONTO, ONTARIO, CANADA M5T 1R5

Tel: **(416) 588-8800; fax: (416) 964-1756**
Best Time to Call: **9 AM–7 PM, Mon.–Fri.**
Coordinators: **Larry Page and Michael Coyne**
States/Regions Covered: **Toronto**

Rates (Single/Double):
  Modest: **$41 / $51**
  Average: **$51 / $56**
  Luxury: **$61 / $85**
Credit Cards: **DC, MC, VISA**
Minimum Stay: **2 nights, holiday weekends**

Toronto's oldest professional reservation service represents twenty-five high-quality homes throughout metropolitan Toronto. All are close to the safe, efficient public transit system; most are situated in charming downtown neighborhoods, within walking distance of many attractions. Larry and Michael match your needs as closely as possible to the right home or guest house, where hosts share advice on local sights, dining, or shopping. A free brochure is available upon request.

PRINCE EDWARD ISLAND

Note: All prices listed in this section are quoted in Canadian dollars.

Woodington's Country Inn ✪
RR 2, KENSINGTON, PRINCE EDWARD ISLAND, CANADA C0B 1M0

Tel: **(902) 836-5518**
Best Time to Call: **Noon**
Hosts: **Marion and Claude "Woody" Woodington**
No. of Rooms: **5**
Max. No. Sharing Bath: **4**
Double/sb: **$44**
Single/sb: **$22**

Open: **All year**
Reduced Rates: **10% after Sept. 15**
Breakfast: **Full**
Other Meals: **Available**
Pets: **Welcome**
Children: **Welcome**
Smoking: **Permitted**
Social Drinking: **Permitted**

Relax on the spacious lawns surrounding this immaculate Victorian farmhouse or stroll to the private beach. You'll feel at home immediately. Marion is a fabulous cook and her table reflects all that is fresh and wholesome. Woody hand-carves the most realistic duck decoys you've ever seen. Marion's spare time is spent making gorgeous quilts. A wood carving or quilt would make a memorable souvenir to take home.

Smallman's Bed and Breakfast
KNUTSFORD, O'LEARY, RR 1, PRINCE EDWARD ISLAND, CANADA C0B 1V0

Tel: **(902) 859-3469, 859-2664**
Best Time to Call: **10 AM–noon; 6–10 PM**
Hosts: **Arnold and Eileen Smallman**
Location: **7½ mi. from Rte. 2**
No. of Rooms: **4**
Max. No. Sharing Bath: **6**
Double/sb: **$25–$35**
Single/sb: **$15–$25**

Suites: **$35**
Open: **All year**
Breakfast: **Full**
Other Meals: **Available**
Pets: **Sometimes**
Children: **Welcome**
Smoking: **Permitted**
Social Drinking: **No**
Airport/Station Pickup: **Yes**

This comfortable, split-level home is just 10 minutes from the beach. The kids will enjoy the backyard sandbox as well as a private track where the family racehorses train. Eileen is a dedicated baker, always ready with coffee and a homemade snack. Breakfast specialties include homemade biscuits and cereals. Many local restaurants serve fresh lobster, clams, and oysters in season. Your hosts can direct you to the better buys in town, as well as the Gulf of St. Lawrence, golf courses, mills, and museums.

For key to listings, see inside front or back cover.

✪ This star means that rates are guaranteed through December 31, 1993, to any guest making a reservation as a result of reading about the B&B in *Bed & Breakfast U.S.A.*—1993 edition.

Important! To avoid misunderstandings, always ask about cancellation policies when booking.

Please enclose a self-addressed, stamped, business-size envelope when contacting reservation services.

For more details on what you can expect in a B&B, see Chapter 1.

Always mention *Bed & Breakfast U.S.A.* when making reservations!

If no B&B is listed in the area you'll be visiting, use the form on page 733 to order a copy of our "List of New B&Bs."

We want to hear from you! Use the form on page 735.

QUEBEC

Note: All prices listed in this section are quoted in Canadian dollars.

Bed & Breakfast à Montréal ✪

P.O. BOX 575, SNOWDON STATION, MONTREAL, QUEBEC, CANADA
H3X 3T8

Tel: **(514) 738-9410**
Coordinator: **Marian Kahn**
States/Regions Covered: **Montreal,**
  Quebec City

Rates (Single/Double):
  Modest: **$30 / $45**
  Average: **$40 / $50–$60**
  Luxury: **$45–$60 / $65–$85**
Credit Cards: **AMEX, MC, VISA**

Marian established the province's first reservation service in 1980.
Most of the fifty hosts in her group have been welcoming guests ever
since and have seen many travelers return for repeat visits. Homes are
located downtown, in the Latin Quarter, in fashionable Westmount,
and in other attractive neighborhoods. Accommodations are in Victorian rowhouses, condo apartments, and even a contemporary ranch-
style house overlooking a golf course. Although the decor in each may
differ, the standard of gracious hospitality is assured in all.

Bed & Breakfast—A Downtown Network ✪

3458 LAVAL AVENUE, MONTREAL, QUEBEC, CANADA H2X 3C8

Tel: **(514) 289-9749**
Best Time to Call: **8:30 AM–6 PM**
Coordinator: **Robert Finkelstein**
States/Regions Covered: **Montreal,**
  Outremont, Quebec City,
  Westmount

Rates (Single/Double):
  Modest: **$25 / $35**
  Average: **$30–$40 / $45–$55**
  Luxury: **$55–$65 / $65–$75**
Credit Cards: **AMEX, MC, VISA**

Bob specializes in downtown accommodations with hosts ready to
introduce you to good shopping, diverse restaurants, and places of
special interest with an experienced eye on good value. After a day of
hectic activity that might include a *calèche* ride through the cobbled
streets of the Old Quarter, or a visit to the futuristic high-fashion
urban area, and samples of excellent cuisine from all over the world,
your hosts look forward to having you return to relax in their homes.
There's a $5 surcharge for one-night stays.

Bay View Farm/La Ferme Bay View ✪
P.O. BOX 21, 337 MAIN HIGHWAY ROUTE 132, NEW CARLISLE WEST,
QUEBEC, CANADA G0C 1Z0

Tel: **(418) 752-2725, 752-6718**
Best Time to Call: **7–8 AM**
Host: **Helen Sawyer**
No. of Rooms: **5**
No. of Private Baths: **1**
Max. No. Sharing Bath: **4**
Double/pb: **$35**
Double/sb: **$35**
Single/sb: **$25**

Open: **All year**
Breakfast: **Full**
Other Meals: **Available**
Pets: **No**
Children: **Welcome**
Smoking: **No**
Social Drinking: **No**
Airport/Station Pickup: **Yes**
Foreign Languages: **French**

A spacious wooden home on the rugged Gaspé Peninsula coast, Bay View Farm is a mecca for folk music fans: there are concerts throughout the year, and an annual festival the second weekend of August. If you choose to exercise your body as well as your voice, the local options include golf, tennis, and waterfront sports. Your hosts serve generous breakfasts of bacon, farm-fresh eggs, toast, coffee, homemade muffins and jam, and fresh seasonal fruit from their own gardens and orchards. Additional light meals are offered at moderate cost.

Bed & Breakfast Bonjour Québec ✪
3765 BD MONACO, QUEBEC, CANADA G1P 3J3

Tel: **(418) 527-1465**
Best Time to Call: **7:30–11:30 AM;
7–8:30 PM**
Coordinators: **Denise and Raymond
Blanchet**
States/Regions Covered: **Quebec City**

Rates (Single/Double):
 Modest: **$35 / $45**
 Average: **$40 / $60**
 Luxury: **$85 / $95**
Credit Cards: **No**

Denise and Raymond's accommodations are in the two districts that border Old Quebec. Their carefully selected hosts delight in making your visit a genuine French experience. The boulevard Grand-Allée is reminiscent of the Champs Élysée in Paris. Historic sites, the St. Lawrence River, charming restaurants, and shops are within easy reach of every B&B.

La Rajotière ✪
14 PRINCIPALE, AYLMER, QUÉBEC, CANADA J9H 3K8

Tel: **(819) 685-0650**
Best Time to Call: **8 AM–12 noon**
Hosts: **Michèle Quenneville and Jean
Veillette**
Location: **5 mi. W of Ottawa**

No. of Rooms: **4**
No. of Private Baths: **1**
Max. No. Sharing Bath: **4**
Double/sb: **$50**
Single/sb: **$40**

Guest Cottage: **$90; sleeps 4**
Open: **All year**
Reduced Rates: **15% weekly; 10% seniors; Tuesday–Thursday**
Breakfast: **Full, Continental**
Other Meals: **Available**

Credit Cards: **MC, VISA**
Pets: **Sometimes**
Children: **Welcome**
Smoking: **No**
Social Drinking: **Permitted**
Foreign Languages: **French, Spanish**

While visiting Ottawa, Canada's capital, experience the hospitality of French Quebec. This large Victorian home is only ten minutes from the center of Ottawa, in a historic setting by the river, marina, beach, bicycle path, local museum, art gallery, and several small cafés. The large sunny rooms, furnished with antiques, overlook perennial gardens. Enjoy the veranda, hammocks, and bicycles. Breakfast, served in the sun-room or on the terrace, includes a fruit platter, freshly baked breads and croissants, ham and cheeses, and homemade jams and patés. The area is renowned for its festivals in summer and cross-country skiing in winter.

Appendix:
UNITED STATES AND CANADIAN TOURIST OFFICES

Listed here are the addresses and telephone numbers for the tourist offices of every U.S. state and Canadian province. When you write or call one of these offices, be sure to request a map of the state and a calendar of events. If you will be visiting a particular city or region, or if you have any special interests, be sure to specify them as well.

State Tourist Offices

Alabama Bureau of Tourism and
  Travel
401 Adams Ave.
Montgomery, Alabama 36103
(205) 261-4169 or (800) 252-2262

Alaska Division of Tourism
P.O. Box E
Juneau, Alaska 99811
(907) 465-2010

Arizona Office of Tourism
1100 W. Washington Street
Phoenix, Arizona 85007
(602) 542-8687

Arkansas Department of Park and
  Tourism
1 Capitol Mall
Little Rock, Arkansas 72201
(501) 682-7777 or (800) 643-8383

California Office of Tourism
801 K Street
Sacramento, California 95814
(800) 862-2543 or (916) 322-0881

Colorado Dept. of Tourism
1625 Broadway
Suite 1700
Denver, Colorado 80202
(303) 592-5510 or (800) 255-5550

Connecticut Department of Economic
  Development—Vacations
865 Brook Street
Rocky Hill, Connecticut 06067-3405
(203) 258-4290 or (800) 243-1685
  (out of state) or (800) 842-7492
  (within Connecticut)

Delaware Tourism Office
99 Kings Highway, P.O. Box 1401
Dover, Delaware 19903
(302) 739-4271 or (800) 441-8846

Washington, D.C. Convention and
  Visitors' Association
1212 New York Avenue N.W.
Suite 600
Washington, D.C. 20005
(202) 789-7000

Florida Division of Tourism
126 W. Van Buren Street
Tallahassee, Florida 32399-2000
(904) 487-1462

Georgia Tourist Division
Box 1776
Atlanta, Georgia 30301
(404) 656-3590 or (800) 847-4842

Hawaii Visitors Bureau
2270 Kalakaua Avenue
Suite 801
Honolulu, Hawaii 96815
(808) 923-1811

Idaho Travel Council
700 W. State Street
Hall of Mirrors, 2nd floor
Boise, Idaho 83720
(800) 635-7820 or (208) 334-2470

Illinois Office of Tourism
310 South Michigan Avenue
Suite 108
Chicago, Illinois 60604
(312) 793-2094 or (800) 359-9294
   (within Illinois) or (800) 223-0121
   (out of state)

Indiana Tourism Development
   Division
1 North Capitol, Suite 700
Indianapolis, Indiana 46204-2288
(317) 232-8860 or (800) 289-6646

Iowa Tourism Office
200 East Grand
Des Moines, Iowa 50309-2882
(515) 281-3679 or (800) 345-4692
(515) 242-4705

Kansas Department of Economic
   Development—Travel and Tourism
   Division
400 West 8th Street, Suite 500
Topeka, Kansas 66603
(913) 296-2009 or (800) 252-6727
   (within Kansas)

Kentucky Department of Travel
   Development
Capitol Plaza Tower, 22nd floor
500 Mero Street
Frankfort, Kentucky 40601
(502) 564-4930 or (800) 225-8747
   (out of state)

Louisiana Office of Tourism
P.O. Box 94291
Baton Rouge, Louisiana 70804-9291
(504) 342-8119 or (800) 334-8626
   (out of state)

Maine Publicity Bureau
P.O. Box 2300
97 Winthrop Street
Hallwell, Maine 04347
(207) 582-9300 or (800) 533-9595

Maryland Office of Tourist
   Development
217 E. Redwood Ave.
Baltimore, Maryland 21202
(301) 333-6611 or (800) 543-1036

Massachusetts Division of Tourism
100 Cambridge Street—13th Floor
Boston, Massachusetts 02202
(617) 727-3201 or (800) 447-MASS
   [6277] (out of state)

Michigan Travel Bureau
Department of Commerce
P.O. Box 30226
Lansing, Michigan 48909
(517) 373-1700 or (800) 543-2 YES

Minnesota Tourist Information Center
375 Jackson Street
Farm Credit Service Building
St. Paul, Minnesota 55101
(612) 296-5029 or (800) 657-3700
   (out of state) or (800) 652-9747
   (within Minnesota)

Mississippi Division of Tourism
P.O. Box 849
Jackson, Mississippi 39205-0849
(601) 359-3297 or (800) 647-2290

Missouri Division of Tourism
P.O. Box 1055
Jefferson City, Missouri 65102
(314) 751-4133 or (800) 877-1234

Montana Promotion Division
1424 9th Avenue
Helena, Montana 59620
(406) 444-2645 or (800) 541-1447

Nebraska Division of Travel and
   Tourism
P.O. Box 94666
Lincoln, Nebraska 68509
(402) 471-3794 or (800) 228-4307 (out
   of state) or (800) 742-7595 (within
   Nebraska)

Nevada Commission on Tourism
Capitol Complex
Carson City, Nevada 89710
(702) 687-4322 or (800) NEVADA 8
[638-2328]

New Hampshire Office of Vacation
Travel
P.O. Box 856
Concord, New Hampshire 03302-0856
(603) 271-2343 or (800) 678-5040
or (603) 271-2666

New Jersey Division of Travel and
Tourism
C.N. 826
Trenton, New Jersey 08635
(609) 292-2470 or (800) 537-7397

New Mexico Department of Tourism
Lemy Building
491 Old Santa Fe Trail
Santa Fe, New Mexico 87503
(505) 827-7400 or (800) 545-2040
(out of state)

New York State Division of Tourism
1 Commerce Plaza
Albany, New York 12245
(518) 474-4116 or (800) 225-5697
(in the Northeast except Maine)

North Carolina Travel and Tourism
Division
430 North Salisbury Street
Raleigh, North Carolina 27611
(919) 733-4171 or (800) VISIT NC
[847-4862]

North Dakota Tourism Promotion
Liberty Memorial Building
604 E. Boulevard
Bismarck, North Dakota 58505
(701) 224-2525 or (800) HELLO ND
[435-5663]

Ohio Office of Tourism
P.O. Box 133
Columbus, Ohio 43216
(800) 848-1300 extension 8844
or (800) 282-5393

Oklahoma Division of Tourism
P.O. Box 60,000
Oklahoma City, Oklahoma 73146
(405) 521-2409 or (800) 652-6552
(in neighboring states) or
(800) 522-8565 (within Oklahoma)

Oregon Economic Development
Tourism Division
775 Summer Street N.E.
Salem, Oregon 97310
(503) 378-3451 or (800) 547-7842

Pennsylvania Bureau of Travel
Development
453 Forum Building, Department of
Commerce
Harrisburg, Pennsylvania 17120
(717) 787-5453 or (800) 847-4872

Puerto Rico Tourism Company
23rd Floor
575 Fifth Avenue
New York, New York 10017
(212) 599-6262 or (800) 223-6530
or (800) 866-STAR [7827]

Rhode Island Department of
Economic Development
Tourism and Promotion Division
7 Jackson Walkway
Providence, Rhode Island 02903
(401) 277-2601 or (800) 556-2484
(East Coast from Maine to Virginia,
also West Virginia and Ohio)

South Carolina Division of Tourism
1205 Pendleton St.
Columbia, South Carolina 29201
(803) 734-0122

South Dakota Division of Tourism
Capitol Lake Plaza
711 Wells Avenue
Pierre, South Dakota 57501
(605) 773-3301 or (800) 843-1930
(out of state) or (800) 952-2217
(within South Dakota)

Tennessee Tourist Development
P.O. Box 23170
Nashville, Tennessee 37202
(615) 741-2158

Texas Tourist Development
P.O. Box 12008, Capitol Station
Austin, Texas 78711
(512) 462-9191 or (800) 888-8839

Utah Travel Council
Council Hall
Capitol Hill
Salt Lake City, Utah 84114
(801) 538-1030

Vermont Travel Division
134 State Street
Montpelier, Vermont 05602
(802) 828-3236

Virginia Division of Tourism
202 North 9th Street
Suite 500
Richmond, Virginia 23219
(804) 786-4484 or (800) 847-4882

Washington State Tourism
  Development Division
101 General Administration Building
Olympia, Washington 98504
(206) 586-2088 or 586-2102
  or (800) 544-1800 (out of state)

Travel West Virginia
2101 E. Washington Street
Charleston, West Virginia 25305
(304) 348-2286 or (800) CALL WVA
  [225-5982]

Wisconsin Division of Tourism
P.O. Box 7970-B
123 W. Washington
Madison, Wisconsin 53707
(608) 266-2161 or (800) 372-2737
  (within Wisconsin and neighboring
  states) or (800) 432-8747 (out of
  state)

Wyoming Travel Commission
I-25 and College Drive
Cheyenne, Wyoming 82002-0660
(307) 777-7777 or (800) 225-5996
  (out of state)

Canadian Province
Tourist Offices

Alberta Tourism, Parks, and
  Recreation
City Center Building
10155 102 Street
Edmonton, Alberta, Canada T5J 4L6
(403) 427-4321 (from Edmonton area)
  or 800-222-6501 (from Alberta) or
  800-661-8888 (from the U.S. and
  Canada)

Tourism British Columbia
1117 Wharf Street
Victoria, British Columbia, Canada
  V8V 1X4
(604) 387-1642 or (800) 663-6000

Travel Manitoba
Department 6020
7th Floor
155 Carlton Street
Winnipeg, Manitoba, Canada R3C
  3H8
(204) 945-4345 or 800-665-0040 (from
  mainland U.S. and Canada)

Tourism New Brunswick
P.O. Box 12345
Fredericton, New Brunswick, Canada
  E3B 5C3
(506) 453-8745 or 800-561-0123 (from
  mainland U.S. and Canada)

Newfoundland/Labrador Tourism
  Branch
Department of Development
P.O. Box 8700
St. John's, Newfoundland, Canada
  A1B 4J6
(709) 729-2830 (from St. John's area)
  or 800-563-6353 (from mainland
  U.S. and Canada)

The Department of Economic
  Development and Tourism
Government of N.W. Territories
Yellow Knife Box 1320
Northwest Territories, Canada
  X1A 2L9
(403) 873-7200 or (800) 661-0788

Nova Scotia Tourism
P.O. Box 130
Halifax, Nova Scotia, Canada B3J 2M7
(902) 424-4247 or (800) 341-6096
  (mainland U.S.) or
  (800) 565-0000 (Canada)

Ontario Ministry of Tourism and
  Recreation
Customer Service
Queens Park
Toronto, Ontario, Canada M7A 2E5
(410) 965-4008 (within Canada) or
  (800) 668-2746 (from mainland U.S.
  and Canada, except Yukon & N.W.
  Territories)

Department of Finance and Tourism
Visitor Services
P.O. Box 940
Charlottetown, Prince Edward Island,
    Canada C1A 7N5
(902) 368-4444 or (800) 565-7421 (from
    New Brunswick and Nova Scotia—
    May 15 to October 31) or
    (800) 565-0267

Tourism Quebec
C.P. 20 000
Quebec, Canada G1K 7X2
(800) 363-7777 (from 26 eastern states)
    or (514) 873-2015 (collect from all
    other U.S. locations)

Tourism Saskatchewan
1919 Saskatchewan Drive
Regina, Saskatchewan, Canada S4P
    3V7
(306) 787-2300 or (800) 667-7191
    (from Canada and mainland U.S.,
    except Alaska)

Tourism Yukon
P.O. Box 2703
Whitehorse, Yukon, Canada Y1A 2C6
(403) 667-5340

BED AND BREAKFAST RESERVATION REQUEST FORM

Dear _____
     Host's Name

I read about your home in *Bed & Breakfast U.S.A. 1993*, and would
be interested in making reservations to stay with you.

My name: _____

Address: _____
     street

_____
     city   state   zip

Telephone: _____
     area code

Business address/telephone: _____

_____

Number of adult guests: _____

Number and ages of children: _____

Desired date and time of arrival: _____

Desired length of stay: _____

Mode of transportation: _____
(car, bus, train, plane)

Additional information/special requests/allergies: _____

_____

_____

_____

_____

_____

_____

I look forward to hearing from you soon.

                           Sincerely,

APPLICATION FOR MEMBERSHIP
(Please type or print)
(Please refer to Preface, pages xxxix–xl for our membership criteria.)

Name of Bed & Breakfast: _____

Address: _____

City: _____ State: _____ Zip: _____ Phone: ( ) _____

Best Time to Call: _____

Host(s): _____

Located: No. of miles _____ compass direction _____ of Major

City _____ Geographic region _____

No. of miles _____ from major route _____ Exit: _____

No. of guest bedrooms with private bath: _____

No. of guest bedrooms that share a bath: _____

How many people (including *your* family) must use the shared
bath? _____

How many bedrooms, if any, have a sink in them? _____

Room Rates:
$ _____ Double—private bath $ _____ Double—shared bath
$ _____ Single—private bath $ _____ Single—shared bath
$ _____ Suites
Separate Guest Cottage $ _____ Sleeps _____

Are you open year-round? ☐ Yes   ☐ No
If "No," specify when you are open: _____

How many rooms are wheelchair-accessible? _____

Do you require a minimum stay? _____

Do you discount rates at any time? ☐ No   ☐ Yes

Do you offer a discount to senior citizens? ☐ No   ☐ Yes: _____ %

Do you offer a discount for families? ☐ No   ☐ Yes: _____ %

Breakfast: Type of breakfast included in rate:
☐ Full ☐ Continental

Describe breakfast specialties: _____
_____

Are any other meals provided? ☐ No   ☐ Yes
Lunch ☐ cost: $ _____   Dinner ☐ cost: $ _____

Do you accept credit cards? ☐ No   ☐ Yes:
☐ AMEX ☐ DINERS ☐ DISCOVER ☐ MASTERCARD ☐ VISA

Will you GUARANTEE your rates from January through December 1994? ☐ Yes   ☐ No

Note: This Guarantee applies only to those guests making reservations having read about you in *Bed & Breakfast U.S.A., 1994.*

If you have household pets, specify how many:
☐ Dog(s)   ☐ Cat(s)   ☐ Other

Can you accommodate a guest's pet?
☐ No   ☐ Yes   ☐ Sometimes

Are children welcome? ☐ No   ☐ Yes   If "Yes," specify age restriction _____

Do you permit smoking somewhere inside your house?
☐ No   ☐ Yes

Do you permit social drinking? ☐ No   ☐ Yes

Guests can be met at ☐ Airport ____   ☐ Train ____   ☐ Bus ____

Can you speak a foreign language fluently? ☐ No   ☐ Yes
Describe: _____

GENERAL AREA OF YOUR B&B (e.g., Boston historic district; 20 minutes from Chicago Loop):

GENERAL DESCRIPTION OF YOUR B&B (e.g., brick Colonial with white shutters; Victorian mansion with stained-glass windows):

AMBIENCE OF YOUR B&B (e.g., furnished with rare antiques; lots of wood and glass):

THE QUALITIES THAT MAKE YOUR B&B SPECIAL ARE:

THINGS OF HISTORIC, SCENIC, CULTURAL, OR GENERAL INTEREST NEARBY (e.g., one mile from the San Diego Zoo; walking distance to the Lincoln Memorial):

YOUR OCCUPATION and SPECIAL INTERESTS (e.g., a retired teacher of Latin interested in woodworking; full-time host interested in quilting):

If you do welcome children, are there any special provisions for them (e.g., crib, playpen, high-chair, play area, baby-sitter)?

Do you offer snacks (e.g., complimentary wine and cheese; pretzels and chips but BYOB)?

Can guests use your kitchen for light snacks? ☐ No   ☐ Yes

Do you offer the following amenities? ☐ Guest refrigerator
☐ Air-conditioning   ☐ TV ☐ Piano   ☐ Washing machine
☐ Dryer   ☐ Hot tub   ☐ Pool   ☐ Tennis court
Other _____

What major college or university is within 10 miles?
_____

Please supply the name, address, and phone number of three personal references from people not related to you (please use a separate sheet).

Please enclose a copy of your brochure along with color photos including exterior, guest bedrooms, baths, and breakfast area. Bedroom photos should include view of the headboard(s), bedside lamps and night tables. Please show us a typical breakfast setting. Use a label to identify the name of your B&B *on each*. If you have a black-and-white line drawing, send it along. If you have an original breakfast recipe that you'd like to share, send it along, too. (Of course, credit will be given to your B&B.) **Nobody can describe your B&B better than you. Limit your description to 100 words and submit it typed, double spaced, on a separate sheet of paper. We will of course reserve the right to edit.** As a member of the Tourist House Association of America, your B&B will be described in the next edition of our book, *Bed & Breakfast U.S.A.*, published by Plume, an imprint of New American Library, a division of Penguin USA, and distributed to bookstores and libraries throughout the U.S. The book is also used as a reference for B&Bs in our country by major offices of tourism throughout the world.

Note: The following will NOT be considered for inclusion in *Bed & Breakfast, U.S.A.*: B&Bs having more than 15 guest rooms. Rental properties or properties where the host doesn't reside on the premises. Rates over $85 for double occupancy. Rates exceeding $35 where 6 people share a bath. Rates exceeding $40 where 5 people share a bath. Beds without headboards, night tables, and adequate bedside reading lamps.

Note: If the publisher or authors receive negative reports from your guests regarding a deficiency in our standards of CLEANLINESS, COMFORT, and CORDIALITY, and/or failure to honor the rate guarantee, we reserve the right to cancel your membership.

This membership application has been prepared by:

_____
(Signature)

Please enclose your $35 membership dues.   Date: _____

Yes! ☐ I'm interested in Group Liability Insurance.
No ☐ I am insured by _____ .

Return to:
Tourist House Association of America
RD 1, Box 12A
Greentown, Pennsylvania 18426

To assure that your listing will be considered for the 1994 edition of *Bed & Breakfast U.S.A.*, we MUST receive your completed application by March 31, 1993. Thereafter, listings will be considered only for the semiannual supplement. (See page 731.)

APPLICATION FOR MEMBERSHIP FOR A
BED & BREAKFAST RESERVATION SERVICE

NAME OF BED & BREAKFAST SERVICE: _____

ADDRESS: _____

CITY: _____ STATE: _____ ZIP: _____ PHONE:( ) _____

COORDINATOR: _____

BEST TIME TO CALL: _____

Do you have a telephone answering ☐ machine?   ☐ service?

Names of state(s), cities, and towns where you have hosts (in alphabetical order, please, and limit to 10):

Number of hosts on your roster: _____

THINGS OF HISTORIC, SCENIC, CULTURAL, OR GENERAL INTEREST IN THE AREA(S) YOU SERVE:

Range of Rates:
   Modest: Single $ _____   Double $ _____
   Average: Single $ _____   Double $ _____
   Luxury: Single $ _____   Double $ _____

Will you GUARANTEE your rates through December 1994?
☐ Yes   ☐ No

How often do you reinspect listings? _____
Do you require a minimum stay? _____
Surcharges for one-night stay? _____
Do you accept credit cards? ☐ No   ☐ Yes:
☐ AMEX ☐ DINERS ☐ DISCOVER ☐ MASTERCARD
☐ VISA

Is the guest required to pay a fee to use your service?
☐ No   ☐ Yes—The fee is $ _____

Do you publish a directory of your B&B listings?
☐ No   ☐ Yes—The fee is $ _____

Are any of your B&Bs within 10 miles of a university? Which? ___

Briefly describe a sample host home in each of the previous categories: e.g., a cozy farmhouse where the host weaves rugs; a restored 1800 Victorian where the host is a retired general; a contemporary mansion with a sauna and swimming pool.

Please supply the name, address, and phone number of three personal references from people not related to you (please use a separate sheet of paper). Please enclose a copy of your brochure.

This membership application has been prepared by:

_____
(Signature)

Please enclose your $35 membership dues.　　Date: _____

If you have a special breakfast recipe that you'd like to share, send it along. (Of course, credit will be given to your B&B agency.) As a member of the Tourist House Association of America, your B&B agency will be described in the next edition of our book, *Bed & Breakfast U.S.A.*, published by Plume, an imprint of New American Library, a division of Penguin USA. Return to: Tourist House Association, RD 1, Box 12A, Greentown, PA 18426.

To assure that your listing will be considered for the 1994 edition, we must receive your completed application by March 31, 1993. Thereafter, listings will be considered only for the semiannual supplement. (See next page.)

INFORMATION ORDER FORM

We are constantly expanding our roster to include new members in the Tourist House Association of America. Their facilities will be fully described in the next edition of *Bed & Breakfast U.S.A.* In the meantime, we will be happy to send you a list including the name, address, telephone number, etc.

For those of you who would like to order additional copies of the book, and perhaps send one to a friend as a gift, we will be happy to fill mail orders. If it is a gift, let us know and we'll enclose a special gift card from you.

_____

ORDER FORM

To:
Tourist House
Association—
Book Dept.
RD 1, Box 12A
Greentown, PA
18426

From: _____
(Print your name)
Address: _____
_____
City   State   Zip

Date: _____

Please send:

☐ List of new B&Bs ($3.00), available July to December.

☐ _____ copies of *Bed & Breakfast U.S.A.* @ $14.00 each (includes 4th class mail)

Send to: _____

Address: _____

_____
City   State   Zip

☐ Enclose a gift card from:

Please make check or money order payable to Tourist House Association.

The Tourist House Association of America is looking for Bed & Breakfasts completely set up to accommodate handicapped guests.

A special section will be incorporated in the 1994 edition of *Bed & Breakfast U.S.A.*

Requirements are comfort, cordiality, and cleanliness at a fair price. Ramps for wheelchairs, reach bars for bathtubs and toilets, doorways wide enough and breakfast table high enough so a wheelchair can fit comfortably. Also activities that are accessible to handicapped participants.

If you or someone you know meets these requirements, please fill out the form opposite.

WE WANT TO HEAR FROM YOU!

Name: _____

Address: _____
Street

_____
City   State   Zip

Please contact the following B&Bs; I think that they would be great additions to the next edition of *Bed & Breakfast U.S.A.*

Name of B&B: _____

Address: _____
Street

_____
City   State   Zip

Comments:

All membership dues collected for the handicapped section will be donated to the Muscular Dystrophy Association.

Just tear out this page and mail it to us. It won't ruin your book!

Return to:
Tourist House Association of America
RD 1, Box 12A
Greentown, Pennsylvania 18426